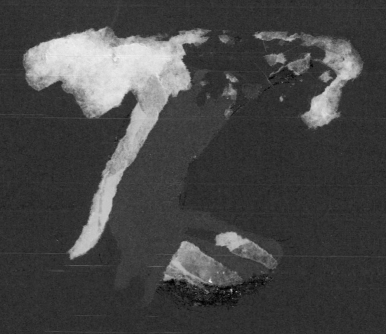

THE ENVY OF THE WORLD

THE ENVY
OF THE WORLD

Fifty Years of the BBC
Third Programme and Radio 3
1946 – 1996

HUMPHREY CARPENTER

with research by Jennifer Doctor

Weidenfeld and Nicolson
LONDON

First published in Great Britain in 1996 by
Weidenfeld & Nicolson

The Orion Publishing Group Ltd
Orion House
5 Upper Saint Martin's Lane
London WC2H 9EA

Humphrey Carpenter has asserted his right to be identified as the
author of this work in accordance with the Copyright, Designs and
Patents Act 1988.

ISBN 0 297 81720 5

A catalogue record for this book
is available from the British Library.

Filmset by Selwood Systems, Midsomer Norton
Printed in Great Britain by Butler & Tanner, Frome and London

ERRATUM

The chapter heading on p.365 should read:

A day in the life of Radio 3, April 1996

500113599

'a service which is literally the envy of the world'
Peter Laslett on the Third Programme, quoted in the
Cambridge Review, *12 October 1957*

Contents

Illustrations

William Haley, the Director-General who was the Third Programme's founding father (BBC)

Etienne Amyot, Leslie Stokes and George Barnes (BBC)

Sir Adrian Boult, chief conductor of the BBC Symphony Orchestra (BBC)

The 150-foot Third Programme mast at Brighton (BBC)

Louis MacNeice, 1942 (BBC)

Richard Strauss talking to Sir Adrian Boult in the interval of a concert broadcast on the Third Programme on 30 October 1947 (BBC)

Dylan Thomas at the microphone in 1948, with Douglas Cleverdon in the background (National Portrait Gallery)

Harman Grisewood, the second Controller of the Third Programme (BBC)

Third Programme Continuity Suite in the sub-basement of Broadcasting House (BBC)

Fred Hoyle giving one of his remarkable Third Programme talks (BBC)

John Morris, Controller of the Third from 1952 to 1958 (BBC)

Watercolour by John Betjeman of the Queen knighting George Barnes in a BBC television studio (Anthony Barnes)

Typical performers on the Third Programme, as seen by a cartoonist in *Isis*, November 1952 (Bodleian Library)

'The Third Programme family' cartoon in the *Daily Sketch* to mark the tenth anniversary of the Third Programme in September 1956

Peter Ustinov and Peter Jones, celebrating the tenth anniversary of the Third Programme in 1956 with *In Third Gear* (BBC)

Samuel Beckett's *Fin de partie* being recorded for the Third Programme, in 1957 (BBC)

The Sound Broadcasting Society (formerly the Third Programme Defence Society) press conference at the home of Ralph Vaughan Williams, 18 July 1957 (Times Newspapers Ltd)

P. H. Newby, the Third Programme's fourth Controller, 1958 (BBC)

Michael Tippett at the microphone in 1959 (BBC)

Hans Keller (BBC)

Radio 3 announcers in 1972 (BBC)

Sir William Glock announcing his last Proms season, in June 1973, with Stephen Hearst, Controller of Radio 3 from 1972 to 1978 (BBC)

Philip French, producer of *Critics' Forum* for sixteen years (BBC)

Radio 3's Controller Ian McIntyre and Robert Ponsonby, Controller of

Preface

Early in 1993, Nicholas Kenyon, Controller of BBC Radio 3, asked if I would be willing to write a book to mark the fiftieth anniversary of the start of its predecessor and progenitor, the BBC Third Programme, which would fall in September 1996. It was a subject I found immediately congenial, largely for personal reasons.

As a child in the mid-1950s, in a television-less household, I had an old valve radio by my bed, and would channel-hop until the late hours between the Light Programme, the Home Service, Radio Luxembourg, and an odd station called the Third Programme, on which one heard the most unpredictable things. I cannot pretend that, around the age of ten, I was a regular listener to the Third, but I certainly tuned in to it quite often. One day, for instance, I picked up on it a strange play about a woman composer and her peculiar friends. I suspected that it was meant to be funny, although it was on the usually serious Third. I had discovered Henry Reed's inimitable Hilda Tablet saga, which I now know to be one of the Third's most memorable creations. It was about the joys and perils of being a biographer. Did it, I wonder, influence my eventual choice of career?

A decade later, in 1968, I joined the BBC staff as a General Trainee. I used to listen to the Music Programme – the daytime occupant of the Third Programme's wavelengths – in the mornings before setting off for work. These were the days of those fine announcers Patricia Hughes, Cormac Rigby and Tom Crowe, who seemed almost more interesting than the programmes they introduced. But during my second year as a trainee I became aware, from a sinister document called *Broadcasting in the Seventies*, that the BBC was undergoing one of its frequent periods of self-motivated and tumultuous change. The Third had already partly metamorphosed into Radio 3, and soon (in the spring of 1970) its name disappeared altogether.

In 1975, soon after I had left the BBC staff, I contributed a programme (my first as a freelance) to Radio 3 about J. R. R. Tolkien, whose biography I was writing. Thereafter, radio producers gradually began to employ me as a critic, presenter, and radio playwright, and in recent years I have become more and more a participant in Radio 3. I am therefore both an insider and an outsider, which is not a bad position from which to write the history of an organisation. To do so while it is undergoing some radical and controversial changes, under Nicholas Kenyon, naturally adds spice to the project. Yet it is a case of *plus ça change*, for the most obvious fact to emerge from this book is that the Third Programme and Radio 3 have been changing, and have stimulated argument and criticism, since the network began.

I could have set out to write a history of half a century of British culture, especially music, as well as of cultural broadcasting during that period. Such a book would have required twice as long to write, and would have been twice the length. I have decided instead to write the story of the Third Programme and Radio 3 as they seemed from inside. Thanks to the BBC's splendid Written Archives, it has been possible to reconstruct the daily life of the network in considerable detail. Histories of broadcasting tend to concentrate on top-level policy rather than the daily lives of programme-makers, but I have tried to show what it was, and is, like to work behind the scenes at Broadcasting House, and have portrayed cultural life as seen from the studio. The view may therefore sometimes be limited, but thanks to the liveliness of my main characters – the Third and Radio 3's Controllers and their programme makers – the picture of the times does, I believe, come alive to a degree that a more Olympian study of the arts and music from 1946 to 1996 might not achieve.

'Unlike France, which believes in the existence of the Republic of Letters,' a retired senior BBC administrator, Gerard Mansell (half French by birth), observed to me when I was interviewing him for this book,

> there is no such Republic in Britain. And there is a widespread latent prejudice against people being too clever, too literate; against people standing out from the mass; in favour of the commonplace, the trivial, as against the adventurous and the special. It's not really surprising that some element of this tendency should be found within the BBC, which is a broad church.

Since Mansell was chairman of the BBC think-tank which helped to kill the old Third Programme in 1970, it might be felt that he is scarcely in a position to castigate the Corporation for philistinism. But there can be little argument with what he says. Some might, indeed, see it as surprising that the BBC ever allowed the Third Programme to be founded, though this book shows it was a logical step at that time (1946), given the high ideals of the Reith era. But the Corporation has had doubts about the Third and its successor, Radio 3, ever since. Hence the drastic 1957 cuts in the Third, the constant neurotic search for a larger audience, the present-day nail-biting about 'accessibility', and all the other anxieties that have so frequently got in the way of the third network performing its hugely important task.

The BBC has never sat down to define 'culture', or what a 'cultural network' should be doing. Nor has it really ever faced up to the fact that if such a network is to do its job properly, it will, by definition, only have a very small audience. But that audience matters. At the very least, it will consist of people who already have 'good taste' and are exercising and enlarging it by their choice of listening. Better still, the young and the not well educated may be introduced to good music and speech – as happened spectacularly in the early years of the Third.

This is a prime function of public service broadcasting, and an absolutely vital task for the cultural health of the country, which is not performed by any other cultural organisation or elsewhere in the media. Opera, concerts, the theatre and lectures are expensive and socially exclusive. Other radio and TV networks only give glimpses of them, and newspapers and magazines treat them chiefly as material for upmarket gossip. To lose Radio 3's direct dissemination of the arts, its constant promotion and relays of live music around the country, and its discussion of vital issues in intellectual life, would be a disastrous blow to Britain.

In these days of 'managerialism' and relentless commercial com-petition – not to mention the BBC's own controversial attempts to compete with its commercial rivals – Radio 3 will continue to be at risk. I hope that this history will illuminate its real value, and thereby contribute to the security of its future.

'THIS IS THE BBC THIRD PROGRAMME...'

CHAPTER ONE

Persons of taste, of intelligence, and of education

'Now there has been a number of claims as to who invented the Third Programme,' Sir William Haley, former Director-General of the BBC, told Frank Gillard in 1978, 'and when Professor Asa Briggs was writing the history of the BBC ... he came and saw me and said he'd seen this minute and that minute. And I said, "Those minutes were written for your history. They didn't know it was coming, but they were written for your history. The heart of the Third Programme was really two decisions of mine."'

Haley was not exaggerating his part in the creation of the Third. Yet the minutes unearthed by Briggs, in his mammoth history of British broadcasting, show that a national network much like the Third had been envisaged since the start of the BBC. In 1924, only two years after the first transmissions, and while the BBC was still a privately owned business,[1] the suggestion came up in a board meeting of a separate wavelength to carry 'highbrow education and better class material'. The separation of highbrow material from general programming was not, however, an idea that appealed to Sir John Reith, the BBC's dictatorial Director-General for its first sixteen years. A son of the manse, who had gone straight from school into an engineering apprenticeship, he was driven by a missionary fervour to educate and sustain the entire listening population, whatever its class and level of education.

Consequently the BBC's radio programmes in the first few years of broadcasting, when listeners had no choice of networks,[2] included much that could be labelled highbrow, mixed up with the more popular material such as dance bands and variety shows. During 1925 Reith received a complaint from a member of his board of directors that there were 'too many uninteresting items, such as Elizabethan music, new fangled songs,

---

[1] The British Broadcasting Company Ltd, established as a private company in 1922, the year of its first broadcasts, became the publicly owned British Broadcasting Corporation in 1927.
[2] At this time, the country was covered by a network of regional stations, led by 2LO in London, the principal provider. The stations broadcast their own programmes for some of the day, and came together for 'simultaneous broadcasts' at other times.

weird quartettes and quintettes, groaning Chamber Music, quite unap-
preciated by the public, readings from unknown poets, etc ... also talks
on subjects which are of no interest to 99% of the listeners.'

In fact talks on classical music proved hugely popular. Percy Scholes,
the 'BBC Music Critic', became a household name by speaking on musical
events in London from 1923 until 1928, as did Sir Walford Davies with
his long-running series *Music and the Ordinary Listener*, which began in
1926. Meanwhile, thanks to Percy Pitt, the BBC's first Director of Music,
who had been trained on the Continent in the 1880s, music programming
was not unadventurous. There were concerts of contemporary music (both
British and continental) from 1926, and early music was occasionally
heard; for example, an opera series in the late 1920s included Monteverdi's
The Return of Ulysses (16 January 1928).[3] Bach cantatas were broadcast each
Sunday afternoon from 1928 to 1931. This series was initiated by Edward
Clark, a member of the BBC music staff who had studied music in Paris
and Berlin, where he had come to know Debussy, Ravel and Schoenberg.
He brought many of the European composers of the day to London,
including Schoenberg, who conducted a broadcast of *Gurrelieder* (27
January 1928), and Webern, who on one of many visits conducted a BBC
programme which included his *Five Pieces*, Op. 10 (2 December 1929); and
he was responsible for listeners hearing, on 14 March 1934, a complete
performance of Berg's *Wozzeck*. It was conducted by the BBC's second
Director of Music, Adrian Boult, who had succeeded Pitt in 1930, and
become the first conductor of the BBC Symphony Orchestra, formed that
year. Boult was an ally of Clark (an erratic individual, who was levered out
of the BBC in 1936), but, in Constant Lambert's words, he conducted
Second Viennese School works like 'a really polite protestant who has
found himself involved in a religious ceremony of some totally different
creed'. The *Wozzeck* broadcast was listened to avidly by the twenty-year-
old Benjamin Britten – who had himself been noticed by Clark and the
BBC Music Department, and would soon have works commissioned by
them, a crucial step in his career.

As to speech programmes, the only modern poet Reith liked was Robert
Bridges; yet T. S. Eliot, W. H. Auden, and many other modernists were
allowed to give talks. The output of the Radio Drama Department was far
more adventurous than the West End. Nevertheless, by the early 1930s
anything that was not comfortably middlebrow tended to be offered rather
apologetically. 'Are Talks Too Highbrow?' asked an article in the *BBC Year
Book* for 1931. Harold Nicolson, a Governor of the BBC, wrote that 'an

---

[3] This was broadcast on the 5GB Experimental station, established in 1927 as (in theory) an
alternative national service, though it was audible only within a radius of about a hundred
miles from the Daventry transmitter. Its title referred to the experiment of running an
alternative network, and its programmes were as mixed in 'brow' as the existing one. However,
its inauguration did lead to an overall increase in the broadcasting of serious music.

oily, unctuous coating of compromise descended upon the presentation of the more difficult items'.

The *Year Book* article suggested that people should 'pick and choose' from broadcasts, but the programme schedules severely limited choice. There were now two networks, the National and Regional, and on some nights they scheduled programmes of serious interest which clashed with each other, while on other evenings there was only lightweight material on both. J. C. Stobart, head of the BBC's Education Department, complained in 1930 of 'good nights when one wants to listen to both sides at once, and bad nights when one is forced to go to bed or the pictures to escape both'. Even on good nights, it was a ragbag. A talk on Beethoven might be sandwiched between the Fat Stock Prices and dance music from the London Palladium. Meanwhile both networks filled up the gaps with interminable light music: 'Suite, *The Humours of Bath* (Herbage) ... *Parade of the Sunbeams* (Maclean) ... '

Stobart's suggestion was to establish a third network which would offer continuous serious listening. He wanted to call it the 'Minerva Programme', after the Roman goddess of the arts. It would present discussions, debates, famous plays, and 'melodious' classical music – in other words, something closer to the present-day Radio 4 than to the Third as it eventually emerged. Stobart wrote that 'Home and Family' would express the character of the network. 'Minerva would not go in for extremes,' he explained. 'She would follow the middle way between Schönberg and Billy Mayerl.' There would be 'no distinctions between brows, high or low, because I believe that both extremes are abhorrent to the clientele I envisage'. Experimental or avant-garde material, such as 'Strindberg, the Sitwells and James Joyce', would be left for another network, the curiously named Venus Programme.

Stobart's proposals were immediately turned down, and for the remainder of the 1930s the BBC muddled along, with its two existing radio networks trying to serve all tastes. Inevitably, the demands of the majority gradually swamped the more intellectually ambitious programmes. By the end of the decade, the 'wireless' was regarded with scorn by most intellectuals, as yet another example of popular bad taste. In a 1938 article, Evelyn Waugh sneered at 'the radio-ridden villas of the Sussex coast'. Virginia Woolf cautioned the young Stephen Spender never to take a job with the BBC.

*

Reith left the BBC in 1938, to be chairman of Imperial Airways, and the radio networks developed by the Corporation during the war, 'For the Forces' and the 'Home Service', concentrated on entertainment. The Forces wavelengths broadcast news, popular music and variety shows, and the Home put out schools programmes, *Children's Hour*, drama, talks and light music, as well as news, with some orchestral concerts. The tone of both channels was relentlessly cheery. In *Horizon* for December 1944, after several years of this sort of radio, Cyril Connolly complained that 'the BBC pumps religion and patriotism into all its programmes; mediocrity triumphs'. Nine months later, Harold Nicolson wrote scathingly to another BBC Governor, Lady Violet Bonham Carter, of 'the BBC's unerring instinct for the second-rate'.

However, outside the Corporation there were signs of a growing national interest in the arts. 'A concert had only to be billed to be sold out,' writes Joyce Rowe in the official tenth-anniversary history of the Third Programme, 'while plays which in peace-time would have struggled for an audience drew packed houses for weeks on end.' In 1940 a Government agency, the Council for the Encouragement of Music and the Arts, was set up chiefly to stimulate amateur music-making in the provinces, but soon also began to subsidise orchestras, the Sadler's Wells opera and ballet companies, and theatres in various parts of the country. In 1945 it was combined with ENSA, the Forces' entertainment organisation, and was restructured as the Arts Council of Great Britain. The 1944 Education Act raised the school-leaving age from fourteen to fifteen, encouraged adult education, and made provision for a considerable increase in university places, thereby increasing the potential arts audience.

Within the BBC during the war, it was felt that broadcasting could be 'the prime re-educative agency of the post-war world', and in March 1943 the Controller of Home Programmes, Robert Maconachie, drew up proposals which recognised the existence of 'a highly intelligent minority audience' with an appetite for 'critical discussions of art, drama, music and literature; poetry and prose readings of the less popular type; experiments in radio drama; programmes in foreign languages etc.' The needs of this audience were to be served by a programme described as 'Cultural (for want of a better word)'. It was given the designating letter 'A'. There were to be no less than four other networks: B would be 'Educational and Youth', C 'roughly on the level of the present Home Service', D like the wartime Forces Programme, and E a Light Programme, competing with Radio Luxembourg (which had begun in 1933) for the popular music audience.

Even at this proposal stage, doubts crept in about the likely success of a cultural network. Maconachie wondered whether 'the really intelligent section of the public, which broadcasting has not yet reached', would respond to it. There was also recognition that the audience would be numerically very small. But, it was argued, it would be influential. The BBC's Charter would come up for renewal in 1946, and the cultural programme scheme had about it a whiff of wanting to make a good impression.

Maconachie's proposals were taken seriously, but five networks were beyond the BBC's resources. A scheme put on paper in August 1943 by Kenneth Adam, then Director of Publicity (later Controller of the Light Programme and then Director of Television), envisaged three radio services: Arts ('it would frankly be acknowledged to be a *minority* programme', wrote Adam), Popular and Regional. This was agreed on.

Two months later, Maconachie's successor Basil Nicolls, whose job was now called Controller of Programmes, produced specimen schedules for 'A', the Arts Programme. He emphasised that it was important to have no 'fixed points' – times when programmes must begin or end, such as the six o'clock news – since these had often made it necessary to cut down concerts or plays 'within absurd limits'. Nicolls's schedules, however, were not adventurous. They included a dramatisation of *The Pilgrim's Progress*, a performance from gramophone records of Walton's *Belshazzar's Feast*, and a live relay of *The Mikado*. There was to be an 'Experimental Hour' once a week, but otherwise the brow seemed distinctly middle.

The network might have gone on the air in this form, if it had not been for the championship and far-sightedness of one man, who, shortly after the Maconachie–Nicolls proposals were put on paper, became Director-General.

*

Reith had been succeeded by F. W. Ogilvie, an academic economist who was incapable of making decisions and sticking to them. In 1942 he was asked to retire, and was replaced by two Joint Directors-General, Sir Cecil Graves (who had been Ogilvie's deputy) and R. W. Foot, a lawyer who had been in charge of the Gas, Light & Coke Co. They became known as 'one Foot in the Graves', and were no improvement on Ogilvie. Graves became ill and resigned in 1943, and Brendan Bracken, the Minister of Information, told the BBC Governors that the War Cabinet insisted that Foot should not be put in sole charge of the Corporation. They responded by appointing William Haley to the new post of Editor-in-Chief, so that he could share power with Foot.

Haley was a forty-two-year-old journalist with no university education. Born in Jersey, he had left school to serve as a wireless operator in the First World War, before joining *The Times* as a copytaker. He soon proved his worth, and became a reporter on the *Manchester Evening News*. By 1930 he was its Managing Editor, and a decade later became joint Managing Director of it and its sister paper, the *Manchester Guardian*. A workaholic who 'simply could not understand anyone not wanting to be at work', as a fellow journalist described him, he would go on holiday 'with an ill grace and an enormous book bag'. Such spare time as he allowed himself was devoted to reading; he was said to get through three Victorian novels a week, and was a compulsive self-educator. 'His reverence for knowledge,' writes the same colleague, 'was all the greater for his not having been to university.'

During 1944, Foot left the BBC and Haley became Director-General. He prided himself on being decisive: 'The one thing a newspaperman has to do ... is to make up his mind on the instant ... I think one of the great things in life is not to be afraid of making mistakes. God knows one's made hundreds.' He was later to say of the Third Programme, when the

Governors were worried that it might be dull: 'Let it often become dull. Let it make mistakes.'

He was in a hurry to get the post-war plans into shape. The three-network scheme was retained, and the Cultural Programme now became known as 'C'. Reminiscing more than thirty years later, Haley claimed that it was he rather than Basil Nicolls who insisted there should be no fixed points in its schedule:

> The heart of the Third Programme was really two decisions of mine. The first was that it should be a programme with no fixed points whatsoever. Up to then, programme-making ... had been carpentering. You just had blocks of things. I remember on one occasion asking why two particularly dull forty-five minute pieces had come one after the other, and I was told this had been the first chance to slot them in. And I said that was no way to make programmes.

It was not just a question of blocks of predetermined length. Conductors of live concerts were put under considerable strain by the demand for tight timings. The wartime announcer Stuart Hibberd describes Sir Henry Wood trying to fit a Beethoven overture and an Elgar symphony into fifty-eight minutes, before the nine o'clock news. 'In the end it became a neck-and-neck race with the clock, the last chord coinciding with Big Ben's first stroke.' One evening in June 1945, the cellist Pablo Casals, soloist with the BBC Symphony Orchestra, caused havoc with the timings in the Home and Overseas Services by deciding to 'put some more rosin on his bow'. Even the *Radio Times* admitted that sometimes a concert had to end in a 'frenzied prestissimo', with a clock-watching conductor hoping to avoid 'that greatest of all radio humiliations – being faded out'.

This humiliation sometimes befell speech programmes. Stuart Hibberd recalls Godfrey Winn giving a talk which over-ran and was faded out before the last paragraph. 'Winn was most upset about it, as it had apparently happened once before, and this talk was planned to rise to a climax at the end, which was not broadcast, and he therefore argued that the whole point of the talk was lost.'

Sir Adrian Boult (who had been knighted in 1937) pointed out that things were done better in America; he recalled 'the night at NBC when I was just walking on to the platform for Part II of a concert, and discovered that my starched collar had collapsed. I was firmly invited to go back and change it while the announcer offered to gag.' However, gagging did not come easily to Stuart Hibberd and his colleagues, and Victor Hely-Hutchinson, the BBC's Director of Music from 1944 to 1947, stated firmly: 'Our concerts must be for *broadcasting*, not for concert-goers.'

Haley recalls that, when the Governors were discussing his and Nicolls's concept of a more flexible network, they suggested that there should at least be a news bulletin at a regular time; but Haley was stubborn:

> I said, 'No, not on your life, no fixed points. The people in charge of it all

shall have a completely blank open space of up to five hours every night, night after night. And if they want five nights to do something in, then have five nights.' And that was agreed. And I said, 'It follows from that that everything the programme does shall be given the time that the man who created it or wrote it or composed the music thought was necessary ... There'll be no cuts.'

Haley was also determined that nothing should be broadcast on the network 'until we are satisfied we have assembled the best body of people capable of doing it at the time. If we can't do a great piece of music or a great play because we have not got the right conductor or the right actor, we will wait until we get them.'

Obviously resenting the notion that Basil Nicolls, rather than himself, might have invented the Third Programme, Haley (talking more than twenty years after the event) dismissed the importance of Nicolls's contribution. He asserted (inaccurately) that 'Nicolls wanted [it] to be called the Minerva Programme, the Arts Programme, every silly name you can think of'. Haley also claimed that his own championship of high-cultural broadcasting had a very idealistic motive:

I have always believed ... that every civilised nation, culturally and educationally, is a pyramid with a lamentably broad base and a lamentably narrow tip. And ... I devised these three programmes with the idea that we would have a Light Programme which would cover the lower third of the pyramid. We would have a Home Service which would take more than the middle third, take everything up to the tip. And then we'd have a Third Programme. Now it has been said that this was stratifying or segregating listeners into classes. Well, it was in a way, but that was only the start; it was not meant to be a static pyramid. And my conception was of a BBC through the years – many years – which would slowly move listeners from one stratum of this pyramid to the next ...

I said I would want the Light Programme to play the waltz from *Der Rosenkavalier*. Then about a week or ten days later I would hope the Home Service would play one act – the most tuneful act – of the opera. And within the month the Third Programme would do the whole work from beginning to end, dialogue and all.

Unfortunately it never really worked out ... I did make a very big mistake ... I did say that each of the programme heads should have control of his own programme ... But of course once he had control ... his only real interest was in the success of his programme, and very unfortunately, certainly with the Light Programme, the measure of success was always the listening figure. And this idea that we would slowly narrow this pyramid, and get the base smaller and smaller, and the middle and peak larger and larger, was obviously against the interests, as they saw it, of the programme heads. And therefore they never really got down to a very active co-operation.

*

On 24 November 1944, Haley made the first public announcement about the new cultural network. He told a luncheon of the Radio Industries Club that, after the war, the BBC would 'give the home listener the choice of three programmes designed entirely for himself'. He continued:

> Programme A (I will use letters for convenience to avoid confusion) will be a programme capable of regionalisation in the same way as programmes were regionalised before the war. Its character will largely follow that of the present Home Service. At the same time a new programme (which I will call Programme B) will be brought into being to cover the United Kingdom on long wave ... It will be ... of a light character.
>
> A few months later, as soon as we can get the wavelengths back from their wartime use and as soon as other considerations permit, it is our intention to bring in yet a third programme (which I will call Programme C).

He said he hoped to get 'this third programme' on the air 'within a year of the end of the war in Europe', and continued:

> You will notice, perhaps, I have said little about the contents of the third programme. They are still being planned. But the existence of this completely additional service must inevitably widen the scope of broadcasting enormously. It will enable us to do many things which mere considerations of space have denied us before, things which ought to find a place in any properly constituted broadcasting service.

After his speech, Haley was asked how soon Programmes A and B would come on the air. 'And I said, "Well, I will guarantee that, unless something completely unexpected happens, in ninety days after the war, peacetime broadcasting will be in." And I can remember somebody whistled and said, "You can't do that." And I said, "We will do it." And we actually did it in eighty days.'

So they did. The refurbished Home Service and the brand-new Light Programme came on the air on 29 July 1945. At a press conference ten days earlier, Haley told reporters that 'the third programme' (*sic*) would probably start 'in one year from VE Day, that is on May 8th, 1946'.

Although nothing was said about it at the press conference, the head of the third network had already been appointed. A meeting of the Governors on 3 May 1945 approved the choice of 'Mr G. R. Barnes to be in charge of Programme C'.

*

George Barnes is described by a BBC colleague, D. G. Bridson, as 'a tall, sandy-haired charmingly diffident man who was much liked by all who worked with him. His humour was as dry as a good Martini, and he even had the ability to see the funnier side of himself.' He had joined the BBC in 1935, aged thirty-one, as a Talks Assistant, rising swiftly to become Director of Talks in 1941. His father had been Lieutenant Governor of Burma, and he had been educated at the Royal Naval College, Dartmouth, before taking a first in history at King's College, Cambridge, where he became a friend of E. M. Forster. He once remarked to an Oxford-educated colleague: 'You Oxford men are the worldly men ... We Cambridge men are without ambitions. We want only to think and read quietly, to live our lives in retreat, by the candles of the eternal verities.' In fact he was by inclination a man of action; only poor eyesight had kept him out of the Royal Navy. Bridson notes that, though there was 'something peda-gogic' about him, he resisted the temptation to make his radio network 'merely an instrument of higher education'. Sir Isaiah Berlin says of him: 'The Cambridge world he belonged to had a kind of aesthetic life which he adhered to, and was faithful to.'

Haley, who had chosen Barnes to run it, portrays him as

> a curious man ... The Governors were always a bit dubious about him ... because he had all the Eton [*sic*] manner and charm. And I remember saying one day, 'Well, gentlemen, remember there's a thin piece of true tempered steel running through that lanky young man.' And that was perfectly true. But every now and then, unfortunately, the steel vibrated too much and things got out, not merely out of hand with what he was doing, but out of his hands.

Around the time that Barnes was appointed, there was some anxiety about obtaining wavelengths for Programme C. In April 1945 Haley noted that it might only reach 'about half the population'. The ideal way of extending, and improving, its transmissions would be to adopt what the Engineering Department described as 'frequency modulated ultra short wave broadcasting'. FM radio transmission had been developed in the United States during the 1930s, for military purposes (to eliminate inter-ference in radio communication between armoured vehicles), and it had been used widely in the war. But the BBC knew it would take a long time to persuade the public to buy 'the necessary receivers or adapters', and the erection of special transmitters would be extremely expensive, so for the time being 'no account of its possibilities can be taken'.

On 18 October 1945 the Governors were told that the Cabinet was being asked to approve the use of 'medium-wavelength 514 for programme C'. Meanwhile Barnes was still working in Talks Department, and it was not until January 1946 that the Cabinet approval was received 'for the institution of the third programme'. Only then could more BBC staff be allocated to it.

It was still hoped that Programme C would go on the air a few weeks later, in May, as Haley had half promised. A meeting in August 1945 had minuted: 'Programme C to start on 5th May, 1946.' Another memo mentioned the hope of beginning 'one year after VE Day' (9 May). On 14 January 1946, Haley approved the network's official terms of reference:

> The Programme is designed to be of artistic and cultural importance. The audience envisaged is one already aware of artistic experience and will

include persons of taste, of intelligence, and of education; it is, therefore, selective not casual, and both attentive and critical.

The Programme need not cultivate any other audience, and any material that is unlikely to interest such listeners should be excluded. Servicing elements, such as special [news] bulletins, will either be absent or take a subordinate place.

Within this formula there should be ample scope for experimental work and the development of new radio forms and technique, as well as for a wide range of programmes.

By the beginning of March, Barnes was 'assuming that the Programme will start in June or July'. But two technical problems were now causing a delay. On 4 April the *Star* reported that 'lack of studio space' meant that Programme C would begin 'at least a couple of months late'. The paper thought it 'hardly credible' that room had not yet been found for 'a national radio service which will benefit millions'; however, 'producers are desperately short of studios, and those places which are available have to be booked up weeks ahead (the BBC was already using premises as far afield as Camberwell in south London to accommodate the needs of Home and Light).

Still more difficult to resolve was the matter of wavelengths. 'There has been no effective reallocation of radio wavelengths,' reported the *Birmingham Gazette* on 20 April, 'either for broadcasting, shipping, or other purposes since 1934, the decisions of the 1939 [international wavelength] conference being impossible to implement because of the war.' The BBC had chosen a frequency for Programme C, but the Government wished to retain it for 'broadcasting to Europe'. But all this was merely rumour, and on 28 April the *Sunday Times* remarked that a public statement about the opening of Programme C 'seems overdue'.

On 7 May a BBC Programme Policy Meeting was told that the announce-ment of the starting date of the 'Third Programme' would be made shortly. But the weeks passed, and in June, when the Finance Department asked George Barnes (who was still in Talks) what foreign currency he would require in the coming months, he wrote back with obvious irritation:

I am afraid that it is impossible to give any estimate, at present, of the requirements for Programme 'C' this autumn, since I have not yet begun to plan the Programme, and have little idea of what is to go in it. I transfer to my new job on July 1st, and expect the orders for the Programme to be approved by mid July; thereafter planning will start, and an estimate for your purpose should be possible. In the meantime, I can only suggest that the Programme will require at least as much foreign currency as does the Home Service.

By 23 July it had been decided that Programme C 'will not actually be going on the air until the very end of September'. Six days later, Barnes informed senior staff: 'The Programme will run nightly from September

29th from 6 pm, probably till midnight ... ' But what was it to be called? On 20 June, Haley noted that he, Nicolls and Sir Noel Ashbridge, Controller of Engineering, needed to discuss 'Title of the third programme', because he had to write a paper on the new network for the Governors. He recalls: 'Various names for the Programme continued to be put before me, and I disliked them all, for one reason: they were all attempting to crystallise some image of the programme ... I didn't want it to be strait-laced by some image.'

In the paper, which is dated 4 July 1946, Haley wrote under the heading 'Title':

> Many suggestions have been made, simple and recondite, and have then been discarded for one reason or another. Arts Programme, Programme C, the Cultural Programme, Droitwich Programme [named after the transmitter which would carry it], Minerva Programme, all have their drawbacks.
>
> In the long run any Programme of character assimilates its title and strips it of any original significance. The main requisite is that a Programme should be christened with something appropriate, something simple, something broadcastable, something that will not deter any section of the public from coming to it, and something that people feel they know already. Under all these heads I think we are not likely to do better than to adopt the already publicly adopted
> THE THIRD PROGRAMME.

Haley recalls that the Governors 'were all delighted because it was a completely non-committed name ... Nobody argued about it, not even Harold Nicolson. They all said, "That's fine, D.G., The Third Programme." '

CHAPTER TWO

Get off 514

'There official Programme and Publicity title of the new programme will be "The Third Programme"', records a memorandum dated 30 August 1946, only a month before opening day.

The Third was born at an exciting time. The previous year, Britain had elected a Labour Government with a huge majority, enabling it to carry out a socialist programme of nationalisation (coal, electricity, gas, public transport, iron and steel) and the creation of the National Health Service (which became law in November 1946). The end of the war had brought a flurry of good things in the arts. Britten's *Peter Grimes* opened at Sadler's Wells in June 1945, and was immediately recognised as the beginning of a renaissance in British opera. The same summer saw the first Cheltenham Festival of British contemporary music, and the first Edinburgh International Festival was being planned for 1947. (The Aldeburgh and Bath Festivals followed in 1948.) July 1946 brought the International Society for Contemporary Music to London for its first festival there since 1938. Universities began to be crowded with returning ex-servicemen, and with the first working-class beneficiaries of the 1944 Butler Education Act, which had instituted a system of grants to provide university places for those who could not afford to buy them. Money and raw materials were in short supply – the war had impoverished national resources – but there was a great hunger for the arts.

The composer Alexander Goehr, who was fourteen when the Third began to broadcast, and who knew many of its original staff (his father, the conductor Walter Goehr, worked often for it), says: 'The Third Programme was founded on Labour England. Its imagined listener was a hard-working, Labour-voting schoolmaster in (say) Derby, who was interested in international theatre, new music, philosophy, politics and painting, and who listened selectively to all these things on the Third. That's what everyone believed in.'

George Barnes had been allocated offices in the former Langham Hotel opposite Broadcasting House, which the BBC had taken over during the war. Whereas the Light Programme and Home Service were run by Controllers, he had been designated merely 'Head of Third Programme', and had been allocated only nine staff, seven of whom were clerks and secretaries. The only people with whom he could share responsibility for creating the Third were the Assistant (Presentation & Publicity) and the Assistant (Planning).

The first of these jobs had been given to Leslie Stokes, aged thirty-six, not a university graduate. He had trained at RADA on an LCC scholarship and had acted professionally, before joining the BBC in 1938 as an announcer. Early in the war he had been in charge of Presentation and Planning for the Overseas Service, then had become a producer in Features and Drama. Philip French, who produced for the Third from 1961, when Stokes was still in the same job, describes him as 'very suave, gay, the brother of the writer Sewell Stokes, and co-author with him of a play about Oscar Wilde that had some success just before the Second World War, with Robert Morley as Wilde. He was a very amusing and slightly Macchiavellian man, immensely funny.'

The Assistant (Planning) was a year older than Stokes, and had a more exotic background than him or Barnes. Born in Cape Town of a French father and a mother who was half Danish and half Dutch, Etienne Amyot had been educated at the University of Cape Town. 'My father died when I was very young,' he explained, talking nearly fifty years after the beginning of the Third Programme. 'He wanted me to be a lawyer, but my mama knew that I was a musician.' He learnt the piano from the age of six, encouraged by the head of the Cape Town music college. Later, 'I went to Berlin. Wilhelm Backhaus liked my playing, and he sent me to do technique for two years with Szreter, a great pianist not much older then me (he was about twenty-five then). And I played a great deal everywhere: in England – my first engagement there, I think, was on the pier at Brighton – and in Europe, Scandinavia and America.'

The outbreak of war in 1939 found Amyot preparing to tour the USA and Canada. Instead, he joined the British Army, and after Dunkirk was seconded to the BBC to be South African Programme Organiser, and then Assistant Director of the African Services. After a while he went back into uniform,

> into a thing called Psychological Warfare. I was abroad, but I used to be sent back quite often, and whenever I came to London, I always saw William Haley. I'd met him when I was running the African Services, and he began to talk to me about this idea that he had. The thing that preoccupied his mind towards the end of the war was how, in the war, the BBC had got this immense prestige all over the world, for telling the truth. How could this prestige be sustained? He said we must think of something no longer propaganda, but more of the mind and spirit, which people can enjoy and become, not more educated, but more enlightened. He wanted the BBC to have a great civilising influence.

When the Third began to materialise, Haley approached Amyot about working for it. 'You don't get a job at the BBC unless you're chosen by a board,' says Amyot, 'but he did think that, as I had a lot of contacts in Europe with musicians, poets, writers and playwrights, I might be "international". He thought I would be a good person to work with whoever was going to do it – with George Barnes.'

Amyot had injured one hand during the war, so returning to the concert platform was out of the question. In any case, he says,

> this was more exciting, something of value. I had lunch with Haley and George Barnes, and the whole thing was discussed. And then one began working at ideas for it at once. And George and Leslie came down to my country house, Little Marsh, on the Solent, and the Third Programme was really planned there. We'd talk, and wander in the woods, or sail – George was a sailor. And he had this idea of having an 'Ideas Cabinet'. When any idea came up, he'd run and write it down on a piece of paper, and it was put in an old box. What's happened to that Ideas Cabinet, I don't know. A lot of the ideas were never used.

Asked to give a character sketch of Barnes, Amyot replies:

> Highly intelligent, very much a product of Cambridge – a delightful man, immensely civilised, with an enchanting wife who helped him considerably. He was very much King's College: E. M. Forster, Dadie Rylands, the rest. All his ideas were first-rate but slightly esoteric. Some-times, Leslie [Stokes] and I would say to George, 'Oh, that's far too grand, that's above *our* heads, so it'll be above everyone else's.'
>
> He thought like a scholar, and yet he was an artist too. The first thing he gave me was all the cantatas of Bach, and he said that when I got exhausted in the evenings, I could play through one of them. He *adored* music. It was very easy to get him to accept all the musical ideas. He was a very smooth channel for them.

Geoffrey Grigson, who had worked as a producer under Barnes in the Talks Department, describes him rather harshly in a poem, written years later to commemorate Barnes and the creation of the Third:

> You would have preferred pursuing knowledge,
> Provost of the best-lawned Cambridge college –
> A cynic? No. Perhaps a compromiser,
> By nurture, between the average and the wiser.
> For which we had the lip to call you shallow,
> And nicknamed you the Pillar of Marshmallow.

Given that Amyot was a musician and Barnes a Cambridge-educated intellectual, it might be supposed that the first proposed the Third's music policy and the second the speech content. Amyot agrees that this is true in broad terms,

> but we all came up with ideas. You mustn't forget Leslie, who knew a great many people in the theatre, as indeed did I. And so did George; his aunts

were Irene and Violet Vanburgh. When George eventually became Vice-Chancellor of Keele University, he wanted to make me an honorary Doctor of Music, and I said I couldn't afford the robes. He told me he had Henry Irving's robes from his Oxford degree. They were rather moth-eaten, but I could use them!

Besides the triumvirate of Barnes, Amyot and Stokes, Haley was keeping a close watch on the plans. 'He'd come over to our office day after day,' recalls Amyot, 'and sit on somebody's table and say, "What ideas have you got?" He kept an immensely alive interest in the programme.'

Asked how the team conceived the new network, Amyot explains: 'I think we thought of it as one of ourselves, or as somebody like us, wanting to listen to three or four things of value each week. And every night there must be one outstanding thing.' Did they want to educate their audience? 'Never. I believe that education is curiosity. I don't believe it is somebody teaching you something.' Did they have class preconceptions, wishing to broadcast chiefly to people of their own social position? 'We wanted to get through to as many people as we could. Because an awful lot of people who had not had the opportunities of a so-called good education were nevertheless curious enough to want to know. Renaissance Man was what we tried to make the Third into.'

Before 1945, Barnes, Amyot and Stokes would have been little more than timetablers, allocating air-time to various types of programme – News, Talks, Variety, Drama, Features, Music, Religious Broadcasting and Sports – but leaving those departments to use the spaces as they wished. Haley had changed all that. Simultaneously with the start of the Light Programme and the new Home Service, he had instituted a new system. This gave editorial veto to the heads of the three networks, who were designated the 'Programme side', and reduced the status of the programme-making departments to suppliers – the 'Supply side'. In the memorandum which outlined the system, Haley explained: 'The heads of the Programme side will be finally responsible for the form and content of their Programmes and will have an absolute right of rejection of the material offered by the supplying units.'

Harman Grisewood, George Barnes's successor in Talks Department, and later to head the Third Programme, thought this an 'absolutely crazy' system. 'One might think,' he says,

> that, coming from the newspaper world, Haley understood that an editor has got to have absolute, complete control over the output in every detail. But in Haley's system there was a very strange kind of no man's land of authority between the Supply departments and the editorial [i.e. Programme] chiefs, so the editorial chiefs couldn't really say, 'This is exactly what I want to have – Solomon playing a Beethoven recital at nine o'clock precisely.' The Supply department could say, 'No, we don't agree, music policy is such-and-such.' Well, in Talks terms this was really impossible ... I loathed the system.

It is still in use in the BBC today.

Even before Barnes, Amyot and Stokes took up their new jobs on 1 July 1946, memos had been flying to and fro between them and the Supply departments, discussing possibilities for the Third, since once they arrived in their Langham offices, time would be very short for planning – a mere three months before the Third went on the air.

Opera was an obvious priority. However, Covent Garden, used as a dance-hall during the war, had not yet reopened. Etienne Amyot felt that 'we should rely, for Wagnerian and Italian works, on the big centres in Europe'. Land-lines for live continental relays were not yet as easily available as they had been before the war, so Barnes asked Engineering if tape recordings could be made on site, and brought back to London. (At this date, most BBC recording was still done on disc, at 78rpm.) He was told that the Corporation had two Magnetophon tape recorders, looted from Germany, but these were 'not up to our programme standards'. Six new ones had been ordered from the German manufacturers, 'but we have not the faintest idea when we are likely to get them'.

The solution seemed to be to organise studio performances of operas by English composers – 'e.g. Vaughan Williams, Benjamin Britten, Delius' – and to broadcast the classics of the European repertoire from gramophone records. However, three months before the Third went on the air, Barnes heard that the Musicians' Union and the gramophone companies would not allow him more than three hours of 'needletime' (broadcasting of gramophone records) per week, which would be used up by a single opera.

Barnes wanted the Third to carry two BBC Symphony Orchestra studio concerts each week. The head of the Supply department concerned, Victor Hely-Hutchinson, Director of Music, thought this could just be managed if the orchestra were enlarged, so that it could be split into two (as it had been before the war). Eventually twenty-two more players were recruited, but Hely-Hutchinson feared it would be a 'tight fit' getting all the necessary performances.

Barnes also scheduled nearly four hours of outside broadcasts of public orchestral concerts each week, but Hely-Hutchinson thought that 'the right sort of programme' could not be easily obtained that way, 'most public Symphony Concerts being built on a strong box-office bias' – that is, consisting predominantly of popular works. Two full-length chamber concerts per week were also on Barnes's list, but Hely-Hutchinson was sceptical as to whether this could be managed. 'There are not many good Chamber Music combinations in the country,' he wrote, 'and extremely few of outstanding quality.'

Hely-Hutchinson added: 'If the music policy of Programme C is to be sufficiently consistent and distinguished, it is essential that its day-to-day management shall be put in the charge of one individual who is free from the distraction of having to plan for other programmes.'

Barnes agreed, and the role was given to Anthony Lewis, who had joined the BBC Music Department in 1935 at the age of twenty, after reading music at Cambridge and studying composition with Nadia Boulanger. 'Anthony was wonderful,' says Etienne Amyot. 'Every idea that we had, he would put into practical form. If I said to him, let's get the such-and-such Quartet to do all the Beethoven quartets, he'd ring me the next morning and say, "I've got on to their agents – they can come," and give a date. Anthony was one of the main props.'

The poor standard of English professional musicians in 1946 is a subject that recurs in early Third Programme memos. In May 1946, Amyot went to hear Schnabel give a piano recital at the Albert Hall. Afterwards he wrote that 'such a standard [has] not been heard in an English concert hall since 1939. With Programme C we can revive that standard.'

Amyot had been told that Schnabel was unwilling to broadcast, so he was delighted, when he contacted Schnabel's London agents, Ibbs & Tillett, to hear that 'on the contrary, he would like to broadcast very much indeed!' He gathered that Schnabel, the violinist Huberman, and the cellist Piatigorsky would be giving six Schubert recitals in London in the autumn of 1947, and that the Third was welcome to broadcast them. 'I think this is splendid news,' he told Barnes. 'It provides us with an admirable small "Festival" for our autumn planning of next year.'[1]

The Third would have to plan its music programmes far in advance of normal BBC practice if it were to achieve the hoped-for standard. 'We should propose to agents,' Amyot told Barnes, 'that they should let us know well in advance when any international pianist, violinist or singer was likely to visit the country, and guarantee at least one performance for Programme C to that artist with the agent.' He also hoped that Music Department staff would 'go abroad and spy out the lie of the land in different countries'. (They had done this before the war.) The vital thing was 'to start planning these music programmes and booking the artists *right away*'.

Music Department began to rise to this challenge. Anthony Lewis promised to 'bring back the fullest information possible' from Prague, Paris and Brussels, which he was due to visit, and one of the staff conductors, Stanford Robinson,[2] promised he would do the same on a trip to Budapest. Lewis was back from Prague by mid-June 1946, and reported that the Czechs would collaborate willingly on live relays or local tape recordings, an attitude which (noted Amyot) 'should solve the Opera difficulty'.

Amyot emphasises that many top international musicians were

---

[1] In the event, Schnabel took part in a series of Schubert, Brahms and Mendelssohn concerts broadcast on the Third (from Central Hall, Westminster) in September and October 1947; Huberman and Piatigorsky did not appear, and the other principal performers were Josef Szegeti (violin), William Primrose (viola) and Pierre Fournier (cello).

[2] A now almost forgotten musician of considerable talent. Joining the BBC in 1924, he trained the groups that later became the BBC Singers and BBC Chorus, and in 1932 became conductor of the BBC Theatre Orchestra, later (1949) renamed the BBC Opera Orchestra and then (1952) the BBC Concert Orchestra. After the war he was the staff conductor of operas.

extremely eager to broadcast in 1946, because they had been 'starved of performances' during the war. 'Bruno Walter came to lunch with me and Haley, and spoke of "the privation of being without music". That was the luck of the Third Programme. It came at the moment when you could have *anybody*, the very, very greatest.'

It was soon clear that the Third should not merely wait to see which foreign performers were due to visit England, but, as Amyot put it in June 1946, 'should take the initiative and *invite* some of Europe's most distinguished artists to this country for special performances'. The BBC had been officially discouraged from this before the war. An artist of Schnabel's reputation would be expensive, but Amyot pointed out to Barnes that booking him for two performances would cost 'no more than a 45-minute show produced by Variety'.

Rather surprisingly, it was assumed that Variety Department would be making regular contributions to the Third, though nobody was clear what form they should take. A BBC spokesman told the *Evening News*: 'If the Marx Brothers had just been invented they would be regarded as the right sort of material.' The Variety staff suggested 'Sophisticated Revue', a 'Full-length Jerome Kern musical comedy', Gilbert and Sullivan, dance band shows, or 'Fantasy, e.g. "Mabel in Metroland"'. The experimental nature of the new network encouraged them to ask, hopefully, 'Will censorship be relaxed?' They admitted to feeling 'apprehension at what 42 extra hours of broadcasting [each week] will mean. Is there any chance of one day's silence per week?'

Meanwhile, in July 1946, the poet Cecil Day-Lewis had a talk with Barnes about an unusual scheme for poetry broadcasts. Barnes jotted it down: 'When there is a great national festival or disaster ... why not invite three or four poets to write a special poem to an agreed length for it. This could then be read during an O[utside] B[roadcast] and would show listeners the use to which poetry can be put.'

*

Francis Poulenc was performing in London in June 1946, and showed the same enthusiasm as Schnabel when invited to broadcast on the Third during his next visit. Meanwhile Anthony Lewis was drawing up proposals for the first few months of symphony concerts. Amyot had declared that these would 'not be planned with an eye to the box-office but with a view to presenting works that [are] new or unfamiliar to a London audience', and Lewis's schedule consisted almost entirely of music in this category. Not only were there to be broadcasts of new works by Britten, Stravinsky and Shostakovich; the Third's listeners were to be treated to Micha, Burkhard, Martinů and Eugene Goossens.

Barnes felt rather hesitant about contemporary music, remarking that it gave the listener nothing that 'one can hum'; he was left 'wondering' about the absence of 'tonic and dominant'. But listeners would have plenty of classics as well. By mid-September, shortly before the Third went on the air, Barnes's office was able to announce that, over the coming months, they expected to broadcast the following:

Madame Renata Borgatti playing the 48 Preludes and Fugues of Bach.
Dame Myra Hess playing Mozart Piano Concertos in March and April 1947.
The Lowenguth Quartet from Paris playing the complete String Quartets of Beethoven in one week (probably in December 1946).
Askenasa and Goldberg playing the Beethoven Violin and Piano Sonatas complete (January/February 1947).
Madame Renata Borgatti playing all the piano works of Debussy (Autumn 1947).
We are hoping to have ... all the Beethoven Sonatas for the pianoforte in the spring of 1947.

The Drama plans were similarly all-embracing. They included a George Bernard Shaw Festival in January 1947, and a Shakespeare Festival the following June and July, to include all the history plays. Drama Department, however, was not being as co-operative and enthusiastic as Music Department. It was headed by Val Gielgud, brother of John. 'His brother was very, very famous,' observes Etienne Amyot, 'and if you have a famous brother, you want to show your own hand. And if *we* had an idea, *he* would rather squash it.'

Gielgud told Barnes that, under present conditions, his department could only provide the Third with a full-length play once a month, which was considerably less than the ideal. On their side, the Third Programme had reservations about the current standard of radio drama. Leslie Stokes told Tyrone Guthrie that most BBC drama producers were only fit for 'producing on Bognor Pier'. He thought the Third might go in for broadcasting 'the sort of play which is not suited to the Shaftesbury Avenue market and which usually goes round and round the agents' and managers' offices until it ends (if it is lucky) with a production on a Sunday night or at the Gate Theatre or some such place'. Guthrie was dubious; he thought there were 'few plays good enough for inclusion in such a series which had not been produced in the theatre ... anyhow the series would not provide good radio'. He emphasised that plays accepted by the Third 'must be suitable for adaptation to radio'. Therefore he could envisage 'no possibility of covering [the] full repertoire of drama as in music'.

No such limitation applied to talks. Barnes told the BBC Governors that he hoped to commission broadcasts by 'the great European thinkers Karl Barth, Jung, Benedetto Croce, Maritain, and others. They would, of course, have to be broadcast in translation.' Talks about music would obviously play a large part. Music Department recommended 'some of the younger men such as Henry Boys, William Glock, [Constant] Lambert, Tippett'.

As to news and current affairs, Barnes wrote to Haley: 'I recommend that there should be no news bulletin in the Third Programme.' He was, however, happy to broadcast 'comment on news which we shall obtain, I hope, both from News and Talks Divisions'. He also said he felt there was no need to include church services on a regular basis, though the Third might relay an act of worship on 'the great Christian festivals'.

By mid-August 1946, a month before opening day, Barnes and his team had drawn up detailed plans for the first week's programmes, and had submitted them to the Director-General. Haley was about to go away, so he handed them to Basil Nicolls, now designated Senior Controller. Although Nicolls had played a part in the creation of the Third, he had no real commitment to it. Harman Grisewood describes him as 'a classical "First" at Christ Church [who] appeared well satisfied by his early intellectual attainments and saw no need to make further efforts'. In 1944 he had sent Haley a memo observing that Programme C could 'be managed on £7,000 a week, as certain types of higher-brow material are relatively cheap'. Now, when Barnes was ready to go on the air, Nicolls lost no chance of sniping. 'The week seems to be rather narrowly highbrow,' he wrote to Barnes, 'and to contain very little to attract the marginal listener.' He gave each day's schedule an alpha, beta or gamma rating, and suggested that Barnes should have included comedy, nature programmes, and light music. 'You can't really expect to maintain a highbrow intellectual level all the time and I should have thought that Offenbach, Gilbert and Sullivan, ballet, and that sort of thing would make a welcome sustaining programme.'

Fortunately, Haley soon returned to Broadcasting House, and Nicolls's interference ceased. But a much tougher adversary now appeared.

*

There had been much discussion, negotiation and argument over the matter of wavelengths for the Third. At one time the merger of the West and Midland Regional Home Services had been proposed, so as to release a wavelength, but a public outcry had led to the abandoning of this plan. Eventually a scheme was drawn up whereby 514.6 metres medium wave, currently in use for the West Regional Home Service, could be transferred to the Third (and replaced by another wavelength for the West of England). The 1934 Lucerne agreement on frequencies, which was still in effect after the war, had allocated 514.6 not to Britain, but to Tunisia and Latvia. The former had never used it, and the Latvian station, which had operated at low power, had been destroyed by the Nazis. The French had 'lent' the Tunisian use of it to Britain during the war, for beaming programmes to Allied troops in Europe. There was no reason to suppose that the Latvian station would go on the air again.

The Third would be broadcast on 514.6 from Droitwich, the big West Midlands transmitter which also radiated the Light Programme on 1500 metres long wave, and the signal would be a powerful 120KW, ensuring that the Third would be widely audible. This main frequency would be backed up by a network of low-powered transmitters situated in the main centres of population, operating on 203.5 metres medium wave – London, for example, would have several. These small transmitters would be situated wherever the BBC could negotiate to have them erected; the masts were up to 150 feet high, and there were sometimes local objections. Sites chosen by August 1946 included the Belfast Water Works and the Bournemouth Refuse Destructor. Many others were far from ready.

On 25 August the BBC Monitoring Service picked up an ominous announcement in Russian from the USSR: 'The building of a new radio station is about to be completed. The station will be called Soviet Latvia and will work on 514.6 metres, the wavelength formerly used by the Madona station destroyed by the Germans.' Moscow Radio added, in its English news broadcasts, that the transmitter was situated in Riga, and that its programme 'will be heard all over Europe'. If this was not just bluff, it would interfere seriously with the Third, and vice versa.

The BBC did not regard it as merely an unfortunate coincidence. The first post-war International Telecommunications Conference was about to be held in Moscow, and the Russians' claim to 514.6 – which could not really be disputed – was their opening move. There could be no doubt that they were deliberately disrupting the BBC's highly publicised new cultural programme. It was an early shot in what, a few months later, came to be called the Cold War.

Sir Noel Ashbridge, the BBC's Controller of Engineering, hurried off to see the General Post Office official in charge of wavelengths, a man named Townshend. He was sympathetic, and said it would be a pity if the Third Programme had to be postponed yet again, or even abandoned, but he would have to summon a meeting of Foreign Office and Privy Council officials to decide on a course of action, for it was undeniable that the BBC had no legal right to use 514.6 metres.

The meeting was held on 4 September. Ashbridge said that in due time the Third could be radiated adequately by the network of low-powered local transmitters on 203.5 metres. But at present, 514.6 was vital if most of Britain was going to hear it. The meeting decided to recommend to the Cabinet that the BBC should remain on 514.6 for the time being; the matter could be reconsidered if and when the Riga station actually came on the air.

If the Russians had had a spy at the meeting, they could not have acted more shrewdly and swiftly than they now did. (Were they being tipped off by one of the British intellectuals who was working secretly for them?) On 17 September, Riga suddenly came on the air, at high power, carrying not just a test transmission but actual programmes. There was no choice for the BBC but to retreat. It was decided that the Third should use 514.6 metres as planned, but at drastically reduced power – a mere 25KW. Meanwhile engineering staff around the country hurriedly marshalled all the temporary wartime transmitting equipment that could be found, and set up makeshift masts on the roofs of BBC premises, so as to increase the coverage of the Third on 203.5 metres.

Droitwich was already sending out late-night test transmissions on 514.6, at 120KW, and on 27 September, two days before the Third was to open, the GPO forwarded to Ashbridge a telegram from Moscow:

NOTRE STATION DE RADIO DIFFUSION MADONA EPREUVE DES GRANDES BROUILLAGES SUR FREQUENCE 583 KLC [i.e. 514.6 metres] OCCASIONNEES PAR STATION ANGLAISE FONCTIONNANT SUR MEME FREQUENCE STOP FREQUENCE 583 KLC EST ATTRIBUEE POUR REPUBLIQUE SOCIALISTE SOVIETQUE LATVIA SELON PLAN DE LUCERNE STOP PRIERE POUR CESSATION DES BROUILLAGES TRANSITER [*sic*] VOTRE STATION SUR UNE AUTRE FREQUENCE.

Haley noted in his diary: 'On Friday the Russians sent us a cable telling us to get off 514. We are staying with it on about 30KW [*sic*].' But he had been obliged to tell the Governors, on 19 September, that the Third would now probably reach less than half the population of Great Britain.

*

The wavelength crisis had caused the BBC to postpone a press conference scheduled for early September, at which detailed plans for the Third were to be unveiled. Meanwhile Fleet Street had been carrying stories all year about the new 'Highbrow Programme', under such headings as 'TIMELESS RADIO FOR INTELLECTUALS' (a reference to the lack of fixed points in the schedule). There had been gossipy pieces about George Barnes ('He is a Cambridge man, tall, willowy, a well-dressed athletic type'), and Marjorie Anderson, who was to be one of the Third's announcers; the *Star* evening newspaper described her as 'one of radio's pin-up girls during the war' – she had worked in overseas broadcasting. Having even one woman announcer in the team was moderately daring at a time when radio presentation was male-dominated; *Woman's Hour,* which was first heard on the Light Programme a week after the Third went on the air, had a male compère, Alan Ivimey. The *Sunday Times* reported that the Home Service was lending the best known of the wartime newsreaders, Alvar Liddell, to be chief announcer for the Third, and noted that none of the network's staff was over forty-five, 'and most are under 40'.

The press conference was finally held on 19 September, ten days before opening night, when the news about Soviet Latvia was released to the press. 'ONLY HALF COUNTRY WILL HEAR BBC "HIGHBROW" PROGRAMME', announced the *Daily Express* next morning:

Although the Russian broadcasts have 'seriously embarrassed' the BBC, who planned to send out the new programme to most listeners, they admit that the Russians have every right to the wavelength ... They have reduced the power of Droitwich station so that the reception will be limited to a radius of 20 miles instead of well over 100 miles ... It is a disappointing start.

However, the *Manchester Guardian* quoted the BBC as stating that coverage would be 'considerably increased by Christmas', and the *Birmingham Mail* saw the funny side:

We may have to take our Shaw and Wagner and much else against a rather glaring Latvian backcloth. The proof of the intellectual pudding, however, will be in the eating. Perhaps when the Russians hear how really good British culture can be, they will soft-pedal Latvia.

On Thursday 26 September, the *Listener*, the BBC's own weekly journal, published a four-page supplement on the Third. In the opening article, Haley promised that it would 'devote to the great works the time they require', and would 'seek every evening to do something that is culturally satisfying and significant'. Next came a piece by Barnes, promising that every night there would be 'a principal item of considerable length demanding sustained attention'. He made a brief allusion to tight resources – 'the limitations imposed by lack of studios, telephone lines and building labour are considerable but should ease as war recedes' – and to the economic necessity of repeating material from other networks, though this would be a boon to 'the busy person' who could not hear it first time round.[3] But the mood of his article was upbeat: 'We hope that from September 29 there will be many broadcasting occasions which you cannot afford to miss.'

Barnes also appealed for contributions to programmes: 'Unless play-wrights and poets, critics and writers, producers and composers can see an opportunity within the scope of the new programme, listeners will not find the stimulus they expect.' This point was also made by the radio correspondent of the *Star*:

> One of the big headaches which face the planners of the BBC's third programme [*sic*], which starts on Sunday, is to find people to write for it.
>   To make radio a more attractive market, officials in charge of the programme propose not to limit works to one performance. It will be possible, therefore, for an author who writes a play for, say, 50 guineas, to receive 150 guineas if his work is repeated twice ... 'There never have been so many demands on the professional writer as today,' said Mr George Barnes, head of the programme. 'We realise it will not be easy to find writers ... '

Meanwhile a debate was going on in the press about the principles

---

[3] The Third Programme's policy of repeating programmes may have been formulated initially for economic reasons, but there were more altruistic motives too. In July 1946 a policy paper by Barnes stated that there would be 'Repeat performances of our own best programmes and the best from other Services'. In November that year, Anthony Lewis wrote that the repetition of performances by the BBC Symphony Orchestra, and the sharing of them with the Home Service, was 'in order to secure a higher proportion of performances to rehearsal' (an economic motive). However, in December 1947 Barnes stated that it was the Third's policy to repeat 'unfamiliar or difficult programmes' so as to help the listener, and eighteen months later Christopher Holme, assistant to the then Controller, wrote that 'the systematic repeating of programmes' was intended to give listeners 'that familiarity which is such an important element in the appreciation of anything new or difficult'. The unpredictable quality of reception also meant that a programme had another chance, quite literally, of being heard.

behind the creation of the Third. *Tribune*, the journal of the left wing of the Labour Party, felt that the network's contribution to 'the cultural and political life of the nation' could be 'tremendous'. It noted that Bertrand Russell was to be given 'the freedom of the air', and that Sartre's *Huis clos* was to be broadcast 'uncensored, although the Lord Chamberlain banned it from the public stage'. Still further to the left, the *Daily Worker* complained about the 'venomously phrased ... anti-Soviet propaganda' in press reports of the clash of wavelengths, and observed that the Third would stand or fall, not by whether it pleased the 'cultural aristocracy', but by the extent to which it could 'attract a mass audience to whom these programmes will be a new experience'.

The *Star*, widely read by that audience, was nervous about so much unadulterated high culture: 'It is to be hoped that the enthusiasts won't overdo it. True, the demand for good music and plays is higher now than ever before. But Wagner and Greek Tragedy digest easier with light seasoning.' *The Times*, on the other hand, welcomed the culture but was worried by putting it in the ghetto of a separate network. It argued that the BBC should be giving everyone programmes of a high standard: 'If the effect of the present experiment is merely to fence off a group of more exacting listeners and encouraging them to ignore, and their special programmes to be ignored by, the general body of listeners, the new programme will not fulfil its high purpose.' To which the politically liberal *News Chronicle* replied, on Saturday 28 September, the day before the first broadcast:

> Criticism of this venture on the ground that it is going to cater only for a small majority of 'highbrows' is both unfair and unimaginative ... We believe that ... many critics and sceptics will be enjoying before long the chance of really solid and worthwhile listening. For our part, we wish the Third Programme the very best of success.
>
> As for the people who don't like the sort of fare that the Third Programme will offer – well, it's a free country and they don't have to listen.

CHAPTER THREE

No time to do anything else
except listen

'This is the BBC Third Programme,' said Patrick Butler, one of the Third's announcers, at precisely 6 pm on Sunday 29 September 1946, into a microphone in one of the drama studios in Broadcasting House. '*How to Listen.* Including how not to, how you ought to, and how you won't. By Stephen Potter and Joyce Grenfell.' Etienne Amyot recalls that it was Leslie Stokes's idea to open the Third with a send-up of highbrow broadcasting. 'He said, "I think we ought to have a laugh at ourselves", and it was he who thought of getting Stephen Potter.'

Potter was on the staff of Features Department. Together with Grenfell, he had already written a string of mildly satirical *How to . . .* programmes for the Home Service, forerunners of his 'Gamesmanship' and 'One-Upmanship' books. Their new script began with an atmosphere of tense excitement:

NARRATOR (*in a hushed tone*): The programme is about to begin. We are rehearsing the opening announcement. The last details are being added. In the studio, last directions from the producer . . . One minute to go . . .

Amyot says there was indeed such a mood as six o'clock approached that evening: 'We were terrified that something might go wrong. I remember George saying to me, before we went on the air, "Well, it'll succeed or it won't."'

In its opening moments, *How to Listen* exposed everyone's anxiety that no one would tune in to the Third. A radio producer, waiting eagerly for his live programme to go on the air, is suddenly granted a dispiriting vision of what is going on in listeners' homes:

NARRATOR: Are they ready? Are they listening? Here, the house is empty – there, the set is switched off – but here, Licence number 865432, Mrs Moss, is she listening?
OLD LADY: Turn up the wireless, Mrs Moss.
MRS MOSS: Yes, dear, it is chilly tonight, let's turn up the wireless a bit . . .

PRODUCER (*anxiously*): Yes, but is she really going to listen?
NARRATOR: On to another radio set. Where are we now? Let's look in at
   the window of Baltimore Gardens.
MAN: It's your call.
WOMAN: I said four clubs.
MAN: Four clubs . . . I say, could we have the radio down a little, please?
WOMAN: Yes, let's have it down a little. It's a bit difficult to concentrate
   on bridge.

This was all too realistic. A survey conducted by the *Daily Telegraph* during
the third evening of the Third gathered these, among other responses:

HOUSEWIFE: Bottling apples when the play started and could not listen.
   Now playing bridge.
BUSINESS MAN: Not the time. I play bridge.

How to Listen went on to poke fun at every kind of BBC cliché, from the
inanities of *Workers' Playtime* on the Light Programme to 'poetic drama'
at its worst. Then, in the final few minutes, it suddenly turned serious,
quoting from *The Anatomy of Melancholy* and Robert Graves on the listening ear, and offering some mock-Shakespearian verse (spoken by Deryck
Guyler) which was presumably thought appropriate to the opening of the
Third: ' . . . Admit me Chorus to this History, / Who, Prologue-like, your
humble patience pray / Gently to hear, kindly to judge our play.'

The *Radio Times* billed *How to Listen* as running from 6 until 6.45 pm,
but it actually under-ran by seven minutes, which would have been
unthinkable on the Home or Light. Such variations from the schedules
characterised the first evening's programmes. 'The timing was slipshod to
say the least,' reported one paper next day. 'Everything started to time, it
is true, but few items finished to time. And the silences! A minute was
common, but the most uneasy lasted from 7.56 until 8 o'clock. This wait
was broken only by a voice which spoke 12 words and then was still – for
three whole minutes.' This voice belonged to Christopher Pemberton, the
fourth member of the Third's announcing team, who was in charge of
'Continuity' that first evening. Continuity announcing – filling the gaps
between programmes, from a special studio manned by an announcer and
an engineer who controlled the network's output – had been instituted by
the BBC during the war, when it was feared that a bomb might put a
programme off the air. Studio S3, an airless box in the sub-basement of
Broadcasting House, had been handed over to the Third after serving as
Continuity Suite for the Forces Programme during the war. Some 'filling'
went on that first evening; the gap after *How to Listen* was bridged by
Pemberton reading from Henry James,[1] which the *Daily Express* found

---

[1] A press report states that Pemberton and Alvar Liddell were both doing Continuity announcing that first evening, but many years later Pemberton told Cormac Rigby that he had read
Henry James as a 'fill' that first night (the choice of author was Leslie Stokes's), and Rigby
thinks it unlikely that two announcers would have been in Continuity. Liddell was probably
introducing the BBC Symphony Orchestra's broadcast from Maida Vale.

'distracting', and a later gap was covered with eight minutes of records[2] – but announcers had been told to leave respectful silences between programmes, and not to imitate the matey presentation style of the other networks.

After *How to Listen* and the James reading came Bach's *Goldberg Variations*, played on the harpsichord by Lucille Wallace, with Marjorie Anderson in the studio to introduce her. The use of a harpsichord for Bach's keyboard works was still a novelty in Britain in 1946. The music critic of the *Birmingham Weekly Post* welcomed it in this broadcast: 'We are likely to forget that the use of a concert grand for early keyboard music is an anachronism, and on this occasion we heard the Variations as Bach himself did.' However, another critic, Philip Hope-Wallace, complained that, because of poor reception, the harpsichord sounded like 'someone distantly thrashing a birdcage'.

Next, at 7.30 pm, came 'Reflections on World Affairs: an address by Field-Marshal the Rt. Hon. J. C. Smuts, CH, FRS, KC, Prime Minister of the Union of South Africa' (the *Radio Times* billed it thus). Etienne Amyot explains the choice of speaker:

> We wanted the Third to be opened by Churchill – again, Haley's idea. And Churchill was approached, but he was very ill. I think I'm right in saying that he had had a stroke or a heart attack – it was all kept very quiet. And so Haley said, 'There's only one other person if we can't get Churchill, and that is Smuts of South Africa.' A very, very great man, rather like Pliny. He was a friend of my mother's, and I was always sent to meet him when he came over here. He gave a marvellous opening address.

While Smuts was speaking, BBC engineers all over the country were listening anxiously to the quality of the signal, especially that radiated from Droitwich on 514.6 metres. The strength of this proved far better than had been feared, despite the drastically reduced power; it was picked up as far south as Bournemouth and as far north as Manchester, and only the report from Exeter mentioned 'cross-talk identified as Latvia'. Next morning's *Times* reported that in London the Droitwich transmission was heard 'very well', and parts of the capital also received the 203.5 metres signal, from local transmitters, 'loud and clear'. Over the country generally, however, 'reception was "patchy", and in certain areas unobtainable'. One bad patch, according to a Manchester newspaper, was in Preston, despite the presence of a temporary mobile transmitter: 'After Field Marshal Smuts had uttered the first ten words of his address his voice stopped suddenly and for three and a half minutes the silence was broken only by atmos-

---

[2] Denys Drower, who was an extra announcer for the Third in the early days, says that Etienne Amyot asked him to pick a Continuity record library of some two hundred discs for stand-by and fill-up purposes. 'What a lovely task! I based many of my choices on my own home library.'

pherics. Then the Field Marshal faded in again with the thread of his argument completely lost.'

Smuts's talk – and the near-silence from Continuity which followed it – brought the Third to 8 pm and its first symphony concert, a broadcast from the BBC's Maida Vale orchestral studio by the BBC Symphony Orchestra, conducted by Sir Adrian Boult. The first item was the national anthem; then came a Festival Overture, commissioned for the occasion from the thirty-two-year-old Benjamin Britten.

Amyot had given Britten and his publisher, Erwin Stein of Boosey & Hawkes, dinner the previous summer, to persuade him to write it. 'It was a sticky dinner,' Amyot reported to Barnes.

> The first half . . . was a tremendous attack against the BBC by Britten which threatened at moments to become quite hysterical. He said he had no faith in the new programme, and that we might for a week or two spend a lot of money and time in trying to get the things we wanted, the service . . . would disintegrate by Christmas and be indistinguishable from either A or B [i.e. Light or Home].

But then he changed his manner and agreed to write the piece.

'It has brilliance,' wrote the music critic of the *Daily Sketch* the morning after the broadcast, 'but is not likely to rank among the composer's important works.' Britten himself seems to have agreed, since he did not allow the overture to be performed again or published during his lifetime (it eventually appeared as *Occasional Overture*). Donald Mitchell, who succeeded Stein as Britten's publisher, conjectures that 'problematic rehearsals' – defective orchestral parts, and Britten's low opinion of Boult – may have been a factor. The overture is a rather lacklustre piece, not remotely equalling his most recent orchestral composition, *The Young Person's Guide to the Orchestra*.

Reviewing the Third's opening concert, *The Times* found no fault with the overture itself, but thought that the technical quality of the broadcast did not give it a fair chance: 'It is impossible to assess critically from the undimensional reduction of it given by radio hearing.' No such reservation was felt about Purcell's *Come Ye Sons of Art*, which (following Handel's *Music for the Royal Fireworks*) concluded the first half of the concert. The soloists included two counter-tenors, Alfred Deller and Charles Whitehead. 'It was a revelation to hear the familiar duet "Sound the Trumpet" sung by voices of this unfamiliar timbre,' wrote *The Times* critic, for Deller's almost single-handed revival of that voice for solo performance had only just begun.

During the interval of the concert, Sir William Haley gave an 'introductory talk' about the Third Programme which was, in effect, its official opening. Most of what he had to say had already been said publicly in the run-up. But he did refer to the wavelength crisis:

> Had our original plan for the Third Programme remained possible we

should have opened with about an 80 per cent coverage and have built up from there. As it is, we have to start with nearly half the listening population uncovered. While we will do all we can to improve the coverage on medium wave, we are pressing on with our plans to develop frequency modulation.

When his fifteen minutes were up, Haley went downstairs to Third Continuity to listen to the remainder of the concert: Vaughan Williams's *Serenade to Music*, Bliss's *Music for Strings* conducted by the composer, and Parry's *Blest Pair of Sirens*. This all-English programme was followed by a heavily scripted discussion (one of the radio genres guyed in *How to Listen*) between 'ex-Servicemen and others', under the title *The World We Fought For*. 'The handful of woolly-minded men discussing . . . around 10 o'clock,' wrote the radio critic of the *Star*, 'were obviously reading it all out and despite careful producing it did not sound real. The Third Programme should be above such posed spontaneity. Why not have a real on-the-spot discussion?' But Haley left Broadcasting House in a contented glow. 'The Third Programme opened at 6 pm,' he wrote in his diary that night. 'At last it is in being. The programme itself promises well; the first six weeks look good.'

*

As the final three programmes were being broadcast that evening – twenty-five minutes of Monteverdi madrigals on gramophone records, conducted by Nadia Boulanger, a repeat of a 1935 talk on London by Sir Max Beerbohm, and '*Epilogue*: readings from the Bible, and organ music' – Fleet Street was preparing its judgements on the birth of the new form of radio. There were some jibes. Noel Whitcomb in the *Daily Mirror* alleged that BBC staff were referring to it as 'Haley's Third Symphony, for orchestra and two listeners', and suggested that the Third would turn the wartime variety show *ITMA* (*It's That Man Again*) into *It Is That Gentleman Once More*. On the other hand the radio correspondent of the *Daily Express* thought that the Third was too much like the existing networks: 'General verdict: Last night's six-hour programme was not all that different from large parts of the First and Second Programmes.'

But most columnists were enthusiastic. 'It would be unjust to offer anything but a very tentative judgement . . . when it is only six hours old,' wrote John Thompson in the *Evening Standard*, yet he went on: 'Personally, I like the look of it.' Cecil Wilson in the *Daily Mail* thought the opening night rather cautious in character: 'It demanded no greater feat of endurance than two hours of choral and orchestral music, with a 15-minute interval . . . and the fragments of talk and music which made up the rest of the evening were easy enough on the ear.' But he warned that 'sterner tests are to come', and he could envisage that people might become 'drastically anti-social' in consequence – 'we might fix a warning light at the front door: "Silence: Third Programme in progress."'

Some of the listeners who wrote to the BBC after the first night's broadcast said much the same. 'It has one drawback,' commented an American woman working at the United States Embassy in London; 'it leaves no time to do anything else except listen and I can see a succession of evenings in which meals will be prepared in ten minutes' time and eaten in five minutes.' An even more exuberant letter came from a doctor in County Cork: 'It was with the utmost expectancy I tuned into 514.6 ... at a little after 6 pm I knew that the Muses had visited and would continue to visit every evening ... Long life to Mr Barnes!' And from Hampshire: 'Today is the high spot in my listening life. Never before have I felt that the BBC gives such excellent value for money as I have felt today ... Keep up this high standard, resist all attempts to commercialise broadcasting, and the public will yet learn to thank you.'

The second night of broadcasting, Monday 30 September, had two highlights. The Third's first 'Public Concert of Chamber Music' was relayed from the Concert Hall of Broadcasting House, with the Griller Quartet playing Sibelius, Bax, Purcell and Matthew Locke, and the BBC Singers performing madrigals. Then came Douglas Cleverdon's production of Milton's *Comus*, with Peggy Ashcroft as the Lady and Dylan Thomas as one of the brothers. The *Manchester Evening News*, conducting a 'vox pop' on the Third a few days later, reported: 'A dress designer said she had never enjoyed anything quite so much as "The Masque of Comus". She voted Dylan Thomas, a new name to her, the most expressive voice in radio.'

The third evening of transmissions was taken up almost entirely by George Bernard Shaw's *Man and Superman*. It began at 6 pm, was punctuated by two interludes – George Thalben-Ball playing organ music by Bach, and a performance of Michael Tippett's *Boyhood's End* – and finished at 11 pm. Listeners had been prepared by a talk broadcast the previous evening by Dean Inge, on Shavian philosophy, and by a full-page article on the play in the *Radio Times*, by Desmond MacCarthy.

It was the longest radio play ever broadcast. Etienne Amyot, who was watching through the window of the control cubicle, remembers the actor Sebastian Shaw, who was playing Tanner, breathing heavily towards the end and undoing his shirt. 'But he was absolutely marvellous,' says Amyot.

> Certain well-known actors whom I won't name – they've all been knighted since – were beastly about him because they wanted the part themselves, I imagine. But Val Gielgud was certain he'd be dead right for it. And he was. The cast brought the play completely to life. It fascinated me so much that a few days later, when I went down to the country, I read it right through again. And we repeated it the night after the first broadcast, not because we wanted to save money, but so people could have a second chance to take it in.

The production of *Man and Superman* was discussed extensively in the press – not the quality of the performances, which was taken for granted, but the question of whether listeners should be given five scarcely diluted hours of Shaw on one evening. (These, it should be remembered, were the days before portable radios were common, and the household wireless set was usually an immovable object, placed by the sitting-room fireside. Nor were meals on trays a part of the middle-class lifestyle in 1946.) '*Man and Superman* riveted listeners to their chairs,' declared one of the popular radio critics, Jonah Barrington,[3] 'to the exclusion of meals and front-door bells ... ' But he complained that the intervals were too short: 'I challenge any housewife – male or female – to get a meal cooked and eaten and cleared in 40 minutes. I tried it myself and it can't be done. Give us an hour.' Another columnist, John Farrell, thought the length of the play was 'thoroughly justified', and added: 'Shaw makes not only good theatre and cinema, but also good radio.' The *Irish Times* critic thought that the broadcast 'raises the question of how long the radio can hold an audience', and suspected that *Man and Superman* had made 'a very sticky evening's listening' – but admitted that he hadn't even turned it on himself, and would like to hear from readers who had. Replying to this, a man from Waterford wrote that he had 'listened to the whole five hours of it' with his wife and a friend, and knew of five others in the town who had also heard it, and 'had enjoyed it'.

However, the *Daily Telegraph* received a reader's letter which suggested that the Third Programme was giving 'undue importance to length ... the medium of broadcasting does not lend itself to such prolonged programmes'. *Cavalcade* magazine gave a satirical glimpse of the Third's staff planning such extended broadcasts:

> These radio-mystique men may be seen any afternoon of the week in certain taverns around and about London's Broadcasting House ... [dressed in] the flowering hand-woven tie, the inescapable patterned shirt, and the delicately contrasted rugged countrified jacket and manly trousers ... A writer approached the programme-arranger and offered him a script running for 45 minutes. The answer was: 'I say, old man, couldn't you make it last longer?'

*

A broadcast by the Paris Conservatoire Orchestra (then visiting London) on Thursday 3 October, the fifth night of the Third, was spoilt for at least one Scottish listener, who reported that Roussel's Third Symphony had been interrupted by 'the unseemly entrance of the Queen of Sheba'. Ten minutes passed before 'this lady and the stentorian baritone who followed in her train' had disappeared – presumably back to Soviet Latvia. No such interference interrupted a relay from a London theatre of Donizetti's *Don Pasquale*, in Italian, by the New London Opera Company, on Friday 4 October. But the same listener – the radio critic of a Scottish newspaper –

---

[3] Jonah Barrington was the pseudonym of Cyril Dalmaine, who had been a BBC conductor in the 1930s.

was still discontented: 'The ... performance ... seemed to be full of sparkle. But it raised for me the old argument about opera in a foreign tongue. Perhaps listeners to the Third Programme are expected to know Italian. But if the BBC is going to keep its promise of an opera week, listeners are going to have to know French, German, and Czechoslovakian [*sic*] in order to avoid my sense of frustration.'

An English translation was used for Sartre's *Huis clos*, broadcast the same evening as *Don Pasquale*, under the title *Vicious Circle*. The cast were from a recent London production: Alec Guinness, Beatrix Lehmann, Betty Ann Davies and Donald Pleasance, directed by the twenty-one-year-old Peter Brook. This had been staged under 'club' regulations at the Arts Theatre, since the Lord Chamberlain would not licence it for public performance. The BBC had decided it was outside his jurisdiction. '*Huis clos* was banned by the censor as being highly indecent,' recalls Etienne Amyot, 'and I did have a great argument about it. But that was solved by Haley, who said, '"Put it on, and see what happens."'

The interval talk between Acts 2 and 3 of *Don Pasquale* was given by a young Oxford history don, Alan Bullock, who had worked in the BBC European Service during the war. He welcomed the arrival of the Third, but was not impressed by George Barnes: 'He was quite an able administrator, but I didn't think that he had a great deal of interest in, or knowledge of, the arts and literature and so on, or even international affairs. I had him to a meeting in my house, with Isaiah Berlin, Herbert Hart, Freddie Ayer, one or two others, and he was totally out of his depth.'

The first week of the Third came to an end with a BBC Symphony Orchestra concert in which Sir Adrian Boult conducted a Mozart symphony, and then yielded the rostrum to Zoltán Kodály, then visiting London. He had conducted the first English performance of his *Missa brevis* on the Thursday evening; now the Symphony Orchestra gave another English première, of his Concerto for Orchestra.

'Every evening,' observed the music critic of the *Birmingham Weekly Post* at the end of the first seven days of transmissions, 'has offered something that must be quite new to the majority of listeners.' The *Irish Times* radio critic judged that the Third 'has not been as pretentiously high-class as many people feared'. A Belfast paper, the *Northern Whig*, was relieved that the Third 'does not force culture – a word detested by the British because of its associations, one supposes, with Kultur – down listeners' throats'. And a young RAF officer serving in Lincolnshire wrote to the BBC: 'For the first time I can spend an interesting and intellectually invigorating evening by the radio ... I especially appreciated the "Contemporary Music and the Listener" survey broadcast on Saturday. This has helped me to reorientate my approach to the subject.' The letter was from John Stonehouse, later to become Postmaster-General, fake evidence of his own death, and be imprisoned for fraud.

The Third's evident success began to raise the question of why the British were frightened of becoming highbrow. The *Newcastle Journal* reported a recent public speech by Haley: 'It is lamentable,' he had said, 'but the surest way to increase the number of listeners is to debase the standards.' The paper commented:

> There it is. We are, in general, a low-brow rather than a high-brow people ... For this it would be foolish to condemn the present generation. Most of them left school at 14, with no foundations for high standards. They have lived through the frenzied, frantic years of two mighty convulsions; and between those two cataclysms were the constant snarlings and thunder-rumblings of an uneasy armed truce ... Sir William Haley's statement ought to shock us into action which will at least mend matters. We should aim, at least, at being soundly-based middle-brow people, with aspirations towards higher planes.

The young music critic Desmond Shawe-Taylor, writing in the *New Statesman* a week after the Third had begun its task, did not concern himself with brows. 'I wonder,' he wrote,

> if music-producers and music-consumers realise how profoundly the whole musical landscape is likely to be transformed by the arrival of the Third Programme ... An immense profusion of public music-making now spills all over London, but a great deal of it consists of vain and endless repetition of a handful of works: I mean the Beethoven–Tchaikovsky–Grieg–Rachmaninov concertos, the Beethoven–Brahms–Tchaikovsky symphonies, and so on ... But consider the listener whose tastes are more catholic or sophisticated ... By dint of going through the Saturday concert announcements with a tooth-comb, he discovers a small number of concerts at which there is to be heard something which is good but seldom given, or something new ...
>
> One or two series of concerts actually cater for this ... off-the-beaten-track kind of taste: for example, the Boyd Neel concerts at Chelsea [and] the Morley College cycle ... But what I have seen ... of the Third Programme's musical plans ... is quite enough to dazzle the eyes ... As far as I can see, for critic and concert-going public alike, the importance of broadcast music is not only catching up with that of the 'live' article, but threatening to shoot well ahead.

A senior member of the BBC Music Department, Julian Herbage, in a 1946 article, gives the same impression of the triteness of repertoire in London concerts at this time, adding that they were 'given almost invariably with insufficient rehearsal and sometimes by indifferent conductors'.

The *Spectator* carried an editorial about the Third, which judged that the first few days had given 'a very pleasing impression ... of *embarras de richesse*'; this was 'a refreshing contrast to the old BBC vices of timidity and monotony ... At the moment everything remains in favour of the Third Programme.' Was there already an ominous note in that 'at the moment'?

CHAPTER 4

Combat psychology

The BBC began to wake up to the existence of its new child. One of
the first letters of congratulation came from a member of the Variety
Department, who saw the potential for humour in the Third; he wanted
it to 'develop something new in radio entertainment ... to reflect the
impact of contemporary life on a witty intelligent person'. The radio critic
Jonah Barrington had the same idea – could not the Third revive the 'lost
art ... of political satire ... Surely a few delicate chuckles about Mr Herbert
Morrison or Mr Aneurin Bevan ... ?' *Personal Points*, a 'light revue' on the
Third, featuring Joyce Grenfell and Arthur Marshall (19 October 1946),
had a go at this – and managed only a tentative sketch about the political
neutrality of the Irish Republic, which offended nobody. Meanwhile the
Third was itself becoming the butt of popular jokes. A *New Statesman*
competition in November 1946 challenged readers to compose an ode to
George Barnes. This was one of the winning entries:

> You, being more appropriately armed,
>> In your own way are striving to surpass
> Samson, who, with the jawbone of an ass,
>> Only laid low a thousand Philistines.

A cartoon in *Punch* on 4 December, alluding to the Third's frequent over-
runs and under-runs (as compared to the strictly timed Home Service,
with its regional variations), showed a musician emerging from the studio
and being admonished by the producer: 'Oh, by the way, Mr Pontifex,
you finished absolutely exactly at nine-thirty – don't you think that's just
a trifle regional?'

After two days of broadcasting, the Third's announcers had been told
by Leslie Stokes that '*no* apology should be made after an over-run for the
late start of the next programme item. It is part of our policy to allow
every broadcast to run its full required length ... ' But there were limits.
'I did feel that the ten-minute over-run of *Music Anthology* on Saturday
night was rather a lot,' Stokes remonstrated to Anthony Lewis, who had
compiled it. On 14 December there was a twelve-minute over-run in a
talk by the pianist Peter Stadlen on *Schönberg and the Twelve-Note Scale*,

preceding a live public concert.[1] The producer complained that the orchestra and audience 'rather strongly resented being kept sitting there'. A week later, there were so many over-runs that the Third closed down half an hour late, at half-past midnight. The philosopher Bernard Williams, who was listening to the Third in 1946 as a schoolboy, says that the chaotic timings added to the air of discovery. 'You tuned in to listen to one thing, and found yourself hearing something completely different. So it didn't simply fortify people's existing tastes.'

Modern music could be heard in profusion. Between October and Christmas 1946, notable performances included: Hindemith's *Ludus tonalis* played by Noel Mewton-Wood (23 October); Eugene Goossens conducting the first performance of his Second Symphony (2 November); Poulenc's Sextet for piano and winds (3 December); Honegger's *Symphonie liturgique* (7 December); and Stravinsky's *Symphony in Three Movements* (21 December). The last three were first English performances. During these three months there were also no less than seven programmes of Schoenberg (including *Gurrelieder*), and Berg could be heard quite frequently.

John Stonehouse's letter had praised the talks series *Contemporary Music and the Listener*. One of the first speakers in it (12 October 1946) was Michael Tippett, whose Third String Quartet had its first broadcast on 29 October. In his talk, Tippett gave a general survey of the contemporary music scene, introducing pieces by Bartók, Berg, Stravinsky, Hindemith and Gershwin. 'I had met Tippett before the war,' says Etienne Amyot,

> when I had given a recital of an unknown French composer – I can't remember the name – and I got a letter from Poulenc, and another from somebody I'd never heard of, called Tippett. He came to see me, and I liked him enormously. I knew none of his music, and he gave me a piece to play, but I had too much other work to learn. But when the Third started, I introduced him to George, and they got on awfully well, and Tippett did a lot of talks.

Barnes was slightly critical of Tippett's talk on contemporary music – 'you packed too much information into the time' – but wanted him to give another broadcast, asking him to expand some remarks he had made about achieving intensity in the performance of Purcell. They met to discuss this. Meanwhile *Contemporary Music and the Listener* also brought to the microphone Mátyás Seiber, on Bartók's string quartets (28 December 1946), and Nadia Boulanger, on 'Stravinsky and Neo-Classicism' (2 November 1946). On the same day she also conducted her own ensemble in a concert of early and contemporary French music.

---

[1] Stadlen, born in Vienna in 1910 and resident in Britain from 1935, became known as an expositor of Schoenberg and Webern, and was frequently heard playing their works on the Third, to the extent that Music Department eventually felt he was being over-used in this capacity. In the late 1950s, when the rest of the British music world had finally come round to serialism, he made a public rejection of it.

On 14 December, John Betjeman made his first broadcast on the Third: a talk on Evelyn Waugh, in the series *Living Writers*. He described Waugh as a consummate user of the English language, and read a passage from *Vile Bodies*; but Waugh himself, who had borrowed his butler's wireless set to listen, was not pleased: 'Too much of it was quotation.' Betjeman had worked for George Barnes in Talks, and by 1946 was almost a member of Barnes's family. He addressed Barnes as 'the Commander' – an allusion to his failed hopes of entering the Navy – and signed many letters to him in the *persona* of Basil Nicolls, who was such an irritant to the Third. Barnes's son Anthony, then a schoolboy, recalls these family jokes: 'My father certainly could have a very commanding manner. My parents were both fairly austere intellectuals, and John was full of fun. I begged them to invite him every holidays, which they did – I think he found them immensely helpful during the difficult time that Penelope, his wife, was becoming a Roman Catholic.'

Besides Betjeman on Waugh, the *Living Writers* series included V. S. Pritchett on George Orwell, Rose Macaulay on E. M. Forster, and Geoffrey Grigson on Wyndham Lewis. In other literary talks, Ralph Partridge recalled Lytton Strachey, and George Rylands read from John Donne. Anne Ridler, who took part in the Third's early poetry programmes, recalls that the poetry editor, Patric Dickinson, told speakers to pronounce Donne's name as 'Don' on the Home Service but 'Dun' on the Third.

In a series called *The Poet and the Critic*, on 7 November 1946, a combative Edith Sitwell swept aside Henry Reed's mild doubts about some of her recent work: 'Mr Reed ... after speaking most generously ... complains that some of my longer poems ... suffer seriously from excessive diffusion of energy ... Now, to me, these latest poems are among the best I have written ... ' Sitwell was enthusiastic about radio, and offered the Features producer Rayner Heppenstall a script for his proposed series of *Imaginary Conversations* between famous characters in history (based on Landor's *Imaginary Conversations of Literary Men and Statesmen*). Her suggestion was an exchange between William Harvey, discoverer of the circulation of the blood, and King Charles I, while Graham Greene proposed to introduce Henry James to Edgar Wallace. Neither of these scripts materialised, but thirty programmes in the series were eventually broadcast over the next few years. Rose Macaulay portrayed John Milton arguing with two Scottish Covenanters, Herbert Read imagined Hamlet talking to the pirate captain who had rescued him from the ship carrying him towards his death in England, and 'Michael Innes' (J. I. M. Stewart) pitted Samuel Johnson against Lord Monboddo, who had anticipated Darwin's discovery that man was descended from the apes.

Science and current affairs were covered by short talks, but the programme which made most impact in both these subjects was a reading in four instalments (14–17 October 1946) of John Hersey's *Hiroshima*, a chilling report on the experiences of survivors of the atomic bomb, which had been published in the *New Yorker* four weeks before the Third began.

'It is the most terrifying series of broadcasts I have ever heard,' wrote the critic of the *Daily Express*.

Three weeks later, the Third broadcast a sixty-minute documentary by Nesta Pain on atomic energy (6 November 1946). But most Features Department contributions that first autumn were literary. Indeed, many were plays – the dividing line between Features and Drama was almost non-existent. Stephen Potter made a radio adaptation of Nevill Coghill's modern English version of some of the *Canterbury Tales* – which had been specially commissioned by the Third – for a series which began on 21 October,[2] and the next night listeners heard the first programme on the Third by Louis MacNeice, *The Careerist: a psycho-morality play.*

MacNeice had been on the staff of Features, as a writer and producer, since the early months of the war, and had created some memorable programmes, among them *Christopher Columbus*, with Laurence Olivier and a William Walton score for the BBC Symphony Orchestra, and *The Dark Tower*, with music by Benjamin Britten. Michael Bakewell, who worked with MacNeice in his later BBC years, describes these and other typical MacNeice scripts as fast-moving quest-stories, in which 'you don't know half the time whether you're in reality or unreality'.

In *The Dark Tower*, broadcast on the Home Service nine months before the Third began, one of the exotic characters who detains the hero from his quest is called 'The Soak'. He may have been inspired by the heavy drinking of some of the Features staff and their hangers-on. The actor Denys Hawthorn recalls that

> the George, near the BBC in Great Portland Street, was a kind of university of life. You would have met Louis MacNeice, Francis 'Jack' Dillon, Donald McWhinnie (a very distinguished radio producer and later theatre director), and of course lots of writers, people like Julian Maclaren Ross and Laurie Lee. It was a place to go, and if you came to London you would make a beeline for the George.

In his autobiography, Rayner Heppenstall provides a *Who's Who* of the department, as seen in the bar of another BBC pub, the Stag's Head in New Cavendish Street (opposite Rothwell House where Features Department worked). Regulars there included Terence Tiller, Jack Dillon, D. G. Bridson, and Heppenstall himself. Bridson admired Ezra Pound and looked rather like him (bearded, in a green corduroy jacket); the others were uniformly tousled, 'none of us getting his hair cut regularly'. They would stay in the Stag (as it was known for short) until closing time at three o'clock, and then troop back across the road 'with the beer running out of our ears'.

Heppenstall says that even in this company, MacNeice stood out as a drinker. 'Louis's characteristic facial expressions, however, were not

---

[2] A second series was broadcast in 1949. In 1951 Penguin published Coghill's text, which became a bestseller and brought Chaucer to innumerable modern readers.

reassuring even when he was sober.' Denys Hawthorn describes him as looking like 'a highly intelligent horse, one of Swift's Houyhnhnms', and adds:

> He would take instant dislikes to people. We were all in the bar one day, and he kept on looking at a man who was nothing to do with us, and saying, 'I don't like the look of that fellow at all.' And the actor Patrick Magee, who was with us, said, 'Well, let's face it, Louis, you're not exactly the norm yourself.' And for some reason or other that upset him terribly. He seemed to think that he wasn't noticeable. But he was!

W. H. Auden (himself a heavy drinker) told Stephen Spender he thought MacNeice had become an alcoholic through the custom of everyone in these BBC drinking groups having to buy a round, 'and if there are twelve people, this means you have twelve drinks!' But Michael Bakewell emphasises that the drinking did not impede the programme-making. 'The fact that you might have recruited your cast in the George that lunchtime gave the whole thing a kind of added spirit – in more senses than one. I don't think it would be tolerated in the BBC now, but then it was felt that this free-and-easy life they were living was the medium out of which their creativity came.' Douglas Cleverdon, arguably the finest and most creative producer in Features, has said much the same: 'The pubs were important. We were very relaxed there. And it meant that if an idea cropped up, it could be discussed and developed in the pub. We never saw people in offices. There was no formality. It was one community.'

The Careerist, written and produced by MacNeice and broadcast on the Third on 22 October 1946, presents the life of a modern Everyman, James Human, largely through different voices inside his own head. He becomes a successful publisher, but is destroyed by his lust for power and money. A week later, on 29 October, the Third broadcast MacNeice's translation of the _Agamemnon_, produced by Val Gielgud. Then on 3 December came MacNeice's _Enemy of Cant_, subtitled 'A panorama of Aristophanic comedy'. MacNeice himself produced, the music was by Antony Hopkins, and Aristophanes was played by Dylan Thomas, who had taken a small part in _The Careerist_.

Seven years younger than MacNeice, and with four books of poems to his name, Dylan Thomas depended heavily on the BBC for cash. He had been broadcasting since 1936, having realised that it was less of a chore than literary journalism. He was a natural for radio. John Arlott, who produced poetry readings for the Far Eastern Service of the BBC, describes him at the microphone: 'He would stand, feet apart and head thrown back, a dead cigarette frequently adhering wispily to his lower lip, curls a little tousled and eyes half-closed, barely reading the poetry by eye, but rather understanding his way through it, one arm beating out a sympathetic double rhythm as he read.' Etienne Amyot says that Thomas 'used to come into my office and ask me for half a crown because he wanted a drink. He could be enchanting.' Thomas wrote to a friend that he was now scraping a living in 'the thin puce belfries of the Third Programme'.

The first script he wrote for the Third was a talk entitled *Holiday Memory*, broadcast on 26 October 1946. It began:

> August Bank Holiday. A tune on an ice-cream cornet. A slap of sea and a tickle of sand. A fanfare of sunshades opening. A wince and a whinny of bathers dancing into deceptive water. A tuck of dresses. A rolling of trousers. A compromise of paddlers. A sunburn of girls and a lark of boys. A silent hullabaloo of balloons.
>
> I remember the sun telling lies in a shell held to my ear for a whole harmonious, hollow minute by a small, wet girl in an enormous bathing suit marked 'Corporation Property'.
>
> I remember sharing the last of my moist buns with a boy and a lion. Tawny and savage, with cruel nails and capacious mouth, the little boy tore and devoured. Wild as seedcake, ferocious as a hearthrug, the depressed and verminous lion nibbled like a mouse at his half a bun, and hiccupped in the sad dusk of his cage ...

The next evening, 26 October, Thomas was one of the readers of Edith Sitwell's poetry in *The Poet and the Critic*. He arranged a selection of Pope's works for Mary O'Farrell to read on 14 November; and five nights later he was heard as Private Dai Jones in Douglas Cleverdon's production of David Jones's *In Parenthesis*.

Cleverdon, a rare-bookseller who had joined the BBC before the war when his Bristol business was hit by the slump, had known David Jones since the late 1920s, and had commissioned him to illustrate a limited edition of *The Ancient Mariner*.[3] For some years, Cleverdon had wanted to broadcast *In Parenthesis*, Jones's epic about the First World War, which he believed would be more comprehensible on the air than on the printed page. The Third now gave him the opportunity.

In Parenthesis was repeated on 11 November 1948, with the young Richard Burton now in the cast as Private Thomas. Reviewing a biography of Dylan Thomas in 1965, Burton recalled his extraordinary performance on that occasion:

> Dylan as an actor and as an explosive dynamic performing force was a dangerous rival for other actors, as I know, for I worked with him a few times or several, and once for instance a director [Cleverdon] said to him, we were rehearsing a radio play at the time, Dylan will you take the words 'Mam! Mam!' and scream them for me; you understand that you are dying in No Mans Land, and when you hear the Royal Welsh [*sic*] sing, I will give you a cue light and then scream for me woodjew there's a good chap. And the Royal Welsh did sing in this rehearsal, it was a record of course,

---

[3] Cleverdon also knew Eric Gill, and Richard Ingrams describes him at a Gill exhibition, peering at a drawing of male private parts, and remarking: 'Good Lord, I think that's me.'

and they sang of what you could see from the hills above Jerusalem, and was in the minor key and sad as the devil or death, and the green light flickered, and Dylan short, bandy, prime, obese and famous among the bars screamed as I have never heard, but sometimes imagined a scream, and we were all appalled, our pencils silent above the crossword puzzles, and invisible centuries-gone atavistic hair rose on our backs. And there was a funny silence and Dylan said that he'd bet I couldn't do that scream like that with a cigarette in his mouth and I shook off all the centuries, stopped staring, smiled a little, noted that he had indeed monumentally screamed with a cigarette in his mouth and went stunned back to my crossword.

In his long poem *Autumn Sequel*, Louis MacNeice describes Thomas's voice as containing

> A whole masque
> Of tones and cadences – the organ boom,
> The mimicry, then the chuckles.

A week after *In Parenthesis,* on 28 November, Thomas read a selection of Blake on the Third, and two days later, in the *Living Writers* series, he gave a talk on the prose of Walter de la Mare:

How many of the nasty ghosts, from the other side of the razor's edge, from the wrong room, from the chockablock grave, from the trespassing hereafter, from the sly holes, crawl over and into the seedy waiting-rooms, the creeping railway carriages, the gas-lamped late Victorian teashops the colour of stewed tea, where down-at-soul strangers contrive their tales and, drop by drop, leak out the shadows of their grey or black, forlorn, and vaguely infernal secrets. The ghosts of Mr de la Mare, though they reek and scamper, and, in old houses, at the proper bad hours, are heard sometimes at their infectious business, are not for you to see. But there is no assurance that they do not see you.

Yet another poet who was on the BBC staff at this time, Roy Campbell, calls Thomas 'the best all-round reader of verse that I ever produced'. Campbell had discovered that, though all the pubs around Broadcasting House opened at 11.30 am (this being the ruling of the magistrates in St Marylebone district), those in St Pancras district could legally commence business thirty minutes earlier. He therefore persuaded a landlord of a pub within two hundred yards of the BBC that the district boundary ran straight through his premises, and that it was legal to serve alcohol at 11 am if customers stood on one side of it. 'It was in his pub that Dylan and I arranged all our poetry programmes ... I used to keep him on beer all day till he had done his night's work and then take him down to the Duty Room where the charming Miss Backhouse or Miss Tofield would pour us a treble whisky as a reward for our labours.' (The Duty Room, on the ground floor of Broadcasting House, was the home of the Duty Officer, whose functions ranged from fielding telephone calls from irate listeners to providing hospitality for distinguished broadcasters.)

Campbell records one occasion when this liquid diet became too much for Thomas's performance:

> I ... found Dylan snoring in front of the mike with only twenty seconds left. He was slumped back in his chair, with an almost seraphic expression of blissful peace. I shook him awake ... [He] was almost sober when he got the green light, though he did bungle the title as *Ode on Shaint Sheshilia's Day;* but after that his voice cleared up and I began to breathe again. When he had finished reading the *Ode* I got another fright: he began to beckon me wildly with his arms and point to the page before him. I got the engineer to switch off the mike and slipped into the studio again. Dylan had forgotten how to pronounce 'Religio Laici'. I told him and slipped out. He had about three shots at it, bungled it, gave it up; and then went on reading. The next day I was hauled up in front of George Barnes, but he was a good boss and had a sense of humour. I promised to keep an eye on Dylan: Dylan promised me to keep an eye on himself – and he kept his word.

Thomas was paid well for his broadcasts, but had usually squandered most of it by the time he got back to his wife Caitlin and their children, who had been given a temporary home in Oxford (in a summerhouse on the banks of the Cherwell) by A. J. P. Taylor and his wife. Sometimes he even hired a car to take him home. His drinking, of course, continued when he got there. 'Had a good Christmas?' he wrote to Roy Campbell after they had been working together on the Third for some while. 'My inside feels like a flooded tin-mine.'

*

Douglas Cleverdon's wife Nest says that her husband was always keen to match a writer with the right composer. Elizabeth Poston provided the score for *In Parenthesis*, while Louis MacNeice commissioned Elisabeth Lutyens to write music for his script *Enter Caesar*, first broadcast in the Home Service in September 1946, and repeated on the Third in November. Lennox Berkeley was chosen for Patric Dickinson's dramatisation of Book 3 of the *Iliad*, with a cast which included the boy actor David Spenser as one of the Trojan children. 'That was for Val Gielgud, in Studio 8,' recalls Spenser half a century later. 'Helen was played by the most beautiful woman I'd ever seen – Margaret Leighton. I remember we had a break between rehearsal and transmission, and she went home and came back in a black evening dress.'

On 8 December 1946, Spenser played the lead in *Panic* by Paul Dehn, billed as 'A radio allegory concerning the adventures of a schoolboy who loved beauty and hated pedants'. Spenser recalls: 'It was a lovely script. A place in Greece is becoming a popular beauty-spot, and the boy decides to stop that. He dresses up as a faun, and jumps out at the tourists, hoping to frighten them away. But huge crowds come, and it's in all the newspapers. And the boy realises that he's harmed the place, and decides to return to his own clothing. But he can't. He's become a faun.'

Panic was written well in advance of transmission, but Spenser says that many programmes were assembled at the last minute:

> Sometimes the script was written during the day – this was true sometimes of Douglas Cleverdon's features, and Jack Dillon's. It was practically making it up as you went along. Louis MacNeice would be writing in the morning a fairy story in which I'd be playing a prince, live that afternoon. But the people who'd been in the wartime BBC Drama Repertory Company were brilliant sight-readers, and it never worried them.

In those pre-stereo days, few instructions had to be given about positions in the studio. Everyone crowded around the front and back of the big microphones, 'though if you were with Sir Donald Wolfit,' says David Spenser, 'he was on one side of the mike, and everyone else was on the other!' One producer, Howard Rose, made actors mark their scripts with coloured pencils – 'yellow for emotion,' says Spenser, 'red for getting excited, and there were purples and greens. By the time he'd finished, I didn't know what I was doing. But about halfway through transmission, he would get up, put on his coat, doff his hat through the window to the cast, and go off – he had to catch his last train home! And suddenly the acting style changed; everyone had been freed!'

If a play was over-running during a live transmission, the producer would have to creep into the studio and indicate drastic cuts. Spenser remembers a production of Maeterlinck's *The Blue Bird* in which he was playing the boy; Felix Felton, the producer, 'suddenly burst in, and pointed a pencil at the end of the speech I was saying. So I stopped there. He then turned over *nine* pages of my script, and pointed again – and I went on.' Actors frequently had to cover for others' lapses. Spenser recalls one elderly lady picking up her handbag and departing during a broadcast, in the belief that she had finished – whereas Spenser knew she had lines in the last scene. 'I was signalling to everyone to stop her. But she went, and Sybil Thorndike got up and played the last scene for her.'

Even without mishaps, the nervous strain of broadcasting an elaborate drama or feature was considerable. 'A sort of combat psychology was brought into play,' writes Rayner Heppenstall.

> There might have been as many as seven or eight microphones ... to say nothing of eight gramophone turn-tables [and] a conductor taking, on headphones, upwards of twenty cues, with an orchestra, a choir and solo singers with whom he would have spent a maximum of three hours, never having seen his score (or they their parts) until that day. As the routine of

'tone', 'level',[4] synchronisation of clocks, listening to the end of the previous programme from another studio which might not even be in London, the flickering red light, the steady red, the first green light,[5] was gone through, it hardly seemed possible that the next hour and a half should proceed without mishap. The build-up of excitement was extreme, the unwinding afterwards at once happy and draining, the let-down during the next few days deflating.

*

From 1926 to 1936, the BBC had broadcast a fifteen-minute five-days-a-week series called *The Foundations of Music*, intended to educate listeners in the basic classical repertoire and some less well-known works. It was decided that the Third should take over this function – though not the *Foundations* title – and a week after the network had begun to broadcast, Barnes sent Haley a chart 'which will show how we are tackling this material in the first eight weeks'. It listed performances of Bach, Mozart, Haydn, Schubert and Beethoven, as well as music under the headings '16th Century Choral', 'Romantic', 'Song Cycles' and 'Contemporary'. Barnes explained to Haley:

> In a few cases we follow the old Foundations method of making concerts out of a number of the same kinds of work by the same composer, e.g. the Mozart pianoforte sonatas, the Haydn quartets, but in most cases we are building varied programmes from these works without losing sight of the overall plan which is to play e.g. the whole of Bach's keyboard music in our first year or eighteen months.

Haley wrote on this memo: 'Good. I think when running series such as the Mozart sonatas, piano concertos etc, we should announce all the dates in the R[adio] T[imes] as soon as possible.' Desmond Shawe-Taylor said much the same in *Picture Post* at the end of November 1946: could the Third 'let us know as far as possible ahead (perhaps in a monthly pamphlet?) the principal dates on the menu'.

In fact from the issue of 22 November, the *Radio Times* had begun to print highlights in the Third for several weeks ahead, showing many of Barnes's plans coming to fruition. Music programmes previewed in this fashion included Bach's *Christmas Oratorio*, spread over a number of evenings before Christmas; the same composer's unaccompanied cello suites, played by Pierre Fournier (14, 18 and 19 January 1947); Purcell's *Dido and Aeneas*, with Joan Cross as Dido, conducted by Constant Lambert (4 and 5 January); Winter Promenade Concerts from the Royal Albert Hall,

---

[4] 'Tone' is the note A (440 cycles), generated electronically in the studio control desk; it is used to set the 'level' (volume) of the studio output and recording equipment.

[5] The red light, operated from Continuity in the case of a live programme, flickers to warn the studio that it is about to come on the air, then goes steady when it does. Green lights give cues to individual performers.

including (on 17 January) the first performance of Patrick Hadley's cantata *The Hills*; Solomon beginning a series of recitals of all the Beethoven piano sonatas (19 January); Renata Borgatti playing Bach's *Well-Tempered Clavier* (from 21 January); two studio performances of Handel's opera *Admetus*, conducted by Stanford Robinson (1 and 2 February); the Concertgebouw Orchestra performing Bruckner's Seventh Symphony (15 February);[6] and Simon Goldberg and Stefan Askenasa playing the complete violin sonatas of Beethoven (from 16 February). Drama highlights included a Christmas Day broadcast of Christopher Hassall's verse play *Christ's Comet*; Tyrone Guthrie's production of Tennyson's *Queen Mary* (8 January); and George Orwell's own adaptation of *Animal Farm* (14 January).

Shawe-Taylor also pleaded: 'Repeat, even more than you do already, especially what is new and unfamiliar; and warn us that you are going to do so, and when.' George Barnes was of the same opinion. 'My own inclination,' he wrote to Anthony Lewis at the end of the Third's first month of broadcasting,

> reinforced daily by requests from within and without the Corporation, is to arrange in January/March [1947] for much of the music that we do to be given a second performance ... Obviously you will plan repeats of new works, and are arranging for rarely heard music to be heard again ... but we would like to go further than this and if possible to repeat up to 50% of our output ... We should want 'live' repeat performances but on occasion we would take recorded repeats rather than miss a second per-formance ... Don't worry about not getting in all the works which you want performed in the Third Programme since we are prepared to plan over a period of three years if necessary.

Anthony Lewis himself believed in even longer-term planning. In a lengthy document headed 'Music in the Third Programme', dated 25 November 1946, he observed that in order to carry out all the Third's musical objectives – that is, to broadcast all the music worth hearing – 'it would be as well to view the task in terms of a five, or even seven year plan. It should not be thought that seven years will suffice for a complete survey of the repertoire, but some such period will serve as a convenient guide.' He suggested that 'the *complete* Beethoven quartets might well appear every three months, the *complete* Haydn quartets every year and the *complete* Bach cantatas every seven years'.

In this document, Lewis reported on the Third's present musical resources, observing that 'the main source of opera' would for some time to come still be 'the permanent continental organisations'. He added: 'Studio Opera has hardly got into its stride yet, but when the question of internal and external orchestral resources is satisfactorily settled, it should be possible to mount important productions under increasingly propitious conditions.' In fact the Third had already mounted its first studio opera.

[6] This was cancelled when the Third went off the air in February 1947; see below, pp. 52–3.

Sir Thomas Beecham conducted *Tristan und Isolde* in German on 24 October 1946, between 6 and 10.45 pm, with a live repeat four days later. Arthur Carron sang Tristan and Marjorie Lawrence was Isolde. Etienne Amyot recalls a last-minute crisis:

> At two o'clock in the afternoon, Tommy said he wasn't going to conduct, and Tony Lewis said, 'What on earth are we going to do?' And I said, 'We're going to go and see him.' He was living in St John's Wood. And we won him round. He was just having a tantrum. He conducted marvellously. It was very exciting to hear that music, which one hadn't heard for six or seven years in this country.

Beecham was back to conduct *Die Walküre* in the studio on 18 December 1946. Lewis observed that, on account of their political overtones, 'the great Wagnerian operas . . . seem unlikely to reenter the normal continental repertoire for some considerable time'; hence the Third's initiative. There was also a studio production of Britten's new opera *The Rape of Lucretia* on 11 October 1946, with Kathleen Ferrier, Peter Pears and Joan Cross, conducted by Reginald Goodall.

Despite the Third's frequent use of guest conductors, Boult – who also took the baton for two or three Home Service orchestral programmes each week – was heard most weeks conducting Third Programme symphony concerts. Haley acknowledges that 'the Third Programme would never have got going without Adrian Boult. He would play anything that was put before him. The most avant-garde stuff, the most hackneyed stuff. And he would give it every time an honest, careful, professional performance.' The programme for a Third Programme Saturday evening public concert conducted by Boult at the People's Palace in East London,[7] on 14 December 1946 (the broadcast delayed by Peter Stadlen's over-run), bears out Haley's observation: Beethoven's *Prometheus* ballet music was followed by Alan Rawsthorne's First Piano Concerto and Bartók's *Deux images*.

This People's Palace series was a bold experiment – the publicity and administration were expensive to the BBC – and was mounted despite George Barnes's dislike of hearing an audience during a broadcast. He asked the BBC's Listener Research Department what listeners preferred, and also inquired:

> How should Song Recitals be presented? Suppose the songs not to be in English, does the listener like to be told the story of the song before it is sung (and of course I assume that it will be well worded and reticently spoken by the announcer), or does the intrusion of a spoken voice giving more than the title of the song destroy the mood induced by the music?

---

[7] This had been used as a concert venue by the BBC since 1927, in order to bring orchestral concerts within the reach of East Londoners who would not have attended the established concert halls.

Personally I have no doubts on the matter at all. I would far rather not know what the song is about than be told its story, because to my mind the spoken voice destroys what I have come to hear, namely, the music.

Research into the size, nature and tastes of the Third's audience was now being carried out. The Listener Research Department discovered that, while the initial publicity for the Third had persuaded more than ten per cent of the listening population to sample it, by the end of three months this number had reduced to six per cent; meanwhile the Home Service attracted forty per cent and the Light Programme fifty-four. By Christmas 1946, the average Third Programme broadcast was being heard by about 700,000 people at any one time – though more than one and a half million were tuning in during the evening.

The report mentioned that some people were 'no doubt listening under duress because sets are shared and ... others in the same room want to listen'. This was alluded to in a *Radio Times* cartoon (8 November 1946) which shows a small boy gagged and bound next to a radio set, while his father says into the telephone: 'No need to hurry back, darling – Julian and I are thoroughly enjoying the Third Programme.'

The audience figures were encouraging, but the report emphasised that they would have been better had the Third been clearly audible all over Britain. Only half of those who had tried to pick it up had 'found reception quite satisfactory'. The BBC had hoped to improve coverage by Christmas, but the only improvement had been the introduction of a low-power transmitter at Hull, and national coverage remained at 'rather less than 50%'. One of the worst areas for reception was the northern half of London, which was badly affected by interference from Latvia. Plans for improvement were uncertain – an engineering report stated that 'several schemes' were being considered – and the long-term solution still seemed to be FM transmission. 'But this will take several years to complete.' Meanwhile the radio critic L. Marsland Gander complained of background noise 'like frying sausages'.

Haley recalls that, by a maddening technical fluke, the Third 'could be heard much better in Switzerland than in the West End of London. And people used to go to Switzerland, listen to it, and come back and say, "How is it you can't let us have it in Mayfair?"' This European audience included one very distinguished listener. Haley remembers receiving 'a message from Richard Strauss, the composer, thanking us for the music he'd heard on the Third Programme, which he'd never hoped to hear in his life'. He would have been able to hear much of his own music. *Metamorphosen*, written the previous year in memory of the destruction of Dresden Opera House, had its first Third Programme broadcast on 6 October 1946, played by the Boyd Neel Orchestra. ('It shows the old hand ... turning away untiringly at the old familiar mill,' wrote Ernest Newman in the *Sunday Times*, with complete insensitivity to the nature of the new work.) And a recording of *Der Rosenkavalier*, made for the Third at the

Hamburg Music Festival, was broadcast on 8 November.[8]

The Third's audibility in Europe led the BBC Governors, at a meeting on 14 December 1946, to consider the suggestion that it should replace the BBC European Service. The youngest Governor, Barbara Ward (a writer and broadcaster in her thirties), was all for it, and so was Haley, who called it a 'bold and imaginative stroke', but the others were against it. In November, the suggestion had been received from a Mr W. N. Weech in Baltimore, Maryland, that 'You should consider beaming your Third Programme to America, on the short waves'. Barnes took the idea seriously, but was told that no wavelength was available, though selected programmes from the Third were already being made available via the BBC's existing overseas services.

It might have been expected that the Third's audience within Britain would be predominantly upper middle class. The first Listener Research report confirmed this: '30% of the upper middle class, as compared with only 4% of the working class, declared that the Third Programme was very attractive to them.' Moreover the typical listener was male: 'The proportion of men who found it very attractive was half as great again ... as among women.' Predictably, too, the Third appealed 'more to the older than to the younger half of the population'. Yet a large number of listeners did not correspond to this stereotype. The report pointed out that 'the numerical preponderance of the working class in the population is so great that ... about one in three were working class listeners'.

One of these was a sixteen-year-old schoolboy called Peter Hall, who was determined to get into professional theatre. He listened eagerly in his small bedroom under the eaves of a railway station in rural Cambridgeshire, where his father worked: 'Nothing widened my horizons so much as the Third Programme.' Another schoolboy who listened, Peter Maxwell Davies, was four years younger than Hall and the son of an optical instrument maker:

> The Third Programme, when I was a boy, was (together with the local library and the Manchester Central Library, particularly the Henry Watson Music Library) of absolute paramount importance. I think I listened to it every evening, more or less from the moment it started till the moment it shut down, while I was doing my homework. And it was the best education I could ever have got. There was I, a working class boy on a

[8] The belief that Strauss had cooperated with the Nazis put the BBC in a quandary when his Oboe Concerto was being considered for the 1946 Proms. Victor Hely-Hutchinson noted that the BBC's policy with composers who had been on the wrong side in the war was to be 'influenced exclusively by artistic considerations', and referred the concerto to Julian Herbage, who was then on the Proms staff. Herbage studied the score, and reported: 'The ostrich has stuck his head in the sand and pretended there has been no world war ... taking us back to an age of innocence in classical old Vienna ... is this escapism par excellence or is it a good bit of salesmanship for charming but outmoded ideas? It certainly is an effective piece of music ... and well deserves a place in the Proms.'

council estate in Swinton, with precious little access through family or friends to anything that would be of interest to Third Programme listeners normally. And the Third Programme was a huge window on all sorts of things, particularly music (obviously), but also drama and poetry.

And the playwright Harold Pinter, who in 1946 was a sixteen-year-old, the son of a tailor in East London, says, when asked if the Third widened his horizons as a teenager: 'Enormously. The Third Programme was a great thing.'

CHAPTER FIVE

Always think big

The critic Edward Sackville-West envisaged thousands of Peter Halls, Peter Maxwell Davieses, and Harold Pinters having their horizons widened. In *Picture Post*, at the end of November 1946, he declared that 'the Third Programme may well become the greatest educative and civilising force England has known since the secularisation of the theatre in the sixteenth century'.

Praise continued in the early weeks of 1947. 'There seems little doubt that it is the best radio programme in the world,' wrote the radio critic of the *Scotsman*, while the magazine *Music Teacher* reported that someone had been overheard saying that if the Third couldn't civilise the British in ten years, 'we deserve oblivion'. The *Time & Tide* music critic was concerned about the standard of some performances – he described Peter Stadlen's playing of Schubert's posthumous A Major Piano Sonata as 'extremely bad' – but was generally delighted: 'On Monday, for example, the Hungarian String Quartet gave the best performance of Bartók I have ever heard.' A columnist in the *Tatler* praised the Third's policy of broadcasting musical rarities:

> To someone living in the country it has come as a sudden boon that is fast becoming a part of one's life – to such a point indeed that last night when about to plunge into the gusty darkness, to go to dinner twenty miles away, and happening to see that Purcell's *Indian Queen* was about to be played, I very nearly doffed my coat, almost picked up the telephone to make halting excuses ... Three nights ago ... there was a magnificent performance of the *Litaniae Lauretanae*, a Litany for Our Lady of Loreto written by Mozart at the age of eighteen. Rarely heard, it is to my mind a work as great, if in a more florid style, as Bach's *Matthew Passion*. Here the performance was exhilarating, infinitely moving.

As to speech programmes, Austin Welland in the *Sunday Mercury* grumbled that the Third was dominated by 'third-rate poets, Bloomsbury intellectuals and BBC producers who should have been schoolmasters', but went on: 'Having chosen your item, don't switch off in disgust if the first few minutes seem dull. I nearly missed one of the most outstanding radio plays of the year – Louis MacNeice's *The Careerist* – because the first 10 minutes were unnecessarily complicated and bewildering.' The current affairs talks attracted criticism for political bias – from both right and left. A correspondent to *Time & Tide* complained that A. J. P. Taylor, talking in a series on British foreign policy, had offered 'A specious, and elaborate apologia for the actions of a certain "friendly" Power' (the USSR), while a reader of the Communist *Daily Worker* described another programme in the same series as 'a tirade of anti-Soviet calumny, distortion and lies'. The Third soon instituted a series called *The Soviet View*, in which the BBC's foreign news staff reported on attitudes expressed in the USSR press and radio. It ran for many years.

The appearance on the Third of such Oxford figures as A. J. P. Taylor stimulated the interest of that university. The *Oxford Magazine* noted that 'senior members are at last beginning to listen to the radio' (though Alan Bullock recalls that the Third was praised by those dons who had been invited to speak on it, but sneered at by those who had not), and informed its readers that 'payment is comparable with that made by the more exclusive literary periodicals'. It hinted at rivalry between universities: 'The Master of Trinity College, Cambridge [G. M. Trevelyan], recently held the attention of his radio audience for an hour, a period of time which the experts thought would be far too long. Have we no one capable of like performance?' Trevelyan's talk (7 January 1947) was on *Society in Roman Britain*. He was back on 28 September with an appreciation of Thomas Carlyle.

Not everyone was accepting the Third's invitations to speak. Sean O'Casey and George Bernard Shaw both declined to join 'a series of famous authors reading their own works', but Thomas Mann spoke on *Germany: her character and destiny* (4 June 1947), and T. S. Eliot was happy for a recording of his British Academy lecture on Milton to be broadcast later on the evening it was given (26 March), and came to the studio to introduce 'a personal anthology of poetry', with a reader, on 13 November that year. The critic Geoffrey Grigson, who was doing plenty of broadcasting himself, complained that the Third was being too deferential to Eliot, whose ultimate fate (he believed) was to be 'a very miniature Cowley, written about by dons in Nebraska and Cambridge'. But the only regular grumble was about poor reception. By mid-January 1947, FM broadcasting of the Third had begun experimentally from Alexandra Palace in north London, on 90.3 mc/s, but the only people with sets that could pick it up were a 'restricted panel of BBC research workers'.

During the Third's fifth month of broadcasting, February 1947, the BBC published a booklet, *The Third Programme: a Symposium of Opinion and Plans*, which included praise from Harold Nicolson and Desmond Shawe-Taylor; but the press observed that its appearance at this time was ironic, since the Third had just been taken off the air. The winter had brought record-breaking low temperatures, and by the beginning of February coal stocks were almost exhausted, and supplies paralysed by the continuing snowstorms. Factories were closed, the domestic use of electricity was restricted, and on 11 February, as part of the Government's measures to conserve power, the Third ceased broadcasting – though the Home Service and Light Programme continued with a limited number of programmes.

Rose Macaulay remarked to the society hostess Sybil Colefax that it was 'monstrous that the BBC had cut the Third Programme because of the fuel crisis, as it is the one good thing we get'. Numerous protests were received at Broadcasting House. 'It seems to be becoming increasingly evident that anything which is not the choice of the vast majority must go,' one angry listener wrote to Haley, while another sent a letter to the Postmaster-General: 'I have not missed more than three important 3rd programme broadcasts since its inception ... I demand that [it] be restored immediately.' The writer Sylvia Townsend Warner pleaded, in the correspondence column of *The Times*, for the Third and Light to be 'given on alternate evenings', which would be 'more creditable to an educated nation', and a Mrs Lily Thicknesse from Surrey saw it as a class issue: 'Could not some of the music hall programmes have been cancelled instead of the 3rd Programme? Or must the lower orders *alone* be considered?'

Etienne Amyot recalls that the suspension of the Third had been ordered by Emanuel Shinwell, Minister of Fuel and Power in the Labour Government:

> Shinwell decided that the new transmitters for the Third would take too much power, and that it was ridiculous, when people couldn't cook a bit of haddock, to listen to Beethoven or Bernard Shaw. So to hell with the Third Programme. And we had a hurried meeting in Haley's office, and he said: 'Do you know anybody in the government?' It so happened that Patrick Gordon Walker [a junior minister] had been in the same unit with me, in Psychological Warfare, and I said, 'We could have a try.' So I went to the House and talked to Patrick, who, after all, had been a history don at Oxford and was very keen on the Third, and he was furious at Shinwell's edict, and went to talk to the head of all the trades unions, I think.

The Third resumed broadcasting on 26 February, 'the BBC having received only six hours' notice from the Government' (reported the *Daily Telegraph*), though for the time being programmes were to end one hour earlier than before, at 11 pm.

Quite apart from the fuel crisis, Britain was still desperately impoverished by the cost of the war. Advertisements in the *Radio Times* advised on how to cook with limited ingredients: 'We're a small household – only myself and my husband, so we only have two ration books. Before the war I used about three times as much fat as I get now ... ' Rationing of food, clothing and petrol lasted a further six years. In such austerity, the Third seemed extraordinarily luxurious.[1] 'Poor we may be, economically,' observed the

---

[1] The BBC licence fee had been increased from ten shillings to one pound with effect from 1 June 1946 (two pounds for a combined radio and television licence). At this period, university professors and senior BBC producers were earning about £1000 per annum; ordinary producers about £700; secretaries about £240.

Labour journal *Tribune*, in an article on the Third, 'but culturally we are probably richer than we have been for a long time.' The programmes for a sample evening (27 January 1947) show what heights the Third could rise to in its fourth month on the air. Broadcasting began at 6 pm with music by Britten, including *A Ceremony of Carols* and *Rejoice in the Lamb*, the latter with Peter Pears and Alfred Deller among the soloists, and Michael Tippett conducting. Then came a programme in a series about the acoustics and technology of music broadcasts. The Hungarian String Quartet followed with Mozart, Bartók and Beethoven, with an interval talk by Eric Linklater on Richard Hillary – one of a series about outstanding people killed in the war. At 9.20 came a production of T. S. Eliot's *Sweeney Agonistes* by Patric Dickinson, and at 9.50 a discussion on the challenge posed to Keynesian economics in a posthumously published book by Etienne Mantoux, a young Frenchman killed on active service. At 10.20 Alec Guinness and the Dolmetsch Consort of Viols combined for a programme, produced by Douglas Cleverdon, on Shakespeare's use of contemporary songs, and the final broadcast, finishing around midnight, was a recital of contemporary music for strings and wind, including chamber concertos by Berg and Elisabeth Lutyens.

*

Early in 1947 Anthony Lewis, who had planned the Third's music broadcasts, left the BBC at the age of thirty-two to become Professor of Music at Birmingham University, and in March, Victor Hely-Hutchinson, Director of Music, died suddenly at the age of forty-five. Etienne Amyot recalls that Basil Nicolls offered him the Director's post: 'He took me to the Athenaeum and said that the job was going, and he whispered, "Of course, it carries a gong" [a knighthood]. But I'd been briefed by other members of the Corporation to say – and I said it – that whoever was Director of Music ought to have control of the Orchestra as well. And Nicolls got up and walked out in a rage.' At this time, the BBC Symphony Orchestra was under the sole command of Boult, and there was a widespread feeling that the quality of its playing needed to be raised.

For the moment, Kenneth Wright became Acting Director of Music, and John Lowe was put in charge of music for the Third. He immediately proposed 'a large scale History of Music (performed, not talked) ... to stretch across the twelve months starting January, 1948'. He also asked each member of Music Department to 'set out on paper a ... scheme for four months' broadcasting of the type of music in which he specialises'. The Programme Builders, as the music producers were then called (because they planned programmes, but often left the actual production to the sound engineers), included Basil Douglas, who later became manager of the English Opera Group for Benjamin Britten. Lowe asked him to plan song recitals (two per week) for the year beginning 1 July 1947. 'When big singers are coming over for opera,' Lowe told him, 'see if they can stay in England a little longer for recitals ... Only first rank singers, from any country. If a singer falls out at the last minute, let us ask for cancellation or gramophone records, rather than substitute a second ranker.' He recommended 'Plenty of use of Pears – plus Britten whenever possible and [Kathleen] Ferrier', and concluded: 'The only limitation . . . is singers who have not yet been de-Nazified, and singers who would need to be got out of Germany at the time you want them.'

The year-long series on the history of music began to be planned. Meanwhile July 1947 saw the start of *Contemporary British Composers*, studio recitals featuring works by Lennox Berkeley, Christian Darnton, Antony Hopkins, Benjamin Frankel and Edmund Rubbra – to name only those represented in the first four programmes.[2] 'The principle on which we have worked,' Lowe told Kenneth Wright, 'was not to include composers like Tippett, Britten and Walton who are pretty regularly performed and not confine ourselves to particularly experimental composers.' Another Programme Builder, the composer Humphrey Searle, was featured in the series in December.

July 1947 also saw the start of *Music of the Sixteenth and Seventeenth Centuries*. Barnes had been approached by the musicologist Ernst H. Meyer, who since the mid-1930s had been doing pioneer research into English chamber music up to Purcell, and it was agreed that he would provide material for ten programmes, to be conducted by Arnold Goldsbrough. Meyer wrote in the *Radio Times*:

> Delving among the ancient manuscripts and prints of English and Continental libraries never fails to fill the discoverer with a spirit of excitement and adventure. The seventeenth century, in particular, produced countless gems . . . Too often has all this music been regarded merely as a period of transition . . . Yet . . . there is a limitless wealth of forms, expressive melodies, and exciting harmonies; there are striking orchestral effects; there is drama, intense joy, and sombre tragedy . . .

The series included Handel's cantata *Aminta e Fillide*, motets by Rameau, and Constant Lambert's realisation of a symphony by William Boyce.

Period instruments were not widely used at this date, but Goldsbrough gave instruction in style to the players hired by the BBC, who included Norbert Brainin (violin), Bernard Richards (cello), Adrian Beers (double bass), Geoffrey Gilbert (flute), and Bernard Brown (trumpet). Among the first violins was Emanuel Hurwitz, who recalls:

> They wanted a house orchestra that would be amenable to learning the style. I eventually became the leader. It was a wonderful experience, but

---

[2] Other composers featured in the series, which ran until the end of 1947, were (in order of transmission) Arnold Cooke, Herbert Howells, Patrick Hadley, Gerald Finzi, Herbert Murrill, Alan Bush, Richard Arnell, Elizabeth Maconchy, William Alwyn, Bernard Stevens, William Wordsworth, Wilfred Mellers, Alan Rawsthorne, Elisabeth Lutyens, E. J. Moeran, Humphrey Searle, Stanley Wilson, Ian Parrott and Phyllis Tate.

bewildering, because Arnold [Goldsbrough] would ask you to phrase it a different way every ten minutes – he kept on experimenting. He'd say, 'That's it!' But you'd come back after the rehearsal break and he'd give a beaming smile and say, 'Forget everything I said! *This* is how we'll do it.' You learnt to mark the parts with very light pencil!

He helped to teach us that the vibrato in Bach had to be different from the vibrato in Tchaikovsky – though some of us knew that already.

The broadcasts were live, and Hurwitz recalls:

Being the Third Programme, you didn't have to stop for the nine o'clock news, but Basil Lam, who was producing, still had to work out timings. And Arnold wouldn't ever do a complete run through until the actual broadcast, so Basil had to time the bits and then add them up. I remember on one occasion him imploring me, only few minutes before we went on the air, 'Can you get Arnold to tell us the *order*?' And Arnold said, 'I'm trying to get this phrasing right – don't bother me with trivialities.' And sometimes when we were on the air, doing (say) some early French opera, and over-running more than even the Third Programme would allow, Basil would tiptoe into the studio and creep between the music desks, putting little notes on them: 'Cut No. 17.' And he'd have to placate some poor baritone who'd lost an aria!

The success of the series led, in 1948, to the orchestra beginning to give public concerts, as the Goldsbrough Orchestra. In 1960 it was renamed the English Chamber Orchestra.

Barnes approved of the trend towards historically authentic per-formances. 'Broadcasting can lead the musical ear back to an appreciation of the subtleties [of pre-classical music] impossible to concert-giving organ-isations where masses alone draw money,' he wrote to John Lowe. Mean-while, among proposals for broadcasts of twentieth-century music, Boult was keen to schedule *Wozzeck*, which had not been heard in England since he had conducted a pioneer concert performance in 1934. He warned John Lowe that Berg's score would need 'a good three weeks' rehearsal with no other serious orchestral music going on'.

Boult also wrote that he had been worried, since he came to the BBC in 1930, about 'the infrequency of performance of some of the greatest masterpieces in musical literature', such as the B Minor Mass, the Passions, *Messiah*, Brahms's Requiem, and Beethoven's *Missa solemnis*; listeners should be able to hear these 'at least once a year', and he hoped the Third would undertake them at regular intervals. On 22 May 1947 he conducted a complete performance – still comparatively unusual – of the *St Matthew Passion* on the Third, with Pears and Ferrier among the soloists.

John Lowe was keen to arrange a Beecham series. Beecham was already on the Third quite often – he conducted the Berlioz Requiem in the studio on 13 May 1947 and *The Trojans* on 2 July – but Lowe had grander plans: 'One orchestral concert per fortnight, starring some of the many out-of-the-way works in which Beecham specialises ... One opera per month ... including one Wagner and one Rameau ... Alternatively the entire Ring with Beecham and the RPO ... ' This was extravagant, considering that it was now known that the History of Music series would be very expensive. But Barnes was keen on ambitious schemes. At a meeting with Music Department, he told them: 'Always think big.'

Another member of Music Department, Denis Stevens, recalls that John Lowe was sometimes the butt of Beecham's jokes: 'Beecham would say, "Come round to the Savoy," and John would run as fast as his legs would carry him. And Beecham told him: "I want to do this opera by Maillart, *Le jeune sage et le vieux fou.*" And John would get terribly excited, and say, "Beecham's going to do an opera." And all the copyists would be alerted, and the cast would be booked from all over Europe – and they'd suddenly find that no such opera existed.'

Some of Beecham's letters to the BBC are masterpieces of invective. In August 1951 he called a financial offer 'preposterously inadequate, thoughtlessly impudent and magnificently inept', and when he received an impassive reply, he wrote: 'It is not my custom to haggle over affairs of this sort with persons whose views differ so widely from my own.'

*

Barnes himself followed his precept of 'thinking big' by sending the music critic William Glock on a fact-finding trip around Europe. During war service in the RAF, Glock had written for the *Observer*, but was sacked from the paper in 1945 for his uncompromising championship of contemporary music. When Bartók died that autumn, Glock wrote of him that 'no great composer ... ever cared how "pleasant" his music sounded'.

Glock had listened to the Third since the beginning: 'I remember the first night, with the Boulanger Monteverdi records, and Smuts – and Joyce Grenfell, wasn't it? It was the great thing of the day.' He had given one of the talks in the Third's series *Contemporary Music and the Listener*, on Hindemith (16 November 1946), playing the musical illustrations himself at the piano during the live broadcast – he had studied the piano with Schnabel in Berlin in the early 1930s. A few weeks after this broadcast, Amyot asked if he was interested in visiting the occupied zones of Europe, and bringing back news and (where possible) recordings of what had been going on musically in the former Nazi-controlled territories. When Barnes put the idea to Haley, the Director-General approved – 'I think we should do this' – and Glock set off at the beginning of May 1947. Six weeks later he was back in London, hastily listening to discs he had collected. The first of his talks on *Music in Post-War Europe* was heard on 3 July. Despite the ruined opera houses and concert halls, and the white, tired faces Glock saw everywhere, there had been a remarkable flowering of music since May 1945, often in tricky circumstances – 'How could one have foretold that in Munich there was an acute shortage of brass players, because they had nearly all been Nazis? How agreeably symbolical!'

The American Music Officer for Bavaria gave Glock 'the best meal I'd had for eight years' at the US Officers' Club, and introduced him to 'Georg Solti, the young Hungarian who is chief conductor at the opera'. When Glock asked to hear records, he discovered the music of Carl Orff. 'I'm not quite sure of the value of such music,' he told listeners, after letting them hear an excerpt from *Carmina Burana*, 'but it would certainly have been quite wrong not to present it to you.' After Munich, Vienna was a delight – 'the best orchestra in Europe' – while Prague boasted 'more scores in the music department of one ordinary bookshop than I'd found in the whole of Vienna'. The annual music festival was in progress, and Glock met Shostakovich, who 'made an unforgettable impression with his nervous movements and appearance of spiritual distress'.

In Berlin, where all the concert halls that Glock knew from his time studying with Schnabel had become rubble, he was heartened by a performance of *Peter Grimes*; he told listeners that 'this opera of Britten's has done incalculable good for English music'. He went to the official de-Nazification centre, which had just cleared Furtwängler, so that Glock was able to attend his first post-war rehearsal with the Berlin Philharmonic Orchestra. The de-Nazification files could be inspected. 'I'd hoped to see the file on Herbert von Karajan,' said Glock, 'but it wasn't there.' At Hamburg, where a new opera house had been erected on the vast stage of the old one, he saw a stunningly simple production of *The Magic Flute*. But he was not excited by contemporary German music. Boris Blacher, whom he met in Berlin, told him: 'Be patient! We may have something to show you in five years' time.' Glock concluded the series by wondering 'whether the greatest lesson of my tour is not this: that you can only have first-class singing and playing if they've grown from the performance and understanding of your own composers ... The most important lesson must be learned at home, and when our own composers have prepared the textbook.'

Two of those composers had been present, on 11 February 1947, at one of a series of dinner parties Barnes and Amyot were holding for people in the arts. The guests that evening were Elizabeth Poston and Alan Rawsthorne, along with Glock himself, Anthony Lewis, and Steuart Wilson, the Arts Council's music director. They discussed applause at broadcast concerts, which Barnes was still fretting about, and agreed that the audience should remain silent at public chamber concerts broadcast on the Third. They then tackled the question of performance standards. The feeling was that these had actually gone down in the few months since the Third came on the air, because it was making so many demands on performers, and there was too little time to rehearse. The solution seemed to be to contract and pay for rehearsals as well as broadcasts. Also, somewhat cynically, it was felt that if the broadcast were repeated (live) on two occasions, this should guarantee 'at least one good performance'.

Besides repeats, there was 'diagonalisation', the sharing of material, on different days, between the Home Service and Third Programme. For example Honegger's *Jeanne d'Arc* was heard on the Home on 15 April 1947, conducted in the studio by Basil Cameron, and again on the Third three nights later. Yvonne Lefébre played Roussel's piano concerto with the BBC Symphony Orchestra as part of the Third's Saturday orchestral concert on 3 May 1947, and repeated it live on the Home Service the following afternoon. (There was one change of item: the Third had Kodály's *Dances of Marosszek*, but the Home listeners were given Mendelssohn's *Ruy Blas* overture.) Drama was 'diagonalised' too. Peggy Ashcroft played Viola in *Twelfth Night* on the Home Service on 10 March 1947, and on the Third on 18 March. John Lowe was worried that the two networks would begin to 'look like copies of each other', but Barnes did not share this concern: 'Diagonalisation of international artists . . . is surely desirable.'

Most of the Third's speech output was not diagonalised – productions like Douglas Cleverdon's *Paradise Lost* were available to Third listeners only. It began on 19 October 1947; Dylan Thomas played Satan, and the *Listener* reviewer, Martin Armstrong, thought this less than perfect casting: 'It swamped Milton, it swamped *Paradise Lost*, it occasionally swamped even the sense, for the louder Dylan Thomas shouts the more his articulation deteriorates.' Another Third Programme poet was attracting great praise. 'MacNeice continues to be the outstanding creative writer in British broadcasting,' wrote the head of Features, Laurence Gilliam, in MacNeice's 1947 annual report (an indignity suffered by BBC staff members then and now). MacNeice's scripts for the Third this year included adaptations of *Njal's Saga* and *Grettir's Saga*, and a version of the Cupid and Psyche story. Another classical text broadcast on the Third during 1947 was Gilbert Murray's translation of *The Frogs* of Aristophanes (20 February); later the same evening, listeners could hear scenes from the play in the original Greek.

Gilliam commended MacNeice for 'stimulating outside writers', but most of the Third's current drama productions were adaptations of classics. Tyrone Guthrie produced Tennyson's *Queen Mary* (8 January) and Henry Reed added some 'verse of my own concoction' to his script of *Moby Dick* (26 January), in which Ralph Richardson and Cyril Cusack were Ahab and Ishmael. Richardson brought his Old Vic production of *Richard II* to the studio on 23 April, with Alec Guinness as the king, and Cusack appeared with the cast of the Abbey Theatre, Dublin, in *The Playboy of the Western World* on 9 March. There was a Shaw Festival (five plays, in January), and on 14 January, Rayner Heppenstall produced *Animal Farm*, adapted by George Orwell himself. There were also plenty of international classics, for example Sartre's *The Flies* (14 May), Robert Donat in a dramatisation of *Don Quixote* (23 October), and Miles Malleson in *Tartuffe* (11 December).

As to opera, Amyot recalls that

Haley came in one day, and said, 'You know, I've just been reading about the influence before the First World War of Diaghilev and the Russian Ballet. Can't we think of something which will have as lasting an influence?' Well, I'd been for a few days to Vienna, and I'd heard *Fidelio*. The opera house had been destroyed, and it was given in the city theatre, and I met the *Intendant* [artistic director], through Lord Montagu's sister Elizabeth, who was then, I think, helping to make *The Third Man*. And now I suddenly thought, I'll get in touch with him – and would the whole opera company, which was superb, come over to London?

And Haley said, 'That's a wonderful idea, but how is it going to be done?' And then, purely by chance, I met Dr Schmidt, who was the Austrian Ambassador to London, and I asked him whether he would be kind enough to lunch with me at Brooks's a week or two later. Which he did, and I said, 'What we want to do is to bring over the whole Vienna State Opera Company.' And he said, 'That would be wonderful, but just to bring them over for some broadcasts?' And I said, 'If they came over, I'm sure they'd be recorded, and they'd be at Covent Garden.'

Then I got on to David Webster [administrator of Covent Garden opera house], whom I'd never met, through a friend of mine, and he was agog – 'Of course we'll put them on.' And then I got on to Walter Legge [then with Columbia Records], and said, would they record the great singers? And the Company came over. And that was one of the great highlights of the Third Programme in its first years. It set London aflame. It was a standard of performance people hadn't heard here for years.

'This is a week for opera,' Edward Lockspeiser wrote in the *Radio Times* for the week beginning 14 September 1947. 'The Vienna State Opera is paying its first visit to England, opening at Covent Garden on Tuesday, and from then till the end of the week there will be broadcasts from the theatre every night on either the Third Programme or the Home Service.' The broadcasts extended to the end of September; the repertoire consisted of *Don Giovanni*, *Cosi fan tutte*, *Fidelio*, *Le nozze de Figaro*, and *Salome*. Josef Krips and Clemens Krauss conducted the Vienna Philharmonic Orchestra, and the cast included Elizabeth Schwarzkopf and Hans Hotter. 'These are performances to hear, and hear again,' wrote Dyneley Hussey in the *Listener*. He was particularly impressed by 'the perfection of the ensemble between singers and orchestra'. It showed up the pitiful inadequacies of the typical British pit musician. For example, the effect of 'the softest and eeriest chords for trombone and wind' in the graveyard scene in *Don Giovanni* was something that 'an English orchestra engaged for the occasion could hardly have accomplished without months of rehearsal'.

The Vienna State Company had, in fact, already been heard on the Third on 8 August, when *Cosi fan tutte* was relayed from Salzburg. From the same Festival came their production of Strauss's *Arabella* (18 August). Strauss himself, now aged eighty-four, came to London in October for a Strauss Festival, arranged by his publishers to earn him some money. 'He is in real difficulty,' noted Herbert Murrill of the BBC's Music Department, 'and it is hoped by means of this visit to put if possible £1000 in his pocket.' In two broadcasts on the Third (19 and 30 October) he conducted *Don Juan*, the *Symphonia domestica*, and *Till Eulenspiegel*.

Festivals and regular concert and opera seasons were beginning to enrich the Third. From Glyndebourne came the world première of Britten's *Albert Herring* (20 June 1947), preceded by a Stephen Potter documentary about the making of the opera (19 June). Edinburgh Festival relays that summer included Bruno Walter conducting Ferrier, Pears, and the Vienna Philharmonic in *Das Lied von der Erde* (11 September). Many of the Proms were broadcast on the Third, for the first time – on some evenings the Prom was split between Home and Third, while on others one of the networks carried it in its entirety – and in January there had been a two-week Winter Promenade season, also from the Albert Hall, and again shared between Third and Home. All this meant that the Third's music expenditure was soon soaring. In May 1947 Barnes told John Lowe that no non-BBC orchestra or chamber group must be engaged without special permission.

Yet when it came to broadcasting all nine Mahler symphonies – two of which had not yet been heard in Britain – between November 1947 and March 1948, Barnes realised that 'foreign orchestras' would be needed, preferably the Vienna Philharmonic conducted by Bruno Walter. He proved available, but the orchestra was not, and he conducted the First Symphony with the London Philharmonic Orchestra on 6 November. The remaining symphonies were broadcast as follows:

Second: Minneapolis Symphony Orchestra, conducted by Eugene Ormandy (on gramophone records), 17 November 1947.

Third: BBC Symphony Orchestra, conducted by Boult, 29 November 1947. This was the first British performance of this symphony.

Fourth: Philharmonic Symphony Orchestra of New York (conductor not known; on gramophone records), 12 December 1947.

Fifth: BBC Symphony Orchestra, conducted by Boult, 20 December 1947.

Sixth: Orchestra of Nordwestdeutscher Rundfunk, conducted by Hans Schmidt-Isserstedt (a recording made in Hamburg), 31 December 1947. This was the first time this symphony was heard in Britain.

Seventh: BBC Symphony Orchestra, conducted by Boult, 31 January 1948.

Eighth: BBC Symphony Orchestra, conducted by Boult, 10 February 1948.

Ninth: Vienna Philharmonic Orchestra, conducted by Bruno Walter (gramophone records of a concert given in Vienna in 1938), 13 March 1948.[3]

By this time the Third's policy of using top international performers had brought protests from the Incorporated Society of Musicians. Kenneth

[3] Michael Kennedy provides the information that Sir Henry Wood had conducted the first British performances of the First (1903), Fourth (1905), Seventh (1913) and Eighth (1930); Bruno Walter had conducted the Second in Britain in 1930, and the same year the Hallé Orchestra under Sir Hamilton Harty had performed the Ninth, which was broadcast by the BBC.

Wright wrote anxiously to Barnes that 'we must not tacitly assume that there are few, if any, British artists who can give us fine performances of a lot of this music which you want'; Amyot believed that it was 'almost futile' to look for world-class musicians in Britain, but the BBC (said Wright) should encourage the raising of standards.

At the dinner on 11 February, Alan Rawsthorne had suggested that the Third should commission a series of works from contemporary British composers, and two days later John Lowe wrote to Michael Tippett, asking if he would consider writing something for the Third's first anniversary concert on 29 September. Similar letters went out to Vaughan Williams, Walton, Britten, Rawsthorne himself, and Patrick Hadley – and also to Poulenc and Strauss.

Walton had written to Barnes in January with suggestions for the Third: Eric Tuxen should be brought over from Denmark to conduct Nielsen's symphonies – 'They are almost unknown here & I was much interested in a rather poor recording of one a week or two ago in a programme of Danish music,' wrote Walton. Also, as the Third 'seems intent on an orgy of atonalism & whatnot', why not (continued Walton) perform some of the works of Kaikhosru Sorabji? 'Though he was supposed to be the last word in the days of my youth it may sound as tame as Schönberg by now.'[4] As to the first anniversary commission, Walton said he had too many other commitments, including a promise to the BBC to write an opera for radio. He accepted £500 for this, and told them he hoped to write it during the next eighteen months.

Vaughan Williams thought that commissioning for the Third's first anniversary was a mistake. '*PLEASE* do *NOT* have specially written works for your celebration,' he wrote to John Lowe; 'they are always DUDS – choose a programme of all the best works of our own & other countries (especially ours) starting with that wonderful mass by an unknown English composer which was done at St John's College Cambridge a few years ago. I wish Mr Tippett would do more of that kind of thing instead of being seduced by his foreign companions into wasting his efforts over the dreary Monteverdi stuff.' (Tippett was performing Monteverdi at Morley College.) Vaughan Williams also recommended Sullivan's 'To a garden full of roses' from *Ruddigore*, and Britten's *A Boy is Born*.

Britten himself was too busy to accept a commission, but Strauss and Poulenc asked about terms, and the BBC Copyright Department offered five to seven guineas per minute. Strauss said he had 'a double concerto' in mind, but the most enthusiastic response came from Poulenc, who had in mind a work for small orchestra, possibly a sinfonietta. 'I think he might be able to do something good with this idea if he continues to remain in the right mood,' noted Edward Lockspeiser, the Programme

[4] Sorabji, then in his fifties, was a self-taught composer of highly complex music which he refused to allow anyone to perform in public.

Builder who was in touch with him,[5] adding that Poulenc did not wish to receive payment until the work was completed. Lockspeiser also suggested engaging Poulenc to 'play and sing himself extracts from his opera *Les Mamelles de Tirésias* ... I have heard him do this to a group of friends and it is exquisitely entertaining.' But Etienne Amyot knew the opera, which is about a husband and wife changing sexes, and felt it 'really sails too close to the wind even for the Third Programme'.

The next communication from Poulenc, a little over a month before the first anniversary, began *'Catastrophe!'*, and explained that the *Sinfonietta*, as it was now entitled, was still unfinished. 'Explain all this as kindly as you can to the BBC,' he asked Lockspeiser, 'but really I should never be ready in time not being a Hindemith or a Ravel – that is to say a slow chap.' It was completed before the end of the year, but did not receive its world première on the Third until 24 October 1948, played by the Philharmonia Orchestra conducted by Roger Désmormière.

Tippett decided not to undertake a commission. 'I am down to the opera at last now,' he wrote to Barnes on 13 July 1947. 'A sort of Magic Flute story that will please Tom Eliot, yourself, I dare say, & few else. But it seems it's got to come.' This was *The Midsummer Marriage*. In the event, no one had accepted the commission, and it was even proving difficult to get Boult and the BBC Symphony Orchestra for the first anniversary concert (now scheduled for 28 September, a Sunday night). Boult was supposed to be on holiday then; he said he would come back for the concert, but asked to conduct works that could be rehearsed quickly. Therefore in the event the anniversary was marked in rather muted fashion, with a concert entitled *Orchestral Music by British Composers* – Walton, Bax, Holst, Purcell, Matthew Locke, Boyce and Rawsthorne. There were no new works.

Despite work on *The Midsummer Marriage*, Tippett was keen to carry out Barnes's suggestion that he give a series of illustrated talks on the interpretation of Purcell. Four programmes were arranged, beginning on 5 April 1947, all of them on Saturday evenings. It was comparatively unusual in the early days of the Third to give a series a regular day, and even in this case there was no uniform starting time – the four were heard at 10.30, 9.20, 9.50 and 7.30. Moreover one week had no programme because of an opera broadcast.

The musical illustrations from Purcell were provided by the amateur choir which Tippett conducted at Morley College, and several professional soloists, including Alfred Deller, whom Tippett had found as a lay clerk in Canterbury Cathedral. They were both back on the Third in November 1947, when Tippett gave four illustrated talks on *Purcell and the Elizabethans*, and on the 21st of that month he directed the Morley College Choir in Tallis's forty-voice motet *Spem in alium*. On 5 December the choir

[5] Lockspeiser (1905–73), a pupil of Boulanger, was an authority on Debussy.

returned to the studio for Monteverdi's Vespers, conducted by Walter Goehr.

Meanwhile Tippett had been listening to Nevill Coghill's modern English version of *Piers Plowman*, which began on the Third on 3 August, produced by Stephen Potter. He told Barnes that he had been 'so strongly moved' by it that he had written to Coghill. He said the Third should consider broadcasting 'some of the more dramatic of the Plato dialogues'. Barnes replied that they had 'already arranged' to do this. The series began on 14 October, produced by Rayner Heppenstall, with Arthur Young playing Socrates.

Barnes had already invited Tippett to take part in a non-musical series, writing to him:

> We have been considering inviting one or two artists to visit some place in the British Isles which they do not already know and which has stirred the imagination of artists or writers in the past, in order to obtain some good talks and perhaps to start a train of creative thinking in the artist for which he would be grateful.
>
> I have spoken to John Betjeman about this and he is delighted with the idea and wants to go to Aberdeen for a week or two to study Scottish Gothic, in which he has always been interested but has never had a chance of seeing. I wonder if there is any place in the British Isles where you would like to go on such a visit ... ?

Tippett did not rise to this, but Betjeman went up to Aberdeen in May 1947, and his talk *Aberdeen Granite* was broadcast on 28 July. 'I had not realised there was so much Scotland,' he told listeners.

> From Waverley station north and north for hours ... The train ran on, over wide brown moors with bluely distant inland mountains and then along the edges of cliffs whose grass was a deep pre-Raphaelite green ... but still no Aberdeen. Could there be such a thing as a great city with tramcars, electric lights, hotels, and cathedrals so far away among empty fields, so near the North Pole as we were going?

Arriving at last, he was conveyed to a hotel with a disappointing 'jazz-modern' interior. 'I might as well have been in Manchester, in Leeds or Salt Lake City. This is progress. This is internationalism.' The city centre was disappointing, but that was to be expected: 'You can never enjoy the beauty of a Western city in its shopping streets ... I would have to turn down side streets to see the real Aberdeen.' There he was rewarded by 'a brick tower and spire opposite the Art Gallery ... so marvellous that only Salisbury is in my opinion a rival'. This, dating from 1844, was the work of Archibald Simpson, 'an architect of genius, a Soane, a Hawksmoor, someone head and shoulders above the men of his time'. Betjeman also praised the renovation of St Andrew's Episcopal Cathedral by a modern Aberdonian, the church restorer and decorator J. N. Comper. He concluded his talk with 'the words of a little known Victorian poet' – probably himself in disguise:

> Farewell Aberdeen 'twixt the Donside and Deeside
> How oft have I strayed through the long summer day
> On the fringe of the links o'er thy wide-spreading seaside
> To see the pink pebbles caressed by the spray ...

Aberdeen Granite did not form part of a series, but during 1947 the Third began to broadcast programmes under the title *Return Journey*, which was based on a similar idea – to send someone back to a place of special significance in their past. The two most successful were by Stevie Smith and Dylan Thomas. Smith's was to 'Syler's Green', the name she gave to the north London suburb to which she had come, from Hull, at the age of four:

> There were two or three large estates in Syler's Green which after a while were sold. One of them is especially vivid in my memory. This estate belonged to a Greek banking family. The Greek family had children of our age, and every year in the summer they used to give an enormous hay party. I remember wearing a stiffly starched white sailor suit and going to this party with my sister and the little boy from next door, who was, we thought, rather a muff. Alan did not live next door, he only stayed there sometimes with his aunts. These two ladies, and their companion lady, were neighbours of ours all through my childhood. The two property-owning ladies were called Jessie and Emmeline, and their companion was always called 'Miss Baby'. They had a stone statue of a Roman boy in their garden, and they also had a white fox terrier dog called Beano. Miss Baby used to do a lot of work for Foreign Missions. She asked us once if we would let her have any old gym stockings that we did not want. 'What do you want them for?' I asked her. 'For the 'eathen,' she said. She used to cut them down and make them into jersey suits.

Return Journey to Syler's Green, produced by Douglas Cleverdon and broadcast on 5 August 1947, was read by Flora Robson, rather than by Stevie Smith herself, but Nest Cleverdon recalls that Smith sometimes read her poetry on the air. 'She became a great friend, and she loved our children, which was nice, because she could be perfectly beastly to children. I once saw her in the Tate with Douglas, pulling a beastly face at a baby, which sent it off in hysterical, fearful cries. She thought that was screamingly funny!'

In *Return Journey to Swansea* (28 June 1947) Dylan Thomas went in search of the townspeople's memories of his younger self:

> He'd be about seventeen or eighteen ... and above medium height. Above medium height for Wales, I mean, he's five foot six and a half. Thick blubber lips; snub nose; curly mousebrown hair; one front tooth broken after playing a game called Cats and Dogs in the Mermaid, Mumbles;

speaks rather fancy; truculent; plausible; a bit of a shower-off; plus-fours and no breakfast, you know; used to have poems printed in the *Herald of Wales*; there was one about an open-air performance of *Electra* in Mrs Bertie Perkins's garden in Sketty; lived in the Uplands; a bombastic adolescent provincial Bohemian with a thick-knotted artist's tie made out of his sister's scarf, she never knew where it had gone, and a cricket-shirt dyed bottle-green; a gabbing, ambitious, mock-tough, pretentious young man . . .

The producer of Betjeman's *Aberdeen Granite* was Anna Kallin, the most remarkable member of Talks. Born to a Jewish family in St Petersburg in 1896, she had studied at Leipzig University, and had joined the BBC in 1940 as a monitor of German broadcasts.[6] After other war-work she became a Talks producer in 1946. Sir Michael Tippett says he was 'more or less taught to do good radio' by her. He describes her as 'a very high-powered bluestocking', and says that when young she had been a 'pin-up girl' for the painter Oskar Kokoschka. (Tippett himself owns a double portrait of her by Kokoschka, on a terracotta plaque.) Etienne Amyot judges her 'one of the most brilliant Talks producers the BBC ever had', and Harman Grisewood, Etienne Amyot's successor, calls her 'an "explorer" . . . her work had something of a personal discovery about it which mattered more than the signs of outward success'.

Grisewood adds that she 'spoke all the European languages with that fluency which seems to be a special gift for educated Russians', and says she liked to refer to the Third as the *Troisième Chaine* – she even persuaded Jacqmar to make her a silk scarf emblazoned with these words. P. H. Newby, who joined Talks after she was well established there, remembers that 'if an idea came up which she didn't feel quite fitted the Third, she had a way of saying *"Ce n'est pas Troisième"* '.

Friends always addressed her as 'Niouta', the Russian diminutive of 'Anna'. Tippett says that this led Alec Robertson, who produced many of the musical talks, to make a mildly risqué joke: 'He had been a Roman Catholic cleric, and had got into trouble, and come out of the church. He said that once, going into Broadcasting House, he had tucked his arm underneath Anna's (who was called Niouta) and said, "Ah yes, two Neuters together." '

*

Harman Grisewood replaced Amyot as Planner, Third Programme shortly before the Third celebrated its first anniversary. Amyot had never intended to stay in the job for long: 'My wife was very ill. And I think you need a new brain every now and then, to think out new ideas. After leaving, I looked after my wife to begin with. Then I went back to music, and to

---

[6] Martin Esslin, who worked in Monitoring alongside Anna Kallin, says that the team also included Ernst Gombrich, William Empson, Geoffrey Grigson, and Gilbert Harding.

writing. And we'd worked frightfully hard at getting the Third to where it was, and I wanted time off to think.' Looking back on those days with Barnes and Stokes, and the rest of the team, he says: 'We were very happy together and worked miraculously well together. It was the happiest job I ever did.'

Grisewood was not entirely unlike Amyot: immensely lively, with an open, enquiring mind and a huge appetite for ideas; a man with many friends in the arts, and himself no mean performer – in his case, as an actor. Born in 1906 into an old Catholic family in Oxfordshire, whose household included a resident priest, Grisewood had gone to Ampleforth and then to Oxford, where he became prominent in the OUDS. 'I did exceedingly badly at Oxford,' he told a journalist in 1951, 'my only asset being some notoriety for a performance as King Lear. So I decided to become a radio actor.' He began to pick up casual work reading stories and acting in plays for *Children's Hour* at the BBC's Savoy Hill studios; then in 1933 he joined the staff as an announcer. These were the days when announcers wore dinner jackets in the evenings, and he explains this practice:

> In the evening most of the people of our sort did change into dinner jackets, if they weren't wearing white ties and going to a really grand dinner party ... And the people who came to speak, who gave the talks, very often in the evening had evening dress themselves. So it would have seemed rather odd in a way to encounter some person who was representing the BBC, who gave them a drink afterwards, and that sort of thing, if they weren't wearing the same kind of rig-out.

But Grisewood, who moved into Programme Planning in 1936, does not deny that in the 1930s the BBC was predominantly stuffy and narrow-minded. He cites Basil Nicolls objecting to his being seen in public with a friend who wore a pink shirt, remarking that this was 'not BBC', and he tells how Ogilvie, the then Director-General, suggested that the Nazis could be persuaded to stop persecuting the Jews if the BBC broadcast 'Beatrice Harrison playing the cello in the woods, so that the nightingale would sing for her' – this was a famous programme at the time. When Grisewood expressed astonishment, Ogilvie replied: 'The Germans are very sentimental about the nightingale; it might persuade them to take a more peaceful view.'

Grisewood found it a great relief to be seconded to a wartime job away from Broadcasting House. In 1941 he became Assistant Controller of the BBC European Service, rising to Acting Controller three years later. Returning to Portland Place after the war, as Assistant Head of Talks, he became restless and unhappy, disliking Haley's new Supply and Programme sides arrangement, and finding some of the Talks producers politically uncongenial – 'so far to the Left as to be real Communists'. Despite his friend with the pink shirt, Grisewood was uncompromisingly Conservative. When nothing was done to curb this leftist tendency, he

submitted his resignation, on 5 July 1947. According to his own recollections, Haley accepted his departure without regret: 'He just said, "Oh
well, all right, if that's what you want to do. You know, I think it's a great
mistake of yours, but still, you do it." Which I did.' Haley tells it rather
differently:

> He did used to get into an awful state. On one occasion he came to me
> and resigned, and said, 'That's the end of it.' ... I didn't want to lose him,
> and I said, 'All right, you've resigned. But I haven't accepted it. I'm not
> going to say a word to anyone ... Until I do something about it, you will
> go on being paid. And I think before very long you will come and tell me
> you have become "unresigned".' And that's exactly what happened.

Grisewood had been taking a close interest in the Third; Amyot recalls
that he often made suggestions for it: 'Harman was somebody full of ideas,
who'd ring one up suddenly, and say, "Have you thought of this or that?"'
Now, Barnes wrote to him asking him to take over Amyot's job as Planner.
'It was a charming letter,' writes Grisewood, 'and pierced through a crust
of distaste which had formed round my thought of the BBC. He told me
he well understood my feelings about leaving and that I would not wish
to join the staff again. But would I come back, he asked, on a personal
and temporary basis to help him? ... He had persuaded the BBC to make
an exception and to take me on, if I'd come, as an outside person to help
him ... ' In fact Barnes's offer was not as informal as Grisewood recalls.
Staff records show that he rejoined the BBC on 15 September 1947, less
than two months after his resignation, as the Third's Planner.

So he found himself installed in the Langham Hotel, which he liked for
its 'mixture of improvisation and ghostliness' (Oscar Wilde had been
among the guests in its days of grandeur). 'Next door to my office,'
Grisewood recalls,

> there was a rather splendid bathroom, and I was delighted to find that
> the bath really worked, and there was hot water, and you could use the
> amenities of an hotel, to some extent, as well as having an office. And I
> was delighted to find one day that the bath had been filled with the most
> beautiful flowers. They were a present from Evelyn Waugh, an old friend
> of mine, rather reluctant to appear on the BBC. He had nevertheless given
> a broadcast, and the flowers were to thank my assistant and me for the
> kind treatment that we gave him. They weren't the most convenient
> offices, and yet it seemed to suit the Third Programme. I liked receiving
> people in the rather splendid entrance of the Langham.

Waugh gave a talk on Californian funeral customs – the background to
his novel *The Loved One* – on 8 May 1948. He was back on the Third on
15 December 1951, giving an introductory talk to Christopher Sykes's
radio dramatisation of *Helena*, his novel about the Roman empress who
discovers the True Cross; this was broadcast the next night, with Flora
Robson in the title role, John Gielgud as her son the Emperor Constantine,

and, in a remarkably imaginative and effective piece of casting, the Light Programme comedian Ted Ray as the Wandering Jew, who in a dream shows Helena where to find the Cross. (Sykes's first choice for the part had been Wilfred Pickles, host of the Light's *Have a Go*.[7])

Once Grisewood was on the 'Programme' side of the fence, Haley's system, which had irritated him so much on the 'Supply' side, proved to have advantages. He was soon, he says, 'exercising a great deal of tact, persuasion and firmness' to get what the Third needed from the Supply departments. He notes with amusement that he met with a great deal of opposition from his left-wing former colleagues in Talks, 'and you can imagine what a pleasure it was for me to encounter and overcome this very opposition'. By the time that he joined the Third, relations between it and the Supply departments had indeed begun to sour. A frequent cause of trouble was over-runs.

'Kirkpatrick's harpsichord recital over-ran by 11 minutes,' Barnes complained to Music Department in October 1947, 'which seems to me excessive for a 30-minute recital, necessitating the postponement until Monday of a very topical and important talk by the Director of the National Gallery on the cleaning of pictures ... ' By the time that Herbert Murrill of Music Department replied to this, he was able to point out that Kirkpatrick's next recital had been preceded by a production of *Macbeth* which had under-run by about half an hour. 'This period was filled,' Murrill wrote to Barnes, 'by a programme of Vittoria Motets, which of course were unannounced in *Radio Times*, and from the musical standpoint were a pretty silly preface to a Bach recital.' Barnes passed this memo on to Leslie Stokes, in charge of presentation, since it was one of the announcers who had devised the Vittoria interlude. Stokes wrote on the bottom of it that it had become the Third's job to preserve listeners from 'the incompetence, or laziness, of the supply depts. The result is that the supply depts have become more lazy and incompetent ... '

The under-running of *Macbeth* (14 October 1947) came a week after a season of Shakespeare's history plays, broadcast nightly. *Henry VI* was performed in a drastically shortened version, and all the texts had been abbreviated (a departure from the Third's principle of no cuts). Barnes wrote to Val Gielgud, Director of Drama, that the experiment had been 'well worth doing', but 'the plays had too many producers and the casting was not as perfect as you had originally intended'. In particular, *Henry V*, produced by Howard Rose (the man who left live transmissions early to catch his train home), had been 'thoroughly undistinguished'; Burgundy's celebrated speech about the condition of France 'was one of the most lamentable performances I have ever heard'. Since Burgundy does not appear in the *Radio Times* cast list, he had presumably been recruited in the George at lunchtime.

---

[7] Pickles appeared as Trimalchio in Louis MacNeice's adaptation and production of *Trimalchio's Feast*, from the *Satyricon* of Petronius, on the Third on 22 December 1948.

Gielgud accepted these criticisms gracefully, but two months later he wrote to Barnes: 'There is no doubt in my mind that the high prestige of the [Third] Programme as a whole is suffering from the "educational and highbrow" labels, and that we are in danger sometimes of pleasing, let us say, the critic of the *New Statesman* rather than listeners.' That journal's radio reviewer, Tom Wintringham, was indeed complimentary to the Third in a column published on 27 September 1947, two days before the network's first birthday: 'From what the "Third" gives us ... I get the feeling that we are becoming a musical nation again.' Yet even he had one major criticism: 'The Third Programme is hampered more than either of the others by the inflexibility of the "educated" English accent.' The *Daily Express* critic, Nicholas Hallam, made a similar comment – 'Must "serious" people necessarily be solemn?' – and added: 'I cannot help feeling ... that the Third would be better for some new blood in its management. Too many of the items smell of the dust of a don's study, and give the impression that they are broadcast because they are highbrow and/or unusual, not because they are good.'

Among the birthday tributes were the usual complaints that the Third could still only be heard by half the population, and was still suffering from interference by Soviet Latvia. One columnist pointed out that it could not be picked up at all in Bloomsbury, supposed heartland of intellectuals, though it was reported that Sibelius was managing to hear it in Finland.

On 6 November 1947, five weeks after the birthday, came a discouraging BBC Listener Research Report, headed *A Year of the Third Programme: some notes on its audience*. This stated that the audience was roughly the same numerically as at the beginning of the year, but that people seemed to be listening to the Third less often than before. Leslie Stokes gave his comments on this to Barnes and Grisewood:

1. What was at first an engrossing novelty has now become commonplace ... its existence is taken for granted ...
2. The programme demands attentive listening ... Variable quality of reception often makes [this] impossible ...
3. It is already possible that the Third Programme may already have done something towards introducing the public to literature, and they may consequently be reading more and listening less ...

On the other hand *Penguin Music Magazine* (September 1947) reported a decline in London concert audiences, and suggested that it had 'dwindled because of the Third Programme'.

Looking at the figures, Haley said he was worried by the fact that only a very small audience was tuning in to the Third's Saturday symphony concerts. 'I must confess,' he wrote to Barnes, 'I do not often find myself attracted to them. Do you think anything can be done without relaxing any standards?' (The previous Saturday's concert had consisted of Mendelssohn's overture *Calm Sea and Prosperous Voyage*, a recitative and aria from Weber's *Der Freischütz*, and Sibelius's Seventh Symphony.) Replying to Haley, Barnes explained that the Saturday concert was the only programme in the week for which the BBC Symphony Orchestra had time to rehearse unfamiliar works; hence it had tended to become 'a miscellaneous collection of large musical items'. If the Symphony Orchestra could be improved, rehearsal time would become less critical and the repertoire could be made more appealing. Meanwhile Barnes himself was becoming anxious that musical works were sometimes being chosen 'for academic reasons', and that there had been instances of 'reviving what is better forgotten'. He added, in this note to John Lowe, 'We should not over do the contemporary.'

An impressive number of contemporary works had been broadcast that year. Some were comparatively 'safe' for the nervous listener, such as Edmund Rubbra's Cello Sonata, Walton's String Quartet in A minor, and Lennox Berkeley's Piano Sonata, which had all received their first broadcasts. But plenty of compositions by serial and twelve-tone composers were being heard as well, including Dallapiccola (*Six Songs of Alcaeus, Two Lyrics of Anacreon,* and other works), Egon Wellesz (*The Leaden Echo and the Golden Echo*) and Roberto Gerhard (his Wind Quintet and Dances from *Don Quixote*).

Stokes affected not to be too worried by the audience figures, but thought it 'would be possible to increase [the] audience by making the programme, while still highbrow, more popular in expression. This would alienate and lose many of its present listeners, but gain a large number of new ones.' Singling out the presentation of music as the chief area in which this change could be made, he thus became the first person in the history of the Third to suggest that the network should be popular as well as serious. There would be many more.

CHAPTER SIX

It must have an audience

'Sir – how many people listen to the Third Programme?' asked a correspondent to a Scottish newspaper on 6 January 1948. 'Certainly nobody I know ... Many have tried and found it unbearably dull and pretentious ... The "Third" has a grand chance, but its producers make the mistake of thinking that what is obscure must be good.' The letter was signed 'No Philistine'. A few weeks later an Ealing listener wrote to the *Daily Telegraph*: 'What enthusiasm there was for it is a rapidly waning quantity ... Its disdain of the average listener is profound. It also affronts him with its dullest offerings, when he has most time to spare.' Another *Telegraph* reader, from Oxford, asserted: 'There are two sorts of listeners to the Third Programme: the genuine and the pseudo intellectual ... The implication that we should be a better nation if we all listened ... is what a half-educated father of a family like me finds so irritatingly complacent and unreal.' Even the previously enthusiastic radio critic L. Marsland Gander was turning against the Third: 'There are some things in it which everybody might like to hear, and there are others which hardly anybody wants to hear. In between these extremes are many other items of interest which the ordinary listener might possibly be induced to hear if he were not repelled by the aura of intellectual snobbery which the Third has somehow acquired.'

Looking at the *Radio Times* for the month in which these complaints appeared, January 1948, one certainly finds a rather less sparkling Third Programme than a year earlier. For example Wednesday 21 January opened with a recital of Brahms chamber music, followed by P. H. Newby giving a talk on *The Thousand and One Nights*. A selection of readings from the *Nights* was heard later in the evening – but not until 10.15 pm. The intervening three hours had been filled with a concert by the Jacques Orchestra (playing Corelli, Gordon Jacob and Malcolm Arnold), a production of F. L. Lucas's play *The Siren*, and songs by the nineteenth-century composer Henri Duparc. Schedules for some evenings looked casually arranged, without a careful alternation between music and speech, and with no effort to relate programmes to each other with common themes.

The only highlight, on Friday 23 January, was a studio production of Handel's *Xerxes*.

The sole new development that the Third could boast at this period was *Ideas and Beliefs of the Victorians*, announced in the *Radio Times* as 'A major new Third Programme–Talks Department project'. It opened on Sunday 1 February with a forty-five-minute symposium featuring Bertrand Russell, G. M. Trevelyan, Lord David Cecil and Christopher Dawson. The *Radio Times* printed a schedule of the programmes (talks and readings) which would follow this inauguration at the rate of several a week, though it was admitted that only the first three weeks' broadcasts had been firmly arranged. Like almost everything else on the Third at this period, the series was not allocated particular days of the week or times. It trickled on for four months. Subjects and speakers were of the highest order – for example Harold Laski spoke on Fabian Socialism (10 February) and Ronald Knox on Newman and Roman Catholicism (29 March). But there were long gaps, and then the series – afterwards published as a book[1] – would suddenly reappear, sometimes with two talks on the same evening.

Many of the jokes about the Third were now coming from the BBC's own comedians; for example, the three networks had been nicknamed 'Slight, Drone and Weird'. Complaints about poor reception included this letter to the *Scotsman*:

> Only recently I spent 30 minutes with my head literally in physical contact with the receiver, straining to pick up the finer points of a most interesting discussion between Lord [Bertrand] Russell and Father Copleston, SJ, on the subject of the existence of God. I have to confess that owing to the difficulties of the reception and to the exasperating nature of the posture I was forced to adopt, I failed finally to gather whether, in fact, the Deity did exist or not, and by then my general indignation was such as to drive all thoughts of the Divine Being from my mind.

Listening to the recording of the early part of this celebrated discussion, broadcast on 28 January 1948, one is left not altogether wiser than this frustrated correspondent. Russell and Copleston set out to dispute the ontological proofs of the existence of God, but soon find they cannot agree on terminology:

> RUSSELL: Certainly the question 'Does a cause of the world exist?' is a question that has meaning. But if you say, 'Yes, God is the cause of the world', you are using 'God' as a proper name; then 'God exists' will not be a statement that has meaning – that is the position that I'm maintaining. Because, therefore, it will follow that it cannot be an analytic proposition ever to say that this or that exists. For example, suppose you take as your subject 'The Existent Round-Square'. It would

---

[1] *Ideas and Beliefs of the Victorians*, Sylvan Press, 1949.

look like an analytic proposition that the Existent Round-Square exists; but it doesn't exist.

COPLESTON: No, it doesn't. Then surely you can't say it doesn't exist unless you have a conception of what existence is. As to the phrase, 'Existent Round-Square', I should say that it has no meaning at all.

RUSSELL: I quite agree. Then I should say the same thing in another context in reference to a 'necessary being'.

COPLESTON: Well, we seem to have arrived at an impasse ...

Russell's and Copleston's style of speaking sounds extraordinarily wooden. This is because unscripted discussions were not yet permitted. The practice was to record the participants talking impromptu on a dictaphone, in advance of the broadcast. This was then transcribed, edited, retyped, and read out by them on the air. The Russell–Copleston dialogue suffered a mishap during this process; Basil Taylor, the producer, had to apologise to them because 'our Control Room were feeding the discussion into the wrong dictaphone for the first twenty minutes and consequently no transcript is available of what was said during that time'. This was all the worse because 'the argument did spring from much of what was said in the first quarter of an hour'. They had to reconstruct it from memory.

Haley listened to the broadcast, and thought much of it 'perhaps a little too difficult for the broad run of even a Third Programme audience. Kant, Plotinus, Sartre and Leibnitz, quoted and poured out at that rate, took some absorbing.' However, he felt it had greatly improved in the second half: 'The greatest tribute one could pay to it was that as it developed one got terribly anxious lest the debate should end at 10.25 as the *Radio Times* said it would.' Certainly towards the end the programme comes alight, as Copleston challenges Russell's assertion that the sense of good and bad is merely a subjective expression of feeling:

COPLESTON: Let us take the behaviour of the Commandant of Belsen. That appears to you undesirable and evil, and to me too. To Adolf Hitler we suppose it appeared as something good and desirable. So I suppose you would have that for Hitler it was good, and for you it is evil.

RUSSELL: No, I shouldn't go quite as far as that. I think people can make mistakes in that, as they can in other things. If you have jaundice you see things yellow that are not yellow. You are making a mistake.

COPLESTON: Yes, one can make mistakes, but can you make a mistake if it is simply a question of reference to a feeling or emotion? Surely Hitler would be the only possible judge of what appealed to his emotions.

RUSSELL: It would be quite right to say that it appealed to his emotions, but you can say various things about that, among others that if that sort of thing makes that sort of appeal to Hitler's emotions, then Hitler makes quite a different appeal to my emotions.

COPLESTON: In your view, then, there is no objective criterion outside feeling for condemning the conduct of the Commandant of Belsen?

RUSSELL: No more than there is for the colour-blind person, who is in exactly the same state. Why do we intellectually condemn the colour-blind man? Isn't it because he is in the minority?

COPLESTON: I would say because he is lacking in a thing which normally belongs to human nature.

RUSSELL: Yes, but if he was in the majority we shouldn't say that.

COPLESTON: Then you would say that there is no criterion outside feeling that will enable one to distinguish between the behaviour of the Commandant of Belsen and the behaviour, say, of Sir Stafford Cripps, or the Archbishop of Canterbury.

RUSSELL: The feeling is a little too simplified. You have got to take account of the effects of actions and your feelings towards those effects. You can have an argument about it if you say that certain sorts of occurrences are the sort you like, and certain others the sort you don't. Then you have to take account of the effects of actions. You can very well say that the effects of the actions of the Commandant of Belsen were painful and unpleasant.

COPLESTON: They certainly were, I agree, very painful and unpleasant to all the people in the camp.

RUSSELL: Yes, but not only to the people in the camp, but also to others contemplating them.

COPLESTON: Yes, quite true in imagination. But that is my point. I don't approve of them and I know you don't approve of them, but I don't see what ground you have of not approving of them, because, after all, to the Commandant of Belsen himself they are pleasant, those actions.

RUSSELL: Yes, but I don't need any more ground in that case than I do in the case of colour perception. There are some people who think everything is yellow, there are people suffering from jaundice, and I don't agree with those people. I can't prove that the things are not yellow, there isn't any proof. But most people agree with me that they are not yellow, and most people agree with me that the Commandant of Belsen was making mistakes.

COPLESTON: Do you accept any moral obligation?

RUSSELL: I should have to answer that question at considerable length . . .

One of the Talks Department producers, Peter Laslett, recalls that Russell never needed a script. A subject for a talk might be proposed to him, and, on the spot, 'that face would set, and his eyes would glint a bit; there would be a moment or two – and then he'd give you twenty minutes of broadcastable prose. You could have recorded a perfect programme from what he said. But we were not allowed to broadcast unscripted material. The curious thing is, this didn't cause the resistance you might expect. Russell would happily go and write it out, and then come back and read it.' Laslett adds:

If you interfered with a man's script when he didn't respect you, you'd had it. I remember a now forgotten figure, an Oxford classics professor, who got so angry with me that he picked up a whisky bottle – we were allowed to drink whisky in the studio – and threatened me with it, and hit one of those extraordinary microphones we used to have, those damn great copper things. Of course it was live. You couldn't reply, 'I'll give you one, you old sod,' because the whole audience could listen.

*

One listener's letter, in January 1948, expressed anxiety about the BBC's reaction to the press attacks on the Third: 'One fears that the clamour and the silly cries of "Intellectual Snobbery" may induce the BBC to give ground.' Indeed, ground was already being yielded. That month, the Third was told that its final hour of broadcasting each evening, from 11 pm to midnight, which had been cut during the fuel shortage the previous year, would be restored in April, but 'will be devoted almost entirely to extra reproduction of recorded programmes' – that is, repeats. No fresh material would be commissioned to fill the extra time. This was necessary because the Third had not been given enough money to finance the extra hour. Its weekly programme budget until the reduction in hours had been £5,000. After the cut, this was reduced to £4,625. 'This gives an average of £132 for each hour of programme time,' noted Harman Grisewood. 'For the extended hour [11 pm to midnight] I am given an additional £365, but I would need £924 extra, i.e. 7 x £132, if these hours were to be planned on the same principle as the remainder of the Programme.' In this memo to Basil Nicolls, Grisewood remarked that the low-budgeted final hour each evening 'does not appear very attractive'.

On 8 February 1948, Grisewood had been appointed Acting Controller, Third Programme, replacing George Barnes. (The title 'Controller' had been granted to the Third's head a short time earlier, bringing its status in line with the other networks.) In a management reshuffle, Barnes had been promoted to a new post, Director of the Spoken Word. In his book on BBC External Broadcasting, Gerard Mansell explains the change:

> Haley was anxious to reduce the calls on the Director-General's time which arose from the large number of officials who reported direct to him. This led him to propose ... the creation of a senior executive body ... the Board of Management, [which] met for the first time on 5 January 1948 under Haley's chairmanship. Its members were five newly-created Directors ... Each ... was responsible for a broad grouping of activities – Administration, Technical Services, the Spoken Word, Home Output and Overseas Services.

Barnes, whose appointment over the heads of the Controllers of the Home Service and Light Programme was something of an accolade for the Third, remained Director of the Spoken Word until October 1950, when he was appointed to the newly created post of Director of Television. In 1956 he left the BBC to become principal of the University College of North Staffordshire, later Keele University, and died in office there at the age of fifty-six. His son Anthony says there had been 'a feeling that he might one day become Director-General', but the strain of running BBC Television, just as competition with ITV was beginning, proved 'ghastly in every way – he wasn't that sort of in-fighter, and I think the cancer that got him a few years later was related to that stress'.

Grisewood was confirmed as the Third's new Controller on 18 March 1948. A magazine article written three years later describes him as

> short, eager, and [he] walks with a stoop. His large hazel eyes have a furrow between them, which probably comes from regarding the lesser-known works of seventeenth-century philosophy as light reading. He is an unorthodox dresser in the usually immaculate BBC, a colleague affectionately remarking that he wears period clothes, 'not only in style, but when they were made'.
>
> He has a house in the country, where he takes his homework – the listener research figures and the two French plays he reads a week with an eye for translation. He rarely listens to the radio – 'except professionally'. He has a taste for good wine and cognac.

Grisewood needed someone to fill the post of Third Programme Planner. 'I was talking to Christopher Sykes about it,' he recalls, 'and he said, "Why not me?"' Sykes, the future biographer of Evelyn Waugh, had written radio scripts but was not yet on the BBC staff (he later became a Features producer and writer). He was allowed to fill the post for three months, during which the job was advertised, as 'Chief Assistant to the Controller'. The successful applicant was Christopher Holme. 'He was an expert on all kinds of things I never was,' says Grisewood, 'a good mathematician, knowledgeable about the Middle East, and so on. We were still a very small team.'

Aged forty-three, a year younger than Grisewood, Holme had been educated at Rugby and Oxford, where he had shared digs with Louis MacNeice. During the 1930s he had been a Reuters correspondent, working, as his widow Anthea puts it, 'in most of the hotspots – Berlin at the time of the Reichstag fire, Abyssinia in '34, Spain, where he reported on the Guernica bombing, and Vienna when the Germans arrived – he and his assistant escaped across the border in Christopher's smashing green Lagonda.' He had then worked in Palestine, and became foreign news editor of the *Observer*, before joining the Third. His spare-time activity was translating German literature.

Grisewood recalls that, at the time when he and Holme took over its leadership, the Third was becoming beleaguered. 'But I didn't mind that. It was what I'd expected. We'd all been brought up by Reith to think that working men should appreciate Beethoven and that kind of thing, but I knew it was a lot of balls.' His conservative and Catholic background had conditioned him to regard culture as something only understood and appreciated by an elite, and he was prepared to defend that elite's right to it. 'The attacks on the Third,' he says, reflect the kind of philistinism which Matthew Arnold and many others have accused the English of. (I don't think you'll find an equivalent of the pejorative English word 'highbrow' in any other language.) It's something to do with the prestige in England of the landed gentry – the people who were looked up to weren't intellectuals, in the way that the French and Germans have always looked up to their intellectual leaders. But I eagerly accepted the role of defender of the highbrow. I think that George Barnes had inherited something of the Cambridge missionary spirit – the general character of Cambridge was more consciously leftish than my circle at Oxford. But I didn't want to missionise. I believe in elites, because they are simply the best. And I think the best is the right thing to have.

Haley felt that Grisewood 'did the Third Programme very well after Barnes, and a lot of its more original ideas were due to him'. However, P. H. Newby, who worked in Talks Department before eventually succeeding to the Controllership of the Third, says: 'When Harman was Controller, it was in fact Christopher Holme who did the work, took most of the editorial decisions, and instituted and energised many of the programmes. Harman was much more volatile than Christopher, who was serious-minded, very good. Harman presided rather than initiated, and it was Christopher who supplied the rock on which the editorial judgement was based.' Anthea Holme says that her husband did not resent this: 'He was very fond of Harman, and never said a word against him.'

*

One of Barnes's last actions on leaving the Third was to circulate a memo about 'the lack of original writing for radio'. So far, the Third had only inspired (he said) a 'trickle' of notable new work. He had discussed it with Laurence Gilliam, the Head of Features, who suggested creating two staff contracts for writers; this would enable him to employ 'a promising writer like Dylan Thomas or G. S. Fraser or Henry Reed for a period of a year'. It is doubtful whether Thomas would have accepted such a contract had it been offered. Later in 1948 he wrote to Richard Hughes: 'I undertake all sorts of little jobs, broadcasting etc., which hinder my own work.' He dreamt of earning enough from film scripts to cut out 'all time-wasting broadcasts'. Actually he was doing very little for the Third at this time.

Grisewood also instigated a competition for listeners to complete Jane Austen's unfinished novel *Sanditon*. The existing portion of the book was read on the air by Leslie Stokes during a week in August 1948, and entries – an outline suggesting how the story might be completed, and an episode from any part of the continuation – were judged by Elizabeth Bowen and two Austen scholars. The winner was announced, and the winning entry read, on 21 October. Publicity schemes such as this were badly needed. In a note to Grisewood in April 1948, George Barnes remarked that his impression as an 'outsider' to the Third was that 'publicity is execrable', so 'no wonder nobody listens'.

This remark came in the course of Barnes's comment on the first programme in a new series, *Serenade*. This had been proposed by John Lowe, who argued that 'Third Programme music needs more *entertainment* of the best sort as distinct from straight recitals of particular works or particular kinds of work ... *imaginative* programmes, so shaped and arranged as to have the spell of real entertainment in them'. The first programme was broadcast at 8.40 pm on 6 April 1948, and lasted an hour. 'We play tonight the first of a new series of Serenade Concerts,' explained the announcer. 'These programmes do not confine themselves to any one period, or composer, or kind of music. Their object is to present, in the evening, a series of beautiful and varied pieces which may follow enjoyably one after the other.' The first piece was a Handel concerto grosso; then came music by Schubert, Bliss, Debussy, Walter Leigh, Dowland and Mozart, with only brief announcements intervening.

'I enjoyed the first Serenade concert,' Barnes wrote to Grisewood. 'I am not certain that the ideal result was achieved, i.e. [a] sequence ... so good that the items were fused together and became almost a work of art on their own ... I thought the presentation poor ... there was little sensitiveness on the part of the announcer.' *Serenade* was made up of live performances rather than gramophone records, and its miscellaneous nature began to cause administrative problems. 'I feel bound to ask you to look into the almost tragic state of affairs at the Serenade Concert last evening (Friday April 23, 9.35 pm),' John Lowe wrote to the Head of Music.

> This difficult and – from a studio and balance point of view – complicated programme was put in People's Palace No. 1 [the main hall of the People's Palace in Mile End Road]. That proved unsuitable for a programme involving, in separate items, a chamber orchestra, a choir with a piano, and a piano solo. We had asked for the Camden Theatre, which *is* suitable. Second, the pianos on which Joan Davies had to play a Chopin Nocturne and the piano part of Brahms' *Zigeunerlieder* were out of tune and had had the guts worn out of them by Dance Bands ... The excellent Grand used at the Proms seems to be kept in store for all the rest of the year. Could it not be used sometimes for special programmes and a 'Brown Coat' [tarpaulin] be stationed over it to keep the Dance Band ivory-thumpers off it?

Looking back over the *Serenade* series a year after it had started, Dyneley Hussey, the *Listener* music critic, was not enthusiastic:

> I do not know how far this series was suggested or influenced by the admirable *Music in Miniature* in the Light Programme, which is said to have had a startling success with people who normally cannot abide anything in the nature of chamber-music ... The charm of *Music in Miniature* lay in its combination of unexpectedness and ... brevity. Extended to an hour's length and with the items formally set out, [*Serenade*] seems a meaningless *mélange*.

The *Sanditon* competition and *Serenade* were, of course, evidence of the Third's determination to win new listeners. This task began to seem desperately important after a Listener Research Report dated 16 April 1948, which stated bluntly that 'the Third Programme audience has diminished considerably and is now so small that it represents only a fraction of those who showed an early interest'. A chief cause of the decline appeared to be 'dissatisfaction' that the Third was 'emphasising unfamiliar works at the expense of known classics'.

A sample evening (Friday, 16 April 1948, the date of the report) shows that unfamiliar works were indeed predominating. The evening's broadcasts began with a radio play by Charles Williams, *The Three Temptations*. The pianist Agnes Walker then gave a twenty-minute recital of Scriabin, and at 7 pm Dr J. Bronowski – one of the great broadcasters of the post-war years – gave the third talk in his five-part series *The Common Sense of Science* ('on the growth of science and its creative ideas in relation to society and the arts'). At 7.30 Ernest Ansermet conducted a programme of Vivaldi concertos, and at 8.40 came *The Great Hunger*, a play by David Thomson about the Irish potato famine. At 9.35 the BBC Chorus and the Boyd Neel Orchestra, with soloists, conducted by Leslie Woodgate, performed Rubbra's *The Dark Night of the Soul* and Bach's Cantata no. 80, *Eine feste Burg*, after which the entertainer Ruth Draper gave one of her comic monologues, 'At an Art Exhibition'. This was followed by a selection of readings from Victorian authors on the emancipation of women, and at 10.55 the choir of the Brompton Oratory provided the musical illustrations to a script by Egon Wellesz on 'Early Christian Music' – the second programme in *A History in Sound of European Music*. The final programme was a selection from the poems of Vachel Lindsay.

The report stated that many programmes were felt to be too long, listeners complaining that they could not 'concentrate on listening for periods of two to four hours at a time'. Many remarked that the Third had lately been 'showing a tendency to become too consciously highbrow, even recherché, and that some of its programmes comprised works of only academic or recondite interest'. A theme which was 'echoed and re-echoed' among those who were questioned was that 'they are looking for programmes which are not so far removed from their experience that they feel hostile'.

One section of public opinion felt that the smallness of the Third's audience did not matter because of the quality of attention given to programmes by those who did listen. The pianist and broadcaster Sidney Harrison wrote in his column in *John O'London's Weekly*:

Our sonata recital on the Third Programme ended at two minutes past midnight. As John Shinebourne put away his cello I asked him how many people he thought had been listening to Delius and Rachmaninoff at that time of day. He said, 'You just give one bad performance and you'll be astonished how many people listen.' That is the beauty of the Third Programme. The few who listen, listen.

Yet even in the musical world there were doubts. 'Will the BBC tell *Musical Express* how much per annum the Third Programme is costing to run,' asked that paper in June 1948, 'and what are the accurate listening figures for it? With this information we could compute the importance of the Third Programme to this nation ... ' No precise audience figures were issued, nor were they given in the Listener Research Report.

Although Grisewood was not making public statements, his internal correspondence betrays a degree of anxiety about the loss of audience. 'I know nothing about the Liapunov Piano Concerto,' he wrote to John Lowe in May 1948, after examining music schedules, 'nor about the Piston Symphony. I presume Piston is a contemporary composer. I spoke the other day about contemporary music "creeping in". This is the sort of instance I have in mind. I don't think we need an extra contemporary music concert this week ... Can something else be substituted, please, on this occasion.' The same memo asked that an *Art of Fugue* recital should be cut from ninety minutes to forty-five.

Contemporary music was not 'creeping in'; it had been there substantially since the start of the Third and now, if anything, its airtime was declining. Edward Clark, the pre-war pioneer of contemporary music broadcasts, had introduced a series called *Turning Points in Twentieth Century Music* between January and March 1949, but this had featured only Schoenberg, Bartók and Stravinsky. Mátyás Seiber's *Sonata da camera* was the only work by a composer associated with the twelve-tone technique to be heard on the Third in May, the month that Grisewood's memo was written. The remainder of the year was equally sparse in this respect. On the other hand Vaughan Williams's Sixth Symphony, which had its first performance in April 1921, received no less than four broadcasts then and in following weeks, two on the Home Service and two on the Third. Britten's newly completed realisation of *The Beggar's Opera* made three appearances on the Third and one on the Home in September.

The BBC had found a new Head of Music (as the job had been retitled), Sir Steuart Wilson, who had previously been director of music at the Arts Council, after a career as a tenor soloist. Grisewood describes him as 'an aggressive kind of man, of great charm, very attractive to women. I didn't get on with him at all well, but he knew his job.' On 26 May 1948, nearly two months after arriving at the BBC, Wilson sent Grisewood a memo which was indeed aggressive. He said he considered that Music Department was taking on more programmes for the Third than it could handle, and reminded Grisewood that for some time he (Wilson) had been saying that 'either I should have to have more staff or cut down on output'. He had now been told that no increase of staff was possible. He went on:

Third Programme music spaces are not filled easily; the nature of the programme and the artist to fill it, is a matter which has to be thought out at some leisure ... At present I consider that my Music Assistants [as Music Department producers were then called] have not got any time for the thought and research which is essential unless your programmes are to become commonplace and hurried.

He therefore proposed that, from August onwards, five live music pro-grammes each week – about three hours of broadcasting – should be deleted from the schedule.

Considering that he had been given no notice of this cut, and his staff were already planning the August programmes, Grisewood replied in surprisingly calm tones. He remarked that the proposed reduction in music was 'altogether too great for me to meet by turning to other departments who are already fully stretched'. In any case, such a drastic reduction in the amount of music per week would 'radically affect the Third Pro-gramme'. But Grisewood took a tougher line with Wilson's superior, the Controller of Entertainment, telling him: 'I cannot accept the cut proposed ... This is a grave situation ... I am threatened with blanks in the weekly schedule that cannot be filled. I suggest that D.H.B. [Basil Nicolls, now styled Director of Home Broadcasting] is immediately acquainted with the situation and is shown H[ead of] M[usic]'s memorandum.' Yet Grisewood allowed that Wilson had a problem: 'His people ... have been overworked for months ... on the brink of breakdown. Now it has come.'

Grisewood also wrote to Nicolls about the urgent 'need to make the Third Programme more attractive'. He said he needed 'one new full-scale drama production per week', and an increase in features – an area in which the Third was 'decidedly under-nourished'. Only Talks Department was able to meet the Third's requirements, probably because its staff had increased since the Third began.

No further correspondence about Wilson's proposed cut in music pro-grammes can be found, and it is evident from the *Radio Times* that no such cut was made, presumably because, by mid-June, Haley had approved the creation of two new staff posts in Music Department. It may be that Wilson's drastic decree was simply a ploy to achieve that end. However, one major casualty among music programmes could not be avoided.

*

In January 1948, the Third had launched a remarkable series of gigantic proportions, entitled *The History in Sound of European Music*. Planning for this had begun a year earlier, in collaboration with the editors of the *New Oxford History of Music*, one of whom, Gerald Abraham, now professor of music at Liverpool University, had been on the BBC staff. He agreed to take charge of the broadcasts. No less than 104 programmes were envisaged, progressing chronologically from *The Oldest Surviving Secular Music* to twelve-tone technique (and the backlash against it). A large number of distinguished musicologists were enlisted to devise them.

Rather than give talks with musical illustrations – the obvious way of covering the ground – they were asked to plan concert programmes of historically informed performances, and write programme notes, which would be read by Alec Robertson, the music talks producer. George Barnes noted that 'the performance will be of the highest professional standard available in this country', and it was hoped that HMV would put selected recordings from the series on sale in the shops.

From the start, there was a subtle conflict of interests. 'Each broadcast should contain a masterpiece,' declared Barnes when drafting the series' terms of reference. He was evidently anxious that the programmes should not be swamped with obscure items: 'In choosing works the importance of the familiar as a bait for the uninitiated must always be remembered.' However, Gerald Abraham, in a printed pamphlet publicising the series, put the emphasis on the discoveries that the series would make:

> It has been worked out by people who believe that the music of every known period contains at least a proportion of living art, well worth listening to if only we can conquer any initial strangeness of idiom. They are not so foolish as to claim that all, or anything like all, the works to be broadcast are masterpieces; the really important point is that none of them are mere museum-pieces.

The BBC producer assigned to the series, Basil Lam, did not get on with Abraham, who began to mutter that the Third Programme staff were 'incompetent'. By late February 1948, when the series had been on the air for nearly two months, John Lowe admitted that the BBC's handling of it had been 'seriously deficient'. Programmes were often being set up at the last minute, without Abraham being 'properly consulted'. The series was due for a three-month break after the twenty-fifth programme, *Early Keyboard Music on the Continent*, in mid-June 1948. In early May, Grisewood expressed concern about the quality of the programmes, writing to John Lowe that

> the presentation and arrangement of the material [has] caused me a good deal of disappointment. What I looked for was some real historical feeling in the spoken material but what I get is a sense that music must have developed *in vacuo*, so to speak, having no correspondence on the one hand with the other arts and none on the other with the great rousing world of events ... Furthermore, I find the style itself in which the material is written for the most part dry and not very well suited to speech. I get the impression that the speaker, Alec Robertson, does his best with it but it still remains as wooden as an academic text book. I would like the whole approach in the light of what I have said above to be considered afresh before irrevocable plans are laid for the autumn series.

Grisewood was also concerned that, as later periods in the history of music were reached, the forces required for proper illustration of big works could not be afforded. Consequently the series was not resumed in the autumn of 1948.

Gerald Abraham's disappointment, indeed outrage, was widely shared in the musical world. 'It is a pity,' Haley wrote to Grisewood, 'these stories are circulating hinting dark deeds by Philistine administrators. *The history must certainly go on*, to confute them. I suppose if necessary we can find a new editor?' Grisewood was prepared for it to resume in condensed form, but this was not acceptable to Abraham. Meanwhile a memo from Steuart Wilson was sarcastically headed 'Quam olim Abrahae promisisti' – 'which you once promised to Abraham' – an allusion to the *Magnificat*.

*

By the summer of 1948 the press was beginning to get wind of the drastic drop in audiences. 'The BBC Third Programme, which costs £1,000,000 a year,[2] is now listened to by only two people in 1,000 – according to listener research figures,' reported the *Sunday Dispatch* on 22 August. 'A year ago,' continued the report,

> nine in 1,000 listened. The figure dropped to seven between October and December 1947. Then from January to March this year, to four. Mr Harman Grisewood, director of the Third Programme, told the *Sunday Dispatch* yesterday: 'We are discussing ways of widening the scope of the programme, but there is no suggestion of diluting it. At present we estimate that only about 50 per cent of the country can hear the "Third", and of these a considerable proportion get poor reception.'

A correspondent to the *Daily Mirror* suggested that 'the ultra-mincing highbrow Third Programme' should be replaced by 'a university of the air', offering 'courses in a variety of subjects, including foreign languages'.

The Third celebrated its second birthday on Sunday 26 September 1948, three days before the actual anniversary, with Bach's B Minor Mass, T. S. Eliot reading *Four Quartets* (on gramophone records), and Harold Nicolson giving a talk on the Third itself. Recalling that 'I was one of the Governors who decided to introduce this programme', he wasted no breath on empty praise, but turned to the sensitive matter of the Third's audience:

> It was a misfortune, I now feel, that we failed to define more precisely the exact nature of the audience to whom this new experiment should address its appeal. I have the impression sometimes that the producers and planners of the Third Programme, being vague regarding the nature of their audience, become vague also in the choice and handling of their subjects. They seem never to have quite made up their minds whether their aim is to satisfy the highly educated or to entice, solicit and inveigle the semi-educated to enlarge the areas of their knowledge and appreciation.
>
> Let me give an instance of this uncertainty of choice and handling. The other day the Third Programme broadcast a version of Plato's *Symposium*;

---

[2] This sum included staff salaries, transmitter and studio costs, and other overheads. The programme budget was around £260,000.

it attracted, it seems, a large number of listeners. Now, if the producers had aimed at satisfying the highly-educated, they would have known that they would not satisfy, but only irritate, such an audience by leaving out the awkward bits. But if they were aiming at an audience ignorant of the *Symposium*, then they were abandoning their own standards in supplying that audience, not with the *Symposium* as written by Plato, but with the *Symposium* as edited in Langham Place. I am not suggesting of course that the *Symposium* should have been broadcast in its entirety; I am only suggesting that if the producers had kept an educated audience in mind they would have known that this masterpiece is not suitable for rendering on the air. They would have left it alone.

Proceeding with this rather sour birthday tribute, Nicolson emphasised that the original concern of the Third had been solely with the quality of programmes, not the quantity of audience. 'In the first year,' he said, 'this principle was strictly adhered to, with the most beneficial results. Of late however I have detected a decline in integrity, a tendency to consider whether the item broadcast can be made more palatable to a larger number of people.' He blamed Listener Research, which he described as a 'temperature-chart', seeping into the BBC's subconscious and ruining its morale. His talk concluded with 'a gnawing fear' that the Third might attempt to be more popular. 'If that were allowed to happen, then assuredly the hopes and ideas which gave it birth will have been doomed to disappointment, and the Third Programme will become merely a third pro gramme on the British broadcasting system.'

A more cheerful element of the birthday was the news, announced on 29 September, that 'after March, 1950, the Third Programme should sound louder and clearer', thanks to 'the new allocation of wavelengths at the Copenhagen conference'. So ran the *Manchester Guardian* report of a BBC statement, which continued: 'The new wavelength of 464 is shared with Kharkov, which is more remote [than the Soviet Latvia transmitter at Riga]. We shall be able, therefore, to raise the strength from 20–25 kilowatts to about 120. The BBC does not guarantee that every listener will hear the Third Programme really well, but nearly everybody should get satisfactory reception.'

Unfortunately a few weeks after this announcement, reception became even worse than ever. On 9 November a transmitter at Tunis came on the air on 514 metres, as it had every right to do under the current allocation of wavelengths. In the next few days it gradually increased in power, so that it was soon stronger than the signal from Riga. By Christmas, BBC engineers had re-sited the Third's 203.5-metres London area transmitter from Nightingale Square, Balham, to Brookmans Park, Hatfield, with satisfactory results; but in those parts of the country dependent on the Droitwich 514-metres signal, the Tunisian interference meant that reception had deteriorated further.

Meanwhile Grisewood and his team continued their efforts to broaden the appeal of the Third without sacrificing quality. At the end of September, Haley announced to a Radio Industries meeting that the Third intended to carry 'a series of Light Music Concerts'. Grisewood attached 'a good deal of importance' to this project, explaining: 'What we want to do ... is to acquaint British listeners with the authentic light music tradition that is flourishing on the Continent and which does not encounter the same lowbrow/highbrow polarisation which always crops up in dealing with the subject here.' Yet he seemed a little anxious about it. Stanford Robinson, the BBC staff conductor of opera, felt that the selection of music 'should not be too lowbrow', and might 'stop short at e.g. Léhar'. Grisewood felt this was 'very sound'.

The series kicked off stylishly, with Beecham conducting the Royal Philharmonic Orchestra in a one-hour programme at 8.30 pm on Tuesday 30 November: Hérold's overture *Zampa*, Saint-Saëns's symphonic poem *Le rouet d'Omphale*, Bizet's *L'Arlésienne* suite, Fauré's *Pavane* (with chorus), and Chabrier's *España*. The broadcast was preceded by a talk by Compton Mackenzie entitled *What Is Light Music?* 'What is the true antonym of light?' he began.

> Light comedy and low comedy, light women and chaste women, light cavalry and heavy cavalry, light blue and dark blue, light opera and grand opera, light music and serious music, the light programme and the third programme. Note that the third programme has not dared to call itself the low programme ...
>
> You see, somebody better equipped than myself might have been tempted to turn his prologue into an apology because the mood of contemporary musical opinion is anxiously serious ... After being considered the most unmusical nation in the world for so long and being by now convinced that they were misjudged, the British public is not going to take any risks of enjoying too obviously the popular music they believe they have outgrown ... There is no doubt that contemporary composers are positively ashamed of melody ...
>
> It certainly isn't quite as easy nowadays to write good light music as ... it used to be in the days before humanity indulged in two world wars ... But whatever the Third Programme gives us, for goodness sake don't let us all sit round our radio sets with a grim determination to feel lighthearted, and then discuss the performance afterwards as if we'd sat listening to it with thermometers in our mouths, as if we were comparing our temperatures. Let us fancy that whatever instalment of some earnestly comic topographical serial[3] we may have missed on the Light Programme or the Home Service we have surrendered to a truer gaiety.

The next *Light Orchestral Concert* on the Third (Wednesday 8 December) was given by Stanford Robinson and the London Symphony Orchestra. It

---

[3] Mackenzie was probably thinking of *Much-Binding-in-the-Marsh*, a Light Programme series starring Richard Murdoch and Kenneth Horne.

included Lennox Berkeley and Benjamin Britten's jointly composed suite *Mont Juic*. John Barbirolli and the Philharmonia Orchestra appeared in the series on Tuesday 14 December at 8 pm and Sunday 19 December at 10.10 pm – oddly, during these months when the Third was struggling to gain new listeners, no one seems to have suggested that all the programmes in a series should be broadcast at the same time and on the same day each week. On Boxing Day, Josef Krips and the Vienna Philharmonic Orchestra played Strauss, Schubert and *Eine kleine Nachtmusik*.

The quality of performance could not have been higher, but the idea of light music on the Third began to cause widespread unrest. An article in the Oxford University magazine *Cherwell* on 31 January 1949 declared:

> These concerts are an unfortunate departure on the part of the BBC. To begin with, they are hardly good advertisements for similar concerts on other Services: the idea that Beecham or Barbirolli, conducting on the Third Programme, will give a better performance of a work than other conductors on the Home Service, creates an entirely false impression of the distinction between the two programmes ... The distinction ... is essentially one of *material*. The Third Programme is nothing if not the Specialist's programme.

The writer then went on to ridicule the idea that the *Light Orchestral Concerts* would bring new listeners to the Third:

> Do the BBC authorities imagine that because a listener tunes in to hear Beecham conducting a popular work of Tchaikovsky at 6.30, he will necessarily switch on again to hear Bertrand Russell on 'Social Cohesion' at 9.15? If the idea of these light concerts is to encourage the man in the street to be a more enterprising listener, then one can only wonder at the BBC's lack of insight into human nature. If, on the other hand, they represent a genuine attempt to reduce the Third Programme to the status of a second Home Service, then a unique opportunity in the history of Broadcasting has been seriously mishandled.

Even stronger objections were raised from Cambridge, by E. M. Forster. Grisewood recalls:

> I was sent for by Haley one day, who told me he'd had a visit from E. M. Forster to complain about how the Third Programme had become vulgarised. Haley said: 'I won't bother to explain what Forster really meant by vulgarisation, because I think it's best that you should see him. Why don't you ask him to lunch?' So I asked him to the Garrick, and Forster said: 'When your predecessor was there, you never would have had light music on the Third.'

As an Oxford man, Grisewood detected in Forster 'this suspicion of Oxford' – Barnes had been a Cambridge man, and traditionally Cambridge suspects Oxford of levity.

Returning from the lunch, which was on 8 December 1948, Grisewood wrote down what had been said:

> Mr E. M. Forster ... wished to know why I personally had embarked on this venture ... I told him I felt these programmes would be likely to justify their inclusion mainly as a result of the performances ... under first-rate conductors ... I added that if the Third Programme could do something to enlarge musical taste on lines that were closer to e.g. the Viennese and the Italian, we would have done something worth while. To this latter point Mr Forster agreed, but asked whether the programmes themselves sufficiently carried out this intention. He looked at the programmes and told me that he thought they were poor programmes for the Third Programme by any standard and inadequate for the purpose that I had in mind ...
>
> Mr Forster asked if I did not regard the inclusion of these programmes as a waste of the limited space available ... I replied ... that the time available was really quite adequate ... to cover the whole repertory of serious music ... Nothing more obviously Third Programme was being excluded ...
>
> I gained the impression that Mr Forster was not intending to leave the matter as it stood but would seek some opportunity to raise the point again.

Grisewood recalls: 'I spoke with great vehemence, to defend the principle of enjoyment. Forster's face clouded a little, and he took out of his pocket a little piece of cardboard. He held it in front of me. On it was written, in large letters, "TEMPER, TEMPER!"'

Doubts were felt about the project even within the Third. 'We are none of us perhaps quite certain what we mean by "light" music,' John Lowe wrote to Grisewood a week after the Forster lunch. By mid-January 1949, Grisewood felt that 'it would probably be best to drop the "Light Music" title for the light music concerts'.

Scarcely had this controversy begun than the BBC announced, in November 1948, that during the following January and February the Third would carry 'six weekly half-hours of swing', performed by Vic Lewis's band. An enraged reader of the *Birmingham Mail* described this as 'almost a disaster for British broadcasting ... I appeal to those who, like me, welcomed "The Third" because of its real quality, to write and protest.' Grisewood was anxious, telling Stokes that 'our interest in Jazz must be limited to the strictly musical. We are not ... interested in modern modifications of the original impulses that gave rise to the Jazz style, believing this mostly to arise from what might be called commercial motives.'

Another innovation announced to the press shortly before Christmas 1948 was the latest result of the Third's search for humour. Leslie Stokes described it to the Head of Publicity:

Third Division, with the sub-title 'Some Vulgar Fractions', is the title of an experimental series of six humorous programmes produced by Pat Dixon which will be broadcast at weekly intervals in the Third Programme, beginning in January. The object of the series is to present humorous material of a nature and in a manner which will appeal to those whose appreciation of satire and acceptance of unconventional presentation is largely unsatisfied by the popular comedy shows at present on the air. The style ... will be mainly satirical ... The narrator will be Robert Beatty and others appearing in most of the programmes will be Benny Lee, Benny Hill, Peter Sellers, Michael Bentine, Patricia Hayes, Harry Secombe, and Carole Carr. The authors will be Frank Muir, Denis Norden and Paul Dehn.

Muir and Norden were the scriptwriters for the Light Programme comedy series *Take It From Here*, which had started during 1947. Muir says it had done something to extend the boundaries of the genre: 'Until then, most radio comedy was end-of-the-pier and pantomime. We were the first to acknowledge that our listeners had read a book. We did sketches in '47 and '48 parodying Jane Austen.' Muir says that Pat Dixon, who produced *Third Division* for the Third Programme, was 'a terrific chap, and a rebel – he used to attend producers' meetings carrying the Confederate flag, which was propped up in his office. He was knocking on a bit, not young, but he started all sorts of ideas and shows. And what he wanted for the Third was a freewheeling amalgam. We [Muir and Norden] got on well with him, and he asked us whether we'd have a go at it. But it wasn't "experimental"; it was what we were doing all the time. There's no such thing as "experimental humour". You can try things, but you can't say, "I don't care whether people like it or not – I'm working up to something."'

The originality of *Third Division* lay in the choice of young performers. 'When you look at the cast list,' says Muir, 'they were all beginning.' Apart from Robert Beatty, an actor who linked the show, most came from the Windmill variety theatre off Piccadilly Circus. 'Peter Sellers was doing impressions there, in funny voices. Benny Hill was the same, and Bentine had an act there called Sherwood and Forest. Secombe was doing a shaving act at the Windmill, very bright and frisky – the way different people shaved, with a shaving brush.'

Third Division was broadcast during January and February 1949, at around 8 pm each Wednesday evening – a rare instance of a programme being given a regular slot. Muir says he and Nordern made their own choice of performers for each sketch, checked that they were available, and then got Dixon to book them. 'We have now completed the six recordings in the series,' Dixon told Leslie Stokes on 30 November 1948, 'and I hope you will agree that they are pretty good entertainment.' Recordings do not survive, but the scripts are in the BBC Written Archives. This is how the first one begins:

EFFECT: DING DONG DING DONG
DING DONG DING DOINK!

BOB: Good evening. This is Robert Beatty. Tonight we make history. Tonight we present a comedy series on hallowed air. The first comedy series ever to appear – and I say it in solemn tones – on the *BBC's Third Programme. (MUSIC)* For no particular reason it is called –

PETER: Third Division.

BOB: With the added subtitle ...

BENNY H: Some vulgar fractions. *(Sniggers vulgarly.)*

BOB: Yes – comedy on the *Third Programme. (MUSIC)* Comedy! Why? It has been claimed that between the BBC's Light Programme and the *Third Programme (MUSIC)* – we seem to be getting some induction from the Sistine Choir – between them, it has been claimed there exists a cleavage as deep as any you will see in a Restoration comedy. But we do not take this view. We believe that humour is *not* incompatible with the intellectual approach. What did Plato always say?

MICHAEL: Lambadia ochontes diadosousin allelois.

BOB: That's what Plato *always* said. It's probably what made him such a bore at parties. However, it *does* underline our problem. The idea of putting a humorous programme on this particular segment of rarefied air was first mooted at a meeting of the Third Programme General Staff. It happened something like this ...

FADE OUT AND IN

PETER: Gentlemen, be seated.

EFFECT: TAMBOURINE AND ALL SIT DOWN.

MICHAEL: Now as I see it, this projected humorous programme should have a definite ... er ... shape. We must go all out along a well-defined ... er ... line ... We must plan with a positive goal in ... er ... mind. And our object should be this – *something original that's been done before.*

HARRY: Quite, quite!

PETER: Point taken.

BENNY H: Admirably put.

BENNY LEE: Very true.

PETER: Hear! Hear!

HARRY: Er, I don't understand that.

MICHAEL: Good, now we're all in ... what did you say, Ffolliot?

HARRY: I don't understand what you mean. To tell you the truth I don't understand half of what goes on on this Third Programme.

MICHAEL: You don't understand! *(pause)* Abdul!

PETER: Sahib.

HARRY: No, no. Not that! Don't, please. Keep him off. No. No. NO!

EFFECT: SCREAM – INTO BOTTOMLESS PIT (ECHO).

BOB: And so the debate continued. It soon became obvious that it was pointless to offer our particular listeners the common or garden music-hall standard of humour. This sort of thing, for example ...

RECORD: ATMOSPHERE

EFFECT: STEAMER SIREN

BENNY H: Lumme, this boat ain't half tossing about something chronic. I feel proper seasick.

HARRY: Don't worry, old man. You'll be all right when the moon comes up.

EFFECT: LAUGHTER
FADE OUT AND IN

BOB: No, plainly it was no use to offer that sort of humour, because our listeners remember the original lines in Ovid!

FADE IN
RECORD: ATMOSPHERE

PETER: Me miserum quanti montos volvuntur aquarum
         Iam iam iacturos, sidera summa putes.

MICHAEL: Heu! Miser es; mox laetus eris mittesque dolorem,
         Cynthia cum radios fuderit alma mari.

RECORD: LAUGHTER

Third Division was the first programme to bring Sellers, Secombe and Bentine together at the microphone. Two years later, with the encouragement of Pat Dixon – though Dennis Main Wilson was the producer this time – they were joined by another young comedian, Spike Milligan, for a series called *Crazy People*, which gradually metamorphosed into *The Goon Show*. Recalling radio in the 1940s and early 1950s, Harold Pinter emphasises the importance to him of this and other comedy programmes: 'It was wonderful stuff. I'm sure that *ITMA* and *The Goon Show* and Arthur Askey influenced me and my work. They had inherited the world of James Joyce.'[4]

*

On 11 November 1948, Haley wrote a four-page 'note' on the Third for the BBC Governors. He observed that in its early months it had 'achieved an outstanding *succès d'estime*', but that 'seriously critical' comments were now being heard, with the theme that, 'in its endeavour to attract an audience', the Third was 'in some danger of compromising its essential character and integrity'. He recalled that the original objective had been to 'give pleasure to a widening audience of all classes and ages', and said that this had not happened:

The Third Programme started off with a quite remarkable degree of listening ... But the figures steadily declined ... Bad reception was undoubtedly a most important factor ... The most faithful Third Programme

[4] A 1958 Audience Research survey showed that the favourite programme of Third Programme listeners on other networks was *The Goon Show*, named by twenty-seven per cent of those questioned.

listeners have been known to give up when after a succession of evenings of quite passable reception they suddenly, often on an evening when there is something of outstanding interest, find the level of interference quite intolerable.

The BBC, Haley continued, could not lay down a 'precise datum line' stating the minimum number of listeners that was acceptable, 'but if the Programme is to achieve its purpose it must have an audience'.

Turning to the programmes themselves, Haley said the problem was 'to keep a proper proportion between the familiar and the unfamiliar'. In the early days, a number of 'all' programmes – all the Beethoven quartets, all the Shakespeare history plays, and so on – had been broadcast. Some of these were 'not intrinsically worth doing'. Meanwhile the Corporation's Supply departments were under considerable strain, and the Third's hopes of obtaining excellent programmes from continental broadcasting organisations had been largely disappointed. 'To take an important relay from France is still not an enterprise but a gamble. You are quite likely to get hooked up to the wrong opera house.' A Musicians' Union ban on live outside broadcasts in Britain, then in force, was depriving the Third of 'ready-made' concerts. The union's 'restrictive policy' in imposing a 'needletime' limit to the use of gramophone records 'means that many first-class foreign performances of great works are denied us'.

The ban had been imposed because the BBC rejected the union's demand that a full broadcast fee should be paid for live relays, rather than about half that rate. The BBC had also been unable to get the union to agree to recorded repeats of music broadcasts without the entire original fee being paid again. Meanwhile the union, in league with the gramophone companies, restricted BBC 'needletime' to twenty-six hours per week, to be shared between all three networks. This was reduced to twenty-two hours during 1949.

Haley hoped that these were 'temporary difficulties', but admitted that 'the strain they have imposed has led ... to a certain contraction of ambitious effort'. He concluded by hoping that the Governors would agree that the Third had 'justified its conception' and 'should be persevered with'. On the one hand it 'should not seek popularisation'. Yet it must also avoid 'becoming *recherché* and recondite'.

Returning to the matter of audiences, Haley felt it 'desirable' that a 50–40–10 ratio should eventually be achieved between Light, Home and Third, but this would 'take many years to attain'. In fact the Third's audiences for important programmes were 'not negligible'; recent productions of Shaw's *Saint Joan* and T. S. Eliot's *The Family Reunion* had achieved figures of around half a million. Meanwhile the BBC should do all it could by means of publicity and 'cross-trailing' (trailing Third Programme material on Home and Light) to 'maintain interest in the Programme among the general public as well as among its natural adherents'.

After reading what Haley had written, Grisewood wrote his own comments. He pointed out that the Third's audience was numerically comparable to the circulation of the *Sunday Times* and the *Observer*. He felt that the 'experiments' in attracting a new audience had shown that 'very little movement can be made in the direction of popularisation without weakening the value of the Third Programme'. He thought that 'we should now regard the period of the experiment as being concluded'. (Since neither the light music series nor *Third Division* had yet begun when he wrote this, it is not clear what 'experiment' he had in mind.)

Haley's comments were discussed by the Board of Management (the new team of 'Directors') on 11 November 1948. The minutes record that they 'considered that the Programme had fully justified itself, and that its present policy was right. They felt, indeed, that the only fault in the Programme was its coverage, and that pending the institution of the Copenhagen Wavelength Plan [giving the Third a new principal wavelength] everything possible should be done in the way of technical advice to listeners on how to make the best of the existing transmissions.'

Haley did not mention another severe problem: rising costs. On 14 February 1949, Christopher Holme noted that in all types of programme – music, features, drama and talks – fees and other costs had risen steeply during 1948, chiefly due to inflation. He estimated that the Third needed an extra £1,319 per week to maintain programmes at their present standards. Grisewood passed a request for this increase to Basil Nicolls, but was told that the Third's weekly Programme Allowance would be increased by only £200. He replied to Nicolls that this meant 'in effect a cut of more than 20%' in the Third's financial resources, and as costs rose the position would become even worse:

We are therefore dealing with a continuously deteriorating situation. I think this cut will be reflected – in spite of the ingenuity we will exercise – in the character of the output. There is a very close relation in the Third Programme between costs and style of programme. There is no doubt that certain types of programme will have to be considerably reduced in number, and others of a simpler sort will have to be increased. A greater use will have to be made of repeats. Some effect of monotony cannot be avoided.

Nicolls was sympathetic, but told Grisewood that 'the plain fact is that the money is not available ... If after further experience you feel that lack of money is really going to affect the T[hird] P[rogramme] adversely I think we shall have to review all the possible expedients. I will always try to help you from Programme Reserve with any special project.' Grisewood thanked him, but could not help remarking that the Light Programme and Home Service had been granted generous budget increases.

During the next month, March 1949, it was decided that the BBC could no longer afford to go on broadcasting four to six studio operas each year, shared between the Home and the Third. The two networks really required different types of opera, and costs were 'exceptionally heavy' in relation to 'listener interest'. The Opera Unit, under Stanford Robinson, was to be closed down. It was a severe blow, especially because the Musicians' Union ban prevented live relays from British opera houses. (The ban was lifted in May.)

Fortunately the BBC was already committed to one exciting opera project. *Wozzeck* was heard in its entirety on the Home Service on Wednesday 16 March 1949, and repeated live two nights later on the Third. Though the broadcast came from the Royal Albert Hall, the BBC had paid for it. Boult conducted the BBC Symphony Orchestra, which had been rehearsing Berg's score for ten days – rather less time than he had asked for in 1947 – and the total cost was £4,000. Much of this had to be paid from Grisewood's programme budget, aided by a grant from Nicolls's Programme Reserve. 'The performance was of the highest order,' wrote Dyneley Hussey, not in his regular *Listener* column but in a BBC internal report, commissioned by Haley, on music broadcasts on the Third. 'The dramatic effect of the opera "came over" extraordinarily well – better, probably, than it did in the actual performance in the Albert Hall, where the spectacle of the performers in formal concert-dress must have been destructive to illusion.' *Wozzeck* was next heard on the Third on 25 January 1952, when the first British stage production, conducted by Erich Kleiber, was relayed from Covent Garden.

Dyneley Hussey was reporting on broadcasts from January to March 1949, before the effects of the financial cuts had been felt, and he was generally enthusiastic: 'That the criticisms I have to offer are mostly concerned with relatively unimportant matters is, perhaps, the finest tribute that can be paid to the planning and presentation of the Programme.' He was delighted that the troubled *History in Sound of European Music* was to resume at the end of May 1949, and judged that 'the balancing of the ingredients' in music programmes had been 'skilfully maintained'. But he devoted no attention to the tricky questions of whether the unfamiliar should predominate over the well known, and how much time should be given to contemporary music. Meanwhile Grisewood was resisting the inclusion of modern composers in more than a handful of programmes. 'Should we not now go back carefully over the whole field of modern music that we have covered in the last two years,' he asked John Lowe, 'and decide what works have been really worthwhile so that we can deliberately decide against a repeat of those that are not?'

On 18 March 1949, the day that the Third was broadcasting *Wozzeck*, Mátyás Seiber wrote to John Lowe, who had been at a contemporary music concert in London when Seiber's Second String Quartet was being performed, to ask if the Amadeus Quartet might have 'the opportunity of repeating the performance on ... the Third Programme'. Lowe passed the letter to Herbert Murrill, who answered: 'Quite frankly, we are able to broadcast only a very little of music so radical as this. The audience to whom it would appeal is, as you know, extremely small ... I cannot hold out any very strong hopes that we should wish to put your String Quartet into broadcast programmes.' Seiber responded that this was

> a rather sad state of affairs that a work cannot be broadcast even in the Third Programme because there is supposedly too small an audience for it ... I must tell you (but you probably know it already) that all over the Continent the Third has a tremendous reputation because it can fearlessly and without making any compromise broadcast music of any school and style, including the most extreme, and has done so in the past. It would be a pity if this courageous policy would be given up.

Eleven days earlier, the *Evening Standard* had printed a leading article headed 'PRETENTIOUS CULTURE: NO WONDER THE "THIRD" AUDIENCE DWINDLES'. It quoted Bunthorne's lines from *Patience:* 'The meaning doesn't matter if it's only idle chatter of a transcendental kind', and went on:

> Look at last night's programme. We started with half an hour of 'Musical Curiosities', a programme of 'unusual music'. Later we were able to hear the first performance in Europe of Alexei Haieff's Divertimento (1944) and some Danceries de la Renaissance by the prolific Anon. Finally some selections by the Modern Imagist Poets, including the notorious Ezra Pound. It seems rather that the obscure is preferred to the intelligible; the esoteric to the beautiful; the peculiar to the classical.
>
> Who listens to this spawn of the musical coteries and the literary bun-fights? ...
>
> Recently the Third Programme has given signs of searching of heart ... An intimate revue has been produced; some programmes of light music have been played. The whole spectacle was like a stately dowager unbending to the third footman on the night of the servants' dance.
>
> But the BBC must make a more radical change than this ... There is ... the massive army of music-lovers who fill the Albert Hall during the Prom season, and the immense reading public which uses the public libraries. The BBC should beam the Third Programme at this audience, instead of confining it to Bloomsbury ...

It was true that things had got into a rather dreary state; there was, as Haley had put it, 'a certain contraction of ambitious effort', with few examples of what Grisewood called 'associative planning' – groups of programmes linked by one topic. On the other hand not all listeners liked a concentration on a single theme; after a Goethe Season, spread over 1949 to commemorate the bicentenary of his birth, Compton Mackenzie remarked that there were 'evenings when I wished that Goethe had never been born'.

Readers of the *Evening Standard* replied to this leader in large numbers, the majority supporting the Third. But on 4 June the *Daily Mail* carried the headline 'BBC CHIEF EXPECTED TO QUIT SOON. A STORM OVER THE THIRD

PROGRAMME.' It alleged that Haley was expected 'any day' to announce his resignation as Director-General: 'He is understood to have been concerned in a great behind-the-scenes battle over the future of his pet project, the Third Programme. This has recently come under heavy fire from Government forces. They maintain it is too expensive a luxury. Its transmissions ... are costing the BBC £900,000 a year. Its listening public is estimated to number only 250,000 ... ' Four days later, Grisewood wrote to the BBC's Head of Publicity, saying that there were 'rumours from various quarters to the effect that the Third Programme is coming to an end'. He hoped that the publicity department would issue 'a firm denial', and would publicise the Third's future plans, as well as reminding the press about the improved prospects for reception.

These plans were issued in outline three weeks later, in a confidential memo to the heads of the Supply departments and the editors of the *Radio Times* and *Listener*. Grisewood allowed that the Third would not have an easy time in coming months; it was entering 'a period which will surely prove to be ... more testing ... than it has experienced since its inception'. But the fact that reception should improve dramatically from March 1950 should give rise to 'a new creative impulse'. The arrival of a new audience, thanks to better reception, meant that the Third should 'perform again some of the outstanding radio achievements in all fields ... at the rate of about one a week'. Furthermore, each quarter of the year would be 'regarded as a "season" to be planned integrally in advance'. It was a very positive response to the financial cuts, the press attacks and the rumours of closure. 'There should be no complacency about the audience figures that exist at present,' warned Grisewood, but he ended the plans optimistically: '15th March 1950 is from now on a target date for all concerned. Work must begin now if what is required for that date is to be ready.'

CHAPTER SEVEN

Clamouring for television

T wo days later, on 30 June 1949, Christopher Holme issued more detailed plans. From October, each quarter would be treated as a 'repertory season', with up to six 'performances' of major programmes – the word 'repeat' was not to be used. Subsequent (live) performances would aim to improve on the first. A schedule of performances would be announced in the *Radio Times* and possibly in a quarterly pamphlet. This repertory system was presented as 'a logical step forward' from the existing practice of repeats, and desirable because radio was 'more ephemeral even than a daily newspaper'. It would also avoid the particular Third Programme danger of 'miscellaneity', which was likely to occur without 'regular news bulletins and fixed points'. No mention was made of one obvious advantage, which indeed was presumably the original motive for the whole scheme, the considerable financial saving. This was admitted by John Lowe in a memo about the musical aspects of the 'repertoire' system. 'I remain convinced,' wrote Lowe, 'that the seasonal-repertoire method as sketched out will represent a considerable saving of money, as well as better planning.'

Giving a lecture to a Workers' Educational Association summer school soon after the announcement of his repertory scheme, Grisewood showed no signs of feeling beleaguered. He compared the Third to the post-war effort to double the number of university places, but saw it as more than an educational venture:

> What is at stake is something fundamental to our civilisation. It is what I call the principle of refinement . . . the attempt at perfection in the Christian sense . . . If such an enterprise as the Third Programme cannot flourish in our society . . . such a rejection would in my opinion be likely to include our whole tradition of refinement and much else that is taken to be essential to civilisation as Europe has understood it.

Despite the fighting tone of this lecture and the fanfare for the 'repertory season', the Third's plans for October to December 1949, announced in a pamphlet – the first of a quarterly series that ran for the next seventeen years – suggested business as usual rather than any major changes. Under

'Talks' it was stated: 'A high proportion of these are topical and therefore cannot be announced in this folder.' Only a few speakers were specified: John Betjeman reading his poems, a medieval disputation conducted by a group of Dominican friars (the first of many on the Third), the head-master of Eton giving the Reith Lectures (repeated from the Home Service), and a few more. There was no mention in the pamphlet of the repertory system as such, though it was stated that two operas, Verdi's *Falstaff* and Vaughan Williams's *Hugh the Drover* had been 'chosen as reper-tory productions for the whole winter season', and would be given six studio performances each between October and May. As to drama, there would now be three rather than two broadcasts of most plays. The dates of these were not given, only the week in which they would be heard.

Despite the widespread press criticism which continued to be directed at the Third during the following months, the increased number of repeats (surprisingly) went almost unnoticed – an exception being the radio critic of the *Birmingham Gazette* (10 April 1950): 'Repetition of programmes is inevitable; but the repeats, particularly of music and plays, could be better spaced. The excellent production of *Alcestis*, with Valentine Dyall, a magnificently virile Hercules, was heard three times in as many weeks. A second performance within a month is enough, the third could be given months later.'

Meanwhile *The History in Sound of European Music* was coming to grief again. Grisewood was so upset by the first programme in the new series – *The Beginnings of Opera*, compiled by Edward J. Dent and broadcast on 28 May 1949 – that he wrote to Steuart Wilson that it was 'well below the standard suitable to any BBC programme'. A week later Basil Lam, producing the series, complained to John Lowe that two of the con-tributing experts, Egon Wellesz and Martin Cooper, had 'caused con-siderable difficulty ... mainly by failing to edit the music itself [for performance] – or indeed to take any active interest in their contributions'. Another supposed expert had submitted, for a programme on the baroque harpsichord and clavichord, 'a most odd and even eccentric selection of music ... and a script which has no programme value'. Lam said he could have put together a better programme on the subject himself, with no trouble. Most of the material in the series was 'very adequately dealt with in available books' and did not require 'the services of a specialist'. He suggested that it would be best to discontinue the use of outside con-tributors, and consult them only when necessary.

Grisewood had a more drastic solution, that 'we should stop at Beet-hoven'. This was eventually accepted, on the principle that the more recent history of music was already well documented and recorded, and the last programme in the series, *Orchestral Music in Beethoven's Time*, was broadcast on 28 March 1950. It then transpired that no recordings of the series had been retained by the BBC Sound Archives, which had been a main aim of the project. Nor had HMV recorded the broadcasts, as had been originally intended, though some of the programmes were eventually repeated in their studios and issued as commercial discs.

As to contemporary music on the Third, the effect of Grisewood's hostility to it could be seen in the schedules. During 1949 there had been plenty of first broadcasts of music by such composers as Rubbra, Bax, Villa Lobos, Copland, Gordon Jacob, Rawsthorne and Britten, whose *Let's Make an Opera* was heard on 7 October. Stravinsky was well represented, but the followers of Schoenberg were little in evidence; Elisabeth Lutyens was one of the few serial composers whose work was heard on the Third in any quantity that year. Tippett was now absorbed in writing *The Midsummer Marriage*, and only made occasional appearances at the microphone. 'The opera completely enfolds me at the moment,' he reported on 25 October 1949.

'Is anything happening about the opera we commissioned from Walton?' Haley asked Basil Nicolls in September 1950. 'The two years' time limit must be almost twice up by now.' A few months earlier, Steuart Wilson had asked Walton if *Troilus and Cressida* – which he had chosen for his subject – would be ready for a concert performance as part of the Festival of Britain in the summer of 1951. Walton replied: 'On the whole I'm not keen ... I don't think it would stand the cold hard light of a concert performance, & it may, with luck, just get away with it on the stage.' He told the BBC he was willing to forego the commission fee (£500), because of the time he had taken, but they decided to keep the commission in force as an incentive – though, as someone in the BBC observed, he did not need the money.

Walton sometimes complained that not enough of his work was broadcast, but by comparison with most contemporary composers he was within the charmed circle of those whose music was performed on the Third without question. Mátyás Seiber was still trying to break into it. His cantata *Ulysses*, with words from Joyce's novel, had been chosen for a broadcast by the London Contemporary Music Centre, which provided a number of programmes for the Third; but the BBC's music reading panel sent Seiber a rejection slip for the work, even though he had not submitted it to them.

This panel had been in existence since 1934. It consisted of Music Department staff and distinguished musicians from outside the Corporation; in the late 1940s and early 1950s these included William Alwyn, Lennox Berkeley, Mosco Carner, John Ireland, Gordon Jacob and Edmund Rubbra. Around 1950, many British-based composers began to agitate that the panel system was not allowing their works on to the air. Besides Seiber, these included Roberto Gerhard, Elizabeth Maconchy, and Humphrey Searle, who had left the BBC staff in 1948. In July 1950 he wrote, in a report submitted to the Composers' Guild of Great Britain:

> Most of the works submitted [to the BBC] have to be read by a panel, but there appears to be no definite ruling as to which composers' works have to go before the panel and which not. Those which do often have to wait

a considerable time to be read, as ... the BBC is inundated with scores ...
Even if a work is passed by the panel, the BBC do not give any guarantee
of performance, and this matter is usually left to the energy and will-
power of the individual composer.

Consequently, continued Searle, it often took years to get a new work
performed. Though much modern British music was broadcast, 'the proportion in relation to music of other countries and older music remains
very small'.

This is confirmed by the BBC files. In October 1950 about ninety new
orchestral works (let alone other kinds) had been approved and were
waiting *sine die* for performance. They included pieces by Havergal Brian,
Elisabeth Lutyens, Daniel Jones and Egon Wellesz. Leonard Isaacs, who
succeeded John Lowe as Third Programme Music Organiser during 1950,
described this as 'a most shocking bottle-neck'. He was told that the
problem was the lack of opportunity for performance; contemporary works
did not usually fit into the BBC Symphony Orchestra's programmes, and
though the regional orchestras were willing to perform a certain amount
of them, 'they are apt to prove lowering to [the Third's] listening figures'.

Even composers who often received commissions from the Third for
incidental music found it difficult to get new works placed. For example
in January 1950 Elisabeth Lutyens offered Lawrence Gilliam a Homeric
'Music Drama for radio', *Penelope*, enclosing a script and piano score, and
saying she would orchestrate it in a fortnight if he was willing to commission the work. The piano score was automatically sent to the music
reading panel, who turned it down because it had not been orchestrated!
This process took nine months – Lutyens complained that 'the BBC have
had as long to say "yes" or "no" as a mother to produce a child' – and
Penelope was never orchestrated or performed.

Mátyás Seiber demonstrated plenty of 'energy and will-power' in trying
to get *Ulysses* broadcast, but when he protested to Steuart Wilson, he was
told that the problem was largely Joyce's words. In fact two of the panel
had also been unenthusiastic about the music: William Alwyn wrote
that 'the unrelieved "coldness" & remoteness makes for monotony', and
Edmund Rubbra thought it 'very radical'. Only Lennox Berkeley liked
Ulysses, calling it 'imaginative, and at times beautiful'; he recommended
it 'with reservations for Third Programme'. Mosco Carner, not then serving
on the panel, wrote to say he had heard a public performance of *Ulysses*,
and thought it a masterpiece which must be broadcast. Meanwhile the
London Contemporary Music Centre refused to offer the BBC any other
work as a substitute; Seiber continued to press Music Department to
broadcast it; and finally Wilson gave way.

Ulysses was heard on the Third on 27 April 1950, conducted by Boult,
who wrote to Seiber: 'I certainly hope there will be many other performances, though I am now to be removed into the world of the Box
Office and I am afraid that it is not likely that I shall have much to do

with it.' This referred to the BBC's decision to replace him as permanent conductor of the Symphony Orchestra. Haley recalls this sad episode:

> The BBC was bedevilled by the fact that before the war Toscanini had conducted it [as guest conductor in 1935, and from 1937 to 1939], and said, 'The BBC Symphony Orchestra is the finest in the world.' And during the war it was split up, and ... did go completely to pieces, and Boult didn't like rehearsing very much anyway. And Nicolls said to me, 'We've got to get this orchestra back ... to being the best in the world. And we must give Boult twelve months to do it.'
>
> So Boult was given twelve months. And before the twelve months were out, Hely-Hutchinson, who was Director of Music, died, and ... Steuart Wilson ... was chosen by the Governors ... He was a colossal mistake. He was a quarrelsome man ... He said to me, 'Quarrelling is great fun.' I said, 'Well, it isn't for me.' Fairly soon after he came in, the year of Boult was up, and we then got various critics privately to tell us, was the BBC Symphony Orchestra now the greatest in the world? And I think unanimously they said, 'No'. And they came to me and said, 'Boult must go.'

Boult had reached sixty, the BBC's retirement age, on 8 April 1949, but Reith had always told him they would 'draw up a new contract' when that happened. His own hope was to continue for another five years.

At this juncture Grisewood let slip an implied criticism of Boult and the orchestra. Following a Third Programme music meeting on 23 November 1949 it was minuted that the Third 'do not object to getting a part of their standard fare (e.g. Beethoven and Brahms symphonies) from the Proms provided standards of performance are high'. Wilson took this as an excuse for an entirely unnecessary quarrel. 'What right have your programme planners to suggest that the BBC Symphony Orchestra, in a Beethoven or Brahms Symphony, will not provide a performance of high standard?' he snapped at Grisewood in a memo, adding that he would accept such criticism from 'music critics of some standard', but not from 'your programme'. Grisewood was not putting up with this; he replied that he found Wilson's note 'offensive' and 'calling into question my authority'. He demanded a withdrawal, and got one. The irony was that, in the meanwhile, Wilson was plotting to replace Boult.

'Wilson came along and said, "I've got Barbirolli in the bag,"' recalls Haley.

> Nicolls was in favour of Barbirolli ... So I gave Sir Adrian notice of retirement. The minute that was done, Nicolls came to me and said, 'Barbirolli's off, because all he did was to go to the Hallé Society and squeeze more money and [a promise of] fewer performances out of them.' And there we were, left without a conductor; and I couldn't ask Boult to come back. We'd given him his farewell lunch ... We tried Kubelik, but he wouldn't come because his wife was terrified – she said that England

was too near Europe, and she feared that they might again be over-run, and she would go nowhere but America. And in the end, willy-nilly, we appointed Sir Malcolm Sargent.

Though it is hard to believe, Haley was unaware of the widely known fact that Boult's wife Ann had formerly been married to Wilson – they had divorced in 1932, and she married Boult the following year. Though there is no evidence of a personal vendetta by Wilson, Boult had moved his office out of Yalding House (home of the Music Department) and into Maida Vale studios as soon as Wilson arrived.

Aged fifty-five, Sargent had made his name before the war conducting the Royal Choral Society and many other choral groups. Knighted in 1947, he had been chief conductor of the Proms since 1948. Later to acquire the nickname 'Flash Harry' for his slick appearance and supposed vanity – a Gerard Hoffnung cartoon shows him using a mirror instead of a music stand – he could not have been a greater contrast to the self-effacing Boult. Haley was doubtful about him from the start: 'I said to Nicolls ... "I do not believe Malcolm Sargent will give up his trips to Greece and other places, and we've only a limited period." Well, he did a wonderful job with the Proms. I don't think he did a wonderful job with the orchestra.'

Boult's last broadcast as a BBC staff member was on the Third on 17 June 1950, when he conducted Bach's *Magnificat* and Vaughan Williams's oratorio *Sancta civitas*. The next year he became principal conductor of the London Philharmonic Orchestra. He continued to enjoy a distinguished career for another three decades, eventually retiring in 1979 at the age of ninety. Haley remained conscious of the 'injustice' done to him by the BBC, and eventually wrote to Boult to apologise. 'And I got a very nice letter back from him saying that all was forgiven.'

Sargent made his first appearance as the orchestra's permanent conductor on the opening night of the 1950 Proms, by which time Steuart Wilson had left the BBC to join the administration of Covent Garden. He was succeeded as Head of Music by Herbert Murrill, an old friend of the Third, who adopted a conciliatory tone whenever he and Grisewood had a difference of opinion. Not that there was much to differ about with Wilson gone. The only nagging problem was, as usual, over-runs.

From his position as Director of the Spoken Word, George Barnes had passed to Grisewood complaints from various sources about unpunctuality in the Third. 'Obvious instances,' he wrote, 'were the hour's over-run of the *Magic Flute* from Salzburg (made no better by the announcer's bland assurance that the programme had "taken rather longer than we thought") and the Sibelius concert by Beecham. It was suggested that if the Third Programme is endeavouring to increase the number of its listeners, it is losing a lot of goodwill by this unpunctuality ... ' Replying, Christopher Holme explained that, with foreign relays, 'we find it quite impossible to tie down these people, particularly the Austrians, to any advance estimate of timings'. However, shortly after this, on 6 January 1950, Grisewood sent Music Department and the other Supply departments a formal notice that the Third was abandoning its policy of never fading out programmes which had over-run. The success of that policy had, he said, depended on 'a thoroughly responsible effort' by producers to calculate the length of a programme and stick to it after the *Radio Times* had gone to press:

> I cannot see that this effort is in fact being made. Timings are being constantly altered ... which causes ... frequent drastic re-arrangements ... The situation is worse than it has ever been. I am by now convinced that the reputation of the Third Programme is sufficiently imperilled for me to terminate the existing system ... Programmes which over-run on transmission will be faded out according to the judgement of those in charge on behalf of the Third Programme.

John Lowe responded that he and his Music Department colleagues 'cannot provide the best programmes and the best available performances' if Grisewood was about to become inflexible about timings:

> We perform many new or hitherto unbroadcast works, and these must be timed by the artists. Many conductors do not arrive at the stage of creative work in their programmes as early as ten weeks beforehand [the date at which timings were expected to be made], and reasonable compromise between the creative artist and the machine is necessary for the health of both ... I am satisfied that the remarkable success of some of the big series which Music Department have provided has been dependent on planners giving a considerable degree of flexibility ...
>
> Personally, I should take a very gloomy view indeed of fading out of Music Department programmes – to me the proud record which T[hird] P[rogramme] has of never having yet faded out a musical performance stands for a certain integrity and decency which is needed in musical life today.

Grisewood did not remove his threat. There were no fade-outs of music programmes, but other Supply departments were told again that flexibility in timing was no longer permitted, and 'timings which have been agreed on after consultation with all concerned must ... be adhered to'.

On 29 January 1950 Grisewood wrote to Lowe praising the broadcast of extracts from Vivaldi's oratorio *Juditha triumphans* two days earlier: 'This sort of music ... is ideal for us since it is delightful to listen to at first hearing and hard to come by from any other source ... We are doing a real work for music, I am sure, in giving currency to music of this date.' Lowe agreed, adding: 'The Schutz series and Monteverdi Vespers will be important contributions in April/June, and Mr Stevens has an important Vivaldi scheme brewing for 3rd Quarter.'

Denis Stevens had joined the BBC Music Department the previous year at the age of twenty-seven. A pupil of Egon Wellesz at Oxford, he had worked as a violinist in the Philharmonia Orchestra until he was appointed to the BBC, 'specifically in charge of what they called "pre-classical" programmes then' (he succeeded Basil Lam, who, says Stevens, had 'gone off to make harpsichords'; Lam left in 1949 and returned in 1960, later becoming Editor, Pre-Classical Music). To his great delight, Stevens was soon able to begin 'producing Vivaldi concertos in dozens'. He explains that this was for a selfish motive:

> I wanted to hear what they sounded like. Fortunately, having had some training at Oxford with Wellesz, I knew where to go, and was able to come up with a dozen Vivaldi concertos, or a French opera, or the entire Telemann *Musique de table* and so on. The Vivaldis were London reprints of an Amsterdam edition, which the British Museum had in quantity. It was all photographed for us, and passed to the copyists. And, though I say this as shouldn't, the Vivaldi concertos have never been done so well again, because I insisted on a rich and varied continuo section. Apart from the cello and bass we had a chamber organ brought in by Mander, and a Goff, the Rolls Royce of harpsichords, played by Thurston Dart, *and* the lute played by one J. Bream, who was then twenty-eight. Nowadays all you get is a little old lady at the back tinkling on the harpsichord.

The cost of the extra players could be met, Stevens explains, because the budget was flexible: 'Nobody asked any questions. Producers were responsible; if I went wild and spent a lot one week, people would say, "Be careful – only do chamber music for the next two weeks." And when in 1952 I was asked to put on a complete Monteverdi opera (Walter Goehr conducted, and I did the editing), we had nine continuo instruments, which is what he specified: two harpsichords, two organs, a bible regal, an arch lute, a guitar, and so on.'

Other members of Music Department were able to create pioneer programmes for the Third in their own specialist areas. For example Robert Simpson, who joined in 1951, organised broadcasts of Haydn's lesser-known symphonies and choral works, which ran throughout 1952. Former staff member Humphrey Searle created series of linked talks and performances exploring the work of Liszt, broadcast in January and February 1950.

Denis Stevens explains that, in the case of works for which no performing edition or orchestral parts existed, Music Department could turn to its 'army' of copyists: 'We had a top floor with about ten men sitting there scribbling away frantically. It was all done by hand.' As to 'authentic' styles of playing and singing early music, Stevens says that he and his colleagues usually managed to impress on string players

> the necessity of being a little different to, say, doing Strauss's *Symphonia domestica*, or something like that. But it was the vocalists with whom we had to work the hardest, because they'd been brought up in the tradition of cathedral singing. I had to teach them about ornaments. Fortunately I had several facsimiles of late sixteenth and early seventeenth century vocal books, and we could discuss them and they'd try them out. We soon

had Deller doing the most magnificent tremolo. He was phenomenal – he could bring tears to your eyes.

Stevens also emphasises the value of outside broadcasts:

> If you got tired of the cooped-up atmosphere of Yalding House, you could say, 'Well, I think we'll go down to King's College, Cambridge and record a choral programme – I've just discovered some Tallis hymns alternating plainchant and polyphony.' So we'd set off there, and help Boris Ord set up the choir. Or another day we might go down to Salisbury or Chichester, because I had a way of tying in the composers with the places, so if it were Weelkes we would go to Chichester, and if we were doing something from the fifteenth century Eton manuscript we'd buzz down to Eton. And I would say to the choir, 'You see that tombstone over there? That's the composer.' And it really did make a difference.

By the beginning of 1950, John Lowe felt that, though the Third had made great musical strides, there was still 'one fairly big shortcoming'. He explained:

> The D[irector] G[eneral]'s original brief said: 'The Third Programme will be international.' ... I'm afraid we haven't got there yet. We relay or record a fair amount from the Continent[1] ... But ... we need someone with the musicality and mental agility of an Amyot, frequently on the move on our behalf in Europe ... As to the general planning, I think we are being reasonably systematic about the period 1700–1900, but too trial-and-errorish about music before Bach, and contemporary music.

Similarly, Grisewood felt that the Third had not 'got there yet' with regard to poetry, and in January 1950 he enlisted three distinguished academics – all of them from his old university, Oxford. John Bryson, Lord David Cecil and Nevill Coghill were to 'act as a planning and advisory group in the field of poetry'. Bryson intended to come to London 'about once a week' to discuss poetry programmes with BBC staff. Around this time Professor T. H. Pear of Manchester University sent Grisewood some comments on the Third, which included this observation: 'On the whole it seems doubtful if the organisers leave London except for Oxford and, occasionally, Cambridge.'

*

With the approach of the date on which the Third would change to new wavelengths (15 March 1950) it was announced that the programme's main signal would be on 463 metres (not 464), radiated from Daventry at 150KW, supported by local transmitters on 194 metres – so low on the medium-wave band that many listeners complained that their sets could not receive it. New transmitting equipment was ordered from Marconi's

---

[1] Listeners could now expect an opera each week. About three-quarters of the performances, at this time, were recordings from continental opera houses.

and installed at Daventry, and it was decided that before the Third came on the air each evening at 6 pm the 463-metres frequency would carry the BBC's daytime broadcasts to Europe, to prevent any other country 'thinking the frequency is free and putting a transmitter on it'. Meanwhile the BBC took considerable trouble to publicise the wavelength changes – there were alterations to Light Programme and Home Service frequencies too.

Work began on building a new Daventry mast, 725 feet high, and the Third accepted the BBC Midland Region's offer of a documentary programme describing its erection. The producer, James Pestridge, decided to climb the mast himself with a microphone; he was 'late Bomber Command' and 'apparently possesses both the nerve and the warm clothing for the job'. After the programme had been broadcast, Leslie Stokes was of the opinion that Pestridge had been wasting his efforts, 'since there was so little said at a height of several hundreds of feet which ... could not have [been] said from the ground'.

The mast and its transmitting equipment were not in fact ready for March 1950, so a temporary transmitter was rigged up at Daventry, coming into service on the evening of 15 March. Even though this was not expected to produce nearly so good a signal as the new permanent transmitter, initial reports of reception were good. Desmond Shawe-Taylor wrote in the *New Statesman* on 8 April that, since the Third had opened in 1946, it had until now been

> impossible ... to receive without fiendish interruption. Addicts of cultural enlightenment have been living for years as though on a small raft surrounded by lashing seas of jazz and political propaganda; let all else fail, and Tunis could be relied upon for a shrill and obdurate version of the Bell Song from *Lakmé* ... And now, has all this changed? Has the reshuffle of wavelengths cleared the European air? It is too soon, apparently, for a comprehensive reply. But where I live, Third Programme reception, though still imperfect, is hugely improved; and I hear similar reports from elsewhere.

When the new permanent transmitter finally came into service a year later, on 8 April 1951, the signal was reported to provide 'ample volume' with 'negligible interference' in many parts of the country. Grisewood noted that 'good reports have been received of reception as far north as Inverness, at Dublin, and in East Anglia'. The Third's coverage was now estimated to have increased to between sixty-five and seventy per cent of the population, though the proportion who could listen was, of course, very different from those who did. A BBC engineering report in Cardiff, a month after the permanent transmitter had begun operating, stated that 'Signal strength is good', but added: 'I have come to the conclusion that comparatively few people in Cardiff listen to the Third Programme ... '

Three months before the wavelength change, on 17 December 1949, the BBC had opened a television transmitter at Sutton Coldfield, bringing TV to the Midlands. On 12 March 1950, under the headline 'THE THIRD

PROGRAMME: PUT AN END TO THIS NONSENSE!', the radio critic of the *People*, Keith Bailey, wrote:

> Every time you pay £1 for your wireless licence you are being taxed a shilling to keep on the air a spate of highbrow broadcasting that only five listeners in a thousand want ... The BBC ... throws money away on this highbrow programme when the whole country is clamouring for television ...
>
> But television programmes occupy only three hours a day; the BBC cannot afford to pay commercial prices for star outside attractions like boxing, so only 200,000 people think that television sets are worth having ...
>
> Sir William Haley could rouse real public good will – which he may soon need – by dropping the Third and showing with no mistake that he has decided to put all the BBC's resources into the development of television.

*

The *Manchester Evening News* noted that, under the new transmitting arrangements, the Third was providing a useful service to musicians. Before the start of transmission each evening, at 5.55 pm, the note A was being broadcast, at the request of the British Standards Institution. 'It gives musicians and instrument makers a reliable and unchanging note for tuning their instruments.' Grisewood also decided to close down each night with the national anthem (the Home and Light already did this). Soon after this practice began, the *Burnley Express and News* (25 April 1951) reported that the radio comedian Gillie Potter was claiming it as a personal success – he had been making representations to the BBC about the lack of 'God Save the King' on the Third, and described his campaign as an 'expression of his loyalty as an Englishman'.

The permanent transmitter came on the air just in time to carry the Third's contributions to the enormous Festival of Britain. 'Music from the Festival,' wrote Grisewood on 9 February 1951, 'represents a heavy programme obligation, and we have had to commit ourselves to a good deal more than is comfortable in the schedule.' Pears and Britten gave the first Festival concert broadcast by the Third, the opening recital in an English song series at the Wigmore Hall, on 7 May 1951; their programme included the first performance of Tippett's *The Heart's Assurance*, which had been commissioned by Pears. From Covent Garden came *Tristan und Isolde* (29 May) and *Parsifal* (2 July), both with Kirsten Flagstad, and *Die Meistersinger* (2 July), conducted by Beecham, with Hans Hotter as Sachs; also the first performance of Britten's *Billy Budd* (1 December); while in the studio Desiré Inghelbrecht conducted Debussy's *Pelléas et Mélisande* (2 July).

As to the spoken word, the Third had commissioned for the Festival a new translation of the *Aeneid* by C. Day-Lewis. The first of twelve episodes, with Alan McClelland as Aeneas and Jill Balcon as Venus, was broadcast on 17 September. W. H. Auden's new translation of Cocteau's *Knights of the Round Table*, also commissioned by the Third, was heard on 22 May,[2] and Eliot's *The Cocktail Party* received its first broadcast on 1 July, with Irene Worth as Celia and Jill Balcon as Lavinia. But Drama Department's main Festival effort for the Third was Henry Reed's adaptation of Hardy's *The Dynasts*, produced by Douglas Cleverdon in six ninety-minute episodes beginning on 3 June. Jill Balcon was again in the cast, as the Empress Josephine.

The Festival of Britain marked the centenary of the 1851 Great Exhibition, and the Third's most remarkable contribution to it was an 1851 Week, which began on Sunday 22 April. It was the brainchild of Peter Laslett, a Cambridge historian who managed to combine a junior research fellowship there with a BBC Talks producer's job in London. 'Everything which you will hear during this week in 1951 was heard in England during 1851,' he wrote in the *Radio Times*.

> All the musical items have been taken from concert programmes belonging to that year, and in some cases whole concerts are to be played again just as they were originally performed. For the plays, we have chosen from the London successes of the 1851 season ... The features are likewise part and parcel of the year in question; the words they use will be those first spoken and written in the course of it. The news will be the news which was printed in the 1851 newspapers and the talks will be spoken versions of pronouncements made in 1851 by the eminent talkers of that generation ... The purpose of this is ... to use the wireless to recapture the aesthetic atmosphere of the Great Exhibition year.

So it came about that the first news bulletin to be read on the Third – for there had been none as yet – was a hundred years out of date.

The week opened with Mary O'Farrell reading Queen Victoria's address at the opening of Parliament in February 1851. Later 'speakers' included Charles Kingsley, George Eliot, Browning, Disraeli, Herbert Spencer (impersonated by Harman Grisewood), Dickens, Thackeray, Ruskin, Carlyle and Berlioz. Henry Mayhew's study of poverty in London was presented as a dramatised feature; Beecham conducted a reconstruction of a Philharmonic Society concert; and there were Victorian versions of two Light Programme series: *Listen with Mama* and *A Pot-pourri for the Edification and Instruction of Ladies at Home* – in other words *Woman's Hour*.

John Lowe, who had left the Third to become Head of Midland Region Music, wrote to Grisewood praising the 'fine planning and results' of the 1851 week, and a Listener Research survey reported that most listeners felt that 'devoting each evening for a whole week to a single theme created the atmosphere of 1851 as no other broadcasting method could'. This

---

[2] Auden was co-librettist of Stravinsky's *The Rake's Progress*, which had its world première in Venice relayed on the Third on 11 September.

report quoted from a number of individual listeners, identifying their jobs, and thereby indicating that the Third still had a wide social range of listeners:

> It was ... a splendid idea to devote the whole week's programmes to this one theme. Usually I hear about six or seven programmes on the Third – this week I heard seventeen ... (*Factory Manager's wife*)

> Not being a Third Programme listener particularly I felt I wanted to listen to this past week about 1851, and I enjoyed it very much. It was carried out successfully, for now I have become a Third Programme listener. (*Tailor*)

> The idea was, to my mind, an unqualified success ... Friday's operatic broadcast was an outstanding item, particularly the *Ernani* ... I cannot recall the Third Programme ever having offered us such a choice of good stuff. (*Police Officer*)

> This has been a most interesting week of programmes on which the people responsible should be congratulated. Could we have some 'history without tears' this way occasionally? ... (*Lecturer in Physics*)

> The atmosphere was brilliantly achieved ... to such a degree that my father thought that the 1851 news item was *Today in Parliament*, till mention was made of the Rt. Hon. W. E. Gladstone. (*Machine Tools Apprentice*)

> ... It was instructive, interesting, amusing and entertaining by turns, and sometimes all at once. It is a pity to have only one week though. The recipe should be repeated. (*Mail Order Clerk*)

That this was a fairly typical social sample was borne out by a Listener Research survey into the 'character' of the Third's audience, completed in the spring of 1953. Researchers discovered that only about one-fifth of those who might (on the basis of education and tastes) be expected to listen regularly were in fact doing so. On the other hand a surprising number of poorly educated people were tuning in at least once a week. *The Economist* commented that 'the odd result emerges that the Third Programme has a far bigger market among the supposedly philistine than among the cultured'.

But though the range of listeners was still wide, the audience was still not growing numerically. Estimates of its size varied, but no figures were impressive. A parliamentary commission on the future of British broadcasting, set up during 1949 under the chairmanship of Lord Beveridge (a principal architect of the Welfare State), was told that, while the average winter evening audiences for the Light Programme and Home Service were 5½ million and 3¼ million people respectively, the Third was 'in the neighbourhood of 90,000'. When a senior BBC engineer was asked to find out, in the spring of 1951, what proportion of the Third's listeners tuned in to 194 metres in preference to the Daventry signal on 463 metres, he replied that it would not be possible to discover this without sending out 'a quite impracticable number of enquiries', because only a very 'small percentage' listened at all.

The Beveridge Committee's report, published in January 1951, paid almost no attention to the Third, though it observed that 'since it began [it] has lost numbers of audience rather than gained them'. The Committee wanted to see broadcasting continue as a public service rather than 'a popular commodity', but recommended that there should be competition against the BBC in the development of television, and encouraged the BBC to use FM radio transmission for local broadcasting rather than for the Third. Among witnesses called by the Committee was Lord Reith, who as well as giving oral evidence, submitted a written memorandum which included these sentences: 'The Third Programme, positively and negatively, is objectionable. It is a waste of a precious wavelength; much of its matter is too limited in appeal; the rest should have a wider audience. Its existence is taken to condone the absence of policy elsewhere; it is an easy way out.'

The press continued to bristle with complaints about the Third, by no means all of them crudely philistine. An article by Roger Pitt in *Public Opinion* (January 1951) pleaded for 'a different kind of Third' – an improvement in the quality of production and presentation:

> Many broadcasts are intolerably badly delivered. Except with music, standards of production are noticeably lower than in either Home or Light ... Why is there so little attention to the contemporary scene ... ? Why no sustained treatment of current affairs ... ? In the arts, should there not be less attention to the past? ... Even within the academic world, it displays a marked partiality for the older universities.

But Pitt did praise 'Mr Hoyle's fine series on the nature of the universe', broadcast in January and February 1950.

Fred Hoyle, then in his early thirties, held a lectureship at Peter Laslett's Cambridge college, St John's. Laslett recalls that the BBC's science programmes editor, Archie Clow, had put Hoyle on the air a little while earlier, but said he must not be used again because of his strong Yorkshire accent. 'So he was my rediscovery,' comments Laslett. He and Hoyle were sitting one day in the Whin teashop in Cambridge,

> eating its famous sticky buns in front of the fire on a November day, and Fred – this large Yorkshireman – murmured, gulping his sticky bun, 'The universe is being created all the time.' And I said, 'Eat your bloody bun, Fred, and don't talk nonsense.' And he set out, there and then, to demonstrate it to me – somebody with no previous interest in mathematics or physics – in a way I could follow. He didn't actually say the sticky bun was being created all the time. But it was the ability to grasp the attention of an outsider. I think he was the best broadcaster I ever handled.

Hoyle's talk *Continuous Creation* was broadcast on 29 March 1949. It began:

> Tonight I want to tell you about some new work on the expanding universe. Together with two of my colleagues, H. Bondi and T. Gold, I have reached the conclusion that the universe is in a state of continuous creation. The reason for such a drastic departure from previous ideas is simply that observations at present available are unfavourable to former theories and give a definite preference for a universe with continuous creation. But before we go into a detailed discussion of the creation process I wish to give a brief outline of what we mean by the expanding universe ...

Laslett emphasises that at this time Hoyle's name was completely unknown, and he, Bondi and Gold had not yet published their research findings.

The following year, Hoyle gave four more talks (beginning on 28 January 1950), again produced by Laslett, which further expounded this 'steady-state' theory and its implications. 'One Saturday night about three months ago,' wrote the book reviewer of *Cavalcade* magazine, Hayter Preston,

> I was twiddling the knob on my radio when I heard the Third Programme announcer introduce Fred Hoyle ... I count that turn of the radio knob one of the happiest accidents of my mental life. From the moment Hoyle's homely Yorkshire accents began to unfold, in clear and simple terms, the stupendous panorama of the stellar universe as revealed by the latest advances in physics I received a shock to my imagination, comparable only to that administered by the poetry of Shakespeare at its most sublime. Thereafter at five on Saturday evenings I listened to Hoyle at once enthralled and humbled ... Faced with such a majestic spectacle, it seems incredible that any intelligence endowed with the sense of comparison should ever imagine that [the creation of the universe] has been staged for the benefit of man.

Hoyle's talks were printed in the *Listener*, which was bombarded with so many requests for copies that Blackwell's issued *The Nature of the Universe* as a book a few weeks later. The first printing of ten thousand sold out in a week. Hoyle writes in his memoirs that he and his wife spent the royalties on their first refrigerator.

There had already been objections to his talks from churchgoers. The Revd Walter Bottoms complained about them in the *Baptist Times*, and when the Home Service repeated them in July and August 1950 a Mrs Olive Offord of Hove told the *Brighton Evening Argus* she had protested to the BBC that 'the agnostic statements made by Mr Hoyle would greatly distress many who found solace and comfort in religion'. The *Church Times* rather nervously described the broadcasts as 'forthright'.

Grisewood hoped that more outstanding academics would 'establish a closer contact' with the Third, so that the audience could be 'in touch with the best minds'. But an article in the *Spectator* by an Oxford undergraduate,

James Matthews, suggested that the Third was not responding properly to new ideas in the academic world. Matthews had enjoyed listening to Hoyle, but was worried by what had – or had not – followed his broadcasts:

> Here was a chance for a unique series of follow-up broadcasts – talks, features, discussions – exploring in the wake of contemporary science. The universe and the imagination of man – are there anywhere two themes comparable in fascination and power? ... What we got [was] *Replies to Fred Hoyle*: calculated essays in narrow disparagement, allegations faintly suggesting academic discredit ... and some colourfully-contrived Christian parables. Then tomb-like silence ...

Matthews judged that, in contrast, the Third's music policy would give it 'an eternally lasting following'. But he cited Peter Laslett's observation in the *BBC Quarterly* that the Third was 'the great instrument of inquisition for the intellectuals', and commented sourly: 'Galileo might have agreed.'

*

When new ideas did penetrate the Third, they tended to do so inconspicuously. On 17 November a Talks producer, Prudence Smith, wrote to her departmental head: 'I have an excellent script for a first talk from Iris Murdoch (brilliant young philosopher, First in Greats, research in Cambridge and Paris, now researching for Ph.D at Oxford while teaching there) ... She has a lovely voice. I can strongly recommend her ... '

Born in South Africa, Prue Smith had been overwhelmed by the Third when it started during her time as an Oxford undergraduate. 'I couldn't believe there were such things on offer, freely in the aether, for the whole population if they so chose.' Recruited to the BBC via the Oxford University Appointments Committee, she often revisited the university, talent-spotting for the Third:

> I knew Iris Murdoch at Oxford; she was senior to me, but she came back from serving in the war. She was a great friend of my tutor, Philippa Foot. Iris was said by her close friends always to have a novel in her suitcase that she had written during the war, and was trying to get published, and everyone thought this ridiculous because Iris was a supreme philosopher, who for some unknown reason considered herself to be a novelist. When I was asked to produce philosophy broadcasts, I thought of her and her lovely Irish voice.

The script she wrote for Prue Smith was entitled *The Novelist as Metaphysician*. It examined the philosophy of the novels of the French existentialists. 'Dear Prue,' Murdoch wrote on 8 November 1949,

> What I had in mind was to discuss the conception certain French novelists now have of their vocation: that they are to picture the 'situation of man', the human consciousness caught in the act of making its own world etc., so that the tasks of novelist & existentialist phenomenological philosopher

converge ... If let loose in two subsequent talks I could discuss all this in relation to Sartre and Raymond Queneau, who represent two entirely different types of 'metaphysical' novelist ... Forgive this wild note, for your private eye ... Salut! Ever yours
   Iris

Eventually one further talk was agreed on, and Murdoch came to London to record them both. 'I don't think you need a voice test,' Prue Smith had written to her, 'having, as I remember, a fine contralto. It's only the sopranos who come over like Minnie Mice.'

The Novelist as Metaphysician and the second talk, *The Existentialist Hero*, were broadcast on 26 February and 6 March 1950, and Murdoch received a fee of forty guineas plus expenses. The first talk was densely written – 'It's high level talking, but perfectly clear,' was Smith's comment. The second was much more eloquent, particularly in a passage where Murdoch compared the heroes of modern existentialist novels with their predecessors in fiction:

> These are people from after the deluge. The values of the nineteenth century are gone. The destruction for which Nietzsche called has taken place. And, on the other hand, there is none of either the satanism or the cynicism which marked the novels of the twenties: Evelyn Waugh's early work, for instance. Cynical frivolity is the reaction of those who are still under the sway of the morality which they deny. But Pierre and Françoise [in Simone de Beauvoir's *L'Invitée*] are something *new* in the immoralist line. They are not uneasy rebels against the social code, nor are they exactly oblivious of it. They are detached from it, and they make their own morality as they go along.

Murdoch's own early novels have often been said to be English versions of French existentialist fiction, but a later passage in this talk demonstrates her lack of affinity with the Sartre–de Beauvoir school of fiction:

> These people [Sartre's and de Beauvoir's characters] are appealing, but they are never enchanting – and the worlds in which they live are without magic and without terror. There is here none of the enticing mystery of the unknown ... and none of the demonic powers we feel in Dostoevsky. There is not even the nightmarishness of the absurd which Kafka expresses. Sartre's nightmares are thoroughly intelligible. This is ... an unpoetical and unromantic literary tradition.

In the light of these remarks, Murdoch's first novel *Under the Net* (1954)[3]

---

[3] *Under the Net* was probably not the novel she was carrying around in the suitcase. Dame Iris Murdoch wrote to the author in 1994: 'My intentions as novelist began rather early, when I was about 8 or 10! My father (civil servant) read novels eagerly, and brought me in on this in early age. I then thought, I will try to do these too! I wrote childish *stories* early on, and certainly hoped to be a novelist. I wrote "novels" probably at age 18. The war took up a lot of my time (and after) but then I certainly attempted "real" novels before, I think, 1950.'

and its immediate successors may be seen as a deliberate attempt to restore romanticism, poetry and Dostoevskian nightmare to existentialist fiction.

Another 'first' for the Third achieved by Prue Smith was Michael Ventris's announcement of his successful deciphering of the Linear B tablets found at Knossos. Smith herself happened to witness the event:

> Michael Ventris worked with my husband – they were both architects at the Ministry of Education – and we knew him and his wife well. As with Iris and the novel in the suitcase, Michael was said to be working on the Cretan tablets – ha ha, a funny thing for an architect to do. But he was; he damn well was.
>
> One night (I shall never forget it) we went to dinner at his new house in Hampstead, which he and his wife – also an architect – had designed. And Michael didn't appear; he was in another room. Bets, his wife, went on serving the sherry and niblets, but Michael didn't appear and didn't appear. And we got a bit hungry. Finally he emerged, looking totally exhausted, saying: 'I'm terribly sorry to have kept you waiting, but I've done it, I've done it!' – as though he'd been putting up a wardrobe or something. 'I *know*,' he said, 'that this language is Greek.'
>
> That was the night his long-precedent suspicions – and those of other scholars (he always paid tribute to the work of others) – were confirmed by a certain detailed finding, tracing a particular symbol through an incredibly detailed grid he'd made. He took me back to the room to show me. l was going to say 'It was all Greek to me' – but it was!
>
> The following week, at the Third Programme Talks Meeting, I rather timidly said, 'I know the man who has deciphered the tablets from Knossos.' 'What do you mean?' said somebody. 'They're indecipherable.' 'Oh no,' I said, 'I do assure you. This is *it*. We must put him on.' And they trusted me, and it was put on; and it was the first public announcement.

Ventris's talk, entitled *The Cretan Tablets*, was broadcast on 1 July 1952. After sketching the history of attempts to decipher them, he went on:

> For a long time I thought that Etruscan might afford the clue we were looking for. But during the last few weeks, I've suddenly come to the conclusion that the Knossos and Pylos tablets must, after all, be written in Greek – a difficult and archaic Greek, seeing that it's five hundred years older than Homer and written in a rather abbreviated form. But Greek nevertheless. Once I made this assumption, most of the peculiarities of the language and spelling which had puzzled me seemed to find a logical explanation, and although many of the tablets remain as incomprehensible as before, many others are suddenly beginning to make sense. As we expected they seem to contain nothing of any literary value, but merely record the prosaic and often trivial details of the palace administration . . .
>
> Most of the phrases are quite short. The longest sentence I can find has eleven words and occurs on a tablet from Pylos which seems to be an

assessment for tithes, somewhat as follows: 'The priestess holds the following acres of productive land on a lease from the property-owners, and undertakes to maintain them in the future.'

Asked whether it was difficult to persuade Ventris to announce his discovery on the Third Programme, Prue Smith says: 'Not at all. He thought this was the right place.'

*

Record Review, a discussion of new gramophone recordings, began to make occasional, irregular appearances on the Third from 8 December 1949. Philip Hope-Wallace and William Mann were the first reviewers, and Mosco Carner, Trevor Harvey, Boyd Neel and Andrew Porter took part in the following months. The programme was not a new idea – discs had been reviewed as part of the Home Service's *Music Magazine*, started during the war – and when Alec Robertson, who was producing *Record Review*, left the BBC in the autumn of 1952, Christopher Holme recommended that it be dropped: 'I believe our approach to new gramophone issues should be much more like that to new books, i.e. not on "space-filling" lines but waiting for anything really worthy of notice and likely to generate a good talk.' Anna Instone, Head of Gramophone Department (from which the programme emanated), disagreed strongly: 'I am astonished that you should propose deleting the reviews at a time when more interesting records are being issued than ever before ... ' But the programme ended, and did not reappear for five years.

The fifth birthday of the Third, on 29 September 1951, earned it more friendly press coverage than of late, with a *Times* leader in firm support – 'The Third Programme ... is ... a main enemy of philistine democracy ... ' – and an angry swarm of *Evening News* readers descending on one Herbert Sheppard of Tunbridge Wells, who had dared to suggest that the Third be axed. 'NOBODY agrees,' thundered the paper, printing a selection of letters in support of it. However, the journal *Twentieth Century* remarked that Harman Grisewood and E. M. Forster, who had both given talks on the Third to mark the birthday, 'sounded like aristocrats making dignified speeches from the scaffold before having their heads chopped off. The execution has been postponed but the baying of the Philistines still lingers in the air.' And although the BBC's Board of Governors, in a minute dated 25 October 1951, may have meant to assure the Third of their support, they actually conveyed anxiety:

... the Board expressed the view that the Third Programme was making an important contribution to culture and thought that it had fully justified itself. They regretted that the numbers listening were not larger, and hoped that, now that the reception had been much improved, every effort would be made to increase the listening figure, with the very clear understanding that standards should not be in any way lowered.

The Chairman, Lord Simon, sent Grisewood a note a few weeks later saying that he had heard that the audience 'is really beginning to improve. I do hope it is true. The programme most certainly deserves it.' It was not true. A Listener Research survey in May 1953 reported that the average audience each evening was now no more than 45,000, though numbers rose considerably (up to 100,000) for certain plays and concerts. Another report from the same department indicated that listening to BBC radio as a whole was declining throughout Britain. Between 1948 and 1951 the average hours per adult per week had diminished from nine and a half to seven and a half, for no discernible reason: 'The coming of TV has only slightly accelerated the decline [which] cannot be laid at the door of [Radio] Luxembourg for it was only in the middle of 1951 that Luxembourg started broadcasting commercial programmes in English on any other day than Sunday ... The search for the beneficiaries of listening's decline [has] proved fruitless ... ' Even if TV was not a principal cause of the decline, the BBC was starting to publicise television programmes much more extensively. From January 1953 the TV billings, released from their ghetto at the back of the *Radio Times*, appeared alongside (though after) the day's radio programmes.

Though the Third seemed to be in jeopardy at home, its reputation was increasing abroad. A member of the United States Federal Communications Commission, Frieda Hennock, began to campaign for a similar radio network in America, telling the *Evening Standard*: 'Ah, if only we had something like your Third Programme!' Italy had already begun its own version of it; starting in October 1950, it broadcast for seven and a half hours daily – ninety minutes longer than the Third itself. Spain established a two-hour daily cultural programme in 1952, and Greece inaugurated a four-hour one in 1954, while by 1955 ORTF in France had merged several existing programmes (*Club d'essai*, an experimental service started in 1946, *Université radiophonique*, and *Radio Sorbonne*, both begun before 1949) into a network called Paris IV, which was broadcasting for six hours on weekdays – chiefly Sorbonne lectures – and for slightly shorter periods at the weekend, when it carried general cultural programmes. West German listeners were treated to experimental Third Programme-type broadcasts during 1955, and in 1957 Bavaria began an evening cultural programme modelled on the Third.

When Sir William Haley visited Rome, he was told that the cultural radio channel had been named *Terza Programma* in honour of its progenitor. 'I was introduced as the creator of the Third Programme,' he recalls, 'and therefore the father of the Italian *Terza Programma*. And I said, what were the other two programmes? And they said, "There's only one!" '

*

During the weeks following its fifth birthday, the Third was largely occupied with planning a series commemorating Schoenberg, who had died in July 1951. In general, BBC music staff at this date were not admirers of his music. After listening to a Third Programme broadcast of *A Survivor from Warsaw*, for speaker, male chorus and orchestra, Leonard Isaacs, Third Programme Music Organiser, wrote:

> This is a pernicious piece of horror. I can find no saving grace in it anywhere. That Schoenberg was deeply moved by the story which he relates is unquestionable, but he related it accompanied by such indescribably weird and horrible sounds, and continues these even through the chanting of the *Shema Yisrael*, that he defeats his own purpose. In any case this is a documentary and not a piece of music.

Music Department took its time deciding whether or not to have a Schoenberg commemoration. Erwin Stein of Boosey & Hawkes wrote to Herbert Murrill the month after Schoenberg's death, explaining that he was Schoenberg's 'oldest pupil alive', and offering his services: 'Few people know really any of his music & the most distinguished critics are writing the basest nonsense when they come to deal with his theories.' But Isaacs advised Murrill against 'subservience to the small group of fanatical apostles of Schönberg', and it seems this feeling was behind the choice, as general editor of a series of talks on Schoenberg, of Michael Tippett.

'I wasn't Schoenbergian,' says Tippett, 'but they turned to me and said, "Look, will you take it over?" And I made conditions. I said, "Yes, provided you let me make Schoenberg the figure he was. I'm doing a cultural biography" – if there is such a term.' Tippett sought out a number of people who had known Schoenberg closely: 'I went to find Kokoschka, for instance, who had been with Schoenberg in Vienna, and I went to Milhaud in Paris.' He did not record them on tape, but used what they had told him in his scripts – 'things about Schoenberg that were amusing: his passion for smoking, his love of Gershwin'.

The series of talks was to accompany broadcasts of some of Schoenberg's music, performed by artists based in Britain;[4] both speech and music covered Schoenberg's career in chronological order. Tippett was paid a fee of two hundred guineas for choosing and supervising the contributors, and writing and broadcasting his own material. Such earnings were vital to him: 'It was almost my only livelihood. I had no private money, and I didn't want to teach music.'

As part of the commemoration, Schoenberg's *Five Orchestral Pieces* were scheduled for performance in a BBC Symphony Orchestra broadcast (26 January 1952), with Sargent as conductor. 'He is very apprehensive about the inclusion of this work,' reported Leonard Isaacs,

---

[4] These included Esther Salaman and Paul Hamburger, who performed the song cycle *Das Buch der hängenden Gärten* (10 January); the singers Owen Brannigan, Sylvia Fisher and Constance Shacklock, who were heard in *Gurrelieder*, conducted by Karl Rankl, with Alvar Liddell narrating (12 January); Peter Stadlen, who played the Five Pieces for piano (29 February); and Antonia Brosa, who was the soloist with the BBC Symphony Orchestra in the Violin Concerto (20 March).

and has asked that a special point be made in the announcement pointing out that its place in this programme is due to the existence of a Schoenberg scheme and not to his own liking of the work. This, of course, is quite impossible to say in an announcement in the form in which he wants it ... I give you fair warning of this because the announcer on duty is likely to meet with some exceptional interest on Sir Malcolm's part ...

Another member of Music Department, Harold Rutland, commented:

It is a little difficult to understand how he came to consent to conduct the Pieces if that is how he feels about them! Has he, I wonder, forgotten that when Sir Henry Wood brought them forward in this country for the first time in 1912, he urged on the players by saying 'stick to it, gentlemen, stick to it; this is nothing to what you'll have to play in twenty years' time'.

On the day of the broadcast of *Five Orchestral Pieces*, Sargent cancelled his appearance, and Paul Beard, leader of the BBC Symphony Orchestra, directed the performance in his place.

The season, entitled *Schoenberg and his Time*, opened on 30 December 1951 with a performance of his Chamber Symphony No. 1 by the orchestra of the English Opera Group conducted by Norman del Mar, and an introductory talk by Tippett entitled *From Vienna to Los Angeles*. Martin Cooper in the *Spectator* had some reservations about the plans for the series, and the talk:

The works of the twelve-note period – the really controversial ones by which Schoenberg stands or falls – are inadequately represented in comparison with those of the earlier years ... In Tippett's introductory talk we heard about Schoenberg's domestic affairs, his relation with his first and second wives, his return to the Jewish faith, his quarrel with Thomas Mann ... and his obsession with numbers. All this is fascinating, but it has little to do with music.

Mann had been asked to contribute a talk about the quarrel – Schoenberg had objected to his appropriation of the twelve-note system for the composer hero of his novel *Doctor Faustus* – but he declined, even though he had recently given a Third Programme memorial talk on George Bernard Shaw (8 January 1951). He wrote to Anna Kallin about Schoenberg's music: 'Searching my mind regarding this topic which occupied me so intensely while I was working on the novel, I find that I have little that is new to say about it ... I am sure you will have enough musicologists at your disposal who will do justice to the high level of the Third Programme.'

Those who did speak on Schoenberg included Egon Wellesz, who had studied with him in Vienna, on Schoenberg's use of words (6 January 1952), Mátyás Seiber – another pupil – on the twelve-note system (17 January), Roberto Gerhard on his studies with Schoenberg in Berlin (19 February), and Darius Milhaud, reminiscing about his visits to Schoenberg

(27 February). Tippett's further talks included, on 27 January, *Moving into Aquarius*. Later published as the title essay in a collection of Tippett's writings, this was subtitled 'Old and New in the Great War', and was described in the *Radio Times* as 'A talk ... on Schoenberg, Picasso, James Joyce, and others, in relation to a crisis'. Tippett did not exactly identify the nature of this crisis; he disclaimed any belief in astrology, but suggested that it was related to the beginning, during the twentieth century, of a new 'world month' under the sign of Aquarius. He regarded Schoenberg as part of the 'catastrophe' that had accompanied this, and felt that in one sense he had gone too far: 'Like Freud his demon drove him down a road of over-simplification, towards a dogma – the law of the twelve-tone system.' Yet he admired Schoenberg's austere dedication to his task: 'That few of us will ever have the purity of Schoenberg is certain ... '

Desmond Shawe-Taylor, reviewing the Schoenberg season in the *New Statesman*, observed that, though Tippett was 'not a Schönbergian composer', he had 'flung himself with immense and commendable enthusiasm into the task', and was evidently attracted by his subject's 'intransigence and "purity" '. However, Shawe-Taylor was not convinced that Tippett had been 'the clearest expositor or advocate that could have been found'. He continued: 'He was always lively, throwing off bright ideas like sparks from a Catherine wheel. Schönberg was described to be "like" Freud, Picasso, James Joyce; we were whirled through bewildering perspectives of art and history, as though by the Red Queen. Sometimes, like Alice, we wanted to cry: "Stop!" ' Shawe-Taylor singled out *Moving into Aquarius*, observing that Tippett's belief that 'we are now in the midst of a crisis in human affairs' was not 'much more than a hunch'. As to the broadcasts of Schoenberg's music, Shawe-Taylor particularly commended *Pierrot lunaire* (12 February), in which the speaker had been Hedli Anderson, second wife of Louis MacNeice and the original performer of the Britten–Auden *Cabaret Songs* – Shawe-Taylor called her 'brilliant'.

Edward Sackville-West, writing an internal report about the Third's music programmes, was less tolerant of Tippett: 'I admire Michael Tippett greatly as a composer, but as a thinker he does not appear capable of any degree of precision, or of choosing his words so that they can only mean one thing. I found his latest talks impossible to attend to, so lacking were they in any sense of direction. They reminded me of lay sermons in an Ethical Church or the Rudolf Steiner Hall.' (Sackville-West also got in a dig at broadcasts of Shaw's plays, which were still frequently bulking out the Third: '[They] always strike me as communicating the boredom of all concerned in their production.')

The final talk in the series, given by Tippett, was entitled *Schoenberg in America*, and was broadcast on 20 March. The next morning, he received this telegram:

OSKAR ADLER NEVER WARNED SCHOENBERG OF ANYTHING WHATSOEVER DID NOT WRITE ALLEGED LETTER DOES NOT BELIEVE IN NUMEROLOGY YOU MUST CHANGE INCRIMINATING END OF YOUR WALK [*sic*, for 'talk'] IN SUNDAY REPEAT LETTER FOLLOWING HANS KELLER

Oskar Adler, doctor of medicine and friend of Schoenberg, had been known to Keller in childhood; they had both played in an amateur string quartet in Vienna, from which Keller fled in 1938 at the age of nineteen. Adler, too, came to Britain a few years later. By 1952 Keller was becoming known as a maverick music critic. His objection to Tippett's broadcast was fully explained in a letter from him to the editor of the *Radio Times*:

> Mr Tippett referred anonymously to what he did not realise was a wrong report in the *Musical Quarterly*, New York, October 1951, according to which Schoenberg had, on the occasion of his 76th birthday, received a letter from his friend Oskar Adler 'warning him that the coming year was critical because 7 and 6 add up to 13.' Schoenberg died on July 13, 1951, at the age of 76, and the report implied, however unintentionally, that Dr Adler's alleged letter contributed indirectly to Schoenberg's death. Mr Tippett made this implication yet more explicit by adding, in an atmosphere which he charged with emotion: 'Poor Schoenberg! What a strange friend!'
>
> With the full authority of Dr Adler (who is of Schoenberg's age and is at present recovering from a serious illness) I wish to state emphatically that (1) *he never wrote the alleged letter;* (2) *he never, on this or any other occasion, warned Schoenberg of anything whatsoever;* (3) *he does not, in fact, believe in numerological superstitions.*
>
> Yours etc.,
>> Hans Keller.

Keller also wrote to Tippett: 'Fortunately Dr Adler's wireless is out of order so that he will not have heard your talk, but he may hear the repeat on Sunday, and if the concluding section remains unchanged, its groundless accusation may kill him.'

Tippett replied: 'What an unforeseen and unfortunate affair! But don't let us get it out of proportion. I mentioned neither Adler's name nor the *Musical Quarterly*, so it can only be such people (very few indeed) who have seen the M.Q. in this country who will know to whom by implication I referred.' He passed the correspondence to Grisewood, adding: 'Speaking off the record now, Keller is as unpleasant as his conduct & his style. He belongs to the more dubious of the clique round Ben [Britten] ... ' Keller had recently, with Donald Mitchell, edited a 'Britten Issue' of their journal *Music Survey*, and this was about to reappear in book form as *Benjamin Britten: a commentary on his work by a group of specialists*. It was widely attacked by reviewers as hero-worship. Tippett told Grisewood that the Adler incident would cause him to be 'hated more than ever' by the Brittenites.

*

The BBC press release about the Schoenberg Season concluded: 'In the second quarter [of 1952] it is planned to broadcast a short series of

statements by leading international personalities on *The Artist in Society*.'
Anna Kallin wrote to Thomas Mann to ask him to take part in this series,
which she described as 'a kind of *profession de foi* from a few of the leading
authors, musicians and painters on the position of the artist in society ...
The other speakers I had in mind were Casals, Stravinsky, Silone [an Italian
author], Picasso, Malraux, and in this country Graham Greene.' Each was
being asked to give a talk of 'anything between 20 and 30 minutes'. This
time Mann agreed to take part – he was the only one on Kallin's list who
did – and a recording session was booked at a radio station near his home
in Pacific Palisades, California. On 15 May he wrote to Kallin that the
recording had been made, but

> if it isn't as flawless as I – within my limited means – might have produced
> it, circumstances very much beyond my control ought to be blamed.
> All had been discussed with both New York and our local Mr Lafrano.
> The latter in particular had been given the exact timing of the speech so
> that the tape could be prepared accordingly. Ten a.m. had been agreed
> upon and everything seemed settled. However, when I arrived at the
> studio at the appointed time, nobody seemed to know of the appointment.
> First, and as 'one Mr Mann', I had to wait for my passage to be cleared.
> Then I had to wait for fifteen minutes while a man who had spent twenty
> or thirty years in prison related his experiences on tape. Following which
> no tape possessing the right length proved to be available and some
> superior ingineer [*sic*] had to be notified, – as though no agreement on
> the subject had ever been reached. And finally, during my own recording,
> nobody was present but a yawning engineer who in no way encouraged
> me to interrupt myself when I had slipped which, incidentally, I myself
> mostly failed to notice while I was doing it.
> This is not meant to be a complaint. I merely wish to say that I would
> have been more successful if conditions had been more favourable ...

Anna Kallin apologised, assuring Mann that the talk was excellent: 'You
do not sound tired or nervous at all, and the couple of very minor flaws
make the talk even more like "real lace" – you know the little knots in
real lace which make it even more precious than it otherwise is.'

The talk was broadcast on 28 May 1952. Mann begins by describing *The
Artist in Society* as 'a ticklish theme'. He judges that an artist 'oversteps his
limits by indulging in ethical, social, and political criticism', and suggests
that public success (such as Mann himself had experienced in abundance
since his youth) is not altogether welcome, 'for he clings to that still quite
personal, quite profitless, quite free-wheeling early stage of his art, when
it was still unconscious of itself as art, when it laughed at itself. At bottom,
the artist would like to keep it like that.'

As some of the Third's critics had remarked, many talks were under-
produced. In the spring of 1952 Noel Annan, then a young don at King's
College, Cambridge, was asked by Mary Somerville, the BBC's Controller

of Talks, to listen to as many of them as possible during April and make a report. These are some of his comments:

> *7 April: J. Enoch Powell, MP, on 'The Social Services, Theory and Practice':* A brilliantly reasoned talk ... Delivery first class – hardly any politician's cant tone: timing good, sense well brought out.

> *10 April: R. R. Braithwaite, Fellow of King's College, Cambridge, on the lectures delivered by Professor Erwin Schrödinger of the Dublin Institute of Higher Studies:* Comical don's voice, but well controlled and modulated and every ounce of meaning given to the text. For philosophers only? But if so, did it say something new? Surely well known to all good Russellites. Nor was it clear what was Braithwaite and what was Schrödinger. It was not a review but a general discourse.

> *12 April: Philip Hope-Wallace on Jean Cocteau, Poet of the Cinema:* Most amusing, excellently done; witty, allusive, cultivated and well-informed. Not profound but not a profound subject. Entertainment value high: good sense and very funny.

> *14 April (Easter Monday): Norman Nicolson on 'The Wheel of Fire' – Bonfire Night discussed as 'a fire festival linking us with our ancestors':* Portentous voice, talking rubbish. Not an anthropologist and his methodology is shocking.

> *15 April: Edgar Wind giving the first of three talks to mark the quincentenary of Leonardo da Vinci's birth:* Miraculous talk of great beauty and ingenuity. Clever diction – interest sustained – very hard subject and great fascination.

Annan put some of his conclusions into an article on 'Talking in the Third Programme' in the *BBC Quarterly* (autumn 1952). Far from feeling that talks were too abstruse, he deplored the fact that 'I have never yet listened to a talk ... which I was constitutionally incapable of understanding.' He wanted to hear such things as scientists talking to scientists on their own terms. 'The fact that I should understand little would not matter a farthing.' He also regretted the Third's lack of 'intellectual gaiety', wanting more speakers like Philip Hope-Wallace and John Betjeman, and remarked that the English could not play with ideas 'with the facility and dexterity of the French'. How different the Third would be if 'for a month' only members of that nation were allowed to speak on it.

Much of the trouble was the tyranny of the script, essentially an unplayful medium. Unscripted discussions and interviews were only just beginning to be heard. They had not been regarded as acceptable material for broadcasting until tape recording and editing had become sufficiently widespread for producers to be able to control such impromptu material. (Live conversation on the air would not be risked for a long while yet.) One of the earliest such recordings to be broadcast on the Third was heard on 15 January 1952. W. R. Rodgers, an Irish poet who worked in Features, had recorded Oliver St John Gogarty and Brinsley Macnamara chatting about 'an unwritten play' (they argued as to which of them was to write it) set in Dublin, to be called *The Wildes of Merrion Square*. According to the *Radio Times* the conversation was supposed to be taking place in a Dublin 'tavern', but after a rather tentative few moments of distant traffic, the location sounded very much like a studio, and at times the participants seemed to be working from a script.

Yet sometimes scripted discussions or interviews worked very well. On 21 February 1949, Ivy Compton-Burnett was heard in conversation with Margaret Jourdain, with whom she had lived for thirty years. The formality of the proceedings was entirely suited to the speakers and their topic:

JOURDAIN: We've often talked over other people's books, but never your books.

COMPTON-BURNETT: It seems an omission, Margaret, as I am sure we have talked of yours.

JOURDAIN: I see that yours are a novel thing in fiction; and unlike the work of other novelists, I see that they are conversation pieces, stepping into the bounds of drama; that narrative and exposition in them are drastically reduced; that there is less scenery in them than in the early days of the English drama, when a placard informed the audience that the scene was 'A wood near Athens'; and less description than in many stage directions. There is nothing to catch the eye in this country of the blind. All your books, Ivy, from *Pastors and Masters* to the present-day *Two Worlds and their Ways*, are quite unlike what Virginia Woolf called 'the heavy upholstered novel'.

COMPTON-BURNETT: I don't see why exposition and description are a necessary part of a novel. They are not of a play, and both deal with imaginary human beings and their lives. I have been told that I ought to write plays, but cannot see myself making the transition. I read plays with especial pleasure, and in reading novels I am disappointed if a scene is carried through in the voice of the author, rather than the voices of the characters. I think that I simply follow my natural bent. But I hardly think 'the country of the blind' is quite the right description of my scene ...

One of the first completely unscripted interviews on the Third must have pleased Noel Annan, if he heard it, for it was in French. On 15 September 1951 listeners heard Ewald Junge speaking to the eighty-three-year-old Henri Matisse, about the Dominican chapel he had recently designed and decorated at Vence. After initially giving a few short, grumpy answers, the old man got into his stride about the use of colour. No translation was provided. (Among other broadcasts in French was Albert Camus talking about his novel *L'Etranger*, heard on 17 July 1954, though it was followed by an English translation. Rayner Heppenstall produced several programmes in which French poets read their work, again followed by translations.)

When Anna Kallin invited Arnold Toynbee to take part in a series on Asia in the spring of 1951, he asked her if they might not have a 'genuine extemporary' discussion. But as late as 1956 impromptu speaking was not encouraged. When Douglas Cleverdon was assembling a documentary on ten years of the Third, he asked contributors to come to the studio four days before transmission, so that their off-the-cuff recollections could be recorded on a dictating machine, transcribed, edited, and read out by the speaker during the live broadcast, just as Russell and Copleston had done some years earlier. By this time, tape was being widely used – though disc recording had not been abandoned – but the BBC's studio managers proved slow learners at editing. 'At present with an inexperienced operator,' Cleverdon complained in October 1954, 'it may take as long as an hour to make six joins.'

*

Like Noel Annan reporting on talks, Edward Sackville-West, who was commissioned to comment on the Third's music programmes in the spring of 1953, was pleased by most of what he heard. 'In the first years of the Programme,' he wrote, 'there was, perhaps, rather too much *musica antiqua* ... I think the balance has become more equitable in the last year or so.' Broadcasts for the third week of February 1953, just as he was compiling his report, included works from every musical era and an astonishing range of names; for example, Charpentier's opera *Médée*, and works by Wishart, Bloch, Agricola, Philidor, Grétry and others who would have sent listeners scurrying for their music encyclopaedias – had not the *Radio Times* provided a commentary on much of what was about to be heard. The issue of 13 February also included a full-page article about Michael Tippett, whose *A Child of Our Time* and the Ritual Dances from *The Midsummer Marriage* were being heard that week (the opera was now finished but had not yet been performed).

William Glock still gave talks on music, his subjects ranging from Monteverdi to Hindemith. He often worked from handwritten scripts, in which he had scribbled the musical illustrations he was to play live at the piano. In early 1952 he delivered three half-hour talks entitled *Some Problems of Interpretation* (beginning on 13 March), and he was back on 16 April with the first of six *Studies in Music Criticism*. In July 1954 Roger Fiske, who had succeeded Alec Robertson as producer of music talks, asked Glock to present another programme on Hindemith. Glock replied:

> What I would very much like to hear myself would be an evening of the best Messaien, an evening of Dallapiccola, perhaps even an hour of Boulez; also Webern! and I wd be happy to be asked to contribute a programme on Stravinsky's latest works ... which seem to me something new and vastly important ... and/or a programme on Elliott Carter ... Will you think about these suggestions?

Fiske replied:

The trouble about the composers you would like to talk about is that there is not so far sufficient of their works recorded to make a programme of the length we want. There is nothing I should like better than an evening of Dallapiccola. We have no recordings at all of Elliott Carter. If you happen to know of any recordings of his piano sonata and string quartet and cello sonata, then certainly we might have a go at him next year, if you can give us the numbers. We only have one work by Dallapiccola, and I don't think anything by Boulez.

The BBC's failure to keep up with contemporary music in the mid-1950s was noted by Alan Frank, of Oxford University Press music department, writing in the *Musical Times* in February 1954:

> ... the appearance of really adventurous music in the Third Programme is in my view too rare ... We have a right to hear samples of the most recent developments ... As it is, programmes contain much that is safe and perhaps rather dull, and seldom anything really advanced or experimental.

Glock knew far more about contemporary music than anyone in the BBC at this time. In his role as chairman of the music section of the Institute of Contemporary Arts, he went every year to the International Society for Contemporary Music festival, held in major European cities, and so became acquainted personally with composers scarcely heard of in Yalding House. Since 1948 he had also been directing a remarkable summer school of music, first at Bryanston School, then at Dartington Hall, where members of the European avant-garde lectured and worked alongside young British musicians. Meanwhile, observes Glock, the BBC 'still gave the impression that contemporary music was led, for example, by Samuel Barber in the United States and by Poulenc in France. It was this middle-of-the-road policy that I was determined to undermine.'

He began this task by helping to promote contemporary music concerts in London, and making the Third feel obliged to broadcast them. 'Producers used to come ashen-faced out of the studio,' he says, 'after concerts which they had abhorred from beginning to end.' But he could only achieve limited success with what he calls his 'musical underground' in the years before he himself joined the Corporation.

*

When Mary Somerville, Controller of Talks, read Noel Annan's report on talks on the Third, she described him as someone 'like ourselves' – that is, with a Third Programme outlook. An uncomfortable reminder that the Third's potential audience was not necessarily so like-minded was delivered by the Oxford undergraduate magazine *Isis* a few months later. In the 12 November 1952 issue its editor, the future novelist David Hughes, wrote:

> On a cheap day [ticket] the younger dons catch trains to London to record eclectic talks; the President of the Union is approached for permission to give a nation-wide hearing to one of his debates; poets are paid more

money than any magazine can manage for their words to be spoken in a throbbing voice. We cannot therefore afford to criticise a national institution which looks keenly towards Oxford for so much of its material. The Third Programme, a Picasso lady with an eye in its forehead and a tubular cheekbone, has pushed open the doors of Broadcasting House to admit the best from a university from which the bulk of its staff has probably hailed.

But at the same time we do not listen much to the Third Programme, which is a curious thing when so much of its work must clearly be directed at us ... [5]

The article was accompanied by cartoons of corduroyed, bow-tied and scruffily polo-necked intellectuals braying into BBC microphones. 'It has now become a cartoonist's cliché,' wrote Hughes,

to speak of corduroys, curly pipes, beards and bundles of scrappy but intellectual papers. But though this outward uniform is still a part of the men who dominate cultured radio, an even more terrifying uniformity of the spirit is being worn. This consists of condemning anything which large numbers of people like (it must be bad), of posturing both in front of the microphone and behind the scenes. They are in charge of a movement to pinnacle a chi-chi art, misguided traders in the obscure.

P. H. Newby, who was in Talks in the 1950s, says that Mary Somerville was responsible for this donnish atmosphere. 'She said her ideal Third Programme talk was the kind of talk that went on at high table. From which I deduced that she hadn't sat at many high tables. Because the talk there is often *not* of the lofty kind you would expect.'[6]

Despite many accusations like Hughes's, the Third was still making no effort to woo audiences with such simple devices as a regular day and time for a series, or a predictable pattern of repeats – of which there were as many as ever, though Grisewood's repertory system had never established itself. *New Soundings*, a monthly magazine programme of new poetry and prose, edited and introduced by John Lehmann, which began on 9 January 1952, might be heard on a Wednesday at 9.25 pm one month and on a Monday at 8 pm the next. *Prospect*, an architectural review, with Nikolaus Pevsner among its contributors, and *Foreign Review*, Alan Pryce-Jones's survey of the arts, science and politics abroad, turned up at equally unpredictable times. Most programmes were not even part of a series, so

[5] Oxford and Cambridge Union debates were frequently broadcast live on the Third. On 23 February 1952 listeners heard Cambridge discussing whether 'the English Channel should be abolished'. Among those in favour of Britain's continuing separation from Europe was the Vice-President, Douglas Hurd.
[6] Newby says she did not approve of 'dons talking to dons', but wanted the atmosphere of a specialist talking to a highly intelligent layman. He adds: 'She claimed to have been the very first talks producer, in the late Twenties or early Thirties, when she scandalised distinguished speakers by editing their scripts to make them sound more like spoken English.'

there was no way of guessing whether a particular evening's listening might include a scientific debate, such as Alan Turing, the computer pioneer, discussing (with others) *Can Automatic Calculating Machines be said to Think?* (14 January 1952), or the theologian and philosopher Donald Mackinnon on a panel arguing about life after death (7 February 1953).

Isaiah Berlin was unusually favoured in being granted, in October, November and December 1952, an almost regular time (9.30 pm, 9.40 pm, 9.15 pm and so on) for six weekly lectures entitled *Freedom and its Betrayal*. Then a thirty-three-year-old Fellow of All Souls, he had made four short broadcasts on the Third since 1946, and had been taken up by Anna Kallin as a potentially brilliant speaker. He explains that he was now keen to give a series of radio lectures 'about the fact that the great eighteenth-century philosophers were ultimately responsible for a lot of intellectual tyranny, ending in the Soviet Union, in the *gulag*; that these good men, who were against superstition, falsification, authority, and were great liberators, had nevertheless preached doctrine which led, albeit in a somewhat perverted form, to tragic consequences.'

He was, however, an extremely nervous speaker. 'I hate lecturing; I'm a very nervous lecturer. Every lecture I've ever delivered has been an agony to me. And I said to Miss Kallin, "Look, I can't, I don't know how to talk, I'm no good at all. I certainly can't talk live, because I'll be absolutely petrified. I can only talk into a machine."' She arranged for him to record. And he did not write a script: 'I wrote fifty pages of notes, and boiled that down to about sixteen. Then I boiled *that* down to about five, then two, and then a postcard with headings. And then I didn't look at it, because I thought I might not be able to read my writing!'

The experiment was a huge success: 'I talked and talked and talked – which I do anyway – and that was the basis of my being thought to be a possible candidate for the chair of Social and Political Theory at Oxford. Because what had I written before that? Only a book on Karl Marx. Nothing else at all that counted. And the broadcasts made my career in Oxford.'[7]

He became a frequent speaker on the Third, and a not infrequent listener; nevertheless when he was asked to contribute an essay about it to a proposed symposium to mark its fifth birthday, he wrote to Grisewood:

I have nothing to say conceivably worth saying about the 3d [*sic*] Programme. I shd be delighted to receive 50 guineas; I shd be proud to appear with Sir M. Beerbohm, Mr Forster, Mr Nicolson & E. Sackville-West & Lionel Trilling; but my thoughts about the 3d programme are either too confused or too trivial to set down; & so, as between the mixture of ambition & greed on the one hand, & shame at exposing my nakedness on the other, the latter wins all too easily. So you must forgive me if

[7] The one surviving recording from the series, a talk on Rousseau, shows that speaking unscripted entirely suited Berlin, who occasionally hesitates a little, but mostly speaks with remarkable fluency.

I demur; & remain (for once) silent; & that on a subject of genuine
importance.

Preparations for the symposium had begun too late, and the book never
appeared.

Jazz, which David Hughes would not have categorised as 'a chi-chi art',
and which certainly appealed to many undergraduates, was beginning to
creep into the Third, but only on rare occasions. One of the earliest was
on 8 March 1952 when Max Jones introduced a selection of records by
Jelly Roll Morton. Humour was now rarely attempted, apart from regular
appearances by Stephen Potter discoursing on innumerable aspects of
Lifemanship, and few who gave talks were under the age of forty – an
exception was John Berger, described as 'a young painter and art critic'
(he was then twenty-six), who on 8 August 1952 spoke about his feelings
while drawing from a life model. However, young writers did begin to
make regular appearances in another literary programme, *First Reading*,
which began on 26 April 1953. It was edited and introduced by John Wain
(who was the same age as Berger), and the first edition included a reading
by thirty-one-year-old Kingsley Amis, then a university lecturer working
on his first novel. Philip Larkin, the same age as Amis, took part in the
programme a few weeks later.

Other ways of presenting and discussing contemporary writing were
tried the following year in *Literary Opinion*, 'a monthly programme of
comment and observation', which began on 14 April 1954, when Angus
Wilson spoke on 'The Future of Fiction'. Kingsley Amis was heard in the
edition of 9 June, giving a talk entitled 'In Defence of Dons':

> From the tone and content of what the journalists say about the dons, it's
> pretty clear that they divide them into two types. One is the port-sipping,
> walnut-cracking pedant of the older universities, perpetually immured in
> oak panelling and saying: 'Well, Fogworthy, I always maintain that old
> Dan Chaucer distils the very spirit of the Middle Ages, eh?' And the
> other one is the nicotine-stained steel-spectacled pedant of the newer
> universities, showing the sleeves of his pullover below his cuffs and saying:
> 'Now, don't give me that, Higgins, where's the sociological significance in
> the *Arcadia*, eh?' Both these antichrists of what's technically known as the
> true literary attitude are, I think, almost entirely creatures of dream.

P. H. Newby, who was producing, received a note from Amis asking if 'it
would be all right for me to put on *special voices* for the "Well, Fogworthy"
and "Don't give me that, Higgins" utterances.' Newby was dubious: 'It
might be effective: it might not.'

John Lehmann's programme avoided some of the sillier solemnities of
the Third. 'When recently Mr John Lehmann asked Mr Cyril Connolly to
talk on Petronius in his programme the result was a delight,' wrote a
correspondent to *Time & Tide*. 'Had this been left to the BBC we should
probably have been offered a disquisition on the Recusant Poets of North

Germany by the Reader in Classical Studies at the University of Pen-y-Pass.' Geoffrey Grigson's poem on George Barnes mocks this tendency:

> George will hire the Greek Ambassador to read, in Greek,
> All Aeschylus, in 99 instalments, week by week.

Far from being concerned about the Third's heavy bias towards the universities, and Oxford in particular, Grisewood wanted to strengthen its Oxford connections. At the end of 1951 he asked the university to set up an Advisory Committee of dons who would give the BBC the benefit of their wisdom. (He issued no such invitation to Cambridge. 'I suppose we thought Peter Laslett was our link with Cambridge,' says P. H. Newby.) It began to meet in 1952, and continued to do so for a few years before being absorbed into a system of BBC Advisory Councils organised by geographical regions. Nothing of real importance was discussed at meetings of this Oxford committee, except the establishment of a BBC General Traineeship for graduates, which began in 1954. Competition for the eight or so places each year was immense – '800-odd applicants for 1954 when the scheme was open to men and women, and 500 this year when it was confined to men,' noted the BBC in 1955, giving no reason for the exclusion of women. The first year's recruits – all from Oxford – included Alisdair Milne of New College, a future Director-General of the BBC.

By the time the Oxford committee was established, Grisewood had been promoted to Director of the Spoken Word, replacing Barnes, who had gone to run BBC Television. Christopher Holme was Acting Controller, Third Programme, from May to November 1952, while candidates for the Controllership were considered. Holme's widow Anthea says that many people would have liked to see him get the job himself, but he had not ingratiated himself with senior administrators, and was passed over. 'It should not be long before the name of the new Third Programme Controller is known,' reported the *Manchester Guardian* on 30 September 1952. 'The appointment is a crucial one, for the strength of the chosen candidate will indicate what the BBC has in mind for the future of the Third. A strong candidate will indicate that the Corporation intends to continue building up the programme in the face of persistent suggestions that it is not worth the money spent on it.'

In mid-1952 Sir William Haley left the BBC to become editor of *The Times*. His successor as Director-General, Sir Ian Jacob, formerly in charge of the BBC Overseas Service, had no personal commitment to the Third, and was thought to favour popularisation of broadcasting rather than striving for higher intellectual achievements on the air. The choice he and the Governors made for the new Controller certainly did not suggest that the BBC considered the Third to be a jewel in its crown. 'Since November,' the *Daily Express* reported on 13 March 1953,

> the Third Programme has been controlled by John Morris, fluent speaker of Japanese and, at 57, within three years of the normal BBC retiring age.

Morris, grey-haired expert on the Far East, spent years as an Indian Army officer. He was with the 1922 and 1936 Everest expeditions. When the Pacific war began he was Professor of English Literature in Tokyo.

From 1938 to 1941 he was adviser to the Japanese Department of Foreign Affairs. After Pearl Harbour [*sic*], for a brief spell, his arrest was overlooked.

He got away, returned to England, and was put in charge of the BBC Far Eastern service.

Morris, who confesses to being a devotee of the 'Third', is the third chief of the £879,000 programme with its nightly audience of fewer than 100,000 listeners . . . But even though the listeners to the 20 stations which broadcast the Third dwindle steadily, the controllership is a path for BBC promotion. Minimum salary: £2,250.

Harman Grisewood did not think much of his successor's qualifications for the Controllership:

He was a nice fellow. Shy, nervous, an oddity in that he had been a Gurkha warrior. Ian Jacob thought well of him as a fellow soldier, and he was not unsympathetic to any of the things I'd attempted to do. But he was not disposed or well equipped to enter into all that world as a participant, which I felt quite strongly to be necessary, just as a publisher must know his writers and go about amongst them. But Morris didn't do any of that. He was an office man.

CHAPTER EIGHT

Two tits and a bum

Two of the original announcers left the Third during 1951. Marjorie Anderson went to the Light Programme to introduce *Woman's Hour* (along with Jean Metcalfe), and Alvar Liddell returned to the Home Service. Announcers working in Third Continuity were encouraged to write comments on the evening's programmes, and on 7 January 1953 the two recent recruits both did so. Peter Fettes (previously with the Light) noted of an American comic operetta, *Boston Baked Beans* by Gail Kubik, that it was 'evidently by Menotti out of Gershwin. More of an abortion than a miscarriage I would say.' The other announcer reacted much more enthusiastically to *Rhondda Reminiscence* by Gwyn Thomas: 'What a magnificent programme! Full of life, humour and spontaneous poetry. I thought the production and performance exceptionally lively. An excellent idea to broadcast on the Third a piece in which such skill goes with humanity and not merely sophistication.' This was signed 'Richard Baker'.

After graduating from Cambridge, where he had read modern languages, Baker had joined the Announcers' Reserve, and worked in various parts of the BBC before being appointed to the Third. He had a wide knowledge of music which sometimes proved useful. One evening he was announcing a piano recital in which the soloist had decided to play Beethoven's *Hammerklavier* Sonata from memory. 'I had fiddled about, as a boy, with the slow movement,' says Baker. 'She went through the first two movements fine, got to the slow movement, and went wrong – I simply *knew* she had gone wrong. The right hand kept going, but the left hand came off the keyboard and pointed to the closed score, at the side of her. So I tiptoed across and opened it, and fortunately knew it well enough to put it in front of her with the right page open.' On another occasion, Beecham was conducting Mozart's Requiem, and Baker was seated next to the rostrum. 'He was quite old and not very well, and after the first two movements he sat down on his stool, very breathless. And he turned round to me, with all the microphones live, and said, "I'm damn tired, dear boy. Why don't you think of something else to say? Don't mind what it is. Recite Macaulay's *Lays* for all I care!"'

Baker's supposedly Cockney vowels had been ironed out during his training as an announcer. He describes the style of presentation on the Third at this period as 'the opposite of chat – you were simply not required to express any personal opinions. It went too far in the direction of formality, but the manner of presentation in the whole BBC was formal. It was an inheritance from the war years, when it had been important to be impersonal.' The guardian of standards was the Third Programme Presentation Assistant, Mrs Elizabeth Blunt. 'Liz was very forthright,' says Baker. 'She didn't know a tremendous lot about music or the arts, but she was hugely professional in the way she dealt with the typing and the rotas, and really one feared a telling off from Liz more than one did from anybody.' She was still in office in 1965. 'Mrs Blunt was acting wholly within her responsibilities in making the suggested corrections,' wrote a member of Music Department that year, after she had saved the Third from a minor disaster. 'Third Programme owes much to her perceptive vigilance in maintaining standards and consistency of style in presentation since the programme began in 1946.'

Like the other announcers on the Third, Baker had plenty of spare time, since – apart from a few daytime recordings – he was only required in the evenings. He spent some of it acting on television, appearing in a children's Saturday serial, *Spanish Gold*, 'in which I played a naval officer, and Graham Stark was the comic relief. And that was live, at five o'clock on a Saturday afternoon. I sometimes had to rush back to do the evening Continuity on the Third Programme.'

Another announcer, Tom Crowe, joined the Third not long after Baker. He came from an Anglo-Irish family. 'I always try and side-step it when I'm asked to classify my family background, because the English love doing it,' he says,

> but I suppose my family would have described themselves as rather like those people in one of Yeats's poems, 'Hard-riding country gentlemen.' I was educated at St Columba's, which was – this sounds dreadful – a school for Irish Protestants, and then I went to Trinity College, Dublin, where I read French and German literature. I didn't complete the course, but left to join the Irish Guards, and went out to Germany just after the war ended. I left that in 1949. I used to speak German quite fluently, and I got an audition for the BBC German Service. I didn't get a job there, but I was launched, terrifyingly, on Continuity in the General Overseas Service at 200 Oxford Street [in 1950]. From there I found myself drifting on to the Light Programme, announcing dance bands in places like Tunbridge Wells. Then at last I saw a post advertised for the Third Programme, and applied for that and got the job.
>
> There were only four of us – Dicky Baker, Christopher Pemberton, Pat Butler and me; and it was a very rare and purified atmosphere. It's almost unbelievable now, but you were allowed two minutes of unexplained silence between programmes. You could just switch off the microphone and sit back!

I thought it was all too dignified. It was like a line in Evelyn Waugh's novel *Helena*, in a scene when she's with her tutor, and he describes her face – I can't remember the exact words – as 'having the expression that British youth habitually have when in the presence of the classics: a mixture of incomprehension and reverence'. I think the management of the Third Programme was a little like that; they felt that you should be solemn in the presence of the arts. And I don't hold that view, because the arts are there to enrich life. They're there to rejoice in. So why should you be solemn about a Haydn quartet, when it's such a joyful thing?

One of the BBC's few women announcers, Patricia Hughes, sometimes did duty on the Third Programme in the early 1950s, while also working on Home and Light. Like Crowe, she found the Third constricting: 'It was very solemn. If you fluffed an announcement even the tiniest bit, you had a sleepless night afterwards, thinking you weren't good enough. Really, you felt you weren't a human being – that you couldn't be yourself.'

The Third's new Controller, John Morris, who arrived in his job at about the time that Tom Crowe joined the network, concerned himself at first more with administration than artistic matters, and it was Christopher Holme who, in January 1953, expressed anxiety about the lack in recent months of 'themes' running through the Third's programme planning. He began to put pressure on the Supply departments to rectify this, with the consequence that a Faust month and a season of Spanish music and drama began to be planned. Meanwhile a ready-made theme was supplied by the Coronation, due to take place on 2 June 1953. The Third's plans included *A Garland for the Queen*, a set of vocal pieces commissioned by the Arts Council from leading British composers, to be recorded at a Festival Hall concert and broadcast two days after the Coronation. In the event this and other Third Programme contributions to the festivities were overshadowed by a live relay on 8 June of the first performance, in the presence of the Queen, of Britten's opera *Gloriana* from Covent Garden. Live BBC Television coverage of the Coronation itself made broadcasting history, attracting an audience of more than twenty million, more than twice as many as listened to it on the radio. George Barnes was soon afterwards conducting the Queen round Lime Grove TV studios when, to his astonishment, she suddenly told him to kneel, and knighted him with a sword that had been smuggled in from Buckingham Palace. John Betjeman sent the Barnes family a drawing he had made of the incident.

Meanwhile John Morris was largely occupied with the possibility of the Third broadcasting on Sunday afternoons, in the winter months only, with a corresponding reduction of half an hour on weekdays. It was decided to canvass various distinguished persons who had broadcast on the Third, to discover what they thought about the scheme. Among them was T. S. Eliot. 'I always look at the Third Programme[1] on the evenings when I am at home and able to listen,' Eliot replied to Morris.

[1] i.e. its billings in the *Radio Times*.

I find that I rarely listen until after 8 o'clock, unless there is something of very particular interest to myself, and that I never listen after 11 pm. I am, therefore, perhaps not one of those best qualified to express an opinion about alteration of the hours. I am, however, doubtful about the advantages of extending the Programme to Sunday afternoon, as it seems to me that it already tends to overlap with concerts worth hearing. For instance, I notice that on Sunday, July 5th you have an interesting symphony concert at 6.15 in the Home Service which overlaps to some extent with a talk on the Third Programme by Mr Shawe-Taylor. These are both programmes which I should like to hear. On the whole, I am somewhat in favour of retaining the present hours of the Third Programme.

The concert, by the BBC Northern Orchestra, consisted of Handel's *Arrival of the Queen of Sheba*, Strauss's Second Horn Concerto (with Dennis Brain as soloist), and Schubert's Ninth Symphony. Shawe-Taylor was giving a talk on nineteenth-century vocal ornamentation, with illustrations on records.

Despite Eliot's doubts, Sunday broadcasting from 3 pm was introduced by the Third on 27 September 1953. Closedown was brought forward by half an hour to 11.30 nightly throughout the year. 'You will notice that over a complete year this schedule will actually amount to a slight cutting down of the present overall time,' wrote Morris in an internal memorandum, 'but I think it is unlikely that many people will notice this. It seems however, short of asking for an increased programme allowance, the only way of coping with the ever rising programme costs.'

Despite the cost factor, Sunday afternoons had a lavish look. There were Bayreuth recordings of Wagner, including the complete *Ring*, and classic drama, including *The Merchant of Venice* (25 October 1953) with Peggy Ashcroft as Portia and Michael Redgrave as Shylock, and music by Julian Slade, then resident composer at the Bristol Old Vic; his musical *Salad Days* arrived in London the following summer. Meanwhile it was suggested within the BBC (and reported in the *Scotsman* on 3 August 1953) that 'perhaps the Third Programme wavelength might be used during the day for a continuous commentary of [*sic*] the Test matches'; but a BBC spokesman said this would 'prove too expensive'.

The strident demands that the BBC should stop wasting money on the Third had continued intermittently in the popular press, but there is no evidence that this was considered seriously within the BBC – until the very month when the Third spread itself into Sunday afternoons. On 22 September 1953, in a memo headed 'Private & Confidential', the Controller of Finance, T. Lochhead, sent Lindsay Wellington, Basil Nicolls's successor as Director of Sound Broadcasting, a note of the costs of the Third for 1952–3, and 'a provisional estimate of the savings which would result from its cessation'. Taking into account such overheads as engineering, rent of premises, and pensions, the Third was now costing £890,000 per annum. Only about half this sum would be saved immediately if the

Third shut down – many of the overheads could not be eliminated at once – but Lochhead told Wellington that 'the savings could be considerably increased' if, for example, the number of BBC orchestras was reduced. He offered to discuss the position with Wellington, but for the time being nothing further was done.

*

'Wit and humour have never been absent from the Third Programme,' asserted the *Radio Times* on 4 September 1953,

> but the right sort of material is hard to find. This week, Henry Reed proves his versatility as a radio writer by contributing a mock-solemn account of a young critic's research into the life of an imaginary novelist, Richard Shewin, 'the Balzac of the twentieth century'. The critic, Herbert Reeve (whose name no one seems able to catch),[2] meets some very odd characters indeed and makes disconcerting discoveries . . . Before long we realise that the title of the programme, *A Very Great Man Indeed*, is a little ironical, to say the least . . .
>
> Here is a sparkling piece of radio satire which will give pleasure to all who relish sophisticated fun at the expense of literary Bohemia. It will be broadcast on Monday and Wednesday.

Henry Reed, born in 1914, came from a working-class Birmingham family. Louis MacNeice had taught him classics at Birmingham University in the early 1930s, where he had got a First, and decided to write a biography of Thomas Hardy. A spell in the Royal Army Ordnance Corps led him to write the most famous poem of the Second World War, 'Naming of Parts', which appeared in his first and only collection, *A Map of Verona* (1946). By the time the Third began, he was trying to work on his Hardy book, and was in love with a would-be novelist, Michael Ramsbotham, five years his junior. He scraped a living reviewing for the *Listener* and the *New Statesman*, and offered the BBC his radio dramatisation of *Moby Dick*, written to while away spare time when he was a cryptographer at Bletchley Park during the later part of the war. It was broadcast on 26 January 1947, on the Third, and thereafter his name appeared frequently in the *Radio Times*, with Douglas Cleverdon producing most of his scripts.

Nest Cleverdon says of Reed:

> Henry was a selfish creature, I suppose, and he liked to be liked. But at the same time he had an immensely catty tongue. He could be intensely irritating, but the results were such that it was always worth it. Every single script was late in being delivered. Right up to the last day! Three pages wouldn't have arrived, and Douglas would be told: 'Don't use that scene, I'm rewriting it.' The actual productions were enormous fun,

---

[2] Henry Reed was always being confused with Herbert Read.

though; everybody loved them – it was a holiday, a party.

As writer and producer, Reed and Cleverdon created several plays with classical and historical settings: *Pytheas* (25 May 1947), about a fourth-century BC Greek navigator, *The Streets of Pompeii* (16 March 1952), which won an Italia Prize, and *The Great Desire I Had* (26 October 1952), which imagines Shakespeare visiting Italy. In the meantime, Reed was failing to get on with his Hardy book. 'My mind would often wander from my subject,' he wrote in 1971, recalling this difficult time.

> Minds often do this. And none more eagerly and rapidly, I came to notice, than those of the people I interviewed who had personally known my Author. They were invariably glad to help. From my encounters with them I would retire grateful and moved, full of tea and sherry, and on one occasion, memories of what must have been almost the complete piano works of Brahms. They were fine men and women. But . . . I would realise that the main content of their disclosures had concerned, exclusively, themselves.
>
>   This struck me as a profoundly interesting fact in itself. After a time I began . . . a small dramatic study of it. It was called *A Very Great Man Indeed* . . .

Reed had befriended the boy radio actor David Spenser, who recalls: 'Henry was already entering that dreaded writer's block. He did a lot of research on Hardy, but gradually it dawned on him that he would *never* write this book. By which time he was writing almost nothing – certainly his poetry had more or less seized up. And the moment he stopped the Hardy, decided to give up the biography, he suddenly found himself writing *A Very Great Man Indeed*. Into it went all that he had experienced while researching Hardy's life.'

Listeners on 7 September 1953 heard Reed's play commence with the dry tones of actor Hugh Burden, giving what sounded like a typical Third Programme talk on a famous writer:

> REEVE: The late Richard Shewin has been justly called 'the poet's novelist'. Other and abler pens than ours have done justice to the work that earned him the title 'the Balzac of the twentieth century'. It is now ten years and more since he died, but his great series of novels are still strikingly relevant to our predicament today . . . But his literary glory is not our theme . . . which is no less than the man himself . . .

There follows a brief excerpt from one of Shewin's novels – a brilliant parody of Henry James[3] – and then Reeve recounts his attempts to track down members of Shewin's circle. His first encounter is with Shewin's caustic brother Stephen, played by Carleton Hobbs, whom he finds in bed:

---

[3] Reed was an accomplished parodist. *A Map of Verona* includes his celebrated spoof of *Four Quartets*, which begins: 'As we get older we do not get any younger.'

'I am not ill, Mr Reeves [*sic*], if that is what you are thinking ... I've never seen any point in getting up, if there's nothing to get up for.' This has touches of Reed himself, who in his later days became deeply reclusive. 'A lunch party had been arranged for him,' recalls David Spenser, 'but no Henry! So the person who'd arranged it rang him up, and said, "Where are you?" And Henry said, "Well, I just *don't* feel like coming." And he didn't.'

Reeve now meets the Misses Adela and Elizabeth Burkley of Shepherd Market, to whom Stephen Shewin has maliciously sent him, though their profession is not apparent to the innocent would-be biographer:

REEVE: I never knew Shewin myself, but ... today one is perhaps beginning to appreciate his real size.

ADELA (*baffled*): But Mr Shewin was never a *large* gentleman ... Betty, the gentleman was saying that Mr Shewin was a *modest* gentleman. (*Gently.*) He wasn't, was he, dear?

BETTY: Modest? My word, no. Nobody could say that. He was an all-the-lights-on man, Dicky Shewin was, every time.

REEVE: Well, of course many writers have an unaccountable fear of the dark.

ADELA: And a looking-glass too.

BETTY: My word, yes. He was very vexed if there wasn't a looking-glass.

Reed notes in his introduction to the published text of *A Very Great Man Indeed* and its sequels that not everything he wrote reached listeners. 'A fair number of passages, accepted by the producer, already recorded by the cast, were sometimes, at a late moment, ordered out by higher assessors, on the grounds of indelicacy.'

A few weeks after the first broadcast of *A Very Great Man Indeed*, the Third got into trouble for allowing the poet George Barker to read his *True Confession* (13 April 1953). This was a typical passage from the poem:

> Good God, let me recollect
> Your many mercies, tall and short,
> The blousy blondes, the often necked,
> And those whom I should not have thought
> given wisely to me;
> Nor let me forget my grateful memory the
> odd consolers,
> Too frequently brunette,
> Who often charged me for your mercies, God.

Sir Alexander Cadogan, Chairman of the BBC, wrote to Lord Balfour, who had complained about the poem in the House of Lords, that those in charge of the Third had been told that they had committed 'a grave error ... I entirely agree this broadcast should never have taken place.'

Henry Reed claimed that in the first sequel to *A Very Great Man Indeed*, entitled *The Private Life of Hilda Tablet* and broadcast on 24 May 1954, 'full frontal nudity was heard on radio for the first time'. The passage in question concerns Herbert Reeve's second meeting with Hilda, whom Stephen Shewin describes as a 'lady music-writer':

> HILDA (*distant, behind door*): Bertie! Is that you, Bertie? ... Come on in!
> REEVE (*apprehensively*): Where *is* Hilda?
> ELSA (*placidly*): She is taking her bath ... This is the way, please ...
> HILDA: Come in, Bertie. Excuse the old bod. Don't mind, do you? ... Do sit down. No, not on *that*, unless, of course, you prefer it. There's a stool just there. (*Splashing.*)
> REEVE: G-good morning, Hilda.
> HILDA: Good morning. Now look. I want your help, desperately. Have you heard of a couple of chaps called Faber and Faber? ... Well, they're both after my life.
> REEVE: After your *life*, Hilda? Good God!
> HILDA: Well, don't be so ruddy surprised, old boy. Damn it, several publishers have asked for it. It's been quite an interesting life ... Now, I'm going to ask you, Bertie, as an old pal – (*Great watery sounds as she gets out of the bath*) – to let me put myself entirely in your hands. Just chuck us that large towel marked 'H. T.', will you? Thanks ... Now, it'll need a goodish bit of research, but of course you're used to that, and the book itself need only be about 350 pages ...

So Hilda hijacks Reed and makes him write her biography instead of Richard Shewin's.

Hilda had dominated the first play, thanks largely to a masterfully masculine performance by Mary O'Farrell. Now she became the central figure in what was to be a whole saga. Superficially, she and her companion the soprano Elsa (played by Marjorie Westbury) were a spoof – and quite a risky one for 1953 – on the composer–singer ménage of Benjamin Britten and Peter Pears. Hilda's all-woman opera *Emily Butter* is of course a dig at the all-male *Billy Budd* (Reed originally wanted to call it *Milly Mudd*). But Hilda was also modelled on Elisabeth Lutyens, whom Reed had come to know well when she wrote the music for a 1950 feature he had scripted on Canterbury Cathedral. 'They had been on reasonably good terms,' write Lutyens's biographers.

> In general outline Hilda might have more obviously resembled Ethel Smyth – in her homosexuality [Lutyens was married], her bluff rural heartiness, and the endlessness of her projected biography. (Dame Ethel's autobiography ran into many volumes.) ... But the details of her characterisation were absolutely unmistakable. Hilda had a father named Sir Eric [Lutyens's father was the architect Sir Edwin Lutyens] ... She had set Schopenhauer (as opposed to Liz, who in 1953 had set Wittgenstein). She talked inexorably of twelve-tone music ... The *Daily Telegraph* was held to have described [Hilda's] music as 'thawed architecture'. This was almost certainly a reference to a running joke Liz had with Constant Lambert,

who had once said that if, as Goethe maintained, architecture was frozen music, it might be a good idea to melt down one or two of Edwin's banks. Reed could perhaps have picked this up in the pub, along with the other fragments of Liz's distinctive and oft-repeated stories.

Insult must have been added by the fact that Hilda's supposed compositions were waspishly funny parodies of twelve-tone music written (and played on the piano) by Donald Swann.[4]

Lutyens and her husband Edward Clark began to talk of suing Reed. Lutyens's biographers comment:

> It is important to know that in Reed's plays Hilda is, despite everything, an ultimately endearing figure ... Far more deadly, though fortunately she never knew it, was the portrait which Dylan Thomas drew after her visit to Laugharne in 1951 ... 'Weasel-eared Lizzie,' he dubbed her in a letter ... 'hissing and gushing and drooling and bubbling about Edward, money, the BBC, twelve tones, Constant [Lambert] and babies ... monologuing herself to death.'

According to Lutyens, Thomas's behaviour during this visit was far worse. On one occasion he was so drunk that he opened her sponge bag and drank her shampoo.

He had made few appearances on the Third after his burst of work in its early days. For a while he lived mainly off writing film scripts (none of them made), then in February 1950 paid his first visit to America to give public readings, spending most of his time there either drunk or recovering from a binge. A few months after his return, Laurence Gilliam (Head of Features) and Douglas Cleverdon took him out to a meal, 'knowing that he was particularly penniless,' writes Cleverdon, 'and asked what he would like to do for quick and easy money.' Thomas suggested a programme based on Edgar Lee Masters's *Spoon River Anthology*, a sequence of poems in which the dead of a town in the American Mid-West speak their own devastatingly honest epitaphs from the graveyard. Cleverdon and Thomas met again shortly before Christmas 1950 to discuss this in detail, and at that meeting, says Cleverdon, 'we also discussed the *Madtown* (as he then called it)'.

This was a project which had originated in 1939, when Thomas, then living with his wife Caitlin in a small house in Laugharne in south Wales, had taken part in amateur dramatics organised by the novelist Richard Hughes, who lived at Laugharne Castle. 'What Laugharne really needs,'

---

[4] In his history of the Proms, Barrie Hall provides some more examples of Hildaisms from Lutyens. When William Glock announced at a press conference in the 1960s that 'by chance' there happened to be five women composers featured in his current Prom season, Lutyens wrote to a music journal that 'by chance' there happened to be eighteen homosexual composers featured too, and just what did it matter? 'She also coined that memorable and deadly sobriquet for English pastoral composers – "The Cow-Pat School".'

Thomas told Hughes after it was over, 'is a play about well-known Laugharne characters – and get them all to play themselves.' Indeed the idea went back even further, to 1932 or 1933, when Thomas had spoken of wanting to write a kind of Welsh version of Joyce's *Ulysses*, with the action contained within twenty-four hours. His 1944 Home Service talk *Quite Early One Morning* was a first sketch for this, a word portrait of a small Welsh town (in this case New Quay, Cardiganshire, where he was then living) in the early hours of one day. The success of this led him to contemplate a full-length dramatised treatment of the subject, and at first there was to be a farcical plot, with a police inspector from London judging the whole place to be insane. The title was to be *The Town was Mad*, or *The Village of the Mad*.

Cleverdon guesses that he wrote 'most of the first half' of such a play during 1949, soon after he had moved back to Laugharne. 'At what stage Dylan drifted from the dramatic form of *The Village of the Mad* to the feature form of *Under Milk Wood* is uncertain. It seems to me probable that when he began to write the long, opening sequence of the dreamers in the "lulled and dumfound town", the feature form imposed itself upon him, and he continued in the same vein.' By 'feature' Cleverdon means the use of narrators to introduce other voices, as in the radio feature programme of that period. He recalls that about a third of the final script was written before 'I suggested the obvious solution – that he should drop the plot altogether, and simply carry on with the life of the town until nightfall. He seemed relieved at this proposal . . . '

Nest Cleverdon recalls a memorable evening at this stage in the project:

He'd written about three quarters of it, and he came to dinner one night, with Caitlin, to read what was done. Richard Burton and his adopted father Philip Burton were there too. It was in our house in Albany Street. And halfway through supper, Caitlin revealed that she'd left all three children alone in a strange flat. The youngest, Colum, was still a baby. And I was so horrified that I couldn't really concentrate for the rest of the evening. But Dylan read marvellously, and we were all bowled over. There was a silence of appreciation when he'd finished, and then Caitlin said, 'Bloody potboiler.'

Douglas Cleverdon writes of the reading that 'its effect was overwhelming', but that in the following months progress was fitful:

From time to time [Dylan] assured me that there was nothing he wanted more than to complete *Under Milk Wood*; but he was obliged to spend his time on small jobs that brought immediate cash returns. I . . . was able to persuade the BBC to take the unprecedented step of offering, on account, five guineas for every thousand words;[5] but this made little difference. On another occasion Laurence Gilliam suggested that I should visit Laugharne myself in order to urge him on. This was equally fruitless ... One accepted the producer's occupational risk of drinking pint for pint with Dylan on an empty stomach until half an hour after closing time; but then, instead of returning to the Boat House [Thomas's home] and supper, we went in again through the back door of the pub and stayed for another couple of hours.

Time passed, and the script lay about, unfinished. In October 1951 Thomas sent what he had written of it to the literary magazine *Botteghe Oscure*, asking for a hundred pounds, badly needed to pay debts in Laugharne. It was published in May 1952 under the working title *Llareggub, a Piece for Radio Perhaps*. Thomas had first used this mock-Welsh name, 'bugger all' spelt backwards, in a short story published in 1936, where there is a passing reference to 'the Black Book of Llareggub'. Over the year that followed, he wrote most of the rest of the play, taking a script with him when he set off for his third American trip in April 1953. In May he gave public readings of it at Harvard University (solo) and in New York (with actors), allegedly writing additional material at the last moment before these performances. In New York he took the parts of First Voice and the Reverend Eli Jenkins.

Cleverdon, hearing that the script was finished at last, thought this 'too good to be true'. So it proved. He arranged to meet Thomas, now back in Britain, with David Higham, Thomas's agent, at Simpson's-in-the-Strand, for a celebratory dinner at which *Under Milk Wood* was to be handed over. Thomas did not arrive; word came that he lacked the money for the train journey from Wales, but Cleverdon was assured that he would bring the script to the BBC the following week. Cleverdon takes up the story:

Dylan arrived at the BBC with the script at lunch time on Thursday [15 October 1953] and explained that he must have it back by Saturday; it was his only copy, and he would need it for the [next] stage-reading in New York; his flight had been booked for Monday evening, the 19th. My secretary, Elizabeth Fox, accordingly typed the script on duplicating stencils, and gave it back to him when he called at the BBC on Saturday morning.

During the weekend he telephoned me at home, in some agitation, to

---

[5] On 26 August 1952, Cleverdon wrote to Copyright Department about Thomas: 'I am aware that the Corporation has decided that no advance payment is to be made to him: so I suggest that we might make some arrangement whereby he is paid at the rate of £5.5.0 for every 1000 words that we receive from him. Then any extra payment could be adjusted when we had received the complete script and estimated the timing. If it is suggested that he might still leave the work unfinished, I have sufficient confidence in him to guarantee the Corporation (by deduction from my salary) against any loss that may be incurred.' This arrangement was accepted by Copyright, and Thomas was paid fifteen guineas under it in October 1952.

say that he had lost the manuscript, either in a taxi or a pub. I assured him that I could get the script duplicated on Monday, and would bring copies to him at the Victoria Air Terminal before he left for New York. I met him on the Monday evening, and, to his evident relief, gave him three copies. As we were having a farewell drink before the coach started for the airport, I said how sorry I was that the manuscript had been lost; he replied that if I could find it I could keep it; and he gave me the names of three or four pubs in which he might have left it. A couple of days later I found it in the Helvetia in Old Compton Street, Soho.

In 1966 Caitlin Thomas sued for the ownership of the manuscript, but lost. Nest Cleverdon says that Douglas eventually sold it for £1,000 at a time when the lease on their Albany Street home had run out, and they were buying a house in Islington.

Arriving in New York, Dylan Thomas directed and took part in two stage-readings of *Under Milk Wood* on 24 and 25 October 1953. The American poet John Malcolm Brinnin, who had organised all Thomas's trips to the USA, writes that at first he seemed in good spirits, talking repeatedly about 'his immense relief in having "escaped" from London'. But by the time rehearsals began, he was running a high temperature, and he agreed to see a Dr Milton Feltenstein, who had treated him for gout on a previous visit, and had suggested he moderate his drinking. Feltenstein now gave him an injection of a cortisone-based drug, intended to sustain him through the strain of performing. This seemed to work, and *Under Milk Wood* went well at its two performances. But after a party two nights later, to celebrate his thirty-ninth birthday, Thomas became deeply depressed, and during the following days his behaviour alternated between exuberance and misery, with hallucinations. Dr Feltenstein was called, and is believed to have administered a sedative of morphine and sulphate. If so, it was probably this rather than alcohol which caused Thomas to sink into a coma and die in hospital on 9 November.

'His body was brought back to Laugharne,' wrote Cleverdon in the *Radio Times* a few weeks later, 'where in his "seashaken home / On a breakneck of rocks" he had written ... *Under Milk Wood* ... Thankfulness that at any rate one such work was completed is mingled with helpless exasperation at the thought of the potential masterpieces of which the tragedy of his early death has deprived us.'

These words were part of an article introducing the first broadcast of the play, scheduled for Monday 25 January 1954, at 7.25 pm on the Third Programme. 'Had Dylan lived,' writes Cleverdon, 'of course, he would have taken the part of the First Voice ... It happened that in January 1954 Richard Burton was acting at the Old Vic; although he was then playing Hamlet and rehearsing for Coriolanus, he undertook to play Dylan's part.' Among the entirely Welsh cast, Philip Burton, Richard Burton's adoptive father, took the part of Eli Jenkins, and Hugh Griffith was cast as Captain Cat. The children's songs and singing games (with music by Daniel Jones) were prerecorded by Cleverdon at Laugharne School. Hearing that school-children were to take part in the play, a reporter from a national newspaper telephoned Cleverdon to ask whether they would be in the studio for the broadcast, with the implication (writes Cleverdon) that 'innocent children should not be exposed to the immoral influences of Llareggub'.

Cleverdon was aware that, in the light of the recent George Barker row, the play might provoke complaints about sexual explicitness. Current BBC practice was for heads of Supply departments to do any necessary censorship, so Cleverdon wrote to Laurence Gilliam a week before the broadcast:

> I have gone through the script of *Under Milk Wood* with some care, and append a list of the passages that might cause offence to those who seek it. These passages are marked in blue in the enclosed script.
>
> In several cases the cutting of these passages would involve also the cutting of larger sections (marked in red) of which the passages are an integral and inseparable part: e.g. if in Cue 604 we cut the line 'Let me shipwreck in your thighs' (rhyming with 'I'll tell you no lies') the two stanzas 603 and 604 would have to go; that would ruin the poem: if we cut the poem (one of the finest parts of the work), Rosie Probart would be left with two sentences only: this (with the loss of 608–617) would destroy one of the main tragic themes – the 'one love' of Captain Cat's life. Similarly to cut the line 'Roll me on the ground' in Cue 491 would lead to the cutting of Polly Garter's song on pages 45, 47, 55, and 70, to the virtual elimination of Polly, and again to the destruction of a major theme. To cut 'Come and sweep my chimbley' in p.70 would mean cutting the whole of 812, Mr Waldo's song. To cut these three poems (two of them crucial) would entirely distort the closely-wrought pattern of the work ...
>
> A few other passages are susceptible of a double meaning to those who look for it; but are no worse than twenty per cent of the dance band songs of the 'hold-me-in-your-arms-tonight' variety.
>
> I cannot help thinking that in view of our earlier broadcasts of *Lysistrata*, *Trimalchio's Feast*, *Venus and Adonis*, *Volpone*, Sartre, and some Restoration comedies, *Under Milk Wood* should be acceptable in uncut form to any reasonable Third Programme listener. The humour is broad, but never dirty; and the whole work is on a plane of poetic imagination which should entitle us to disregard the pettifogging hypocrisies of those who never listen to the Third, but whose hostility will be encouraged rather than placated by timidity on our part. Moreover (as I understand that Leslie Stokes has pointed out), to leave Dylan's script untouched, as the work of a major poet of our time, is a defensible position; but to cut half a dozen sentences leaves us open for not cutting two dozen more.

Gilliam hastily consulted Sir Ian Jacob, the Director-General, who in turn talked to Grisewood (Director of the Spoken Word), Lindsay Wellington (Director of Sound Broadcasting), and John Morris. The decision was made that the broadcast should proceed – with cuts 'at the discretion of Features

Department', which put the matter back in Gilliam's hands. He did not wish, as he put it, to 'weaken the force of a very considerable work of broadcasting art' and 'alienate the true Third Programme audience without satisfying the prudes'. Nevertheless he was inclined to 'make minor alterations to meet the spirit, as we understand it, of the DG's directive', and he submitted to the Controller of Entertainment (Sound) a list of three small cuts. Cleverdon describes these as 'two tits and a bum', and so they were: 'wriggle her roly poly bum', 'the nipples and the bees', 'draws circles of lipstick round her nipples'. Everything else was left untouched – except that the word Llareggub was not printed in the *Radio Times;* Cleverdon's article simply referred to 'the town'.

After four and a half days' rehearsal, *Under Milk Wood* was recorded on Sunday 24 January 1954, the day before transmission. Richard Burton had not been able to rehearse with the cast until that morning, because of his Old Vic commitments, so Cleverdon had pre-recorded his narration for use in the earlier rehearsals. There was disagreement in the studio between Cleverdon and Daniel Jones, who, as Thomas's literary executor, refused to agree to the restoration of words Thomas had cut from the New York performances, but otherwise all went well, and after the recording Cleverdon took some of the cast to the Globe Theatre in Shaftesbury Avenue to repeat twenty-five minutes of the script on stage, as part of an evening entitled *Homage to Dylan Thomas*.

After listening to the broadcast next day, Martin Armstrong wrote in the *Listener*: 'I was spellbound from start to finish ... Both production and performance were nothing short of perfect ... In this poem it seems that Dylan Thomas was entering on a magnificent development of his powers.' The *Daily Sketch* radio critic wrote: 'If this is not a masterpiece, then I have never heard one.' And the reviewer in the *Tablet* was painfully conscious that this was Thomas's final work: 'As the last line died away and the silence seeped in we thought: there will be no more.'

Those who missed the broadcast, and the repeat two nights later, could soon buy it on two long-playing records issued by Argo. Cleverdon notes that the entire cast signed away their rights in this for the benefit of Caitlin and the Thomas children. The record became a bestseller, and a stage production, directed by Cleverdon and Edward Burnham, transferred from the 1956 Edinburgh Festival for a seven-month run in the West End. J. M. Dent published the text immediately after the first broadcast; Daniel Jones, who edited it, gave the name of the town as Llaregyb.

In his book on the genesis of the play, Cleverdon makes no assessment of it. In the *Radio Times* just before the first broadcast, he allowed himself to describe it as 'a major work'. Cleverdon's colleague D. G. Bridson, in his book *Prospero and Ariel*, writes of it as 'radio's greatest script'.

*

Paradoxically, the huge success of *Under Milk Wood* caused a row between the Third and Drama Department. When, a few months later, John Morris complained to Val Gielgud that Drama was not offering the Third enough plays, Gielgud snapped back that Features, to whom Douglas Cleverdon belonged, were 'running a private drama sub-section of their own', and the Third was taking plays from them without letting Drama know. To the Controller of Entertainment, Gielgud complained that Morris 'prefers Cleverdon acting in an unofficial capacity as a source of drama supply rather than Donald McWhinnie [Gielgud's deputy] or myself . . . It amounts to a vote of little or no confidence in this department.' The situation was smoothed over by the appointment of Raymond Raikes as 'Third Programme Specialist' within Drama. But when two years later Morris was asked to contribute to a BBC European Service feature marking the tenth birthday of the Third, he mentioned only two specific Third Programme achievements, *Under Milk Wood* and the Hilda Tablet plays, all produced by Cleverdon.

The Private Life of Hilda Tablet, broadcast four months after *Under Milk Wood*, contained even more jokes than its predecessor at the expense of the musical world. Like Tippett,[6] Britten, and Elisabeth Lutyens, Hilda takes time off from composition to participate in the Purcell revival:

> HILDA (*confidingly*): Oh yes, Herbert, I realised a lot of Purcell in my early days.
> REEVE: Sorry, Hilda, but – realised he was what?
> HILDA: What was what?
> REEVE: You said you realised Purcell – ?
> HILDA: Course I did. Everybody knows that. I realised a lot of Palestrina, too, if it comes to that.
> REEVE (*lost, but sympathetic*): Yes, well, of course, we all have to realise such things, when the time comes, I suppose.

Real-life musical goings-on in the Third frequently had a Hildaesque character. A memo headed 'Isaac Stern, Igor Markievitch and the Philharmonia Orchestra', dated 5 January 1954, could almost have been written by Henry Reed. Stern was to have been the soloist and Markievitch the conductor in a concert to be recorded in Poplar Town Hall – a 'last resort', since no other big orchestral studio was available – three days before Christmas, and to be transmitted on the Third on Christmas night. Leonard Isaacs's memo continues the story:

> On December 20th Markievitch, because of fog, was late returning from Madrid and missed his first rehearsal altogether. This was, rightly or wrongly, interpreted in an unfavourable light by the orchestra, who were thus from the beginning a little 'put off'. During the afternoon rehearsal, at which Dr Simpson[7] was present, it became apparent that the studio was

---

[6] A lustful priest who appears in a Graham Greene parody (another supposed extract from the writings of Richard Shewin) in *A Very Great Man Indeed* is given the name Father Tippett.
[7] Robert Simpson, the producer.

unsuitable. (S[enior] S[tudio] M[anager] writes that he always knew it was, but this warning was not transmitted to me until after the event.) Dr Simpson and the Studio Manager started enquiries, with the result that the recording session itself was transferred ... to Maida Vale 1, at 9.30 pm on December 22nd ...

Stern could not be found and therefore had to be told [about the change of time and venue] when he turned up to rehearsal. He arrived in a distrait state, as he had just heard that his wife had been taken ill and had been removed to a hospital. This was a bad start, and to find that Markievitch was not very interested in a soloist in any case, did not improve matters. Markievitch's attitude throughout has appeared casual except where he himself was concerned.

The rehearsal went through and Markievitch called Stern for 10.30 pm on December 22nd, saying he would be ready for him. How he could have imagined this, when the session only began at 9.30 pm and the Symphonie Fantastique itself lasts over 45 minutes I cannot think. At any rate Stern turned up as required to find that only the first movement of the Symphony had been recorded – and he had to wait until the other four movements were completed. He thus started again in a bad frame of mind but did his best, with rather poor support from the conductor. Stern was under the impression that this was a 'run-through': only afterwards was he told that this was in fact the recording itself – and that our terms for pre-recording did not permit of repeating whole movements (our agreement with the M[usicians'] U[nion] precludes this). None the less, the overture was then recorded twice, because Markievitch was dissatisfied with the first playing.

Stern thereupon asked for a repeat of the first movement of the Concerto, and was supported by the leader of the orchestra. However, at this point (11.50 pm) some members of the orchestra said that they required to leave before midnight (they asserted that they had been told that the session would be over by 11.45 pm, but as I have not been able to discover any reason for the statement I believe it to be typical orchestral wishful-thinking) and no Corporation employee has the authority or right to require an orchestra to repeat a performance in a pre-recording session. It therefore had to be left as it was.

Dr Simpson had gone up the previous day to Birmingham ... to supervise another recording session – and was himself taken ill there, which prevented his being present at the Markievitch recording. His secretary ... stayed on for the session, giving all the help in her power. Had I been phoned I would have come down immediately but I only learned of all this after the event ... I have heard from one or two other sources of Markievitch's dislike of virtuoso soloists – and it explains his rather strange attitude at my recent interview with him in regard to his concert for us next May, when he said 'This is for me an important occasion and I should wish for no concerto in the programme.'

*

William Haley, the Director-General who was the Third Programme's founding father. 'The heart of the Third Programme was really two decisions of mine.'

The Third Programme's original triumvirate: (*left to right*) Etienne Amyot, Leslie Stokes and George Barnes.

Sir Adrian Boult, chief conductor of the BBC Symphony Orchestra. Sir William Haley said: 'The Third Programme would never have got going without Adrian Boult.'

(above, right)
Louis MacNeice in 1942.

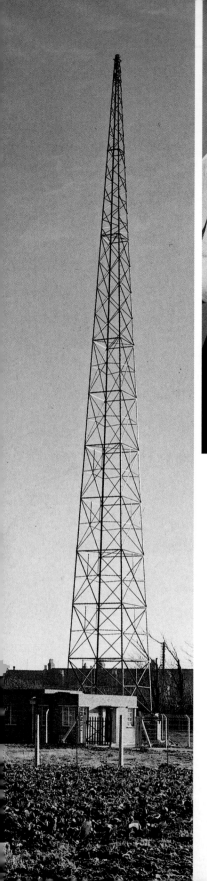

The 150-foot Third Programme mast at Brighton, one of a network of local transmitters radiating it on 203.5 metres medium wave, to combat the interference from the USSR.

(right)
Richard Strauss (*right*) talking to Sir Adrian Boult in the interval of a concert broadcast on the Third Programme on 30 October 1947, in which Strauss conducted *Till Eulenspiegel*.

Dylan Thomas at the microphone in 1948, with Douglas Cleverdon in the background.

Harman Grisewood, the second Controller of the Third Programme; he called it 'fundamental to our civilisation'.

(right)
Third Programme Continuity Suite, in the sub-basement of Broadcasting House, in 1951. The lady is the programme engineer in charge of the network; the announcer's studio is beyond the window.

Fred Hoyle giving one of his remarkable Third Programme talks: 'I have reached the conclusion that the universe is in a state of continuous creation.'

John Morris, Controller of the Third from 1952 to 1958. 'He was an office man.'

ROYAL VISIT TO
T.V. STUDIOS

Cmdr GEORGE BARNES
KNIGHTED

A watercolour by John Betjeman, painted for the Barnes family, of the Queen knighting George Barnes in a BBC television studio. Betjeman has changed 'Mr George Barnes' to read 'Cmdr.', since he always addressed Barnes as 'Commander'.

Delicious guineas for poseurs

Typical performers on the Third Programme, as seen by a cartoonist in *Isis*, November 1952.

'The Third Programme family': a cartoon in the *Daily Sketch* to mark the tenth anniversary of the Third Programme in September 1956. 'The television set is not there for viewing,' reads the original caption, 'the brow of the dog is high.'

At Stern's request, the concerto recording was not broadcast. He was paid his fee (£210), but since the recording had not been used, John Morris asked if he could recover this sum from central reserves. The Third was still terribly short of money, and Morris noted in August 1954 that this made it impossible to embark on 'any ambitious projects' during the coming autumn and winter. Fortunately, big works were coming on the air almost unbidden. Britten's *The Turn of the Screw* was relayed from its opening night in Venice on 14 September. (Five days earlier, the Third broadcast a dramatisation of the Henry James novella on which the opera is based, with Flora Robson as the Governess, and the night after the Venice relay listeners could hear *A Call at Bly*, a 'dramatic epilogue' to the story by 'Michael Innes', the Oxford don and novelist J. I. M. Stewart.) Walton's *Troilus and Cressida* and Tippett's *The Midsummer Marriage* both had their premières at Covent Garden on 3 December 1954 and 27 January 1955 respectively.[8] Lennox Berkeley's *Nelson*, first performed in 1953, was relayed from Sadler's Wells on 30 September 1954, and Berkeley's *A Dinner Engagement* had its first broadcast on 1 July 1954 from the York Festival.

For many listeners, the operatic broadcast in the autumn of 1954 which remained most in memory was the première of Hilda Tablet's magnum opus, on the night of 14 November. Entitled *Emily Butter: an occasion recalled*, the programme was a delicious spoof not just of *Billy Budd* (Hilda's alter ego Donald Swann came up with some excellent musical parodies) but of the Third's style of relaying opera premières. Herbert Reeve, who of course introduces the programme, explains to us that *Emily Butter* has been the subject of no less than nine pre-performance talks on the Third. The opera itself consists of ten acts, so that the relay takes most of the night, and at one moment (as at Poplar Town Hall) the orchestra refuses to do any more overtime. Set in a department store, *Emily Butter* has an all-woman cast, one of whom, a last-minute replacement from La Scala, sings in Italian. The climactic moment is the entrance of a plain-clothes policewoman, come to investigate shoplifting; her voice is in the *basso profundo* range.

The 'real' Hilda Tablet, Elisabeth Lutyens, was meanwhile taking up arms against the BBC. During the early 1950s there had been a growing number of complaints from composers about the bottle-neck of scores which had been passed by the reading panel, yet had failed to receive a broadcast. In August 1953, *Musical Opinion* published a letter from Richard Howgill, who the previous year had been appointed to the new post of Controller of Music at the BBC. He explained that it had now been decided to grant 'panel-free' status to quite a large number of 'established' contemporary composers, which meant that a member of Music Depart-

---

[8] In Walton's opera, Richard Lewis sang Troilus, Magda Laszlo was Cressida, and Peter Pears was Pandarus; Sir Malcolm Sargent conducted. Tippett's cast included Richard Lewis as Mark, Joan Sutherland as Jennifer, Adele Leigh as Bella and John Lanigan as Jack, with Otakar Kraus as King Fisher; John Pritchard conducted.

ment could schedule performances of their works without reference to the panel.

Lutyens thought little of his reassurances. In 1947, the Third had broadcast a programme of her works which she had selected herself, as part of a series organised by Humphrey Searle. This, though, was exceptional; normally her submissions had to be scrutinised by the panel, whose reports were usually unfavourable. 'I have never believed that Elisabeth Lutyens had the real stuff of a composer in her,' wrote Leonard Isaacs in 1952, after reading her Chamber Concerto No. 6, and she continued to find it very difficult to get works broadcast, though she was regarded as a firmly established composer in British contemporary music circles. 'My own experience, therefore,' she wrote to Isaacs in 1953, after reading Howgill's bland promises, 'does not seem to agree with Mr Howgill's statement of the case.' Howgill was shown her letter, and unwisely wrote to her that 'Your work for documentaries and features is much appreciated and possibly is more the real Elizabeth [*sic*] Lutyens than that of your music which shows you as a disciple of Schoenberg.' Lutyens replied with indignation that Howgill 'should prefer a mature composer to write pastiche'. Her letter continued: 'Richard, you know this jungle world. It is difficult enough to earn a living as a composer, but *never* getting a broadcast is making it almost impossible ... I am sick to death of self-interested, self-pitying composers with chips on their shoulders working & intriguing for performance and so I'm sure are you.' Howgill consulted his staff about her complaints; Leonard Isaacs commented: 'The BBC is not anti-12–tone – it takes decisions on its readers' reports ... '

Lutyens continued the struggle; but, despite the new 'panel-free' system, she and many other contemporary composers did not get real support from the BBC Music Department during Howgill's term of office.

*

John Morris's memo about the Third's 1954 autumn and winter plans mentioned, rather lugubriously, that it was becoming 'increasingly difficult' to find classic English plays which the Third had not yet broadcast. With this in mind, 'Mr John Barton, a young Fellow of King's College, Cambridge, whose work with the Marlowe Society has been outstanding' had been commissioned to choose and edit for broadcasting a series of early English plays. In fact Barton's series, *The First Stage*, consisting of thirteen plays from the beginnings of English drama to the 1580s, was not ready until the autumn of 1956, when it ran once a month on Sunday afternoons. By that time the Third had discovered a new, rich seam of contemporary drama.

Modern English novels had often been dramatised on the Third. Among those in 1955 and 1956 were *The Fellowship of the Ring*, the first book of Tolkien's *The Lord of the Rings* (with Terence Tiller as producer and adapter, in serial form beginning on 14 November 1955), Mervyn Peake's *Titus Groan*, adapted by the author (1 February 1956), and William Golding's

Lord of the Flies (28 August 1955), with a cast of schoolboys. 'In order to obtain sustained performances in long and difficult parts from very young actors,' announced the BBC's publicity department, 'producer Archie Campbell has borrowed from film-making technique. He is rehearsing and recording the play scene by scene, and then editing the whole into a final broadcast form.' (This was to become the standard studio technique for radio drama.)

Though it was Golding's first novel, John Morris recognised his 'considerable reputation as a writer', and encouraged him to do 'original work for the Third Programme', offering 'more than the fees usually given to a writer new to broadcasting'. Golding was delighted by the broadcast of *Lord of the Flies*. 'It seemed to me to be wholly convincing, moving and frightening,' he wrote to Archie Campbell. 'The effort to give character by differentiation between boys' voices was successful to a degree I should not have thought possible. I suppose no one would suggest that listening to such a play for two hours is a pleasure, but you made me experience something very real and obsessive.' In a later letter, to a Talks producer, Golding wrote: 'I'm glad of the chance of telling you how much I appreciate many of the talks on the Third Programme, let alone the plays, music and the rest. I'm ingenuous enough to be grateful for getting so much for so little.'

The radio adaptation of *The Lord of the Flies* had been made by a thirty-seven-year-old actor and playwright, Giles Cooper. It was his first script for the Third, but he had been writing for Home and Light for some years while 'resting' from stage work. His wife's sister was Nest Cleverdon, who describes him:

> Giles didn't look like a playwright; he looked like a regular army officer – handsome, blond, quite tall. He came of an Anglo-Irish family, who'd had a castle in Sligo. He was educated at Lancing, and when he was eighteen he went and fought in the Spanish Civil War. He then went briefly to drama school, but he was never going to be a good actor – he was too much the self-conscious Englishman. He then had a long, bloody, beastly war in the Far East, and I always thought that lay at the back of his black comedies. He came back to find his girl-friend had left him, and it took him a long time to get going as a writer.

Alongside his script of *Lord of the Flies*, Giles Cooper submitted a synopsis and some sample scenes for an original radio play. 'At Mathry Beacon on the Welsh coast,' explains the Drama Department Script Reader's Report, dated 11 February 1955,

> an assorted group of people are placed in charge of a rocket deflector, when V2s started coming over England about 1943. They are a little Welshman, [an] educated non-commissioned man, a West Indian negro and a North Countryman, and two young women. Isolated in their little community, they form a strange self-contained society of their own; one

of them discovers that the war is over, but doesn't want to break up their contentment, so does not tell the others. As time goes on children are born to them, and their isolation continues; the natives only speak Welsh and no news comes to them anymore. Ultimately they learn the truth and turn against one of their number who taunts them. He is killed, and the others with their belongings, cattle and children march off back to the outside world.

The Script Reader who wrote this, Mollie Greenhalgh, had not liked *Lord of the Flies* – 'the most gruesome piece I have ever read, and I cannot think that anybody will be other than repelled by it' – but she was delighted by *Mathry Beacon*, though its story bore an obvious resemblance to Golding's novel: 'A brilliant idea, carried out with equal brilliance in the excerpts given here. Mr Cooper should certainly be encouraged to go ahead with it as soon as possible.' It was broadcast on the Third on 18 June 1956, produced by the Assistant Head of Drama, Donald McWhinnie.

Nest Cleverdon describes McWhinnie, who was to contribute so much to the Third in the next few years: 'Donald was a thin, haggard-looking Scots boy, a wonderful jazz pianist, who drank a great deal. He had a great appreciation of modern writing, and found himself in a Drama Department which was being run by Val Gielgud as if it were the days of Henry Irving. And he and Barbara Bray worked immensely hard to change things.' P. H. Newby describes McWhinnie as 'a very silent, reserved man; co-operative, very sensitive, and a marvellous producer of drama. He could do more with a silence than other producers could do with background music, even speech.'

The first half-hour of McWhinnie's ninety-minute production of *Mathry Beacon* seems slight by comparison with Golding's masterpiece, but then it swiftly asserts its individuality. The eerie sound of the rocket deflector punctuates each scene, as the little community metamorphoses from a disciplined army unit into a free-loving, free-thinking utopia – and then slides into violence.

Cooper soon followed *Mathry Beacon* with *The Disagreeable Oyster*, a black comedy which again caught Mollie Greenhalgh's fancy. She summed up his storyline in a memo to the Drama Script Editor, Barbara Bray:

> Fantasy about a little clerk called Bundy who is sent on a mission to another town – his first night away from home since his marriage. Arriving, he finds that he is not wanted after all but decides instead of going home to make the most of his night of freedom. Unfortunately instead of adventure he meets trouble – an encounter with the local eccentric, the local prostitute and the police leads him into a situation where he is almost arrested for nudism. He arrives home in a collection of extra-ordinary garments, still clutching the loaf his wife had asked him to buy.

> An ingenious fantasy which Mr Cooper could no doubt bring off with his usual verve. It doesn't seem to me quite as amusing as some of his other plays, but there is very little dialogue here [in the material Cooper

had submitted] and it may get funnier as it goes along. For a sixty minute Loosebox placing.

The Loosebox was a reserve of scripts awaiting production, and it soon began to seem unlikely that *The Disagreeable Oyster* would emerge from it. 'It is hardly Home Service material,' observed Donald McWhinnie, 'and to our distress it has been turned down on the script by Third.' He described it as 'a genuinely experimental programme of quality' (its style was much more impressionistic than in *Mathry Beacon*), and he sought permission to pay for a production out of the Controller of Entertainment's Experimental Fund. *The Disagreeable Oyster* was heard on the Third (which had been persuaded to change its mind) on 5 March 1957.

Lord of the Flies had suggested yet another plot to Cooper, and on 7 December 1956 Mollie Greenhalgh reported on a synopsis he had submitted entitled *Unman,Wittering and Zigo*:

> Mr Ebony goes as a master to the Upper School at Chantrey – 'an old school with new ideas, Spartan and Liberal'. The atmosphere in his form puzzles him. Constant references are made to his dead predecessor Pelham, and he finally hears from the boys that they murdered Pelham. He cannot believe them, but is deeply worried and affected by the problem, which influences his private life and his life at school. 'Everything is infected by this spirit of evil.' Then he hears that one of the boys, a nervous weakling, has committed suicide, leaving a confession of Pelham's murder. Ebony discusses the problem with a friend. Who murdered Pelham? If the boys did, who was the leading spirit? If Pelham's own personality gave them a corporate will and led to his death, why doesn't it happen all the time – to all the leaders?
>
> A fantastic, gruesome story, strongly allied in subject and feeling to *Lord of the Flies*. I found it, in synopsis, unconvincing, and weak in conclusion, and unlikely to be of great entertainment value. However, it is difficult to tell how it would work out without more dialogue.

Donald McWhinnie read it too, and commented: 'The synopsis doesn't convince. On the other hand, with re-thinking, there might be something interesting here.' The debate about it continued.

A few weeks earlier, a thirty-three-year-old barrister, John Mortimer, sent Features producer Nesta Pain a synopsis of 'a dialogue between a very old prisoner and a very old barrister. I'm sure,' his letter to her continued, 'it would make a very good short radio play and long to hear what you think of it.' A script was commissioned, and Mortimer told Pain: 'I think it might be right for the Third, but of course I'll leave it to you.' *The Dock Brief* was finished by the beginning of February 1957, and was broadcast on the Third on 16 May, with Michael Hordern as the barrister and David Kossoff as the criminal; it won an Italia Prize. It was also seen on BBC Television on 16 September 1957, with the same cast and Nesta Pain directing. Mortimer's writing career was launched.[9]

Another playwright acquired by the Third during this period was already a cult figure, but his work had not yet reached a wide audience. When Samuel Beckett's *En attendant Godot* was staged in Paris early in 1953, Rayner Heppenstall went to see it with the BBC Paris Representative, Cecilia Reeves, in the hope that it might suit the Third. 'The first part of it is extraordinarily effective,' Reeves wrote to Donald McWhinnie, 'but it ceased to be convincing after we had a drink at the interval, so that it would probably be easier to hold the attention with a radio version.' She sent the script with this note. McWhinnie passed it to a Drama Department producer, E. J. King Bull, who reported that it was

> in French, but by a follower, in some sense, and/or compatriot of James Joyce. It is pretty funny. Performed visually by a troupe of genius, it might be supremely funny. It is something of a Ted Kavanagh script in style,[10] with suggestions of a René Clair production, as well as the more intellectual passages of Lewis Carroll. On top of all this there is, presumably, a philosophic or even religious allegory, which is sure to make some people mention Kafka. The title might even be translated *Waiting for Nobody* . . .
>
> I think it would be culpably unenterprising not to undertake the project. It might fail in effect, but it could scarcely fail in interest, because it is entirely suited to an English audience in nearly every respect . . . It is very much for consideration whether production should be left to stand on flat comic dialogue, or treated in the full-dress surrealistic convention of *ITMA*. Probably the latter . . . The more I think, the more I feel that it is a major task which ought to be attempted . . . I should like to undertake it . . . Is one to think of Jimmy Edwards and Dick Bentley, or Tommy Handley and Deryck Guyler, or two actors with comedian talent, but intellectual background? . . .[11]

It would, of course, have to be broadcast on the Third. John Morris said he was 'quite interested', but Val Gielgud smelt something 'basically "phoney"', and advised Morris that 'we should do well to drop the project'. Meanwhile Beckett sent his own English version, which he insisted must be used, and when he read it, Donald McWhinnie's reaction was the same as Gielgud's: 'we . . . feel that there is something basically phoney about the piece. We have accordingly dropped it.' E. J. King Bull explained to

---

[9] During this period, the Third Programme also discovered Rhys Adrian. The first of many plays by him on the network was *The Man on the Gate* (19 November 1956). John Tydeman calls him 'a miniaturist – in many respects I think he's better than Pinter, but he's never written a "big" play'.

[10] Kavanagh was the scriptwriter of *ITMA*.

[11] Edwards and Bentley starred in *Take It From Here*; Handley and Guyler had featured in *ITMA*. (Guyler was General Gland in the Hilda Tablet plays.)

Leslie Stokes that 'Beckett's own English version' was 'far less funny, and less racy' than the French text; it appeared that 'Beckett has had Irish inflections and idiom in his mind', as opposed to the BBC's music-hall reading of the play. He added that Beckett's 'agent and publisher, whom I saw in Paris, described him as *"un sauvage"*, with whom collaboration would be out of the question'.

A year and a half later, in August 1955, *Waiting for Godot* was staged at the Arts Theatre Club in London, directed by Peter Hall. The popular press dismissed it as rubbish, but Harold Hobson and Kenneth Tynan insisted that it must be seen. Hobson wrote: 'At the worst, you will discover a curiosity ... at the best something that will securely lodge in a corner of your mind for as long as you live.' The production transferred to the Criterion Theatre, where Raymond Raikes of Drama Department went to see it on the instructions of Val Gielgud. He reported as follows:

Let me say at once that I am quite sure that if the present company were asked to perform this play for the microphone, with only such radio production as would be necessary to transfer the play from the theatre to broadcasting, I believe that it would be as vital in radio as it is on the stage. Of the five actors involved, Peter Woodthorpe, Hugh Burden, Timothy Bateson, Peter Bull and Michael Walker, all but the last are experienced in our medium and would be capable of making the necessary changes in technique; and Michael Walker is a boy who gives the most sincere performance of any child actor I remember seeing for many a long day. This small company has been brilliantly directed by Peter Hall, and his direction extends to a studied control of the dialogue, with its extraordinary contrasts of rhythms and its compelling climaxes ...

May I suggest that we record and broadcast this production as soon as possible lest it be said that the BBC has once again 'missed the boat'. It seems to me a minor tragedy that on the strength of the report that this play obtained when it was received from Paris in April 1953 (a report I have only now just read after seeing the play itself) it was not then given on the Third Programme.

This, however, proved difficult to arrange. Donald Albery, impresario for the Criterion production, wanted to delay a broadcast until the play had been fully exploited for the stage. Nothing had happened by the following June, when John Morris noticed the *Sunday Times* reporting that Beckett had completed a one-act play, *La fin du jeu*, which would be seen at a festival in Marseilles. Morris asked Val Gielgud to make 'immediate enquiries', so that 'if it turns out to be suitable, we may get an option on it before the rats get at it'. Cecilia Reeves left her Paris office and went in search of Beckett. She wrote to Gielgud that he was 'an elusive character' who spent much of his time away from his Paris base. Nevertheless she made contact with him. On 4 July 1956 Beckett wrote to her:

As I explained to Mademoiselle Poulain I should like very much to do a radio play for the Third Programme, but I am very doubtful of my ability to work in this medium. However since our conversation I have, to my surprise, had an idea which may or may not lead to something.

It now seems unlikely that my new play, the title of which I have not yet found, will be performed at Marseille. I do not wish to have it translated for some time. It is a very visual affair and I am afraid quite unsuitable for broadcasting.

I hope I shall have the pleasure of meeting you when you are back in Paris. I shall ring you at your office towards the end of this month.

John Morris moved quickly, and in a few days he had made an appointment to meet Beckett at the BBC Paris office on 18 July. Later that day he wrote to Gielgud:

As arranged, I saw Samuel Beckett in Paris this morning. He is extremely keen to write an original work for the Third Programme and has indeed already done the first few pages of his script. I got the impression that he has a very sound idea of the problems of writing for radio and that we can expect something pretty good. He says his output is unpredictable; sometimes he works slowly, at others very fast; but he does not wish to be tied down to any definite date but says he will keep in touch and let me have the script as soon as it is finished.

The play which was to have been done at the Marseille Festival has now been cancelled owing to some sort of muddle with the organisers. It will now be done, he hopes, in Paris in the autumn. He himself, contrary to previous reports, does not necessarily think it will be too visual for sound radio. He will not however permit the play to be done in English until it is done in Paris in the original French version, but he has promised the Third Programme the first chance to do an English translation immediately the French stage production is fixed up.

Beckett completed the script in just over two months, sending it to Morris on 27 September 1956. 'It calls for a rather special quality of bruitage [sound effects], perhaps not quite clear from the text,' he told Morris. 'I can let you have a note on this if you are interested in the script for the Third Programme.' Morris replied that he was 'delighted' with the script, and had requested the Copyright Department to get in touch with Beckett about fees. He asked for the promised note on sound effects. Beckett replied on 18 October: 'I find it difficult to put down my thoughts about the bruitage. And I am not sure that what I want to say is worth saying. I feel it might be no more than an amateur's statement of what is common radio practice. For the moment I think I had better hold my peace. By far the best would be for us to meet, or for me to meet the bruiteur, before production, and talk it over. I hope this will be possible.'

Despite his earlier doubts about Beckett, Donald McWhinnie agreed to produce *All That Fall*, as the new script was titled. During a visit to Paris in late October he discussed it with Beckett, who reported to Morris on 16

November: 'His ideas about the sound agreed with mine and I am sure he will do a very good job. I hope indeed I shall be able to do something else for the Third Programme ... ' Beckett considered coming to London for rehearsals and recording, but on 18 December he told McWhinnie: 'I have finally decided that I should be very definitely less a help than a hindrance. I am very slow and go wildly and repeatedly wrong before arriving at something that resembles what I want. I'd only bother and upset you all. And I'm not worrying, having talked with you here and felt your feeling for the thing, its ruinedness and stifledness and impudicity.' He was, however, concerned at McWhinnie's decision that the noises of farmyard animals which the play required should be made by the actors:

> I may be quite wrong, but it seems to me a rather gratuitous complication. But then I don't know what is in your mind. Perhaps your idea is to give them the unreal quality of the other sounds. But this, we agreed, should develop from a realistic nucleus. I think the absurd apropos with which they occur, and their briefness, are enough to denaturalize them. And if not could they not be distorted by some technical means? But perhaps you are thinking of something quite different. If they are badly imitated the result will be atrocious. And if well, what do we gain? Do you lack recordings of the animals involved? Do not let the above weigh with you unduly. I am simply perplexed and should be grateful if you would let me know a little more fully what is in your mind.

In fact the exaggerated pantomime style of the animal sounds imitated by the cast makes a brilliant opening to *All That Fall*, broadcast on 13 January 1957. Similarly the very ordinary noises heard by Mrs Rooney (Mary O'Farrell, in a very different role from Hilda Tablet) on her laborious way to the railway station to meet her blind husband (J. G. Devlin) are initially heard in nightmarish distorted form, so that we only gradually recognise them as a donkey clip-clopping, a bicycle bell, a car approaching, and so on. McWhinnie had used the BBC's new experimental 'Radiophonic' equipment to give Beckett's play a strange aural landscape. Having developed this technique for *All That Fall*, he often employed it in other productions, including Giles Cooper's *The Disagreeable Oyster*.

The BBC had arranged an advance playback of *All That Fall* to the radio critics, who wrote about it at length. 'The production by Donald McWhinnie was a miracle of exquisite timing,' wrote 'K.Y.' in the *Daily Telegraph*; 'the acting by Mary O'Farrell and J. G. Devlin was beyond praise.' Philip Purser in the *Spectator* called it 'an extremely cunning piece of writing for radio, with provision for such evocative noises as the whirr of self-starter, the squawk of slain chicken and the far off strains of Schubert's *Death and the Maiden* played on an ancient gramophone.' Philip Hope-Wallace said much the same in *Time & Tide*:

> Donald McWhinnie's production of *All That Fall* was ... a miraculous web of sound effects and I could listen to Mary O'Farrell for ever in any part

whatever, though best of all as Nurse Rifferty-Rafferty in Ted Kavanagh's *ITMA*. Here she was a wheezing old woman puffing to the station to meet a train which arrived late because it had run over a child. The incident, like a dull bad dream recounted to you by some forcible old bore in a Dublin pub, had a tiresome way of penetrating one's aural imagination all next day. This is a feather in the cap for sound drama, a thing *sui generis* not at all eclipsed by television, though now wholly ignored by the Press.

Beckett himself listened to the broadcast, or tried to, in the BBC's Paris office. 'Bien travaillé,' he wrote to McWhinnie next day.

Though the reception on Sunday was very poor I heard well enough to realize what a good job. I did not agree with it all, who ever does, and perhaps I should have if I had lost less of the detail. Things I liked particularly: the double walk sound in the second half,[12] Dan's YES and their wild laugh (marvellous). O'Farrell and Devlin I thought excellent most of the time, the latter a little perfunctory in parts (his long speeches), but this perhaps due to distortion. Miss Fitt [played by Sheila Ward] very good indeed. I didn't think the animals were right. I shall send you more considered appreciation if I succeed in hearing it better on Saturday [the first repeat]. In the meantime to yourself and the players and all others concerned my very warm thanks and congratulations.

A month later John Morris wrote to Beckett thanking him for a copy of his new play, now called *Fin de partie*, and asked 'if you yourself would prepare an English version of it for radio'. Beckett replied: 'I am afraid *Fin de partie* would be as unsuitable for radio as *All That Fall* for the stage. I am not even sure that I can translate it as it stands.' But he said he would discuss it with McWhinnie, who was about to come to Paris. When they met, he told McWhinnie that the Paris stage production of *Fin de partie* had been postponed for lack of a theatre. 'He feels that it is impossible to render it into English,' McWhinnie told Morris, 'cannot do it himself and has not yet found anyone in whom he has confidence.' McWhinnie suggested that the BBC might be able to help, and when he got back to London, he gave the French text to Barbara Bray, the Script Editor in Drama Department, who translated a few specimen pages. McWhinnie sent these to Beckett: 'They are, of course, only a first draft, but if you felt they were at all promising I think we could evolve something of which you might approve.' He added: 'May I add, incidentally, what a magnificent piece of work I think *Fin de partie* is? A shattering experience even on the page; in the theatre I should think it would pulverize them.'

A Paris production of *Fin de partie* now took place, and the cast also performed it at the Royal Court Theatre in London. Morris engaged them to repeat it, in French, on the Third, and it was transmitted on 2 May

---

[12] Beckett means the sound of Mr and Mrs Rooney walking together down the road, done surrealistically by McWhinnie.

1957, preceded by a talk on *Samuel Beckett: poet and pessimist* by A. J. Leventhal. When writing to Beckett to inform him of the date and time of these broadcasts and their repeats, McWhinnie added: 'Incidentally, John Morris was asking whether there was any possibility of getting from you both a new text with music to open the new style Third Programme for October.' During the months in which the Third had been advancing its relationship with Beckett, it had been overtaken by a crisis. 'New style' was a euphemism for a savage reduction in broadcasting hours.

CHAPTER NINE

Little short of vandalism

During 1955 Sir Max Beerbohm, aged eighty-three, was offered $3,000 to be filmed giving a talk for American television at his home in Rapallo. He refused, describing himself as 'quite incorrigibly opposed' to being televised. A representative of the TV company assured him that everything would be very simple: he need only sit in his chair and tell his audience how happy he was to be speaking to them. 'Do you wish me to start with a lie?' asked Beerbohm politely.

In Britain, the Independent Television Authority was established during 1954 to issue licences to commercial television companies, which were to start broadcasting in the autumn of 1955. The BBC watched this development with paralysing anxiety. Meanwhile the BBC Audience Research Department, having failed to record any improvement in Third Programme listening figures, turned its attention to gathering opinions from those few people who did make up its audience. In late 1954 it recruited a Listening Panel of people who tuned in regularly. They would be asked to provide detailed comments on individual programmes – flattering, it was hoped. However, the 1,500 panel members (selected from more than 7,000 who had applied after seeing press advertisements) were told sternly not to exaggerate their positive feelings when completing their questionnaires, and not to listen more often than they would normally do – 'No duty-listening, please,' said the *Third Programme Panel Members' Guide.*

In fact when comments started to come in, they were by no means universally complimentary. 'The announcers are all cold, grey and impersonal,' wrote a research student, answering a request for comments on presentation. 'Are we allowed no gaiety, nothing but the most toneless standard English?' 'It's so smug and full of CULTURE,' complained a civil servant. A retired grammar school teacher observed: 'I wish they did not all speak in the manner of a smug high-class undertaker curbing his spirits in the presence of Death.' This report of the panel's comments, in May 1956, suggested that the Third's audience was now predominantly middle class; those answering the questionnaire included school and university teachers (the largest group), a doctor, a civil engineer, managers and housewives. A woman correspondent to the *Daily Worker* a year earlier had objected to the suggestion, by one of the paper's columnists, that the Third was designed exclusively for the upper classes: 'As a member of the working class and a listener to the "Third", I do not altogether appreciate the implication that this is an impossible combination.' But a speaker at a Communist-organised meeting on 'Culture and the British People' in St Pancras Town Hall in February 1955 described the Third as 'undemocratic and undesirable' because it presented culture as a 'minority' occupation for 'a closed circle of superior sensibilities'. He admitted that he enjoyed many Third Programme items, but *The Goon Show* seemed to him the true cultural expression of 'progressive people'.

On 3 August 1955 Leslie Stokes wrote to John Morris that though the Third had given up celebrating its birthday since the fifth anniversary, 'I suggest we should do something for our tenth'. It was due to fall at the end of September 1956, by which time 'competitive television', Stokes's term for the new commercial stations, would probably have caused 'a considerable reduction in press publicity for sound broadcasting', so that 'an event like our tenth anniversary' would be all the more valuable in attracting attention back to radio. Douglas Cleverdon was among the first to offer programmes for the anniversary: 'In December [1955] I produced a radiophonic poem by David Gascoyne, *Night Thoughts*, with music (some of it concrete[1]) by Humphrey Searle.' It had portrayed London by night. Cleverdon proposed a new collaboration between Gascoyne and Searle for the celebrations. He also mentioned that the next Hilda Tablet play, *A Hedge, Backwards*, to be broadcast on 29 February 1956, would contain 'some examples of Hilda Tablet's *musique concrète renforcée*, based on comb and paper, Marjorie Westbury's zip fastener, etc.'

In the passage in question, Hilda is describing her incidental music for *Antony and Cleopatra*:

HILDA: *Musique concrète.* Concrete music. You know about it?
REEVE: No.
HILDA: You tape it ... Needless to say, I have my own little line on the thing ... My own brand is called *musique concrète renforcée*; reinforced concrete music ... The opening section is largely based on Elsa's zip ... Now, Bertie, you see this zip-fastener. Now, note the sound it makes when I pull it sharply down. Like this. (*Zip.*)
ELSA (*winces loudly*): Oooh!
HILDA (*mildly*): Elsa. Don't be silly. Now the sound it makes when pulled *up* is quite different ...

Reed and his latest script soon proved troublesome. On 28 February 1956, the day before transmission, Leslie Stokes wrote to John Morris:

---

[1] *Musique concrète* is made up of recorded natural sounds and noises, often manipulated electronically.

I understand you have not read the script of Henry Reed's *A Hedge,
Backwards*, which is to be recorded this afternoon at 2.45, and which is to
be broadcast in the Third Programme this week on Wednesday and Friday.
It is, of course, the duty of the Supply Department to censor programmes,
but you may remember that there was some disagreement over Henry
Reed's script of *A Very Great Man Indeed*.

The new programme is extremely amusing, but it is mainly concerned
with the production of a play by Richard Shewin with a homosexual
theme. A brief scene from the play between two men is given in speeches
719–725. It is continued with a woman substituted for one of the men,
which emphasises the nature of the scene, in speeches 731–735.[2]

Apart from this there are a number of improprieties. Taken separately
only one or two may appear really objectionable, but the number of them
will, I think, give the whole programme a flavour which many listeners
would find unpleasant – among them, perhaps, the Governors, to whom
you recommended it. The following is not a complete list:–

Speech 93. Reference to pubic hair.

Speech 101. 'piss'.

Speech 159. 'tit'. (description of a bell-push).[3] ...

There were several more such items in the list, which concluded: 'Speech
626. "Antony (in Shakespeare's play) is a big butch queer."'

To make matters worse, as Laurence Gilliam pointed out next day to
Michael Standing, the Controller of Entertainment, Reed had only just
delivered the script, so there had been no chance of considering these
lines in advance. Gilliam complained that this was 'merely the latest in a
long run of such incidents' involving Reed, and suggested that

the only possible hope of a cure is the radical one of telling Henry Reed
that his scripts will not be scheduled until they are delivered. He suffers
from the writer's chronic malady of deadlineitis to an extremely acute
degree. He is naturally lazy, like most writers,[4] finds working for the BBC
the easiest way of making an income and takes a peculiarly malicious
pleasure in writing as close to the date line and to the decency line as he
can. These characteristics are, of course, symptomatic of his peculiar
psychological make-up.

On the other hand there is no doubt that over the past ten years Reed

[2] Herbert Reeve observes that the play, found among Shewin's papers but never yet performed,
'did unquestionably deal with a Certain Subject'. A production is nevertheless mounted, by
the expedient of changing one of the male lovers into a woman. Henry Reed must have
known that Leslie Stokes, himself homosexual, was co-author of a play about Oscar Wilde.

[3] General Arthur Dowd Wilbraham Dowd Corke Gland, just 'back from the East' (played by
Deryck Guyler), has not heard the doorbell when Reeve arrives, and asks: 'Did yer press the
tit, or anything?'

[4] It should be borne in mind that Gilliam employed Louis MacNeice and other members of
Features Department who considered themselves to be primarily writers, and who undoubtedly sometimes used this excuse to limit the amount of work they did for the BBC.

has been the outstanding individual contributor to Third Programme, particularly in the sphere of original comic writing. I feel that Third Programme would be very reluctant to endorse a tough line with Reed, as they will be running the danger, if not of killing, at least of offending a particularly touchy goose.

I would be grateful for your guidance in this matter ...

Michael Standing, Controller of Entertainment, replied: 'I share your view that we should not henceforward schedule these programmes until a script has been delivered and accepted ... If Reed is chronically infected with deadline-itis let us set the deadline further back – at any rate to a point that is short of real disaster.' Gilliam passed the whole matter back to Cleverdon, asking him to recommend 'the best way of carrying out this directive, without losing Reed's interest & services'. Cleverdon – who had never complained about Reed's behaviour – simply let it rest. A year later he wrote to Reed:

> My dear Henry,
> This is to confirm that Third Programme have agreed to make a payment of £200 to you for a trip to Greece, so that you may collect material for a programme on cultural tours by Hilda Tablet and General Gland. This will be an outright payment, and there will be no need for you to account for subsistence or other expenses; so we leave it to you to make your own arrangements ...
> Yours ever,
> Douglas.

Some years later, David Spenser, who had graduated from boy actor to radio drama producer, was directing one of Reed's scripts, a translation:

> The script was meant to be ninety minutes, and I knew it would run for three hours. For two months I was ringing Henry, and visiting him, and he kept saying, 'Yes, yes, I'm going to do the cuts.' And still no cuts. And he wouldn't allow me to do them for him. We had about five days to rehearse and record it – it was a complicated stereo production – and the script was *still* running at three hours. On about the third day of rehearsals he came in with the cuts. We all sat down with those creakingly heavy scripts, and Henry sat down too, puffing away at a cigar. And he said, 'Page 176.' And we all turned to page 176. 'Speech 3,' said Henry, 'half way down. There's a comma missing.' And I said: 'Henry, that's not a cut. It's an *addition*.'

*

Among those invited to appear in Cleverdon's feature on ten years of the Third Programme was Bertrand Russell. 'I am persuaded that the Third does an admirable work,' he replied, 'but in fact I never listen either to it or to any other broadcast and therefore I have not enough knowledge to do what is required.' Also invited to take part in the celebrations was Marilyn Monroe. She was in England to film *The Prince and the Showgirl*, and the Third had invited her to play the title role in *Lysistrata* – the leader of the Spartan women who force their men to cease war by refusing to sleep with them. 'I am familiar with the *Lysistrata*,' Monroe told *The Times*. 'I think it has a wonderful title role, and I would certainly like to play it some day.' However, the filming made this impossible, and Dudley Fitts's new translation of another Aristophanes play, *The Frogs*, was scheduled instead, for 1 October 1956.

In advance of the tenth-anniversary celebrations, the BBC issued the press with copies of a forty-four-page account of the Third's first ten years, written by Joyce Rowe, Sound Publicity Officer. This proclaimed some very impressive statistics for music broadcasts. For example, the Third had now put on the air '*all* the songs of Hugo Wolf, the symphonies of Honegger, Bruckner, Mahler, Dvořák and Sibelius, the piano sonatas of Schubert and Beethoven, the string quartets of Haydn and Beethoven, the chamber music of Hindemith, Schumann, Brahms, Dvořák and Fauré. Bach's complete *Klavierübung*, Byrd's three Masses and the orchestral works of Schumann and Brahms.'

Such broadcasts could be heard in their full frequency range and without interference by possessors of FM receivers, now available commercially, who lived within a fifty-mile radius of the BBC's Wrotham transmitter in Kent. Since 1 May 1955 this had been carrying the Home, Light and Third, and by the end of 1956 nine other transmitters were due to begin doing so in England, South Wales and Northern Ireland. 'VHF' (Very High Frequency), as the new service was then known, was already being picked up by thousands of listeners.

John Morris edited a celebratory anthology of scripts from the last ten years, which was published by Nonesuch Press, and new works were commissioned from ten composers to be performed during the months following the anniversary. Kenneth Leighton's String Quartet was the first commission to be heard, on 1 October. The others were Boris Blacher's *Fantasy for Orchestra* (12 October), Phyllis Tate's cantata *The Lady of Shallot* (24 October), Peter Racine Fricker's Cello Sonata (14 October), Jacques Ibert's *Bacchanale* (2 November), Anthony Milner's *The Harrowing of Hell* (14 November), Alan Hoddinott's Septet (8 December), Vagn Holmboe's *Symphonic Metamorphosis: epitaph* (28 December), Andrzej Panufnik's *Rhapsody* (11 January 1957), and Goffredo Petrassi's *Invenzione concertata* (9 September 1957). Michael Tippett agreed to write his Second Symphony but would not accept a deadline.

The tenth birthday itself, 29 September, was marked by Otto Klemperer conducting Beethoven's *Missa solemnis* from the Royal Festival Hall, a recording of W. H. Auden's inaugural lecture as Professor of Poetry at Oxford (given a few weeks earlier), and a satirical programme written and performed by Peter Ustinov and Peter Jones, already well known as a comedy duo in the Home Service. Entitled *Third Gear: a homage to their betters*, it began:

> USTINOV: Well, Peter, promotion has come our way. No longer do we have to endure the clatter and bustle of the Home Service. The portals of Olympus have been opened to it; we have graduated into the Shadow Cabinet of life itself. We are to be heard on the Third.
>
> JONES: Yes. Pity they've reduced the fees.
>
> USTINOV: Well, it's much less effort. Here, the frontier between obscurity and nonsense finally disappears. All we've got to do is be above their heads and we're home. Or we would be if we could find the building ...

They manage to discover the entrance to the Third's offices and studios, and, passing a commissionaire who is wearing a hand-woven uniform and reading Proust, get into a lift.

> LIFT MAN: Going up. First floor: Talks, Features, *The Soviet View*, Twelve-Tone System, Reith Lectures, hospitality room, Nevill Coghill, Dr Pevsner, archaeology, anthropology, public relations and shower baths ... Second floor: London Baroque Ensemble, medieval poetry, Toynbee, Aramaic mosaics, minor Elizabethans, recreation room, critics' cavern, Philip Hope-Wallace, Balinese gongs, canned laughter, Edward Sackville-West, oyster bar ... Fourth floor and roof garden: Director-General's play-pen, astronomy, canteen, Sanskrit rolls, pre-Columbian relics, string quartets ...

Getting out of the lift, they find themselves watching a broadcast which consists of two actors looking at each other in total silence. This proves to be an *Imaginary Conversation* between William the Silent and the Sphinx. 'This programme was recorded,' drones the announcer, 'and will be repeated *frequently*.'

Next, they stumble into the Third Programme's version of a Light Programme favourite, *Old Time Dancing*, in which couples perform an ancient Far Eastern dance step and an Elizabethan *coranto* entitled 'Sir Ian Jacob's Fancy'. They get trapped in a children's programme, *Listen with Stepmother*, in which a nine-year-old boy is reviewing a new edition of *Crime and Punishment* 'for the very young', then escape in a taxi driven by an ardent Third Programme listener, who refuses to take them to Covent Garden to hear *Carmen*:

> TAXI DRIVER: You don't want to see that hackneyed old thing ... My kids get no supper till they've studied their Bartók on the upright. The wife don't get 'er 'ousekeeping till she's learnt 'er Dylan Thomas by 'eart ... We're gonna book you tickets at the Arts Educational Establishment in Islington. Michael Tippett's lecturing there tonight, and there's a little concrete music in the interval ...

On the day after the tenth anniversary, listeners heard another comic programme commissioned for the occasion, the first of six daily episodes of *The Memoirs of Mrs Cramp: being episodes in the family life of a professional man of letters*. This was a spoof of the Light Programme's *Mrs Dale's Diary*, in which (introduced by swirling harp arpeggios) a London doctor's wife confided her daily worries. The Third's Mrs Cramp, played by Patience Collier and scripted by Angus Wilson and Christopher Sykes, was introduced by a harpsichord, played hesitantly in the background, and poured out her anxieties just like her Light Programme original:

> It all began on the Monday when Henry was busy powdering his wig. He's making a comeback with a huge new novel – at least not a comeback really because of course discerning people have never stopped reading him, but still there has been a kind of lull for the last fifteen years. It's his first historical novel – eighteenth century – and Henry's never happy until he's felt right into his material. That's why he's taken up practising on the harpsichord. But the wigs were rather a failure ...

So was Mrs Cramp, and the programmes were not repeated.

Press coverage of the tenth anniversary was extensive. Yet, of the leading national papers, only *The Times* – edited by the Third's founder, Haley – and the *Manchester Guardian* refrained from criticism. Two of the many commentators who expressed reservations about what had been achieved since 1946 were insiders. In a Radio and Television Supplement to *The Times* a month before the anniversary, Christopher Sykes recalled Edward Sackville-West's prognostication that the Third might become 'the greatest educative and civilising force England has known since the secularisation of the theatre', and commented: 'It was hoped above all that it would give rise to a whole school of new writers. After 10 years this hope cannot be said to have been fulfilled ... To this there are some partial exceptions, notably Henry Reed ... [But] discovery [of writers] remains in the province of the publisher ... '

Sackville-West himself, writing the leading article for the *Listener* in the anniversary week, was even sharper. He began by praising one of the Third's principal features, 'the opportunity to hear forgotten music', but observed that this had not always been an enjoyable experience: 'For example, not many listeners, I imagine, can much have enjoyed Schumann's *Genoveva*; but now they can at least say to themselves, what few could have said before: "I know that *Genoveva* is a dull and stupid opera which I never wish to hear again."' The Third in its early days had been 'thrilling', and 'could not be expected to continue indefinitely on quite the same level'; also 'familiarity breeds contempt'. Tastes varied among listeners, 'and if we are bored to tears by Telemann's *Tafelmusik*, or the plays of Claudel, or the agricultural policy of Chile, we should have enough imagination to realise that others are not'. Whatever its shortcomings, 'the Third has become an institution, a necessary part of life to those who wish to make an intelligent use of their leisure'.

Sackville-West continued with even harsher criticism. He went on that the danger had become apparent of

a certain rigidity – a sameness in the mere aspect of the weekly programmes that implies a failure to *evolve* on the part of the Third as a whole ... As a symptom of what I mean, I should instance the tendency to fall back again and again on certain kinds of programme that have been successful in the past but to which the law of diminishing returns quickly applies. For example, several complete performances of a routine symphony by different orchestras and conductors, spread over a week and masquerading as 'Interpretations', serves no useful purpose, for differences of interpretation in such cases can be demonstrated only within the limits of a single programme. Similarly, it is hard to resist the conclusion that, where music is concerned, the planners succumb with too great alacrity to the lure of *musica antiqua*. I would not for a moment suggest that it was a mistake to explore the pre-classical periods, but for every one such programme that has held a high content of beautiful and interesting stuff, there have been at least two that resembled a monastic diet of pumpkin soup and lentils ...

Sackville-West concluded the article by asserting that, nevertheless, his prediction that the Third would usher in a golden age was 'in process of fulfilment'. Certainly 'enrichment has taken place'. Despite this kindlier ending, the article struck the editor of the *Listener* as so negative that he sent John Morris an advance copy before publication.

Harman Grisewood was asked to write a report for the Director-General (whose Chief Assistant he now was) on the press articles about the anniversary. He summed them up as 'superficially pleasant in their congratulation, and rather blunt but unpenetrating in their criticisms', not, therefore, 'illuminating for us – who have "heard it all before" and yet who do have perplexities about the Third and who would be glad of some light thrown on them'. Two questions (continued Grisewood) were crucial: first, 'the nature and size of the minority to be served', and second, how the Third was supposed to relate to the BBC's other networks. Each Controller of the Third had been aware of a dilemma: if he broadened the appeal of the programme, it would overlap 'wastefully' with the Home Service, yet if the Third was too different from its neighbours, 'it becomes too confined and loses its point as broadcasting'. The BBC itself, like the press commentators on the anniversary, had 'provided very little help in resolving this dilemma'.

John Morris made similar remarks in a speech to a UNESCO conference of 'cultural programme specialists' in Paris a few weeks later. The delegates, several of whom came from behind the Iron Curtain, had nothing but praise for the Third, yet Morris admitted to facing the dilemma that Grisewood had described. He said the Third was sometimes criticised for aiming too high intellectually, 'and indeed by lowering the standard it would doubtless be possible considerably to increase the number of listeners. If we adopted this course, however, the Third Programme would ... become a mere extension of the Home Service, and would therefore cease to have a *raison d'être*.' He told the conference that 'we are still experimenting. The final pattern has not yet emerged; probably it never will, since the very life of a programme such as the Third depends on a constant re-adjustment of the point of view'.

Even as Morris spoke, readjustment was going on, but not of the positive, beneficial sort that he implied.

*

On 28 September 1955, a week after ITV had come on the air, the Controller of the Light Programme, Rooney Pelletier, wrote in the course of some notes about the future of his network: 'Haley said: "The robots are on the march." His foresight was phenomenal. The robots are now marching.'

By the following summer, ITV had inflicted huge damage on the BBC's viewing and listening figures. Sixty per cent of the television audience had been captured by the opposition, and the decline in radio listening had been hugely accelerated by the choice of television channels. The BBC was thrown into a state of panic. P. H. Newby recalls a senior man at Broadcasting House, George Camacho, guessing that 'radio would last out his time in the BBC, but he didn't see it surviving much longer than that'.

Among those concerned with high-level BBC strategy was Richard D'Arcy Marriott, who at the age of forty-eight had just relinquished the post of Controller, Northern Ireland to become Chief Assistant to the Director of Sound Broadcasting, Lindsay Wellington. During July 1956 Marriott jotted down his thoughts about the BBC's predicament. 'However much we are concerned with sound broadcasting and however much we believe in its future,' he wrote, 'it would be unrealistic to shut our eyes to the fact that the BBC's reputation and possibly its very existence are going to depend on its success in TV. One of the objects of sound broadcasting, therefore, ought to be to serve TV.' This could be done in a number of ways: by exchanging ideas between radio and TV, by radio making its staff available to TV, and 'above all by making economies which can help to supply the needs of a TV service in competition'.

Economies (Marriott continued) could be achieved most easily by reducing radio programme hours. One possibility was to merge the existing networks at certain times of day. Another was 'a reduction in evening hours on one of our three programme services'. Indeed, the very idea of separate BBC radio networks in competition with each other now seemed 'out-dated'. What was needed, Marriott asserted, was 'complete integration' of the three networks so as to maximise the total audience – 'and I mean all three'.

There was nothing wrong with the three having 'certain general characteristics', which might be defined as 'Light, Medium and Serious'. But there was no question of allowing the Serious programme to go its own way irrespective of audience figures: 'It is all very well to record the triumphs of the 3rd Programme ... but we are concerned with broad-casting. The very high-brow representing only one fraction of one percent of the population are entitled to be catered for ... but not to ... the extent of one-third of our total output.' Marriott was well aware that his aim of attracting and appealing to a mass audience – as he put it, meeting 'the tastes and needs of all our listeners' – involved a dramatic break with the BBC's history and the principles on which it had been founded. He had no regrets about this:

> The programme policy that I advocate implies the rejection of an attitude that many of us have grown up with, of having a mission to educate, to up-lift, to lead people on to better things, to give them what we think they ought to want rather than what they do want. We ought to ask ourselves what a commercial sound broadcasting organisation would offer the public – it is not impossible that there may be one – and then make sure that we can do the same kind of thing only better, without any baseness or vulgarity or lowering of standards (standards can be main-tained at any level of appeal). We ought to remember that about half the population consists of very simple people, with not very much education, who look to radio for their entertainment and relaxation – and who shall say that they are wrong?

Marriott's startling views met with agreement by somebody, very likely Lindsay Wellington, with whom he discussed them. 'I believe (roughly),' wrote this person in an unsigned memo on 5 October 1956,

> there was general growing agreement in [the] 19th century that 'the people' should have 'the best' – working-class leaders joined with Liberal aristocrats in clamouring for this. What was missing was any working-class experience (on a mass scale) of 'the best'. Once this was experienced through the BBC it became clear (around 1950) that 'the people' didn't desire 'the best' at all. So, much of the Reithian/Haleian preconceptions are now proved to be false assumptions.

On the other hand this person was not in favour of scrapping the Third – it was 'an asset to the BBC and ... is likely to outlast much else that will be drowned in the rushing waters of TV'.

Marriott's views found general favour among his superiors, and on 18 October they were passed to the Director-General, Sir Ian Jacob, in a memo headed 'Future of Sound Broadcasting' and signed by Wellington. 'The whole output of Sound Broadcasting should cease to be so heavily weight-ed in favour of the highly educated and serious minded,' Jacob was told, 'and should be redirected to giving a much fairer representation to the great majority of people whose tastes are simpler and less intellectual.' To this end Wellington wished to establish a small working party to examine the implications of the policy change. Meanwhile he wanted to waste no time in increasing the appeal of radio at peak hours. The expense of this could be offset by merging Home and Light at off-peak periods, although an alternative was 'to reduce the Third Programme hours in the evening'. As to the character of the Third, as envisaged by Wellington and Marriott, it was defined curtly alongside the Home and Light: 'one wholly "lowbrow" programme, one "middlebrow" programme, and one serious (but not consistently "highbrow") programme'.

Wellington did not explain to Jacob how one could manage to be serious without being highbrow. Nowhere in this document, nor in the hundreds of pages that were written on the reorganisation of radio during the following months, was the nature and function of the Third discussed in any detail or wider context. There was no examination of what it had achieved since 1946, nor of the effect it might have had on listeners' lives and British culture in general, and no definition of its aims and whether it had met them.

The working party proposed by Wellington was set up less than three weeks later. Marriott was chairman, and the other members were Richmond Postgate (Assistant to the Controller of the Home Service), Michael Standing (Controller of Entertainment, Sound), and Frank Gillard (Controller, West Region). It read and listened to comments by those running the Third, and by other senior BBC staff. Among these was Christopher Holme, who had been a crucial member of the Third's team for the past eight years. Strikingly, he thought that the Third's hours could be reduced somewhat without its functions being seriously impaired. 'A starting time of 7.00 pm on most evenings would be adequate,' he told the working party, 'but freedom must be retained to open at 5.00 pm or earlier for important relays etc. (e.g. Glyndebourne).' Holme felt that the Third's difference from the Home was best defined as that 'between Malcolm Muggeridge and Isaiah Berlin'.

One of the few notes of caution in the rush to cut the Third's hours was sounded by Andrew Stewart, Controller of the Home Service. He had noticed that those listeners who had abandoned radio for television were chiefly those who had been addicted to the Light Programme. In comparison the Home's audience was dropping very little, and 'the Third Programme does not drop at all'. He urged the working party to 'keep the Third Programme in being as a working entity' rather than merge its administration with that of the other networks, as Marriott had proposed. Otherwise, he said, the BBC might have to go to the labour of creating it all over again, if it found that only 'serious' people had remained loyal to radio.

In contrast, the Third's own Controller, John Morris, seemed to have little interest in his network's survival. Interviewed by the working party, he told them that the trouble had been his lack of adequate control over the Supply departments. He could turn down their suggestions, but could not propose programmes himself. Features Department were doing a good job, but relations were bad with Drama. If he rejected any of their offers, they took it as 'a personal slight'. Music Department was staffed by 'paper musicians' out of touch with the real world of concertgoing. Ideally he would manage all the producers who contributed to the Third himself.

This would 'electrify proceedings'. It was 'personalities' who had made things 'go astray'. As to his target audience, he defined it as 'the readers of the *Sunday Times*, the *Observer* and the weeklies'.

In contrast with BBC staff, listeners had plenty to say in support of the Third. Leslie Stokes sent the working party a bundle of letters received during the past few months. 'They are fair examples of the kind of appreciatory letters which come in constantly,' he explained.

'I am in no way "high-brow",' wrote Mrs H. M. Wood-Smith from Dorset, 'but such plays as *Mother Courage*, *Lord of the Flies*, *Mathry Beacon*, *Siegfried*, etc. are a privilege to have heard ... ' A teacher from Horsham High School for Girls offered to 'support a fund to bolster the finances of the Third', and felt that closing it down would be 'one more blow to the cultural life of this country and, indirectly, of the world'. A hospital porter in south London said he would be 'considerably less content with my lot without the Third'; Joyce Winson, also from south London, asked for 'repetitions, as soon as possible, of all the Henry Reed satires'; and a listener within the range of the Wrotham transmitter reported: 'Since I obtained a VHF set a year ago I have kept a list of operas and choral works to which I have listened, and the total is 50.' The mood of these letters was summed up by Patricia Begley from Kent, who wrote: 'The Third Programme ... for me, makes life worth living.'

Only one member of the BBC staff told the working party that he felt as passionately about the Third. His memo is unsigned. 'I would be ashamed,' he wrote, 'if what was conceived in war as an act of faith were jettisoned by the Corporation as an act of despair.'

*

The working party wrote its report at speed, and submitted it to the Governors during January 1957. Over a hundred pages in length, it concluded that three radio networks were still needed, and that the Third 'ought to be maintained'; but 'it both can be and should be altered'. In this view 'we are supported by the almost unanimous view of our colleagues and by the present Controller of the Third Programme'. The Third's target audience should be 're-assessed and re-defined'. The fact that listening had shrunk to less than one per cent of the radio audience showed that there had been 'a deviation' from the original aim of the Third. Morris's suggestion that the potential audience should be equated with the readership of the serious Sunday newspapers and weekly magazines was accepted. 'We estimate that this audience might not be far short of two million adults and that the target ratio to be aimed at should be 5%.'

The report accepted that criticisms of the Third for being 'too much occupied with minorities within a minority', and the use of such epithets as 'precious', 'esoteric' and 'donnish', had 'some measure of justification'. Too many people had been 'put off by the general character of the Programme and ... made to feel that the Third Programme is too difficult and too high-brow and altogether outside their reach'. A 'considerable effort' was now required 'to regain the goodwill of this section of the audience and to attract them as regular listeners'. But nowhere was it suggested how this should be done. Nor was any mention made of a previous attempt to popularise the Third, Grisewood's light music series, which had turned out to be an embarrassment to the BBC. Grisewood himself was not consulted by the working party; nor were Barnes, Amyot or Haley, who had created the Third.

The report urged that the Third should be shortened drastically:

> The present length of 40 hours per week is not only extravagant of our money and resources, it is also extravagant in terms of the amount of attention that intelligent people, who tend to have wide interests outside broadcasting, are prepared to give to radio. The obligation to fill five hours every evening imposes unnecessary strain on planners and producers and results in the inclusion of the second-best. We propose an average of 2½ hours each evening, normally between 8 and 10.30 pm, with freedom to extend whenever necessary. The aim would be to give one major pro-gramme each evening, which with suitable publicity could be made to stand out as the prestige radio programme of the day.

Moreover all programmes on the truncated Third must be 'subjected to the test of whether or not they are good radio'. This would mean 'an end of those programmes whose real place is ... in the learned quarterlies'. This was not a limitation of Third Programme freedom, but 'a removal of a freedom which ought never to have been taken'.

The hours removed from the Third were not to be left as silence. The next section of the report was headed 'A "Third Network"'. To anyone who had assumed that a principal purpose of reducing the Third was to save money, the contents of this must have come as a surprise. The axed hours were to be used 'to accommodate a number of spoken word items, some from the general programme field and some in the sphere of Further Education', which would be displaced by 'the popularisation of the Light Programme and Home Service'. These items, to be heard on the Third's wavelengths in the early evening (but to be planned by the Home Service), could be given the label 'BBC Third Network'. It should include such existing programmes as *Science Survey*, *Talking of Books*, and *The Night Sky*. As to further education programmes, these would find 'greater elbow-room' on the Third's frequencies than they were getting at present on Home and Light.

To facilitate all this, and to eliminate pointless rivalry, there would no longer be separate Controllers of the networks. They would be replaced by 'two principal lieutenants' to the Director of Sound Broadcasting, to be called Controller of Programmes and Controller of Programme Services, the former supervising programme content and the latter managing staff and facilities. Though not mentioned by name, the post of Controller, Third Programme would disappear along with the rest, and the Third would be managed by the central hierarchy.

Despite the advance of television, the working party judged that there was 'no likelihood of Sound broadcasting disappearing completely'. But its future role, in the age of car and battery-powered radios, was envisaged as 'a much reduced one ... a companionable background [for] the driver, the housewife, the man at his hobby, the beach-party and so forth', though there would still be 'attentive' listening to 'high-grade music ... news and information in a wide sense, and possibly ... a small amount of imaginative radio writing'.

The BBC's Board of Management discussed the report on 25 February 1957, and generally endorsed it, though it was felt that reducing the Third by more than fifty per cent, to a mere two and a half hours each night, was too severe. Three hours of airtime was felt to be more appropriate. Members of the Board were enjoined to strict secrecy until a public statement could be made.

In fact there had already been a statement on 31 January, warning that some 'adjustment of the existing pattern of sound broadcasting' was on the way, and on 1 February *The Times* carried a rumour that the three sound networks might be merged into two. A few days later the *Radio Times* moved BBC TV programmes to the front of its billings section, and relegated radio to the back.

*

Among the first to get wind that the Third might lose its independence within the BBC was Peter Laslett, who had now resigned his radio job to become a full-time Cambridge don. On 11 February *The Times* carried a letter from him protesting that this would be disastrous:

> Gone would be the freedom from fixed periods of broadcasting. Gone would be the opportunity and the urge to experiment. Gone would be the sense of its own unique identity, a name which is rightly famous ... The courageous and the correct policy for the BBC is to merge the Home and the Light and leave us the Third as what it is – the most interesting and important broadcasting in the world.

Three weeks later *The Times* Personal Column carried an advertisement calling on those interested in preserving the Third to contact Peter H. Needs, a primary school teacher from southeast London. 'The response was so heartening,' reported the *Manchester Guardian* on 11 March, 'that he has now decided to organise a society and put the campaign on a formal basis ... He says: "I felt it was up to those who appreciate the Third to do something about it ... I am pleased to say that out of 700 people who have sent me their names so far, the great majority say they are ready to pay an increased licence fee if that will ensure the continuation of this service."' Three days later the same newspaper reported that Needs was now receiving letters of support at the rate of about 150 a day, and had called a public meeting at the Charing Cross Hotel on Sunday 24 March.

That day, about 250 people turned up, among them Peter Laslett, who agreed to be chairman of the Third Programme Defence Society, with Needs as secretary. Many of those present testified to the importance of the Third in their lives, most notably a woman who, according to the *Daily Mirror*, 'said in a foreign accent: "I come from Central Europe. When I had a choice of country to live in I chose Britain – because of the Third Programme."'

The only note of disagreement among those present came when Needs compared the Third to the 'completely banal' omnibus edition of *The Archers*, at which point one of the audience protested hotly: 'I listen to *The Archers*.' Two days later the *Birmingham Post* quoted one of the cast of *The Archers*, Norman Painting, who had often acted on the Third, saying that any curtailment of it would be 'only a little short of stupid'.

The matter now came up in the House of Commons, where on 16 March the Labour MP Kenneth Robinson collected 130 signatures from Members of all parties on an adjournment motion that 'This House would deeply regret the passing of the British Broadcasting Corporation Third Programme'. The *Manchester Guardian* noted that the list was 'heavily weighted in favour of Labour members, who outnumber the Tory signatories by about three to one'. The Labour weekly *Tribune* gave Peter Needs the space to state his case. 'Now the time has come,' he wrote, 'for us to make ourselves heard, and we shall have to be vociferous if we are to drown the all-pervading jingles and other Ad-Mass fodder. Let us fight to save for posterity Britain's greatest post-war contribution to living ... '

On 8 April, Sir Ian Jacob held a press conference to announce the new arrangements for programmes which would come into effect in October. The Third would be 'shortened to some three hours every night, starting at 8 pm', though its starting and closing times would be varied on occasions. A new service called Network Three would occupy the Third's wavelengths from 6 to 8 pm nightly. This would accommodate 'many of the spoken word programmes that will be displaced from the Home and Light under the BBC's plans', and would also carry minority-interest programmes. In contrast to the Third's cuts, two hours per day would be added to the Light Programme, which would start at 7 am and close at midnight. The Home and Light 'will join to form a single programme at some periods during the day'. The new Controller of Programmes – the job with responsibility for overseeing Home, Light and Third – would be Rooney Pelletier, at present Controller, Light Programme.

The Third Programme Defence Society immediately issued a statement describing the BBC's new policy as 'a retreat on all fronts', which would do 'irrevocable damage' to the Third. The Society would now launch a national campaign, 'aimed at securing a change of this policy before it comes into full effect in the autumn'.

The press, formerly so critical of the Third, now took the side of its defenders. *The Times* punned on Goethe's last words, 'More light', commenting: 'They must not be the BBC's.' The *Daily Telegraph* accused the

Corporation of trying to hide the damage to the Third beneath 'bureau-cratic double-talk'. On 18 April the adjournment debate in the Commons was opened by Kenneth Robinson pointing out that the BBC's Advisory Council, to which many MPs and other public figures belonged, had not been consulted. He described the new-look radio schedules as 'a policy which is wholly wrong in intention and mistaken in logic . . . The BBC has begun to think in numbers. The disease is spreading from television to sound radio . . . ' The next evening, three out of four panellists in the BBC's own *Any Questions* condemned the cuts in the Third. In *The Times* on 26 April a letter of protest appeared over the signatures of Lord Beveridge, Sir Arthur Bliss, Sir Adrian Boult, the Bishop of Chichester, T. S. Eliot, E. M. Forster, Christopher Fry, Sir John Gielgud, Victor Gollancz, John Masefield, Harold Nicolson, Bertrand Russell, V. Sackville-West and Ralph Vaughan Williams.

The BBC's response, on 3 May, was to publish a letter in *The Times* signed by the Chairman, Sir Alexander Cadogan, asserting that three hours each evening was enough to 'provide a first-class Third Programme', whereas approximately seventeen hours a day 'will be devoted to the majority audience' on the Light. Peter Laslett complained in the same columns on 9 May that Cadogan's letter offered no possibility of discussion or concession. He also reported that the 'important post' of Chief Assistant to the Controller of the Third Programme had been axed, which was yet another indication of the damage that was being done. Christopher Holme's post was indeed abolished later that month – he moved to Features Department as a producer, soon becoming Assistant Head of Features – but the BBC had quietly made one important concession to the protesters. The Third would retain its own Controller, with John Morris staying in the job, and Leslie Stokes as his Assistant.

Early in June, while the Third's wavelengths were, for the first time, carrying Test Match commentaries during hours of play (until 5.15 pm, when the Light took over), Richard Marriott, original architect of the cuts, took time to write down his thoughts on the criticisms. It was, he stated, 'an inescapable fact' that the Third would lose the 6 pm to 8 pm airtime, but this

> need not in itself mean that any of the kinds of programme now contained in the Third Programme will no longer be broadcast. It need only mean that they would appear rather less frequently, and, in view of the large scale use of repeats on the Third Programme, even this might be more apparent than real . . . We do positively want to shorten the programme in the belief that a smaller quantity of broadcasting will enable us to maintain the high quality . . . We refuse absolutely to accept the elevation of the Third Programme into a symbol as if it alone represented what we were doing in the cultural field. It is on our total output that we intend to be judged . . .

Certainly the plans for the 1957 autumn and winter programmes which

John Morris circulated internally at the end of June gave no appearance of serious reduction in either quantity or quality. They included plenty of operas, a BBC Symphony Orchestra concert every Saturday, and several sets of linked music, including pieces inspired by *Don Quixote*, a series on masterpieces of eighteenth-century Italian string music, French song from Berlioz to the present day, and *lieder* recitals by Fischer-Dieskau. Speech programmes included six talks by Karl Popper on 'the dangers of an over-specialised world', a production of Kafka's *Metamorphosis*, and a new Samuel Beckett piece, *Molloy*, 'suggested by the author himself'. There would be scripts from Kingsley Amis and John Mortimer, and an adaptation of William Golding's new novel *Pincher Martin*. On paper it looked like the best season the Third had arranged for a long while, though Morris added a warning that 'some of the items might be held over', or indeed might 'never materialise'. But he asserted that the list was 'sufficiently representative of the sort of thing which will be found in the Third Programme in its shortened form'.

On 12 June, *The Times* carried another letter of protest against the cuts, signed by a number of French intellectuals, including Albert Camus and Jean Cocteau, who had themselves all broadcast on the Third. Meanwhile on 6 June, Peter Laslett had been given an interview with Sir Ian Jacob and Sir Alexander Cadogan at Broadcasting House. 'There were only three of us present,' he has recalled.

> 'Damn it, Laslett,' said Sir Ian, stubbing out his cigarette in Cadogan's ashtray, 'who are you to appoint yourselves the representatives of the English highbrow? You can only be a tiny minority, however much you talk of the poets and playwrights, professors and composers who support you. Why won't you trust us? We are the people who have been entrusted with British broadcasting policy.' And the grave Sir Alexander nodded his head. 'If you wanted to go round beating up all these people to support high level broadcasting, why didn't you do it in 1954 when the commercial television service was pushed through Parliament?'

By 'these people', Jacob meant T. S. Eliot, Sir Laurence Olivier, Michael Tippett and Ralph Vaughan Williams, who had agreed to support Needs's and Laslett's pressure group, which had now been renamed the Sound Broadcasting Defence Society. On 18 July, Laslett was back at the BBC, bringing them all to meet Cadogan, Jacob, and two Governors, Sir Philip Morris and Lord Rochdale. Olivier had agreed to present the Society's case, and he told the Governors, Chairman and Director-General:

> The Third Programme is in relation to broadcasting what the theatre is to other branches of the entertainment world. I have just been abroad all over Europe. Everywhere they are building theatres. I return to England and find they are pulling them down.[5] I have always had the greatest

---

[5] There was a spate of West End theatre closures and demolitions around this time.

admiration for the work of the BBC ... By far its most valuable jewel in its crown is the Third Programme, and that is going to be cut up, we are told.

Eliot, too, made a speech, demanding (according to *The Times*) that 'a statement be issued to the public to dispel the fear that the BBC was preparing a catastrophic abdication of its responsibilities, lowering the standards of culture at home and lowering the prestige of Britain abroad'.

Another source (a 1963 *New Yorker* 'profile' of the Third) records Eliot as giving a far more impassioned speech than this suggests:

> I ... allowed myself to be persuaded by the official assurance that the shorter time would mean a better Third Programme. But two hours a day is seven hundred and thirty hours a year, and this *could* mean that two thousand one hundred and ninety less talks were broadcast each year. Even when the proportions are balanced out between drama, music and the spoken word, it is clear that that innocuous little two hours in fact represents a catastrophic blow to the entire Third Programme, and it is likely that the spoken word will be among the heavier sufferers ...
>
> This seems to me a plan to pander to the more moronic elements in our society, and to drive the minority further into its corner at a time when, as never before, there is an opportunity to increase the numbers of the minority. The day of bread and circuses is over; the BBC should provide more and more leaven.

Laslett vividly recalls the effect of Eliot's words: 'Eliot made a speech to Jacob, and I'm glad nobody will ever make a speech like that to me. Poor old Jacob withered under this treatment. They were being made to feel that they were nobodies in their own country by a man who, of course, was originally an American.' Faber and Faber, of which Eliot was a director, had by now published for the Sound Broadcasting Society a fifty-page pamphlet called *Sound Broadcasting*, which set out the objections to the cuts.

Replying for the BBC, Cadogan told the deputation that the Corporation had been 'impressed' by the support for the Third, but the BBC could not 'conduct its policy in the columns of the press'. He assured the delegation that what they had said would be considered very carefully. The visitors then left the BBC and went to Vaughan Williams's house overlooking Regent's Park, where they gave a press conference and posed for cameras. Eliot had slipped away, but a picture in *The Times* next day shows Tippett at one end of the table and Vaughan Williams at the other, holding an ear trumpet. The eighty-five-year-old composer, who died the next year, asked reporters: 'Shall we beat our violins into cricket bats and our bows into golf clubs? No – we are musical and we shall go on being musical, perhaps because of and perhaps despite the BBC.'

The day before the delegation had met the Governors, the BBC Advisory Council had at last met to consider the proposed changes. Its members included Alan Bullock, who said that Oxford was puzzled about the thinking behind the cuts, and Isaiah Berlin, who, according to the minutes, 'said that in his view any attempt by the BBC to compete with commercial broadcasting would fail; ought it not therefore to do something which commerce would not do so that it would not be in competition?' A similar point was made by Gerard Hoffnung, cartoonist, broadcaster and tuba player, who wrote to Sir Alexander Cadogan: 'It is ... particularly difficult to understand why sound radio should be encouraged to lower its status in order to compete with Television, rather than doing exactly the opposite in order to delight the interested and enlightened listeners ... The decision to chop down the Third ... seems to me ... little short of Vandalism.'

On 2 August the *Daily Telegraph* announced: 'BBC YIELDS ON THE "THIRD". THREE HOURS MORE ON SUNDAYS.' Cadogan had written to the Sound Broadcasting Society announcing that the Third would broadcast for six hours each Sunday. But there would be no other concessions, and he had refused to recognise the Society's right to negotiate with the Corporation in any official capacity. The Society responded that it would redouble its national campaign. It had asked the BBC to broadcast a debate on the changes on Network Three, the new miscellany which would occupy the Third's wavelengths from 6 to 8 pm, when it came on the air at the end of September. Cadogan refused this too: 'No useful purpose would be served by broadcasting such a discursive discussion.'

The Third's autumn plans were published at the end of August, when John Morris spoke off the cuff to the press. He agreed that music would be 'the chief victim' of the cuts, 'because we do more of that than anything else', but it would still occupy about fifty per cent of the Third's airtime. Pressed to say exactly how much music would be lost, he answered 'roughly an hour a day'. When asked if he had expected the furious public reaction to the cuts, he laughed and said: 'The BBC is always interested in the views of listeners.' Later the same day the Sound Broadcasting Society described Morris's autumn plans as 'making the best of a bad job, but they cannot alter the fact that the Third Programme cannot give a full coverage in three hours a night'.

A month later, on Sunday 29 September 1957, the Sound Broadcasting Society marked the eleventh birthday of the Third with a funeral. 'As it lived, so did it die,' reported *The Times* next day. 'The Third Programme in its old form having ceased to exist, the Sound Broadcasting Society, mixing nostalgia with protest, came to the stage of the Royal Court Theatre last night to bury and to praise.' T. S. Eliot, who 'apologised for not being able to attend in person', had contributed a recorded speech in which he said he was frightened by the BBC's assumption that 'a minority is less important than the majority'. The Allegri Quartet played Elizabeth Maconchy's First String Quartet, C. Day-Lewis and Jill Balcon read a selection of twentieth-century poetry, the Allegri returned to the stage to play Mozart, and Sir John Gielgud recited Shakespeare, Dryden, and a passage from *The Duchess of Malfi*. 'It is a pity,' observed *The Times*, 'that such an original entertainment was produced only by the sense of outrage; must a Third Programme die again before we may mix our media so boldly and so successfully?'

During the evening Peter Laslett made a speech. 'Let's look at what has happened,' he told the audience. 'The BBC founded eleven years ago a service which is literally the envy of the world ... Then somebody at Broadcasting House got worried about money, or television, or Radio Luxembourg, and suddenly the BBC started taking up this extraordinary attitude about "culture" and "cultural minorities". Why did they do this thing? Was it because their nerve failed, or did they never really believe in it?'

The next evening, Monday 1 October 1957, the new schedules came into effect, and the Third's nightly broadcasting hours were reduced by forty per cent.

PART TWO

1957–1970

RUDELY TRUNCATED

CHAPTER ONE

Dodecaphoneys

Network Three, the cuckoo in the Third Programme's nest, was introduced to listeners by Lindsay Wellington, Director of Sound Broadcasting, in the *Radio Times* for 29 September 1957 (the eleventh birthday of the Third), which covered the first week of the new schedules. It would, he explained, 'be used for programmes which we believe will be of interest to many other minorities which have a place in the total community'. This was exactly the point which Peter Laslett had been making throughout the campaign to save the Third: that the BBC was regarding culture as merely one of a whole range of minority interests – of no more importance than a hobby.

An unsigned article in the same issue of the *Radio Times* defined Network Three's audience as

> minorities who are enthusiastically devoted to some form of self-expression ... the jazz-fancier or the pigeon-fancier, the man or woman who wants to learn, say, Spanish from scratch, the fisherman or cyclist or collector of LP records ... the bridge player or the naturalist, the more sophisticated film-goer, the ardent motorist or the enthusiast for amateur dramatics.

All these 'will be able to find a programme, broadcast either weekly or monthly, with their special interests in mind'. Other programmes would tackle 'the wide interests and many problems of parents and the younger generation'.

Network Three came on the air at 6.15 pm on Monday 30 September 1957 with a programme of this latter sort, *The Younger Generation*, a magazine of the *Woman's Hour* type which had been transferred from the Light Programme. This was followed at 6.45 by *For Collectors*, in which an art-dealer was questioned about buying 'modest-priced pictures'. At 7 came half an hour entitled *Parents and Children*, a weekly programme in which parents would 'discuss and hear discussed the difficulties and pleasures of bringing up a family'. This edition included an item on when and how children should be told about sex. The first evening of Network

Three concluded with fifteen minutes of *Starting Spanish*, before the wavelengths were handed over to the Third.

The next evening, Tuesday 1 October, there was no Network Three; the Third came on the air early to relay *Siegfried* from Covent Garden. *Götterdämmerung* was heard at the same time on Friday. But this was exceptional – far more so than the advance publicity had suggested – and for almost every evening from Monday to Saturday, Network Three used the Third's lost airtime for its relentlessly jolly middlebrow mixture of hobbies, 'family programmes', and undemanding forms of further education.

Ironically it was Network Three that established *Record Review* on the air (after earlier tentative efforts). The first of the new series was heard on Saturday 5 October 1957, when Trevor Harvey spoke on 'Building a Library', and Martin Cooper and Mark Lubbock reviewed new releases. The presenter and producer, John Lade, had begun to broadcast on the Home Service's *Music Magazine* in 1947, when he was still a student at Trinity College of Music. In 1953 he joined the BBC Gramophone Department as a producer on a short-term contract: 'They paid you in cash. I was supposed to be doing gramophone programmes for the Third, but that didn't take up all the time, so I'm afraid I produced *Housewives' Choice* as well! And it didn't do me any harm, I think. My quarterly offers to the Third would include new recordings of complete operas, long works or works needing special placing, and series like Schnabel's complete Beethoven sonatas when reissued on LP, or Bach's 48 (Rosalyn Tureck) and the *Little Organ Book* (played on neo-classical organs in Austria by Peter Hurford).'

Lade describes the origins of *Record Review*:

When Network Three was planned, Anna Instone, Head of Gramophone Programmes, without my knowing, suggested a weekly review of new records and asked me if I would like to produce it and also introduce it (this saved money). I agreed and to begin with I was warned not to be too highbrow, in order to catch as wide a range of listeners as possible for Network Three. That is why we were announced as 'a programme for all record enthusiasts'.

The first reviewers were often people I already knew from *Music Magazine*, but I see that very early on (November 1957) I gave first broadcasts to Stephen Dodgson and Edward Greenfield. The programme gradually took a definitive shape. The first contributor to cause a bit of a storm was John Carewe, when in 'Building a Library' he played in swift succession the opening bars of Beethoven's *Eroica* which were all at a slightly different pitch.

Although at that time there were far fewer versions to compare, we had to take into account the rapidly increasing LP market, calling for new studio equipment to add to the 78 rpm decks, and a little later came the important development of stereo.

Other than *Record Review,* there was little on Network Three which would have been allowed on the Third, and the producers of the hobby programmes searched energetically for determinedly non-cultural activities which they could feature. One senior programme official drew up this list:

1. Wine making.
2. Tropical fish.
3. Making music in the home (recorders, piano players, duets, and home orchestras).
4. Amateur dramatics.
5. Decoration of walls/floors/ceilings, i.e. mosaics, frescos, murals, etc. This might make three programmes.
6. Specialised cooking.
7. Indoor gardening, e.g. window boxes, pot plants, Japanese gardens, etc.
8. Pub games, e.g. shove-halfpenny, darts with the various variations on the game, snooker, skittles.
9. Exotic cats.
10. Cage birds, with special reference to their training, e.g. budgerigars.
11. Painting and sketching.
12. Enthusiastic amateurs: astronomers, meteorologists, seismologists, etc.
13. Photography and cine cameras.
14. Making models.
15. Conversation and letter writing: the lost arts of communication.
16. Pottery.
17. Parties and party games (to be placed near Christmas).
18. Chess, bridge and other indoor games. I would not propose that these should be included in one half hour. Chess and bridge might well stand a short series of three. But I shall have to talk to the experts before making a firm recommendation.

Writing a few months after the start of Network Three, Peter Laslett was particularly scathing about its hobbies programmes: 'Here you can learn how to acquire a taste for old glass; quite easy, you know, and all done in a dull little talk lasting a quarter of an hour. Or how even you, with your rather modest income ... can become a collector of pictures; rather bad ones of course, but think of the fun of it; lots of boring little prints, all alike.' Within the BBC, cynics soon dubbed Network Three 'the fretwork network'.

Meanwhile the *Radio Times* tried to reassure the Third's supporters that nothing of importance had been lost. It promised that there would be 'at least one opera' and 'an average of one play and one feature' each week. Play and feature would each be broadcast twice during the seven days, but there would be fewer subsequent repeats than in the past, though policy in this respect would not be settled 'until experience shows what listeners prefer, and the planning of the Third Programme should be regarded as experimental in this respect during the next few months. It is thought preferable to reduce the repeats of talks rather than drama and other productions which cannot, by their nature, be printed in the *Listener.*' Several recently inaugurated series, including *The World of Industry*, *Law in Action*, and *Research* (discussions on the latest scientific work), would continue to be heard monthly. There was also now a fortnightly arts magazine, *Comment*, which took the form of three scripted reviews of a film, a play, an exhibition or an opera; also two quarterly literary programmes, *New Books* and *Recent Novels*.

Rayner Heppenstall writes that the chief effect of the cuts on listeners was

> the lack of string quartets with the first gin at six o'clock. This was a serious deprivation ... To me as a writer–producer, the curtailment made less difference than I should have expected. One saw, indeed, that in general programmes ought now to be shorter, but in the first curtailed year I did a quite interminable *Caleb Williams* [by Godwin] ... while ... since my friend-at-court [Leslie Stokes] remained as Assistant to Controller of Third Programme, I continued never to have a programme suggestion turned down.

There were signs that the BBC was trying to improve the publicity for, and indeed the internal organisation of, what remained of the Third. On 6 December 1957 the *Radio Times* carried, for the first time, a pull-out supplement giving the Third's plans for the next quarter (which were also still being issued as a pamphlet); and shortly before the cut in airtime John Morris had instituted a Third Programme Committee which would meet every week to discuss offers for programmes, and if necessary initiate them itself. This was his solution to the Controller's previous powerlessness to commission programmes, as opposed to passively accepting offers from the Supply departments. Representatives would attend from Talks (P. H. Newby), Music (Peter Crossley-Holland), Drama (Donald McWhinnie) and Features (Douglas Cleverdon). 'The purpose of the weekly meeting,' Morris explained, 'will be to bring a collective judgement to bear upon Third Programme output as a whole.'

At the first meeting, three months before the new schedules began, there was some reference to the cuts. Several programmes which had been accepted before 'the announcement of the shortening of the Third Programme' now had to be rejected. On the other hand the committee recommended giving more airtime than had been requested to a programme on the pre-First World War 'little magazines', which had been suggested by Malcolm Bradbury, then a twenty-five-year-old university lecturer. Also in the minutes was this note: '*Molloy* by Samuel Beckett. The author's suggestion of a solo reading of the last section of Part I with music by John Beckett was accepted.'

Donald McWhinnie had pleaded that Beckett should be sent a recording of *All That Fall*, but weeks passed after transmission before the discs reached him. When he finally heard the production loud and clear, he was astonished by the creaking sing-song voice of Mr Slocum, the race-course clerk who gives Mrs Rooney a lift in his car. It was, Beckett said, a voice that he had been hearing already in his own head as he wrote. It belonged to the actor Patrick Magee.

He therefore was the obvious choice to read Beckett's prose on the air. Under McWhinnie's direction he recorded an extract from the novel *Molloy* (1951), with music by Beckett's cousin John, who had been studying in Paris. Magee also taped a recently written Beckett fragment, *From an Abandoned Work*. These were broadcast on 10 and 14 December 1957 respectively. Beckett's biographer Deirdre Bair writes that Magee's voice so delighted Beckett that it prompted him to start writing in English again – most of his recent work had originated in French.

The Third Programme Committee provided an opportunity not just to discuss specific programme proposals, like *Molloy*, but also for general criticism. On 19 August 1957, P. H. Newby voiced the feeling that talks were becoming 'too specialised' – there were too many on academic subjects and not enough first-class contributions which were 'just "talk"'. He wondered if Michael Tippett might be willing to do another piece. Tippett accepted the invitation, and gave two talks under the title *Too Many Choices* (5 and 12 January 1958), discussing 'the multiplicity today of contradictory ideologies, cultures, traditions ... and now this necessity of personal choice leads as often to a sense of frustration as to a sense of direction'.

In many respects it was business as usual for the Third, but the Sound Broadcasting Society did its best to puncture any complacency that might have set in now that the public was getting used to the new schedules. At the beginning of February 1958 it issued a report which made it clear that the reduction in airtime had been disastrous for music, drama and talks. Music had been cut by thirty-seven per cent (and forty-one per cent less contemporary music was being heard), talks had dropped by over half, and though drama had only been reduced by twenty-two per cent many of the Third's plays were now 'refugees from the Home Service', adaptations of novels and middlebrow original scripts. 'Major theatrical items' such as Greek drama, Shakespeare and European classics had been reduced by more than half. 'The Third Programme has, in fact, been maimed,' stated the report. 'It can no longer hope to do its full job: a job which over 10 years earned it world renown. The new Network Three ... has done nothing to compensate for the damage that has been caused.'

The BBC sent the Sound Broadcasting Society a brief formal acknowledgement that it had received the report, but made no comment; so the Society sent a letter to *The Times*, published on 19 February, challenging Sir Arthur fforde, who had succeeded Cadogan as Chairman of the BBC, to state the Corporation's views. The *News Chronicle* reported that 'the man who actually drafted the letter ... was T. S. Eliot'. This did not deter

Eliot from accepting an invitation from D. G. Bridson in Features to inaugurate a series of personal-choice poetry programmes in the Home Service. Indeed, Eliot's tone was playful as he discussed details with Bridson: 'If it would make any difference to your arrangements I repeat my offer to do one of the two men's voices ... I don't know whether that would be an infringement of union rules, but if not ... I should quite enjoy taking part in this performance and offer you my *voice* completely without charge.' The playfulness was possibly the result of his recent second marriage, to his former secretary Valerie Fletcher. 'I want very much to bring my wife with me to witness the proceedings,' he told Bridson, 'as she has never been behind the scenes at the BBC.'

Sir Arthur fforde's reply to the protest, published in *The Times* on 24 February, rejected 'the particular strictures' made by the Sound Broadcasting Society, and gave no sign that the BBC would budge. The Society then issued a statement that it was 'convinced that feeling in this country is still strong and widespread; and that, although the work has made heavier demands on the active voluntary officers than they can easily continue to meet, *this work must go on* ... WE ASK YOUR IMMEDIATE FINANCIAL SUPPORT TO DO WHAT NEEDS TO BE DONE.'

On the same day that he received the Society's report, Sir Arthur fforde had to deal with a challenge to the BBC from Samuel Beckett. The Royal Court Theatre was planning to perform his English text of *Fin de partie*, under the title *Endgame*, but the Lord Chamberlain refused to license it unless Beckett changed the wording of a reference to God: 'That Bastard – he doesn't exist.' Beckett refused. As the BBC was exempt from outside censorship, Donald McWhinnie pointed out to John Morris that 'if we were to broadcast this play in the Third Programme we should almost certainly excite a good deal of publicity'. It was just the sort of thing the Third needed to restore its reputation – though McWhinnie added hastily: 'It would be indefensible for us to allow any considerations other than artistic ones to influence us.'

The script of *Endgame* was passed to Richard Marriott, instigator of the cuts in the Third. He discussed it with the Head of Religious Broadcasting, who said he had no objection. Marriott was in favour of going ahead: 'If we were to refuse to broadcast [*Endgame*] it would certainly be known to a considerable number of people whose respect for the intellectual integrity of the Third Programme we value and whose respect would thereby be lessened.' But Marriott's superior, Lindsay Wellington, felt it necessary to refer the matter to the Director-General, Jacob, who in turn passed it to the Chairman with the comment: 'Having read the play I find it difficult to understand why it should be thought to be so brilliant, but I do not think that the Third Programme should be debarred from broadcasting it if they want to. The audience to whom Beckett appeals will find nothing to shock them in it, & I doubt whether others will listen. Do you agree?' Sir Arthur fforde did not. 'I think he should be asked to find an alternative for the word,' he told Jacob, adding: 'Generally speaking, I do see that a lot of the lines are very well put together ... '

Beckett again refused to make the change. 'He feels that, having taken such a firm stand over the Lord Chamberlain's objection to the play, he cannot make any compromise to please the BBC,' Leslie Stokes told Marriott. McWhinnie, supported by Val Gielgud, suggested that the Chairman might be satisfied if the play were accompanied by a talk or discussion airing different views about it; but nothing came of this, and eventually the Lord Chamberlain was persuaded to lift his ban on the grounds that the play had already been performed in French at the Royal Court, when the equivalent word, *salaud*, had been used. *Endgame* opened there in October 1958, followed each night by a new Beckett piece, *Krapp's Last Tape*, written for Patrick Magee and directed for the stage by McWhinnie. Beckett had questioned him anxiously about the workings of a tape recorder, but McWhinnie was scarcely able to help, being still more accustomed to disc recording.

Meanwhile Magee had read from another Beckett novel, *Malone Dies*, on the Third on 18 June 1958. This was the subject of an Audience Research survey, which reported that '0.1% of the adult population of the United Kingdom' had been listening, and that the broadcast had excited 'sharp divisions of opinion ... ranging from intense disgust to great admiration and excitement, with a substantial proportion of listeners ... reduced almost to incoherence when confronted by Beckett'. Many listeners found Magee's voice 'strange, strangled, and bubbly', and some were 'moved to strong revulsion against what they considered most depressing studies of "man at his lowest"'. But many approved, including a psychotherapist who wrote: 'Beckett has the courage to express what many people dare not acknowledge ... He seems ... greater than any [writer] I can think of during the last thirty years or so.'

Also causing disagreement within the BBC was Giles Cooper's *Unman, Wittering and Zigo*, about the schoolmaster who finds that his pupils murdered his predecessor. Leslie Stokes did not think it good enough for the Third, but P. H. Newby, whom John Morris consulted, stuck up for it, comparing it to Kafka. Morris therefore accepted it, and it was broadcast on 23 November 1958, with McWhinnie producing and David Spenser playing one of the boys, Wittering. Its evocation of an isolated public school made it one of the most memorable plays done on the Third.

Although he had been helping to run the Third since its beginning, Stokes seemed inclined to treat the cuts as a joke. At the Third Programme Committee, three months before the start of the new schedules, he had suggested that, since the Third had opened in 1946 with *How to Listen*, they might commence the reduced Third with *How to Listen in Half the Time*. 'Miss Kallin,' noted the minutes, 'suggested that Henry Reed might be asked to write a calypso on this theme.' Reed did not need to be prompted to write something about the cuts. When the next Hilda Tablet play, *The Primal Scene, as it were ...*, was broadcast on 11 March 1958 (following repeats of previous episodes in the saga) Herbert Reeve had much to say on the subject. At least, it *seemed* that he had much to say:

> *(Fade in the bells of Algeciras. They are heard from time to time behind Reeve.)*
>
> REEVE: We – we are sorry to have to mention it so early, but the still admirable Third Programme has in recent times been rudely truncated. We shall return to this point later. We mention it now merely to explain why we must move hurriedly forward to the first happy day when we all assembled at the beautiful and romantic port of Algeciras, in Southern Spain, to join Mr Aphanasis's splendid yacht, the *Jokasta* . . .

Aeschylus Aphanasis, a Greek millionaire plotting to steal the Elgin Marbles from the British Museum, has invited Hilda and her cronies on a Mediterranean cruise (the play was the fruit of Reed's expenses-paid trip to Greece). Although throughout the voyage Reeve refers intermittently to the 'Third Programme that has recently been . . . so rudely castrated', he somehow never gets round to discussing the issue.

On 20 August 1958 the BBC announced what looked like a small concession to the opponents of the cuts. 'The BBC Third Programme is to broadcast for two hours more on Saturdays,' announced *The Times*.

> After October 4 . . . it will start at 6 pm instead of 8 pm . . . Mr John Morris . . . explained that the extension would permit greater contrast with what the Home Service was offering at the same time, especially in music. 'It will also allow greater flexibility in programme planning.' . . . Network Three . . . will be moved back into Saturday afternoon . . . it will start at 4 pm. Mr Morris also announced that successful programmes would not be henceforth repeated so soon after their first hearing. He said that a recent survey had shown that 'while most listeners are glad of a second chance to hear an important broadcast the majority would prefer a longer interval between the original broadcast and its repeat'. Productions will now be repeated after an interval of three weeks.

But there was disappointment when, a month later, the Light Programme and Home Service were allocated an extra half-hour each day, but there was no further restoration of airtime to the Third. The Sound Broadcasting Society protested that this would 'only further weaken the substantial elements in British public broadcasting and encourage the lighter sort of listening'.

If it had not been for the Society's continual protests, the Third might have been given extra time instead of the Home. No sooner had the autumn 1957 cuts come into effect than Marriott told Wellington he was concerned about the lack of 'late night serious music' – something which the uncut Third had provided in abundance. He suggested extending the Third again from 11 to 11.30 pm, but pointed out that this would seem to be 'as demanded by the Third Programme Protection Society' (*sic*); so the Home was chosen instead for the new series *Music at Night*, which began in the autumn of 1958. This meant moving *Market Trends* (the stockmarket report) to the Third, where it scarcely belonged. It was heard nightly just before closedown.

Not knowing this, Peter Laslett regarded the Society as having been at least an effective watchdog. Surveying the situation a year after the cuts, he guessed that any further BBC threats to the Third would cause 'a rumpus on a national, even an international scale', though he added: 'Obviously too much should not be made of this success. We may be too sanguine in supposing that no Director-General will ever venture again to reduce the time allotted to high level broadcasting, or to abolish the Third Programme.'

*

John Morris retired from the BBC at the end of 1958. Laslett's feeling that the BBC was now taking the Third seriously again was borne out by its choice of his successor as Controller, Third Programme, a man who was unashamedly an intellectual – an 'Uncommon egghead' as the *Manchester Guardian* dubbed him.

'Mr Newby is undoubtedly an egghead,' explained this article on P. H. Newby,

> – his background as critic, novelist, and university lecturer qualifies him amply for the title – but in looks and temperament he does not tally with the popular image of eggheadedness. There is nothing about him of the tousled don, or of the circumspect Establishment man. He is approximately the size and shape of Sir Gordon Richards [the jockey], even down to the bright, darting eyes, the aggressive chin, and the head of smartly cropped hair.

Ved Mehta, interviewing Newby for the *New Yorker* after he had been Controller for four years, noted that – like Haley, the Third's founding father – 'Newby is more or less a self-educated, self-made man [who] discovered culture for himself. [His] father was a baker in a small English village, and Newby himself has never taken a degree.' Mehta described him as

> a quiet, unworldly, rather sphinx-like man, whose large head and tightly drawn mouth gave him a cerebral look. At first, his eyes appeared as inexpressive as the grey walls and the modern furniture of his office,[1] but as he talked on into the afternoon about the Third, he began radiating good cheer, though his voice maintained the neutral quality of a formal broadcast.

Ernest Warburton, who began to produce music programmes for the Third later in Newby's time as Controller, writes:

---

[1] The Controller's office was now in Broadcasting House.

On first acquaintance Howard seemed aloof. He gazed at you with 'novelist's' eyes. He was slow to comment on programmes, so that when he did congratulate or castigate, it really did mean something. When you knew him better, he emerged as a very sharp man with a wry sense of humour. I think he enjoyed people underestimating his range of sympathies and width of knowledge. He never put them right in this regard; I think it appealed to his sense of humour – as did having a teenage daughter who pranced around the house to the sound of Radio 1.

Val Gielgud, whose relations with the Third had been sticky, soon developed a considerable admiration for Newby. 'There are few recollections of the BBC that I cherish more warmly than my relations with Howard Newby,' he writes in his memoirs.

> We disagreed almost invariably. We argued lengthily and inconclusively. I have never known a man prepared to go to such lengths and spend so much time in making sure that justice was done to an opposing point of view. His courtesy was completely disarming. I have no doubt that he found me tiresome, just as on occasion I found him obstinate. But he never exploited his position in the official hierarchy, and I did my best to encourage personal relationships between him and producers more in tune with his ideas than I was. I enjoyed working with him almost as much as I have enjoyed his novels – which is saying quite a good deal.

On one occasion Drama Department proposed a radio adaptation of one of Newby's novels for the Third, but Newby himself turned the idea down.

Percy Howard Newby had first approached the BBC in 1946, at the age of twenty-eight. 'Now about myself,' he had written to the Talks Department,

> Born 1918. Served with RAMC 1939–1942 ... Then I was seconded to Fuad University, Cairo, as lecturer in English literature, a post I have just been able to relinquish in order to live in England once more; also the cost of living in Egypt was crushing me. Published a novel, *Journey to the Interior* (Cape, Dec. '45). This is being translated into French and Swedish and has also been published in USA. Given an Atlantic Award in Literature (Rockefeller Foundation) covering the period 1946–47 ... Forthcoming publications: *Agents and Witnesses* – a novel to be published by Cape. *The Spirit of Jem* – a book for children to be published by John Lehmann.

He continued to write fiction throughout his BBC career, eventually winning the first ever Booker Prize in 1969, for *Something to Answer For.* 'I look back on it with some amazement,' he says of his literary productivity while he was also Controller of the Third, 'but the writing was always done either at night or weekends. Writing is a compulsion. When I retired, I thought, "Now I'm quite free to write, so I can write three books a year instead of one every two years." But in fact the output was exactly the same.'

Philip French, who was a Talks producer working for the Third from 1961, describes Newby's fiction as 'very quiet, with a dry humour. The best of the novels are set in the Middle East, mostly Egypt. He has a fascination with the British abroad, very ordinary people who find themselves in extraordinary places. Forster is a great influence, and I think Henry James as well. His only novel which touches on the BBC is *Feelings Have Changed* (1981), in which Louis MacNeice and Laurence Gilliam make appearances.'

Newby says that he was brought to the BBC by Geoffrey Grigson. 'He'd read a novel I'd written, thought well of it, and . . . dropped a note to Talks Department with the consequence that I was invited to write and read at the microphone a short story. Which I did and this led to other broadcasting, book reviewing in the Home Service, for example, and then regular talks broadcasting on the Third Programme.' He joined the staff in 1949, as 'the short story expert' in Talks.

He supplied both Home and Third with stories, and he emphasises that, whereas all suggestions for the Home had to be sent via the Head of Talks, offers to the Third were made directly to the Controller at a weekly meeting, which he describes as it was in his early BBC years:

> The talks meeting was held every Monday afternoon, and it often went on till seven o'clock in the evening, and the conversation ranged very wide. There was no agenda; the theory was that, if the conversation round the table was good, the broadcasting that resulted from it would be good. Peter Laslett would be hammering a point about social patterns in the seventeenth century,[2] and being disagreed with by Alec Robertson, who looked at it from a religious point of view and said the family was not quite like that in the 1680s; and you realised that what you were listening to was not a conversation designed to produce broadcasting, but one that might have been broadcast itself.

Newby says that when he took over as Controller, Third Programme late in 1958, he found the staff 'in a state of shock' from the cuts, feeling that the BBC 'had no confidence in them'. He knew it was 'necessary to build up morale'. He was 'anxious to increase the audience, of course', and he told the *Manchester Guardian* that he was concerned to meet his listeners and 'sound out their views'. He had letters sent out to members of the Third Programme 'Panel' of listeners, inviting them to a series of meetings at Broadcasting House. These were only a limited success; Newby wanted to meet the sort of people who ought to be listening to the Third but were not, whereas by definition those who came to the meetings were devotees.

---

[2] Newby is speaking of the period when Laslett was on the staff of Talks Department. In March and April 1960, some years after he had resigned from the BBC staff, he gave three talks on the Third about 'the social order before the coming of industry'; the first was on the family as social unit in pre-industrial Britain. The series subsequently formed the basis of his very highly regarded book on this subject, *The World We Have Lost* (1965).

Moreover they would not listen to each other, or to him. 'When I succeeded to this job,' he recalled four years later,

> the first thing I did was to invite the research panel down to Broadcasting House. This ... panel [is] like a reservoir with a tap at the top and a leak at the bottom; the water gets changed every two years. I thought the panel would be intimidated, so I prepared a story of my life: 'I am Newby. I was born in 1918. I spent some time at St Paul's [School], and was in the Medical Corps during the war. I live in Buckinghamshire, twenty-five miles from London, with my wife and teenage daughter. I am not a very social person. I get to the BBC early in the morning, work here until late in the afternoon, listen to the Third in the evening at home, and fit my writing into the time between work and listening to the Third.' But as soon as the panel arrived, I hardly had a chance to say anything. They went at each other, now talking about a play they didn't like, now about an opera they did like.

Retreating from this disillusioning glimpse of his audience, Newby turned his attention to improving his image in the minds of the Supply departments. He knew that producers tended to regard the Controller and his deputy as 'abominable no-men' dedicated to turning down imaginative programme ideas. He said he was going to encourage producers to make suggestions and criticisms of all kinds, even if they were outside their own specialist fields. With this in mind he instituted fortnightly meetings with all the producers in Features and Drama (such meetings already took place with Talks and Music), and reduced the meetings of the general-purpose Third Programme Committee to once a month. He says of this: 'The whole energy of the Third Programme came from the Controller having direct contact with producers, not with heads of departments. That was the crucial difference between Third Programme editorial control and Home and Light, where all the offers went through the heads of department.'

Philip French, who attended the Talks meetings with Newby, agrees that the character of the Third under Newby was profoundly affected by his frequent contact with producers, and the extraordinary degree of democracy with which the meetings were conducted:

> Everybody in Talks could attend, and you didn't have to put ideas on a proposal form. You could just float an idea, which might even be accepted straight away, or you might be told to put it on paper and re-submit it in more detail. And there was no dictatorship by Howard. It was collegiate. He had, ultimately, a veto, but it was rare for him to exercise it in the face of general enthusiasm for a suggestion. And he would accept being overruled in a generous way.

French – himself an Oxford graduate – suspects that Newby adopted this policy partly because of his own lack of intellectual self-confidence:

> There was a degree of uncertainty about Howard, because he hadn't had

a proper university education – it was the kind you got before the war at a teacher training college. In fact he'd become an academic himself, in Egypt; he was very much a British Council sort of man. But he had this feeling that he lacked something educationally, which made him unduly cautious, unnecessarily defending high standards. And he couldn't let his hair down; he lacked levity.

French says that, when he joined Talks in 1961, there were still some remarkable characters at the meetings: 'I had rarely come across or kept company with people of such obvious distinction, like T. S. Gregory, who had been a Methodist minister and had converted to Catholicism. He was a philosopher and a theologian of some distinction, and he knew all the philosophers and theologians.' Prue Smith (the Talks producer who had brought Iris Murdoch to the microphone) says that Gregory 'used to come out with very long and very complex sentences about the nub of the question he would like to see examined by five philosophers that none of us had ever heard of. He brought it off, as a rule. We respected his judgement.'

Another Talks producer admired by French was Leonie Cohn: 'She had been Herbert Read's secretary and amanuensis, and her particular area was the visual arts. She produced a remarkable series of conversations with artists. And then there was Anna Kallin! By then she must have been well beyond retirement age, but she had some special contract which allowed her to stay on. She knew *everybody*!' French says that these individuals, and others in the same mould, imposed 'a certain kind of exclusivity' on the Third. 'At meetings, somebody's name would be suggested, and someone around the table would say, "Yes, but do you think he's got a Third Programme mind?" Or someone might be dismissed as a "journalist" – which I think is an honourable calling. It meant that a lot of people who should have been on the air were shut out.'

Third Programme talks were still being reprinted, more often than not, in the *Listener*, and French says that this made it much easier to persuade people to give them. 'Any script of quality was almost certain to get in.' All the producers still made programmes for the other networks, and there was no obligation to contribute to the Third if they had no ideas to offer. 'The great thing about the Third,' says French, 'was that if you didn't want to do something, then you didn't have to. Nobody ever made you do anything you didn't believe in.'

*

In March 1958 William Glock (then aged fifty) was invited to a party at the Guildhall, during which he was asked if he would consider becoming a candidate for the directorship of the Guildhall School of Music. He decided to put his name forward, and among those whom he asked to provide references was Richard Howgill, currently the BBC's Controller of Music – a post that had been created a few years earlier.

Howgill, a BBC administrator rather than a musician, had been Controller of Music for six years, during which he had pursued a middle-of-the-road policy. Under him, Music Division had regularly commissioned music from such British composers as Rubbra, Alwyn and Bliss, and had supported Tippett, Walton and Britten, though not the younger generation. Nicholas Kenyon, in his history of the BBC Symphony Orchestra, writes: 'When it was suggested in August 1956 that the music of Henze, Boulez and others was not receiving sufficient attention on the air, there was a discussion as to how it was possible to establish whether their music was of a sufficiently high quality to be broadcast. "On balance it was felt that to broadcast a few of their better works would not blunt our reputation for acute critical assessment." This sentence might stand as a memorial to the BBC's insular musical policy in the 1950s.'

Howgill replied to Glock's letter asking for a reference for the Guildhall job: 'Please come to lunch next Wednesday. I have got a better idea.' He told Glock he was retiring next year; would Glock consider succeeding him? It could be far more influential than running the Guildhall. Glock left the lunch table 'in a state of some turmoil'.

It was a daring suggestion. From several bases – the Dartington Summer School of Music, his chairmanship of the ICA music section, and his editorship of the magazine *The Score* – Glock had been running (in his own words) a 'campaign of insurrection' against the British musical establishment, challenging it to pay serious attention to contemporary music.

The BBC took a long time to make up its mind to offer him the Controllership. By the time it eventually did, Glock had rather gone off the idea; he told Lindsay Wellington that 'my really profound interest was musical education, not broadcasting, of which I didn't know enough'. Then he went home and rang Michael Tippett, to see what he thought. Tippett said: 'You're a bloody fool to give up a job which could have infinitely more influence on music in England.' Glock relented, and the news that he was to be put in charge of the BBC's music caused consternation in many circles. On the other hand the impresario Walter Legge wrote to him: 'I don't know whether I am more surprised or delighted. I feel rather as though ... Luther had just been elected Pope.'

At first he was kept on a tight rein: 'Richard Howgill told me to report to him every morning for six weeks.' Nevertheless he had a clear mission in mind. 'What had gone on for eleven years, starting at Bryanston and Dartington, and in the ICA and my magazine, had really conditioned me to try and achieve something in the BBC which would be on a grandiose scale, but along similar lines.'

Before the war his mission would have been unnecessary, for the BBC had broadcast plenty of contemporary music. 'Many times I sat in my office in Yalding House,' recalls Glock, 'looking through the *Radio Times* of the 1930s and saying to myself, "I'll never reach that."' But the 1950s were a time of drought. 'I hardly went to the Proms, for example, because each season seemed to be a rather spiritless variation on the one before.'

The Proms, promoted by the BBC, were planned by a committee, 'and I didn't believe in planning by committee'.

In his history of the Proms, Barrie Hall confirms Glock's picture of them in the 1950s. Critics reported 'dissatisfaction and boredom', and called the programme 'feeble, hackneyed and flatulent'. First performances were rare – Howgill argued that the duty of the Proms was to provide second and third performances of works, 'the most important to a composer', rather than premières. In 1955 a critic wrote that, since the war, the Proms had fallen into a 'Slough of Despond'. Julian Herbage, who did much of the Prom planning, wrote: 'There is no doubt that this vast audience is attracted mainly by the standard fare.' He claimed that a proportion of the programme showed 'what is going on abroad', but this meant music by Kodály, Prokofiev, Milhaud, Copland, Shostakovich, and Samuel Barber. In a Last Night speech, Sargent told contemporary composers: 'If music be the food of love, play on – if not, shut up!'

Glock says that these 'narrow horizons' were partly the fault of Howgill's deputy, Maurice Johnstone, Head of Music. Glock found him 'likeable', but says he dismissed Schoenberg and the other members of the Second Viennese School 'in a spirit of almost moral indignation', and was even more affronted by the avant-garde. These opinions would have carried more weight if Johnstone had not mentioned casually to Glock that he had never heard the *St Matthew Passion*, and 'didn't care' about chamber music. This seemed almost unbelievable in a successor to Edward Clark, who had programmed music from Bach to the contemporary with 'judgement and enterprise'.

Glock's first step was to ask that the Proms committee should be disbanded, and the concerts be planned by Music Division (that is, chiefly himself). Though some spoke of him as 'a Hitler', this was agreed to, and Glock then embarked on a much more adventurous Proms policy: 'What we tried to do – and we all seemed to agree on this, I and the new members of staff – was to choose works that were really worth hearing, even if they might be a chamber of horrors from time to time.' He was not able to make many changes in his first Proms season in 1960, apart from beginning to break down 'the old segregation of past and present', but in 1961 came the first semi-staged opera performance at a Prom (a Glyndebourne *Don Giovanni*), and new Prom works began to be commissioned in some quantity from young British composers.

One of the first was the *Fantasia on an In Nomine of John Taverner* by twenty-eight-year-old Peter Maxwell Davies. Glock knew Davies well from Dartington, and wrote to him in November 1961 asking if 'you might have anything suitable ready for the next season's Proms'. Davies, who had given a talk on the Third three years earlier about the position of the young composer in Britain, received £300 for the commission. He conducted the *Fantasia* himself at the Proms on 15 September 1962. The rest of the evening was under the baton of Sir Malcolm Sargent, who was still chief conductor of the Proms; he stood down willingly on such occasions. 'I think he was my ally in wanting to see something fresh,' says Glock. 'On the other hand it wasn't he who was going to supply it.'

Sargent had been removed from the chief conductorship of the BBC Symphony Orchestra in 1957, and replaced by Rudolf Schwarz. Glock describes Schwarz as 'a fine musician and a very civilised man'. However, 'the press was fanatically against him', and the orchestra 'needed cleaning up and strengthening'.[3] Schwarz's contract would end in 1962, so Glock began to plan the orchestra's 'rejuvenation', paying attention to its annual Royal Festival Hall winter season of concerts as well as its role in the Proms.

As to Glock's new recruits to Music Division, they included the musicologist David Drew and the composer Alexander Goehr, son of Walter Goehr and a member, with Maxwell Davies and Harrison Birtwistle, of the Manchester Group of composers. Goehr and Drew were both still in their twenties, and were sharing a flat at the time. 'We wanted to have absolutely nothing to do with the BBC,' says Goehr. 'It was the enemy, and we were anti-establishment. But William offered us a sum that, at that time, we were unable to refuse. And the two of us joined, sharing one job. David lasted only a short time,[4] but I stayed for several years.' Glock was also able to rely on the judgement of Maurice Johnstone's deputy, Eric Warr, whom he had known at Cambridge. And further recruitment went on. 'No doubt,' writes Glock, 'the most controversial decision was to invite Hans Keller on to the staff.'

Keller, now aged forty, had been in Britain since 1938, when he had arrived as a young Jewish refugee from Austria. His father, a Viennese architect, was a keen amateur musician who had played much of the standard orchestral and operatic repertoire with Hans in piano duet arrangements. 'Indeed,' writes Christopher Wintle, editor of a Keller memorial symposium, 'when one learns of the Kellers' life-style in their early nineteenth-century house in outlying Döbling (the Austrian Hampstead), it is hard not to invoke precisely that legend of Old Vienna that Hans himself set out so assiduously to dispel.' Soon after war broke out, Keller was interned on the Isle of Man, along with many other Germans and Austrians in Britain. Vaughan Williams, who had somehow heard of his violin-playing, eventually secured his release. Hans's father had died before the war; now, he lived with his mother in London, took an LRAM, and picked up work as a freelance musician. His widow, the artist Milein

---

[3] One of its worst moments had come on 5 February 1958, when it gave the première of Tippett's Second Symphony – the work that Tippett had been asked to write for the Third's tenth anniversary in 1956. Boult was brought in to conduct it, but the complicated opening bars collapsed, and he had to stop the performance, apologise to listeners, and begin again.

[4] Drew says he stayed for a few months, while also writing music criticism for the *New Statesman*. He describes himself as a 'low-grade' music producer, and says he was also detailed to investigate the 'notoriously confidential, not to say classified, reports of the Music Reading Panel, going back at least a decade and perhaps even as far as 1945'.

Cosman Keller, says he took the LRAM exam without attending any classes, and was offended when he was only awarded 99%. The examiners explained that 100% was never given on principle.

Meanwhile psychology and psychoanalysis occupied his mind almost as much as music. He began to contribute to psychological journals, and, wishing to be psychoanalysed but being unable to afford the fees, undertook the task himself (writes Wintle), 'engaging in free association every day for five years ... His aim was to acquire a deeper knowledge of his own aggression, and hence of how to put that aggression to constructive use.' A leading psychoanalyst entrusted him with a schizophrenic patient, with whom he attempted 'musical-psychological treatment'. It was not successful.

Wintle explains that Keller thought about music largely in Freudian terms: 'He defined Stravinsky's artistic personality in terms of its "suppressive exhibitionism" ... and apart from finding sado-masochistic elements in Stravinsky, Webern and even Dallapiccola ... diagnosed "aggressive narcissism" in Boulez, schizophrenia in Schumann, and a "violent repressive counter-force against ... sadism" in Britten.' Put like this, such diagnoses sound comic. In fact they were powerfully argued and, in the case of Britten, probably on the right track.

Admittedly, Keller did sometimes write criticism which sounded like a parody of Freud. His 1951 essay on the 'Harry Lime Theme' from the film *The Third Man* could be the work of one of the spoof music critics in the Hilda Tablet plays. He analyses this hit tune, poker-faced – 'The striking, indeed the only feature about this "tune" is its submediant obsession which, avoiding any Aeolian insinuation, creates an extended *appoggiatura*' – and then suggests that it is the musical equivalent of *coitus interruptus*, corresponding to 'a relatively unsublimated amount of, perhaps, infantile sexual energy'.

As Wintle remarks, 'Hans could not make a living' from this kind of writing, and his income from playing was never substantial. During the 1950s he supported himself by contributing to a number of magazines, both in English and German. From 1949 to 1952 he co-edited, with Donald Mitchell, the journal *Music Survey*, which was characterised by what Keller called 'positive aggression'. This characteristic was also displayed in a book on Britten which Keller and Mitchell edited in 1953. Glock, reviewing it on the Third (29 January 1953), called it 'adolescent' in its grandiose claims for Britten, and said that the editors 'ought to know better'. This was the sort of fighting language that Keller himself liked. The previous year he had sent Glock a note about the Schoenberg memorial issue of his magazine *The Score*: 'Could have been worse, could have been better.'

Further correspondence between Glock and Keller followed, 'invariably aggressive on his side', says Glock. Soon Keller, with his high forehead and moustache, became familiar to Glock among concert audiences, 'animated and note-scribbling'. Eventually Glock enlisted him to write for *The Score*, and to teach at Dartington – though their friendship was spiced by many differences of musical opinion. For example, Glock could not agree with Keller's assertion that Gershwin was a better composer than Webern – 'as though in purpose and ideals they inhabited the same universe!' commented Glock – and Keller also 'valued Britten above any limit I could then aspire to'. Nevertheless they were united over fundamentals, and Glock admired Keller's gift of making 'pronouncements which at their best have almost the authority of proverbs'.

Glock suggested to Keller that he should apply for a job in Music Division. Maurice Johnstone said he would be appointed 'over my dead body', but he arrived at Yalding House in September 1959, four months after Glock. His first title was 'Chief Assistant (Chamber Music and Recitals)'; over the following years he held a variety of other jobs, and by 1977 could write that he had been 'in charge of more or less everything, with the sole exception of opera' – not that he was inexpert on opera, or 'all that marvellous in other areas'; it had just happened that way. In any case, under Glock, music staff were encouraged to undertake projects of almost any sort that appealed to them. 'I don't think I ever interfered with programme-making by my staff,' says Glock. 'I tried to do some things myself, and they could either follow or counteract. They were jolly good staff.'

Howard Newby notes that Keller had one blind spot: 'He had no interest in old music, or even a lot of eighteenth-century composers, until you got to Haydn. I had an immense liking and admiration for Keller, although if anyone had heard me say this at the time they would have been amazed, because he used to insult me in public – to a degree that now amazes me – and our rows were tremendous. But he insulted anyone in authority that he could.' Keller himself always insisted that emotion played no part in his outbursts. 'I wasn't in the least offended,' he wrote reassuringly to a BBC colleague who had skirmished with him. 'As almost invariably, I simply meant what I said.'

*

One of Keller's earliest memos that survives in the BBC files is headed 'Functional Analysis'. Dated 8 March 1960, it refers to a method of ana-lysing musical works which Keller had developed in the mid-1950s, and which he had explained in an article in *Music Review*:

> Tautology is the greatest insult to the dignity of human thought. Yet most so-called 'analytical' writings about music, from the humble programme-noter who has absolutely nothing up his record sleeve to the great Tovey who may or may not have withheld a lot, boil down to mere tautological descriptions ... During my work on Mozart's chamber music ... I have developed ... a method of analysis [which] aims at ascertaining the *latent* elements of the unity of *manifest* contrasts.

Keller's first Functional Analysis broadcast had been given on the Third the year before he joined the staff, on 7 December 1958, and was devoted to Mozart's Piano Concerto in C, K503. In the first part of the programme, a performance of the work, movement by movement, was (in the words of the *Radio Times*) 'linked with analytic music designed to show how the contrasting themes and the movements hang together'. There was then a three-minute silence, to allow the listener to contemplate what had been heard; then the entire concerto was repeated without the 'analytic music'. The whole programme took sixty-five minutes. The 'analytic music' had been composed, or at least arranged, by Keller, and consisted of snippets from the concerto, in a form which he believed would demonstrate the structure of the work. There was no speech in the broadcast, other than the introductory announcements.

When the violinist André Mangeot heard Keller applying Functional Analysis to Haydn at Dartington, he deplored the 'analytic music', which he described as 'bits of so-called Haydn that Mr Keller had composed to show us Haydn's inner thoughts'. But Deryck Cooke thought the method 'brilliant', and Keller claimed that among its admirers was Sir Adrian Boult. However, the initials of Functional Analysis tended to invite derision. A letter to the *Musical Times* about analysing *Carmina Burana* was headed 'FA and Orff'.

Keller was more sceptical than Glock about the avant-garde. On 19 July 1956, giving a talk on the Third about the annual International Society of Contemporary Music Festival, held that year in Stockholm, he considered the case of *Kontra-Punkte* by Stockhausen:

> Now, while this music did not get a prize, it didn't get the opposite of a prize either. Everybody was pretty polite about it, at any rate in public although, so far as I was aware, nobody understood it. When something is incomprehensible to some people, or even many people, it is either their own fault, or the composer's fault, or the fault of either party. When something is incomprehensible to everybody, the likelihood is that it is the composer's fault alone ...
>
> Now, a generation or so ago, the articulate inhabitants of our musical world made fools of themselves by rejecting Schoenberg ... The contemporary 'dodecaphoneys', as I irreverently call them, think that Schoenberg, though admittedly a technical innovator, was at heart a banal romantic, old-fashioned enough to believe in expressive music ...
>
> I wonder ... when it will strike the advocates of the new, or rather fashionable style that they have never yet discovered a bad work written in it. Every single dodecaphoney piece is praised for some reason or other; apply to Webern and you can't go wrong.[5]

Keller put this damning assertion to the test five years later, on 5

---

[5] The earliest Third Programme broadcast of Stockhausen appears to have been on 5 October 1955, when Peter Racine Fricker introduced *Darmstadt and the Young Composer*, a programme about the summer courses for composers held at Darmstadt. It included Stockhausen's *Klavierstücke*, 'recorded at Darmstadt last June'.

June 1961, when the Third broadcast, as part of a chamber concert of contemporary music, a performance billed in the *Radio Times* as *Mobile for tape and percussion* by Piotr Zak, a twenty-two-year-old Polish composer. The piece was played twice during the broadcast, and was reviewed next day in *The Times* by Jeremy Noble:

DISAPPOINTING MOBILE

The BBC's policy of giving the musical *avant-garde* a hearing needs no justification, but there are bound to be occasional lapses; Piotr Zak's *Mobile* for electronic tape and two partially improvising percussion players, broadcast twice in the Third Programme last night, sounded like one of them.

The composer's refusal to publish a score suggests that he considers a consciously analytic approach a waste of the listener's time. It was certainly difficult to grasp more than the music's broad outlines, partly because of the high proportion of unpitched sounds and partly because of their extreme diversity ('the tape exploits the full range of the aural spectrum'). Without some idea of what could be irrelevant, it is not easy to say what is not. It was more disappointing that such recognisably musical events as did occur seemed trivial, and that the texture made so little sonorous appeal. Beside it Nono's early *Polifonica-Monodia-Ritmica* shone as the model of clarity and controlled fantasy.

The *Mobile* was also reviewed in the *Daily Telegraph* by Keller's friend and co-editor Donald Mitchell:

The first performance in this country of a *Mobile* (ominous title) for tape and percussion by Piotr Zak, a Polish composer, proved wholly unrewarding. He exploited the percussion with only limited enterprise and his tape emitted a succession of whistles, rattles and punctured sighs that proclaimed, all too shamelessly, their non-musical origins.

There was nothing, one felt, to 'understand' here. It was only the composer's ingenuousness that was mysterious.

Two months later it was revealed that there was no such composer as Piotr Zak, and that the performance (in the words of the *Daily Telegraph*)

was arranged by Hans Keller, head of the Corporation's chamber music and recitals department, with the help of Susan Bradshaw, concert pianist.

Miss Bradshaw, 29, said last night: 'The idea struck us as we listened to the faintly melodious sounds produced by the moving of chairs after a concert. It was a serious hoax to set people thinking.'

The *Daily Express* quoted her as saying that she and Keller had created the recording by 'banging about at random. We used drums, xylophones, cymbals, glasses, ashtrays, and anything else handy. At one time we were whistling, using an echo effect. We didn't rehearse at all, and it was fun reading the critics.'

On 5 August, in a programme on the Third entitled *The Strange Case of Piotr Zak*, Keller gave his own account:

Miss Susan Bradshaw and I myself went into a studio and bashed about on percussion instruments for about twelve minutes. We also had a special mike in a corner screened off and put through an echo chamber, where we produced the electronic noises ... and the purpose of it all, and here I'm getting serious, was not a hoax. It was really an experiment, or if you like I wanted to pose a problem. How far would this kind of thing be taken seriously? Well, I'm glad to say that the critics whose reviews I've read, reacted roughly in the same way in which I would have reacted. In other words they thought it was a lousy piece, but they took it seriously, as indeed I would have taken it seriously. The problem I'm posing is: why and how is this kind of thing possible nowadays, and could it have been possible at a previous historical stage?

Keller then discussed this with Noble and Mitchell, the two critics he was referring to. Mitchell thought it was a pity the piece had been so bad; the hoax would have had more point 'if one had tried to manufacture a work of quality, which ... would have borne some closer resemblance to the kind of work it was parodying'; but Noble felt that 'Hans has shown in a very vivid way that there is no difference ... between the non-work and the bad work, in a situation of total compositional freedom such as is accepted by today's composers.'

The Zak hoax had been authorised by Newby – 'I took a deep breath and said "yes"'. It caused a great deal of correspondence in the press and musical journals. Writing to the *Daily Telegraph*, G. H. Bosworth from Kent commented: 'The revelation of the hoax itself contains another hoax. Mr Piotr Zak *does* exist. Under a variety of aliases he continues to contribute works to our broadcast programmes. He is a great friend of the BBC's Controller of Music, and lives in a private apartment in Broadcasting House.' Keller himself, talking to Noble and Mitchell, was more tolerant: 'There are many creative people who write in a style which fundamentally is phoney, because it hasn't got precise and spontaneous terms of reference for the recipient, but who nevertheless are creative enough to get something across.' Turning to Stockhausen, he said: 'I've changed my mind in as much as I think he has a highly artistic mind. [But] he hasn't in my opinion faced this problem of communication ... Boulez is, for instance, more worried about it, I think.'

*

Boulez's *Le marteau sans maître*, conducted by John Carewe, was the second item in the Third's first Thursday Invitation Concert, broadcast at 8 pm on 7 January 1960, eight months after Glock had become Controller of Music. The Boulez was, as he recalls, 'sandwiched between ... two great Mozart string quintets'. The intention was to provide a foretaste of 'quality and boldness' in what was to be the Third's most important music series for many years to come.[6]

The *Radio Times* (1 January 1960) explained:

> The Thursday Invitation Concerts ... will be given at the BBC's Maida Vale studios before an invited audience of about four hundred ... Anyone glancing at the programmes will notice that the majority of them include more than one kind of instrumental sound, or else a contrast of instrumental and vocal. They have been built on these oppositions, in fact, and on the further principle that equal importance should be given to past and present.
>
> The new series has two main ambitions – to provide a repertory of outstanding works, ranging from the fourteenth century to the twentieth, such as could never be heard in the ordinary run of concert-going; and to make sure of the highest standards of performance.

Glock explains that the Invitation Concerts had their origin at Dartington, where 'I had tried out a few programmes in which works of very different periods were placed side by side, in the hope that they would combine with each other in an illuminating way'. Alexander Goehr was present at the first concert:

> It was in Maida Vale Studio 1, and extra chairs had been put out on ground level, to get more people in. *Le marteau* was the flagship of the avant-garde, and to juxtapose it with Mozart was seen by some as a kind of abuse of the audience – people who had come for one didn't want the other. But that was the kind of thing my father had done at Morley College, and William himself at Dartington. We were fighting the idea of 'New Music'. We didn't want to see the kind of thing that had happened in Germany, where people committed to new music were interested in nothing else. The *one-ness* of music lay behind William's policy. I remember him saying that all the London new music organisations would become redundant within a few years, because we were trying to make a revolution. We posited a Third Programme intelligent music lover who would respond enthusiastically if presented with good performances of music from *any* period.

The same principle was carefully observed as the Invitation Concerts continued, with works by Janáček and Berg (14 January 1960), Debussy and Messaien (21 January), Purcell, Bach and Britten (28 January) and Dowland, Beethoven and Henze (4 February). Other contemporary composers whose works were heard early in the series included Nono, Berio, Maderna, Stockhausen and Elliott Carter. Later came John Cage (16 No-

---

[6] The earliest Third Programme broadcast of Boulez seems to have been on 18 March 1957, when Yvonne Loriod and Boulez himself played the two-piano work *Structures,* livre 1.

vember 1961, the first British broadcast of his *Winter Music* for two pianos, played by Cornelius Cardew and John Tilbury).

Glock writes that some people criticised the Invitation Concerts as being 'planned only for four hundred initiates'. He allows that the atmosphere among the audience of roughly that number who filled the seats at Maida Vale each Thursday was often electric. Yet 'the audience at home often reached a total of 100,000, twice the usual Third Programme figure, and enough to have filled the Wigmore Hall or St John's, Smith Square, 150 times'.

Alexander Goehr says that the policy behind the Invitation Concerts had as much to do with pre-twentieth-century music as with the contemporary:

> The programming of the two Mozart quintets with *Le marteau* was a message: this was the beginning of the re-establishment of Mozart, slightly to the detriment of Beethoven – the big Beethoven nights at the Proms were dismantled – and of Brahms, who had been the big composer of the previous generation. William brought in a proper treatment of the Middle Ages and the Renaissance, of Bach and the classical period, and of the twentieth century, with a slight decline of the nineteenth century giants.

Some Thursday Invitation Concerts came from the regions, but they were all announced by Alvar Liddell, who 'is ... as much a part of the show as are the artists who take part' (wrote Leonard Isaacs of Music Division). Tall and silver-haired, in an impeccable dinner jacket and seated at a table covered with green baize, Liddell introduced the broadcasts in his sonorous style. In some regions, even the technicians were similarly clothed. A 1967 memo from the Head of Music, Scotland, complains that the producer sent up from London for one of the concerts, Tim Souster (himself a composer of the Stockhausen school), was 'the only person who had not troubled to put on evening dress ... I just felt that it let the side down a bit ... '

Sir John Manduell, who in 1960 was a music producer, recalls a rare occasion on which Liddell's authority was challenged, not in an Invitation Concert but during a recording by Julian Bream. Liddell was reading the introductory announcements, which had been written by Deryck Cooke,

> and Deryck had put in that a piece which Julian was going to play 'is thought to be by Bach'. And Julian slapped down his guitar, and in his lovely Cockney accent said: "Ere, Alvar, what do you mean, *thought to be*? It's so bloody good it '*as* to be by Bach.' And I can see Alvar absolutely thrown that this young guitarist with a Cockney voice would actually dispute the validity of what he'd said.

Manduell admired the Invitation Concerts, but like some other members of Music Division he became aware that Glock's passion for the avantgarde was keeping out other kinds of twentieth-century music: 'There were quite individual voices like Alan Rawsthorne, who became rather

sad, simply because they were being cold-shouldered, or felt they were.'
Robert Simpson, another BBC music producer, also suffered from this
prejudice by his Controller. An expert on Nielsen and Bruckner, whose
own music was firmly based on tonality (his works included seven symphonies and eight string quartets), he found himself in entrenched opposition to Glock. 'I'm a great admirer of Bob,' says Manduell. 'His Second
Symphony is such a fine piece for more or less classical orchestra. But we
had great difficulty in getting it programmed. And Bob's own predilections
in music – the Nordic composers like Nielsen – tended to be neglected
too. It was to our great good fortune that he was around to fight for them,
otherwise they might not have been heard for quite a while.'

Simpson managed to include some of their music in *The Innocent Ear*, a
series he created for the Third in 1960. 'The names of the composers in
this programme will be announced only after the performance of their
works,' explained the *Radio Times*. It proved hugely popular with listeners.
'The function of the programme,' wrote Simpson, 'at least as I originally
conceived it, was to fix the listener's attention, in a way not possible
otherwise, on works he normally might give a miss if he saw them billed
... It's a marvellous and valuable way of listening ... '

Simpson has written of Glock's 'unjustifiable exclusion of much valuable
twentieth-century music that was either not fashionable or failed to meet
with [his] approval'. Glock himself denies this. 'What do you mean by
"excluded"? There are one or two composers whom I've been accused of
ignoring. But when I look at the programmes since I've left the BBC,
they're still ignored now. I left my staff – all senior, and with distinctly
interesting attitudes and beliefs – to get on with their work. If they thought
these composers were worth putting in, they would have put them in,
and I would not have said no.'

Howard Newby greatly admires Robert Simpson: 'Bob was a traditionalist
in the best sense of the word, and incidentally a very good composer. He
also had a marvellous critical mind. To hear Bob talking about Beethoven
was a revelation.' Yet Newby reserves his greatest praise for Keller: 'If I had
to answer the question, "Have you ever met anyone whom you think was
a genius," I would say "Yes", and it would be Hans Keller.' Alexander
Goehr describes Keller as 'ninety per cent genius and ten per cent show-
off and fraud, and when the ninety per cent was operating he was magnificent'.

As Chief Assistant (Chamber Music and Recitals), Keller was responsible
for the Invitation Concerts in their first two years; he then took over
'Orchestral and Choral' programmes. On 30 August 1960, Paul Huband,
Head of North Region Music, wrote to Keller about a Mr Cox, the secretary
of the Manchester Institute of Contemporary Arts, which was jointly
promoting one of the Invitation Concerts with the BBC: 'I think we may
consider ourselves fortunate that Mr Cox is an understanding man who
does not wish to fall out with the BBC here. Otherwise he would not have
agreed to a programme which, from his point of view, is not altogether

suitable for the occasion.' Keller was having none of this. 'I am quite overwhelmed by Mr Cox's generosity of heart,' he wrote to Huband. 'It is surely on such spirit of self-sacrifice that the continued existence of the BBC, the country, and possibly the world, depends. I shall ask the Chamber Music Group to stand in silence for a minute, in view of the fact that our programme "is not altogether suitable for the occasion from Mr Cox's point of view". Whose occasion is it anyway?'

Huband, who had not met Keller and was unaware of his 'positive aggression', wrote back explaining that Mr Cox's Institute, as co-promoters, were 'entitled to some consideration' about the content of the programme, and concluded: 'I now suggest that we should not take any further an argument for which neither of us has the time nor, I assume, the inclination.' But Keller had both: 'Thank you for your memo of September 13, whose second, crucial point is fallacious. It was never agreed that the concert should be presented *under the auspices* of the Institute.' Wearily, Huband replied that the Institute was 'bearing local costs', and so deserved consideration. Again, he pleaded for the cessation of the argument. Keller responded: 'You must not forget that from my point of view, this whole correspondence (which you started) centres on my defence of C[ontroller of] Mus[ic] ... Personally (as distinct from departmentally), I happened not to be concerned in this matter at all.'

Though he was quick to defend Glock from criticism, Keller was also quick to attack him on matters of principle. In the autumn of 1962 he was urging Newby to broadcast a Gershwin musical on the Third, and was trying to persuade Glock to include Gershwin preludes and piano arrangements of his songs in a Thursday Invitation Concert. When Glock refused, Keller wrote:

On an issue of this kind (which is not without its mythical aspects), it is essential that musical realism should be conscientiously retained. Towards this purpose, may I submit these factual questions:

1 Which of the preludes and/or piano arrangements were known to any of those who rejected the idea?
2 What, in hard musical words, were the reasons for rejection?
3 Why did you support a major Gershwin operation for Third Programme three years ago but do not feel like accepting a comparatively minor one now?
4 Why is jazz in a T[hursday] I[nvitation] C[oncert] – as you once said – possible, and Gershwin impossible?

I think my questions deserve an answer *sine ira*.[7]

More consistent opposition to Glock came from Robert Simpson. In 1969, after the première of Maxwell Davies's *Worldes Blis* had caused a mass walk-out and booing at the Proms, and had greatly over-run its

---

[7] Without anger.

estimated performance time, Simpson exploded to Glock:

> What kind of composer is it that can miscalculate the length of his own
> work by some 45%? The curious thing about such a piece is that whereas
> the composer proclaims his anxiety to get away from the past, he succeeds
> only in producing an almost featureless mass of squashed Schoenberg,
> some of it not far in 'advance' of the more distraught parts of Mahler's
> Ninth. Most of this piece could have been written forty years ago. The
> one minimal point of interest lies in the fact that it is an attempt at
> composition – unlike many of Davies's things. But if you wish (as he
> suggested) to create an impression of incompleteness at the end, you must
> suggest in the music itself that completeness is a possibility, and if you
> are to compose on this scale you must achieve some sense of movement.
> Neither of these conditions was even remotely met, and the shoals of
> people who left the hall were not, I'm convinced, doing so because of the
> 'bizarre effects' mentioned in the South-East News, but because there were
> indeed no effects, bizarre or otherwise. It was pure tedium engendered by
> lack of invention and lack of genuine emotion that drove them out . . .

*

Alexander Goehr says that Glock devoted all his attention to the Proms,
the Invitation Concerts, and the BBC Symphony Orchestra, leaving his
staff to get on with the rest of the programmes without interference:

> There was cheerful, productive anarchy; everyone did what they loved
> best. I was doing orchestral concerts. Leonard Isaacs was the head of
> that section, and I looked after the broadcasts by the non-BBC London
> orchestras. I could put on what I wanted, more or less, and hire the
> conductors I liked. For instance Reginald Goodall had been reduced more
> or less to being a coach at Covent Garden. John Carewe rang me up about
> this, and said, 'He's the only person round here who really understands
> Wagner. Can't you do something?' And I brought the Covent Garden
> orchestra into the studio, and followed the concept of mixed pro-
> gramming. They started with Dukas's overture *Polyeucte*, which is an
> imitation of *Tristan*; then came the *Ascension* by Messaien (the idea that
> Goodall could conduct this was thought remarkable), and after the interval
> was Schumann's Fourth Symphony. The manager of the orchestra tried to
> stop this; he wanted to do the Vaughan Williams *Dona nobis pacem*, with
> Douglas Robinson, the Covent Garden chorus master – or alternatively
> wait for Solti or Britten to conduct them. But it was the beginning of the
> revival of Goodall's career.

This concert was broadcast on 21 December 1961.

Many British composers whose work had been rejected by the pre-Glock
BBC, or had remained unperformed, now began to experience a sense of
liberation. Among these was Elisabeth Lutyens, who received a large
number of BBC commissions during Glock's Controllership, and in conse-

quence at last achieved a secure reputation. In 1963 Anthony Payne in the *Listener* judged that she had 'become a considerable artistic force'.

Though Howard Newby says he got on well with Glock – 'We met socially and there was never the slightest tension between us' – he notes that Glock was not a good administrator of his own department:

> William took the planning of the Proms entirely into his own hands, and he gave them a fresh burst of life; they were marvellous. But unfortunately it took up too much of his time ... He did not effectively communicate with members of his department, and there were extraordinary scenes sometimes at the Third Programme Music Meeting. William never came; he was represented by other senior members of his department. I remember one occasion when I said, when a performance of a particular work was suggested [by a music producer], 'But we're going to have that in the Proms.' And they didn't know!

As to his own managerial style, Newby describes himself as more confident of his own editorial judgement than John Morris had been. But as time passed during his Controllership,

> the offers that came from the speech departments – from Features, in particular; to a lesser extent from Talks Department – withered. They were not sufficiently compelling, even from Drama Department. The Head of Drama would say, 'I know, let's do a new production of *Hamlet*.' And you would say, 'But why? What's new about that?' And there was no good answer other than it was filling space. So as time went by, the amount of speech in the Third naturally diminished, and the amount of music increased.

There were, nevertheless, significant discoveries and achievements in drama during this period. 'An entirely new school of avant-garde dramatists has come into being during the last two years,' wrote a drama producer, Charles Lefaux, to Val Gielgud on 19 November 1959, 'but our listeners have not yet been given an opportunity of judging this kind of dramatic work for themselves, except for the plays of Samuel Beckett.' He sent Gielgud two examples, both by N. F. Simpson: *A Resounding Tinkle*, which had won a prize in an *Observer* competition, and *The Hole*, which Kenneth Tynan had praised when it was staged at the Royal Court. Both plays, which had far more in common with Ionesco and the Goons than Beckett, had in fact already been turned down by the BBC, but when Newby read *A Resounding Tinkle* he decided that the Third should broadcast it, which it did on 20 July 1960. Meanwhile he was, for the second time, commissioning a script from Harold Pinter.

That name had first been heard in Broadcasting House in 1950. The son of a tailor in the East End, Pinter had shown promise as an actor when a Hackney schoolboy, and had managed to get a London County Council scholarship to the Royal Academy of Dramatic Art. But he disliked RADA, and left after two terms. In 1950, at the age of twenty, he was trying to

get work as an actor. The Features producer R. D. ('Reggie') Smith, who
had been on the committee which awarded Pinter his scholarship to
RADA, gave him a list of BBC staff who might be willing to employ him,
and Pinter wrote to all of them, in handwriting which veered between
copperplate and a childlike ball-and-stick. The BBC habitually misread his
signature. 'Dear Mr Puiter,' wrote Frank Hauser of Drama Department.
'Dear Miss Pinter,' began John Arlott, who was producing a poetry programme. And when he finally obtained an audition, somebody wrote him
down as 'Herbert Pinta'.

It was Reggie Smith himself, always a friend to needy actors (his casting
was said to be done on the basis of people's misfortunes rather than their
talent), who gave Pinter his first BBC job, as a voice in two Home Service
features, *Focus on Football Pools* and *Focus on Libraries*. Pinter did well
enough for Smith to cast him as Abergavenny in Shakespeare's *Henry VIII*,
broadcast on the Third on 14 January 1951. 'I ... hope you found my
performance satisfactory,' Pinter wrote to Smith afterwards. 'I listened
to the recording, and to me, my voice sounded almost unrecognisable.
However, I feel I am beginning to understand what is needed in microphone technique, and working with you has been a most interesting and
valuable experience.' He had now returned to drama school – this time
the Central – but when he auditioned for Features Department later in
January 1951 he did not create a very strong impression. The notes on his
four audition pieces are: '1. Not much attack. 2. Produceable. 3. Not
attractive. 4. Fair.' Under general remarks is written: 'Cockney. Good quiet
approach.' He was sent a standard rejection letter.

Nevertheless the BBC gave him some acting work in the North of
England Home Service, and, while trying to scratch a living in the theatre
during the 1950s, he kept writing doggedly to Smith and other BBC
producers reminding them of his existence. In 1954 he took the stage
name of David Baron. 'I think you must be mad,' Smith told him. 'What
a name to call yourself.' It had little effect. 'A very bleak spring,' Pinter
reported to Smith in May that year.

He had had poems published in a literary journal, but did not think of
writing for the theatre until 1957, when a friend in the Bristol University
drama department asked him for a script at a few days' notice. The result,
The Room, attracted some attention, and Pinter submitted it to the BBC.
Barbara Bray, Drama Department Script Editor, turned it down, but asked
to see anything else he had written. She was sent *The Party*, later retitled
The Birthday Party; she rejected it. A few months later Donald McWhinnie
read a short story by Pinter, *The Examination*. 'I find it a brilliantly compact
piece of writing,' he told Pinter, 'but unfortunately it is too close in style
and feeling to Beckett to make a really successful broadcast in its own
right. This is, of course, a compliment.'

The West End impresario Michael Codron daringly mounted a London
production of *The Birthday Party*, announced for the spring of 1958, and
it was in the wake of this news that the BBC decided to commission a

half-hour radio play from Pinter. He wrote a script called *Something in Common*, of which the first draft would run for an hour. On 21 May 1958, just after *The Birthday Party* had flopped (it ran for only a week), he sent a revised and shortened version of this to McWhinnie. 'The play has come a cropper, as you know,' he wrote. 'What else? The clouds. They are varied, very varied. And all sorts of birds. They come and perch on the window-sill, asking for food! It is touching.'

Something in Common, in which an upper-class husband gradually changes places with the mysterious old match-seller who stands each day in the road outside the house, was read by a young Drama Department producer, Michael Bakewell. 'I think we could do this,' he reported. 'It would make a terrifying yet extremely moving piece of radio. A few speeches need to be tidied up, otherwise I think this would make excellent material for Third Programme.' McWhinnie agreed, adding: 'Pinter is just the sort of writer to whom we should extend our patronage ... I am sure that if we were to do so, we should ... make some contribution to Pinter's development as a writer.' But John Morris, then nearing the end of his time as Controller of the Third, strongly dissented. 'I agree that Pinter writes vivid dialogue,' he commented. 'But this is not enough: dialogue must be about something, & in my opinion this piece is entirely pointless. The comparison with Beckett is false: whether you like or hate his work, or cannot understand it, it is beside the point, since he is a very considerable literary artist, which Pinter is not.'

Morris let McWhinnie refer the matter upwards to Richard Marriott, who did not particularly like the script, but was aware that a general principle was at stake. Simpson's *A Resounding Tinkle* and *The Hole* had just been rejected by the BBC (Newby had not yet rescued the former), and Marriott (writing to Morris) observed of Simpson and Pinter:

> Both these authors ... are writing for an intelligent audience, their work is discussed by intelligent critics and they are part of the contemporary theatre scene. Should this not then be reflected in our Third Programme? I quite take your point about Beckett ... but surely it would be wrong if our Third Programme waited until reputations were established. We have taken some pride in our readiness to be at the front, to experiment, to have failures, etc., and would one not expect the Third Programme to be dealing with the same sort of plays that interest the Royal Court ... ?

Val Gielgud, who did not like Pinter's script either, was of the same mind, arguing that 'whatever the individual opinions might be ... of plays of this kind, pieces which achieve a certain intellectual réclame and are balanced on the razor edge of indecision should in general be given the benefit of the doubt and the chance of presentation on Third Programme'. Morris yielded, and the play, now retitled *A Slight Ache*, was accepted.

It was broadcast on the Third on 29 July 1959, produced by McWhinnie. The castlist in the *Radio Times* gave 'David Baron', Pinter's own stage-name, as the actor playing the mysterious seller of matches, but this character never speaks. Maurice Denham and Vivien Merchant, Pinter's wife, gave outstanding performances as the uptight couple whose barren lives are gradually invaded by their obsession with the match-seller. But the reviewer in the *Listener*, Ian Rodger, was unimpressed, finding himself uncertain what the play was about, and adding: 'no amount of brilliance in dialogue makes up for the dearth of a clear plot'.

A month before *A Slight Ache* was broadcast, Barbara Bray read Pinter's recently completed one-act stage play *The Dumb Waiter*, and told McWhinnie that it could make 'very effective radio'. Meanwhile Pinter was offering other ideas conceived for broadcasting: a synopsis (untitled) about a man subjected to psychological tests in a scientific research establishment, and another, called *A Night Out*, in which an insurance clerk, browbeaten by his mother, turns on the female sex. One of Bray's readers, Bryan Izzard, reported to her of this second proposal:

> Mr Pinter is certainly trying to break new ground here, it is most unlike his previous efforts in having what could be called a very strong story line. Perhaps it is a story line which we have met many times before. I am not entirely happy about it for that reason, but Mr Pinter gives very little clue as to how he intends to treat it. Certainly some fascinating things do arise out of the synopsis ... Let us go ahead and ask for more.

Howard Newby, who had now succeeded Morris as Controller of the Third, saw the synopsis and agreed. 'Please go ahead,' he wrote to Bray on 31 July 1959.

A Night Out was broadcast on the Third on 1 March 1960, with Pinter and Vivien Merchant again in the cast; Barry Foster played the hero and Mary O'Farrell his mother. McWhinnie, who produced, had now been invited to direct Pinter's new stage play *The Caretaker* at the Arts Theatre. 'I am most anxious to be able to accept this invitation,' he wrote to Val Gielgud, 'particularly in view of the fact that the Third Programme has played an active part in bringing Pinter to the attention of the public as one of the most interesting of our younger contemporary dramatists.' Permission was granted.

The Caretaker made Pinter's reputation. BBC Television had turned down *The Dumb Waiter* as 'too obscure', but ITV now snapped up *A Night Out*, in which the BBC had not thought to retain television rights. Fortunately for the Third, Newby had lost no time in commissioning another radio play from Pinter, who chose to adapt his unpublished novel *The Dwarfs*, which he had already shown to Barbara Bray in typescript. Newby read this new Pinter text in October 1960. 'I think I can see what he is up to,' he assured Val Gielgud, who had expressed doubts about it.

> Perhaps [continued Newby] one should judge it less as a play than as a poem. It does then, I think, take its place naturally in a certain sequence of existentialist and quasi-religious statements. Its concern is whether or not the world is meaningful. Or is meaning simply an attribute of habit?

We have all experienced the phenomenon of saying a word over and over again until it becomes strange. As I understand it Len is hovering on the edge of this meaningless world ... where he tries to take a grip of himself by naming chairs and tables. But worse is to follow. He becomes unsure of his own relationship to the external world and as Pete says ... falls prey to a flux of sensation. He can only perceive; he cannot form concepts. This terrifying regression to the world of a newly-born infant (who doesn't know which is his own toe and which the corner of the sheet) is an extreme form of not knowing. At this stage the Freudian analysis turns into medieval story; mystical accounts of the so-called 'dark night of the soul' sometimes tell of devils. In this case the devils are dwarfs and they are shown not so much as malign beings but rather people who *know*. The 'horror' and 'disgust' passages can be paralleled in mystical writings.

Another account of the play would be to say it is an account of Len's mental breakdown and restoration to health in a mental hospital. There is such quasi-religious complexity in the text that I don't think this would be an adequate account. From one point of view Len is Christ on the Cross ('They make a hole in my side'). He says 'I've lost a kingdom'. But I don't think you can reduce the text to any single meaning. There are some very funny lines, I thought. Of one thing I am sure: it is deeply serious writing and I've no doubt we should try to give it as effective a production as possible. I have not discussed this with Mrs Bray because I thought you would like my own unguided response.

Despite this brilliant analysis of the play, Gielgud replied that he still found it 'incomprehensible'. Moreover there were 'several passages in it which I feel should in no circumstances be broadcast at all'. He argued that an author's reputation should not be an excuse for the BBC to 'abdicate our critical and editorial function' (as if Newby had done any such thing), and suggested that once again the matter be referred to Richard Marriott for arbitration. But Newby would not budge. 'I believe *The Dwarfs* to be a seriously considered piece of writing and my reason for asking you to carry on with the production is based on that judgement,' he told Gielgud, adding:

> You will remember that our commissioning of this play has been pub-licised in our [quarterly] pamphlet and in *The Times*. Our suppression of the play would bring it under close scrutiny from the outside world and I do not think any claim that the play is incomprehensible is going to carry much weight. I am naturally concerned about this because the good repute of the Third Programme is in question.

McWhinnie had now left the BBC to work full time in the theatre; he was replaced as Assistant Head of Drama (Sound) by Martin Esslin, an expert on Brecht. Gielgud responded to Newby that no one but McWhin-nie would be capable of producing *The Dwarfs*, so Newby offered to bring him back at the Third's expense. However, Gielgud gave the task to Barbara

Bray, and the production was heard on 2 December 1960.

For a little while longer, the Third provided Pinter with a useful platform. He adapted *The Caretaker* and his television play *The Collection* for it (they were broadcast on 20 March and 12 June 1962), and his short story *The Examination*, previously rejected by McWhinnie, was heard on 7 September that year. But the theatre, and the cinema, were soon taking up all his time.

The failure of radio to retain its hold on those it had nurtured did not surprise Louis MacNeice, who was still on the staff of Features. For some time, he had taken a dejected view of the medium's future, while still valuing it for what it could do. It was a while since he had created any of his best work for the Third, and when Newby became Controller he took MacNeice out to lunch at the Zoo and encouraged him to write something that would be the equal of *The Dark Tower*. MacNeice was not in good shape; his second marriage was deteriorating, and he was drinking heavily. At first, nothing came of Newby's encouragement, though during 1960 MacNeice and a junior producer in Features, Anthony Thwaite (also a poet), organised a new series of translations from the *Odyssey* by contemporary poets, including MacNeice and Thwaite themselves, and Ted Hughes. They were broadcast on the Third on twelve successive Thursdays from 6 October.

Thwaite says that, where such programmes were concerned, 'there was no puritanical nonsense about budgeting: one was encouraged to go for excellence. When Richard Hoggart introduced a selection of D. H. Lawrence poems, I hired Albert Finney (who was excellent) as the reader; when E. J. Scovell rather wistfully said she admired Peggy Ashcroft as a verse-reader, I hired P. A. to read Scovell's poems.'

MacNeice also offered Newby an Arthurian project, *The Remorse of Sir Gawaine*, but this was turned down. Then in September 1961 he submitted the outline of a new quest-story for radio:

> The programme will be entitled *The Mad Islands* and would be based upon various Irish legends dealing with strange adventures in the western seas ... I would like to make the thing timeless ... The hero visits a succession of unknown islands which are so peculiar that they can symbolise almost anything one wants. I might, of course, invent some brand-new islands ...

He did. In *The Mad Islands*, broadcast on the Third on 4 April 1962, the hero, Muldoon, who is searching for his father's killer, comes to the Island of the Rival Beds, in which two Welsh witches, Olwen and Branwen, vie with each other to make love to any man who crosses their threshold – and then turn him into one of their household cats. MacNeice was probably alluding to his own situation not long before the script was written, when he was torn between his wife, Hedli, and the radio actress Mary Wimbush. By the time the play was broadcast, he had chosen Wimbush, and had also gone freelance, leaving the safety of a BBC salary.

In the summer of 1963 he wrote another quest-script for the Third, *Persons from Porlock*, the equally autobiographical story of a painter who fails to achieve his full potential because of the distractions of life, and eventually dies in a pot-holing accident. MacNeice chose to accompany a BBC engineer down a Yorkshire pot-hole to record sound-effects for this scene. He got wet, caught a chill, developed pneumonia, and died on 3 September 1963, a few days after *Persons from Porlock* had been broadcast. The Features Department, which had made his and so much other radio writing possible, only survived him by a few months, being disbanded during 1964 as part of the BBC's continuing efforts to accommodate itself to the age of television. Its demise further deprived the Third of imaginative speech.

Two other Third Programme playwrights came to grief during the 1960s. Giles Cooper, though writing prolifically for television, was still supplying the Third with scripts, though none of them had equalled the imaginative achievement of *Unman, Wittering and Zigo*. One night in December 1966, returning to his Sussex home after a London dinner, he got to his feet in the train compartment, opened an exterior door, and fell out. The coroner's verdict was death by misadventure, but his sister-in-law Nest Cleverdon is sure it was suicide.

Henry Reed, meanwhile, had reached the end of the Hilda Tablet saga. The story had really been wound up in *The Primal Scene, As It Were ...*, and the final play in the series, *Not a Drum was Heard: the war memoirs of General Gland* (6 June 1959) was a rather sub-standard offering, though there was a memorable performance by Marjorie Westbury as the General's mad sister. Reed created one other programme in the series, *Musique Discrete*, not a play but a recital of music by Hilda (27 October 1959). Donald Swann wrote some amusing parodies of current musical fashions, and Derek Jacobi played the gushing music critic Angel Bish, but the satire was gentler than the Piotr Zak hoax.

After the conclusion of the Tablet saga, Reed contributed a few translations to the Third, but his output soon dwindled to almost nothing. Literary editors would send him books to review, and he would talk about them entrancingly to friends, but he seldom managed to commit anything to paper. In July 1971, Newby had dinner with him and suggested he should give a talk on the Third to mark P. G. Wodehouse's ninetieth birthday. Reed accepted, and *Wodehouse at Ninety* was billed in the *Radio Times* for Friday 15 October. Alan Haydock, the producer, takes up the story in a memo to Newby:

We had arranged weeks ago that he would record on Monday, October 11th. He telephoned on that day to say that the talk wasn't ready and to ask if he could do it later in the week. A studio was booked for the Friday afternoon. On Friday morning he telephoned again. He was obviously overwrought. He asked if he could do the broadcast live. I thought this was inadvisable and suggested we record at six that evening ... Mr Reed

arrived at 6 pm and was clearly unwell and unsteady on his feet. He had
written only one and a half foolscap pages of script and proposed to
improvise the rest, bringing in substantial extracts from the Wodehouse
books he had brought with him. We attempted to record but it was very
soon apparent that there was no possibility of getting an acceptable talk
from him that evening. I explained to him that we did have a stand-by
programme ready ... I listened for some time to his confused account of
his creative problems which seemed to me genuine and deserving of
sympathy ...

The Hilda Tablet plays were published that year, and continued to be
repeated on the air at frequent intervals, but Reed's writing career was
over. Hard-up in his final days, he died in 1986 at the age of seventy-two.
In an obituary, Richard Boston judged Hilda Tablet, Herbert Reeve, General
Gland and the others to be characters 'rivalled in our times only by those
of Beachcomber'.

*

In *Not a Drum Was Heard*, Gland deludes himself that the BBC interviewers
who have come to record his memoirs are actually there to offer him the
post of 'Controller-General' – a reference to the impending retirement of
Sir Ian Jacob. When he left the BBC in 1960, the choice of successor as
Director-General fell upon Hugh Carleton Greene, Director of News and
Current Affairs. From then on, news began to play an increasingly large
part in the BBC's output, and by August 1963 it was mooted that even the
news-less Third should carry at least one bulletin every day.

Frank Gillard, who had succeeded Lindsay Wellington as Director of
Sound Broadcasting, discussed the idea with Newby. 'He begs us not to
force a mid-evening bulletin on him,' Gillard noted, 'but is keen to take
on a late-night news programme ... under such title as *The World Today*,
at the end of his evening transmission.' Newby wanted an open-ended
programme in which the BBC's foreign correspondents and other experts
could discuss significant world events. But this request was not granted;
instead, it was decided that the Third would close with a fifteen-minute
news bulletin each night. It was intended that this should contain only
'significant news', excluding those 'human interest' stories which would
not appeal to 'a serious-minded citizen'. Special attention was to be given
to 'science, education and foreign news', and to 'obituaries of writers,
artists and other specialist celebrities'. The BBC's Diplomatic Correspondent, Thomas Barman, felt that there should be emphasis on 'the
whole of that vast area that links politics with economics; e.g. the
Common Market, EFTA, the IMF, GATT, Comecon, etc. etc. On these topics
the Third Programme would have the field largely to itself, since only the
Financial Times does full justice to them, with *The Times* and some quality
provincials, bad seconds.'

The first bulletin was broadcast at 11 pm on Monday 14 October 1963.
By the end of a month, Newby felt it was

becoming a magazine with, it must be confessed, some not very significant contributions from outsiders. Last night, for example, we heard Sir Denis Brogan talking for just under three minutes about Thomas Paine. This was à propos the putting up of a statue to Paine in Thetford. The occasion was, I should have thought, of marginal news interest and certainly what Sir Denis said could scarcely have been illuminating to a Third Programme audience. The thought that a reporter had been sent to Cambridge specially to get it is a bit damping.

Were we right to give as much space as we did to the obituary on Adolphe Menjou? And once again the rather pious piece about the Red Cross running to nearly two minutes at the end of the bulletin seemed of little interest or importance to me.

There were interesting news happenings in Europe yesterday of which we heard nothing. Two that come to mind are the 35th congress of Left-Wing Socialists in Italy, a congress which authorised its leader Nenni to participate in a centre-left government, and secondly, it seems that a quite important decision was taken at the Vatican Council. Could we in fact make a greater effort to get more significant European news?

A month later, Gillard expressed displeasure to Newby that the news had started a few minutes late on several occasions. 'I take the view that this bulletin should be broadcast at 11 pm precisely,' he wrote, 'except when we are subject to circumstances entirely beyond our control.' This meant abandoning Haley's principle, on which the Third had been founded, of 'no fixed points'. Newby replied at length to Gillard's demand:

We have, to date, broadcast 43 bulletins in Third: of these six have been planned to start after 11. Had these late starts not been allowed it would have been impossible to maintain the system of planned repeats of productions which is an important feature of Third Programme. A good example of this occurs this evening. Rhys Adrian's play *A Nice Clean Sheet of Paper* begins immediately the Invitation Concert ends and runs to 11.05. There is no other place I could have put this repeat during the week. The particular evening to which [Gillard] draws attention ... was a planned over-run: I could have secured an 11 pm News by asking for a five minute cut in the second broadcast of *Verlaine in England* or reducing the amount of time given to *Interpretations on Record* which had been placed at 45 minutes because, before planning it, we judged that this was the ideal length ...

My reason for earnestly hoping that [Gillard] will reconsider his decision is ... that it will damage the Programme itself. The basic problem is that all items ... are designed ... not to fill a pre-ordained space ... The important question is 'what is the optimum duration for this particular broadcast?' ... A strict 11 pm guillotine will introduce a rule into this game that will make it terribly hard to play ... A nudge in the direction of 'space-filling' would, I am convinced, diminish the variety not only of Third Programme but ... of radio as a whole.

Gillard did not give way, and though in practice the bulletin often started a little late, Newby's freedom of planning, with only three hours at his disposal each evening, was indeed further restricted. A note about the Third in the *Radio Times* (26 September 1963) stated, with no evidence of irony: 'It is in the nature of the Third Programme that it should have fewer fixed points than the other services.'

*

Newby was determined to maintain the linked series of music and speech programmes which had been such a distinctive feature of the Third. 'I completely failed to get off the ground,' he recalls, 'a whole series on the contribution of Judaism to the contemporary world ... Hans Keller ... was very much in favour of it. But two other Jews were totally against it – they thought that, since it was based on racial considerations, it should not take place.' No such objections were raised to *The Negro in America*, a series broadcast in the autumn of 1964 to mark the passing of the Civil Rights Bill in the USA. Designed to give 'a coherent picture of the main events in the struggle for integration during the last ten years', and jointly edited by the black American poet Langston Hughes and D. G. Bridson, it included programmes of black music, a discussion about current black writing, and several relevant plays, recorded by American casts. The success of this led to Bridson masterminding *America Since the Bomb*, twenty programmes broadcast in the last quarter of 1966, surveying the American way of life in the nuclear age.

Unlike his predecessors, Newby tried to allocate regular weekly or monthly days and times to broadcasts which formed part of a series. *Comment*, the Third's review of the arts, found a permanent home on Thursday nights in the interval of the Invitation Concert. Philip French recalls that it had started in 1955 almost by accident:

> It was decided at the beginning of the Third that there wouldn't be any regular magazine programmes – 'We're not going to have spaces to be filled'. Even series like *Law in Action* had always to be up to the standard of something that would be published in a law journal, otherwise the programme would be dropped for the time being. But in 1955 there was a national newspaper strike, and it was decided to have a programme to perform a service that had been lost – to provide theatre and arts reviews. So *Comment* began, and David Sylvester and Robert Kee were brought in as 'advisers' for it, but it was just a staff announcer introducing the pieces, which were written scripts commissioned from the people whose newspaper columns were in abeyance. But it kept going after the strike was over, and then George MacBeth came to run it, and in 1961 it became *New Comment*, and had interviews. In fact it was the beginning of topical interviews on the Third.

With the arrival of *New Comment*, the *Radio Times* (which had never supplied advance details of *Comment*) was able to announce that, for instance, Christopher Isherwood would be heard in conversation with his old collaborator on the Mortmere stories, Edward Upward (21 June 1961), that Ted Hughes had been recorded at the Mermaid Theatre's poetry festival (26 July), that Peter Cook would be talking about satirical cabaret 'in his night club The Establishment' (9 August), and that L. S. Lowry was to be interviewed by Tom Rosenthal (8 November). Anthony Thwaite, who was responsible for organising these interviews, recalls that the novelist Richard Hughes was 'the most taciturn fellow I have ever had professional dealings with – he took hours, so it seemed, to say either "yes" or, more frequently, "no"'.

George MacBeth, editor–presenter of *New Comment*, was a dull broad-caster but a colourful individual who wielded extensive power. At Oxford he had done his best to be a 'character', dressing in spats. Arriving at the BBC he was for a time an inconspicuous junior producer at Bush House, and then, as Anthony Thwaite puts it, 'suddenly seemed to establish himself as the central figure in the broadcasting of poetry'. Philip French gives a sketch of him:

> George always wore a three-piece suit. He was one of the people I had in mind when I once said that the Third Programme was run by bohemians disguised as civil servants, whereas the BBC nowadays is run by civil servants disguised as bohemians. George looked like a civil servant, or a classics don, which he could have been, because he was a brilliant classics scholar as well as a very gifted poet.
>
> He was also fascinated with evil and perversity, with the Bomb, Samurai swords, polymorphous sexual activities, dangerous games such as bull-fighting, and the Gestapo. He was definitely attracted by fascism. Yet he encouraged the Beat Poets, or their equivalent in England, and performed himself at Sixties poetry 'happenings'. He had a great desire to *épater les bourgeois*, while remaining tremendously cool, both in his demeanour and writing, which was very controlled.

The danger of any one individual being given authority in this area had been recognised by Patric Dickinson, the Third's original poetry editor. 'Wherever there is a single judgement,' Dickinson had written to George Barnes in the spring of 1946, 'there is bound to be prejudice and limitations of taste.' The 1950 experiment of putting editorial decisions about poetry in the hands of Oxford dons (Bryson, Cecil and Coghill) had been aban-doned after a few months, but in 1957 an internal BBC Poetry Committee had been set up to oversee programmes. Its original members included D. G. Bridson, Rayner Heppenstall, Louis MacNeice, Howard Newby and Terence Tiller. 'I think that this Committee will prove sufficiently catholic to ensure fair representation of all contemporary poetry whose work is suitable to broadcast performance,' wrote Bridson before the first meeting. After Newby became Controller of the Third, George MacBeth replaced him on the Committee. 'Mr Gittings[8] asked if the Poetry Committee was keeping itself informed of the progress made by John Wain in the writing of his long poem,' reads a typical minute, on 8 February 1963. 'He said that Mr Wain always turned up at the pub next to Moss Bros on Tuesdays with poetry in his pockets.' In other words, the commissioning of poetry broadcasts required a good deal of inside knowledge; and George MacBeth certainly had that.

He had published the first collection of his own poetry, *A Form of Words*, in 1954 when he was still an undergraduate. 'The important thing,' he once said, 'is to thrust out huge quantities of fairly well-written poetry. If it doesn't last, who cares?' This policy might have doomed him to obscurity if he had not enjoyed the support of 'The Group', a circle of writers who had come together at Oxford, and met once a week in London to read and discuss members' work in progress. In the satirical pamphlet *Bluff Your Way in Literature* (1966), Martin Seymour-Smith gives this scathing portrait of them:

> THE GROUP, OR THE POETRY WORKSHOP, OR TEDDY'S FRIDAYS
> If you write verse, you can get in on this ... The Group is a loose conglomeration of not promising versifiers who meet every Friday night, 'in somebody's congenial flat', 'without drink to distract us' ... The Group's two founders and leading spirits [are] Philip Hobsbaum and Edward ('Teddy') Lucie-Smith ... The leading lights in it are ... Peter Porter, an Australian poet who writes about anything that takes his fancy and is an advertising copywriter, George MacBeth, a BBC employee who writes about concentration camps and nasty relatives (do not quarrel with this man: he edits much of the verse that goes out on the Third Programme), and Alan Brownjohn, who is a clean and often distinguished poet ...

Seymour-Smith also wrote, under the heading THE BBC LUCIE POETS: 'This phrase ... is a vague term, and can be used to cover any poet who has his verse broadcast regularly on George MacBeth's *New Poetry* on the Third Programme. Some obvious BBC Lucie Poets are Edward Lucie-Smith, Peter Porter, Anthony Thwaite ... Alan Brownjohn ... B. S. Johnson ... and ... MacBeth himself. It is unsafe to say anything direct about these poets ... Do not run them down on any account.'

Philip French agrees that MacBeth was 'very much part of the Group, and he put them on the air a great deal, but I don't know of any really distinguished poets that he kept off the air. He had Basil Bunting reading Wordsworth, Betjeman reading Tennyson, and Larkin broadcasting on a number of occasions.' Nevertheless a typical edition of MacBeth's *New Poetry* tended to feature at least a couple of the poets listed by Seymour-Smith, and on one occasion (8 December 1961) MacBeth devoted an entire twenty-five-minute edition to his own poems. Twice (23 August 1963 and

---

[8] Robert Gittings, poet and biographer, then working for the BBC.

18 February 1964) he took an outside broadcast van to Lucie-Smith's home in Chelsea, so that the Friday evening meeting of the Group could be relayed live on the Third.

On the other hand, as French says, he was in touch with Sixties trends. On 9 January 1960, long before such things became common, Jack Kerouac read his poems on the Third to a jazz accompaniment, and there were further broadcasts by the Beat Poets. The Third's microphones were at the Royal Albert Hall in June 1965 when Allen Ginsberg opened a poetry festival by intoning his poems to a pair of Tibetan prayer cymbals, and the following year recordings were made at the Nottingham Poetry Festival, when Adrian Mitchell and Brian Patten were among the stars. MacBeth also campaigned on behalf of Ted Hughes, whose short story *Sunday* was turned down by Newby in 1960 because it described cruelty to a rat. 'I'd be happy to try again,' MacBeth wrote to Hughes, 'if you care to let me see the others you spoke about.'

MacBeth's obituarist in *The Times* judges him to have been 'the single most influential official in the field of British poetry since T. S. Eliot' – influential, that is, not as a poet but a dispenser of patronage. Within the BBC there were unsuccessful attempts to reduce his power. Newby tried for some time to have him taken off *New Comment*, in view of his 'lack of distinction as a broadcaster', and offered the money to pay an outside presenter. But the memo cited 'MacBeth's temperamental unwillingness to share the responsibility for the programme', and not until 1964 did Philip French take over (presenting as well as producing, despite a marked stammer). Meanwhile MacBeth continued to introduce poetry programmes, and as late as 1972 Newby's successor, Stephen Hearst, was trying to unseat him from these. He clung on for a further four years, after which he left the BBC and slipped into relative obscurity, though his 1991 novel *Another Love Story*, which appeared a year before his death from motor neurone disease, attracted critics' mockery for its self-pitying portrait of the break-up of his second marriage, to the writer Lisa St Aubin de Teran.

MacBeth's programmes, though cliquey, could not raise the sneer, often levelled at the Third, of 'dons talking to dons'. Yet even in the mid-1960s much of the Third's output was still exactly that. Ved Mehta's 1963 *New Yorker* article on the Third was largely devoted to *Dunford Dialogues*, of which the second series was then being recorded. The programme's presenter, Renford Bambrough of St John's College, Cambridge, told Mehta how the series had originated:

David Edge [a talks producer], on one of his talent-scout visits to our Senior Common Room, asked me what I thought of the Third's philosophical offerings. I said that they seemed to be so careful and scripted that they left an impression of artificiality ... After some discussion, Edge and I arrived at a scheme for gathering – for a few days each year – a number of thinkers in a country house and catching their words and thoughts on a tape recorder. For a first general topic, we settled upon 'The Brain', and decided to ask some philosophers and scientists to come out to Richard Cobden's estate, in Dunford, to talk about it. Our first assembly, in the spring of 1961, yielded a rich harvest – twelve hours of tape. In subsequent months, Edge edited the script and recordings down to four forty-five-minute *Dunford Dialogues*. They came over the Third like a charm.

Mehta went to Dunford House in Sussex, where Cobden, apostle of free trade, had lived a century earlier. He watched the new series being recorded: 'In the library and the drawing-room, where the philosophers and theologians reclined in easy chairs and talked, and in a side room, where the BBC engineers were stationed, the mood was one of gentility and dispassioned thinking.' The participants included Donald MacKinnon and John Wisdom, both Cambridge philosophers. As MacKinnon talked, 'he continuously sharpened pencils with a razor blade; he carried a supply of blades in his pocket, and the pencils, thanks to the BBC, awaited him wherever he turned. He often inadvertently dropped a used blade on the floor and Edge picked up after him as inconspicuously as possible.'[9] In contrast with MacKinnon's 'booming voice', Wisdom was retiring and taciturn, and when the after-dinner recording began he said little at first; but gradually 'his voice, not much louder than a whisper, mesmerised all. Though his halting sentences came across like so many raps on a door of knowledge, his words ... suggested those of a medium more than those of a professor.' The participants 'talked on into the night', while Edge 'took notes, marking the knotted and smooth passages in order to shape and polish the broadcast on the BBC's anvil'.

Dunford Dialogues were certainly an improvement on the scripted conversations of the Russell–Copleston era, but they were still stilted and self-conscious, and singularly uninformative to the layman. Bernard Williams, who took part in another philosophy series on the Third, a series of discussions, chaired by Stuart Hampshire, on *Equality* (beginning on 25 November 1961), says he was told that he should speak as if he were addressing fellow philosophers, rather than talk to a lay audience. Williams also recalls, after a philosophy broadcast on the Third, one of the BBC staff joking unconcernedly about the smallness of the audience: 'He said it would probably have been cheaper to have telephoned each of the listeners individually!'

The Third was doing its best to keep up with the times. One of the *Dunford Dialogues* was about the effects on the mind of the drug LSD. Yet it still had a reputation for lofty exclusivity. On 10 June 1961 the *Guardian*

---

[9] MacKinnon had had this habit since teaching at Keble College, Oxford (where he lived on the top floor of the Warden's Lodgings; the present writer was then a small boy living downstairs).

printed this squib: 'Overheard at a BBC Third Programme publicity reception: "But why on earth does the Third Programme *need* publicity? Mightn't it attract the wrong type of audience?"'

CHAPTER TWO

An almost continuous service
of good music

B y the beginning of 1959 the BBC was beginning to realise that
Network Three had been a mistake. Marriott, writing to Wellington,
claimed that it had 'almost doubled the audience of Third Programme a year before'; but Wellington, replying, quoted an Audience
Research survey which had reported that the average Third audience was
'consistently bigger' than those for Network Three, which was also getting
a bad press. The hobbies magazines took some interest in it – demanding
more airtime for their particular hobby – but Fleet Street columnists
mocked it. Tom Driberg in the *New Statesman* called it 'an unobtrusively
worthy little miscellany', but added: 'I do not myself know anybody who
listens to it.' A correspondent in *The Times* described it as 'invertebrate',
while Robert Robinson wrote of its language programmes in the *Sunday
Times*: 'The people in the Spanish lesson (so nice they might be made out
of cake), preparing to meet Spaniards who will turn out to be Spanish
but not too Spanish, they are my favourites. Then the "experts" on sex,
so jolly and unaffected, it's hard to believe they're not talking about
fretwork.'

In September 1958, a year after the inauguration of Network Three, the
BBC announced that the *Younger Generation* programme which contained
the sex-talks would be dropped. Five months later, Marriott wrote to
Wellington: 'The present Network Three audience ... size is beginning to
worry us.' Rayner Heppenstall puts it bluntly in his memoirs: 'The non-
highbrow-minority idea didn't work. Ideas cooked up by administrators
don't work.'

Marriott proposed that Network Three programmes be dropped on
Saturday afternoons. But what should be put in their place? 'Before we
give up entirely,' he wrote to Wellington on 21 April 1959,

> it might be worth trying something different and one possibility that
> suggests itself is to give a long programme of good music of the classical
> repertoire such as the *Music of the Masters* series previously broadcast in
> the Home Service ... This would mean ... an extension of broadcasting
> hours ... and also the use of the third network for something which was

neither Network Three nor the Third Programme. This is not necessarily impossible ...

Wellington liked the idea: 'I favour ... putting out a music programme on Network Three on Saturday afternoons. It is a sensible expansion of broadcasting, and the money can be found.'

They chewed over the idea during the spring and summer of 1959, and brought Rooney Pelletier, now styled Controller, Programme Planning (Sound), into the discussions. He began to feel that the Saturday afternoon music programme would appeal to a different sort of audience from the old-style Third Programme listener. On 21 July he wrote:

Objective: To please people who 'like music' but don't pretend they possess a musical education – people who already know quite a bit of the so-called 'familiar' repertoire of good music and are pleased to hear this repertoire in excellent performances ... For most, these programmes will serve as an accompaniment to some sort of Saturday afternoon occupation; work in the kitchen or nursery, sewing, woodwork, gardening, tinkering with the car, even letter-writing. The music will not interrupt the flow of activities within the home – it will become part of it ... The 'brow' is somewhere between the best of light music and the most popular Promenade Concerts.

Pelletier felt that the experiment required more than a ninety-minute *Music of the Masters*, which 'just isn't compelling enough, either in billing or in length'. He suggested that the three hours (2 to 5 pm) should be allocated to different items. The afternoon could start with a piano recital, after which there could be a repeat of some other music programme, before *Music of the Masters* began at 3.30.

Meanwhile a listener had pointed out to the BBC that the amount of serious music on day-time radio[1] had declined during 1959 by about twenty per cent. 'I checked this,' Marriott noted after seeing the letter,

and found him to be roughly accurate ... So far from reducing the amount of music in the day-time, I think it ought to be our tendency to move in the other direction and I wonder if we have given enough thought to this. We know, of course, that good music is no audience builder and that music lovers are a very favoured minority. We accept this situation in the evening; are we doing as much as we can in the day-time?

At the beginning of 1959 Marriott had convened a committee of senior BBC programme planners to consider the possibility of area and local broadcasting on FM. Its report, delivered in September that year, also considered the future of the three national radio networks, and urged that these should be 'used to their full capacity by providing three separate

---

[1] It perhaps needs to be emphasised that the Third Programme did not broadcast during the day (except on Sunday afternoon). This decline refers to the Home Service and Light Programme.

programmes throughout the daytime and evening; otherwise, it was feared, commercial radio (which had not yet begun in Britain, but was certain to do so) might move into any gaps, laying claim to BBC frequencies while they were lying idle. As things stood, 'the unused time on the Third Network was a standing invitation for a take-over bid by commercial operators and ... it was essential to close the door'.

The report recommended that the Third's frequencies should carry

> throughout the daytime an almost continuous service of good music, except on weekdays during term time for Schools broadcasts and at weekends for some of the programmes at present carried by Network Three, which could be so labelled if desired. In the evening from 6 pm to midnight it could continue to carry all that is at present broadcast in the Third Programme, together with some additional good music and a number of programmes likely to appeal to all intelligent and educated people with a wide general interest in contemporary affairs.

Looking for models for this 'almost continuous service of good music', BBC management, early in 1960, scrutinised two Canadian radio stations which were already providing this: CKVL Montreal, which 'though known as a "good music station" ... clearly transmits great quantities of music which we would label "light"', and CFRA Ottawa, whose programmes included everything 'from prom type orchestral to salon music, pops, jazz and even a Saturday night dance party'. The BBC had different ideas. In May 1960 Peter Gould of Music Division submitted a scheme which would provide programmes of serious music from 7 am until the Third began at 8 pm. It included a series to be called *This Week's Composer*, a mid-morning miscellany, a midday orchestral concert, and a teatime *Music in the Evening*.

It was decided that such a scheme – which would depend upon the consent of the Government to the extension of broadcasting hours, and of the gramophone companies and the Musicians' Union to the increased use of gramophone records – should be introduced by stages. Phase I would consist of daytime music broadcasts on Saturdays and Sundays only. Phase II would extend them to weekdays. Marriott did not expect things to move fast – 'it may be a long time before [the music network] applies to anything more than weekends,' he wrote in November 1960.

Meanwhile the Saturday afternoon music broadcast on Network Three, envisaged since the spring of 1959, began on 8 October 1960. It consisted of a two-hour *Music of the Masters* (2.30 to 4.30), given each week by one of the BBC's house orchestras, with a chamber music duo providing a contrast in the middle. On alternate Saturday mornings from 10.15 to 11.15 the network also carried *Stereophony*, a programme of stereo gramophone records. Listeners wishing to hear both channels had to place their radio receivers near their television sets, for the right-hand channel was carried on BBC TV sound and the left on Network Three.

As another experiment, four hours of 'good' music – mostly recorded repeats – were broadcast on Network Three on two afternoons during

Christmas (26 and 27 December 1960). This was judged a success. 'I thought that the selection of music was admirable,' wrote Marriott on 2 January 1961, 'and if we could keep up anything like this standard for our Third Network music service when it comes we should not do badly.'

During 1960 the Government had convened a committee to make recommendations on the future of British broadcasting, under the chairmanship of Sir Harry Pilkington, and in February 1961 the BBC submitted to it the proposal of using the Third's frequencies in the daytime and early evening for 'programmes of serious music'. Meanwhile William Glock, who had become Controller of Music after the scheme had begun to take root in the BBC's collective mind, was privately dubious about it: 'I didn't like it. Because I didn't like the idea of a continuous stream of music, with people only half, or a quarter, listening to it.' He thought there was some truth in Benjamin Britten's assertion that the loudspeaker is an enemy of music, and that great works should only be heard on appropriate occasions; also in Auden's observation that in a consumer society things are heard and then forgotten. Glock foresaw the 'danger of musical wallpaper'. Yet he could also perceive that 'it gave radio a chance [of] an entirely new kind of programme'.

The Pilkington committee reported in June 1962, noting the BBC's music scheme, and concluding that 'on balance' the case for an extension of radio hours for this purpose had been made. But the Musicians' Union was now blocking the BBC's attempt to negotiate more 'needletime' (broadcasting of gramophone records), which was essential to 'the new Music Programme' as the venture was now being called informally. No less than four phases were now planned for its introduction. 'But as the weeks pass,' Glock wrote to Lindsay Wellington on 26 November 1962,

> and as the M.U. maintain their objections and look like pushing back the first two phases further than we had foreseen, I've had time to become more and more convinced that we should launch the whole scheme at one blow, and not sidle into it step by step. If we could set ourselves to begin perhaps on January 1st, 1964, prepare for it thoroughly, and make it an anxiously awaited event, I believe this new programme could have a tremendous impact . . .

February 1963 had been chosen for the introduction of Phase I, now planned as Sunday daytime only, but when that month came there was still no agreement over needletime. 'The Union say that there is not the slightest prospect of their agreeing to anything approaching the 47 hours a week additional time needed by the Corporation,' noted a Programme Contracts official. 'They reasserted their view that the entire plan for an extension of sound broadcasting should be dropped in spite of the fact that it would mean a very substantial increase in the amount of employment available to their members.'

Meanwhile Glock, assisted by Gerald Abraham who had rejoined the BBC in 1962 as Glock's deputy, had prepared a report on the Corporation's music policy, which (making no mention of Glock's private doubts) looked forward to the 'tremendous challenge' of the Music Programme, and promised adventurous planning:

> We shall have to consider the special problems of broadcasting to a daytime audience – for there will be many listeners who are unable to give the concentrated attention that they would naturally bring to evening programmes; and this will mean avoiding (during the morning at least) music perhaps which makes a violent physical impact, or whose procedures are unfamiliar, or whose expressive intentions are not yet generally understood.
>
> Nevertheless we intend to plan this vast new network with the same aspirations that we try to bring to our present output. As may be imagined, a magnificent range of music will be open to us; we shall be able to explore the repertory more completely than ever before. At the same time, the very magnitude of this new programme will mean that if, once again, we are to try to ensure that 'the promise (as we hope) of the printed page is translated into actual experience', then we shall quite certainly have to enlist the help not only of every talented artist we can find, but also of gramophone records. Otherwise we could not possibly sustain such a daily output of music and offer it in good performances – and nothing else is worth while.
>
> It is an exciting prospect that lies ahead, a prospect not without its dangers, including that of musical saturation. But whatever else may happen, there is one thing we intend to maintain; and that is liveliness.

The Music Programme would also depend heavily on the BBC house orchestras, and the report emphasised that the 'rejuvenation' of the Symphony Orchestra was an urgent priority. It soon began. After some months of trying out different conductors to replace Rudolf Schwarz, Glock and his colleagues chose Antal Dorati, who (writes Glock) 'had a great reputation for re-vivifying orchestras'. He was offered a two-year contract, but insisted on four if he were going to achieve a real change in the orchestra. 'He was a brilliant animator of the orchestra,' Glock has observed, 'but I don't think he was the sort of conductor who would have broadened and deepened the playing of the orchestra in the long run. And he also accepted, after the four years, the fact that this was enough, and made a typical Dorati remark: "I wasn't sorry to leave, I shouldn't have come at all." '

Dorati believed that the orchestra needed to be freed from 'the slavery of the microphone' and be exposed to more concert audiences; so it 'started going abroad more often', says Glock. Meanwhile the search was going on for better players – hampered by poor BBC orchestral salaries. Glock recalls that many players from other orchestras were keen to work for the BBC, 'because of the dull programmes they themselves were doing and the amazing variety, by comparison, that the BBC was doing ... They were willing to drop ten per cent of their salaries, but not twenty-five ... So we used to lose all sorts of potentially very good players.'

*

The Music Programme was to have no administrative connection with the Third, but would be run by a Chief Assistant in the Music Division, answerable to the Controller of the Home Service[2] – implying that management thought of it as a chiefly middlebrow service, and regarded it as not deserving its own Controller. The man chosen for the post was thirty-five-year-old John Manduell, who had been born in South Africa and educated at Haileybury, Cambridge, and the Royal Academy of Music, where he studied composition with Lennox Berkeley. He joined the BBC in 1956, and in 1961 became Head of Music, Midland Region – scarcely settling in at Birmingham before he was recalled south to set up the Music Programme. He found the delay caused by the Musicians' Union 'very frustrating – you couldn't see the end of the tunnel'.

On 27 March 1963, while this stalemate continued, Manduell issued some 'Statistics and Observations'. He had been promised a programme allowance of £500,000 a year when the Music Programme became fully operational, and this would mean that a generous proportion of the broadcasting hours could be devoted to live music, or BBC recordings. Only a third of the output would have to be provided by gramophone records, and repeats would not be broadcast until some weeks after the original transmission. Draft schedules had been compiled on the assumption that 7.30 to 9.30 am should provide music for 'a time of energy and activity'; the lunch period should cater for 'relaxation'; and Wednesday and Thursday afternoons were to have special attention, 'since, with early-closing [of shops] primarily still falling on these days, a potentially larger and more attentive audience should exist'.

More than six months after this document had been drawn up, the Musicians' Union was still stonewalling. 'The point has now been reached when there seems no chance of further negotiations being fruitful,' stated a memorandum to the BBC's Central Music Advisory Committee. Not everyone in the BBC felt that the Music Programme was a worthwhile venture. The Head of Talks and Current Affairs (Sound), George Camacho, pleaded for the airtime to be used instead for educational programmes, which he thought would meet a more important national need. But the BBC continued to negotiate with the Union, and in the summer of 1964 an agreement was finally reached. In return for an increase in needletime, the BBC would maintain its house orchestras 'for the foreseeable future', and would also set up a new Training Orchestra, 'with a view to training ... about 65 young players ... for future incorporation into the regular BBC orchestras'.

The Music Programme was at last able to go on the air, and it was announced that Phase I of the scheme would start on Sunday 30 August

[2] Home and Light had had their Controllerships restored by this time.

1964. A month in advance, Frank Gillard, who had succeeded Wellington as Director of Sound Broadcasting, issued a warning to Glock:

> If we fail to find an audience of reasonable size for the Programme, we shall before long become embarrassed by it. In general, therefore, the Music Programme should not be regarded as a channel for new, difficult and advanced music. Where that element is included, I would like to see it presented ... at a regular placing each week. It should not be inter-mingled with more familiar works in the normal run of concerts.

The BBC's advance publicity for 'the new Music Programme' emphasised that it would 'maintain a regular pattern' of programmes, 'so that people know what to expect'. But there would be 'room for special broadcasts', such as Britten's *War Requiem* from Germany on 6 September. The *Birmingham Post* article on the new service was headed 'A SERIOUS SOUND FOR THE THIRD – ALL DAY', and quoted Richard Marriott saying that the emphasis would be on 'music which is easily enjoyed rather than what is difficult'.

The first day's broadcasting certainly observed that criterion. After a short inaugural talk by Glock, at 8 am, a programme of newly released recordings began with ballet music by Delibes. Then came Gluck, Ravel, Haydn, Handel, Scarlatti and Vaughan Williams, filling the time until *Music in Miniature* at 10.30 am – a popular Home Service chamber music series which had transferred to the Music Programme. At 11 am listeners heard a recording of the final round of Italian Radio's competition for young opera singers, followed by the violinist Manoug Parikian playing Bach and Mozart with the English Chamber Orchestra. At 12.55 Lennox Berkeley made the first of several Sunday appearances, talking about forthcoming items in the Music Programme. After a ten-minute news bulletin at 1 pm, Alec Robertson previewed the week's Proms. The after-noon recital (Schubert and Beethoven) was given by Rudolf Serkin, live from the Edinburgh Festival, with Lord Harewood, the Festival director, in conversation with Hans Keller in the interval. Finally at 4.30 came *Music Diary*, described by John Manduell in the *Radio Times* as 'a widespread weekly survey of music-making in Britain'. The Music Programme ended at 5 pm, when the Third opened its evening broadcasts with more music – a Dvořák piano trio.

John Manduell sat in the Continuity studio for the whole of the first day – 'I felt as the chap responsible I'd better hear everything that hap-pened.' His own reaction, communicated to colleagues by memo, was that there had been 'too much talking'. Spoken links were cut down for the second Sunday of broadcasting, 7 August, and satisfaction at this was expressed next day at the Music Programme's new weekly meeting, though it was observed that 'the delivery and the announcers' own embel-lishments to the script had often been unfortunate'. Frank Gillard, mean-while, thought it 'absolutely vital for the speech content to be reduced as quickly as possible', even to the extent of removing *Music Diary* from the schedule. Manduell persuaded him to wait a little.

This anxiety not to alienate listeners who wanted wall-to-wall music tended to distract senior BBC staff from scrutinising the musical content of the new network. Not so Hans Keller. On Monday 12 October, the day after listening to a broadcast of the first half of *La Bohème*, and discovering that, because of tight schedules, he would have to wait until the following Sunday for the remainder, he wrote to Manduell and others:

> Is it not ironical that at the very point when a Music Programme is being established, operas can no longer be presented *in toto*? (That, at any rate, is the impression created in the outside world.) Is it not ironical that so far as I can foresee, everybody on my present distribution list will agree with my rhetorical question anyway? Isn't this the time to inhibit the operation of *vis inertiae* [the force of inertia] in Music Programme planning?

On 11 November 1964, six weeks after the Sunday broadcasts had begun, Manduell was able to report that detailed planning of Phase II of the Music Programme was well advanced:

> One of the most important features will be two-part symphony concerts at lunch-time each day from Monday to Friday [divided by the 1 pm news]; they will be given all over the country, usually before invited audiences. It is hoped that many people who might otherwise never have thought of buying a concert ticket will thus be induced to become patrons of evening concerts as well.

Turning to general policy, Manduell emphasised that 'while inevitably the programme will often [be] background listening for many busy listeners, we must never regard the service as providing merely a giant auditory backcloth. It is our intention that it should beguile and absorb the listener's attention.'

One of the first substantial outside comments on the Music Programme was by William Mann, chief music critic of *The Times*, on 27 November 1964. Observing that the Phase I programmes were already 'broadcasting a quantity of music that may not yet have become part of a listener's experience', he turned to the 'wallpaper' issue:

> Some high-minded souls firmly believe that music is too sacred an art ... to be degraded into any background role: it must remain always a special occasion to be planned in advance and prepared for so that its full splendour is apprehended, when at last the Holy Grail, so to speak, is finally unveiled ... A part of history, at least, is against this view, the part in which composers worked for princely employers and never imagined that their works would ever be listened to in silence ... In our own age, when so much of the music we hear is long familiar, there are two ways of listening: the way of complete surrender for special occasions, the intellectual way; and the sympathetic but not completely engaged recep-

tive faculty, which may extend to no more than sensuous apprehension of the music.

Mann added that he could not himself 'listen to music while I am reading or writing', but liked to hear it 'when I am tidying a room or distempering the ceiling or simply getting dressed'. He concluded that Mozart and Haydn would 'not, I believe, turn in their graves' at such use of their work.

Another comment came from the music journal *The Strad*, which complained that there had been so far too little, rather than too much, talking about music on the Music Programme – an exception being the discussions in the intervals of the afternoon concerts, which were 'usually overpowered by Mr Keller' (who was often the interviewer). The writer felt that spoken commentary on the music was essential; otherwise the new service would become 'the feared-for background, with incalculable complications for our musical life'.

Meanwhile, at the end of September 1964, a month after the start of Phase I, the Third's broadcasting hours were brought forward by thirty minutes daily from Monday to Friday, so that it would now open at 7.30 pm. The extra time had been lopped off the Network Three programmes (though the Network Three title had been dropped a year earlier, and replaced by the vague name 'Third Network' as an umbrella for *Spanish for Beginners*, *Parents and Children*, and the other early-evening survivors of the original fretwork network). This restoration of some of the Third's territory was not drawn to the public's attention by the BBC, nor did it attract any notice in the press.

*

On Saturday 12 December 1964 the Music Programme entered Phase II of its development, broadcasting from 8 am to 2 pm on weekdays, and on Saturdays from 8 am until sports programmes came on the air at 12.30 pm. Regular Saturday programmes included, at 9.30 am, *Record Review*, which returned from a sojourn on the Home Service, with John Lade still presenting.

Humphrey Lyttleton's *Jazz Record Requests* was heard at midday on Saturdays. Although this was the first time that jazz had been given a weekly slot on the Third's wavelength, regular jazz broadcasts in the Third itself had been going on since early in 1963, although they had been announced in very solemn fashion in the quarterly brochure: ' ... four programmes devoted to the work of the American William Russo ... The works performed in these four programmes will be receiving their first public hearing. Among the interesting facets of William Russo's work are the extreme details of notation and the wide range of voicing ... '

Music Magazine, a 'weekly review' of events in the musical world, now moved from the Home Service to become a fixture of the Music Programme at 11 am on Sundays. Begun on 24 May 1944, it had been edited from the beginning by Anna Instone and Julian Herbage. 'Anna was marvellous,' says John Lade. 'She had long black hair and a terrific stammer. By the time I first broadcast for her in 1947, she'd married Julian (he'd been divorced before the war). They were really rather an odd pair, though they were devoted to one another. They'd devised *Music Magazine*, and Alec Robertson introduced it at first.' By 1964 Herbage had taken over as presenter. An expert on Purcell and Haydn, he had been on the BBC music staff for twenty-one years before going freelance in 1946. Instone, Head of Gramophone Programmes, held a powerful position, since Gramophone Department produced all music programmes built around records (including such popular perennials as *Desert Island Discs*) without reference to Music Division.

'*Music Magazine* was a national institution,' says Manduell. 'And a lot of people depended on it. Some of the best coverage of what was still then a fairly limited recording industry was given by that programme and by John Lade's *Record Review*, which was linked to it. And we were jolly glad in the Music Programme to have them.' Of the programme's team, he recalls: 'Anna was the front-runner, the leader, but she would always say in a meeting: "What do you think, Julian?"'

Another Home Service favourite transferred to the Music Programme in December 1964 was *Talking About Music*, which took up residence after the Sunday lunchtime concert. It had first been heard on Sunday 26 September 1954 at 7.15 pm, when the thirty-three-year-old composer Antony Hopkins (much of whose work had been, till that date, writing incidental music for BBC radio plays) discussed 'some of the music to be broadcast during the week'. This programme, too, soon became a national institution.

On weekdays from December 1964, Music Programme listeners could hear *This Week's Composer* after the 9 am news, from Tuesday to Friday. *Your Mid-Week Choice*, a selection of listeners' requests, followed the 8 am news on Wednesdays. As Manduell had promised, there was, on most weekdays, a midday concert beginning at 12.15 pm and coming live from different parts of the country, with *Concert Calendar* and the one o'clock news in the interval. The choice of music remained safe for the time being. Avant-garde composers made no appearance, and little was heard from the early repertoire. There were programmes of French light music and Viennese operetta. In the second week of Phase II, *This Week's Composer* was Offenbach.

David Drew (no longer on the BBC staff) reviewed the first two weeks of Phase II in the *New Statesman*, taking by and large the opposite view from Mann in the 'wallpaper' controversy:

The listener ... risks an addiction which ... reduces to the level of the undifferentiated what is in itself highly differentiated. Applause for the Music Programme's present project of broadcasting the complete series of Haydn symphonies must be tempered by the thought that unless the listener is willing to use his ears the series for him might as well, or better, consist of 104 broadcasts of the same symphony.

The argument that even if 'serious' music is treated as 'background' music the general environment is somehow improved seems insidious. Granted that there is an evident need for musical wallpaper of a higher quality than that provided by Radio Luxembourg or the increasingly Luxembourgeois Light Programme, the fact remains that such a use of 'serious' music is contrary to its nature and symptomatic of the very devaluation which it is supposed to counteract. The only 'good' background music is creative light music, which is light precisely because the melodic, harmonic and rhythmic foreground is more or less free of complexity ...

The musical profession has reason to be enthusiastic about the greatly increased opportunities afforded by the new programme. But it would be a bad thing for everyone, and above all for music, if the programme, and the Third Programme which follows it, were to become a kind of musical ghetto, while the Home and even the Light are quietly stripped of what little music remains to them ...

Hans Keller replied to Drew in a letter in the *New Statesman*:

1. Mr Drew raises the acute problem of background music. Speaking as one who is constitutionally incapable of background listening, I would yet point out that the problem is more complicated than Mr Drew makes it appear: we do not yet know enough about musical perception and cogitation. A musician personally known to me once went to sleep in the course of a boring piece, and was afterwards able to put considerable stretches of it down on paper with a surprising degree of accuracy – a feat of which he would have been quite incapable had he remained awake.
2. There is a considerable body of opinion according to which background listening is positively recommendable in cases where there are resistances to the music in question. People who assimilate a musical language pre-consciously may thus learn to absorb the musical substance more readily.
3. ... As a matter of fact, the Haydn symphony series has produced the most active listener reactions to any series of studio concerts since I became responsible for orchestral broadcasts in 1962.
4. ... While daytime Home Service music is being taken over by the Music Programme, evening music on Home Service remains unchanged ...

Desmond Shawe-Taylor joined the argument in the *Sunday Times* the next month, on the same side as Keller:

Voices have been raised in dismay: the new scheme has been attacked as a further profanation of the sacred art. One can see why; yet the protests hardly bear serious investigation. The indignant creative musician, happily exercising his craft at the hub of things, ought to make the effort to put himself in the shoes of a distant music-lover who may be old, incapacitated, or alone for a great part of the day; what a blessing is the new programme for him! And why should we assume that the kind of intelligent listener at whom it is aimed will not be intelligent enough to exercise his own power of selection? I cannot see that he is any worse off than a lover of literature given the run of a well-stocked library.

That said, Shawe-Taylor had some criticisms of recent Music Programme planning; for instance, Strauss's *Also sprach Zarathustra* at 9 am ('it would be hard to imagine a less fortunate choice'). Yet he admitted that such carpings were subjective, since 'excerpts from *Aida*, alarming to me at any time before noon, were enthusiastically welcomed by a writer of my acquaintance as the perfect adjunct to the process of getting dressed'.

One question not raised during the 'musical wallpaper' controversy was the character of the Music Programme's audience. Whereas the Third, in its early days, had appealed across the social spectrum and introduced many working-class people to a wide variety of music and ideas, two BBC Audience Research reports, in 1963 and 1964, suggested that this would not happen with the Music Programme. 'There were striking associations between listening and social status,' said one of them. People's tastes became more 'serious' with 'each step up the social scale'. The other report emphasised 'the comparative distaste of the working class for serious music of all kinds'.

Phase III of the Music Programme was to start on Saturday 20 March 1965, extending broadcasts from 2 pm on weekdays until adult education programmes came on the air at 6.30 pm. (These were now given the overall title 'Study Session', replacing 'Third Network'.) Extensive trailing in other networks would help to publicise it. 'I have arranged to have references to the Music Programme written into *The Dales*,' wrote the Microphone Publicity Assistant – this was the successor to *Mrs Dale's Diary*. Meanwhile, despite his spirited defence of the Music Programme in the *New Statesman*, Hans Keller had substantial reservations about the way it was being planned. He expressed these in a memo to Glock on 12 January 1965:

> Sunday is supposed to be the new Programme's most important day. Yet, on January 10th, there was no substantial and consistently characteristic music between 9.30 am and 2.40 pm ... What was wrong was the construction of the day as a whole. So long as the overall editorship is not approached ... as a continuously imaginative task, we shall be open to the criticism we get: I have not yet seen or heard a single word of enthusiasm from the musical world for the actual Programme, though individual items as well as the sheer idea of it have been praised ... If we had a face, even those who disliked it would acknowledge its existence and seriously discuss its character ... The only characteristic Programme at the moment – little as I like some of it – is the Third.

Keller's own suggestions for the Third in recent months had included 'a psycho-socio-anthropological programme on The Beatles', who had come to fame in 1963. When this was turned down, he offered it to the Music

Programme. Manduell was keen on the idea, but Keller was told to refer it to Gillard, Marriott and Glock. 'There is substantial musical opinion, my own included,' he told them,

> in favour of the Beatles – or, at any rate, of some of their tunes. I am fully aware of the fact that such an operation would be felt to be controversial ... But it is this very circumstance which I want to utilise ... Nobody will feel indifferent about this programme: we cannot go wrong ...
>
> In lectures up and down the country, in which I have analysed, to audiences which expected a purist exposition of contemporary music, various Beatle tunes, I have come to the definite conclusion that there is not a single member of our music-loving public who is not spontaneously interested in this problem – positively or negatively or, more often, both.

Marriott wrote back to Keller that the proposal was 'not an acceptable one ... This view of the Beatles is a highly sophisticated one and would be unintelligible to the broad general audience of music lovers we are trying to reach with our Music Programme ... On the other hand [it] could very well find a place in the Third Programme ... '

John Manduell sometimes tried to match Keller's positive-aggressive style of memo-writing. 'This memo concedes a corner,' he wrote to Keller when they were having a comic disagreement over the composer Franz Schmidt; 'whether you turn it into a goal kick or head it into the net I shall wait with interest to see.' After music, football was Keller's greatest enthusiasm and expertise – he sometimes interviewed footballers for BBC sports programmes. 'A corner cannot be turned into a goal kick,' he admonished Manduell. 'See my lecture to the British Association of Football Referees.'

*

'This is a milestone for the BBC,' declared Frank Gillard in the *Radio Times* for the week beginning 20 March 1965, in which Phase III began. 'The Music Programme ... reaches full development.' He pointed out that there had been changes too in the Home Service, which was now 'pretty much a spoken-word programme in the daytime', while the Light 'concentrates ... mainly on entertainment music'. In fact light music played a regular part in the Music Programme's new weekday afternoon schedules, with a popular orchestral concert, or a selection of musical comedy recordings, filling the 2 to 3 pm slot. Marriott told Manduell that 'light music of the widest possible appeal' was required at this time because there were speech programmes (schools' broadcasting and *Woman's Hour*) on the other two networks. It was true that, after six weeks, there was still 'virtually no audience' for these afternoon light music broadcasts. However, Phases I and II had managed to attract audiences at peak times of up to 250,000, 'and it is hoped,' stated *The Times* just before Phase III began, 'that they will soon reach a million or more'. Manduell recalls that we used to scan dutifully those yellow sheets that came up from Audience Research, and if we saw a digit before the decimal point instead of a zero, then of course the excitement was immense! But we had something of a mission. We knew that what we had to offer those who were disposed to listen was something we believed in passionately; and we were going to offer it. And persuading others to listen was rather more incidental.

Sports programmes still occupied the Third Network – as the BBC was now calling the frequencies which accommodated the Music Programme, Study Session and the Third Programme – on Saturday afternoons, and it was agreed that Test Match commentaries would elbow music aside on many summer weekdays. John Manduell did not mind this interruption, because his budget was not affected, and he could save the money and spend it elsewhere.

Instructions were issued that, when rain stopped play in a Test, 'music of the "Family Fare" type' was to fill the gaps. When this began to happen in July 1965, a *Daily Mail* columnist complained of the 'Light Programme uproar' which arose from the Third Network on rainy days, and *The Times* pleaded with the BBC to 'find another wavelength for sporting commentaries'. But the plain fact, stated by Marriott after the Music Programme had been running for more than two years, was that 'the audience for ball-by-ball commentaries is anything from 5 to 50 times as great as the audience for the Music Programme'.

Frank Gillard anxiously monitored the quantity of difficult con- temporary works that the Music Programme broadcast, and occasionally sent reproving memos when he thought it had intruded too much. John Lade, who sometimes produced the early-morning record programmes, recalls: 'I put the Bartók *Divertimento* in one day – a harmless piece, but it absolutely frightened Frank. It was alleged that he'd had a silencer put on his shaver so that he wouldn't miss anything!' New music now had its own ghetto on the network, for *Music in Our Time*, the contemporary music series founded in 1942 by Sir Arthur Bliss, had joined the Music Programme from the Home Service in March 1965, initially occupying a slot on Friday afternoons.

The audience for jazz – which, from Phase III, was also featured in Steve Race's *Jazz Scene* on Wednesdays at 5.30 pm – was small but vociferous. 'There is a steady trickle of correspondence complaining about the inad- equate amount of time allotted to jazz,' Marriott noted after eighteen months of the full Music Programme.

> A recent letter . . . complained about the fact that jazz programmes . . . are frequently dropped or cut . . . Most other countries give much more time to jazz than we do . . . Taking account of the attitude to jazz here, I don't think we can do more, but the interested minority – and they really are interested – regard it as a derisory amount. If we cannot do more for them we should at least protect what they do get.

Others complained about the style of the Music Programme's daily pattern. Gillard, listening at leisure while on leave in Somerset, felt that 'the afternoon schedules are too broken up. Half-hour blocks produce a disjointed, jerky, broken-up effect.' One of the BBC Scottish Region staff, Donald Calder, listening in hospital in the spring of 1965, noted 'a somewhat mechanical feeling developing when all or most of the day's programmes was made up of gramophone records or prerecordings. The appearance of a programme which was live, or a recording of a live performance ... made a welcome break.' And the *Financial Times* music critic, David Cairns, wrote: 'There are days when the programme seems to be composed of neat little aseptic, homogenised packages of music ... enervating stretches in which the intellectual level sinks to that of a superior Muzak'.

There were grumbles too about slipshod announcing. John Holmstrom, who had himself been a Third Programme announcer (and who rejoined the announcing team later), complained in his radio column in the *New Statesman* that 'Only a musical ignoramus could refer, for instance, to "the Adagio by Bach" (who probably wrote several thousand Adagios)'. Since the 1957 cuts, the Third had had to share announcers with other networks, and similarly the presentation of the Music Programme was not confined to the musically knowledgeable. Yet some of the absurdities in the announcements were the fault of Music Information Unit, who wrote most of them. 'I thought we had got it established beyond the possibility of misunderstanding that meaningless biographical details were not wanted,' grumbled Marriott in October 1965.

> In the 7 to 8 am period this morning in the Music Programme, the announcer, speaking of a little known composer, told us that he died in Versailles at the age of 83. If he had written the work at the age of 83, or if he had been influenced by better known composers living in Versailles at the time, there might conceivably have been some interest in telling us, but what on earth is the purpose of announcing the age and place of his death? It is another example, though brief in itself, of talking for the sake of talking, which must be put an end to.

In *Punch*, Basil Boothroyd parodied this tendency of the Music Programme:

> This is the BBC Music Programme, the programme for listeners who are sick to death of the human voice and longing for the relief and refreshment of the wordless world of music.
>
> The work which we are discussing today is Galvani's ballet music to *Trisotta*. This little-performed ballet tells the story of Trisotta, a poor Genoese laundry-maid, who finds a gold coin in the underpants of Prince Corazio, the heir to the throne of Italy. Her father is old and drunken and her mother scrapes a precarious livelihood repairing fishermen's nets on the seafront. Trisotta knows that the coin can keep all three of them in luxury for many weeks, and her thoughts as she momentarily yields to

the temptation to steal the coin are conveyed in the early *pas de deux*, which she dances with the underpants to the plaintive cry of the oboes, while the contrapuntal thrumming of the double-basses brilliantly represents the deeper tug of her conscience. After a flurry of clarinet cadenzas depicting her indecision, the horns sound forth nobly as the voice of –

(Listener decides to go up the garden and empty the rubbish ...)

Meanwhile the announcers entered their own complaints in the Continuity logbook. One on 2 December 1965, identifies a potential problem in these days before computers were used to check duplication of items:

This morning seems to be a Mozart morning. Having begun with the *Magic Flute* overture at 0704, at 0732 we had the Symphony No. 39; at 0804, separated from the foregoing by the News and Weather, we had the Symphony No. 33; to round the morning off at 1015, there was the Symphony No. 29 ...

Another strange piece of planning occurred on Tuesday, November 30th. Again – Mozart. At 1030 Nina Milkina played his (according to the *Radio Times*) 'Fantasia in C minor (K.475).' The *very next programme*, at 1100, *Music Making*, had as its second item, at about 1117, what *Radio Times* referred to as the 'Fantasia in C minor for fortepiano'. Disguised like this it was nonetheless in the recording report designated as K.475. The same piece as before, in fact.

In my humble opinion, this *is* bad planning: and was connived at by *Radio Times*.

Still, I like Mozart.

But the only serious cause for concern was the lack of listeners. An Audience Research report issued in March 1966 alleged that five million people were listening to the Music Programme 'fairly regularly', but Gillard described this as 'a comforting assessment of a catchment pool' rather than a measurement of how many were listening at one time, and Marriott had noticed that on many days there was 'no measurable audience in the afternoons'. Figures given by David Cairns in the *Financial Times* (11 January 1966) showed that audiences rose to 200,000 for the Haydn symphonies series, which he called 'quite encouraging', but he noted that by and large the Music Programme had 'attracted little public attention'.

Donald Calder, listening in hospital, discovered that the nursing staff had not heard of the Music Programme, or confused it with the Third, which they said was 'not for us'. Yet those who did listen regularly seemed different in character from the Third's audience. 'Only a minority ... are truly selective,' reported Audience Research. The majority who were listening seemed to be doing so 'not because of their interest in serious music as such, but because they prefer it to any of the other radio services'.

*

Using the 'catchment pool' approach to audience figures, Howard Newby stated, in a public lecture at Broadcasting House in October 1965, that 'A million and a half people regard themselves as Third Programme listeners.' The biggest audience the Third had at any one time was roughly 'on the quarter-million mark'. At the other end of the scale a poetry reading might attract 'an audience that is numbered in thousands'. Newby felt that, in this respect, 'the Third has stood up very well to the inroads made [on radio] by television viewing. The audiences have remained steady for years. I should like to see them go up, of course, but the fact that they have remained steady is a great tribute to the quality of life in these islands.'

Television was not the only rival to the Third. The 1960s had brought a huge growth in the record industry, and in newspaper coverage of cultural matters. In his lecture, Newby mentioned 'the stress set up by the surely unparalleled claims to our attention put out by television, radio, newspapers, books, LP records, journals and magazines. Never has there been a time when such a flood of information, propaganda, literature, art, and music has been poured out. Indeed, you begin quite deliberately to ignore a lot of it.' In this increasingly media-dominated world the Third was finding a role as a home for current affairs discussions. Newby's lecture mentioned the Third's broadcast of 'the Oxford Teach-in on Vietnam' in June 1965, which had attracted a big audience. Looking back on this period, Newby explains:

> I was very anxious to increase the serious coverage of current affairs in the Third Programme, and this coincided with the appointment of George Fischer to Talks Department, as the senior producer who particularly worked for the Third. He was Hungarian, with the Hungarians' energy, intelligence, and perseverance. And it was George who largely instituted these current affairs programmes.

The youth cultures and sub-cultures of the 1960s received a share of the Third's attention, for example in *Portrait of a Young Girl* (8 April 1963), about a young woman's experience of prostitution, and *The Young Affluents* (24 April 1963), in which a London School of Economics sociologist, Alan Little, surveyed the new teenage consumers. A fortnightly series of Saturday night current affairs talks, *Personal View*, given live on an up-to-the-minute topic chosen by the speaker, reached its hundredth edition in August 1967. 'We broadcast more talk about current affairs in the Third Programme than about any other subject,' wrote Newby in the *Radio Times* that month. By this time the Third had also experimented with live 'open-end' discussions, such as one on the Common Market (5 March 1967), when the programme was given unlimited airtime from 9 pm, with a break for the news at 11 pm.

At a Third Programme Meeting in January 1967, Newby observed that 'subjects for "open-end" or extended "live" discussions had to be of a very special character and not many were put forward by producers willing to carry them out'. Richard Marriott had already noticed a 'shortfall' in

Third documentaries on political and social matters. Survivors from the disbanded Features Department, dispersed among Drama and Talks, were still offering plenty of 'historical and literary subjects', but these were no longer wanted; times and tastes had changed.

Indeed the BBC was striving openly to attract a new audience to the Third. On 21 February 1966 the *Daily Express* reported that 'blonde model Jean Ollis' had posed for a poster, intended for distribution to schools and colleges, with the caption: 'People like me like the Third Programme. Whenever there is something I want to hear on the Third I slip away upstairs.' The *Express* had traced the model, who told them: 'I wouldn't call myself a real Third Programme listener ... My picture is on the poster ... because I have a friend at the BBC.'

Newby's lecture mentioned that the Third was now the single largest source in Britain of copyright payments to poets – a reflection of George MacBeth's achievements – but he was less upbeat about drama, and at a meeting two months earlier he had reported a comment by a young drama producer, John Tydeman, on 'the lack of interest shown by English writers in the writing of plays for radio'. In fact the Third had kept up very well with changes in British drama during the 1960s, reflecting – if not leading the field in – the taste for gritty plays about working-class life. Bill Naughton's West End hit *Alfie*, filmed in 1966 with Michael Caine in the title role, began life as a Third Programme script, *Alfie Elkins and his Little Life* (7 January 1962), described in the Third's quarterly brochure as 'a study of a Bermondsey spiv'. Thanking Newby for his congratulations on the broadcast, Naughton reminded him that 'it was a talk we had at the Cleverdons that set me off on the idea' (Douglas Cleverdon had produced it). Newby recalls the conversation:

I remember being present with Douglas and Naughton at lunch one day, and Douglas was trying to prise out of Naughton some idea for a feature. And Naughton confessed that he'd kept a diary, in detail, of his activities over the years; and Douglas asked if he could get a sight of it. And out of this came *Alfie*. But that was typical of the way that Douglas went to work.

Drama Department's enthusiasm for contemporary theatre was largely the consequence of Martin Esslin succeeding Val Gielgud as Head of Drama in 1963, with Michael Bakewell as his deputy. Philip French says of Esslin that 'radio drama took a big leap' when he began to run the department. 'Esslin had had very little practical experience in the theatre, or even in radio drama production,[3] but he had established a reputation as a scholar of the theatre, with his book on Brecht [1958], and another on the Theatre of the Absurd [1961], and he was able to build on the work that had

---

[3] Esslin, who had come to England in 1939 as a Viennese refugee, had been trained in direction at Max Reinhardt's drama school. At Bush House he had worked in the German and European Services, producing a certain amount of drama as well as other programmes.

been done by McWhinnie and Bakewell, to which Gielgud hadn't been particularly sympathetic.'

Young writers now received considerable encouragement. Caryl Churchill, aged twenty-four, had her first radio play, *The Ants*, broadcast on the Third on 27 November 1962. This and other radio scripts helped to sustain her through the 1960s, when she was bringing up a young family; stage success did not come for many years. Joe Orton, aged thirty-four, experienced his first breakthrough as a playwright when *The Ruffian on the Stair* was accepted for the Third late in 1963. Martin Esslin recalls that the script 'arrived in an envelope marked "H. M. Prison, Wandsworth" – Joe was then serving his sentence there for defacing library books'. John Tydeman, who produced it, asked Orton if he had written for the stage, and was shown *Entertaining Mr Sloane*. Hugely impressed, Tydeman passed the script on to the agent Peggy Ramsay, who showed it to the impresario Michael Codron. It had become a West End hit by the time that *The Ruffian on the Stair* was broadcast on 31 August 1964.

Tydeman emphasises that Drama Department did not try to keep an exclusive grip on talented young writers. 'I would always encourage them to write for the theatre – rather than TV, which seemed to do them less good on the whole.' Consequently, some passed through Broadcasting House swiftly on their way to the West End. However, yet another young writer of promise seemed to be more committed to radio than were most of his contemporaries.

'Dear Mr McWhinnie,' wrote a twenty-four-year-old journalist living in Bristol in 7 December 1961, 'I thought the play herewith might interest you. I do hope you'll find time to look at it.' Michael Bakewell acknowledged the script (explaining that McWhinnie had left the BBC), and sent it to a reader, Michael Hardwick, who reported that it was a dialogue between an uncertain hangman and his victim; he judged it 'A diffuse, wordy nonsense by a writer who doesn't know what he's trying to say, and can't say it instinctively'. Bakewell returned the script to the author's agent, softening the rejection as much as he could: 'There is a great deal in this that is very good, but it is much too diffuse and rambling to work in terms of sound alone. I think Stoppard is a writer well worth encouraging, and I would be very interested to hear of any ideas he may have for original radio plays ... '

Born Tomas Straussler in Czechoslovakia, Tom Stoppard had taken his English stepfather's surname after his father was killed in the Far East. He had been working in journalism since he was seventeen. The BBC heard nothing more from him until 1963, when Drama Department accepted a fifteen-minute radio sketch called *The Dissolution of Dominic Boot* for a late-night Home Service series. The reader's report summed up the brief plot: 'In a mad, Evelyn Waugh world, Dominic takes a taxi & doesn't have the fare on him. He goes round & round in the taxi trying to borrow enough to pay for it. And ends up ruined.' At the same time Stoppard also submitted *A Walk on the Water*, his first full-length play, eventually staged as *Enter a Free Man*. 'Little plot, mostly conversation – but *what* conversation!' reported the reader, Cynthia Pughe. 'This held me from beginning to end with its humanity, humour and the pathos of non-communication. A brilliant piece of work, really better suited to sound where the words will have their way uncluttered by vision.' It was accepted for the Home Service. Stoppard next turned his attention to the Third.

'The basic idea,' he wrote in February 1965,

> is for a series of comedies with a unifying theme; roughly, each play would involve an imaginary 'joke occupation', a man/woman with a job which does not actually exist in life, but has a plausibility on an absurd or satirical level. The intention is to treat this idea 'seriously' enough to make it viable as a Third Programme series ... allowing it to make a comment, by implication, on society as it exists.

He gave as examples 'a man who advises people how to Keep Up With The Joneses'; 'a freelance Spokesman' who has been trained 'to deliver, cash on delivery no doubt, a comment on any situation which comes up'; and a designer of Liquorice Allsorts. He observed that

> the extent which distinguishes Third Prog humour from L[ight] E[ntertainment] is that in the former case the humour is inadvertent as far as the participants are concerned. To clarify, N. F. Simpson and the Goons are said to have much in common (and they have), but what separates them is that while the Goons *know* that they are being absurd, and play it up, Simpson's characters are engaged in serious and familiar situations and would be surprised – offended – by the laughter if they could hear it.

The proposal rambled on, bursting with ideas:

> Two cowboys shooting it out in the main street is a mythic cliché. Two cowboys shooting it out in Oxford Street is absurd. Two men dressed up in cowboy clothes to advertise baked beans and killing each other in a quarrel over a woman living in Bayswater, is real. (Though, of course, that job is not imaginary.)
>
> Possibilities: A firm called Boswell Inc. If you wake up feeling witty, they send a man round to write down everything you say anywhere you go during the day, for posterity ... A firm called Fame Inc., guaranteed to make you famous, rich. Call in without appointment; they will advise you on various methods of getting involved in a situation whereby you can sell your story to the papers ...

Drama Department decided to commission a single script as a pilot for this series, and chose 'the one about "Fame Inc."'. Stoppard, however, wrote an entirely different play, about a bus driver who recognises the telephone's Speaking Clock as the voice of his long-lost wife Gladys. *If You're Glad, I'll Be Frank* was broadcast on the Third on 8 February 1966, produced by John Tydeman, with Timothy West and Patsy Rowlands as Frank and Glad.

By this time Stoppard had submitted a lot more. A synopsis about a man intending to jump from a high building gradually evolved into *Albert's Bridge*, broadcast on the Third on 13 July 1967. He had also sent Drama Department a stage play, *Rosencrantz and Guildenstern are Dead*. This was the reader's report, signed 'N.B.' and dated June 1965:

> Not my sort of play at all. There are a few good, striking lines, but I found the script in general long, wordy and rambling. The play seems to have run away with itself ... some very visual bits ... it must last three hours and it would have to be cut in half for the Third to consider it. I don't think it's on. No.

By the time that *Albert's Bridge* had been transmitted, *Rosencrantz and Guildenstern are Dead*, produced on the Edinburgh Festival Fringe by an Oxford student group after numerous rejections from professional managements, had earned a rave review from Harold Hobson in the *Sunday Times* which led to it being staged by the National Theatre in the summer of 1967. 'This is a very considerable play,' wrote Martin Esslin when one of his producers suggested a radio version, but it was now too late – 'the radio rights are very unlikely to be available as a Broadway production is now being arranged'.

As with Beckett and Pinter, the Third had played an important part in Stoppard's early career, but had failed to pick up the crucial play (*Waiting for Godot*, *The Birthday Party* and *Rosencrantz and Guildenstern are Dead*) which made the writer's reputation. As early as 1953, Donald McWhinnie had expressed 'the uneasy feeling that ... we have in some cases applied wrong standards of criticism to potential Third Programme material ... decisions at Controller level have sometimes been taken on grounds of purely personal preference'. There was also the inherent drawback to radio drama that it vanished after a single performance and a repeat or two. So did television drama, but the audience was far bigger. Pamela Hansford Johnson, who wrote six plays for the Third based on Proust, once described writing for radio as 'like shouting into a hole in the ground', and V. S. Pritchett used the same metaphor: 'If I write a radio programme it vanishes after two or three performances into a hole in the air.'

When asked if he minded losing writers whom the Third had helped to establish, Newby says: 'Oh no. It was a matter of pride to us. We regarded the Third Programme as a launch pad. We certainly did not feel we had any proprietorial rights over the writers we had encouraged.' Tom Stoppard liked the way BBC radio had treated him, and in consequence often wrote for radio in later years. 'Portland Place dignifies writers,' he wrote to Richard Imison of Drama Department, 'by seeing them as a genre, a force-without-which, whereas the TV people are more concerned with proven individuals.'

*

During 1969 the Third acquired its first live arts programme (*New Comment* had always been recorded) with a full range of interviews, discussions, written scripts and arts news. Philip French suggested it to Newby, who agreed on the spot. 'We never had a pilot for the programme,' says French. 'We just did a dry run before we went on the air. Bryan Magee was the presenter – an experienced live broadcaster, though more on television than radio. And I produced ninety-two editions of it, till it came off the air in the summer of 1971.' French recalls that *The Arts This Week* (first heard on 2 April 1969) got off to a controversial start:

In 1968 Norman Mailer's book about the anti-Vietnam protests was published in America (but not in Britain), and there was a talk on the Third about it by David Caute. In the course of it, he quoted a passage which contained any number of four letter words. The day before it went out, the script was seen by George Camacho, Head of Talks. He decided this passage must be cut. And Caute refused to cut it, so the talk was withdrawn. Julian Mitchell got up a letter to the *Listener*, signed by a number of writers, in protest about this – he got some pretty classy signatures, like John Updike.

Well, come April 1969 and the first edition of *The Arts This Week*, Mailer's book was published in Britain, and was the subject of a live discussion on the programme – with Julian Mitchell among the participants! I had an idea what might happen, but I didn't discuss with Julian what his strategy was going to be. A couple of minutes into the discussion, Julian said, 'I don't think we can go on discussing this book without giving listeners an idea of what it's like. I'm going to read a passage from it, and anybody who might have objections to the kind of language Mailer uses has ten seconds to get over to the wireless and switch off.' He then proceeded to read, and the discussion went on – there were certainly no protests around the table. There were two or three phone calls about it, no more than that, and I'm sure that one or two people phoned up to say they approved of it.

Howard Newby phoned me up in the studio when we came off the air, to say how much he liked it. And the following morning, at the Talks Meeting, everybody spoke favourably about the programme. But George Camacho said: 'I think there's something serious we have to discuss. A few months ago we prevented Caute from doing just this.' And Howard said, 'No, George. Caute was reviewing a book that hadn't been published in this country, and there may have been doubts then as to whether it was even publishable here. But this time they were discussing something that is available in the bookshops, and I think Philip was wholly justified in allowing it.'

I remember that when the Talks Meeting was discussing Camacho's decision about Caute, in 1968, Howard said, in his quiet studious way, 'How many people around this table have ever used the word "fuck" in print? And immediately George MacBeth said, "I have, of course." And I hadn't, but immediately that night, reviewing a novel for the *New States-man*, which contained the word, I did!

The arrival of the Music Programme had not, of course, deprived the Third of its own music broadcasts. John Manduell took care to liaise with Newby. 'Howard and I always got on very well,' he recalls. 'We had offices almost adjacent, and would wander into each other's and compare notes on what we were doing. I found him an immensely civilised person. We used to have dinners together and talk over what we might do.' Despite this friendship, the Third and the Music Programme remained very separate entities. When Manduell organised 'A Weekend of Music in Cambridge', from Saturday 26 to Monday 28 October 1968, the Cambridge outside broadcasts and recordings were only transmitted during Music Programme hours, and did not trespass into the Third's airtime. (In retrospect this weekend can be seen as the ancestor of Radio 3's many days and weekends devoted to music and the arts in different cities and countries.)[4]

A rare case of collaboration has been recorded in his diary by Cormac Rigby, who joined the BBC in 1965 as an announcer, and in 1968 was also on attachment as programme planner for the Third. It concerned the outstanding Sadler's Wells production of *Die Meistersinger*, conducted by Reginald Goodall, which had already been broadcast live by the Third on 10 February 1968, shortly before the opera company moved to the London Coliseum.

Wednesday 4 September 1968: Today has without any doubt been my most creative day with the BBC & I feel a remarkable sense of elation ... The main part of the morning was the [Third Programme] Music Meeting ... Yesterday I gave Howard [Newby] the cutting of [Peter] Heyworth's review of *Mastersingers* & asked him to read it, as I would like to bring it up at the Music Meeting. I deliberately didn't say any more then, as I wanted him to absorb the *uniqueness* of this production ... Come the day, & at the meeting were Newby, in the chair; Julian Budden [in charge of opera broadcasts]; John Lade; Peter Gould; Hans Keller; Robert Layton; & myself.[5]

To my dismay Julian brought up – rather aggressively – the placing of our Bayreuth recording of *Tristan*. Wagnerians had pointed out that it coincided with a *Götterdämmerung* at C[ovent] G[arden]. Howard said it was a pity but we cdn't alter our plans for a theatreful of people ... Julian charged in with an accusation that Howard was prejudiced & anti-

---

[4] Soon afterwards, Manduell left the BBC to become Director of Music of the recently founded University of Lancaster; in 1971 he was appointed Principal of the new Royal Northern College of Music, which eventually earned him a knighthood. He was succeeded as the planner of the Music Programme by Peter Dodd.

[5] Robert Ponsonby describes three of those who were at this meeting: 'Peter Gould – pianist, Chopin expert and old BBC hand ... Julian Budden, admirable broadcaster and internationally respected expert in Verdi and nineteenth century Italian opera; Robert Layton, master of all gramophone catalogues and of Scandinavian music, practical joker ... '

Wagnerian. Howard indignantly repudiated the charge. I came in & told Julian that it wd be an awkard & considerable bit of replanning, but I would look into it & do my best. Both were mollified. (Later, I did this, switching *Tristan* with a Russian *Boris*, & spending my afternoon on all the consequent modifications.)

Then, that clash over Wagner averted, blow me if Julian didn't say he wanted to give prior warning that Covent Garden were going to do *Mastersingers* in January & a live relay wd cost us £4000. Howard said 'Well I'm afraid we can't take it – we simply can't afford it.' Julian began to expostulate . . . I intervened & asked Howard if I could speak. He nodded, & I said that if £4000 were the cost of *Mastersingers* I would rather not spend it on an ordinary Solti effort, but spend it on putting out again the Goodall one. Julian looked startled, but from the other end of the table came Hans' voice: 'I couldn't agree more.' Julian said 'Oh but Covent Garden have a very starry cast.' I said even if it *were* very starry, the important thing was the music & its reading. Hear, hear & a quasi-papal arm-raising from Hans.

Thus encouraged, I pleaded that the Goodall performance was an historic one. I certainly regarded it as one of the great experiences of my life, but it was not merely personal. Critics & musicians all regarded it as one of those performances that occur once in a lifetime. It would never occur again. We had broadcast it once admittedly, but since then, the move to the Coliseum had made an already unique impact beyond question an historic one. We ought to broadcast it again & had a duty to do so. If we did not, Goodall's *Mastersingers* would be gone for ever, beyond recapture. Hans added that this was true not only because the Wells had no plans to revive it, but that Goodall was going blind & might never conduct Wagner again. I urged that our brief, as a programme to provide the best, demanded that we take it a second time. Hear, hear from both Robert & Hans. Julian, still rather perplexed, said he was all for doing it again, but didn't see how.

Howard – who had been looking very thoughtful – spoke into the silence: 'Well, you convince me that this is such an exceptional performance that we ought to relay it a second time: but we can only do so live – we can't afford to record.' (It costs twice as much to record as to do a live relay.) This was half-way. I had dates at my fingertips. The ideal performance wd be Tuesday 10th [September] – the last with [Alberto] Remedios as Walther. But we would need two listening tests,[6] not the usual one, because this will be our first relay from the Coliseum; so that meant either 14th or 18th. Julian rang his office to get details from the Wells, while we debated whether to break *Radio Times*.[7]

Howard was willing to do so. But the 14th is a Saturday & we cd not take a relay at 5.15 – Sport, which is utterly sacrosanct, does not end till

---

[6] A listening test is a 'dry run' by the BBC sound engineers, with microphones erected, and a sound balance carried out in the control van.
[7] i.e., to cancel the advertised programmes.

6.00. That left the 18th. Opera on successive evenings, for we had a relay of *Giovanni* on the 17th. Julian & Howard & Hans were all for dropping this relay of the disastrous *Giovanni*, & taking *Mastersingers* instead. I had to be my own enemy there & point out that *Radio Times* had gone to press with *Giovanni* on the 17th. However disastrous we cd hardly break faith with listeners by cancelling at this stage. It wd have to be opera on two successive evenings. How, asked Howard, will you replan a whole evening thus displaced – it will be impossible. I said fervently that if that were the only obstacle to broadcasting this *Mastersingers* again I would work till midnight to replan.

So we considered breaking *Radio Times* to take a live relay. Agreed. Problems – it began at 5.15. Music Prog. wd surely replan to let us start early. But between 6.30 & 7.30 there is Study Session, & try as we could, we could see no way of replacing that to allow the live relay. It simply wasn't possible. And so a live relay was out. We shall have to record.

Oh no, said Howard, even for a performance as memorable as this, I simply can't afford £4000. It simply can't be justified. Even then I would still have done it myself. But I could understand Howard's decision.

Then, on the very brink of abandoning it, Peter Gould had a brainwave: if it were recorded, he mused quietly it wd take a whole evening on Third – why not spread it on a Sunday, say from 3 till 9, across Music Programme & Third Programme – & get both to share the cost – £2000 each. There was a little cry of jubilation from Hans & a yelp from me ... Julián rang John Manduell then & there, from the conference room. John was on leave, at home, but enthusiastically agreed to the scheme. I was jubilant.

A recording of *The Mastersingers* was duly made at the Coliseum on 18 September 1968, and was broadcast on Sunday 2 February 1969. This collaboration between the Third and the Music Programme was a foretaste of the future of the Third Network.

CHAPTER THREE

'The ... Third Programme
will disappear'

On 29 September 1966 the *Sheffield Morning Telegraph* wished the Third a happy twentieth birthday, noting that listeners in the South of England had, since July, been able to hear some Third and Music Programme broadcasts in stereo, from the Wrotham transmitter.

A week later the same paper announced that the Third's quarterly brochure, which since 1950 had publicised forthcoming programmes free of charge to anyone on the mailing list, was to cease because of costs. Originally a plain fold-out pamphlet, since 1962 it had been a much more lavish production with an imaginative cover in two colours; the issue for the last quarter of 1962, for instance, had been drawn specially by Jean Cocteau. It was replaced in 1967 by a quarterly supplement in the *Listener*, but after a year, Leslie Stokes – still the right-hand man to the Controller – said he was 'not happy' about the very restricted space this afforded. He told the Third Programme Committee that he would like to see a monthly publication put on sale, 'but this would mean extra staff'.

That ruled it out. Within BBC radio, the emphasis was now chiefly on winning a new young pop music audience away from the pirate radio stations which had sprung up in recent years. In 1966 a government white paper on broadcasting had given the BBC permission to open its own pop channel on 247 metres medium wave, and Radio 1 came on the air on Saturday 30 September 1967. That day, the Light Programme and Home Service were renamed Radio 2 and Radio 4 respectively, while the 'Third Network' umbrella title for the Music Programme, the Third, and the various sport and further education programmes that shared the frequencies with them, became Radio 3. However, its component programmes, including the Third, retained their own names. Newby remained as Controller of the Third, while the Music Programme continued to be the responsibility of Controller, Radio 4.

Almost a year later, in August 1968, Charles Curran, whose appointment to succeed Sir Hugh Greene as Director-General the next spring had just been announced, told the press: 'Hitherto our main effort has been in identifying programme excellence. Now we are trying to get as near as we can as a non-commercial organisation to basic business management.'

Colour television transmissions were due to begin on BBC1 in November 1969, and the *Sunday Telegraph* (23 February 1969) alleged that cutbacks in radio would help finance the extra cost – though the BBC later denied this strenuously.

The Corporation had already, in April 1968, appointed a leading American firm of management consultants, McKinsey & Company, to carry out a study of its administrative structure. In September that year McKinsey's presented their first main report to the Chairman of the BBC, Lord Hill. It pointed out that senior radio management had proliferated to the extent that there were now sixteen people reporting directly to Frank Gillard, Director of Radio. McKinsey's recommended realigning all radio departments under network controllers. They also turned their attention to the future role of radio, and gave a list of alternative strategies for satisfying listeners' needs 'within budget limitations'. These included 'Combination of Third Programme with Radio 3/Radio 4', and even 'Elimination of complete network, e.g. Radio 3'.

This first McKinsey report was kept secret among a few senior BBC staff, and the management consultants were retained for a second round of scrutiny of resources and confidential discussions about the future of radio. Meanwhile a BBC working party of senior radio personnel, including Howard Newby and Gerard Mansell (now Controller of Radio 4 and the Music Programme), with Richard Marriott (Assistant Director of Radio) in the chair, had been meeting for almost a year, to discuss the future of radio. On 4 November 1968 Newby told the Third Programme Committee that this group would shortly be approaching producers 'for information and advice'.

The Marriott working party presented a confidential report to Gillard during January 1969. Gillard described it as 'an unfinished job' because, by then, the working party had been replaced by a Policy Study Group, chaired by Mansell. Nevertheless the report had a lot to say about the Third Programme.

It observed that during its first ten years the Third had tended to 'spiral upwards into ever more esoteric regions', but that during the 1960s it had broadcast 'programmes of great interest and distinction', paying increased attention to 'political and social developments and current affairs in general', so that it 'can no longer fairly be reproached for living in an ivory tower'. The report also commended the achievements of the Music Programme: 'The only complaints have been that continuous good music is not available during the evening as it is in the daytime, that the Music Programme is not broadcast on Saturday afternoons (because of the Sports Service) and that it is interrupted on about 25 days out of 365 by the Test Match ball-by-ball commentaries.'

The working party recommended that, administratively, the Music Programme and the Third should be 'brought together under single Controllership'; that Further Education programmes and Saturday sport should be transferred to other wavelengths; and that during the evening 'the ratio of music to speech [should] be increased', with an emphasis on 'mainstream popular orchestral music'. The quantity of 'difficult contemporary music' should be reduced. This part of the report concluded:

> We recommend dropping the names 'Third Programme' and 'Music Programme' and uniting the whole network and programme service under the single title 'Radio 3'. The Third Programme in particular has made a great name for itself and the loss of this title will be deprecated by some but it undoubtedly has connotations which discourage a large number who might have enjoyed many of its programmes from tuning into it. A new title will help to emphasise that we are making changes and that we intend to be free from past commitments.

Asked why he was willing to see the name 'Third Programme' disappear, Howard Newby says:

> I thought it opened the way to control of the whole network – not only the Third Programme, but Network Three and the daytime Music Programme. I didn't think the words 'Third Programme' merited a great battle. And one has to recognise that, by this time, the speech element in the Third had declined in quality. I was finding it very difficult to get the material I wanted, so I was increasing the proportion of music at the expense of speech.

By the time the report was written, Mansell's four-man Policy Study Group was at work in conditions of strict secrecy. The other three members were senior staff from engineering, television resources, and the Monitoring Service; in other words, programme-makers were conspicuously absent. The secrecy was in the hope of avoiding the leaks and public arguments which had scarred the 1957 reorganisation of radio. Much of the Group's time was spent consulting representatives of the broadcasting and musical trades unions, who were themselves sworn to secrecy. Looking back a quarter of a century later, Mansell says that all this was a mistake; it engendered quite unnecessary fears and anxieties in BBC staff. He adds that the McKinsey team and the BBC men had some difficulty in speaking each other's language; the bringing in of the management consultants was, he says, a political move, designed to impress the Government with the BBC's up-to-dateness.

During March 1969 the Group issued a highly confidential interim report which stated: 'If rising costs cannot be contained, it will be necessary to adopt a three-network system. Day-time serious music would be the casualty.' The plan was to broadcast Radio 1, Radio 2 and Radio 4 in the daytime, and in the evening to combine Radios 1 and 2 on one wavelength, leaving Radio 3 and Radio 4 to occupy the other two channels.

The Group had finished work by the end of May, when it presented its proposals to the Governors: 'The term "Third Programme" would be dropped, to reflect the increase in music and to minimise the disadvantage of the "highbrow" image of the Third Programme.' The option had been considered of 'making Radio 3 an entirely serious music network', that is, dropping all speech programmes; but this was 'considered too drastic a step to take at this point', though 'the possibility of taking it at some later date was not ruled out'.

*

Meanwhile within the BBC rumours were flying around, exacerbated by the very secrecy that was supposed to prevent them. At the Third Programme Meeting on 13 January 1969 one producer complained of 'the lack of communication between producers and the Policy Study Group'. Newby replied that 'a whole series of investigations' was going on, and the proper channel of communication between individuals and the Group was via departmental heads. As it happened, this was Douglas Cleverdon's last Third Programme Meeting, and the Committee wished him well in retirement. 'Few people have played a more creative role in radio over the past thirty years,' said Newby. Nest Cleverdon says that her husband 'was very happy to go back to publishing, which he did for the last eighteen years of his life [1969–87]. His last big book was the collected engravings of David Jones, on the most beautiful handmade paper.'

Three weeks after this meeting the BBC announced that the Home Service weekly arts discussion, *The Critics*, was to be axed after a twenty-two-year run. The *Guardian* suggested that the decision was 'probably inspired by the fact that a study group's findings are soon to be submitted to BBC heads which could even recommend such drastic changes as the abolition of Radio 3 or at least its merger with Radio 4' – though it admitted that the axing of *The Critics* was nothing to do with the study group. A few days later the *Sunday Telegraph* broadcasting correspondent, making his own enquiries in Portland Place, was advised to ' "scotch the rumour" ' that they are planning to abolish the Third Programme'. He speculated that, since the Third was 'cheap to run' and was done 'extremely well', the axe might fall instead on Radio 1, 'which is expensive and ludicrously out of character' (for the BBC); arguably, commercial radio could do that kind of broadcasting much better.

By mid-February senior programme staff had been consulted by Gerard Mansell in his role as chairman of the Policy Study Group. The Third Programme Committee had been told that 'a wide-ranging discussion' had taken place, but no information was vouchsafed. Meanwhile Audience Research had been asked to give an estimate of current listening to Radio 3. They reported that it had 'always been difficult, if not impossible' to do this 'with any precision', since an audience of (say) 50,000 might not show up at all in a typical survey, which questioned only about 2,000 people. They admitted that only a tiny fraction of the population (about 0.2%) listened to Radio 3 exclusively, but as many as 17.3% tuned in sometimes. This was an impressively high figure – but in the penultimate paragraph the report explained that 'a very high proportion' of these people were listening only to the sports programmes.

Observing that, excluding the sports broadcasts, the Radio 3 audience 'rarely touches 200,000', the *Guardian* (8 April 1969) judged that there was a very strong 'statistical case' against the network in the current climate of financial cuts. Yet it quoted Charles Curran, the new Director-General, saying that audience figures were 'not really relevant to the decisions you take about the Third Programme. What is decisive is whether there is a worthwhile audience, and I mean by worthwhile an audience which will get an enormous satisfaction out of it.' Curran questioned whether large amounts of money should be poured into 'relatively esoteric productions'. But this seemed to imply a change in programme policy rather than the axing of the entire network, and three days later the same newspaper quoted Curran saying specifically: 'There is a rumour that Radio 3 is for the chop. This would be quite contradictory to the aim of the BBC, which is to provide a comprehensive radio service.'

The Board of Governors' meeting on 29 May, to consider the Policy Study Group's recommendations, was of course sworn to secrecy. The following weekend the *Sunday Telegraph* alleged that this cloak-and-dagger atmosphere was creating a climate of 'distrust, mounting rumour and declining morale' within the BBC. Three days later *The Times* carried a letter signed by a dozen Cambridge dons, including the distinguished sinologist Joseph Needham, expressing

> our apprehension about the rumours that the Governors of the BBC propose, among other economies, to close down Radio 3 ... Radio 3, and particularly the Music Programme, makes a uniquely valuable contribution to the life of this country. For many people it is the only constantly available and easily accessible source of great music. In its attention to drama, literature, political and social discussion, it plays a vital role in upholding cultural standards, and providing cultural sustenance to the community at large.

Other protests put the same emphasis on the threat to music – there were also rumours of BBC plans to disband its regional orchestras. Bernard Levin, writing in the *International Herald Tribune* (10 June 1969) was one of the few commentators to distinguish between the Music Programme – 'a diet of serious music all day – wonderfully balanced, imaginatively planned and excitingly free of the pressures of time and fashion' – and the Third Programme, which he described as 'music, theatre, philosophy, poetry, science, talks'. The Third, he said, had 'enriched countless lives in the 23 years of its existence'.

On 22 June the *Sunday Times*, which had evidently picked up a leak from the BBC's General Advisory Council meeting a few days earlier, stated confidently that the Music Programme was 'certain to emerge unscathed' from the present crisis. The biggest victim was likely to be 'English regional sound broadcasting'. There was no mention of the Third Programme.

*

The public version of the Policy Study Group's report, a thirteen-page pamphlet called *Broadcasting in the Seventies*, written (anonymously) by Ian Trethowan,[1] who had been appointed to succeed Gillard as head of radio, was issued to the press and BBC staff on 10 July 1969. The foreword, by Lord Hill, the Corporation's Chairman, began: 'The BBC is a public service and wishes to remain one.' But it was necessary, he continued, 'to adapt our service to a changing world to meet changing tastes and needs', and 'to live within our prospective income for sound broadcasting in the next five years'. This would involve 'both gains and losses'.

Hill's foreword was followed by some paragraphs setting out the problems facing the BBC, not least the 'fundamental change in the nature of the radio audience', which meant that – thanks to television – peak listening now took place in the daytime rather than at night. *Broadcasting in the Seventies* then announced that Radio 1 would be retained as 'an all-pop network', while Radio 2 would be gradually converted into 'another all-music network ... presenting all that is covered by the umbrella of "light music"'. Then came a section headed 'Radios Three and Four'.

'Few aspects of British broadcasting have aroused more passion than the Third programme [*sic*],' began this passage,

> so we had better again make it clear that we are not abandoning programmes for minorities. What we have needed to consider is whether this function is best fulfilled within a single enclave. There is a good deal of evidence that some listeners are deterred by the label 'The Third'. Programmes originated on the Third invariably attract bigger audiences when repeated on Radio Four. An evening concert of standard classical music will win more listeners on Radio Four than on the Third.[2]
>
> We have also had to consider finance. The Third costs much more per hour than any other network, yet it has by far the smallest audience. At a time of stringency it would obviously be nonsense to pay less attention to the cost of minority programmes than to the money spent on programmes heard by millions. It is essential to produce programmes for minorities, but it is only common sense to reconsider what proportion of scarce resources should be devoted to these programmes, how they might be made available to the widest potential audience and whether some of the more specialised are really appropriate to the medium of broadcasting.
>
> With these points in mind, we propose to realign Radios Three and

---

[1] Gerard Mansell says that Trethowan had little understanding of the Policy Study Group's findings, and that he (Mansell) would have written quite a different document. Trethowan's was clumsily and tactlessly worded.

[2] This was borne out by the McKinsey consultants' separate final report, presented to the BBC Governors in February 1970, which showed that the average audience for Third Programme broadcasts in the 1968 Prom season had been 250,000, whereas Prom concerts on Radio 4 had attracted 600,000. Similarly Tom Stoppard's *Albert's Bridge* had only attracted an audience 'too small to be measured' when first broadcast on the Third, but its repeat on the Home Service won it 700,000 listeners.

Four. On Radio Three the separate labels of Music Programme and Third Programme will disappear and the entire output of the network be put under the single heading of Radio Three, which will concentrate wholly on music and the arts. The day time stream of music will be maintained and it will now be extended more into the evening. At the same time, Radio Three will continue to carry, in the evening, some of the more specialised drama, poetry, and other cultural programmes which have been a feature of the Third.

The more factual programmes which have been broadcast on the Third – documentaries on current affairs – seem likely to fit better into a reshaped Radio Four ... our aim is to make this largely a speech network. There will be a strong emphasis on news and topical programmes, but ... Radio Four will continue to carry general entertainment programmes.

Broadcasting in the Seventies then moved on to local and regional radio. The BBC hoped for a big expansion, from the existing eight experimental stations to an eventual total of forty. The old English regions were to be replaced by smaller news-gathering areas, and by Network Production Centres at Birmingham, Bristol and Manchester. The report then turned back to frequencies. The BBC was prepared

to consider reallocating the medium waves now used for Radio Three as part of a general pattern of providing improved medium-wave support for the other networks and local stations. This would leave Radio Three on vhf [*sic*] only. Such a high-quality output is, in fact, best heard on vhf, but we recognise that, in the short term, some listeners would be deprived if it were taken off the medium wave, and we would only wish to make the change if we were satisfied that there was a clear balance of advantage to the reception of BBC radio services as a whole.

There was also the question of musical resources. Five orchestras would be retained, but the BBC Scottish Symphony Orchestra, the BBC Northern Dance Orchestra, and the London Studio Players could no longer be financed; neither could the BBC Chorus (a group of twenty-eight singers). The BBC Training Orchestra would disappear after its current players' contracts had ended. It was hoped that the financing of three other orchestras – the BBC Concert, the BBC Welsh and BBC Northern Ireland – could be partly taken over by the regional Arts Councils. (In fact an increase in the licence fee, approved by the Government a few months after *Broadcasting in the Seventies* was published, obviated the necessity of many of these cuts.)

The final page of *Broadcasting in the Seventies* repeated, briefly, the distinguishing characteristics of the new-style radio networks. Radio 3's terms of reference were to be 'a larger output of standard classical music, but with some element in the evening of cultural speech programmes – poetry, plays'. It was hoped that the changes would take place 'next spring', and that 'full rationalisation' would be completed during 1971.

*

A leader in *The Times* on the morning after the publication of *Broadcasting in the Seventies* (11 July 1969) uncovered the BBC's real motive for the proposed massive expansion of local radio. With a Conservative government likely to replace the present Labour administration 'within a couple of years', the Corporation was determined to anticipate the Tories' declared intention of licensing local commercial broadcasting by getting in first. It was the cost of this expansion which had led to the proposals to axe orchestras and restrict Radio 3 to FM.

The leader made no specific reference to the loss of the name 'Third Programme', but quoted the assertion in *Broadcasting in the Seventies* that 'listeners now expect radio to [offer] one particular type of programme, meeting one particular interest'. The leader-writer commented: 'That may be a good way of satisfying existing tastes: it is not well designed to broaden a listener's horizons. It used to be the special glory of British broadcasting that it paid full attention to the second as well as the first of these responsibilities. It would be sad to think that this is no longer the case.'

Other newspapers did not share this concern for the disappearance of mixed programming, but the *Daily Telegraph* was anxious about 'the future of the more serious talks and discussions now put out on the Third Programme', and Peter Porter in the *New Statesman* asked what would happen to speech that was neither drama, poetry, nor current affairs discussions: 'What about the many programmes on history, literature, travel, reminiscence, etc, which the Third found a home for?'

Five days after the publication of *Broadcasting in the Seventies*, Gerard Mansell and Charles Curran went live on the air, on the Third Programme, to answer questions about the proposals. Curran rejected the assumption that the Third was a victim of the axe, and Mansell said that the changes to Radio 3 would have been made even without financial necessity. Writing in the *Observer* the following Sunday, Paul Ferris dismissed this as 'the tiny nibbling sound of compromise disguised as improvement'.

Ferris had interviewed Newby – 'the quiet and somewhat withdrawn figure who is Controller of the Third Programme (with a separate career as a novelist[3])' – and suggested to him that the shift of many programmes to Radio 4 would mean that many of the Third's achievements would be emasculated. '"No," says Mr Newby, because "it would be a mistake to think that Radio 4 in the future will be like the Radio 4 of today. It will be less rigid in planning. What is aimed at is the reviving of Radio 4 with some of the old conventions broken down."' Ferris was not convinced. 'In any case,' he concluded his article, 'the essence of Third Programme

---

[3] This was the year in which Newby won the Booker Prize. The *Times Literary Supplement* (21 November 1968) called his prizewinning book *Something to Answer For* 'brilliantly resourceful'. It was about a professional swindler who loses his memory, and was the fourth novel he had published since becoming Controller of the Third.

patronage has been that a core of producers has a broad, secure base from which to operate. The Third no longer seems so broad or secure.'

Others were even more sceptical. By September a Campaign for Better Broadcasting had been set up – the initials CBB were printed in a logo parodying the BBC's – with the participation of such distinguished persons as Professor Max Beloff, Sir Adrian Boult, James Cameron, Sir Tyrone Guthrie, Frank Kermode, George Melly, Jonathan Miller, Henry Moore and Sir Roland Penrose. Its first public document included this paragraph, supposedly spoken by the BBC:

> We are going to dismantle the Third Programme by cutting its spoken word content from fourteen hours a week to six, keeping a token air-space for drama, poetry and the arts which will do splendidly to fill in the concert intervals. All current affairs and news currently handled on the Third at length will be 'translated' to Radio 4 (i.e. shortened and simplified) as will 'more factual programmes' (presumably those on the Law, Theology, Psychology, Social Science, Architecture, Planning, Environment, Science, Medicine, Education, History and Political Economy). These will be joined on Radio 4 by the speech output of Radio 2 (*Waggoners' Walk*, *Woman's Hour*, *Top Team*, *The Big Business Lark*, light drama etc). Our serious music output will be maintained, though relying more on the standard classics and, of course, only on Radio 3 which will be restricted to VHF so that it will actually be heard by even fewer people than it is now – and serious speech programmes by hardly anybody at all. This will enable us to prove what we have suspected all along, that nobody wants to listen to this serious stuff and we will have every justification for finally washing our hands of it.

The BBC's official response, on receiving this document, was to invite leaders of the Campaign for Better Broadcasting to come and hear the Corporation's case. Unofficially, tempers were rising at Broadcasting House. Ian Trethowan, now Managing Director, Radio, wrote a draft reply which dismissed the kind of broadcasting valued by the Campaign – that is, the old Third Programme – as 'a private playground for elitists to indulge in cerebral masturbation'.

Meanwhile the *Daily Telegraph* broadcasting correspondent, visiting the Director-General's office, asked Curran why the full reports by the Policy Study Group and McKinsey & Co. had not been published. In reply, he was shown 'two immense piles of documents' totalling perhaps half a million words, and was told: 'If you will guarantee to publish it all, we will let you.' But Curran added: 'A lot of it is out of date.'

He was evidently becoming concerned that the whole of *Broadcasting in the Seventies* might go out of date if this period of so-called public discussion was not brought to an end very soon. On 16 October he told BBC staff that the time had come for 'further action'. Twelve new local radio stations would come into operation in the autumn of 1970, with the remaining twenty being introduced four years later. As to Radios 1, 2, 3 and 4, 'the

Board of Governors has now decided that development should begin on the general lines proposed in *Broadcasting in the Seventies'*. Detailed changes would be announced soon. This was followed by an announcement from Trethowan that the first phase of changes would take place in the week beginning 4 April 1970. He also had some good news for listeners to the Music Programme: the Saturday afternoon sports broadcasts would be moved to Radio 4 – though Test Match commentaries would remain on Radio 3. 'If people say this is illogical, so be it. At least they can't at the same time accuse us of rigidity.'

These abrupt announcements that the changes were to go ahead caused a sudden flare-up of resentment and objection among BBC staff themselves. On 23 October 1969 *The Times* reported that two hundred of them had signed a memorandum to the Director-General expressing 'disquiet' at the changes to Radio 3. 'There will ... not be enough adventurous broadcasting,' stated the protesters; 'risks will not be taken or the necessary proportion of failures accepted. The Third, widely praised and emulated abroad, is being emasculated.' Other protests came from staff in the regions, and on 28 October the main BBC trade union, the Association of Broadcasting Staff, announced that it had joined the Campaign for Better Broadcasting.

The *Guardian*, reporting that the National Union of Journalists had joined the protest too, was of the opinion that only parliamentary intervention could cause the BBC to change its plans. But its correspondence column continued to carry pleas for clemency. 'The Third Programme ... is one of the best things that has happened in postwar Britain,' wrote Geoffrey Strachan on 19 November.

> It is D. G. Bridson, Martin Esslin, George MacBeth, and a mighty host of producers, playwrights, poets, composers, critics, scientists, singers, politicians and people of all kinds who have been given enough time to begin, continue and finish what they had to say ... For some years now we have devoted great efforts to increase the number of people who receive higher education. Is this the moment to dismantle the Third?

Writing in a special issue of the BBC staff magazine *Ariel* (1 December 1969), Gerard Mansell tried to persuade the protesters that nothing vital was being lost. There would be 'seven hours of speech each week on Radio 3 – three or four hours less than on the present Third Programme'; this would be used for 'two major play spots each week', both 'world classics' and 'new writing', which left about three hours each week 'in which Radio 3 can continue to play its part in reflecting new thinking, new ideas, and new attitudes to contemporary issues'. As to the assertion that 'mixed' programming was being abandoned for streamlined, generic networks, 'If this is true then it happened quite a number of years ago, with the creation of the Music Programme – and not many of the one million people who listen to it at some point each day would agree that that was an undesirable development.' Meanwhile Curran, Trethowan and other senior management dined and lunched with crucial figures in the Campaign for Better Broadcasting, endeavouring to make peace. Newby, too, had a session with them. He reported to Trethowan on 6 January 1970 that they remained 'uneasy and unconvinced'.

In mid-January, Newby unveiled his plans for the second quarter of 1970, when the changes would come into effect. Radio 3 was to carry 'a higher proportion of mainstream orchestral music' than before, but there would be plenty of contemporary music too, and a wide range of drama. His terse statement produced a three-page response from the Campaign, pointing out that much of the Radio 4 airtime which was to be devoted to former Third Programme speech material would clash with the remaining speech content of Radio 3, so that it would not be possible for the same person to hear it all. The Campaign's rejoinder continued:

What is left of speech on Radio 3? Only drama that demands a special interest or knowledge, or that is too long or too difficult for Radio 4, and the remainder of its programmes shorn of their most popular and entertaining material. In other words speech on Radio 3 becomes what it has never been before – an area confined to difficult, demanding, 'really heavy esoteric stuff'.

How can you attract young producers, young writers, young con-tributors and young listeners to such a small area of broadcasting, left with no identity, no prestige, no discernible character and no loyalty in the public mind? This is what should be the arena, the leading edge, the pacemaker in cultural, scientific *and* current affairs. The one place where the BBC can make a mark that it cannot make anywhere else, on radio *or* television. The one place which initiated a radio revolution which the whole of Europe followed.

The Campaign suspected that, in the long run, speech would disappear altogether from Radio 3: 'The feeling among production staff is that robbed of a stimulating context and identity it is unlikely to survive for more than five years.'

The protests continued, with *The Times* publishing many letters from distinguished people pleading for a stay of execution on the Third. The Provost of King's College, Cambridge, Edmund Leach, hoped that the BBC would retain the name Third Programme for the new Radio 3: 'The consumers' confidence has been shaken, we need an *appellation contrôlée*.' Dame Peggy Ashcroft, Harold Pinter, Benjamin Britten and Bertrand Russell were among forty leaders of the artistic and intellectual world who pleaded for 'further discussion of the BBC's plans', and hoped that the Third could be 'expanded' rather than deleted. Geoffrey Grigson asked: 'Why does Mr Curran suppose that even the vocable *Third Programme* has exerted a kind of magic, white magic, in this country and abroad? Why, in this case, is a "new structure" – and not simply a new energy – required?' And on 14 February *The Times* carried a letter signed by 134 BBC staff, both current and retired, who were thereby breaking one of the terms of their employment – not to comment on BBC policy in the press. 'What we object to,' stated the letter, 'is the abandonment of creative, mixed planning in favour of a schematic division into categories … and … the refusal to devote a large well-defined area of broadcasting to a service of the arts and sciences … The Third Programme, the outstanding creative achievement of BBC radio, will be abolished, and no project of comparable vision will take its place.' The signatories included, from Drama, Douglas Cleverdon, Nesta Pain, R. D. Smith and John Tydeman; from Talks, Philip French and George MacBeth; from Music, Hans Keller and Robert Simpson; from Third Programme announcers, Tom Crowe, Patricia Hughes and Cormac Rigby; and Leslie Stokes. On the front page of *The Times* an anonymous BBC 'prominent figure' described the signatories as 'disenchanted Radio 3 people', and said that the Corporation would not pay the slightest heed to the letter.

This proved correct. On Friday 3 April 1970, *The Times* reported: 'The Third Programme, welcomed in *The Times* soon after its start in September, 1946, as a "powerful newcomer among the agents of enlightened democracy", ends in name, and to some extent in form, tonight.' It noted that the final evening's broadcasts included a production of *All's Well That Ends Well*. This time there was no funeral at the Royal Court.

In the opening paragraphs of *Broadcasting in the Seventies* it had been stated that the 'reassessment of radio' had become urgent because of the BBC's 'money problems'. But during the autumn of 1969 the Government had agreed to an increase in the licence fee, and at the press conference to announce the schedules for BBC radio without the Third Programme, Ian Trethowan admitted that they would 'cost slightly more than last year's'.

RADIO 3

CHAPTER ONE

Away from the black tie

'The new Third-less world of radio arrived yesterday,' wrote John Woodforde in the *Sunday Telegraph* on 5 April 1970. 'Yet, despite the protracted and angry public discussions, few listeners will notice much change.' In the edition of the *Radio Times* which carried the new schedules Howard Newby told an interviewer that 'the very first evening of Radio 3 under the new plans' would sound exactly like 'the old Third Programme':

> From 6 until 7 we're going to have Denis Matthews talking about Beethoven, particularly with reference to the 9th Symphony. From 7 until 8 we're going to have a philosophic discussion between Sir Karl Popper, Warnock, Strawson and Bryan Magee, who's going to be the steering chairman.[1] They're discussing Bertrand Russell's contribution to philosophy and the extent to which the issues he raises have still philosophically to be tackled nowadays. This is going to be as rigorous as anything the Third Programme ever broadcast. Thereafter at 8 we're broadcasting the Beethoven concert with the orchestra of the size that Beethoven had been familiar with; the 8th Symphony in the first part, *Personal View* in the interval, and the 9th Symphony in the second part. After that we have a repeat of a talk on Frank Lloyd Wright, for 20 minutes, and chamber music between 10.25 and 11.30.

The remainder of the first week's evening programmes on the 'Third-less' Radio 3 included Christopher Hampton's dramatisation of Isaac Babel's *Marya* (Sunday 5 April), *Wozzeck* from the Royal Opera House, conducted by Colin Davis (Monday 6 April), a talk on *Cicero's Religious Dilemmas* (Wednesday 8 April), and a repeat of a Hilda Tablet episode, *Musique Discrete* (Friday 10 April). Only current affairs programmes were absent, transferred to Radio 4. 'What remains,' stated the *Radio Times*, 'is

---

[1] Magee was back in the autumn of 1970 with thirteen *Conversations with Philosophers*, beginning on 8 November. This interview series, in which he spoke to A. J. Ayer, Gilbert Ryle, and other leading philosophers, was so successful that it was eventually repeated on BBC Television.

great classic and modern drama, new and adventurous writing for radio, and the expression of original thinking in the arts and sciences.'

A BBC 'fact sheet' issued to the public in February had put it even more forcefully:

> *The Third Programme label* will go. *The Third Programme concept* is *not* being abandoned. We want a larger audience for good programmes, but there is absolutely no question of abandoning minority programmes, except those that have commanded only the smallest 'coterie' audiences, below the reach of audience research sampling. Such programmes are few[2] and the total speech content of Radio 3 will be reduced by only 1½–2 hours per week. These changes are *not* radical.

The principle of 'no fixed points' had not been abandoned. 'The programming remains flexible so that important relays can be included,' pointed out the *Radio Times*. Moreover an extra half-hour's airtime had been granted, so that Radio 3 now closed down with a news bulletin at 11.30 pm.

Nevertheless there had been one major policy change, as announced in *Broadcasting in the Seventies*. Ian Trethowan explained in the *Radio Times*: 'Radio 3 will be strengthened by music becoming the dominant factor in the evening.' Strikingly, this was attacked, in a symposium about the changes in the *Radio Times*, by Peter Maxwell Davies. Explaining that in his schooldays he had tuned in to the Third to hear music, but had picked up 'other forms of culture' in the process, he said he feared that people would now 'lose whole realms of experience' through the introduction of 'generic' broadcasting (music on one channel, speech on another). Newby replied that the speech content of the new Radio 3 would 'exactly match the expectation that you have described', apart from the loss of current affairs. To which another participant in the symposium, the music critic Edward Greenfield, responded: 'Why, then, the recent enormous fuss, with so many producers writing to *The Times*, and risking their jobs?' No one offered an answer. In retrospect, *Broadcasting in the Seventies* was beginning to look like an enormous botch in public relations, which had had little effect on the national radio networks it was supposed to have reorganised.

'The keystones of the former Music Programme remain,' stated the *Radio Times*, referring to Radio 3's daytime broadcasting. Here, too, there was an expansion of hours: Saturday afternoon sport passed to Radio 2, and was replaced by *Afternoon Sequence: a personal choice of records* (the first edition, on 4 April, was presented by Edward Greenfield). *Choral Evensong*, which had moved to Radio 3 from Radio 4, was initially heard only once a month, but after about 2,500 protests were received from listeners it

---

[2] It may be doubted whether there were any programmes that came strictly into this 'minority' category, except the hobbies broadcasts on Network Three. It is notable how, throughout the *Broadcasting in the Seventies* brouhaha, and indeed around the time of the 1957 cuts, the BBC consistently confused cultural programmes with broadcasting for minorities.

became, from July 1970, a weekly broadcast, on Wednesday afternoons.

The Proms were now all to be carried on Radio 3 (with the exception of an occasional Sunday Prom, which clashed with Radio 3's regular Sunday night play, and so was broadcast on Radio 4; also Gilbert and Sullivan Proms were heard on Radio 2). William Glock was a little anxious about this change – he told the *Radio Times* he had 'no idea how many people are going to listen' – but there was now much greater flexibility of timing in planning each Prom, since the first half no longer needed to end in time for Radio 4's news bulletin at 9 pm.

At the end of the 1970 season it became clear that the Radio 3 Proms audience had indeed been much smaller than that which Radio 4 had attracted. On the other hand the average evening audience for Radio 3 had doubled from 50,000 to 100,000 because the network was now carrying mainstream classical music at night. Most evenings, the principal item was a concert in which the names of Mozart, Schubert, Beethoven and Brahms were much more likely to feature than they had in Third Programme days. The audience for this was 'about 80% middle class', and 'about half the listeners were over 50, equally divided between the sexes'.

Radio 4 was getting up to four times Radio 3's evening audience, but radio critics and other press commentators seemed to feel that the two networks now offered a welcome choice of high-quality alternatives – speech or music – rather than the old division by brow level. Inevitably, though, there were some grumbles from the old guard. D. G. Bridson, retired from a long career in Features, wrote in his memoirs that *Broadcasting in the Seventies* had ushered in an era designed 'for the Yahoos', and regretted that 'confining all good music to the narrow groove of Radio 3 ... has merely made doubly sure that none but the already converted will ever hear good music again'.

There was also some anxiety about the future, fuelled by rumours that Edward Heath's Conservative Government, elected in the summer of 1970, would take away the BBC's medium wavelengths and give them to the commercial radio stations they planned to license. The press speculated that Radio 3's medium-wave coverage might disappear very soon. In fact it had many more years to run, and from the beginning of 1971 it was Radio 3's FM wavelengths which had to be handed over, for brief but significant periods each week, to the Open University.

*

The concept of a 'University of the Air', open to all, first became public in 1963 when Harold Wilson, leader of the Labour opposition, proposed it as a consortium of existing universities that would use broadcasting and correspondence to bring tuition to adults in their own homes. Behind the scenes the project was led by the educationist Michael Young, with Peter Laslett, the former Third Programme producer and leading figure in the Sound Broadcasting Society's 1957 campaign, playing a prominent part. 'Michael Young and I became friends,' Laslett recalls.

He and I agreed about breaking the monopolies of universities, and broadcasting was clearly the manner of doing so. A submission, signed by distinguished names, persuaded [Harold] Wilson that the University of the Air was not only practicable but an obvious Labour Party policy. We knew even then that it had to be a mixture of television, open circuit sound broadcasting, closed circuit recording, correspondence and teaching. We wanted broadcasting because it would be an immediately and completely transparently available source of instruction to every citizen with a wireless or television set. It's been the most remarkable success in British educational history.

Asked whether he sees a historic connection between the Third Programme and the Open University, Laslett replies: 'The Third Programme was not intended for education at all. There was a strong feeling against education in the original Third.' However, talks producer Prudence Smith disagrees:

Peter is using 'education' in a pejorative sense. I'm one of the few people who does see a link between the Third and the Open University. Two of us from the original Third Programme, Helen Rapp and myself, were appointed in 1970 to train the new intake of producers – young graduates, straight from university – for the Open University. We'd both spent most of our BBC careers in the Third, and we naturally brought to bear on it the experience we had gathered there. Also those Third Programme meetings, where ideas were discussed, were simulated at the Open University by the way in which academics and broadcasters sat at the same table – it wasn't the academics telling the broadcasters what to do. The broadcasters themselves often moulded what was in the academic mind. That was the Third Programme tradition.

The first Open University programme on Radio 3 was *Arts Foundation Course 1*, broadcast on Monday 11 January 1971 from 7 to 7.30 pm, on FM only. Thereafter the floodgates opened, and the OU was soon occupying Radio 3 FM in the early morning and early evening on most days each week in term-time, complicating the lives of programme planners and necessitating the use of a separate Continuity studio. The BBC's own 'Study on 3' further education programmes – the descendant of Network Three and Study Session – continued as before in the early evening, but on medium wave only while the OU was in session.

There was, however, a substantial benefit to Radio 3 from the Open University. Programmes broadcast on medium wave while it was on FM were low-cost – the news, *Concert Calendar* and the stockmarket report – and Newby was able to persuade Trethowan that the money saved could be used to extend Radio 3 to midnight on Fridays and Saturdays. This extension began in January 1972, restoring after fifteen years all the evening airtime that had been lopped off the Third in 1957.

In theory Newby now had control over all the network's choice of music.

In practice he left this mostly to Music Division. 'My role,' he says, 'was limited to saying, if they had chosen Schoenberg as *This Week's Composer* [at 9 am each weekday], was that a wise decision – shouldn't it be someone more accessible? That was the kind of remark one made, but certainly I didn't get involved in any decision-making before the event.' He did, however, hold regular meetings with Music Division, and at the first of these after the *Broadcasting in the Seventies* changes, on 8 April 1970, there was some discussion about a proposed 'Afternoon Sequence' of music: 'Stephen Dodgson and David Munrow were among those suggested as future presenters.' Dodgson, a composer, was already a frequent broadcaster. Munrow, a newcomer to radio, was about to make a dazzling impression on listeners.

He had first approached the BBC in 1966, when he was twenty-four and earning a living in the Royal Shakespeare Company's wind band at Stratford-upon-Avon:

> I play renaissance and baroque recorders [Munrow wrote], crumhorns, dulcian, kortholt, rauschpfeife and rachett ... I have given broadcast solo recitals abroad on Czech radio and Peruvian television. I lecture part-time in the history of early music at Leicester University and teach early woodwind instruments at King's College, London. I am particularly interested in organising programmes of early music.

He also offered himself as a solo player, and as one half of a recorder and harpsichord duo with Christopher Hogwood, who was currently presenting *The Young Idea*, a programme of records chosen by young people, on the Music Programme at teatime on Wednesdays.

During the late 1960s Munrow became a frequent performer on Radio 3 as a musician, and by 1970 his Early Music Consort, in which Hogwood was the keyboard player, was well enough established to perform at the Proms. But it was not until May 1971 that he had his chance as a presenter, recording four twenty-minute pilot programmes for a series to be called *Pied Piper*, subtitled 'Tales and Music for Younger Listeners'. The first broadcast in the series was heard on Monday 30 August 1971 at 4.40 pm. It soon became clear that Radio 3 had acquired one of the most brilliant and appealing broadcasters in the BBC's history.

The producer of *Pied Piper* was Arthur Johnson, a young Scot in Gramophone Department. He had never encountered Munrow before they made the pilots. 'People had been talking about this vivacious young man,' he says.

> David and his wife Gill had been making ends meet by going round music clubs, schools, with a bag of instruments, and giving lecture recitals – she would help out the odd bit of percussion, or a medieval harp, and he would blow away. I had already been producing *The Young Idea*, with Christopher Hogwood, and David and Chris had been at Cambridge, and

worked together. Chris said, 'What about David Munrow?' So I was sent off to speak to David.

In appearance, he was the most unprepossessing person I'd ever met – very small of stature, maybe just over five feet high, and his face was like a boy from the fourth form. He was frequently mistaken for a juvenile. But he was the most fascinating and extraordinary person I've ever known. He was totally untaught in music, but he'd got hold of a bassoon at school, and taught himself to play it, and it started from there.

Between school and university, Munrow had spent time in Peru, working as a teacher, and in spare time had travelled widely, encountering village musicians playing wind instruments that had been brought to Latin America by conquering Spaniards centuries earlier, and had remained essentially unchanged ever since. He returned to Cambridge with a bag full of them.

There, he read English, but began to organise early music concerts. After taking his degree, he got a job from Guy Woolfenden, musical director of the Royal Shakespeare Company, who was happy to write parts for Munrow's medieval wind instruments, which he was still discovering, acquiring, and teaching himself to play. Eventually his outside commitments became too numerous and he went freelance.

Pied Piper grew out of a suggestion by Peter Dodd, successor to Leslie Stokes (who had retired in the spring of 1970) as Chief Assistant, Radio 3, that there should be 'music programmes aimed at children in the 6 to 12 age-group'. Arthur Johnson says that neither he nor Munrow had expected a long run:

> We'd initially planned a quarter's programmes – four a week for thirteen weeks – just to see how it would go, and then, like *Desert Island Discs*, it just continued, for week after week, except for a summer break. There was one theme each week, and one programme was an interview (it wasn't always a musician). The main age-group who were listening were 14–20 – older than the children we were supposed to be aiming at. People who are now successful professional musicians often say they cut their teeth on *Pied Piper*. Roy Goodman, who conducts the Hanover Band, says he used to make a point of listening to it.

Each twenty-minute programme, introduced with a suitably Pied-Piperish signature tune for sopranino recorder – played of course by Munrow himself – was packed with information and anecdotes to introduce the musical illustrations, delivered in a relaxed manner, but actually the fruit of extensive research. 'We were one presenter, one producer, one secretary, and no researcher,' says Johnson, 'though David's wife Gill helped a lot, finding books and records, and even typing scripts at home, because there wasn't time for them to be typed in the office – David was doing so much else beside the programme that he would have to write them at the last minute.' Munrow's frequent absences on tours with his

Consort meant that up to thirty programmes might have to be recorded in advance at the rate of four per day.[3] 'Meanwhile,' adds Johnson,

I was still expected to do my regular stint on *This Week's Composer* and *Morning Concert* and all the rest of it. And *Pied Piper* was a big strain – on me as well as David. I wouldn't call him a manic depressive, but he was obsessive, and he was driven. He was a perfectionist, and he wanted to do everything himself – he would even put up the music stands at a Consort recording session, and they said that he did it faster and better than anyone else! In the *Pied Piper* studio, he would be setting up LPs on the grams decks, and finding the right groove, though it was someone else's job.

By the spring of 1976, when the programme was coming to the end of its fifth year, 'the pressure had built,' says Johnson, 'and it began to show in him, physically and emotionally. He was only in his early thirties, but looking at photographs of him, you can see it taking its toll. He wasn't sleeping. But what finally happened to him wasn't only due to *Pied Piper*. There were domestic pressures too.' The previous year, Munrow had been hospitalised following an overdose, but he had managed to complete a book on early musical instruments, and besides *Pied Piper* was also recording a five-part series on the same subject for BBC2. Then on Saturday he was found dead by his wife at their Buckinghamshire house. 'I was in the garden, cutting the grass that Saturday morning, and Gill rang me,' says Johnson. 'She had found his body hanging. The next week's programmes had already been recorded, but it was decided to cancel them. I spent the Sunday and Monday preparing a memorial programme to him, with Christopher Hogwood and others in it, and that was put out on the Monday instead of *Pied Piper*. I counted up, and we had done six hundred and fifty-five editions of it.'

*

At the end of 1971, after thirteen years as Controller of the Third Programme and then Radio 3, Howard Newby was appointed Director of Programmes, Radio; he was succeeded as Controller on 1 January 1972 by Stephen Hearst, head of arts programmes in BBC Television.

Born in Vienna immediately after the fall of the Austro-Hungarian Empire, Hearst says that 'therefore I've always described myself as an expert in imperial decay'. The son of a prominent dental surgeon, he began to study medicine at university, but then Hitler came, 'and I disappeared in the first three days, because I was not merely Jewish, but had distributed pamphlets, and stuck labels for the Patriotic Front on to the backs of

---

[3] Ironically, while Munrow was being over-used, the BBC was reluctant to put most other early music performers on the air, on the grounds that they were not yet technically good enough.

Nazis'. His father eventually became a Harley Street dentist, but Stephen arrived in England by himself, 'with ten pounds in my pocket. Yet that very evening I found myself in the Savile Club, being introduced to H. G. Wells'. He was interned early in the war, like so many German-speaking refugees, 'and in the next tent were three members of the Amadeus Quartet'. He then joined the Pioneer Corps, fought in the beach landings in Italy, and became commandant of a camp for Italian prisoners of war in Palestine. In 1946 he went to Brasenose College, Oxford, to read history; then became a Marks & Spencer trainee; then achieved his long-desired aim of joining the BBC.

He was a devoted listener to the Third from its earliest days – 'The whole of the *Ring* – one had never heard this before on radio!' – but found himself in television, writing newsreel scripts. 'Then I became Richard Dimbleby's scriptwriter for documentaries, and a writer–producer for ten years, and eventually Executive Producer of Arts Programmes, under Huw Wheldon – Huw was a great champion, and I was in his slipstream.' Two outstanding series, Alistair Cooke's *America* and Kenneth Clark's *Civilisation*, were made when he was head of the department.

Howard Newby says that Hearst 'was not initially very enthusiastic about coming over to radio'. Hearst himself recalls:

People like Alisdair Milne and Huw Wheldon thought it was preposterous, after this highly interesting life, to go into what they thought was a decaying medium. But I thought that Radio 3 was culturally as important as anything the BBC did; it was the touchstone on which the public service of the BBC would be judged. Secondly, I'd spent a lot of my life in music – my father knew the Mahler family well. I didn't actually think I would get it, but when Ian Trethowan phoned I agreed to stand.

Subsequently I found out that Martin Esslin [another candidate], who had tremendous qualifications, had said to the board that it wasn't the business of the Controller of Radio 3 to think of the size of the audience. Given the importance of the cultural material that Radio 3 was broadcasting, he said, the audience figures played absolutely no part in it; it was an anti-cultural and deeply divisive idea.[4] I was asked the same question, and I said, 'We are financed by public money. I regard Radio 3 as immensely important, but it does soak up (at that time) £42 million, and there is therefore a need to consider a minimum of audience. And I said that for any one programme it needs to be between 50,000 and 100,000. And it could be enlarged, given an understanding of the audience, and a lively style of broadcasting.' That apparently went down well. I think it reassured Lord Hill.

---

[4] Esslin says that Curran, the Director-General, had 'more or less told me I would have the job', but Lord Hill, Chairman of the BBC, treated him at the appointment board as 'a nasty foreign intellectual'. Esslin adds: 'The Third Programme was being destroyed from the day that Hill became Chairman.'

Hearst says that on his arrival at Radio 3, he was regarded initially as an outsider, not because he was a foreigner, but because he came from TV. 'They thought I would be a populist, and change a great deal. But I had a profound respect for it.' Cormac Rigby, who became a key member of Hearst's team, describes him as 'an enthusiast who loved to get things fizzing – to ginger up ideas. And if people were enthusiastic about what they were doing, by and large he would let them have their head. He was never a wet blanket.' The producer Philip French describes Hearst as mercurial:

> Stephen was tremendously charming, but he was always up and down. Some supposedly cataclysmic event would have happened in the world, and Stephen would come into B.H. [Broadcasting House] and explode, in his heavy Viennese accent, 'R-r-rome is bur-r-rning, and what are we doing but fiddling?' And then he could become totally contrite.
>
> Also, like all people coming to radio from television (John Drummond was the same later on), Stephen had a degree of contempt for it, never made absolutely explicit – but it's like a carnivore descending into a world of herbivores. Television people also believe that they have a superior understanding of radio, but actually all they can think of is how to increase audiences, and make it less 'elitist'. Yet Stephen was ambivalent about this. He also believed in high standards, and was an extremely intelligent and cultured man. And he created a relaxed atmosphere – in the sense that he might have a row with you, but he always made it up with you afterwards.

Just before taking up his Controllership, Hearst asked the Head of Presentation, Television, to take every opportunity to 'trail' forthcoming opera broadcasts on Radio 3: 'Since something like half the adult population now watch television, the occasional reference ... can do Radio 3 a great deal of good.' The same memo mentioned that there was 'a slightly new situation in that each radio channel now has its own Presentation Editor'. As in the early days of the Third, Radio 3 would have its own team of announcers. The man chosen to head them, and to oversee Continuity and other aspects of presentation, was Cormac Rigby.

After taking his degree at Oxford, Rigby had gone to Rome to train for the Roman Catholic priesthood, but had found the regime at the English College in 1962 – the year before the Second Vatican Council – to be 'narrow and constricting'. He lasted a year. His decision to leave was 'triggered by the Rector's request that I cancel a subscription to the *Times Educational Supplement* because such reading was a needless distraction to a seminarian'. Departing from Rome 'in some distress', he returned to Oxford, where he worked at a doctoral thesis on the Victorian headmaster and preacher Edward Thring. When his grant expired after three years, 'I opened the *New Musical Express* one morning and found they were looking for announcers for the new Music Programme. Next to it was an advertisement for disc jockeys for Radio Caroline, and the two successful applicants for those two advertisements were Tony Blackburn and me – we're broadcasting twins.'

Rigby later learnt that one of the original Third Programme announcers, Christopher Pemberton, had gone in the opposite direction, leaving the BBC in the late 1950s to become a Catholic priest, serving for part of each year at the English College in Rome. After Pemberton's death in 1983, Rigby wrote that he felt 'Radio 3 would now have its own patron saint in Heaven'.

Rigby joined the BBC five years before the demise of the Third Programme, and had to serve an apprenticeship on the other networks before he was allowed to be heard on it:

> What I was joining was a Presentation Department that served all the radio networks. So you might do an overnight shift reading the news and *Today in Parliament* on the Home Service, and then open up the Music Programme the following morning. I had no specialist knowledge of music – I don't play an instrument and I can't even read music – but I *love* music. And that's what they were interested in. They wanted somebody who would be able to mediate between the musicologists and the people who loved music but didn't quite know what it was about it that they loved.

After a while, Rigby was admitted by Leslie Stokes into the inner sanctum of announcers permitted to do Third Continuity. 'On my first night in Third Programme,' he recalls, 'I had to leave a full minute of silence between one programme and the next. The idea was to discourage people from casual listening. They were expected to look at their *Radio Times*, choose what they want, listen to it, and then go away and do all the other interesting things that their lives were full of.'

Rigby's own area of enthusiasm was ballet, which had never been given much airtime on the Third. He persuaded Newby to let him compile and present a series, *Royal Repertoire*, about the music in the current season at the Royal Ballet, at first using records, but subsequently with the BBC Concert Orchestra. It ran throughout the 1970s, and when Rigby left the BBC in 1985 the *Dancing Times* lamented the departure of 'this dance-informed person within the sacred walls of the classical music department'.

Having done a stint as its programme planner towards the end of its life, and also having taken over Leslie Stokes's task of compiling the quarterly Radio 3 supplement in the *Listener*, Rigby came to know the Third extremely well; yet he feels that *Broadcasting in the Seventies* did not destroy its essential character: 'By the time Radio 3 had settled, five years down the road, I think in effect we got back to the Third Programme – in effect the old Music Programme, that awful hour of Study Session, and then Third Programme in the evening. I think Third Programme continued long after the title had gone, largely in the motivation of the people who were producing programmes for it.' However, as Radio 3's Presentation Editor, he was required to move away from the distancing chill of the old

Third Programme atmosphere: 'My brief was to shift away from the black tie, to do a lot of thawing, to move away from the golden voices of the Alvar Liddell era.'

Nevertheless Rigby did not want too much informality. A 1972 memo from him to his announcing team complains of

announcements much too close on the heels of the music ... The music, its reverb[eration] and its afterglow must be treated with due respect by us. Music needs space to breathe ... Great music needs more space still ... please have some regard for listeners who need a recovery period after a performance of a major work. To hurl in a fill[5] ... within a couple of minutes of – say – a late Beethoven quartet is offensive to some. Better indulge in a little gentle trailing.[6]

Announcers of Alvar Liddell's generation had not been expected to do much more than read words written for them by other people. Rigby recalls that Liddell himself, who was still on the staff when he joined, 'would expect to have everything prepared for him: the script would be carefully typed up, and all the problems would have been sussed out in advance of his arrival'. In contrast, announcers of the Radio 3 Wednesday lunchtime series *Concert Hall*, featuring young and virtually unknown artists live from the concert hall of Broadcasting House, had to write much of their own scripts, and at the last minute. 'I did the first five years of those,' says Rigby,

before Peter Barker took over. The announcer had to go along to the green room to talk to the young artists beforehand, chatting largely to relax them. You'd ask them about their background, largely as a way of countering their nerves. It meant that you had to rely on your handwriting, because what you were writing down about them at twenty to one you had to give out on the air, and sound as though you knew what you were talking about, at five past one.

Concert Hall presented some of the most successful applicants to the BBC's frequent series of auditions for singers and instrumentalists. The accompanist Graham Johnson, who was in his early twenties when *Concert Hall* began, was among these. 'I can't exaggerate the awe that a young musician felt about the BBC,' he says.

Passing an audition and getting on the BBC's books was something you took deadly seriously. (You couldn't make records in those days – only God's chosen few made records.) You had to wait in a green room, somewhere near Broadcasting House, and then you were taken in. The panel was invisible, somewhere in a listening room, and blinds were drawn. You didn't know who they were – it could have been Hans Keller.

---

[5] A short gramophone record to fill up a gap.
[6] Reading trailers for forthcoming programmes.

The performers were equally invisible and anonymous to the panel. Anthony Burton, who was one of the auditioning producers in those days, says: 'I remember hearing Paul Goodwin, the baroque oboist, at an audition – and hearing the absolutely finished article, somebody who was moving us, even with the blinds down in the control cubicle so that we had no idea who this was, or what he looked like.'

Among others who came successfully through this process and appeared in *Concert Hall* and other Radio 3 programmes during the early 1970s was the tenor Anthony Rolfe Johnson, who writes:

> My audition was not conventional. In 1971 when still a student at the Guildhall School of Music and Drama, I was invited by Peter Wishart, then professor of composition, to be the tenor soloist in the *Nocturne* by Benjamin Britten. The BBC were running their series *Youth Orchestras of the World* and we were invited to perform the same programme for this series. I realised that I would soon have to sing an audition for the BBC and had heard many tales of horror about this process. After some discussion with Wilfred Stiffs of Ibbs and Tillett [his agent] we decided to suggest to the BBC that since I had already broadcast for them, they should take the tape of the programme and consider it as my audition. Much to my amazement they did and I passed!

Everyone who participated in *Concert Hall* praises the skill of its original producer, Eleanor Warren, and of her colleague Paul Hamburger, who sometimes took part in it as accompanist. Warren had been a well-known cellist, and was the first wife of the conductor Walter Susskind. 'As Chief Producer, Artists,' explains Ernest Warburton, 'she was responsible for the auditions procedure, and the development of young performers. She did a terrific job in both capacities.' Graham Johnson says: 'Eleanor Warren did more single-handedly for the careers of young musicians, particularly string players, than anyone else in this country.'

Johnson recalls that live *Concert Hall* broadcasts were 'the most stressful thing one ever did. The thought of going out there, and playing, in the heat of the moment, wrong notes which would be disseminated throughout the country by the BBC, was appalling!' And he recalls that the stress did not end when the programme was over:

> There was a kind of KGB watch kept on your broadcasts. Producers put in reports which evaluated them. Paul Hamburger once told me that I'd got a succession of 'B's. I was rather cut up, because I thought I might occasionally have managed an 'A'. But he said, 'No, "A" means "better than expected"; "B" means "as expected", and "C" means "worse than expected".' And therefore the most distinguished artists usually earned a 'B'. This seemed to be a rather absurd piece of bureaucracy at the time, though nowadays I regret that it's gone, and that there doesn't seem to be the same ruthless insistence on standards.

Files in the BBC's Written Archives contain reports exactly as described by

Johnson. On the other hand, Johnson emphasises the care that producers would lavish on artists they particularly admired: 'The young Margaret Price, for example, was completely taken over and encouraged by Leo Black, who asked her to do all sorts of Schubert songs that she sings to this day – and challenged her to do Berg for the first time, which she sings to this day.'

Paul Hamburger, mentioned by Johnson, was an important member of the *Concert Hall* team, both as a producer and an accompanist. 'Paul was not only a very gifted pianist but marvellous at bringing on young artists,' says Cormac Rigby. Anthony Burton points out that Hamburger was technically the BBC's 'staff accompanist' – the last person to hold that long-established title – as well as a producer.

Burton emphasises that, at this period, everyone was able to exploit their particular skills and enthusiasms: 'One was encouraged, in those days, to do what one was interested in. I could produce an edition of *Music in Our Time*, a choir singing Renaissance music, and on Saturday morning I could go down to the Festival Hall and do a Robert Mayer concert.' But Graham Johnson points out that producers sometimes seemed to be doing their jobs with less than full attention:

My first broadcast was with a highly eccentric, elderly violinist; I think Eleanor Warren had decided to give me a chance with him. (At the rehearsal, he told me he'd found a means of travelling at twenty thousand miles an hour, on some sort of carpet, and lots of people were after him for the secret.) The producer was one of the real old school, and he threw at us the Schubert *Fantasia*, which is one of the hardest pieces of chamber music ever written for the piano, some Paganini pieces, and Guy-Ropartz's Second Violin Sonata, which is about eighty pages of post-César Franckian difficulty. And all that could be seen of the producer, as we ploughed our way through this, was the back of the *Daily Telegraph*. At the end, he put the paper down and said, 'Not such a good piece as I thought, really.'

*

Another weekly lunchtime live concert series, the Monday recitals from St John's, Smith Square – also the creation of Eleanor Warren – became one of Radio 3's most popular programmes, not the least factor being the announcer who always introduced them, Patricia Hughes. Cormac Rigby describes her as

the most successful of all women announcers – her personality is a combination of dignity and friendliness. There had been female announcers on the Third from the very beginning – Marjorie Anderson, and also Joy Worth, who had a lovely, slightly 'ginny' voice. You've got to be a very special woman to have a good broadcasting voice – the male voice is, normally, much harder and clearer. I brought Patricia back after her maternity absence. Later I brought in Elaine Padmore, and Susan Sharpe.[7]

Patricia Hughes had left the BBC in 1962; she returned to announcing in 1969, initially as a freelance. She found the atmosphere on the Third 'much more relaxed' than it had been when she left, and was 'thrilled' when she was asked to announce the St John's, Smith Square concerts, which began on 8 December 1969. 'I was absolutely terrified at first, having had a long break from announcing. The first one was the Amadeus Quartet, with William Pleeth, playing the Schubert quintet in C major. But people were very kind – some who were regularly in the audience gave me invitations to dinner, and I made a very great friend of someone who used to come each week from Cheltenham.'

Rigby recalls that Stephen Hearst did not initially share his enthusiasm for Patricia Hughes: 'He took me out to lunch, and we were talking about reducing the starch in the network, and Stephen said: "My dear Cormac, you have to get rid of that terrible woman with the Kensington voice." And I realised he meant Patricia, who was the most popular individual member of my announcing team, and I said, "You must be joking." He wasn't, but he was always a big enough man to rethink his own prejudices.' Hearst himself confirms that he soon came to admire her greatly. Tony Scotland, a later recruit to the team, says that Rigby was an unfailing defender of his staff against the whims of successive Controllers – and also meticulous in trying to meet their needs with regard to shift, overtime, 'and even the numbers of blankets in the announcer's bedroom in the Langham. And he was always ready to step in and do an extra shift himself, to help us out.'

In contrast with Patricia Hughes's flawless style at the microphone was the eccentricity of another member of the announcing team who, too, had returned to the BBC after several years' absence. 'The divine Tom Crowe!' exclaims Rigby.

During eight years away, Crowe had travelled in the Middle East and written a memoir of an Arabist friend, Owen Tweedy, called *Gathering Moss*. It was published in 1967, by which time Crowe was back at the BBC. 'When I came back to the Third,' he says, 'I thought, "I'm simply not going to be frightened by this peculiar object in front of me, the microphone." And so I broke loose. I became notorious – the BBC shivered whenever I went on the air! But the audience seemed to like it. And I got rid of all that reverence.' Crowe's announcing, in the faintest of Irish accents, was indeed distinguished by its witticisms and mishaps. Hans Keller became a particular admirer of his humour. For example he noted that, one morning in June 1971, Crowe had opened up Radio 3 for the day with the remark: 'Good morning to you. It's seven o'clock, I'm afraid.' To which Keller commented: 'Inspired.'

---

[7] And briefly Moira Shearer, who says she found Continuity announcing daunting, and is remembered as having an excellent voice but sounding a little too theatrical.

Peter Ustinov (*left*) and Peter Jones, celebrating the tenth anniversary of the Third Programme in 1956 with *In Third Gear*.

Samuel Beckett's *Fin de partie* being recorded for the Third Programme, in 1957, by the French cast of the Royal Court Theatre production. (*Left to right*) Betty Johnson, BBC studio manager (sound effects), Jean Martin (Clov), Christina Tsingos (Nell), Georges Adet (Nagg) and Roger Blin (Hamm).

The Sound Broadcasting Society (formerly the Third Programme Defence Society) holds a press conference at the home of Ralph Vaughan Williams, on 18 July 1957, to protest against the BBC's proposed cuts in the Third. (*Left to right*) Michael Tippett, Paul Sieghart, Peter Laslett, Roy Walker, Sir Laurence Olivier, Peter Needs and Vaughan Williams (with ear trumpet).

P. H. Newby, photographed in the autumn of 1958 just as he had been appointed the Third's fourth controller. He was to stay in charge until 1971.

Michael Tippett at the microphone in 1959.

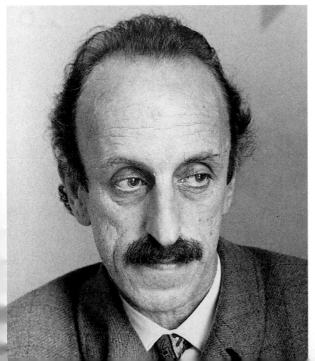

Hans Keller. 'The most controversial decision was to invite Keller on to the staff,' said William Glock.

(right)
Philip French,
producer of *Critic's Forum*
for sixteen years. 'There
were accusations that it
was my fiefdom.'

Radio 3 announcers in
1972. (*Standing left to
right*) Jon Curle, Victor
Hallam, Tony Scotland,
Donald Price, Cormac
Rigby. (*Seated left to right*)
Tom Crowe, Peter Barker,
Patricia Hughes, Robin
Holmes, Norman McLeod.

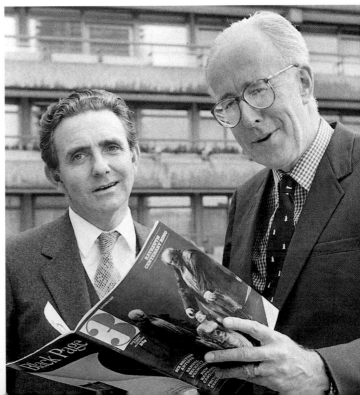

(right)
Radio 3's Controller
Ian McIntyre (*left*) and
Robert Ponsonby,
Controller of Music, at
the launch of *3: The
Radio Three Magazine* in
1982. 'We fought,
inevitably,' says
McIntyre.

Sir William Glock (*left*) at the
press conference announcing
his last Proms season, in June
1973, with Stephen Hearst,
Controller of Radio 3 from
1972 to 1978.

John Drummond, photographed in 1984 when he had just been appointed as the BBC's next Controller of Music. 'I said that what I wanted to do was become Controller of Radio 3.'

Nicholas Kenyon, appointed Controller of Radio 3 in 1992, with a drawing of Henry Purcell at the launch of *Fairest Isle*.

Sir John Gielgud as King Lear and Emma Thompson as Cordelia, in the Radio 3 production to mark Gielgud's ninetieth birthday in April 1994.

(below)
Conductor Andrew Davis with members of the BBC Symphony Orchestra at the Royal Albert Hall, to mark the opening of the 1995 Proms.

Brian Kay presenting *Brian Kay's Sunday Morning* from a Continuity suite in 1995.

Paul Gambaccini, whose Radio 3 programme *Morning Collection*, beginning in September 1995, caused fierce controversy, and ended a year later.

As to the mishaps, Rigby describes the most widely remembered of them:

> The best of all Tom Crowe stories is that wonderful moment when, on a *Morning Concert*, somebody had mistimed the final record, which I think was the *Hebrides* overture, and it over-ran its slot, and they weren't fast enough to suppress the Greenwich Time Signal at nine o'clock. And so the closing bars of the music and the Time Signal coincided, and there was a sort of shocked silence from Tom, and then he came on the air and said: 'Radio 3. The time is nine o'clock, and I do hope that the Mendelssohn didn't interfere with your enjoyment of the pips.'

Crowe says: 'Occasionally one played the wrong record, or played it at the wrong speed, or made other dreadful mistakes. My policy was not to cower when that happened, but to turn the apology into an art-form. And the apology was usually more outrageous and memorable than the mistake!' Towards the end of his years on Radio 3, the *Listener* chronicled some of the best moments: 'There are his laborious, sometimes wildly haywire readings of the studio clock; the back-announcements – "That was Bach's Partita in G, and while you were listening to it I was eating a scrambled egg" – and the incredulous interjections, like the muttered "How repulsive!" in a news story about a dead whale whose stomach exploded, sending tons of rotten blubber all over the beach.' Admittedly, some of his asides bore the mark of premeditation: 'When the clock next misbehaves,' added the *Listener*, 'and he overruns, he will be heard to say that he is *"À la Recherche du Tom Perdu"*.' Patricia Hughes says of these gags: 'I used to tease Tom about his mistakes – "Have you rehearsed them for the morning yet, Tom?" It used to make him very cross.'

In the 1970s, Radio 3 Continuity was in the extension to Broadcasting House, overlooking Duchess Street and visible from it. Cormac Rigby recalls that this caused 'a great scare at one stage because people thought there could be a sniper in the office window opposite, who might train his rifle on the back of the announcer's head and then ring him up and say, "I'm going to shoot you unless you say something rude – or inflammatory – on air." So we had venetian blinds installed, and that was considered to make us safe!'

The other networks had their Continuity suites alongside, which, says Rigby, created a feeling of camaraderie: 'You would get John Peel wandering in from Radio 1 to borrow your dust-bug, to clean a particularly grotty record. That meant that we all felt ourselves to be part of the same enterprise.' Later Radio 1 was moved to Egton House, opposite the main entrance of Broadcasting House, and Continuities for Radios 2, 3 and 4 were installed in more clinical suites in a new wing. 'Something was lost,' says Rigby.

When Rigby became Presentation Editor he and Stephen Hearst decided to revive, on Radio 3, the old Third Programme tradition, which had lapsed for some years, of the Continuity announcer giving readings as planned interludes between programmes. 'It became a great success,' he says. 'Tony Scotland, for example, reading Saki, or Robin Holmes reading from John Clare, were delights.' Perhaps most memorable was Patricia Hughes's performance, in the character of a garrulous Victorian dame, of some late nineteenth-century monologues, *Mrs Caudle's Curtain Lectures*. 'What I wanted to do was to go on the stage,' she says, looking back at her early years. 'That was the thing I always longed for.' These readings (and the recordings she has made since retirement from the BBC of books on cassette) show what an outstanding actress was concealed in her Radio 3 microphone personality.

Tony Scotland joined the announcing team by accident. While working as a sub-editor in the Broadcasting House newsroom, he noticed the numbers of news items about the arts around the world which were not getting into the bulletins. He mentioned this to Cormac Rigby, and found himself invited by Stephen Hearst to compile (with Nigel Lewis) a weekly programme, *The Arts Worldwide*, in which these news stories were read by two announcers. Since this was considered to be a half-time job, it was arranged for him to spend the remainder of his time announcing.

When announcers left the staff, Rigby made it his policy that new appointments should bring down the average age. During 1974 Michael Berkeley, twenty-six-year-old son of the composer Lennox Berkeley, joined the announcing team. After studying composition at the Royal Academy of Music, and privately with Richard Rodney Bennett, Berkeley took a job at London Weekend Television, on the Saturday morning children's programmes. He was then playing keyboard in a rock band called Seeds of Discord, and he says that he and his colleagues at LWT 'virtually invented the pop video – we put together sequences of still photos of pop stars cavorting, which could be screened while their records were playing. And people got the idea for videos from that.' He found his job gave him no time to compose, so he took a BBC voice test and was enrolled into Rigby's team at Radio 3. 'It was full time, but some days the shifts didn't begin till five o'clock, so you had the day free. The trouble is, sitting in Radio 3 Continuity for five hours puts you off music – it took me about three years, after I had left, before I could go to a concert.' Also, there was resistance in Music Division to broadcasting his music – Ernest Warburton says he was thought of as 'just an announcer, and Lennox Berkeley's son'.

The only appointment made by Rigby which caused problems came in 1973, when a young studio manager with an Aberdonian accent, Alma Bickerton, was taken on as a temporary Radio 3 announcer. Her regional voice caused many listeners to send enraged letters. Rigby recalls that they would say

'Remove her – she's not what we're used to. She's not Received Pronunciation, she's not Standard English.' And I had to write back and remind them that we were the *British*, not English, Broadcasting Corporation. I was supported by Stephen Hearst, but Disgusted of Tunbridge

Wells wrote in such droves that Ian Trethowan ordered us to take her off the air. And I always regret that I was overruled.

*

Because Radio 3 was now primarily a music network, most of the programmes were being supplied by Music Division,[8] who had to make their own decisions about live relays of concerts and operas months in advance of the planning of day-by-day schedules. Arriving as Controller, Stephen Hearst found that he had relatively little control of this aspect of his network. To have both a Controller of Music and a Controller of Radio 3 seemed to him 'an institutional nightmare', even though William Glock passed much of the responsibility for Radio 3 music programmes to him. It was obvious to Hearst that there should be 'a Controller of Radio 3 who knew enough about music' to run it all, but nobody listened when he suggested this.

Hearst's strategy, therefore, was to hold weekly meetings with Peter Gould, Head of Music Programmes (Radio),[9] to get some grips on the advance schedules. Another problem was the presentation of music. Howard Newby recalls that, in his time at the Third, 'it was very difficult to get Music Division to be interested in writing introductions that would prepare listeners for new works'. By the 1970s, Music Information Unit was providing material for announcers to read. Anthony Burton explains that 'when I arrived in 1974, the norm for Radio 3 studio music programmes was that the producer asked Music Information Unit to provide a script. The Unit was headed by Deryck Cooke, the world-respected Mahler scholar, an extraordinarily knowledgeable musician.[10] And I think the system of having good specialist scriptwriters writing good scripts for good specialist announcers has more to be said for it than people will now admit.'

The Unit, however, did tend to provide rather densely worded information,[11] and Cormac Rigby tried to institute a system by which their scripts would be rewritten in collaboration between producers and announcers. In practice, however, announcers often filed complaints

---

[8] Some of the music programmes came from Gramophone Department, including the breakfast-time *Morning Concert*.

[9] Ernest Warburton explains that this post had been created by Glock, and Gould was its first holder: 'Peter was a quiet but shrewd character and well respected by those not of the Keller faction.' Gould took early retirement in 1975, and was succeeded by Eleanor Warren, who (says Warburton) 'hated the job' and soon left to become Head of Strings at the Royal Northern College of Music.

[10] Robert Ponsonby describes Cooke as 'inspired, intuitive re-creator of Mahler's Tenth Symphony, jazz pianist, and author of what would have been – had his needless early death not prevented it – a magisterial study of *The Ring*'.

[11] Its scriptwriters tended to give the name of a musician followed by that of the instrument. A present-day music producer, Jeremy Hayes, points out that this could lead to such verbal felicities as 'Iona Brown, violin' and 'Ivor Bolton, organ'.

about scripts that were obstacle-courses of foreign languages, which had arrived shortly before transmission, when the Pronunciation Unit was closed for the evening. One of Rigby's team, Donald Price, noted that he had been given the script for a Dietrich Fischer-Dieskau recital in the Festival Hall just before the broadcast – '15 songs in 55 minutes, all with German titles and descriptions, several typing errors and an underrun to boot!' German proved a hazard for many announcers. In July 1975 Hans Keller complimented one of them on unusually correct pronunciation: 'My wife and I actually understood what was being said.'

Slack timing was as common as ever. In March 1972, Peter Dodd, Chief Assistant, Radio 3, alleged – with slight exaggeration – that the current state of efficiency was '75% of programmes overrunning and 25% under-running'.

There were frequent debates about the sort of language that should be used to introduce music. Lionel Salter, Assistant Controller of Music, complained to Rigby that an announcer had interpolated such comments as 'a delicious finale', 'a lovely slow movement', and 'this most beautiful of Bach's lullabies' into a script. When Rigby investigated, he found that these words – or something like them – had been written by the Music Division producer responsible for the programme. Salter felt that the BBC should not introduce 'value judgements' like this unless 'a named individual is giving his point of view'. On the other hand Stephen Hearst greatly disliked the academic approach favoured by Music Information Unit and many music producers. 'Is music an art form that requires six years' study at a musical academy?' he asked in a memo to Music Division. 'For its total understanding, yes; for its enjoyment, no. We must seek to widen understanding through enjoyment.'

When Robert Simpson gave an interval talk on *The Key System of 'Fidelio' and its Dramatic Significance* (16 July 1972), Hans Keller praised it as 'Absolutely outstanding – one of the talks of the decade', and judged Simpson's use of technical language to have been 'masterly', adding: ' "Dominant" and "subdominant" can be expected to be known, or looked up.' Hearst disagreed:

> I myself, who have listened to music with amateur passion for over 40 years, vaguely know what 'dominant' and 'subdominant' mean without being able to give a definition. I ought not to be expected to look things up ... I think you take too much for granted. The technical language of music is no more comprehensible than the new language of sociology ... It may be an arrogant thing to say but I have been to three universities, have two academic qualifications, and believe that if I don't wholly grasp something then there isn't much of a general audience left who would.[12]

---

[12] Hearst had broken off his studies in medicine in Vienna because of the *Anschluss*. He had then taken a diploma in horticulture at Reading University (refugees were encouraged to learn practical subjects) before going to Oxford to read modern history.

To which Simpson himself replied:

> Stephen H. may have a point – BUT – this talk was billed as about keys,
> and one can't embark on a technical lecture at the beginning ... What
> disturbs me most is S.H.'s implication that only purely emotive talks on
> music should be broadcast. There's room for those, too, but you can't
> analyse music by merely emoting – and my experience of intelligent
> listeners in W[orkers'] E[ducational] A[ssociation] classes, Gramophone
> Societies, etc, etc, is that it is amazing what they *do* grasp.

The matter had already been raised by Hearst at the Radio 3 Committee –
successor to the old Third Programme Committee – earlier in 1972:

> C.R3 [Hearst] said that too often speakers were addressing themselves only
> to initiates of their specialisation. He complained that the second sentence
> of an otherwise fascinating talk by Dr Vernon Reynolds, entitled *The
> Language of Love*, contained the phrase 'ethological paradigm'. Were we
> trying to put off listeners by language that was bound to be beyond their
> comprehension? He asked the Editor, Pre-Classical Music whether he knew
> the meaning of 'ethological paradigm'. He did not. C.R3 subsequently
> asked the Chief Producer, Science Programmes, whether he knew the
> meaning of 'Cantus Firmus'. Chief Producer, Science Programmes, did not
> know the meaning of 'Cantus Firmus'. C.R3 concluded that here was one
> of the dilemmas of Radio 3 broadcasting: if the talks producers did not
> understand the language employed by music producers, and music pro-
> ducers equally could not comprehend what was said in our general talks,
> how many of the public could understand the output of both?

Hearst was keen that this whole question should be debated in a symposium on music talks, which he proposed should mark the fiftieth anniversary of the first broadcast talk on music, by Percy Scholes in 1922.
Keller seized on the idea, and proposed that one topic to be debated should
be 'the desirability of unscripted talks versus the rigid convention of
scripted talks'. He asserted that there were 'only two speakers in the
country prepared to talk without script or notes, the other one being
Isaiah Berlin' – he obviously meant himself as the first. 'Yet,' he went on,
'a Deryck Cooke talking in The Stag[13] can often be more interesting than
when he sits with his script in front of the microphone.'

The obvious solution, to interview experts rather than commission
scripts from them, was not usually adopted. Nor did the symposium take
place. Hearst recalls that, in the meanwhile,

> I asked Cormac Rigby to tot up the musicological introductions that were
> being read out by announcers, and he did, and it came to an hour and a
> half a day. It seemed that, if you listened to Radio 3, you needed a degree
> in music. There was a cycle of Haydn quartets with an introduction by

---

[13] A pub near Broadcasting House.

Misha Donat that was twenty minutes long! So I said that if any of the announcers found an introduction was too long, or full of terms they didn't understand, they were to cut it ruthlessly.

Hearst also says that the Music Division staff quarrelled incessantly with each other:

You had Basil Lam, who was an expert in eighteenth century music, whose fundamental belief was that Bach had to be played on original instruments, and that the only person who was fit to conduct it was Paul Steinitz. And he was at such odds with his colleagues that I had a fortnightly pub lunch with him in order to console him, and listen to his complaints. Then there was Robert Simpson, a distinguished composer, backer of all sorts of still living composers – I don't know whether he got reconciled to me in the end, but he had tremendous suspicions at first. Julian Budden was one of the world's great experts on Verdi. He was the chief producer of opera.[14] In the middle of the 1970s, there was a *Rosenkavalier* production at the Royal Opera House. I went, and I thought it was pretty good. Julian turns up, and produces a list of operas for broadcasting which doesn't feature it. He said, 'You surely don't want to put second-rate music in front of your public.' I was so incensed by this that I picked up the receiver, rang John Tooley [Covent Garden's administrator] and said, 'We're coming on Saturday.' And I cancelled a concert by the Vienna Philharmonic to do it. Julian never forgave me for this. When I left in 1978, he sent me a note saying, 'I want you to know how proud I am not to have to work for you any longer.' And I thought that was splendid! No one would dare to do it these days.

Hearst's meetings had a reputation for being explosive, and he does not deny this himself: 'There were meetings when Keller said, "We should vote on this." And I said, "Democracy's a wonderful thing, but we're not going to vote on whether Beethoven is preferable to Bach. I am here to take the ultimate responsibility." And I picked up my papers and said, "Either you leave this meeting or I do." So he settled down.' Hearst describes trying to cope with Music Division as 'like being a cox in a boat in which the other seven members are continually trying to catch crabs.'

Some people suspected the existence in Radio 3 of a Central European mafia – Hearst, Keller, Martin Esslin (Head of Drama), who was also from Vienna, and George Fischer, a Hungarian (Head of Talks and Documentaries); but Hearst denies that they ganged up together: 'No, I think I established a very good working relationship with George, but with Keller there was a continuous fight. I view his being a member of the BBC as a profound mistake. He was a most remarkable man, who ought to have been a freelance.' Esslin says that the predominance of himself

---

[14] Budden's predecessor in this job had been Brian Trowell, who left in 1970, returning to the academic world because he disliked the changes brought in by *Broadcasting in the Seventies*.

and the other two Viennese refugees reflected 'the fact that the English educational system doesn't produce universalists' (Esslin himself had studied English literature and philosophy at Vienna University as well as drama). John Tydeman observes that the 'mafia' were 'much greater supporters of British culture than the British were!'

Discussions about the presentation of music usually became heated when *Music in Our Time* was mentioned. This weekly programme of contemporary music, which gave a thorough airing to the avant-garde, tended to inspire caustic entries in the announcers' log book. On 30 November 1972, a few days after an edition of the programme featuring Stockhausen and Messaien,[15] Patricia Hughes wrote that it was 'my (personal) weekly nightmare ... we have to read long, sometimes incomprehensible notes, which I don't believe anyone remembers – even if they understand'. She suggested that it might be better to devote each edition to just one work, which would be clearly introduced and explained, section by section, before listeners heard a complete performance. Cormac Rigby thought this 'eminently reasonable', and added: 'One of the most fascinating hours of my life was one day on tour [with the BBC Symphony Orchestra] when Michel Beroff[16] took me through some Messaien – and when I heard it complete thereafter it was suddenly within my reach.' However, the producer of *Music in Our Time*, Stephen Plaistow,[17] was unsympathetic, replying that if Patricia Hughes found it a 'personal weekly nightmare', could not Rigby rearrange her duties, 'and give me an announcer able to take more interest in the programme?' Plaistow asserted that *Music in Our Time* had a 'serious regular following', emphasised that he wrote the scripts himself, and ignored Miss Hughes's suggestion.

Stephen Hearst felt much the same about the programme as she did, and wrote to Plaistow:

I think we can take it as read that the broadcasting of contemporary music must be a major concern for us. It must be our object not just to play it but – because of the difficulties the untutored ear and mind encounter – to make it comprehensible.

I listen to *Music in Our Time* as often as I can and am bound to say that – despite having listened to music with some concentration for over thirty years – I am often baffled if not wholly alienated ... Could you do more in the explanatory presentation ... ? Pierre Boulez is virtually incomprehensible in his evening concerts. It would be arrogance and folly not to bend all our energies to explaining why musicians believe that the

---

[15] Other composers featured in *Music in Our Time* this month were Penderecki, Berio, Elliott Carter, Anthony Payne, Duncan Druce, Martin Dalby, Ligeti and Nono.

[16] A pianist specialising in Messaien.

[17] Ernest Warburton writes: 'Stephen Plaistow is a Cambridge man and an accomplished pianist. He is mild mannered and modest, but also a man of strong character and principles, with a delightful, totally unmalicious sense of humour. I first met him in 1968 when he was already becoming an expert in contemporary music, encouraged by William Glock.'

contemporary music they perform has lasting value. The phrase I get thrown at me most often is: 'It's a confidence trick.' I generally proceed on the principle of defending a producer's efforts, if I can understand them myself. Can you offer any help?

Plaistow replied at length:

The presentation of contemporary music is a problem that will always be with us. I don't want to sound defeatist, but it will. It is impossible to give information about new music which will be instantly comprehensible to the ordinary average-intelligence listener and which at the same time will satisfy listeners with a more serious interest ... There is of course no substitute for experience of the music itself, which suggests that the presentation should always be as short as possible; on the other hand ... to throw *new* music at the listener without any help, as many foreign radios do, usually at dead of night, seems to me almost worse than throwing none ...

I don't think it would be wise to ignore the core of regular listeners in order to catch a few more on the fringe by slanting the presentation more in the direction of what Berio has for breakfast.[18] ... Please, don't let's talk down to them. When listening to a cricket commentary I don't expect the commentator constantly to remind me what over the wicket means or what a leg-spin bowler is ...

Next time someone tells you that modern music is a confidence trick tell him to go and get himself educated, perhaps by listening regularly to *Music in Our Time*. After that he may be in the position to judge – or at least to realise the extent of his previous ignorance and self-satisfied philistinism.

Hearst's remark about Boulez being 'virtually incomprehensible in his evening concerts' refers to *Boulez at the Round House*, a series which began on 17 January 1972, when Boulez introduced the first British performances of works by Maderna, Justin Connolly, and Stockhausen (*Mixtur*), performed by the BBC Symphony Orchestra, with electronics. Stockhausen had been heard often before on Radio 3; in his history of the BBC Symphony Orchestra, Nicholas Kenyon gives a hilarious account of a performance of his *Setz die Segel zur Sonne*, which was broadcast live from a specially darkened Maida Vale Studio 1, on Radio 3 on 14 January 1970:

The entire score for the piece consisted of the following English translation of a text by Stockhausen:

> Play one note long enough
> for you to hear its individual vibrations
> Sustain it

---

[18] The standard question used by BBC interviewers to test recording equipment before beginning to record an interview used to be 'What did you have for breakfast?'

and listen to the notes of the others
– to all of them simultaneously, not to individual ones –
and move your note slowly
until you reach perfect harmony
and the total sound turns into gold
to pure, calmly radiating fire

The Orchestra was split around the studio. In the middle, Stockhausen and four assistants controlled potentiometers which directed the sound into loudspeakers around the room ... There was much uncertainty among the players about what they should be doing. In the *Financial Times*, Dominic Gill reported that ' ... not all of the BBC SO seemed willing. A number of their sounds, indeed, seemed specially remote from the spirit of the text: some brass cat-calls and raspberries ... one or two suppressed giggles ... The lights went up to reveal a marvellous tableau of studio doormen in one corner, huddled together in stunned disbelief.'

Boulez, who had become Chief Conductor of the Symphony Orchestra in 1971, gave a full-page interview to the *Radio Times* a few days before the start of *Boulez at the Round House*. He said he intended to have 'a dialogue with the audience', and would 'introduce and explain each piece. Then afterwards we will have a discussion ... ' Nicholas Kenyon writes that Boulez's introductions 'rambled slightly' and the discussion was 'less than cohesive' (the introductions were broadcast live with the concert; the discussion was recorded for possible future use). The quality of works premiered later in the series was variable; Kenyon says that Boulez

refused to be drawn into judgements of quality. He saw the function of the series as that of simply presenting works and talking about them. Critics ... began to be irritated by Boulez's offhand manner during question-time. The conductor laughed at an objection to his performance of the Ligeti *Ramifications* (that he had not observed the silent bars which the score indicates that the conductor should beat at the end of the piece), saying that there was no point beating when there were not notes   a curious attitude to rests in music. Questioners who had submitted their written questions were sometimes asked to come to the front of the hall and reword their query: a disconcerting experience which inhibited rather than enlivened the proceedings. Slowly, it was discovered that 'informal concerts' were more difficult to run than formal ones.

The argument about the presentation of contemporary music spread throughout Music Division. 'This is a central problem,' wrote Robert Ponsonby on 5 December 1972. He had just arrived at the BBC to succeed Sir William Glock (knighted in 1970) as Controller of Music. Ponsonby, an Etonian, former guards officer, and Oxford organ scholar, had worked at Glyndebourne (1951–5), directed the Edinburgh Festival (1955–60), served with the Independent Television Authority (1961–2), and had most recently been administrator of the Scottish National Orchestra.

Ernest Warburton, who in 1972 was Head of Music at BBC Manchester, describes Ponsonby as

> very tall, very patrician, very proper and very unprepared for the shark-infested waters of Yalding House. In the view of Keller, Simpson & Co he was 'not a musician', notwithstanding an Oxford organ scholarship! He also had the enormous problem of following William Glock, who had not only been knighted by the Queen but virtually canonised by the music profession. But unlike William, Robert actually took his responsibilities for the whole of Music Division seriously.

Ponsonby himself writes: 'While William was clearly a musician in administration, I saw myself as an administrator in music.' He soon found that it took twice as long to get things done in the BBC; he recalls a friend warning him that 'working for the Corporation is like having sexual congress with an elephant – there is no pleasure involved, and no result of one's efforts for two years'.

Howard Newby agrees that Glock's weakness had been 'the administration of his own department'. Consequently

> when William left I was very anxious to have a Controller of Music who didn't devote half his time to the Proms. And when Robert Ponsonby was appointed, I thought he had accepted that point. But not a bit of it! He did exactly the same – spent half his time running the Proms. He was a better administrator, I suppose, than William, because he was more interested in it, but he was never happy in his domestic relations with producers in Music Division. Indeed, there were turbulences, when his authority was challenged, particularly by Hans Keller and Robert Simpson, who thought it was wrong that Ponsonby – whom they did not regard as 'a real musician', whatever that is – should be in charge of such an operation as the Proms. And they created pressure to have the editorship of the Proms broadened in some way. But they did not succeed.

Newby adds that Ponsonby and Hearst were often in conflict: 'Stephen was a much more volatile person than I am, and he quickly got into stand-offs, particularly with Ponsonby, over various things which should have been happening in Music and were not.' Hearst does not deny this:

> There was a constant fight between Ponsonby and me. I believed in the supremacy of broadcasting; Music Division believed that broadcasting was immaterial – it was standards that mattered. For example, the *Radio Times* would give the names of the composers and the works only. It looked like a telephone directory. I changed that; I said that every programme must be made into an occasion. Or when we did a relay from Milan, I put in, 'Live from La Scala' – and only then came the title of the opera. Or I might put Janet Baker in the title billing. And it did increase the audience. If you called it 'A Viennese Evening' you doubled the audience. And I felt this

was not the worst thing to do. But Keller, for example, would behave as if the end of the world had come. So I did fight, yes.

One of Glock's achievements had been to increase vastly the amount of music commissioned. He had hoped that Messaien would write a piece for the BBC's fiftieth anniversary concert, on 14 November 1972, but this did not materialise, and the evening was a rather muted occasion, made up of works by Vaughan Williams, Elgar, Ravel and Berlioz. There was, however, one innovation: the event was broadcast simultaneously on television (BBC2) and Radio 3 – very much Hearst's own achievement, and a technical 'first' which caused a lot of fuss in the engineering departments, but went without a hitch. Cormac Rigby announced for radio and Richard Baker for television, and the two were in vision side by side for a few minutes. Hearst says that the success of the evening led to plans for future simultaneous broadcasts – and to more arguments with Music Division: 'I found that simultaneous broadcasting with television doubled the audience for Radio 3. But Robert Ponsonby complained that a centrally placed camera in the Albert Hall would deprive fifty Promenaders of space. I said, "Robert, we're dealing with three million viewers." This was the difference between someone who thought of concert-going and someone who cared about broadcasting.'

While defending *Music in Our Time*, Stephen Plaistow had asserted that not enough music by living British composers was being heard on Radio 3 outside that programme. New works submitted to the BBC were still being considered by a panel of outside readers, who in the early 1970s included Lennox Berkeley, Mosco Carner, Edmund Rubbra and Hugh Wood, but a log-jam of scores had again built up. Many well-known composers were regarded as 'panel-free' (exempt from this procedure), but no one in Music Division seemed absolutely clear who they were. In 1970 those still having their works read by the panel included Stephen Dodgson, John Gardner, Wilfred Josephs, John Joubert and Kenneth Leighton. When, three years later, an official 'panel-free' list was at last drawn up, there were some odd inclusions and exclusions – most notably in the latter, Peter Maxwell Davies, who still had to be vetted.

Soon after this, the panel system was abandoned, and thereafter Keller, who became Chief Assistant, New Music in April 1973, made his own decisions about most of the scores – and did his best to see that music which had been accepted actually got on the air. Meanwhile Stephen Plaistow noted acidly that many of the scores which had been passed for broadcasting were rubbish: 'Why should we rush to put on Dr X's cantata, at considerable expense, simply because he submits it to us and it's a "worthy" work? We're here to make programmes, aren't we, not to have a tender conscience . . . ? And don't let's forget that no one does more for modern music than the BBC.'

*

By the end of 1972, after nearly three years of the Third-less Radio 3, Hearst was able to report to BBC management that 'a great deal of new creative work' had been broadcast in the network's speech programmes. Notable features had included two programmes about Tennyson and the Arthurian legends (3 September 1971 and 24 March 1972), written and produced by Terence Tiller; T. S. Eliot's *Four Quartets* had been read by Alec Guinness, with music specially composed by Peter Maxwell Davies and performed by the Fires of London (17 November 1972); and the BBC's fiftieth anniversary had been marked by *Poems for the BBC* (13 November 1972), a programme of verse specially commissioned from W. H. Auden, Seamus Heaney, Adrian Henri, Ted Hughes, Adrian Mitchell and Peter Porter. Drama Department had produced first plays by Malcolm Bradbury (*A Very Hospitable Person*, 23 July 1971), Susan Hill (*Lizard in the Grass*, 12 November 1972), Jonathan Raban (*A Game of Tombola*, 30 June 1972), Peter Terson (*The Fishing Party*, 3 October 1971) and Fay Weldon (*Spider*, 13 August 1972). Samuel Beckett's *Lessness* had been broadcast on 25 February 1971, and Tom Stoppard's *Artist Descending a Staircase* had been commissioned by the European Broadcasting Union, to be performed in several languages; the Radio 3 broadcast was on the BBC's fiftieth anniversary day, 14 November 1972.[19]

There were still many people working for Radio 3 who felt that the change to a predominantly music network had been a mistake. During the autumn of 1972, Hearst agreed to the setting up of an informal working party of eight programme staff to consider whether it was 'desirable to have a cultural network instead of a predominantly musical one'. Hearst himself did not feel that the official eight-hours-per-week limit of speech on Radio 3 was 'inviolable', but said that it would cost about half a million pounds a year to finance something that resembled the old Third Programme; and the idea came to nothing.

Meanwhile Hearst was planning several major changes, which he announced at a press conference on New Year's Day 1973. These included a new weekly bulletin of 'good news' from around the globe, *The Positive World*, intended to counteract the negative or depressing nature of most news programmes. Hearst explains how this idea had germinated:

> There was a great deal of *good* news about which, thanks to the doctrinal assumptions of journalists, never figured in newspapers. So we started *The Positive World*, at lunchtime on Saturdays. Unfortunately it had to be compiled by the News Division, and the only person there who thought it was a good idea was Donald Milner [a senior BBC journalist]. And he

---

[19] Martin Esslin and John Tydeman both single out for mention a play which was broadcast shortly afterwards, David Rudkin's *Cries from Casement as his Bones are Brought to Dublin* (4 February 1973). Tydeman says that the question of censoring its very strong language showed the BBC at its best; Howard Newby, Ian Trethowan and the Board of Governors all came out in favour of retaining every word.

did it on his own. But it only lasted a year. A thing like that needs some grass-roots support.

Another innovation was 'French Sunday', to take place six days after the press conference – described as the first day since the start of the Third Programme to be 'entirely devoted to one theme'. *Music Magazine* was to end after a run of twenty-five years – Anna Instone had reached the BBC's retiring age of sixty, and Julian Herbage was eight years older. It was to be replaced by *Music Weekly*,[20] and this would be preceded at 9.05 am each Sunday by 'a classical music phone-in request programme'. Hearst told the press conference: 'We can no longer be regarded as having a terribly tiny audience. During last summer we had more listeners than Radio Luxembourg.'

Three days later, Robert Ponsonby sent Hearst a grumpy memo: 'We read that you held a Press conference on January 1. Careful research reveals that no member of [Music] Division was invited. This confirms the growing impression we have that our output is becoming decreasingly important in your eyes.' Hans Keller had a sight of this memo, and wrote to Ponsonby:

I sympathise with you, but don't worry, there is still some life in this Division left [*sic*]: I myself shall be giving a press conference about C.R3 [Hearst] on February 29. Nothing will be said behind his back. He will be seated at a separate table, with D.P.R. [Newby] on his right and your-self on his left. Each time he is about to interrupt me (as is his wont), one of you two gentlemen will bang him on the head, by courtesy of Tim Souster, [21] who will provide the instruments for the purpose. Meanwhile, let us all be harmonious, constructive and uncontroversial.

Newby saw Ponsonby's memo, too, and pacified him by explaining that it was 'normal practice' for network Controllers to give press conferences without inviting representatives of other departments. Ponsonby was mollified, but pointed out to Newby: 'The public ... are inclined to think that Music Division ... have the final responsibility for programmes of music on Radio 3. It is not so many months since I thought this myself. I am learning fast (but I dare say not fast enough)!' Ponsonby had also been astonished to discover that Controller, Music had no control over the Gramophone Department, which provided a large proportion of Radio 3's music programmes, including those at breakfast time, a peak listening time.

French Sunday, 7 January 1973, was an ambitious project, to be pre-

[20] *Music Weekly* was first broadcast on 1 April 1973, presented by Dominic Gill. Other pre-senters in its early days included Alan Blyth, Stephen Walsh, Christopher Grier and John Amis. Michael Oliver, the best-remembered presenter, first introduced an edition on 16 June 1974.
[21] Music Division producer and contemporary composer.

sented live from Paris by Richard Mayne, in stereo.[22] The quarterly Radio 3 supplement in the *Listener* promised that it would be 'a kind of day-long single programme in which music, poetry, documentary, drama and all the ingredients of radio are integrated as far as possible into one composition'. The day included a live concert by the ORTF Symphony Orchestra, broadcast simultaneously on France Musique; Theodore Zeldin on *Are the French Immoral?*; ORTF's recent winner of the Italia Prize, the play *Récit Combine-Hearing* by Severo Sarduy, which made much use of radiophonics; and John Peel introducing French jazz and pop from midnight to 1 am – extra airtime had been allowed for this special occasion.

At the Radio 3 Committee next day,[23] Michael Mason, one of the producers of French Sunday, observed that it was 'the first time there had been such a collaboration' between different programme departments. Stephen Hearst felt it had been 'a fairly demanding day intellectually', but there was enthusiasm for future theme days. German, Polish and Italian Weekends were envisaged, and Hans Keller suggested that there could also be a 'Women's Lib' event. Indeed the *Guardian* had already got wind that Radio 3 was planning this. Since it was Keller's idea, said Hearst, he could produce it himself, and added that since there were 'few women composers' it might be an uphill task.

Keller and others got to work, and the 'Women on Three' day (30 September 1973) was a considerable success. Elaine Padmore, at that time a music producer, found enough women composers, from medieval to modern times, to fill several programmes.[24] A number of women poets took part in a commemoration of the tenth anniversary of the death of Sylvia Plath, and the main evening event was a play specially commissioned from Caryl Churchill, *Perfect Happiness*, taking 'a wry look at the situation of women now'. Again, Hearst was critical at the post-mortem on the day, saying that 'the theme of Women had proved restricting and there had been times during the day when he personally had been bored'; but he praised the programme on Nadia Boulanger. Many Radio 3 staff felt that this and other theme days meant more to the people making the programmes than to the listeners. Hearst agrees: 'I think that's a good point. They never had very large audiences. On the other hand, a lot of excellent programmes would never have been made without them.'

On Sunday 1 April 1973 the phone-in request programme, *Your Concert Choice*, came on the air. The *Listener* explained that it would be

A weekly two-hour programme in which listeners will have the oppor-

---

[22] Nine months later, on 29 September 1973, Radio 3 relayed the opening concert from the Sydney Opera House, again in stereo.

[23] Tom Crowe remembers that it was raining that morning, and he opened up Radio 3 at 7 am with: 'My friends, this is an English Monday.'

[24] The living composers whose music was heard during the day were Nicola Le Fanu, Elizabeth Maconchy, Thea Musgrave, Phyllis Tate and Grace Williams.

tunity to telephone their 'concert choice' and also to discuss with either Denis Matthews or Humphrey Burton (who will be presenting the programme alternate fortnights) some specific aspect or question arising out of their choice ... listeners who would like to take part can ring on Sunday mornings ... or send a postcard with their request and phone number ...

The day after the first programme, the leader writer in the *Bristol Evening Post* was enraged:

Radio Three, a channel once the Corporation's – and indeed the world's – proud standard bearer in matters of art and taste, launched a Sunday series on the lines of a classical *Housewives' Choice*. Two hours of prime listening time is given over to a pot-luck programme with one of Britain's finest pianists [Matthews] reduced to the role of disc jockey. Once Mozart's music could speak for itself. Now apparently it needs the prop of a flabby phone-in chat. What is the BBC up to?

At Music Division the following Friday there was some cautious praise for the programme – which emanated from Gramophone Department. Robert Ponsonby said he thought that Matthews had presented it 'simply and clearly', but Peter Gould (Head of Music Programmes, Radio) felt that 'the programme concentrated on packaging at the expense of the product', and after further discussion Ponsonby agreed that it had been 'too trivial'. Meanwhile listeners had sent in their reactions letter and telephone. All the calls had been 'highly critical', and most correspondents complained of 'trivial pieces, banal chat, boring homely patter'. John Lade recalls that 'the callers had nothing to say – "I remember that piece so well, it was on our honeymoon and we were walking over the Downs ... " '

Hans Keller had not been at the Music Division meeting at which *Your Concert Choice* was discussed, but three days after the second phone-in he wrote to Ponsonby: 'I have not encountered anyone ... who heard last Sunday morning without considering it a disgrace ... It must be remembered ... that ... I described the project as a rotten idea.' When he saw this, Hearst was so furious that he complained to Ian Trethowan (Managing Director, Radio), and sent a copy of Keller's memo to Newby as well. 'I regard this conduct by a senior official ... as wholly unprofessional,' he told them. 'We cannot go on with Keller as if he were an unimportant gadfly.' Newby had put up with years of being snapped at by Keller, and he discussed the matter with Ponsonby, who felt he 'could not muzzle a member of his staff'; in any case he was inclined to agree with Keller. So Hearst was told that 'the wisest course' was 'to ignore the memo'.

Newby added that the row was 'an illustration of the kind of isolation that has always bedevilled Yalding House'. The BBC's lease on the building that housed Music Division was now running out, and the management were thinking of moving the music staff to an even more remote location, at Maida Vale studios. It was Keller who pointed out, at a departmental meeting, that this would have the 'disadvantages' of lessening 'contact with artists' (in central London) and of 'daily meetings with Planners'. But as yet, no other scheme was proposed.

Meanwhile dissatisfaction with *Your Concert Choice* increased. One music critic complained of 'crackly voices going on about when their grandmothers lived next door to Elgar'.[25] At the end of October 1973, after seven months, Hearst announced that 'the phone-in element' would shortly disappear from it. At this meeting there was also a lengthy discussion about the general aims of Radio 3, during which Michael Mason (co-producer of French Sunday) said he feared it was 'not felt to be the great cultural institution that the Third Programme had been'. Hearst agreed that '1946–1955 had probably been the heyday of the Third Programme as a cultural institution', when there had been less competition from TV and from LP records'. Some months later, at another Radio 3 Committee meeting, Hearst was asked what was the place of a cultural network within the intellectual life of a country. He replied that 'it should not just reflect that life but initiate new life'. To which a producer, Daniel Snowman, wondered whether 'fewer risks were taken now'.

*

On Friday 4 January 1974 at 8.50 pm, Radio 3 broadcast the first edition of a programme of which the old Third would have been proud. Philip French, its producer, says that it originated in a conversation with Hearst, who asked him if he had any fresh ideas: 'I said, something like the old *Critics*, which I had produced myself for some years, but in a slightly different form. Stephen said: "I loved *The Critics*. I don't know why it ever came off." So *Critics' Forum* was born.'

The critics who discussed a selection of the week's arts events in the first programme were Julian Mitchell (chair), Paul Bailey, Dilys Powell and Edwin Mullins. Six months later the programme moved to early Saturday evenings, and remained there for sixteen years. French was given a free hand to run it:

> I never had to check with anyone about whom I could invite to appear on the programme. There were accusations, indeed, that it was my fiefdom. But the only people within the BBC who really complained were producers whose programmes were savaged by us! Martin Esslin even tried to prevent some of his department's plays being discussed by us.[26]
>
> Stephen Hearst had asked me what day and time I would ideally like for it, and I said I'd like it to come on Saturday evenings after *Jazz Record Requests*, because that was a programme I always listened to myself. And we did very well there – we actually got better audience figures than *Stop*

---

[25] The present writer's grandmother played the violin for Elgar in a string orchestra he was conducting in Worcester during his young days. I did not phone *Your Concert Choice* to say so.
[26] Esslin says he objected to the 'camp' style of *Critics' Forum*, and the reviewers' lack of interest in radio drama. 'I wanted better reviewers.'

the Week, which was on the air at about the same time on Radio 4.

The original *Critics* had tended to consist of members of the older generation, such as Marghanita Laski and Harry Craig. For *Critics' Forum*, French turned to much younger people. 'Clive James paid me a nice tribute when he wrote, in *The Metropolitan Critic*, that I was "one of the hidden presences behind the career of almost every serious literary journalist for two generations". And certainly a great many people did their first broadcasts for me.'

Robert Carver, a frequent participant in the programme and the editor of a *Festschrift* to mark French's retirement from the BBC, recalls

the sacramental lunch before [the recording], at which no mention must be made of the sacrificial offerings to be dissected afterwards; the austere Quaker use of both Christian and surname during recording (to prevent the listener feeling excluded by a chummy first-name-only coterie); the post-prandial 'quick flash of the cards' over lukewarm BBC ersatz coffee, at which the assembled critics (often queasy with wine, nerves, or both) tried to say what they were going to say, without actually saying it, to prevent thunder being stolen, shafts purloined, aphorisms heisted.

Another regular critic on the programme, Michael Coveney, remembers

a memorable hand-to-hand fight over Judi Dench's *Mother Courage* between Waldemar Januszczak and Philip Oakes; a surprising effusion of enthusiasm for Andrew Lloyd Webber's *Starlight Express* from both Hilary Spurling and John Carey; the cross-disciplinary gyrations of Marina Warner, Anthony Curtis and Michael Billington; the torrential Edinburgh Festival round-ups of Owen Dudley Edwards; the dismemberment of Peter Brook's televised *Carmen* by my old Oxford tutor, Christopher Ricks.

For the participants, the lunch was always enjoyable but reminiscent of a slight lull before a pretty tough examination ... And there was Philip to compete with over the salad bowls ... Then the slow trudge across Portland Place to the recording studio ... Afterwards, anti-climax: a cup of tea and last week's travel expenses. Farewells and exits, perhaps a shared journey across town with a fellow panellist and glum mutterings about two new Hemingway biographies in the book slot next week, not to mention a nine-hour film about the Polish death camps at the Curzon.

Despite the excellence of *Critics' Forum*, Michael Mason's remarks about Radio 3 not being the great cultural institution which the Third had been were symptomatic of a general malaise that affected Radio 3 in the mid-1970s, after the relief at having survived *Broadcasting in the Seventies* had worn off. Hearst's inclinations were towards a broad-based Radio 3 much like the old Third, and on more than one occasion he was warned by senior management that the network was not doing its primary evening job of providing mainstream classical instrumental music. 'Where, in all this, is Beethoven, Schubert, Brahms, and the rest?' Howard Newby wrote to Hearst at Easter 1974, after examining two weeks' schedules in which evenings were mostly taken up by opera, some of it contemporary. The *Daily Telegraph* radio critic, Sean Day-Lewis, made the same complaint in his column on 6 November that year, under the heading 'MORE MAINSTREAM MUSIC, PLEASE':

> For myself, I use Radio 3 most in the hour before setting out to work ... and the last hour of the night ... Part of me would like *This Week's Composer* always to be Handel and Vivaldi[27] and the last hour of broadcasting concentrated entirely on Bach and Monteverdi[28] ... It is ... all to the good that there should be fairly regular transmission of Schoenberg's music and that of his followers ... All the same, the channel could afford to spend more time in the mainstream, and recognise that music-lovers are creatures of habit ... It should be possible to organise a mainstream concert ... starting at the same time, 7.30 or 8 pm, on four evenings a week.

Meanwhile Hearst himself disliked most of the modern works which Music Division put into his schedules. He told Ponsonby that he believed most of it was 'rejected not just by the general listener but by the committed music-lover', and pointed out that Alexander Goehr's opera *Arden Must Die*, relayed from Sadler's Wells on 19 April 1974, had failed to retain most of the tiny audience it had attracted – figures suggested that three-quarters of them had switched off before the end. But Ponsonby would not accept that anything was seriously wrong with this situation. The only comment in the Audience Research report on the Goehr which interested him was that 'television would have been the better medium for a first-time broadcast'. He wrote to Hearst: 'This is blindingly obvious, and yet we totally neglect it, such is the gulf ... between BBC Radio and BBC Television. We get almost no help at all from Television where contemporary music is concerned. Could not you and I together contribute something positive in this direction?'

Meanwhile Hearst began to notice that few of the BBC staff contributing to Radio 3 actually seemed to be listening to it themselves. At the Radio 3 Committee on 10 June 1974 he 'wondered how often those sitting round the table' tuned in. There was no rush of enthusiastic replies. On 3 February 1975 the same committee was told that, at a recent Talks Meeting, a producer, Angela Tilby, had 'said she rarely listened to Radio 3 and found much of the output, e.g. the music talks and the science talks, indigestible. Most of her friends preferred listening to Capital Radio.' [29]

Morale was raised now and then by theme days, which were becoming a regular feature of the network. The 125th anniversary of the death of

---

[27] *This Week's Composer* in November 1974 featured Handel, Elgar, Palestrina, Shostakovich and W. F. and J. C. Bach.
[28] Late-night music broadcast on Radio 3 during the week following this article was by Matthew Locke, Fauré, Bach, Dufay, Ysaye and Maderna.
[29] This had come on the air in October 1973.

Chopin was commemorated by a Polish Evening (12 October 1974), and eight days later American Sunday, devised by Elaine Padmore, marked the centenary of the birth of Charles Ives. Later came a Welsh Evening (27 September 1975), a Hungarian Evening (6 February 1976), and a Northern Weekend (15–16 May 1976) to mark the opening of New Broadcasting House, Manchester – one of the Network Production Centres envisaged in *Broadcasting in the Seventies*. But Hearst noted that these theme evenings and days required an enormous effort, because of 'lack of communication' between programme departments.

Indeed there was often open hostility. Music Division complained about Presentation – Ponsonby wrote to Cormac Rigby that Patricia Hughes's words at the start of one concert, 'You join me in the Royal Festival Hall', were verging on 'the cult of personality in announcers'[30] – and Presentation sniped at Music. Rigby sent Yalding House a complaint about a narration for Verdi's *Don Carlos*, which had been written by an outside contributor, a distinguished music critic; Rigby called the phraseology 'hideously limp-wristed', and gave examples, with comments by Tony Scotland, who had had to read them:

'she bestows a golden chain'. *Isn't 'gives' much simpler?*

'Carlos kindles a fire . . . ' *Is he too grand to* light *one like everybody else?*

'On recovering, he clasps Elizabeth in his arms, defying the world. "First kill your father," she exclaims, "then drag your mother to the altar!" Carlos runs off, with a cry of "Accursed son".' *You try reading that, without sounding like Gracie Fields.*

*

By the beginning of 1975 the BBC was again seriously short of money, 'screwed down', as the Chairman, Sir Michael Swann, put it, thanks to Harold Wilson's Labour Government, which had refused to raise the licence fee (last put up in 1969) despite the fact that inflation was running at about ten per cent a year. In January programme budgets were severely reduced. However, Hearst was able to report to his team that Radio 3 had 'emerged almost unscathed' from the cuts. It would close down half an hour earlier each night, at 11.30 pm, and on Saturday afternoons Radio 3 and 4 would combine, to carry Radio 3's programme *Man of Action* – a series in which public figures chose their favourite music. ('When Isaiah Berlin did it,' says Hearst, 'it was terrific! Why allow *Desert Island Discs* the monopoly of someone talking about his life and choice of music?')[31]

---

[30] Patricia Hughes says that Tom Crowe had handed over to her with the words: 'And now we join Patricia Hughes', so she had naturally responded: 'And you join me in the Royal Festival Hall . . . '

[31] John Lade recalls that when Tom Driberg was recording *Man of Action*, a bottle of gin had to be sent for at 9.30 am.

Later this combined Radio 3/Radio 4 airtime was occupied by a record programme introduced by Robin Ray.

Indeed Radio 3 benefited from this merger. Five months later Hearst was able to report 'an increase in the R3 audience and a sharp decline in R4's' on Saturday afternoons. Another combining of the two networks, on Tuesday evenings, began in March 1975, and proved equally beneficial, Radio 3 achieving up to 850,000 listeners. This was for a Viennese-style concert. Yet it was noted that early music was now getting extremely high audience figures too. Robert Ponsonby observed that more people had been listening to Byrd, Palestrina and Gibbons than to *The Ring*, *Die Fledermaus* and *The Magic Flute*, and remarked that a large number could now be relied on for 'Lassus; Josquin; and even Dufay, with whom David Munrow scored an amazing success in the Albert Hall (of all places!)'.

After an uncertain start as Controller of Music, Ponsonby was feeling optimistic. Despite the financial cuts, he applied to senior management for an increase in the fund for commissioning new music, pointing out that the BBC's fees for this were deplorably low by international standards. For example, composers such as Elisabeth Lutyens and Malcolm Williamson only netted £200–£300 for a Prom commission, whereas the BBC had to pay at least £1,000 to obtain anything from Boulez, Messaien or other foreign composers of that stature. The fund was now increased, says Ponsonby, 'from about £3,000 to about £30,000'. Among the many works commissioned during his remaining years at the BBC were Michael Berkeley's Guitar Sonata (first broadcast in 1982), Harrison Birtwistle's *Earth Dances* (1986), Pierre Boulez's *Rituel in memoriam Bruno Maderna* (1975), Elliott Carter's *Triple Duo* (1983), Brian Ferneyhough's *La terre est un homme* (1978), Alexander Goehr's *Babylon the Great is Fallen* (1979), Jonathan Harvey's *Inner Light III* (1976), Robin Holloway's Viola Concerto (1985), Oliver Knussen's Third Symphony (1979), Elizabeth Maconchy's Second Clarinet Concertino (1985), Colin Matthews's Cello Concerto (1984), David Matthews's Third String Quartet (1980), Nicholas Maw's *La vita nuova* (1979), Dominic Muldowney's Piano Concerto (1983), Thea Musgrave's *An Occurrence at Owl Creek* (1982), Nigel Osborne's Sinfonia No. 1 (1982), Paul Patterson's *Stabat Mater* (1986), Robert Saxton's Concerto for Orchestra (1984), Alfred Schnittke's Second Symphony (1980), and Hugh Wood's Symphony, Op. 21 (1982).

Ponsonby's regime saw a considerable increase in Radio 3's participation in European Broadcasting Union concerts, though he says that these were not without their problems:

> The EBU international concert seasons were a rare example of international co-operation, live – which is extremely complex. Between twelve and twenty countries would participate in a simultaneous broadcast, controlled from Brussels. We did American broadcasts via the EBU as well, and there were some disasters! Solti was conducting Mahler's Eighth Symphony from Chicago, and I was so determined it should go well that

I sent Leo Black out to supervise it. It was a wonderful performance, and I was in the audience. At the end, I went down to the control cubicle, and Leo's face was absolutely ashen. After about an hour, some subordinate person down the line had assumed that no symphony could last more than an hour, and had disconnected it. Lady Solti, sitting at home in St John's Wood, listening to her husband's marvellous performance, had suddenly got out of her two stereo loudspeakers two separate American radio commercials!

Graham Johnson, who had made his first broadcasts a few years earlier as an accompanist, gives an example of the standard of excellence that Radio 3 was often achieving in the late 1970s:

In 1977, I proposed to Elaine Padmore that we do the complete songs of Poulenc – I said, 'I'm in love with these songs, and there are over two hundred of them.' They really weren't known then; the BBC Music Library didn't have many of them. The result was that I wrote and introduced thirteen ninety-minute programmes, on Sunday afternoons [starting on 23 October 1977]. Bernac came over and did *Babar the Elephant,* all sorts of singers and pianists were commissioned, and I did a programme on the Eluard songs. That one was listened to, on her car radio, by a lady called Sidney Buckland, who was an expert on Eluard, but she didn't know Poulenc's settings of his poems, and suddenly she heard the words clothed with this great music. As a result, she became overnight a Poulenc enthusiast, and made a wonderful translation of his letters – which in turn led to the definitive French edition of them, which places him as one of the great composer-letter-writers of all times. It was a wonderful instance of horizons being broadened.

*

In June 1975 the resentment that Radio 3 should be chiefly restricted to broadcasting music, which had bubbled away among many of the older programme staff since *Broadcasting in the Seventies,* came to the boil. Six of them – Susannah Capon, Leonie Cohn, Deryck Cooke, Hans Keller, George MacBeth, Hallam Tennyson and John Tydeman – wrote to Newby (thereby going over Hearst's head), asking to see him as soon as possible 'in order to discuss the critical situation'. At first Newby said it was a matter for Hearst and the Radio 3 Committee, but after a while he agreed to meet the deputation, with Hearst also present. Meanwhile Hearst was furious at this implied loss of confidence in him.

The meeting, on 13 October 1975, was followed by a session of the Radio 3 Committee, attended by Newby, at which the protesters repeated much of what had been said (but not minuted) earlier in the day. They said they felt that the present restriction on speech programmes resulted in 'a lack of cultural impact of the network as a whole'. Newby's response was: 'Show us the excellence that would drive us to increase the speech output.' He told them that as Controller of the Third and Radio 3 he had been conscious 'from about 1964 onwards' of 'diminishing vitality' in speech broadcasts. Hearst assented to this view of a lack of talent among speakers, compared to the early days of the Third, and asked if anyone present knew of 'a case where talent had failed to emerge because of administrative obstacles'.

Heads of speech-programme departments were also present. George Fischer said that Talks and Documentaries – which also provided Radio 4 with such programmes as *Kaleidoscope* – was too stretched to increase its contributions to Radio 3 without extra staff. Later he wrote privately to Hearst that most of his producers were not good enough to give Radio 3 the kind of material it needed, and he could not do anything about this 'short of criminal acts'. Martin Esslin, Head of Drama, could have pointed out to the meeting his department's recent successes on Radio 3, which included Paul Scofield as Prospero in *The Tempest* (17 November 1974), Alec Guinness as King Lear (15 December 1974), and *Conversations with a Cupboard Man* (6 May 1975) by twenty-eight-year-old Ian McEwan, whose first book had not yet been published. Instead, Esslin complained that Radio 3 was 'neither the serious music programme it was meant to be nor, in the evening, the equivalent of the old Third Programme'.

Newby asked Esslin what he meant by not a serious music programme. Esslin said that there were jazz programmes, and *Homeward Bound*, a sequence of light classical pieces. This had begun in July 1973 at 6.10 pm, on medium wave only, while the Open University was on VHF (Bayan Northcott in the *New Statesman* sneered at it as 'that muzak of the speeding executive'). Newby replied that many people thought there was too little jazz on Radio 3, while *Homeward Bound* was 'a convenient solution' to early-evening planning problems – he longed for the day when there was a separate network for the Open University and other education programmes. But in the end it all came down to the question of generic broadcasting. Most senior BBC staff now accepted this as a fact of existence. The few who did not were powerless to change the system.

Michael Mason told the meeting that generic broadcasting was 'anti-cultural', Deryck Cooke complained that Radio 3 was 'largely listened to mindlessly' by those who wanted musical wallpaper, and Martin Esslin exhorted everyone to 'read Sir William Haley's brief for the Third Programme'. But Hearst said that 'the great days of the Third Programme were before television'. Cormac Rigby chipped in with the observation that everyone seemed to have 'talked themselves into despair', and Esslin suggested that senior management should 'sit down and rethink the whole philosophy of broadcasting'. Whereupon the meeting petered out.

Nothing came of it for a while, apart from a few ideas for speech programmes, and it looked as if the BBC's financial cuts would get worse. Meanwhile Alexander Solzhenitsyn appeared on Radio 3 to air his well-known pessimism about the Western world; George Fischer describes his half-hour talk, given on 24 March 1976 (with the actor Richard Pasco reading an English translation) as 'a brilliant essay on the intellectual and moral feebleness of the West'.

By the summer of 1976 the Corporation's finances were in better shape, so in the autumn the thirtieth anniversary of the Third Programme was celebrated in style, with the *Radio Times* printing interviews with Sir Michael Tippett and Harman Grisewood – who was *Man of Action* on Radio 3 on 2 October; a new work from Samuel Beckett, *For to End Yet Again*, broadcast on 4 October; and a simultaneous relay with BBC2 of *The Barber of Seville* from La Scala, Milan (2 October). Then in March 1977 the latest white paper on the future of broadcasting – the work of a commission chaired by Noel Annan (Lord Annan), who many years earlier had written an internal report on the Third's speech programmes – reflected the views of the Radio 3 protesters.

The white paper praised Radio 3's music programmes, and dismissed suggestions that it should 'return to the form of the old Third Programme'; moreover meetings with BBC staff gave the impression that 'they thought that talk as a genre was moribund because they could no longer obtain thinkers and debaters of the eminence of Bertrand Russell and Fr Copleston'. The Annan committee members themselves did not want Radio 3 to be 'the medium for don to commune with don'. Yet, the report went on, an increasing proportion of the population were university graduates, many of whom wanted to hear 'talks on arts and sciences, and ... on political and social issues', which Radio 3 was not currently providing to any great extent. There was a need for 'high seriousness and intellectual rigour' which TV could not deliver.

The Annan Report's major recommendation – of new authorities to control the new Channel 4 and the whole of local radio, BBC as well as commercial – was not accepted by the Government, and its observations on Radio 3 went entirely unnoticed. Seven years after *Broadcasting in the Seventies*, generic radio was here to stay.

CHAPTER TWO

Mainly for pleasure

I n 1975 the young and widely admired Controller of Radio 4, Anthony
Whitby, died of cancer. His job was taken over briefly by Clare Lawson
Dick, who then retired. The Governors and management chose as her
successor Ian McIntyre, forty-five-year-old presenter of Radio 4's evening
current affairs programme *Analysis*. Howard Newby says that he himself
was 'largely responsible' for this appointment; he liked McIntyre's 'deep
commitment to radio broadcasting, and his belief, unlike most of his
contemporaries, that it really did have an important part to play in the
future'.

However, within a few months McIntyre had earned the nickname 'Mac
the Knife' for his cuts in several Radio 4 flagship programmes, such as
Today and *The World this Weekend*. 'What was proposed,' he says, 'was that
the so-called sequence programmes should do a little less and do it better.'
By the summer of 1978, pressure from News and Current Affairs (the
department in charge of these programmes) led to the top-level decision
to move him sideways, 'to create smoother waters in Radio 4', as Newby
puts it. Stephen Hearst was made head of a BBC think-tank, the Future
Policy Group, and McIntyre became Controller, Radio 3. The implication
that Radio 3 was less important than Radio 4 did not please staff serving
the network. In fact McIntyre had been encouraged to apply for the Radio
3 Controllership in 1971, when Newby relinquished the job.

Born near Aberdeen in 1931, McIntyre had been educated at a Lancashire
grammar school, and at Cambridge, where he read modern languages
and was elected President of the Union; *The Times* described him as 'a
formidable debater with nerves of steel'. After National Service, he entered
the BBC in his mid-twenties as a current affairs Talks producer, sometimes
contributing programmes to the Third. (He has vivid memories of Anna
Kallin, T. S. Gregory, and other characters of that era, but describes the
network as poorly managed in those days.) He rose into middle management before leaving to work for the Independent Television Authority.
He then spent a few years on the staff of the Conservative Party in Scotland,
and was their parliamentary candidate in Roxburgh, Selkirk and Peebles
in 1966 (the seat was retained for the Liberals by David Steel). He also

made some programmes for the Third as a freelance during the 1960s, presenting documentaries on Israel and India. In 1970 he accepted a full-time BBC contract to present *Analysis.*

McIntyre's detractors were inclined to label him a zealot; to which he replied: 'I reflect that the outfit [the BBC] was founded by one.' Certainly he had a Reithian confidence in his own judgement. He had brought up his children with some strictness: for every half-hour of television they watched, they had to spend an hour reading. He infinitely preferred combat to compromise, and was deeply critical of those who did not give of their intellectual best.

For his first few months at Radio 3, McIntyre took things quietly, meeting staff and listening to the output. He may also have been recovering from his Radio 4 bruising, though he said he had a 'strong peasant constitution' and did not mind criticism. (He was, however, scathing about Newby's lack of support for his changes to Radio 4 – 'Howard took up a position under his desk'.) In July 1979 he held a press conference to announce his plans for changes in Radio 3. It was attended by John Woodforde of the *Sunday Telegraph*, who found Mac the Knife surprisingly pleasant: 'Wearing blue serge and the striped summer tie of St John's College, Cambridge, he handled his press conference ... with such precision, charm and tact you wondered how on earth he managed to annoy so many colleagues ... '

Paul Ferris of the *Observer* was similarly surprised by McIntyre's candour; he told Ferris that he thought some of the current Radio 3 programmes 'very bad'. Music, he said, had become 'so predominant' in the network that everything else tended to be regarded as 'high-class Polyfilla'. He added that the Governors and Board of Management had given their approval to his making Radio 3 'a rather more mixed channel'.

He had written them a paper called 'Pleasure and Enlargement'; this was a phrase Howard Newby had once used to some Americans, explaining that the Third was not educational, but was for 'pleasure and enlargement'. McIntyre's paper began: 'Taking over Radio 3 is a bit like inheriting a stately home.' He had now examined 'Castle Hearst', and concluded that it did not need such popularisation as 'a safari park in the grounds'. He did not agree with those who thought it a pale shadow of the old Third; archive recordings of programmes from the supposedly golden age were often a disappointment. Recently there had been several triumphs, such as Michael Charlton's documentary series on the Vietnam War, *Many Reasons Why* (which began on 18 September 1977) and Alec McCowen reading the whole of St Mark's Gospel (31 December 1978). But this standard of excellence, said McIntyre, should be aimed at in *all* speech programmes, and documentaries and plays would then be worthy of providing – as he desired they should – the main event on many evenings. McIntyre concluded the paper: 'Any properly brought-up Controller's eyes naturally glisten at the prospect of bigger audiences.' But he did not suggest how to get them.

However, a recent BBC internal paper on Radio Programme Policy had identified a formula for a considerable increase of audiences for Radio 3; and it had nothing to do with speech programmes. Observing that daytime Radio 3 audiences were low, and contained few women, it asked:

> Should we be concerned about this and seek to broadcast a 'format' which would fit the 'lifestyle' of the busy housewife with a taste for classical music? Should Radio 3 feature the top-selling classical music records during its main weekday daytime programmes, streamed and presented for background listening, and reserve its main 'foreground listening' offerings for the evenings and weekends? ... We believe not. In the words of our Head of Music Programmes [Ernest Warburton]: 'The temptation to turn Radio 3 into a "Top 100 (or 500) Classics" must be resisted.'

Warburton writes of this: 'What was being proposed at the time was much more radical than happens now even on Classic FM. Radio 2 had been very highly structured for a time in the early 1970s; every programme had its own formula, and heaven help a producer who showed any flair or imagination. My remark needs to be read within the context that such barbarities were being mooted for Radio 3.'

In contrast, McIntyre's detailed plans, revealed at his press conference, were solely concerned with speech. A new weekly survey of world affairs, *Six Continents*, would draw on the resources of the BBC Monitoring Service. Special sub-editors would be assigned to Radio 3 news bulletins to select appropriate items and write in the appropriate style. (A journalist visiting Radio 3 Continuity for an article in *Harpers and Queen* found the duty announcer, John Holmstrom, having to rewrite the bulletin to make it literate – 'altering verbs to agree with their nouns'.) There would be a weekly critical commentary on Radio 3 music programmes, *One Pair of Ears*, and the ever-controversial *Music in Our Time* would be moved to a late-night slot, 'so that it can't drive people away from what comes next'. Finally, two programmes made by Cormac Rigby's Presentation Unit, *The Arts Worldwide* and *Playbill*, a preview of forthcoming radio drama, would both be axed; McIntyre said he found them 'self-indulgent'. Speaking today, he refers to them as 'a cottage industry', and describes some of Rigby's team as 'giving the impression of glancing at themselves in a mirror when they were on the air'.

Rigby says that this got McIntyre's regime off to 'a dodgy start' with the announcers. Meanwhile music producers objected to having their work criticised in *One Pair of Ears*, especially since they had no right of reply. They realised that McIntyre believed they were often simply giving airtime to their friends. 'Of course many musicians we broadcast had become our friends,' says Anthony Burton, 'but that was the result of working with them successfully in the studio.'

McIntyre also took Drama Department to task for what he considered to be slack ways, and met with the same resistance there. 'They didn't like being told that I regarded some of their offerings as Radio 4 rejects,' he says. 'Anything that Radio 4 didn't want, and had a good deal of strong language in it, tended to come to Radio 3. I felt that if people turned on to listen to a concert, they shouldn't have to put up, in a longish interval, with a play about lesbians in Namibia.' Stephen Hearst had this problem too: 'What I did find odd was the division of plays between Radio 3 and Radio 4. It wasn't based on the difficulty of the play but, sadly, four-letter words.' On the other hand John Tydeman, who was Assistant Head of Drama during McIntyre's regime (and became Head in 1986), says McIntyre 'had a fuckometer – he used to count up the four-letter words pedantically. He was terribly adversarial, asking us to *justify* every play, as if it was politics. We found him terribly difficult to deal with. On the other hand after a meeting he would say, "Let's have a drink", and be absolutely charming.' Ernest Warburton says much the same: 'Ian could be warm and relaxed and very good company, but also – sometimes without warning – exactly the opposite. He was usually very polite in a stiff, slightly pompous way, but there was also the memorable occasion when – in front of a roomful of producers – he told Robert Ponsonby to "bugger off".'

The features producer Piers Plowright, who had recently begun to make programmes for Radio 3, says: 'I got on quite well with Ian. Some of those meetings were very painful, but I was almost the only one from Drama Department[1] who kept going to them, on the grounds that we had to have a dialogue. Ian's style of running Radio 3 wasn't comfortable, but it was stimulating – in the way that censorship can be!'

Those whom McIntyre targeted for criticism found it was no good arguing with him. As Howard Newby puts it, 'He had a temperament which didn't accept strong points of view which were not in harmony with his. It was this which made him difficult to work with. The exception was George Fischer [McIntyre's former producer on *Analysis*]. McIntyre and Fischer were hand in fist. It led to their being regarded with considerable suspicion by other people.'

Philip French describes Fischer (father of the novelist Tibor Fischer) as 'politically, very different from most East European *emigrés*, who tend to be liberal – George was a conservative anti-Communist'. French continues:

McIntyre was one of the most calm and articulate people I've ever met – almost frighteningly so; he never lost his temper. It always made him seem absolutely reasonable, even when he was not. He usually finished up winning arguments, as much through his manner and character as through the quality of his mind. And Fischer, too, was very powerful in discussion; he drove people into corners, so that they had to give in. People often felt crushed and humiliated by him. A bad atmosphere developed.

'George was an important ally,' says McIntyre, while Fischer – a man of

---

[1] At this date Plowright belonged to Drama Department – a legacy from Drama's absorption of some of Gilliam's producers after Features was closed down.

immense charm as well as conviction – speaks of McIntyre with total admiration.

Anthony Burton, recalling the unpleasant atmosphere in Radio 3 meetings at this time, stresses that it was largely due to the increasing emphasis within the BBC on post-mortem discussion of programmes, rather than advance planning. 'One of the things I loathed was Review Boards and the other meetings discussing programmes that had already gone out. There was a huge amount of ganging-up, and a lot of the time people who were no longer making programmes would take every opportunity to criticise those who were. You could be made to feel very small.'

Robert Ponsonby was angry that, as Controller of Music, he had not been consulted about the change of Radio 3 Controller, and wrote about this to Douglas Muggeridge, Deputy Managing Director, Radio, who responded testily that it was not the job of one Controller to help appoint another. Ponsonby, refusing to be snubbed, said it would have been 'good manners' to consult Music Division informally. He and McIntyre were soon at loggerheads over McIntyre's attack on what he regarded as Music Division slackness. McIntyre describes Ponsonby as 'a person of quality, a civilised man', but admits that they fought: 'We did, inevitably. But nothing like as much as Stephen and Robert had fought before my time.'

The degree of aggression displayed by McIntyre to Ponsonby is revealed by an exchange of memos in June 1985. Ponsonby came back from holiday to find that McIntyre had – not for the first time – been criticising broadcasts of the Robert Mayer Concerts for Young People. Ponsonby wrote to McIntyre:

> When Ian Trethowan and I agreed with Robert Mayer that the BBC would take over the Concerts[2] ... our understanding with him was that our commitment would be indefinite. I believe you think the method of presentation and performance old-fashioned. Well, of course, most symphony concerts are also old-fashioned in their formality. But the method is also well-tried – and self-evidently well-liked.

Ponsonby quoted high appreciation figures from Audience Research, and described the concerts as 'an excellent way of gaining new young listeners for Radio 3'. He concluded his memo: 'The producer of the concerts, Anthony Burton, has been absent from your meeting on both the recent occasions when, without warning, you have raised the matter. I hope that when it is next considered you would make sure that he was able to be present. For that matter, I should like to be there too.'

McIntyre replied:

> Many thanks for yours of June 11th. A remonstrance rather than a mem-

---

[2] Robert Ponsonby explains that the BBC had taken over the concerts (begun in 1922) for the 1974–5 season, when Mayer was ninety-five. 'And it is shameful that the BBC later abandoned them.'

orandum perhaps, but it's good to keep these older literary forms alive. I particularly liked the passage about your early life, the history of the concerts and the General Immutability of Things. Moving stuff.

Do please come to the Radio 3 Music Meeting whenever you find yourself in the country. The 53 bus passes the door. The conversation is generally about programmes rather than public events, but I expect you'd get the hang of it quite quickly ...

Do you remember *Listen With Mother*, by the way? It ran for many years, but Radio 4 eventually took it off because they discovered it was listened to mainly by long-distance lorry drivers.

Anthony Burton says he has kept copies of these memos, since leaving the BBC staff, 'as an awful warning never to go back into an institution in which grown men can behave as childishly as that'.

Ponsonby and his staff had a scheme to commission new operas for each of the major British opera houses from distinguished composers. Ligeti would be asked to write something for English National Opera, Nicholas Maw for Kent Opera, Richard Rodney Bennett or Thea Musgrave for Glyndebourne, Peter Maxwell Davies for Scottish Opera. More remarkably, the Welsh National Opera would be offered Stephen Sondheim. The BBC would pay the commission fee, and the companies the production costs. Negotiations began, with the support of Aubrey Singer, now Managing Director, Radio – another ex-television man, who particularly approved of the choice of Sondheim, because he would attract big audiences.

Costs began to look high; Ligeti, for example, wanted a staggering £30,000; Sondheim's price is not known. The Finnish composer Aulis Sallinen agreed to write *The King Goes Forth to France* jointly for Covent Garden, the BBC and the Savonlinna Opera Festival. It had its first Radio 3 broadcast on 12 April 1987. Opera North contracted Wilfred Josephs to turn Daphne du Maurier's *Rebecca* into an opera. But they had failed to liaise with Ponsonby, who objected to the choice of Josephs as too conservative musically. *Rebecca* went ahead without BBC support, and was first staged in 1983. None of the other projects materialised, but a little later Oliver Knussen was jointly commissioned by the BBC and Glyndebourne Touring Opera. His *Higglety Pigglety Pop!*, based on a Maurice Sendak children's book, was first broadcast, simultaneously on Radio 3 and BBC2, on 3 January 1986.

The new Managing Director, Radio, was keen that Radio 3 should try to increase its daytime audience by offering music for background listening. 'It is snobbishly satisfying,' Singer wrote,

to be the 'Radio High Table' of British culture, but it does seem that the dialogue between those above and those below the salt has been breaking down over the years ... I do not worry about the figures for Radio 3 [still averaging between 50,000 and 250,000 listeners in the evening, less in the daytime], but is it not wrong for a radio channel so frequently to reach 'no measurable audience' [a phrase often found in the audience research reports]? ... Should we on Radio 3 accept as our daytime role the provision of a stream of classical music rather like that provided by an American FM station? It's all very well for C[ontroller] Mus[ic] to describe this as a 'Gadarene rush to mediocrity' – it depends how it's done.

Ponsonby and Ernest Warburton were by no means the only members of Music Division to deplore the prospect of American-style music-broadcasting; one of the producers, Misha Donat, a friend and admirer of Keller, said he thought 'programmes should not be made for those people who were doing something else while listening, but for those whose attention was wholly on the programme'. But Richard Shead, Chief Assistant, Radio 3, warned in January 1979 that 'if anyone were to start up a classical music channel of a popular kind, Radio 3 would be bound to lose listeners', and, while this need not influence the network's style yet, 'it might be wise to keep the matter in mind'. Capital Radio and LBC were now well established, and Singer told Ponsonby: 'I already hear talk of commercial stations opening in London on a classical music format. I don't want to wait until they open before we start some programmes with a streamed format. I would rather be in first, than always having to counterpunch and lose. So, what do you recommend?'

In fact Radio 3 already had a 'continuous stream' music programme, *Homeward Bound*, the early evening 'drive-time' sequence of music. Ernest Warburton recalls: '*Homeward Bound* was a thirty-minute two-part programme; the pieces were identified at the end of each half. It was performed by a small studio orchestra, the London Studio Players. The music was short attractive "salon" pieces. It provided an opportunity for young conductors to make their broadcast debuts.' Cormac Rigby says that great care was taken with the key-relationships within the sequence, to avoid unpleasant clashes between pieces. 'A lot of people remember *Homeward Bound* with nostalgia, because there was very little talking,' says Anthony Burton.

Ponsonby pointed out to Singer that it had a poor audience, but Singer responded that this was because 'the Open University tends to queer its pitch' by occupying the FM frequencies, leaving it on medium wave alone. 'I want you to invent a streamed classical music programme that is different, up-market and which people will be able to copy from us,' he told Ponsonby in July 1979, adding sarcastically: 'I would like you and your producers to be thinking about the problem and really do some creative work, instead of the excellent Japanese flower arrangements you are doing at the moment ... '

Learning that the Open University was about to vacate Radio 3 FM on most early evenings, Singer decided that this would be a good place to try out a more sophisticated 'streamed' programme. *Homeward Bound* would be extended, renamed *Mainly for Pleasure*, and given an executive producer, Gordon Stewart, with all Music Division producers taking turns to produce it. There would also be a rota of freelance presenters, live at the micro-phone, who would bring their own personalities to the programme. Ernest Warburton sent round guidelines for all who would be involved. *Mainly for Pleasure* was to be

> a sensitively compiled anthology of good music of all types and styles ... Since no one is likely to be able to give his full attention over a very long period ... the musical works played would have to be short. But there is a huge repertory of magnificent short works – and there is no law as far as I know which demands, for example, that Chopin Mazurkas have to be played in batches of six.

Nevertheless there was absolutely no question of playing individual move-ments from a long work.

Mainly for Pleasure began its regular Mondays to Fridays, from 5 to 7 pm, on 2 January 1980. The first edition was introduced by Jack Brymer, and Michael Berkeley (who had left the BBC staff the previous year, to have more time to compose), Bernard Keefe and Steve Race were among the other regular presenters. Meanwhile on Saturday afternoons (from 29 September 1979) Radio 3 had begun to broadcast a two-hour musical equivalent of Radio 4's *Pick of the Week*, called *Play it Again*, in which presenters selected and introduced repeats of musical items broadcast on the network during the preceding seven days. As with *Mainly for Pleasure*, the *Radio Times* carried no advance details of what would be heard in the programme.

Hans Keller had not been asked to comment on plans for 'streamed' music broadcasting, for he had retired. At least, he was supposed to leave the BBC in March 1979, when he reached his sixtieth birthday; but in August, Ponsonby found him still at work in his old office, and had to write to him, saying it was time he left. After *Mainly for Pleasure* had been on the air for nearly a year, Keller reviewed it scornfully in the *Listener*, calling its title 'inane' and its presentation 'drivel', and asking: 'Is unbilled car-radio utility what Radio 3 should devote more time to ... than to any specific artistic purpose?'

In the *Spectator*, on 30 June 1979, Keller marked his retirement with an article headed 'Fare better, BBC', in which he looked back over his twenty years in the Corporation:

> My first decade at the BBC was paradise ... through my elementally artistic collaboration with William Glock ... while ... in the seventies, [my] status [was] that of a weirdie ... an intermittently loveable Corporation witch ...
>
> It would appear that, at this stage in the history of Broadcasting, the BBC's radio philosophy is determined by fear – where previously, adven-ture was an indispensable requirement ...
>
> The Third Programme, whatever was wrong with (i.e. snobbish about) it, was adventure, and ... earned the BBC a reputation in the world on which it is still living, the earnings becoming gradually immoral. At the

time of the Third Programme, it was considered downright indecent to talk about audience figures ... whereas our present Radio 3 ... fears every listener that isn't listening ... That one has to satisfy audience demands goes without saying – but culturally, the most essential demands are the future's, which the BBC is in a position to make present: the Third Programme here shines as factual proof. On the cultural level (i.e. Radio 3 and Radio 4) there is something wrong with every programme which, instead of provoking thought, fully satisfies – as thought-killing background ...

Without Third Programmes ... the 20th-century classics would still be odd-minds-out. But before an odd mind becomes a classic, your most outstanding programme might well have to be content with 49,999 listeners, which is an audience too small to be recorded ... The BBC rightly prides itself on not being commercial; the trouble is that again and again, it plans as if it were.

BBC terms of employment forbade staff to comment on the Corporation's policy in the press, even when they had left or retired. The Legal Department considered taking action over this article; but Ponsonby persuaded them that silence was the best policy.

Keller had a busy retirement, being much in demand as a visiting lecturer. He virtually ignored the fact that he had developed motor-neurone disease. After his death in 1985, his old friend Susan Bradshaw, collaborator in the Piotr Zak hoax, wrote: 'He was the only person I ever met to whom everything (particularly, of course, musical things) really mattered.'

*

1980, which began with the inauguration of *Mainly for Pleasure*, was a difficult year for Radio 3. All live opera relays had to be cancelled from early January to late March because of the BBC's need for financial stringency (Radio 3 was still closing down each evening at 11.15 pm, and was joining Radio 4 for a concert once a week). Meanwhile the Corporation had begun negotiations with the Musicians' Union over staff orchestras. An internal BBC paper had recommended the disbandment of the Northern Symphony Orchestra, the Concert Orchestra, the Northern Ireland Orchestra, the Academy (the former Training Orchestra), the London Studio Players and the Scottish Radio Orchestra. Ponsonby believed strongly that no symphony orchestra should be disbanded, but thought that the reconstitution of the Northern into a chamber orchestra made some sense. Internal debate raged for many months, and Ponsonby says that, by the time that proposals were put to the Musicians' Union, 'the light of battle' gleamed in Aubrey Singer's eyes.

Negotiations soon broke down, and the Union called a strike which disrupted music broadcasts, from May to August; Radio 3 had to fill up airtime with tapes from the stockpile, and the opening of the Proms was postponed. ('Alternative' Proms were given at Wembley by the BBC Symphony Orchestra and other London orchestras.) It was a traumatic episode; Ponsonby says his staff were 'outraged' by Singer's handling of the negotiations.

> They threatened to write a dissident letter to *The Times*. I had to tell them they must exhaust all proper internal procedures before they publicly attacked their employers. Robert Simpson would take no more and resigned – with sensational, but characteristic, vehemence – during a meeting at which Singer was explaining his position to Music Division. Outside Broadcasting House our own musicians played daily under the portico of All Souls, Langham Place, while the pickets were supported by many distinguished figures – all of them my friends – among them Evelyn Barbirolli, Lennox Berkeley, Charles Groves and Geraint Evans. We were condemned by broadcasters around the world . . .

Meanwhile within Music Division itself there were redundancies, which lowered morale still further.[3]

Ian McIntyre's September 1980 press handout on his network maintained a bright façade, mentioning such successes as plays by Athol Fugard and Vaclav Havel, and a comedy series by Rowan Atkinson, who had since been taken up by television. *The Atkinson People*, co-written by Atkinson and Richard Curtis, and produced by Griff Rhys Jones (then a young Light Entertainment producer), anticipated some of the future *Blackadder* television scripts – and at times bore a striking resemblance to the Hilda Tablet plays:

> DUPONT (*Rowan*): Oooooooooooooooooo (*the sound of a man thinking*).
> INTRODUCER: A musical revelation from Schopenhauer, or the sound of a rare Nigerian bird? Neither: the sound that you just heard was the last recorded evidence of the philosophic career of French thinker and philosopher, George Dupont . . .
> INTERVIEWER: Professor Parker, how do you rank George Dupont?
> PROFESSOR: As a philosopher, or as a man?
> INT: As a philosopher.
> PROF: Ah, because if you'd asked me how I rank him as a man, I should say, very highly indeed. He was a very attractive man. Beautiful, I should say, in his peculiarly French way.
> INT: No, I meant as a philosopher.
> PROF: Yes, I think the word is beautiful. His skin had that marvellous texture that we English just don't seem capable of attaining, that tender

---

[3] Agreement was finally reached that (1) the Scottish Symphony Orchestra would be reduced by 7 players; (2) the Northern Ireland Orchestra would continue, but discussions would begin about its amalgamation with the Ulster Orchestra (this was eventually achieved); (3) the London Studio Players would continue on a contract more advantageous to the BBC; (4) the Scottish, Northern and Midland Radio Orchestras would go, but their members would be guaranteed sixty-six per cent of their current salaries for five years.

smoothness, as though it had been conditioned daily with olive oil.

INT: And his philosophy, Professor Parker?

PROF: He had this marvellous way of talking, this smooth guttural mono-
tone, something like the croak of a frog – well, of course, it *was* the
croak of a frog – but I'm speaking similitically. No, that isn't right. What
is the adverb from 'simile'?

INT: I'm afraid I don't know.

PROF: I don't know either. I remember we used to sit here day after day,
our lithe young bodies brazen in the sun, thinking about that. I used to
suggest things like 'similaciously', and he'd throw back his long neck
and laugh and call me a stupid old homosexual goat, and then he'd
suggest 'similarly', and I'd leap on top of him, giggling and yelling
things like 'The old frog can't even speak English yet.'

INT: Ha ha, yes. But now, turning to his philosophy, how do you rank
him as a philosopher?

PROF: A what?

INT: A philosopher.

PROF: Oh, so that's what became of him.

Despite these and many other recent Radio 3 highlights, Paul Ferris felt
that McIntyre was turning out to be a disappointment; where were the
promised exciting new speech programmes? 'Week by week,' wrote Ferris
in the *Observer*,

> I have searched the *Radio Times* eagerly ... *Playbill* has gone. A critical
> column on broadcast music has come. *Six Continents* selects from and
> comments on foreign broadcasts. But there is little else in the way of
> innovation ... In the past two weeks ... about 18 out of 40 [speech]
> programmes were being heard for the second time. There are respectable
> arguments for repeating good material, but at that level it becomes dis-
> piriting.

Ernest Warburton was now writing, in a submission to a BBC working
party, of 'the failure of Radio 3, both to capture a bigger audience and to
retain the prestige of the old Third Programme'. In a short book mainly
devoted to criticism of the running of the Proms, Robert Simpson had this
to say of Radio 3:

> Some of the programmes that now occupy the air ... would have been
> rejected by the Third Programme either with contempt or as poor jests –
> especially the increasing number shorn of published details, with insen-
> sitive, disc-jockey like removal of breathing spaces between speech and
> music, [and] the bland superficiality of some of the smoother comperes
> ... By such pseudo-commercial behaviour is Radio 3 losing more and
> more of its character ... This is the fault not of the music production staff
> (though it could do much more to fight philistinism) but the responsibility
> of the BBC's regime.

Aubrey Singer, of whom Simpson was undoubtedly thinking, was pleased with *Mainly for Pleasure*, but felt that the rest of the daytime music planning showed music producers desiring to impress each other with their erudition, rather than aiming to please non-specialist listeners. Controller, Radio 3 had no real control over them; they came under Controller, Music. ('The whole structure of the BBC has always been preposterous,' observes McIntyre.) This dual management would no longer serve. Singer decided to disband Music Division and create a Radio 3 Music Department, answerable to McIntyre rather than Ponsonby. Christine Hardwick (from the previously independent Gramophone Department) would head it;[4] Ernest Warburton would become Editor, Music, Radio 3; and Ponsonby – still called Controller, Music, but with most of his staff taken away from him – would be left with responsibility for the house orchestras, discovering new performers, commissioning composers, and programming the Proms.

It was a serious blow to Ponsonby – Alexander Goehr remembers seeing him looking shattered after he had received the news – and as usual he had not been consulted. John Drummond thinks Singer was depriving him of power because he had criticised Singer's aggressive stance during the 1980 musicians' strike, and Ian McIntyre is sure Singer's action was personally motivated. Ponsonby protested to Singer, remarking that 'personality problems' created by these proposed changes (he may have meant McIntyre's autocratic style) would cause difficulties for the music staff. Singer answered that 'music producers have had a comparatively easy life and it is important now to get the best out of everybody'.

McIntyre says it had never been part of his scheme to take over the music producers. Meanwhile he proposed to Singer that the new Radio 3 Department should include speech as well as music, and George Fischer should be put in charge of this department as Deputy Controller of Radio 3. But Singer rejected this.

The reorganisation took place in the autumn of 1982, and was soon followed by an increase in computer technology, which at first created as many problems as it brought benefits. 'Orpheus', Radio 3's computer system, was supposed to clash-check music selected for transmission, and to provide timings and other information useful to producers. However, the system frequently failed to deliver its promised services. 'It is a very clever system,' wrote a member of the department to Christine Hardwick in October 1985. 'But ... whenever a new [terminal] is connected, back-up lines adopted or whatever technical "improvement" introduced, we seem to be spending an inordinate amount of time in trying to help sort

---

[4] John Lade, who succeeded Anna Instone (and preceded Christine Hardwick) as Head of Gramophone Programmes, believes that his department's independence from Music Division had been a good thing: 'There were so many things we could provide which they could not. We lived above the huge Gramophone Library with people to whom a discography read like something from Mills & Boon.'

out the problem rather than getting on with our work ... Office morale is
sinking – the feeling is that we are fighting a losing battle ... '

Aubrey Singer emphasised that the new department was being established in the hope of attracting a much bigger audience to Radio 3 in the
daytime. 'In the current financial climate,' he said, 'and considering that
45 times as much is spent on the Radio 3 listener as on the Radio 1 listener,
BBC Radio must be seen to be responding to the need for more Radio 3
listeners.' And he told the Board of Management that 'In future the output
[of Radio 3] would be carefully planned and *programmes would no longer be
made in isolation* to fill possible slots in the output.' The words here
italicised were a total repudiation of the Third Programme policy of 'no
fixed points', with programmes only being made when somebody felt that
they deserved to be.

This change had not yet been implemented. January and February
1982 – to take a random sample – brought the Radio 3 listener as rich and
diverse a collection of music and speech programmes as ever. The year
began with a simultaneous broadcast with BBC2 of *Aida* from San Fran-
cisco, with Pavarotti and Margaret Price (2 January). Other opera relays
included Cavalli's *L'Egisto* from Scottish Opera (16 January) and *The Flying
Dutchman* from the Coliseum (13 February). The James Joyce centenary
inspired many programmes, including a feature by Craig Raine (26
January) and Anthony Burgess's musical version of *Ulysses* (1 February).
Pierre Boulez conducted the BBC Symphony Orchestra in Paris, playing
his own music and Webern (6 January), and early music enthusiasts were
offered seven programmes of the Penitential Psalms of Lassus, beginning
on 24 February. Drama included a repeat of John Osborne's *A Patriot for
Me* (28 January), Brian Friel's *Translations* (31 January), and Bernard Kops's
play about Ezra Pound. Six successive nights, from 4 January, were devoted
to readings from *Beowulf*. There were features on Nikolaus Pevsner (30
January) and the history of the Nobel Prize (9 February), and Andrew
Motion introduced his new long poem *Independence*, which was read by
Alan Howard (12 February). Behind the scenes, negotiations were in progress for BBC participation in the recently inaugurated Huddersfield Contemporary Music Festival – though the BBC noted that the proximity of
the city's inner ring road to the halls used by the Festival 'makes it
impossible for us to record anything but the loudest music'.

Among later musical achievements of 1982 was the marking of the
Royal Wedding Day – the marriage of the Prince of Wales and Lady Diana
Spencer on 29 July – with a three-part programme entitled *Bavarian Royal
Wedding of 1568*, featuring music composed for the wedding of the heir
to the throne of Bavaria, and other appropriate contemporary pieces.

To counter the impression that the speech content of Radio 3 was still
disappointing, McIntyre asked Philip French to make a book out of some
recent talks scripts. *The Third Dimension: Voices from Radio 3*, published in
1983, contained twenty-five, entertaining but lightweight. They included
John Sparrow fulminating against dogs – 'what I dislike about them is, if

I may put it so, their *dogginess'*; Bernard Levin, whom McIntyre and Fischer had commissioned (at considerable cost) to report on international festivals, describing a rainy night at the open-air Santa Fe Opera House – 'As I went to my place . . . I saw the patrons of rows K to S baling pints of water out of the concave seats'; Edward Norman recalling 'the exact moment at which I began to see Mexico through the eyes of Graham Greene . . . a man kicked a dog . . . with such force that it fell over onto its side'; and Salman Rushdie exalting in the novelist Elias Canetti – 'Do I really want to share him with the world, or even with that small but exquisitely formed part of the world that listens to talks on Radio 3?'

The Third Dimension ignored poetry, but Radio 3 was doing a great deal for it. Fraser Steel, who edited and produced the network's poetry programmes after the departure of George MacBeth in 1976 until 1985, writes:

> It was a period when the network charted the emergence of almost every new poet of note, from Andrew Motion to Simon Armitage. There were some notable commissions, mainly of verse translations of longer poems, where poet and composer collaborated. But if a historian had to pick a single highlight, it should probably be the broadcast of Geoffrey Hill's *The Mystery of the Charity of Charles Peguy*, read by Paul Webster under Geoffrey's and my direction (1 February 1983). I regard it as the most important English poem since *Four Quartets*, and the broadcast was coordinated with its first publication, by the *TLS*. And my personal choice would include one of *The Living Poet* programmes, on W. S. Graham. It apparently made the difference between life and death to a Glasgow poet who was listening in a hospital bed, with the headphones on, after a narrowly unsuccessful suicide attempt.

*

David Cairns, writing about Radio 3 in the *Observer* on 31 January 1982, concentrated chiefly on the changes made by Aubrey Singer, whom he described as 'a dedicated populariser'. Cairns continued: 'We owe to him that toothless programme of unscheduled pap, *Mainly for Pleasure* . . . I suspect that Mr Singer would be happy to turn Radio 3 into a non-stop programme of popular classics, on the American lines, if it meant quadrupling the ratings.' However, Cairns allowed that Radio 3 was 'still a magnificent network', and welcomed the news that there was to be a monthly magazine devoted entirely to it.

This idea had come from Ian McIntyre. BBC Publications turned it down as not commercially viable, so McIntyre took the proposal to the publishing group IPC. Hoping that it might give them access to BBC television and radio advance listings (which, at that date, only appeared in the *Radio Times*), they agreed. The launch was arranged for the autumn of 1982, with Denys Gueroult, a former Third Programme announcer and producer of archive programmes, as the magazine's editor. 'Ian got me back out of early retirement,' he says. 'I'd never edited anything before in my life, but I was good at meeting deadlines, which I suppose is why he chose me.' McIntyre says: 'Denys did a noble job.'

The first issue of *3: The Radio Three Magazine* appeared in October. Gueroult's opening editorial claimed that the old Third Programme had been indifferent to publicity, and observed that the magazine's launch signified a move into 'the sunlight of the market-place'. It would attempt to interest 'those readers who do not automatically switch to the network as well as those for whom no other exists'. There would be criticism of Radio 3 as well as promotional material, and also plenty to entertain.

The first article was written by McIntyre himself, who clearly hoped that the magazine would increase the number of listeners: 'The audience has always been small, but over the last dozen years or so ... Radio 3 is the only national radio network whose share of the audience has remained rock-steady. I've no reason to think that Fortune is planning to cease to smile, but I don't think she would be offended if we took out one or two life assurance policies.' On the other hand he distanced himself implicitly from the 'continuous stream' programming policy preferred by Singer: 'A wag once said that one of the marks of a good Radio 3 talk was that it could persuade a listener to switch off and read a book. In television circles, that is an observation calculated to induce cardiac arrest ... We are not there to offer wall-to-wall muzak ... '

Much of the magazine was occupied by selected highlights of the month's programmes, described chattily by Natalie Wheen, now a regular presenter of *Mainly for Pleasure*; for example:

> *This Week's Composers: Spohr and Hummel* – They sound like a well-known firm of solicitors, in fact they're important figures on the side streets off the main roads of Haydn, Mozart and Beethoven. They were both performers, Spohr on the violin, Hummel a pianist – and they both wrote yards of music. Starting with two of their most lasting creations, Spohr's Nonet and Hummel's Trumpet Concerto, the week contrasts small and large-scale works.

The first issue of *3* also included a guest celebrity's choice of forthcoming programmes – in this case the sculptor Elisabeth Frink, who told the magazine that she had Radio 3 on all day in her studio – and an Orwellian fantasy by Paul Jennings, 'Dissident's Diary':

> *Friday:* Getting increasingly worried about Benson. On Wednesday he sidled up to me in a most ostentatious way, in a street where the Music Police patrol constantly, and hissed at me from the side of his mouth: 'Aylesbury, the Mozart E flat, K428, and Peterson's got a tape of the new Bruckner 5 from Seoul.' I know Bruckner and Mahler aren't actually on the Criminal Listening file (yet), but the authorities won't turn a blind eye, or rather ear, for ever ...

> Aylesbury was adopted as a Radio 3 base after the brave Southern Sinfonia were taken in the raid on the Bell at Aston Clinton, only four

miles away; they copped sentences of two to five years Pop Re-education ... I must say I think it's very brave of Peterson to keep coming back here ... An oboist of his quality would have no difficulty in defecting to Korea, now the world centre of western classical music. Yet still he brings these treasures back to us, still he helps the brave boys of the Radio 3 Resistance to keep on the air.

The issue of *3* for January 1983 marked the retirement from announcing of Patricia Hughes, who was now sixty. McIntyre later recalled that, when it was time for her to 'pack away her cut-glass tones', he received many letters of protest from listeners, including one from Bamber Gascoigne, calling him a 'barbarian' for letting her go. In fact she continued to announce as a freelance; a few weeks after her official retirement, a presenter of *Music in Our Time* complained that she had followed his programme of avant-garde works[5] with the words: 'Well now, if you're still with us on Radio 3 *(chuckle)* after *all that*, we have enough time before the news at a quarter past eleven to hear some more familiar-sounding – *music* ... ' But the lives of Radio 3 personalities did not attract sufficient cult-following to support a lavishly produced magazine (these were the days before free CDs were used to market such publications), and by February 1984 IPC had lost more than £100,000 on *3*. McIntyre claimed that it had achieved 'a considerable critical success', and sales had reached the respectable figure of 15,000 copies a month; but the issue of April 1984 was the last.

Public anxiety about the future of Radio 3 continued. *The Times* devoted one of its 'Profile' columns to the network, observing that it 'appears to be in a state of unusual embattlement, with producers fretting over censorship and control, contributors worrying about their future, and listeners complaining that Radio 3 is no longer ... meeting their particular tastes'. Reference was made to McIntyre's 'tough' meetings with producers, 'at which past programmes were analysed'. (Tom Crowe says: 'Those meetings were like show trials; everything had been decided beforehand', and several other Radio 3 staff from these years agree, but McIntyre dismisses the accusation as 'absurd', and says: 'Nothing was *ever* decided beforehand.') Yet the profile concluded: 'While the other three BBC stations have lost listeners steadily over the last 15 years, Radio 3 thrives ... Figures ... suggest that about 600,000 people a day tune in ... '

However, BBC top management continued to be concerned about audience figures, and Alisdair Milne, now Director-General, asked in March 1984 if the style of Radio 3 presentation was not 'too stodgy and old-fashioned'. McIntyre replied that the average age of announcers had been much reduced – a former King's Singer, Brian Kay had just joined the

---

[5] The programme, broadcast on 17 March 1983, consisted of Morton Subotnick's *The Wild Beasts*, for trombone, piano and an 'electronic ghost score', and Tristram Cary's *I am Here*, for soprano and tape.

team – and he was personally keeping all of them up to scratch; 'the one who gives greatest cause for concern vocally I have recently sent to a speech-therapist'.

Tom Crowe (who had retired in 1982) feels that McIntyre was by nature a programme-maker rather than an administrator; and in July 1984 McIntyre threw himself eagerly into setting up a Russian Season for Radio 3, planned two years in advance, which would open and close with live concerts from the Soviet Union. In the pre-*perestroika* political climate, this was a challenging task; McIntyre made an exploratory trip to Russia in the spring of 1985 with Richard Imison of Drama Department, and met with enthusiasm for his plans, but a few weeks later several Russian diplomats were expelled from Britain for spying, and the Soviet state artists' and copyright agency VAAP suspended all co-operation with the BBC. The *Sunday Times* reported that the Radio 3 Russian Season would have 'given Russian arts their greatest airing in Britain for years', and continued:

> The season was to have introduced work by externally unknown and officially approved Soviet dramatists and composers. The BBC had begun to adapt several theatre plays for radio – the art of radio drama being undeveloped in the Soviet Union – and intended to broadcast two plays weekly for a month ... McIntyre was intending to return to Moscow next month with two of his music producers ... 'I am probably saddest about losing the current affairs element,' [he] says ... 'We were going to cover – with the Russians' full knowledge – the Party, foreign affairs, education and science.'

This press report caused the Soviet Embassy in London to intercede with Moscow, and a month later VAAP telexed McIntyre asking 'someone from Radio 3 to get in touch ... and give us some of your wisdom'. Cordial relations were resumed, and McIntyre went to Moscow in December with the two music producers (Jane Bevan and Gordon Stewart) and George Fischer.

After this, everything went smoothly. Meanwhile Radio 3 was also planning a two-week Weimar Season, reflecting the culture of the Weimar Republic. This took place in February 1986, and Malcolm Hayes in the *Listener* judged it 'one of Radio 3's big successes of recent years', complaining only that too much had been packed into too short a time. Several rarities of German music theatre were broadcast, including Ernst Krenek's *Jonny spielt auf* and Max Brand's *Maschinist Hopkins*, but Hayes was most impressed by a production of Brecht and Weill's *The Threepenny Opera* (8 February 1986), in which Julia Mackenzie played Jenny – 'her delivery of both her set-piece ballads remains fixed in the memory'.

The month-long Russian Season opened on 2 November 1986 with a live relay of the Glinka Kapella Choir from Leningrad, which had reduced McIntyre, Fischer, and the others to tears when they attended a rehearsal. The season was the most popular 'theme' event so far with listeners – 'It's the first season we've ever done which hasn't produced a single complaint about swamping the network,' McIntyre told Singer. Russian visitors to London included the pianist Tatiana Nikolaeva, who played Bach's *Goldberg Variations* live from St John's, Smith Square (10 November), and during the next few days performed Shostakovich's twenty-four Preludes and Fugues. The Borodin Quartet came to give the complete cycle of the same composer's string quartets, as well as three by Schnittke. New works had been commissioned by the BBC from two younger Russian composers, Sofia Gubaidulina and Elena Firsova, and more contemporary Soviet works were heard in *Music in Our Time*. There were productions of classic Russian dramas ('I rather think we overdid the Chekhov,' wrote McIntyre afterwards), but most plays heard during the month were by contemporary dramatists. The season closed on 30 November with the Gostelradio Symphony Orchestra live from Moscow, with a programme including Yuri Bashmet playing the viola concerto written for him by Alexander Chaikovsky. This concert was broadcast simultaneously throughout the Soviet Union, and 'caused quite a stir', wrote McIntyre. He believed the Russian Season 'could well be helpful when the P[rime] M[inister] goes to Moscow in the spring', and said that Moscow Radio 'do seem keen on reciprocating, perhaps with a week of British music'. He was in Moscow himself for the final concert and a reception at the British Embassy, and when he got back the music producer Gordon Stewart sent him a note saying: 'Now we must find new mountains to climb.'

CHAPTER THREE

Tidal wave

On 12 August 1958 the Third had broadcast the Cambridge Marlowe Society's production of *Edward II*, performed by students and dons, including (in the title role) Derek Jacobi, John Barton, John Bird (later to make his name in television satire), John Tydeman (future head of BBC Radio Drama), and John Drummond. 'It happened because Peter Wood saw it at the Lyric, Hammersmith, where we were doing it,' says Drummond, 'and he recommended it to a producer at Broadcasting House. And we went there and did it in a studio on a Sunday, like that, without any production. By the time we did that, I'd got a BBC General Traineeship, and was within a few weeks of starting work.'

Then aged twenty-three, the son of a master mariner in the British India line and an Australian *lieder* singer, Drummond had been brought up in Bournemouth and sent to Canford public school, where his friends included the organist Simon Preston. In spare time he studied piano and composition. After National Service with the Navy, he read history at Cambridge. Joining the BBC, he was attached to many departments before he settled in BBC TV's Music and Arts, as one of the celebrated team led by Huw Wheldon. There, he created some memorable programmes, including Paul Tortelier masterclasses, documentaries on Diaghilev, Kathleen Ferrier and the Leeds Piano Competition, and *The Spirit of the Age*, a series about British architecture. 'I was not a very good director,' he says of these projects, 'nor did I want to be. What I really cared for was research – I'm a historian by inclination – and I found rewards in producing.' He became assistant head of the department. 'But younger people like Melvyn Bragg were promoted over me, and I was twice passed over for departmental head. I have a reputation for being aggressive and arrogant, and certainly I have a quick tongue. And in Music and Arts there were certain people who were bloody lazy, and I said so.' One journalist profiling him has written: 'He is a formidably large man, known for having opinions and a loud voice with which to express them.' He has been described as speaking at '200 words a minute'.

His failure to achieve promotion led him to leave the BBC at the end of 1977 to become director of the Edinburgh Festival. Here, he made a huge impact with his 'themed' Festivals, in which exhibitions and performances in all the arts were linked by one topic, an effect achieved most brilliantly in the 1983 Festival, which was entitled 'Vienna 1900'. Drummond says of this: 'It was the best demonstration I've ever been able to give in my life of my belief that the arts are all related to each other, not in separate boxes. I *loathe* the ghettoisation we have in this country. There are even subdivisions in music – the chamber music audience doesn't ever go to the Royal Opera House. I *hate* that. I've always worked across the frontiers; I'm as interested in, and knowledgeable about, literature and architecture as I am about music. And I think one should be.'

He left Edinburgh after this Festival because he wanted responsibility for fundraising to be shared between the Director and the Council, and they refused. While he was taking some time off, in Australia, to consider his future, 'Alisdair Milne rang me up and said, "What are you doing?" I said, "I'm having a pause." He said, "Come and see me when you get back." So I went to see him, and he told me that Robert Ponsonby had reached retirement age and was leaving – which was not true (they'd got his birth date wrong) – and asked me if I would like to be Controller of Music, and I said no. It wasn't the right job for me. I wasn't a professional musician in the tradition of Glock.[1] So it went into limbo for a couple of months, and then we had another conversation, and I said that what I wanted to do was become Controller of Radio 3. And they said that wasn't on offer. So there was a lot of to-and-fro, and ultimately I agreed to become Controller of Music on the understanding that the ludicrous existence of two Controllers on the same patch would be addressed.'

Ian McIntyre, who thought it was ludicrous too (as Stephen Hearst had done), wanted the double job himself. 'The time to do something about it,' he says, 'would have been after Robert's retirement. In fact Robert was called in one day, two years before he was due to go, and was told that they'd like him to leave early, so that Drummond could have his job. Robert was outraged by this, and for once dug his heels in, and there was a messy compromise. He was allowed to stay on for a year, with him and Drummond in harness together. And Robert finally went away feeling very hurt, with good reason.' Ponsonby himself says: 'I minded very much when it was first put to me, but actually I was beginning to get stale over the Proms. However, I was outraged by the *way* it was done, and by the fact that there was no competition for my job from among my senior colleagues.'

Drummond arrived at Broadcasting House, as Controller Designate, in the spring of 1985. 'I had a three-day-a-week secretary,' Drummond recalls, 'and a room in the Langham, and access to the Music staff, but I had no contact with Ian McIntyre or Robert Ponsonby. Several senior people in Music Department had protested that I was the wrong appointment. I

---

[1] Ernest Warburton agrees, and describes Drummond as an amateur musician.

could see their reasons, but it seemed to me that I knew a great deal more about some aspects of broadcasting than they did.' He had been told by Milne that he would have authority over television music programmes. 'Alan Yentob, then head of Music and Arts, welcomed my involvement as long as we agreed about everything, but when we didn't, he said, "I wasn't hired to work for John Drummond." '

While kicking his heels, Drummond wrote a report about music in the BBC. *The Times* got wind of this, alleging on 19 July 1985 that it suggested 'ways in which the splintered music department might be re-united under his Controllership', and adding that Drummond was expected to cause a 'tidal wave' in Broadcasting House. Ian McIntyre thought it strange that Drummond should not have consulted him when writing the report. Drummond says: 'It didn't mention him at all, but simply said that the presence of two Controllers on the same patch was not very good – and I may have added that relations were not good between the two occupants [Ponsonby and McIntyre].'

They were not good between McIntyre and Drummond either. After Ponsonby departed, Drummond began to find McIntyre 'bloody-minded and obstructive. And yet in other ways he behaved generously and pleasantly, and face to face we always got on.' McIntyre invited Drummond to attend the Radio 3 meetings at which music programmes were discussed, but (says Drummond) 'I had no power over the schedules, over the network, so what was the point? I usually wouldn't go to them.' When he did, he too found the atmosphere unpleasant – 'so unpleasant that very many contributors to the network refused to attend it. I found the whole tone of McIntyre's management, in that respect, repugnant.'

Drummond was soon making his mark on the Proms. He began with themes, as at Edinburgh: 'I did that simply to focus the mind. It's an enormous canvas, the Proms – fifty-five, sixty, sixty-five, eventually seventy concerts. I chose dance the first year, 1987, partly as a red rag to a bull, because I knew it would upset the musical world! They're so contemptuous about dance, and I simply wanted to point out that some of the greatest music of the twentieth century was written for dance. The literary theme, in 1988, worked best. It was a sensible Radio 3 kind of theme. It allowed us to do things like the four versions of *Pelléas et Mélisande* (Debussy, Schoenberg, Fauré and Sibelius) on consecutive days, linked with a radio production of the Maeterlinck play in a new translation by Timberlake Wertenbaker – to have some really thought-through things. And the following year, 1989, there was a sort of preoccupation with mythology, story-telling, things of that kind. But it was weak, because I wanted to let the themes tail off; I didn't need them any longer.' Meanwhile audiences were going up. In 1987, 76% of seats were sold; in 1990, when a large number of contemporary works were included in the programme, the figure reached 86%. The following year, the Association of Professional Composers praised Drummond for having done 'more than any other single person to promote the living composer ... Our cultural scene would indeed be poorer without him'.

He was running the Proms, as he ran everything, very much as a one-man band. He explains that 'Glock had had a sort of committee [to programme the Proms], and so did Ponsonby.[2] That's not my way of working. I preferred to do it *ad hoc* – I liked to use people where and when, in areas where I was weak, like early music, both inside and outside the BBC.' He emphasises that, though he eventually acquired a full-time Proms Planning Assistant, a huge amount of the work still had to be done by himself – 'phone calls, endless meetings. But I knew the music scene inside out, internationally.'

He says that the biggest change he made to the Proms was 'vastly extending the range of international orchestras. It had started in Glock's time, but only one or two a year. And through Edinburgh I knew all the foreign orchestras. And they didn't cost an arm – they were supported by touring sponsorship, and they sometimes cost less than British orchestras.'

By the spring of 1987 McIntyre had been Controller, Radio 3 for more than eight years, longer than anyone except Newby, and his network's standing within the BBC was currently not high. In March 1987, David Hatch, Director of Programmes, Radio, visited Radio 3 to discuss the network's 'accessibility' to listeners. ('It's a constant theme in Radio 3, the terrible word "accessible",' says McIntyre, 'though not everyone who used it knew how to spell it.') Hatch told a producers' meeting that other BBC staff tended to regard Radio 3 as 'off-putting, exclusive and unwelcoming'. George Fischer immediately sprang to McIntyre's defence, telling Hatch that it was 'galling' to hear this sort of comment from people who 'never listened' to Radio 3 and who ignored its brief. Philip French added contemptuously that 'accessibility' was just a trendy piece of management jargon, and McIntyre (always adept at quoting from his predecessors) recalled that George Barnes had said that the Third 'would not provide crutches for its listeners'.

Hatch said very little in reply, though McIntyre recalls that he wrote him 'a tetchy little note, suggesting that I had mischievously not intervened to prevent the troops giving him a roasting'. Meanwhile McIntyre had done nothing to ingratiate himself with the top level of BBC management. 'I was thought to have said numbers of rude things about television,' he recalls. 'On one occasion I called it "radio's autistic younger brother". This did not go down well.' A 1981 letter from Aubrey Singer to McIntyre asks if he and George Fischer had not been 'disloyal' in criticising Alisdair Milne (then Managing Director, Television, and Deputy Director-General) to his face.

A month after the meeting with Hatch, a small piece of paper signed by

---

[2] Ponsonby says it was not a committee; he consulted experts, both inside and outside the BBC, but made the decisions himself.

the Director-General, Michael Checkland, was pinned on all BBC notice-boards: 'The Board of Governors has agreed that the posts of Controller, Radio 3 and Controller, Music should be merged. The new post will be advertised internally.'

Drummond explains what had been going on: 'I had accepted the job on the understanding that the possible merging of the Controllerships would be discussed. And it wasn't. And a year or more went by, and I was acutely frustrated. I was sitting out in Yalding House just running a concert series [the Proms], which wasn't what I came back to the BBC for. So I applied for the General Administrator's job at the Royal Opera House, very publicly. I didn't want it, but I wanted to see what the BBC would do about it. And they reacted rather quickly.' McIntyre says that the actual decision to merge the Controllerships was made by Brian Wenham, Managing Director, Radio.

BBC-watchers in Fleet Street sprang into action. 'Contest for the control of Radio 3,' announced the *Daily Telegraph* on 30 April 1987, and its radio critic Gillian Reynolds reported:

> Today is the closing date for applications for a key new post. The person who gets it will be the biggest patron of music in this country and one of the most powerful in the world as well as architect of the national agenda of high culture.
>
> The two principal applicants are Ian McIntyre ... and John Drummond ... The fusion of their two functions was the result of deliberations by the BBC's Board of Governors at their meeting on April 9 when they set about 'the general rationalisation of management within the BBC'. With one hand, they tidied up the top of Radio 3 and, with the other, abolished the job of Controller, Local Radio.

Reynolds reported that, besides McIntyre and Drummond, other possible contestants were Alan Yentob, various senior members of the Radio 3 Music Department, and Piers Burton-Page, who had become Radio 3's Presentation Editor when Cormac Rigby left in 1985 to resume training for the Catholic priesthood.[3] However, Drummond and McIntyre agree that the four people interviewed were themselves, Burton-Page and Ernest Warburton.[4] Reynolds continued:

> Ian McIntyre says he proposed the merger of the two jobs three years ago ... But John Drummond was subsequently appointed and, to many

[3] Burton-Page, who was Music Organiser for the BBC World Service before joining Radio 3, writes: 'Ian McIntyre's search for intellectual rigour and his hatred of self-indulgence were in the best Reithian tradition. But he frightened people, and they often under-performed as a result. The manoeuvres that went on to get rid of him were some of the most sickening things I have seen in the BBC.'

[4] Warburton had been made redundant as Editor, Music, Radio 3 in June 1985. He became External Services Music Organiser at Bush House, and was eventually promoted to Editor, World Service.

observers, seems to have arrived at the job on the understanding that any future merger of the two jobs would leave him in total control. Whether any such promise was made by the late George Howard, who was Chairman of the BBC at the time, or the recently departed Director-General, Alisdair Milne ... the open contest for the job now appears to have put these undertakings back into history ...

Drummond says of this: 'No such promise was made to me. Alisdair said I would have to take a chance on it.'

If Drummond does not succeed [continued Reynolds] he does not have long left of his five-year contract to serve. Although he was pipped for the top job at Covent Garden by Jeremy Isaacs, his gifts as an impresario and his formidable range of international contacts ... would surely find him a major job in the arts elsewhere.

McIntyre is a staff man. At 55 (two years older than Drummond) he could perfectly well take early retirement ... But ... there are still those who fear both his political bark and practised bite.

The previous Sunday's *Observer* had printed an article on the contest which also examined the condition of Radio 3. It was by the paper's music critic, Nicholas Kenyon, who also wrote previews of music broadcasts in the *Listener*, where he had frequently scourged Radio 3 for unimaginative programming; for example (on 9 January 1986): 'A dull week, in all conscience, with a distinct under-representation of first performances, rarities and skilfully balanced programmes which make Radio 3 command attention as more than aural wallpaper.' Now he wrote:

Few deny that Radio 3 badly needs a shake-up ... Under the McIntyre regime, imagination in music programming has stultified and creativity has been stifled ....

Some would suggest that the new Controller of Radio 3 needs to be above all a creative musician who can motivate the staff under him or her and reclaim music's corner within the corporation's thinking. They might also conclude that such a person is scarcely likely to be found by advertising only within the BBC.

Drummond's outspokenness had already acquired him enemies in Portland Place, for Kenyon added that 'a deputation of music producers' had made it clear that they did not want him to be chosen for the new job. Similarly in the *Daily Telegraph*, Alan Blyth alleged that Drummond was 'not the soul of popularity'. However, McIntyre describes the appointment proceedings as 'a bit of a charade – everyone knew the result that management required'. Drummond agrees: 'They organised this run-off between Ian and myself, which was difficult for both of us. It was unfair to Ian, because it was perfectly obvious that the key pre-occupation in Radio 3 was music. And if they were going to advertise one joint job, it was perfectly obvious that the person doing it had to be primarily musical.' Sure enough, on 22 May a notice went up: 'The Board of Governors has appointed John Drummond, at present Controller, Music, to the new post combining Radio 3 and BBC Music in the single job of Controller, Radio 3. He will take up his appointment on 1st June.' His contract would run for five years.

Drummond told *The Times*: 'I relish the challenge offered by this new combined job. Radio 3 has long been the BBC's most single-minded contribution to the cultural life of the United Kingdom. We shall keep it that way.' McIntyre, who had been given a week to clear his desk, made no public statement; within the BBC it was announced that he would be taking a period of grace leave while his future was considered. He opted for redundancy, and soon afterwards joined the staff of *The Times* for a while, as Associate Editor responsible for leading articles. Later he wrote a vivid biography of Lord Reith, and an equally readable life of Robert Burns, and also reviewed books. He says he does not complain about the ending of his BBC career, 'although I did not admire the manner of it'.

*

Drummond now had to try to do three jobs at once: Controller of Music, directing the Proms, and running Radio 3. He recalls that he took over Radio 3 on the eve of the Proms, 'in the middle of ten hours of meetings each day', and was 'having to listen to huge quantities of Radio 3 output at the same time as the Proms'. He says he nearly killed himself doing all three jobs. 'You couldn't fail to cope with the Proms – they had to float to the top of the pile, and anyway they only occupied about a quarter of my time (I work quickly, and I had very efficient back-up).' As to the running of Radio 3, Drummond says that 'Brian Barfield was a tremendous support.' Barfield, a former announcer and producer, had joined Radio 3 as Planning Editor towards the end of McIntyre's regime. 'The actual programming of the network – what specific programmes went into what slots – was done by him, in collaboration with Christine Hardwick,' explains Drummond. 'But I had to draw up the schedules. And it was very hard to be Controller of Music on top of it all.'

Much of his time had to be spent attending to the needs of the BBC orchestras. 'There were constant problems about (for example) how big the Scottish Orchestra ought to be, and whether we could get another couple of desks in the cello section to beef it up. And was I being Controller of Music or Controller of Radio 3 when discussing those matters? Both, because if we were going to use the Scottish Orchestra on Radio 3 for a hundred hours a year, or whatever it was, we wanted it to be a better orchestra.'

He decided to give the orchestras their own programme on Sunday mornings. 'It caused a few problems, because the BBC Symphony Orchestra's repertoire contained quite a lot of contemporary music, which some people found difficult. But I wanted us to be proud of the orchestras – and I insisted that people stop calling them the "house orchestras", which made them sound like pit bands. We also needed to recognise that they had an important role to play in their own communities. The Philharmonic's concerts at the Royal Northern College, the Welsh playing in St David's Hall, Cardiff, or the Scottish at Stirling, all needed to be seen as part of the BBC's public profile. Each orchestra only costs what BBC television spends on a couple of drama series, but seen as part of the radio budget they do cost a lot. And I wanted to get the BBC to realise that the orchestras are a national resource, not just a running expense for Radio 3.'

During this period, salary increases negotiated by Drummond and his colleagues put the BBC orchestras back in the position of being able to get the best players. Meanwhile Yan Pascal Tortelier and Andrew Davis were appointed principal conductors of the BBC Philharmonic and the BBC Symphony Orchestra. 'At its best,' says Drummond, 'the BBC Symphony Orchestra is the equal of any orchestra in the world. But radio orchestras cannot do what other orchestras do, which is to repeat the same repertoire over and over again. Of course, when the Symphony Orchestra goes away on tour, it does give the same programme six or seven times. But how many of those concerts can you broadcast on Radio 3? The regulation was that more than half the tour had to be broadcast – within a ninety-day period. Now, how do you do that without making the network seem repetitive? This kind of editorial problem about music on Radio 3 could not be effectively addressed before the merging of the Controllerships. I'm not at all sure that we solved any of them in my time, but at least there weren't two Controllers involved in the dialogue.'

Despite his close interest in the orchestras, Drummond says he could spare far too little time to visit the regions and keep in close touch with the Philharmonic, the Welsh and the Scottish orchestras. David Hatch was aware of this. After some months of Drummond holding the two Controllerships, Hatch wrote that he was doing 'a fine job for the BBC in both running the network and the Proms'. But 'what is not working so well, however, is his Corporate responsibility for music'. Because of Drummond's lack of time to pay attention to them, 'the regional orchestras are declaring a form of UDI. Tours take place of which we know nothing ... Concerts [are] divorced from what [Radio 3] requires.'

Ironically, one of Drummond's current tasks was defending the BBC's musical resources against attack from Hatch's colleagues. 'Michael Checkland, when he was Deputy Director-General, questioned the need for the Music Library,' Drummond recalls. 'And when I asked what was going on, two of the Governors said to me, "We thought musicians played from memory." And three times during my time as Controller, an attempt was made to get rid of the BBC Singers.'

Drummond, who was unmarried, was now often working for eighteen hours a day, and had little time to choose tactful words when dealing with his superiors or his staff. But he also cultivated firmness as a principle: 'The fact that I am confident in public should never allow anyone to believe I'm confident in private. There are whole areas of self-doubt, but I can't stand people who agonise in public, because then *everyone* feels nervous.'

One of the first Radio 3 producers to come into conflict with him was Philip French. 'He immediately abolished all the regular open meetings,' says French.

> He decided that it was not necessary for his staff to question his decisions. He did occasionally get meetings together, but they were in the spirit of a dictator holding a rally. People were expected to come and wave flags. And he'd have decided things in advance of the meeting, and say to everyone, 'I've asked so-and-so to give a talk. Now, who will produce it?'
>
> I complained to David Hatch about the way Drummond was behaving. I don't know what was said to Drummond, but it had an immediately chastening effect. And he asked me if I'd like to do a programme on Australian cinema, for that country's bicentennial, so I got a trip around the world!

Drummond responds: 'Philip French may say that if he wants to, but I think it's grossly unfair. People claim I used to dominate meetings by talking too much, but nobody else had anything to say. What people wanted to do was to play their own games with their own little projects, walking around the battlements of their own existing knowledge. It was very hard, my first year as Controller. I said, "I want change. And I want change of *this* kind." And then we discussed *how* it could be embodied. But the idea of discussing *whether* we needed change was not on.'

Drummond adds: 'Philip French used to spend half the week as the film critic of the *Observer*.[5] He was also the most productive producer around, because he did *Critics' Forum* every week, and lots of documentaries. But he wasn't there all the time.' French dismisses this: 'I went to Broadcasting House five days a week, usually arriving before 8.30 am ... On Mondays and Tuesdays I would go out in the mornings and afternoons to press shows that were held within ten minutes' walk – and I'd have been going to most of those films anyway in connection with my BBC work.'

Drummond continues: 'I had some meetings with individual depart-ments. At the meeting with Talks, George Fischer contradicted everything I said. So I told him, "George, *I'm* the Controller. And quite frankly you're not going to win." He ridiculed things – for example, I said I saw absolutely no reason why Radio 3 shouldn't do programmes about food and drink – eating and drinking well was a pre-occupation of most of our audience. (And we eventually did *Table Talk*, with Leslie Forbes. It was popular and successful, and in no way diminished the network.) But after about a fortnight, George Fischer went to see David Hatch and said it wouldn't work, and he thought he'd better go.'

---

[5] Stephen Hearst had been opposed to French taking up this position while on the BBC staff, feeling that he could not be both the impartial producer of *Critics' Forum* and a critic in his own right; but Hearst was over-ruled by Howard Newby.

Fischer disputes Drummond's version of events: 'Yes, I did take early retirement at the age of fifty-seven in November 1987. But my disagreement with John Drummond was not the cause of it. I had been thoroughly disillusioned by the circumstances of Ian McIntyre's departure.' He adds, however, that Drummond's 'rather garrulous lack of trust in Talks and Documentaries' was a bone of contention between them.

One of Drummond's onslaughts was against the irrelevance of most interval talks to the concerts and operas which they punctuated:

> During the time I was Controller of Music but not yet running Radio 3, there was a Brighton Festival, in May 1987, at which the Finnish Radio Orchestra played all the Sibelius symphonies. Five concerts were broadcast; one had no interval; in the interval of another was *Six Continents*, which I thought was immensely dull; and the others were filled with a reading from Stanford's memoir of Sterndale Bennett, and two talks called *Aspects of Egypt* and *'Dynasty' – Romanian Style*. Sibelius studies were then at an interesting stage, and we had Robert Layton, one of the world's greatest experts on Scandinavian music, on our staff. Yet I could only find one instance at that time of an interval-related talk. That was when the BBC Symphony Orchestra went to Turin, and there was a very good talk in the interval of one of their concerts about arts funding in Italian cities. And I thought, *that* is what we should be doing.
>
> But it was tremendously strongly contested by Talks Department, because it meant that some speech programmes would be produced by Music Department. And the only talking about music (apart from introductory notes) that had been allowed in the period immediately before I took over was in *Music Weekly*, or whatever it was called by then. No conductor was ever interviewed, no composer ever talked, no one was ever allowed to speak about music, because musicians could not be trusted to speak. So vast amounts of time and money were spent on academics like Edward Norman talking at great length about whatever took their fancy. And I remember asking one of the music producers what he did in the interval when he was listening at home, and he said, 'I take the dog for a walk, or make a cup of tea – I certainly don't listen.'

Six Continents, the programme of news reports from foreign radio stations instituted by McIntyre, was discontinued at the end of 1987. (The simultaneous broadcasting of BBC World Service news bulletins on Radio 3, introduced experimentally twice a day by McIntyre a few weeks before his departure, was stopped too.) Within a year or so, Drummond had managed to co-ordinate the interval programmes with the music output. 'It worked best with opera,' he says. 'The opera people saw it made sense. We did a *Wozzeck* from Glasgow in which one interval was George Steiner talking about Büchner [author of the play *Woyzeck*] and the other was about opera in Scotland. And with the Proms, from the second year, we had interviews with conductors and soloists and composers built into the presentation.' Since then, the majority of speech programmes in the intervals have been relevant to the concert or the opera being broadcast.

Drummond also thought – as Stephen Hearst had, some years earlier – that the presentation of music programmes was hidebound. In the press, he complained that many of the scripts written for announcers sounded like 'hand-outs from the Ministry of Music'. He explains that the trouble lay largely in the indiscriminate use of the Music Information Index. Compiled by the Music Information Unit, this was a database of introductory notes on musical works, for use by producers. 'It was a very false friend,' says Drummond.

> Young producers would go there and get pages of undigested musicological facts about some work, and dish it up unedited to the announcers. I wanted people to write their own material. I was trying to liberate the network into feeling more comfortable with itself: giving producers much more say in what they did, and giving the presentation people a real role – because it seemed to me that much of what they did was too tight, too Olympian and cold. And I wanted *enthusiasm* to be communicated, the feeling that we *cared* about what we were broadcasting. But meeting after meeting would go by with people sitting there sullen and po-faced, feeling that their lives were being infringed, because I just wanted them to *do* things rather than cranking the handle.

He admits that he was contentious – 'I *had* to be, in a situation where there was a lot of suspicion of me, and I had to justify myself. And my first year in the double Controllership was very, very difficult, for other people and for me. But after a while, because the heads of department – Christine Hardwick and Anne Winder [running Features, Arts and Education][6] in particular – saw what I wanted to do, it suddenly became better. And I don't feel that the later part of my time was confrontational.'

Anne Winder says of Drummond: 'He was inspirational. And it did settle down – you got used to his rather arbitrary decisions, because of all the good things about him.' Piers Plowright found him 'warm, encouraging, chatty – though he could be pretty acerbic as well'. If he liked producers' ideas, he would take them up at once. Derek Drescher, who had been in charge of Radio 3's jazz programmes for some years – and had found that the amount of jazz broadcast depended entirely on the Controller's whim – 'went along to him to say, "It's time we had some jazz in the Proms", and he took the words from my mouth. I thought, "Good God, this is a breath of fresh air." That year was the first Proms season which included jazz. We had Loose Tubes (30 August 1987), which was amazingly successful.' Proms historian Barrie Hall notes that it was 'a late night Bank Holiday [Prom] which went on well past midnight, hugely enjoyed. The bust of Sir Henry [Wood] sported a Loose Tubes T-shirt throughout.'

---

[6] When George Fischer left in 1987, Talks and Documentaries was absorbed into a new department called Features, Arts and Education, Radio. Continuing Education programmes were later removed from the department, which is now Arts, Science and Features.

Drummond says that there was less confrontation when Donald Macleod became Presentation Editor.

Piers Burton-Page had been in the job when I arrived, and there were people on his staff who disliked what I was trying to do, and who protested vocally. Announcers like Tony Scotland, Malcolm Ruthven and Peter Barker didn't like the idea that they were expected to become people in their own right. But they already were. They had very distinctive styles. And I just wanted a more natural feel. Once I appointed Gordon Stewart as Assistant Head of Music, with responsibility for scripts, and Donald took over Presentation, the whole thing eased and became much more flexible.

Another Drummond appointment, in May 1990, was of Adrian Thomas, Professor of Music at The Queen's University, Belfast, on a four-year contract as Head of Music, Radio 3, on the retirement of Christine Hardwick.

A simple way of increasing the personal element in music presentation was to enlarge *Record Review* on Saturday mornings. Drummond doubled its length: 'It seemed to me a marvellously good programme, wonderfully authoritative. Once we'd got Richard Osborne as a presenter, and later Anthony Burton, who became such a good broadcaster after he stopped being my Chief Assistant[7] and went freelance, I think that worked very well.'

In 1989, two years after taking over Radio 3, Drummond wrote in an internal memo complaining about a dull scripted programme: 'I have been doing my best for the past two years to *stop* people reading on the network. I am sick of being *read at*. I want to be *spoken to*, which is why *Third Ear* was invented and is so successful.' Setting out his plans for the network in 1987, Drummond had told David Hatch that he wanted to have 'a daily strand of serious talk about the arts'. *Third Ear*, twenty-five minutes long, began to be heard from Mondays to Fridays in the early evening from 19 September 1988. Most programmes in the series consisted of a single interview with a leading figure in the arts who was in the news; for example in the programme's second week, on 27 September, Hermione Lee interviewed Salman Rushdie about his new novel, *The Satanic Verses*.

'The initial plan for *Third Ear*,' explains Drummond,

was that all the production departments should contribute editions. At first, nobody was used to the idea of a twenty-five-minute conversation – it took them time to adjust to something so long. But the subject in which it came out right almost from the start was the visual arts, almost entirely produced by Judith Bumpus. Week after week, sculptors, designers, archi-

---

[7] Burton had combined being Chief Assistant to the Controller of Music (appointed by Ponsonby just before he left, against Drummond's wishes) with producing the BBC Singers.

tects and painters would come in and talk about their work in a way that was totally meaningful. The music side wasn't bad. Drama Department had a great deal of difficulty producing anything other than 'luvvie' chat. But the 'issues' editions, on the current affairs of the arts (funding and so on), which Robert Hewison presented most of the time, were, I thought, marvellous.

Radio 3 drama came up for review by David Hatch not long after Drummond had taken over the network, and he remarked that it seemed 'somewhat lacking in identity'. Richard Imison, Deputy Head of Drama, responded: 'That is hardly surprising. The extraordinary thing is that there has been any drama on Radio 3 at all after 7 [*sic*] years under a controller [McIntyre] who has consistently failed to define his policy and ultimately blocked every effort on our part to find one for him.' In fact one very distinctive drama series, which would not have found a place on Radio 4, had continued intermittently during the 1980s: *Barnes's People*, a set of short plays, mostly monologues, written for the network by Peter Barnes. Performers included Simon Callow, Sean Connery, and Lionel Jefferies, and the offbeat nature of the subject matter is indicated by a review, by Nigel Andrews in the *Listener*, of a play in the 1989–90 series:

> *Billy and Me* [29 December 1989] ... was a virtuoso performance by the brilliant Alan Rickman, playing a ventriloquist and his little company of dummy characters ... The vent, who owes his art to a mental breakdown, is fighting off depression with this bizarre colloquy ... This was Barnes at full throttle, playing a dangerous game and getting away with it brilliantly, while also putting over some rich jokes (*Vent to dummy:* 'When we went on that tour of Israel, didn't I remember to pack a pencil sharpener for you?'). Pure radio, stunningly well played ...

Drama successes during Drummond's regime included the return of Tom Stoppard to Radio 3, with *In the Native State*, starring Felicity Kendal. Broadcast on 21 April 1991, this was afterwards reworked by Stoppard into the stage play *Indian Ink*.

Despite these achievements, Drummond says:

> I found Drama Department very difficult to deal with. They were very nice people, but they reasoned with their hearts, often passionately defending thoroughly dull ideas. Producers treated anything that fashionable writers like Howard Barker wrote like holy writ, though to me there was less in it than met the ear.[8] I felt the general level of plays was gloomy, doom-

---

[8] Two of Barker's plays were accepted for Radio 3 during Drummond's Controllership: *Early Hours of a Reviled Man* (16 January 1990) and *A Hard Heart* (18 February 1992). The network had previously broadcast *Herman with Millie and Mick* (10 March 1973) and *Scenes from an Execution* (14 October 1984). John Tydeman says that Barker was 'very appreciated by the young but totally intransigent. I think we were over-protective to Howard – though *Scenes from an Execution* was very good'.

laden. There was practically no humour, and not enough classical drama – 'We can't do *Hamlet* because we did it nineteen years ago,' they would say. 'It has to be *Pericles* because it's the only one we haven't done in the past twenty years.' Yet no one in the country was able to see Shakespeare unless they went to Stratford or the Barbican, and Radio 3 ought to be doing the major canon all the time – Sheridan, Wilde, Shaw, Synge, the great dramatists. And if that meant dragging recordings out of the cupboard and repeating them, fine.

So we did quite a lot of that; we got out the old Scofield *Othello*, and so on, and ran them again. And we had *Critics' Choice*, recognising how very few people ever see a play which has a successful run in the West End, or at the National Theatre, compared to a radio audience. So we asked people like Michael Billington and Michael Coveney to get together with Ned Chaillet of Drama Department, and make a list of plays which had been well reviewed but hardly seen. And that was a strand of drama which I thought often worked better than things written deliberately for radio.

Another of Drummond's anxieties was Radio 3's imminent loss of medium wave. It had been known for some while that it would eventually be confined to VHF (or FM as it was now more generally known), and in July 1987 Drummond had told Hatch he was anxious about this: 'The public are not convinced of the superiority of VHF ... We must be able to demonstrate it's highly desirable for people to get better quality through VHF, even if it costs them a bit.' Warnings that Radio 3 would soon lose its medium-wave coverage were received with as much hostility as Drummond had feared. Car-radio users complained that FM required constant retuning, some listeners were puzzled by terminology ('My local shop says FM and VHF are different'), and few agreed with a Mr Jones from Lancashire who telephoned the BBC to say: 'I have been using FM for the last fifteen years and I can't believe that there are so many people without it. It is another example of the stupidity of the British people. They cannot cook and they cannot listen to good music. They would be better off in the Mediterranean.' Meanwhile the date of the changeover kept being postponed by the Government.

In the midst of all this, Drummond felt a persistent lack of support – even of interest – from top BBC management: 'I had no brief; I was not told what to do by anybody. I can't remember ever having a serious conversation with anyone above me in the BBC about Radio 3. Neither the Director-General nor successive Managing Directors of Radio had any interest in contact with it. They were only worried that I might do something that would cause them to have an inflated postbag, as when I changed the schedules and then changed them again, and said to the press that I'd got it wrong (which shocked everybody at Broadcasting House, a Controller admitting error, but I *had* got some of it wrong).[9] There was no intellectual context whatsoever in which one was working; there were no discussions about the need for Radio 3, or what it was about. I was left alone. It was nice that people trusted me, but I would much rather have had the feeling that they thought that it mattered what Radio 3 did.'

*

Drummond's five-year plan, on taking over the network, had included the promise of 'special projects or seasons', which he knew would encourage departments to work together and – very importantly – attract attention from the press. 'McIntyre had been the politician,' says Tony Scotland, 'but Drummond was the PR man. He ensured that everyone knew that Radio 3 existed. He put it on the map.' Drummond agrees: 'I think that's true. It's a matter of temperament. The actor side of me liked things like *Call the Controller*.[10] And it meant one could put a face on Radio 3, could bang the drum. But it generated an enormous correspondence. The first *Call the Controller*, linked to one of my schedule changes, led to 1,400 letters, every one of which I answered, though it took me from January to Easter.'

Three of Drummond's special projects were devoted to great figures in the history of the Third Programme. Sir William Glock's eightieth birthday, on 3 May 1988, was marked by a day-long celebration, as was Sir Michael Tippett's eighty-fifth, on 2 January 1990. Sir Isaiah Berlin's eightieth, on 6 June 1989, was celebrated with an evening that included Drummond interviewing him. Berlin was heard on the network several times during Drummond's Controllership; he says: 'John Drummond took me up, and decided I was fun.' Drummond says it was more than fun: 'I can remember getting permission to come out of homework at school, and go back to my study and listen to Isaiah Berlin on the Third. He opened my mind to an entirely new dimension of intellectual life. When I became Controller, I couldn't persuade him to lecture any more, but he was prepared to be interviewed. So we built an evening around his eightieth birthday. We subsequently recorded some other conversations about some of the people he'd known. It was one of those links with the past that I like – the kind of mind that ought to be on Radio 3 all the time, with a range of cultural reference that went wider than just the discipline of one subject. He was a symbol of what Radio 3 had failed to continue from the Third Programme – we'd got Edward Norman and we'd lost Isaiah Berlin.'

A Scandinavian Season ran for seven weeks from February to April 1990, and a Japan Season during October and November 1991. Drummond

---

[9] Drummond explains: 'I caused a lot of offence by moving the early morning news bulletins to the half hour – 7.30 and 8.30 am. Radio 4 had news on the hour, so why shouldn't we have it on the half hour? I also wanted to start *Composer of the Week* earlier, to get it on at 8.30. But this schedule wasn't much liked, so eventually it was abandoned; I was quite flexible about it.'

[10] A phone-in programme in which listeners could talk to the network Controller.

himself took a very active part in Radio 3's Berlin Weekend, on 5 and 6 May 1990, to mark the reunification of Germany. 'We had a small commando of producers from different departments,' he says. 'It was exhilarating and fascinating. We used studios in East and West – rather a lash-up, and it was tremendously exciting. And I came back to London, and not one single senior person in the BBC had listened to any part of it.'

Drummond says that this weekend gave him a chance to break down the barriers between the different production departments: 'I had investigated all sorts of ways of structuring Radio 3's programme-making, other than by departments, which I felt worked against producers' knowledge and enthusiasm. I looked at whether we couldn't put teams of producers together, to produce a day – a Tuesday team, a Saturday team, and so on. Of course there were great big rocks in the way of that. But the Berlin Weekend gave us a chance to do it. You suddenly saw a group of music producers and talks producers, and several executives like myself and Brian Barfield, all working *together*. And when we got back to London, a young producer called Elizabeth Burke sent me a postcard which said "Why can't London be more like Berlin?" What she meant was, why couldn't we work this way in London?'

The following year, on Saturday and Sunday 1 and 2 June 1991, Radio 3 presented a 'Twin Cities Weekend' from Minneapolis-St Paul. A press handout stated that 'broadcasting history' was being made by 'transmitting a whole weekend live from another continent'. Minnesota had been selected, according to the handout, because its character was 'relatively unknown' to British listeners, and it had an excellent public radio station, reflecting thriving local arts. Brian Barfield told David Hatch: 'We have had an enormous amount of help and cooperation from our colleagues at Minnesota Public Radio and they intend to carry the entire weekend on the Minnesota network and … on other stations nationwide. An important aspect of our broadcasts … is the reflection of MPR's local programming and … we intend to broadcast their regular Saturday morning programme … as well as the Garrison Keillor show "live".'

Presenters for the weekend included Drummond himself and John Tusa, head of the BBC World Service, which carried some of the weekend's programmes. (Drummond explains that Tusa, one of his oldest friends, was also on the board of National Public Radio in the USA, which had made the weekend easier to arrange.) They had to 'fill' considerably between programmes while the Americans were broadcasting sponsorship credits. Radio 3's audience researchers noted that Garrison Keillor went down particularly well with British listeners – one of whom asked that he should broadcast regularly on Radio 3 – while Paul Donovan in the *Sunday Times* praised the 'many quiet delights' of the weekend:

There was baseball, Prince, Betty Crocker cake mix, the Prairies themselves – their bison gone but blue orchids still hiding in the long grass – and music, much of it live, ranging from Debussy and Beethoven to a

Dominick Argento opera. An edition of Choral Evensong was jointly led by a woman priest, probably for the first time since it began ...

More important ... was the opportunity of contrasting the styles of the two partners, BBC and Minnesota Public Radio ... As far as the microphone approach is concerned, we have more to learn from them than they from us. Minnesota Radio evidently goes out of its way to make good music accessible, something to be participated in, rather than put on a pedestal and worshipped in awe. This is achieved by lack of jargon, a chummy and direct presentational style ... and interviews with musicians before they played and between their pieces. It brought both them, and their music, closer ...

When it comes to content, range, innovation, quirkiness, commissioning new works and maintaining orchestras, the BBC wins hands down. Anyone who thinks, as Douglas Hurd [then Home Secretary] once said, that the licence fee is not immortal and that US public radio could be a model for the future here, ought to dwell on [that].

*

Drummond continued to introduce new programmes. 1 October 1990 saw the start of *Mixing It*, a late-night show aiming to 'reflect the way in which much contemporary music is crossing the boundaries between styles, and to promote genres of music currently unrepresented on other radio programmes'. That same autumn, *Critics' Forum* was replaced by *Third Opinion*, in which Christopher Cook introduced interviews and scripted items as well as critical discussions. Drummond admits that this 'never quite caught on', but defends his decision to axe *Critics' Forum*: 'It was smug – the same little gang of people saying the same sorts of things for years. All right, it had some following, but it wasn't bringing in new voices. And it never covered architecture or dance, and music only rarely. I'd taken part in it as a performer, in my year out between Edinburgh and the BBC, and I'd enjoyed it. But there were people on it who were very boring, and when I asked Philip French not to use them again, I'd turn the radio on a fortnight later and there they were.'

French deplored the loss of the programme he had produced for sixteen years, and took early retirement from the BBC, amid some protest from listeners and participants in the programme; but the response to Drummond's changes since he took over from McIntyre had generally been enthusiastic. Some even felt they had not been sufficiently drastic. An *Observer* columnist, Andrew Stephen, visiting Radio 3, described it as continuing much on its old lines:

The [Continuity] studio seemed wonderfully serene: there were pot plants in the corner, and Peter Barker (Radio 3 senior announcer) was sitting in front of the microphone, pipe in hand, shoes discarded ... Later, Barker took me up to the Pronunciation Unit, which is precisely the sort of thing the BBC does much better than any other organisation in the world. Two ladies sat indexing cards ... When I [saw] John Drummond ... I quickly felt reassured ... It seemed like 40 minutes or so before I succeeded in squeezing in a question ... He goes to every Prom (he missed only one last year, and will miss only one this year), and clearly cares intensely about what he does.

This article observed that Radio 3 was now costing the BBC £40 million a year, seventeen per cent of its radio budget, while only two per cent of the radio audience listened to the network – the peak was still about 250,000 listeners at any one time, while many programmes still had an audience 'so small it is statistically unmeasurable'. Drummond said he was perfectly happy with this; he pointed out that a very popular Royal Academy exhibition might be seen by 100,000 people, roughly the number that listened to many of Radio 3's programmes. He implied that BBC management took an insufficient interest in what was actually being broadcast, and suggested that all the Government wanted was 'a lot more radio networks to sell off to make money' (a reference to current threats of privatisation). 'But these are unfashionable things to say,' he added, 'and I'm not supposed to say them.'

Drummond was not usually so restrained in his public remarks. In November 1988 he was widely quoted criticising Prince Charles's conservative views on architecture, describing them as an example of 'the heritage industry and a Laura Ashley civilisation'. And in June 1991, the *Independent* reported a speech he had made some weeks earlier to the British Association of Concert Agents. It had not been intended for publication, but a tape recording of it had been passed to the newspaper. It was on the subject of the marketing of classical music, and included an attack on the violinist Nigel Kennedy for paying more attention to his image than his music. Drummond compared Kennedy's punk clothing to the vulgarity of Liberace, and described him as appearing 'in a blue dressing gown, with purple shoes, a green face and black lips, with a vampire bite stuck in rubber on one side of his neck'. (To Drummond's embarrassment, this turned out to be a genuine ailment caused by the pressure of the violin.) Drummond also spoke out against the Radio 3 audience, which he said was 'characterised by profound conservatism and deep contempt for everything it doesn't know, including almost the whole of the twentieth century'.

Kennedy replied, in the press, that to judge people by their appearances was no better than apartheid, and though popular feeling was mostly on Drummond's side he was accused by some commentators of elitist arrogance. 'For how long can John Drummond justify a budget of nearly £60m [*sic*] a year when he has such contempt for his customers and their tastes?' wrote Corelli Barnett, adding, with reference to the growing prospect of a commercial classical radio station: 'Once "Radio Vivaldi" gets on the air, he will find his audience will dwindle from little to nothing.' Gillian Reynolds, reporting the Drummond–Kennedy affair in the *Daily Telegraph*, made the same connection:

Meanwhile ... the new national commercial radio franchises are waiting
in the wings. One of the three applicants is a consortium called Classic
FM. Its programmes would feature music by classical composers; but from
6 am to 6 pm there would be no piece played which lasted longer than
four and a half minutes ... We will know next month whether Classic FM
has put in the highest tender for the licence.

Drummond had been asked about this some months earlier, and had said
that such a station 'will not be a rival to Radio 3 ... We commission music
and drama and features. Radio 3 is a foreground network, not a background
channel.'

Tom Sutcliffe of the *Guardian* reported one anonymous Radio 3 producer's
opinion of Drummond, now that he had completed four years as its Controller: 'He gets up our noses. But he's done a terrific job in raising the profile
of our network and making it more accessible.' Sutcliffe agreed – 'Drummond has made things seem serious but not so recherché that dwindling
audiences turn the network into a target for bovver-boy accountants
who think Reith is something you stick on a coffin' – and added:

Drummond's machine-gun patter, at the annual Proms launch, is as fast
as Sir Isaiah Berlin's and far easier to grasp. He's a natural showman and
compere ... The latest outburst, however, may have rather more to do
with the fact that Mr Drummond's contract as Radio 3 boss runs out next
year. He has made no secret, his colleagues say, of the fact that he's not
looking for a renewal. What he wants is to be kicked upstairs and sideways
to a newly created post as the BBC's Director of the Proms – in other
words, keeping the bits of his present job that are fun, and unloading the
boring administrative and committee work.

Drummond says of this: 'They asked me to go on in all three jobs, to do
another five years, and I said no, I'd kill myself doing that, but I wanted
to do the Proms centenary. So the idea of detaching the Proms from the
Controllership came up – though I was initially doubtful, because it would
make the job much less attractive to anybody coming after me. But that
would only be temporary.'

The Kennedy affair prompted the *Independent* to publish an editorial
about Radio 3. 'Mr Drummond has made the channel less pompous and
patronising in tone than it used to be,' declared the writer,

though some relics from the old Third Programme linger on. Those who
listen all day no doubt find a fair cross-section of music of all periods. But
such listeners form a minority. What maddens many classical music
enthusiasts is not the choice of music but its absence. Mr Drummond is
apt to be scornful of user-friendly foreign classical radio stations of the
sort found in France and the United States. Why does he assume that
their output is being *heard* rather than *listened to* – a typical Drummond
distinction full of intellectual snobbishness?

It is not his job to provide classical music around the clock. But it is hard to believe that there is not a market for a commercial station that combines the pluses of Radio 3 without its minuses.

Drummond himself explained the background to his remarks about Kennedy, in a letter to the *Independent*:

> The conference [at which Drummond spoke] was entitled 'Expanding the Market' and was about the marketing of music. In my view, marketing is in danger of becoming a substitute for understanding and its manifestations seem increasingly grotesque.
>
> I have a high regard for Nigel Kennedy's musicianship and a personal friendship with him going back many years. Nevertheless, I believe he is misguided in allowing himself to be promoted in the way he does . . .
>
> There are good and bad ways of seeking a new audience . . .

*

A month after the Kennedy incident, it was announced that Drummond would indeed direct the Proms for a further three years (1993–5) after stepping down from the double Controllership of Radio 3 and Music. Meanwhile the Independent Radio Authority had awarded the country's first national commercial radio licence not to Classic FM, but to Showtime Radio, which had put in a higher bid (to public outrage, the bids were being judged on purely financial grounds). But Showtime failed to raise the necessary capital within the allotted time, and on 19 August 1991 it was announced that Classic FM, the next highest bidder, would have the franchise. Among distinguished persons who had given their names in support of its bid were Dame Kiri Te Kanawa and André Previn. Its chief executive stated that it would 'drift on the Pavarotti wave' – meaning that it would attract the many people who were now purchasing popular classical CDs who had little knowledge of serious music.[11] The new station was to come on air in the late summer of 1992.

Writing a diary column in the *Guardian*, Drummond himself observed of Radio 3 that 'everybody knows exactly what they think ought to be done, but the demands are so contradictory as to be completely irre-concilable'. On another occasion, he remarked that 'Radio 3 broadcasts to about thirty minority tastes, each of which is characterised by its intense dislike of the other twenty-nine'. He says that innumerable letters he received during his Controllership of Radio 3, though from highly edu-cated individuals, were

> of unbelievable idiocy, selfishness, and bigotry. Someone would write and say, 'It's perfectly obvious that what Radio 3 needs is a ninety-minute organ recital every evening.' The head of one of the larger polytechnics demanded that I take all piano music off the air. Then there were the

[11] The specific allusion is to Pavarotti's recording of *Nessun dorma* from Puccini's *Turandot*, which was used as the theme song of the 1990 World Cup.

people who loathed twentieth-century music, or authentic instruments, or opera in a foreign language. I would spend most of Saturday afternoon and Sunday morning at home answering them – after doing a seventeen- or eighteen-hour day during the week. And occasionally my temper would fray, and I would write a rather testy reply, and then they would write to the Director-General or the Chairman to complain.

There's no such thing as 'the music audience'. They like the organ, or they like chamber music, or they like symphony concerts, or they like opera, or the nineteenth century, or new music. But they don't like each other. There is a mass of different audiences. So any schedule you put together is going to displease more people than it pleases.

CHAPTER FOUR

Strategy

On 17 January 1992, the BBC announced that John Drummond's successor as Controller, Radio 3, would be the *Observer* music critic, forty-year-old Nicholas Kenyon. The post had been advertised publicly, and Kenyon's application had consisted of what he described as 'two sharply honed sides of A4'. Afterwards, he said he had not expected to get the job: 'I had thought I was putting down a marker for later on, but when I was offered it immediately, having thrown bricks [at Radio 3] for so long, the least I could do was have them thrown at me.' Asked what was on the two sides of A4, he answers: 'I do remember the thrust of it, which was that Radio 3 can change without sacrificing quality. And that has been a part of everything I have tried to do.'

As soon as he was appointed, an interviewer asked him about Classic FM. He replied: 'I don't see it as a problem. There's big potential for expanding the market and increasing the audience generally. It doesn't lie within my philosophy to move downmarket.'

Kenyon's musical career had begun as a Catholic choirboy in Cheshire, where his father was a Customs and Excise officer. He played the piano, cello and bassoon, but treated music as a hobby and read history at Oxford. He took the Arts Council's arts administration course, then worked for Lina Lalandi, director of the English Bach Festival. In 1976 he joined the BBC's Music Information Unit as a scriptwriter, under Deryck Cooke, whom he admired, but he regretted the Unit's 'lack of any contact with the programme-making process'. He was soon asked by Robert Ponsonby to write the official history of the first fifty years of the BBC Symphony Orchestra. This was published in 1981, and Kenyon followed it with a biography of Simon Rattle. By this time he and his young family were in America, where he was writing music reviews for the *New Yorker*, but he wanted his children to be educated in England, so he returned to London as music editor of the *Listener*, and a music critic of *The Times*, before joining the *Observer* in 1985. He also did some freelance broadcasting for Radio 3, but his microphone style was not liked by Ian McIntyre, who said after he had introduced a magazine programme about the Proms: 'Can't we find anybody better to do this?' Kenyon explains: 'I tended to come across as a very light-voiced, rather squeaky broadcaster.' In spite of this, he was widely used on *Record Review*, presented *Early Music Forum* and *Prom News*, contributed regularly to Radio 4, and was the classical music critic of the Radio 2 Arts Programme.

Paul Donovan, radio critic of the *Sunday Times*, thought Kenyon an unlikely choice for the Controllership: 'He has never been a BBC executive, and is now suddenly a senior one in a place notorious for its Byzantine complexities. He has never produced a programme, and is now in ultimate charge of dozens who have. He is, however, steeped in music ... ' Kenyon agrees that he was not as obviously qualified as several experienced 'broadcasting professionals' who were competing for the job, but says that 'there wasn't anybody among them with enough stature in the musical world'. He adds: 'Remember that the job was not as attractive as it might have been to senior musical figures, first because it didn't include the Proms, second because of the imminent arrival of Classic FM – which was viewed as a potentially terminal danger; many people assumed that it would immediately remove the need for Radio 3.'

At his interview for the job, he offered to go on a management course if the BBC thought it necessary. 'So I was duly despatched on one, and it was full of extremely high-powered people, taught by a very brilliant chap, who spent most of his time, when examining my case, shaking his head sadly and saying, "It's a very strange appointment." '

'Actually,' Kenyon continues, 'I *had* run things – the *Mozart Now* Festival for the South Bank in 1991, and the magazine *Early Music* for Oxford University Press, which involved budgeting and people and so on – but obviously nothing on this scale. I had the freelance outlook.' Gillian Widdicombe, arts editor of the *Observer*, described him as 'inclined to lope into the office with duffel and satchel'. Taking up his job at the BBC, he donned a dark suit.

Just before Kenyon began his five-year contract as Controller, at midnight on Friday 28 February 1992, Radio 3 surrendered its medium wavelength to the Independent Radio Authority.[1] The first day's transmission on FM only was marked by a live relay from the Metropolitan Opera, New York, of *The Barber of Seville*. Broadcasts of Met matinees had begun on Radio 3 in 1990, and were made available at very low cost to European Broadcasting Union members by the sponsors, Texaco – though most of the sponsor credits were blanked out by the BBC.

Kenyon told journalists that he was in no hurry to declare himself on changes to Radio 3 – 'I have an enormous amount to learn, so for a while I will keep quiet.' Yet after he had been Controller for only two weeks, the

---

[1] The removal of the medium wavelength meant that in the summer of 1992, Radio 3 lost many hours of broadcasting because *Test Match Special* was occupying its FM frequency, despite extensive protests. This happened again the following year, though this time coverage was shared with Radio 5 (which carried the morning sessions). From 1994, Test Match coverage went to Radio 4 long wave.

press learnt that three senior members of the Radio 3 Music Department, Clive Bennett, Anthony Cheevers and John Evans, had already been sent to America to listen to classical music radio stations. 'I felt it was worth opening our ears a bit,' Kenyon explained. 'But I don't want to panic listeners. What they hear might be something to react against as much as to follow.'

In fact, as soon as he was appointed, Kenyon had begun to discuss and implement an urgent agenda for altering Radio 3. 'I think its character had to change,' he explains.

John Drummond had begun to alter it in quite significant ways, but when I arrived, what I found was an absolutely overwhelming thirst for change, on the part both of senior management, who were frustrated that so little had happened, and staff who were equally frustrated that their imaginative ideas seemed to count for little. It was rather like a pent-up dam being released. If anything, what we did was go too fast, because of that enthusiasm. But I wanted to make changes *before* Classic FM came on the air – I did not want to be perceived to be changing Radio 3 in response to a style that they had initiated.

What sort of changes were wanted? 'I well remember,' answers Kenyon,

a very distinguished person from the musical world ringing me up when I'd got the job and saying, 'Get rid of those effing announcers.' That was the flashpoint for what people felt about Radio 3 – the announcing style, which had remained unchanged since the Cormac Rigby and Patricia Hughes days. It had been exactly right for that era, but times had now changed beyond recognition. I think the real issue was whether you regarded Radio 3 as something that could be comfortably anachronistic, a rather fuddy duddy old-fashioned radio station. I knew, from the people I knew who went to concerts and did not listen to Radio 3, that this was not a sensible option to take. And so we embarked on the process of taking apart that style and trying to create something different. And I had a very clear brief to move quickly and decisively, in an area where possible change had been discussed for years.

Three weeks after Kenyon's arrival, the *Daily Telegraph* reported that Radio 3's announcers had been summoned by Kenyon and told that 'not all of their services will be required in future'. The report continued: 'For many, the chief reason for listening to Radio 3 is the presence of such announcers as Malcolm Ruthven, Tony Scotland and Peter Barker, who seem to have been there since Marconi's days. But they may not fit in with Kenyon's brave new world. The Controller is said to believe that Radio 3 needs a good jolt to meet the challenge of Classic FM.' A month later, Paul Donovan reported in the *Sunday Times*:

A third of all the announcers on Radio 3 are being made redundant by the new Controller, Nicholas Kenyon. With their perfect diction and graceful manners, they are often regarded as among the last vestiges of civilisation in the BBC ...

What are we to make of the dismemberment of [the] announcing team? It is hard to imagine any controller acting in such a short-sighted way so quickly. The seven men and two women announcers are among the most companionable people on the air today. They introduce concerts, recitals, records and programmes in a calm, pleasant and rational tone now almost unique in broadcasting ... Over the years [they] have dropped what was once a self-conscious snootiness ...

But [Kenyon] has formally proposed that three of them are to be turned into 'presenter–producers'; three to remain as announcers; and three to be made redundant ... Kenyon says the three producer-presenters will need both 'musical knowledge and production experience'. Since there are exactly three who meet these requirements (Piers Burton-Page, Chris de Souza and Andrew Lyle), that appears to ensure their future. Who goes and who stays out of the remaining six, says Kenyon, will be decided by the extent to which producers want to use them and how much they have been involved in live relays.

Speculation suggests that the three who will be picked to stay are Penny Gore, Paul Guinery, presenter of *Your Concert Choice*, and Susan Sharpe, presenter of *Midweek Choice*. That means Peter Barker, who has been in BBC Radio nearly 30 years, Malcolm Ruthven and Tony Scotland will be pushed out. But nobody knows for sure ...

Kenyon denies making the redundancies on financial grounds. 'It seems to be quite wrong that there is one clump of people making programmes and writing scripts, and another clump of people reading material designed by others. We want to knit the two sides together ... '

The announcers should be kept. They are part of what makes Radio 3 great. However many extensions you want to add to a house, you do not strengthen it by ripping out one of the best rooms.

Two months later, on 21 June 1992, Donovan had more news of another drastic change: 'Radio 3's *Music Weekly*, which has covered the musical world with quiet distinction for 17 years, is being taken off the air next month ... *Music Weekly* goes out on Sunday mornings, with a Tuesday afternoon repeat. Michael Oliver presented it for many years and Peter Paul Nash has done so for the past two ... It reports on specialist musical issues ignored or trivialised elsewhere on the air.' Donovan speculated that the loss of the programme would provoke a furore. 'After the revelation in this column eight weeks ago that a third of the announcers were to go, I received more letters than on any other topic for four years ... Incensed listeners also wrote to the BBC, and *The Times* carried a protest from Bamber Gascoigne and Viscount Norwich.' Their letter, published on 5 May, had protested that Kenyon's policies were 'totally at variance with all the principles of public broadcasting'.[2] (Kenyon points out that none of his policies had yet been agreed or announced.)

---

[2] Lord Norwich, under his usual name, John Julius Norwich, later became a presenter for Classic FM.

Donovan also revealed that one of the announcers now definitely selected for redundancy, Peter Barker, had in fact been due to retire in a few
months. Another – again as predicted by Donovan – was Tony Scotland,
while Malcolm Ruthven departed about a year later.

Donovan had been publishing leaked information. It was not until all
union negotiations were completed, and plans were finalised, that on 29
June 1992 the BBC officially announced 'BBC Radio 3 FM's New Look',
and Kenyon gave a lengthy interview to Richard Morrison of *The Times*.
He began by responding to accusations of secrecy: 'Am I taciturn and
secretive? Only possibly in comparison with my predecessor ... I had to
get everything into shape before we announced it. There are big knock-
on effects internally: the reduction in drama, changes in the presentation
department. Those were leaked, and seen out of context.'

He explained that most of the changes were to create 'access points' for
new listeners – as Morrison put it, 'the people who buy classical music on
compact disc, who enjoy it on television, but who at present would not
dream of tuning to Radio 3'. Kenyon's aim was to 'convince Radio 3's
current audience that the wooing of these new listeners does not mean
some ghastly descent into *populism*'. There would, however, be a more
concerted effort than ever before to market the network. Saatchi & Saatchi
had been appointed as its advertising agents, and the autumn would see
the launch of *BBC Music Magazine*, a glossy classical music monthly, which
would give away CDs recorded by BBC orchestras.[3] By the beginning of
1994, it had become the best-selling classical music magazine in Britain,
with a circulation of 75,000, and more than twice that in America.

Kenyon gave an assurance that 'there is no hidden agenda about meeting
listening figures ... We will still be running orchestras, doing *Music in Our
Time*,[4] relaying operas from around the country.' What was under review
was 'whether all *this* material is approachable on the air. And whether
there are sufficient ways into Radio 3 for the whole new audience for
classical music that we know is out there.' It was this 'approachability'
issue that had led to the replacement of old-style announcers. 'I want
presentation to be much more involved,' Kenyon explained, 'more knowledgeable, and to be able to explain to people why there is such enthusiasm
for putting this particular piece of music on the radio.' Therefore the
current breakfast sequence of records, *Morning Concert*, would be replaced
by *On Air*, while the teatime *Mainly for Pleasure* would become *In Tune*.
The BBC press handout described these as 'two weekday programmes with
named presenters, of mostly popular classical music with news headlines,
weather, traffic information, previews, news of the music world'. *In Tune*
would include 'a guest interview'.

[3] Kenyon explains that terms were negotiated with the Musicians' Union by which the BBC
orchestras could record simultaneously for broadcasting and commercial release, which has
led to the issue of CDs of rarely performed works which are in the orchestras' repertoires.
[4] The contemporary music programme was later given a new and longer format, as *Hear and
Now*.

Third Ear was to be replaced by what Kenyon called 'a new, late-night version', to be called *Night Waves*. 'It will be able to do instant reviewing of opera and theatre first nights,' he explained to Morrison, 'much needed, now that you newspaper critics have so pathetically given up on overnight reviews'. As to *Music Weekly*, it was temporarily disappearing to make way for a three-hour Sunday morning record programme introduced by Brian Kay, whom Morrison described as 'a treacle-voiced former King's Singer' (for some years he had been a Radio 3 staff announcer). This was to be the principal programme for 'wooing new listeners', and would include 'tasters' from the coming week's choicest programmes. 'Kenyon agrees that he is taking advantage of Kay's "very direct following, built up through Radios 2 and 4",' wrote Morrison,

and that Kay will generally be playing more popular classical pieces. 'That doesn't mean he won't be playing extracts from more challenging repertoire, so that people can make up their minds about it. We want people to find their own "mix and match" across the network ... ' This is why Kenyon has regimented the Radio 3 week more thoroughly than hitherto. The new late-night music programmes are rigorously labelled according to the day. Tune in at bedtime on Tuesday, for instance, and you will always find vocal music. 'A lot of people say that they don't know where to find what they want on Radio 3. So it's important to have a focused approach to the schedules. I want lots of fixed points.'

Kenyon made no reference to the fact that the Third Programme had been founded under the motto 'no fixed points'. (Challenged on this, he says: 'Different times need different methods of reaching the intended audience.')

He explained that his own catchphrase for the network was 'Music Plus'. Morrison observed that this could be a euphemism for 'Drama Less', though Kenyon said that a reduction in drama was part of an overall BBC strategy which defined Radio 4 as 'speech' and Radio 3 as 'music'. Paul Donovan had alleged that Radio 3's drama output would be halved under Kenyon's new schedules, and this had provoked a letter of protest to *The Times* (30 June 1992) signed by, among others, Harold Pinter, Tom Stoppard and Fay Weldon; David Hatch had replied that drama was being reduced by 'a quarter, not a half'.

Concluding the *Times* article, Morrison observed that Kenyon had achieved a remarkable amount during a mere four months – he had been furiously 'juggling, commissioning, and (in the case of two announcers) sacking', wrote Morrison. He ended with another quote from Kenyon: 'One of the nice things I have discovered about radio is how quickly you can change things ... Though of course you bruise a few egos in the process.'

That day, Tony Scotland wrote to Kenyon, with a copy to his own solicitor:

To clear up any misunderstanding, I should be grateful if you would ask *The Times* to publish a correction, pointing out that Peter Barker, M.B.E., and I are not being sacked but made redundant – in the case of Peter, only five months before he would have retired naturally anyway.

There is a difference between 'bruised egos' (© N. Kenyon 1992) and defamed ones.

Kenyon now admits that the departure of the announcers was 'rather badly handled', but emphasises that it was 'vital to have the new programmes on the air, with new presenters, in the summer of 1992. It was the most decisive thing anyone had done to the style of Radio 3 for years, and we all believed it was overdue.'

He insists that the motives for this change of style were entirely positive:

I came to the network as a passionate enthusiast for classical music, and I was dismayed by the distanced and frankly precious style with which it was, with some exemplary exceptions, presented. I wanted an approach which drew people in, an approach which combined authority with energy, so that everybody who spoke on Radio 3 did so from a position of knowledge and enthusiasm. I loathed the system of X writing scripts for programme Y, and their being read by Z, whom he had never met. It meant achieving a far greater overlap between producers and presenters.

We started by asking three announcers with extensive experience of production, Andrew Lyle, Chris de Souza and Piers Burton-Page, to create a new breed of producer–presenter. Happily, that overlap has become much more common now. For example, Paul Guinery produces and presents his own programmes, including some excellent *Composers of the Week*. But it was a huge change of culture, and I underestimated how long it would take to settle down.

*

The leader-writer of the *Guardian* guessed that Kenyon's plans would alarm those 'who feel that the BBC's music output is heading towards wall-to-wall Vivaldi', but felt that Radio 3 must do something to change its image. 'Sixty-two per cent of its listeners are male, 73 per cent belong to the top social classes, and 72 per cent are over 45 ... These figures suggest that it has not kept pace with the growing general interest in classical music ... Mr Kenyon's plans ... deserve to be given a chance.' The *Independent* agreed: 'Nicholas Kenyon ... has rightly decided to embark on modest change ... The test will be whether he can scoop up ... newcomers without losing the faithful following that he now has.' Some of the faithful were already protesting in the correspondence columns. 'Let Classic FM do its worst – but please, Nicholas Kenyon, let Radio 3 continue doing its best,' read a typical letter from a listener in *The Times*. Paul Donovan in the *Sunday Times* wrote that he had asked the chief executive of Classic FM what he thought of Kenyon's changes: ' "I do feel," he said, "that we set out our stall quite early on and that they are now changing to a format which is obviously closer to ours. That convergence will contribute inevitably to a reduction in listener choice." I put this to Kenyon. "Absolutely untrue," he said. Let's hope he's right.'

On Air, In Tune and *Brian Kay's Sunday Morning* began in mid-July 1992. Gillian Reynolds in the *Daily Telegraph* (14 July) welcomed the new breakfast show:

> *On Air* stepped lightly into place yesterday morning at 7 am ... with Piers Burton-Page introducing European weather and nationwide traffic reports as if he had been doing so forever. There may be some muttering up the road at Camden Lock, where Classic FM is even now girding up its loins for its national launch in September ... Nicholas Kenyon ... has lived long enough in New York to know a good pattern when he hears it, which is why the new Radio 3 model follows it, with news on the hour, headlines every twenty minutes ... and carefully timed bands of music between ...

Classic FM came on the air on Monday 7 September. Its press launch a few days earlier had provoked some scorn; Stephen Pettitt in *The Times* called its style 'grotesquely saccharine', and mentioned that one disc jockey, Henry Kelly, would be giving racing tips, while another, Paul Gambaccini, promised 'music for lovers'. The *Guardian* pointed out that the station's programme controller Michael Bukht had a 'curious double identity': he had once been a TV chef under the alias Michael Barry. In fact Bukht had an excellent broadcasting pedigree: starting out as a BBC general trainee, he had worked for the Corporation in radio and TV before experiencing commercial broadcasting in Jamaica. Returning to England, he had helped to found the hugely successful Capital Radio in 1972, and had later started up other projects in the commercial radio sector.

Bukht had hired Robin Ray to create Classic FM's record library and play-lists. He devised a system of coding and star rating – 'One star means for the committed specialist,' he explained, 'and one in a bracket is for the musically adventurous; two means pretty safe to programme depending on what with; three, tremendously likeable; three, and one in a bracket, can't go wrong; four, everybody knows it.' He also provided each piece with a 'mood rating', indicating 'happy, sad, neither happy nor sad, or both'. Ray's analysis was fed into a computer, which could then answer producers' needs for a specific mood, period, and length, printing out a list of pieces which met the criteria. As to Classic FM's policy of playing individual movements, Ray observed:

> I ... wouldn't include ... the 'bleeding chunk' – something ripped out of the middle of something. I don't approve either of playing movements of works when it doesn't make musical sense. The Liszt piano sonata is, depending on how you look at the manuscript, either in one continuous or eight different movements. It's an experience, a spiritual journey, and it wouldn't make sense to pull out a movement ... However I do think it's perfectly all right to play the rondo from Mozart's horn concerto on its own or the slow movement of Beethoven's seventh symphony ... Why

should I deny people the opportunity to hear wonderful music by insisting they hear the whole work? In fact, I think they will come to the whole work later ...

Scorn for Classic FM persisted for a while. There was widespread joking about the disc jockeys' mispronunciations and other gaffes – to the extent that Tony Scotland found himself being hired by Bukht to give tutorials to the presenters. But the station's informal manner earned praise from the outset. 'My heart was won by Susannah Simons,' wrote Alexander Waugh in the *Evening Standard*, 'whose exclamations of "wonderful, isn't it" and "don't let anyone ever tell you that opera is boring" were unaffectedly natural. Classic FM's genuine, relaxed style will undoubtedly win millions of new and hopefully young converts to classical music.' Richard Ingrams in *The Times* wrote:

> Of course the main criticism of Classic FM is that because of its need to carry regular advertisements, it is unable to broadcast full-length symphonies or concertos (at least during the peak morning and early evening periods) and is therefore, of necessity, limited to snippets, short works or extracts ... But – looking at it from the point of view of the working man or woman tuning in for a short time in the bath or over breakfast – the last thing he or she feels inclined to do is settle down for a leisurely appreciation of Mussorgsky's *Pictures at an Exhibition*. And there is a perfectly respectable tradition for programming snippets, as you can see if you look at the concert programmes of the last century, when it was quite rare for a long work to be performed in its entirety.

By the beginning of 1993, the station's success was beyond dispute. The first official listening figures, released in January by Radio Joint Audience Research (RAJAR, a jointly agreed system measuring both BBC and independents), showed that, in the words of the *Independent*, 'Classic's recipe of classical "hits" is winning an audience as high as 10 per cent [of the population] each week – equivalent to 4.5 million people. Radio 3 can expect only half that figure.' The same paper reported that Kenyon was 'undismayed' by these statistics, and quoted him as saying: 'Classic FM set out to be popular and it is not playing anything that anyone doesn't like. It has to deliver an audience to advertisers, while we are extending choice by the breadth of our repertory.' Michael Bukht insisted that he was not aiming to poach Kenyon's listeners: 'Radio 3 has never been my concern. We're a mainline popular music station competing for the big mass-market audiences of Radios 1, 4 and 2.' Robin Ray agreed: 'If we are successful, Radio 3 will get our listeners sooner or later.' Kenyon told another reporter: 'Radio 3 still has 2.5 million listeners which is more than the audience in this country for live orchestra, opera and chamber music performances. The Classic FM figures are great news to us because they also show that the audience is coming from the world of Pop as well and will create listeners for us.'

Two BBC documents from this period demonstrate the difficulties that were afflicting the Corporation with the arrival and success of Classic FM. The station had come on the scene just as the BBC found itself struggling with a privatisation-mad Conservative Government for its survival as a publicly funded non-commercial organisation. In a 1992 glossy brochure called *Extending Choice: the BBC's role in the new broadcasting age*, which was in fact an early bid for the renewal of the Charter four years later, the Corporation committed itself to Radio 3 in strongly worded terms, describing it (and Radio 4) as 'truly distinctive and unlikely ever to be matched in the commercial marketplace', and praising 'Radio 3's commitment to cultural patronage and excellence across a wide range of audience groups'. However, in the same paragraph, it stated that 'Radio 3 should be more accessible and appealing to classical music listeners'. Similarly an internal BBC document dated 30 March 1993 states that the BBC's strength lies in providing 'high quality programmes which extend choice beyond that available in the commercial sector', yet it should also provide 'access for all through licence fee funding' (that is, not be exclusive or elitist). It stresses that Radio 3 is unlikely ever to be 'matched in the commercial marketplace', yet it 'should be more accessible and appealing to classical music listeners'. Kenyon was having to walk along a very narrow line.

Radio 3's new morning and evening programmes, *On Air* and *In Tune*, had been attracting profuse criticism in their first few months for including too many news bulletins and phone-ins, and for excessive speech. The *Spectator* attacked this tendency under the headline 'DIMINISHED THIRD'. Kenyon says he had to agree with much of the criticism. 'Our presenters talked too much,' he admitted in a press interview in February 1993, seven months after the changes. 'I now tell them to be economical with words. I also accept that perhaps we went slightly too far and threw out too many well-known programme labels.'

*

As well as changing Radio 3's style of presentation, Kenyon took a new approach to the job of Controller. He says of this:

> My own experience of radio production was rather limited. Practically everyone who worked for me was more expert than I was. I saw my own task as setting the strategy for the future, rather than giving lofty judgements on programmes. I don't think during all the time I was at the *Observer*, the editor communicated directly with me about any of the material I wrote. One dealt with the arts editor – and any feedback came via that route. Now the culture of the BBC was entirely different: only by the yes or no of the Controller did anything happen, or was any programme judged good or bad. And that's something that I've been trying to change, by giving editors more responsibility for feedback, and with the contributors feeling that they ought to depend on their editors.

By 'editors' Kenyon means, in the music area, six staff in Radio 3 Music

Department who look after particular types of programme. John Evans, who during 1993 succeeded Adrian Thomas as Head of Radio 3 Music Department,[5] explains the system:

> I myself look after the BBC Singers, and the non-BBC orchestras. I also co-ordinate *Composer of the Week*, and look after all the festival relays. Then there are five editorial units, which are staffed with an editor, producers, and assistants. The first editor, William Robson, is also my deputy, who looks after Chamber Music. Andrew Kurowski edits New Music. Andrew Lyle is the editor of the sequences – that's the morning programmes up to midday, and *In Tune*. Gwen Hughes is the Opera editor, and Graham Dixon is the editor of Early Music.

The speech departments have their own editors who deal closely with Radio 3 through Brian Barfield. These include John Boundy for arts pro-grammes, and Richard Bannerman for documentaries. Others look after drama, religion, science and occasionally light entertainment.

Kenyon says that producers and presenters 'will certainly get a more expert view from their editor, who listens to all that output, than they will from me, who occasionally may catch something, or will listen if it's something that I find particularly interesting. But I'm not able to give an expert view across the range of a network that's on every day of the week'. He adds: 'I am not good at the *post mortem* tearing apart of programmes which my predecessors went in for – it was an unnecessarily humiliating process which was not in the end productive. And I always believe that preparing the next programme is more important than disembowelling the last.'

In the spring of 1993, the lives of all BBC staff were changed drastically by the introduction of Producer Choice, a new internal accounting and management system. It was intended to 'demonstrate both to the public and the Government that the licence fee provides value for money' by giving producers responsibility for 'the full cost of the programmes they produce' (that is, capital costs and overheads as well as programme budgets). They could choose 'whether to use internal resources or to purchase them externally'. There would be 'a new structure of business units and production tariffs', with 'all departments ... aiming to break even annually', enabling 'the BBC to relate to the open market', and to 'operate efficiently to best industry standards'. Network Controllers 'must prepare their programme strategies and choose how to disburse resources to internal and external [i.e. independent] producers'. BBC Radio was now being obliged by the Government to buy a quota of its programmes from independent production companies.

John Evans contrasts Producer Choice with working methods only a few years earlier:

---

[5] Evans had worked for Sir Peter Pears and the Britten–Pears Library at Aldeburgh before joining the BBC.

When I joined the BBC in 1985 as a producer, you could do virtually anything you wanted. It was like going into a sweet shop, and somebody closing the till and saying, 'Help yourself.' If I had an idea, I could do it. And you didn't have to wait till the next financial year to get it approved. I did a project about Serge Koussevitzky, making a documentary that involved foreign travel, and a thirteen-part archive series. I worked on and off at that for about four years, and I've no idea to this day what it cost – and probably it could have been done with much more financial efficiency.

Producer Choice came into operation in April 1993, a few weeks after John Birt had become Director-General, and Liz Forgan had succeeded David Hatch as Managing Director, Network Radio. Ben Woolland, Finance Manager, Radio 3, says that before Producer Choice 'we really had very little control – and very little idea – of who was spending what, or what the network was really costing'. (Radio 3's current costs of about £7,250 per hour are in fact lower than those of Radio 4, which costs £10,000; music may be expensive, but news-gathering is even more costly.) Woolland, Nicholas Kenyon and Brian Barfield (now styled Managing Editor, Radio 3)[6] much prefer having their hands on the network's purse-strings. However, the increased amount of paperwork that Producer Choice generates tended to make it very unpopular with production staff in the early months, while those who had worked in the old-style BBC tended to be contemptuous of it; for example, Gerard Mansell, who rose to be Deputy Director-General before retirement, dismissed it as 'half-baked Thatcherite nostrums imported from the United States'. *Private Eye* (15 December 1995) gives an example of Producer Choice at its worst: 'The BBC Singers ... sought a rehearsal hall for two weeks [and] were told that their usual BBC studio in Maida Vale would be available – for £1,800 a day ... According to the management, market forces dictated that the paper sum was appropriate and should change hands in the BBC's internal market. So with the entrepreneurial spirit so praised by the new BBC, the Singers turned down the BBC and hired the Salvation Army's hall nearby for a mere £400 a day – and ... the BBC lost £4,000!'

Anne Winder, head of Arts, Science and Features, Radio, agrees that Producer Choice has sometimes produced absurdities, but argues that its introduction has made a lot of sense:

I think it had to be drastic to start with. When I took over my department, it had overspent its annual budget – because it was too successful! People were accepting lots of programmes from it, yet *we* had to pay the cost of them! It might have discouraged us from doing our job. Now if we sell ideas to the networks, *they* have to pay for them, and that's a much more

---

[6] Barfield has two responsibilities: planning the schedules, and commissioning speech programmes.

sensible relationship. And I think we're now all much more confident with handling our own budgets, so the atmosphere has started to loosen up again.

Kenyon explains that, where Radio 3 is concerned, Producer Choice replaces

the absolutely vertical structure by which the Controller of Radio 3 managed the Head of Radio 3 Music Department, who ran the producers. There was a chain of command there, which has been replaced by an internal trading mechanism which means that I don't have anything to do with the personnel matters of Radio 3 Music Department. They do not work to me. They work to a Controller of Production (Caroline Millington), who is the head of all the production department heads. The departments, as it were, sell their product to me, and I have a range of suppliers from which to choose.

John Evans's Radio 3 Music Department must now compete with other suppliers of music programmes. 'Nick Kenyon wants to buy the best possible programmes for his network,' says Evans. 'And he now has a choice – he can choose from us, or from the regions (there are five regional music departments) or from the independents.'

Independent producers now provide a substantial proportion of the network's programmes; for example one company, Classic Arts, was responsible for Radio 3's coverage of the Bath Festival for two years, and co-produces *Private Passions*, Radio 3's current version of *Desert Island Discs*, in which Michael Berkeley interviews distinguished guests about their choice of music. This has not brought about any radical change of style, for the simple reason that many independent producers are former BBC staff members.

Kenyon thinks this sort of competition among suppliers is good for Radio 3: 'It's certainly introduced an element of competitiveness which has been to the good. And I am now getting better offers to the network than I think there have been before. Previously, there was an assumption that I would have to take everything that Music Department, as a monopoly supplier, offered, willy-nilly.'

Under Producer Choice, these programme 'offers', which producers had formerly made at frequent meetings with Controllers, can only be submitted for the following financial year. 'We assemble programmes for the network at six-monthly intervals,' explains Kenyon,

because we know the slots that are going to be available. Essentially, we are looking at what we are going to be able to place on the network within the next year. If one did it face to face with producers, it would take most of the six months. So we do it by looking through a large number of offers, which are now made on computer, with a system (that will eventually replace Orpheus, and cover the whole of radio) called Trivium. We accept some offers straight away, reject some straight away, and discuss with producers those that needed further elucidation.

This may sound a cold and calculating system, but I honestly think it's preferable to the old system, when Music Department would record programmes 'on spec', which would often sit on the shelves for ages – and might finally be broadcast three or four years later, by which time the performers had moved on artistically. Every programme that we commission under Producer Choice is guaranteed to be heard in the course of the following year.

John Evans agrees that this is an enormous improvement, but emphasises the bad effect on producers' morale when their ideas are rejected:

There's a limit to how much the network can take, and the producers don't like to see half or three quarters of their best ideas coming back rejected. But it's not unique to Radio 3. If you talk to staff anywhere in BBC network radio round about the annual commissioning period, you get the same response – ideas have been thrown out without enough explanation or feedback. Sometimes they'll be told 'Yes, but not in this financial period.' A producer can be waiting eighteen months to start a project.

Kenyon agrees that there has been frustration and bitterness.

Ironically, back in 1979 Kenyon wrote in the *Listener* about the changes to Radio 3 proposed by Ian McIntyre:

I can't help thinking that the current intended revolution is in danger of concentrating on image at the expense of content – an attempt to be popular which will misfire completely because it will lose the respect both of our audience and our potential audience ...

The great achievements of the Third Programme ... were only possible in a flexible framework where the broadcasting was built around the programmes the producers (chosen for the balance of their fiercely individual tastes) wanted to make, not vice versa ...

What was great about the Wheldon *Monitor*, or the Goldie *Tonight*,[7] or the Glock invitation concerts, was that one person of genius fostered the creativity of his team ... That ... seems the compass on which ... Radio 3 should lock its course.

Such a working method has not been possible for Kenyon himself, in the era of Producer Choice. But he takes a positive view of the situation, saying of the restricted nature of his contact with production staff: 'I think it's right to be fairly "hands-off", in that the Controller has always got to be taking the long-term view, looking further into the future.'

Kenyon has admitted to sometimes feeling trapped by the BBC's current style of management – there are, he has said, 'too many people involved

---

[7] Huw Wheldon edited *Monitor* and Grace Wyndham Goldie *Tonight* in the 'golden age' of BBC Television.

in whatever decision it is you have to make. The creative thinking gets done at very odd times and the conclusions come in odd moments.' But he argues the need for network Controllers to be involved in the BBC's long-term planning:

> We are part of a radio directorate which is having to think about where radio, and the BBC, are going to be in ten years' time; and unless someone's doing that work, there won't be programmes to be made in ten years. I would not like to be a network controller in a BBC where everything like that is being decided by someone else. Of course how one prioritises one's time is one of the more difficult things about the job.

John Drummond has been scathing about the BBC's new style of internal management. 'It's all strategy,' he remarked, in a newspaper interview some while after handing over the Controllership to Kenyon. 'What is strategy? Strategy is nothing. What you have is programmes and programmes come out of people's heads. This McKinsey view of the world has taken over everything. Nobody is sitting around doing things because they believe in them: they're doing them to see if they can make the business strategy work.' Anthony Burton says much the same:

> I remember at one point in the Seventies, we were all asked to write a paper on what we thought we were doing. And one quite senior member of the department drafted one which began: 'Our purpose is to serve the art of music.' This would create hysterical laughter if it were put at the top of any Radio 3 discussion paper these days. Where, they would ask, are the demographics, the listening figures, the assessments of the strengths and weaknesses of the opposition?

However, John Evans is emphatic that programme standards are as high as ever:

> I think the discipline of Producer Choice often stimulates and liberates ideas. It certainly needn't inhibit producers. In Radio 3 Music Department we've recently won two very prestigious awards: a Sony award for *Music of Madagascar*, one of our world music programmes, and a Prix Italia special prize for *Monument* – a radiogenic piece commissioned from the composer Ian Gardiner (5 October 1993). It's a tribute to the City of London, which uses bits of speech from the Sound Archives, ordinary people talking about the City, interwoven with a specially composed score.

And Kenyon says:

> All that 'strategy' means is having your priorities absolutely clear. We are committed to Radio 3 being the leading broadcaster of classical music and cultural programmes in this country. How you deliver that strategy requires endless discussion and debate. And I am an advocate of clarity. There are many ghastly management-speak terms swirling around the BBC at the moment – 'efficiency visions', 'reprioritization exercises', and

so on – but 'strategy' is not one of them. Without strategy, in a competitive environment, you're finished.

*

Producer Choice has put the future of the BBC orchestras at risk once again. In the spring of 1993, Kenyon had to put the case for their survival to John Birt and other senior BBC management. Thanks to Producer Choice, the orchestras were now 'expected to meet competition for the services they provide internally and externally, and to become more active in the commercial world'. Kenyon wrote a confidential policy document on the orchestras which argued that this was impossible; by all means, he said, 'maximise the external income' (from public appearances and foreign tours), but it was 'not viable' to apply the other criteria of Producer Choice to the orchestras – making them competitive trading units. Looking back, he admits that this was 'a battle', and says: 'Three weeks after I was appointed there was a front page story in the *Independent* saying that, as a result of one of the internal task forces, the BBC orchestras were for the chop. And I went in on the basis that this was absolutely *not* what we were going to proceed with. And I think some people in management needed intellectually convincing that it needn't be so.'

Management had to be shown that 'our orchestras could provide something which could not be supplied elsewhere'. They eventually accepted Kenyon's point that their 'wide and distinctive repertory' marked them out from the other British orchestras, but asked whether 'others could not be paid to take that on'. Kenyon pointed out that in Europe, 'all major Public Service broadcasters run radio orchestras, and indeed a recent study by the E[uropean] B[roadcasting] Union identified radio orchestras as "a key element which distinguishes Public Service broadcasters from commercial broadcasters"'. Eventually, says Kenyon, the argument was won. Liz Forgan made a public statement that the orchestras would continue to be supported, but this was conditional on working practices changing and more income being earned by the orchestras. 'But I have absolutely no illusion,' Kenyon adds, 'that the range and scale of everything we do orchestrally is something that can survive another ten years of the kind of financial pressure the BBC will be under – I think it's deeply unlikely.' (John Drummond is even more pessimistic about this.) Kenyon would like to see more funding partnerships to support them, so that the BBC does not have to bear the full cost:

> This is a system that has worked well in Wales, where the BBC National Orchestra of Wales is partly funded by the Welsh Arts Council. There ought to be other possible partnerships that can be developed. I was totally supportive of the proposal to merge the BBC Scottish Symphony Orchestra and the Scottish Opera Orchestra, because you would have had a better orchestra at the end of it, and there would have been a financial benefit. But this apparently proved impossible. I see no problem at all with the role of the BBC Orchestras, if we can sort out the matter of how

integrated they are with the concert life of the country.

The joint review of the orchestras which we conducted with the Arts Council was a good start to the process, but got blown off course by their desire to do something about the London orchestral situation [an abortive attempt to reduce the number of London-based symphony orchestras], at which point the BBC had to draw back. I very much hope that dialogue with them can be revived.

*

By the time that Kenyon's battle over the orchestras was going on, in the spring of 1993, Classic FM had abandoned the pretence that it was not competing with Radio 3. It negotiated to take a share of the Saturday relays from the Met in New York, and, when this failed, it broadcast several operas on CD before Radio 3 was due to carry them live.

Meanwhile Radio 3 was running a 1920s season, as part of the nationwide *Towards the Millennium* festival, which features a decade every year up to the year 2000. (Seasons devoted to the 1930s, 1940s and 1950s have followed in 1994, 1995 and 1996.) Easter Monday 1993 was a Leonard Bernstein Day, co-presented from New York by his biographer Humphrey Burton and his daughter Jamie Bernstein Thomas, who introduced classic Bernstein recordings and discussions of his work. On 25 April, Kenneth Branagh, Samantha Bond, Judi Dench, Sir John Gielgud, Simon Callow and Ian Holm were heard in *Romeo and Juliet*, co-produced with Branagh's Renaissance Theatre Company. As with Branagh's *Hamlet* on Radio 3 (26 April 1992) and Gielgud's ninetieth birthday *King Lear* (10 April 1994), the recording was afterwards put on sale by Random House Audiobooks. And in May 1993 there was a celebration of the twenty-fifth anniversary of the *annus mirabilis* 1968, including a reading of John Lennon's poetry. Meanwhile at the end of April it was announced that Classic FM had won the Sony Radio Award for national radio station of the year.

'I am not going to talk about Classic FM,' said John Drummond when the *Sunday Telegraph* interviewed him about the 1993 Proms. 'The business of running a radio network is no longer my responsibility, and I don't want to have to be *constantly* reacting to what my successor is doing.' Just as the Proms were ending, Kenyon announced another round of changes to the schedules. These included the decision that *On Air*, the earlymorning record programme, would have just one presenter, Andrew McGregor; there would also be a new magazine programme to replace *Music Weekly*, called *Music Matters*, 'concerned with opinion, debate and issues from the national and international music world', heard on Saturday evenings, with a Sunday repeat; and, from January 1994, there would be 'a new weekday 15-minute strand . . . for younger listeners'. This was *The Music Machine*, a 1990s-style *Pied Piper*, heard at 5 pm from Mondays to Fridays, with Tommy Pearson as chief presenter.

Andrew Clements in the *Guardian* described the latest changes as

a tweak here and there, part of Kenyon's increasingly delicate balancing act: to respond to the pressures upon him to access and to hold on to a bigger share of the radio audience (he has already nudged the Radio 3 fraction up from 5 to 6 per cent) while remaining faithful to the widest possible range of programming ... There was no mention [at the press conference] of the future of the BBC's regional orchestras, but Kenyon did touch on the continuing commitment to new music (a new work commissioned every two weeks). Little mention of Producer Choice either, which is bound to affect Radio 3's output as savagely as it has elsewhere in the BBC. At the moment the balance seems to be holding; certainly Kenyon is as buoyant and bullish as ever.

A surprise popular hit during 1993 was a recording of the Third Symphony of the Polish composer Henryk Górecki, written in 1976. In the *Sunday Times*, Hugh Canning described Górecki as a 'holy minimalist' (the symphony draws on early church music), and noted that Kenyon had 'devised a Radio 3 Polish festival that aims to place Górecki ... in a national and historical context ... "The Polish season [Kenyon explained] is the first important project where we have put together all of our orchestras to give a picture of post-war Polish music – Górecki, Lutosławski, Penderecki – and all those will be public and studio concerts throughout the country." ' *Polska!*, as the season was called, ran for two weeks from 19 November 1993. Though it had actually been devised long before the British craze for Górecki, it included his sixtieth-birthday concert, live from Warsaw (6 December), with the composer in attendance.

Although Radio 3 had broadcast Górecki's Third Symphony more than once, and Kenyon (before becoming Controller) had written favourably about it and Górecki in the *Observer*, its popularity had been achieved by 'plugging' a very brief excerpt on Classic FM. In general, however, the commercial station's success was not being translated into classical recording sales, which were dropping steadily, as they had for some years. A senior executive at EMI complained that Classic FM was only a 'sampler' of music. Similarly Graham Sheffield, director of music at the South Bank, observed: 'Classic FM encourages the soundbite culture, the compilation CD culture.' Ticket sales were 'at best static', and the managing director of the London Philharmonic Orchestra said: 'We haven't cracked how to get the Classic FM audience into concerts yet ... ' Meanwhile Classic had announced that it would sponsor the subsidy-starved Royal Philharmonic Orchestra with £500,000 a year. (Later reports questioned the accuracy of this figure.) Classic was relaying more live concerts than previously. 'Classic FM is, in other words, moving directly into Radio 3 territory,' David Lister noted in the *Independent*. It was also invading Radio 4's space, acquiring, at the beginning of 1994, *Gardeners' Question Time*, due to a dispute between the programme's chairman and the BBC. 'Whatever next? *Classic Archers*?' asked Gillian Reynolds in the *Daily Telegraph*.

RAJAR was reporting fluctuations in Radio 3's audience figures, but it was difficult to discern a trend. Christmas 1993 brought a marked increase;

the following summer there was a drop. Edward Pearce in the *Guardian* wrote of this:

> Nicholas Kenyon ... must be tempted up and down market sim-ultaneously. Did he over-react to Classic FM by losing old-guard DJs like Malcolm Ruthven and Tony Scotland? Did he not compound alienation by bringing in ... the naffly named *Brian Kay's Sunday Morning*? It is an insulting programme ... [Kay's] style, half cringe, half puff, a combination of ego-tripper and cathedral greeter, suggests something seeping under the door and does not ingratiate ... At the other end of the spectrum ... humankind can only take so much of an avant-guard [*sic*] mandarin in serious conversation with the appreciative professional friends of an avant-guard mandarin ...

At the end of 1994 Kenyon announced something that only Radio 3 could have done: an entire year featuring British music. David Lister wrote in the *Independent*:

> The idea for the year came to Kenyon when he was thinking how to mark the Purcell tercentenary ... 'We know his greatest hits ... but there's a vast body of work more honoured in the breach than in the observance.' And then there's Tippett's 90th birthday, the 100th birthday of the Proms, the centenary of Sir Malcolm Sargent, and the 50th anniversary of the first performance of *Peter Grimes* ... 'It is,' says Kenyon, 'the biggest con-centration on an area that Radio 3 has ever attempted ... It's a serious piece of exploration. I say only Radio 3 can attempt this.'

Fairest Isle, subtitled *BBC Radio 3's Year of British Music and Culture*, was launched by the Prince of Wales at a concert and reception at Kensington Palace in November 1994. It began on 1 January 1995, with a day of live events and broadcasts culminating in a production of Purcell's *The Fairy Queen*. David Lister wrote that the year promised to bring

> a series of weekly concerts; music documentaries every Sunday lunchtime; a series of evenings devoted to the musical life of each of the six BBC regional centres; invitation concerts; a Monday lunch-time slot of opera highlights including extracts from several little-performed operas such as Sullivan's *Ivanhoe* and Bliss's *The Olympians*. And, among other things, a competition for young composers to write for youth choirs and orchestras. There will also be an impressive array of British dramas ... as well as programmes on poetry and British comedy.

Looking back a year later, after literally hundreds of 'Fairest Isle' pro-grammes, Kenyon picked out his own favourites:

> Three of the biggest events were the simultaneous broadcasts we did with television: January the 1st, in the Banqueting House, Whitehall; March the 5th in Westminster Abbey; and the big Purcell concert on the 21st of November in the Abbey. But I think what really came through was the

amazing richness we found in British music by going into the highways and byways. Specific things for me were Anthony Payne's talk about Elgar's Third Symphony, which included the first orchestral performance of the few sections which he had completed.[8] That sat alongside the BBC Symphony Orchestra's Elgar series at the Festival Hall, where Andrew Davis conducted Elgar with contemporary British composers. And there were things like John Eccles's *Semele*, the first English opera after Purcell, never done in his time, completely overtaken by Handel and the Italian opera, which Richard Hickox put on for us in the City of London Festival. And the invitation concerts that we put on specially, which stretched from contemporary classics like Brian Ferneyhough's *Transit* right back to John Taverner (the old one) – the 450th anniversary of his death fell in 1995, and the Sixteen did a wonderful concert of his music. Whenever you switched on, there was some neglected, fascinating British music.

Kenyon argues that Producer Choice enhanced the quality of the 'Fairest Isle' programmes: 'I outlined the scheme, tried to bring the various partners together, and eventually we had a whole round of special planning and offers meetings, at which those ideas were put on the table and sifted. There was an excellent co-ordinator in Music Department, David Gallagher, who brought all the musical ideas together.' The Royal Philharmonic Society gave *Fairest Isle* its award for the broadcasting event of 1995.

RAJAR figures in October 1995, ten months into *Fairest Isle*, reported that Radio 3's catchment pool was back to 2.6 million listeners, much the same as it had been before Classic FM came on the air. Hints were now being dropped at the top of the BBC that this was not good enough. In the Corporation's annual report, John Birt wrote that Radio 3 must be 'welcoming to the widest possible classical musical audience', while elsewhere Marmaduke Hussey, then the BBC's Chairman, had been describing the network as 'frankly elitist'. Kenyon says that, as so often in the network's past, there was now pressure from the top of the BBC to improve audience figures, in order to help justify the cost of Radio 3:

> Every BBC network has had to look at how it is going to maintain and increase its audience share in a time of competition. Now, Radio 3 has never depended exclusively on audiences, but the clear feeling from management was that we should not get stranded on too narrow an audience base. So an exercise was undertaken – a Reach Strategy – to identify times of day when there were a lot of floating voters who might leave BBC radio and go to commercial services. As far as we were concerned, 9 am and the ending of *Today* on Radio 4 was identified as an opportunity for Radio 3. We had *Composer of the Week* starting at that time, but quite often it offered difficult, or rare and unknown music. So the idea emerged that 9 am presented an opportunity to Radio 3. That was the only concept that emerged from our Radio Directorate discussions. The rest was left to me.

[8] The talk and performance have since been released on CD by *BBC Music Magazine*.

He initiated what he calls 'an extremely exhaustive and fair process of suggestions from Radio 3 Music Department and from independents', though he admits it was all done very fast, during July 1995, with the new programme due to start a few weeks later. 'It was a very rapid but thorough exercise,' he says.

The announcement of the result, during August, was greeted with widespread disbelief, followed by derision. Radio 3's new 9–10 am programme would be called *Morning Collection*, and would be presented by Paul Gambaccini, the transatlantic-born disc jockey whose 'music for lovers' programme on Classic FM had been a target of some mockery in the station's early days. He would now join Radio 3 – and be replaced on Classic FM by Richard Baker, taking his first step into the commercial sector after forty-five years with the BBC. *Morning Collection* would be produced by an independent company, Mentorn Radio. Other independent producers greatly resented this news, for Mentorn had been given an enormous proportion of their quota.

Kenyon emphasised that Gambaccini had worked for BBC Radio 'long before Classic FM was in rompers', and was chosen because 'his connection with film and pop music makes him unintimidating to people who want to try classical music but are unsure about it'. A BBC publicity handout headed *From Puccini to Gambaccini* stated that Gambaccini's programme would consist of 'classical greats . . . from Brahms to Britten, from Strauss to Stravinsky . . . Paul brings his relaxed but knowledgeable style to programmes full of complete works by all the major composers . . . *Morning Collection* takes you on a stimulating journey through 500 years of the classics.'

The music critic Bayan Northcott noted that Gambaccini's presentation style on Classic FM was characterised by 'refraining from any information, commentary or judgement of the slightest musical interest whatever'. After *Morning Collection* had begun on Radio 3, listeners' reactions to it were aired on Radio 4's *Feedback*. 'The outrage was instant,' reported the *Daily Telegraph*.

> Comments on [Gambaccini's] velvet voice and sugary commentary . . . ranged from 'unctuous', 'totally inane', 'ingratiating', 'schmaltzy', to 'egregious and patronising'. One listener complained that 'he sounds as if he's selling raspberry ripple'. Another said listening to him was 'like wallowing in warm blancmange' . . . Gambaccini's accent, however, is only the tip of the iceberg according to his opponents. They are alarmed at the decision to shunt *Composer of the Week*, which has long occupied the morning slot, to noon to make way for *Morning Collection*.

Kenyon appeared on *Feedback* and described Gambaccini as 'a knowledgeable and informed presenter of classical music'. He admitted that the programme was 'a big change of culture and it's meant to be, because we're trying to open up a potential new audience to classical music'.

The Labour MP Gerald Kaufman, who had previously criticised aspects of Kenyon's policy, went on the attack in the *Guardian* and elsewhere, declaring that he was so disgusted by 'the deliberate degradation by the BBC of Radio 3' that he intended to ask the Government to delay the renewal of the Corporation's Charter in 1996. (Renewal for ten years, with funding to continue through the licence, had already been agreed by the Government, but the Charter still had to be presented formally to Parliament.)

Paul Gambaccini's place on Radio 3 did not last long. In May 1996, after sustained attacks from listeners and critics, he announced that he would not continue to present *Morning Collection* when his contract expired later in the year. Kenyon said that the programme's format had been welcomed by listeners but its presentation had been criticised strongly. Mentorn, which had been re-commissioned, began to look for alternative presenters.

*

John Drummond agreed with Kaufman that Radio 3's concerns with 'accountability, accessibility, what the audience wants' cast doubt upon whether the BBC deserved to continue in its present form:

> The BBC has been an organisation which has seen itself as leading society, not following taste. If it no longer wishes to be that, I can't see any justification for its existence. The licence fee can only be justified if the BBC continues to be daring. And its central vision, its confidence in its public role, seems to be very shaky now. It's been undermined in the last fifteen years by the political situation and the fact that accountants and administrators have been the dog wagging the programme-making tail, rather than the other way round. I don't think that anyone at the top has a vision of what radio can be and should be.

Kenyon replied to Kaufman, in an article in the *Guardian*:

> Kaufman is right to say that there is no future for a Radio 3 in copying Classic FM ... but there is also no future for a Radio 3 that does not change. Both Classic FM and Radio 3 will soon be challenged, as will the record companies ... by the proliferation of digital music services via cable and telephone, by the easy availability of high-quality sound at a moment's notice in whatever specialism the listener wants. There are some clear responses to this future: one is digital audio broadcasting, which the BBC is putting its full weight behind, and which will at last replace FM reception with CD quality classical music sound. Intelligent presentation and programming, and the sense of live music-making which is at the centre of Radio 3's broadcasting, are others.

Responding to Drummond, Kenyon said:

> I entirely disagree with those who feel that the BBC is not leading taste any more. What they tend to mean is that the BBC is not doing what *they* want. For heaven's sake, we commissioned fifty new works in 1995, in styles ranging from Harrison Birtwistle and Simon Bainbridge to Michael

Nyman and Richard Rodney Bennett. The BBC orchestras are playing better than ever, all around the country, and the BBC Symphony Orchestra's Charles Ives Weekend at the Barbican, in January 1996, was unanimously praised as something that no other organisation in the country could have put on. John Drummond's Centenary Proms in 1995 were magnificent. The BBC has been the most decisive influence on musical taste in this country for the best part of this century, and I intend it to continue as such.

*

A year before the row over Gambaccini, the BBC had announced that it would launch a Digital Audio Broadcasting (DAB) service in September 1995, carrying the five existing networks: 'The BBC is the first broadcaster in the world to make a firm commitment to launching a DAB radio service ... The BBC plans to start DAB transmissions in key population areas and hopes to reach 60% of the population within four years of the launch ... Liz Forgan outlined the advantages for listeners ... : "The Proms will be crystal clear – even in a car ... " '

With the retirement of Sir John Drummond from the BBC in 1995 – he was knighted that year for services to music – Kenyon took over the directorship of the Proms. Drummond said: 'Nick was uncertain whether he could do both jobs – but I rather persuaded him. And I also rather persuaded the BBC. And I think with the changed nature of the Controllership it's not impossible.' Kenyon himself felt that, despite the extra workload, it made sense to have this responsibility: 'Structurally, it is the right way to do it. We will do more integrated programming than has been possible for the last few years – we're going to put on a series of chamber music concerts linked to the themes of the Proms. We'll have Proms *Composers of the Week*, Artists of the Week, and so on. What the Proms are is the jewel in the crown of Radio 3.' Kenyon's contract as Controller of Radio 3 would run until March 1997; whether or not it was renewed, he would continue to direct the Proms until the year 2000.

In November 1995 it was announced that, from the following summer, schools' broadcasting, which had been occupying Radio 3 from 2 to 3 pm on weekdays in termtime since April 1994, would be transferred to 3 am, to be taped by teachers from radios with timers. Kenyon's staff were grateful to him for clawing back a precious hour of their airtime. It was also announced that, from 4 May 1996, Radio 3 would be on the air for twenty-four hours a day. Kenyon explained that the gap between the former late-night closedown and the 6 am start of *On Air* would be filled with 'low-cost' material, repeats and European Broadcasting Union recordings of live performances rather than originations.[9] But since the

---

[9] It was announced that the MasterControl computer system would operate the network between 1 am and 6 am. Former Presentation Director Donald Macleod was named Editor, Night Time Broadcasting, and Cathy Wearing became Head of Presentation.

needletime restrictions ended in 1990, Radio 3 was free to broadcast gramophone records round the clock should it so wish – though it had to pay for the privilege.

Brian Barfield explains that the introduction of twenty-four-hour-broadcasting means that there has to be one 'fixed point' at which programmes must end and begin; otherwise cumulative over-runs could displace the following day's programmes. Ten pm has been chosen as this point, at least for the present. Otherwise, Haley's 'no fixed points' rule still holds for the evening programmes. The current pattern is drama on Sunday evenings, concerts from Monday to Friday, and an opera on Saturday. All of these are broadcast at whatever starting time and length is required. A forty-five-minute documentary is heard on Sundays at 5.45 pm, and each weekday after the evening's concert there is a different five-part series of short talks, features or poetry readings. Kenyon singles out for particular mention, among the many 'post-concert' speech programmes that have been broadcast in the last few years, *Inherit the Truth*, a series of talks by the cellist Anita Lasker-Wallfisch (4–8 October 1993), about her experiences as a Jewish teenager at the hands of the Nazis. Her life was saved by her music, for she was enrolled in the camp orchestra at Auschwitz. A book based on the series was published in the spring of 1996.

Asked if he believes that the network will still have a role to play in the long-term future, Kenyon repeats what he said in reply to Gerald Kaufman:

> CDs are very cheap,[10] and in the future you'll have digital services with a Schubert or Mozart channel at the flick of a switch. But I think what people always turn to radio for is *surprise* – something that they haven't heard before, which astonishes or delights – and the companionship of intelligent presentation. And on both those fronts I believe that Radio 3 has a very important role to play. The other essential thing will always be its commitment to live music, bringing concerts from around the country to listeners who cannot get to them. That's a vital public service role.

Radio 3 is celebrating the fiftieth anniversary of the Third Programme lavishly; 29 September 1996 (the actual anniversary) is being marked by a day of live concerts, including the BBC Symphony Orchestra giving the first performance of a work commissioned from Colin Matthews. Many other programmes have been made to mark the occasion. Yet Kenyon says he does not look back at the Third with nostalgia:

> We are continually reinventing Radio 3; it continually changes. Yes, it has an umbilical cord back to the early days of the Third Programme. But I personally feel just as great a link with all those adventurous music programmes of the 1930s – those concerts that Edward Clark planned, with Stravinsky and Bartók and Webern coming to the BBC Symphony

[10] Graham Johnson remarks: 'There are now so many small record companies providing us with CDs of obscure works, which you could formerly hear only on Radio 3.'

Orchestra and performing in the Queen's Hall in the Thirties. That seems to me just as much the important tradition that we are recreating and nurturing today as does the Third Programme image.

Anne Winder, who as head of Arts, Science and Features is responsible for much of Radio 3's speech output, is similarly unwilling to indulge in nostalgia for the Third:

The golden age is really a myth – there were some terrific features, but there's now a bigger range of cultural programming. Science has largely gone to Radio 4, but we do have *Blue Skies*, presented by Steve Jones (a former Reith Lecturer) – it's a science–arts programme, and it'll take themes like sexuality or symmetry, which can be debated in scientific or artistic terms; and it mixes the two. There never used to be a frequently heard arts review programme on the Third or Radio 3; *Night Waves* has that role, and does it splendidly.

Many people feel that poetry never has enough space, but we have a new poetry magazine called *Best Words*, which I think is the best stab at it so far – it goes out on a Saturday night, roughly once a month, and is presented by Michael Rosen. One of our 1995 poetry programmes, *Sorrow of Sarajevo*, in which Alan Rickman was one of the readers, was described by the Guardian critic as 'the best programme about Bosnia I've yet heard'. And we've commissioned poems, such as Fred D'Aguiar's *1492*, commemorating the quincentenary of Columbus's voyage.

Then there were the Royal Society of Arts Lectures, on the state of Britain, during the *Fairest Isle* British Music Year – there hadn't been anything like that on Radio 3 since I don't know when. And, though most interval talks now relate to the music, they often do so quite laterally – and we still make the one-off twenty-minute talk when a good idea and the right speaker come up. And we're still not tied to fixed length. If something naturally fits a slightly odd length, Radio 3 can accommodate it, just as it always used to – whereas Radios 4 and 5 simply can't.

It can also still accommodate odd subject matter. Piers Plowright's programmes include a study of the different songs of Japanese cicadas (*Insect Musicians*, 20 June 1988), a spoof about a one-armed jazz bagpiper (*Piping the Blues*, 25 January 1992) and a surrealist-style evocation of a painting by Miro, to celebrate his centenary (*Mirooo*, 20 April 1993).

The foreign weekends, always a highlight of Radio 3, continue at intervals; a very successful Prague Weekend in 1994 (28 and 29 May) has been followed by a Tanglewood Weekend, from the celebrated American music festival, on 12–14 July 1996. Radio 3's own Stravinsky Festival will run from February to April 1997, using the BBC orchestras and other in-house resources. Kenyon is also planning a three-year series (1997–9) built around the great monuments of twentieth-century music.

He says he looks with 'unabashed pleasure' at the range of programmes he has introduced to the network:

Of course much of the public and press comment has been about programmes like *On Air* and *In Tune*. They will always be a problem for some listeners. But look at the other innovations of my time so far, in which we've tried to develop new forms for our regular subject matter. *Spirit of the Age* has found two marvellous presenters for early music, Chris Page and George Pratt. *The Music Machine*, with Tommy Pearson, has carved out a completely different style for teenagers – and if we can only get the programmes on to cassette as well, they will reach exactly that young GCSE audience we should be nurturing. *Music Matters* (a marvellous title, thought up by Fiona Shelmerdine in Music Department) has reinvented the tradition of *Music Magazine* and *Music Weekly*, with Ivan Hewett as a continually curious, probing, intelligent interviewer. Then the late-night programmes, *Voices, Ensemble, Music Restored* – which we're going to bring forward to 10 pm – have found marvellous presenters like Iain Burnside, quirky, witty, involving. Jazz has developed apace with Brian Morton and the new programme *Impressions* (alongside the indispensable *Jazz Record Requests* with Geoff Smith, who could give anyone a lesson in presentation skills). All these are new programmes, which sit happily alongside *Composer of the Week*, the features, documentaries and drama. Whatever Gerald Kaufman may say – and it's difficult to think which fraction of the output he listens to – the range and quality of these programmes is something of which I'm very proud.

*

Just as this book was going to press, the status of Radio 3, and of radio in general, was once more called into question within the BBC, with the announcement by John Birt on 7 June 1996 of a huge reorganisation. The Radio Directorate was to be abolished, with its Managing Director. (This seemed to explain the abrupt departure from the post, four months earlier, of Liz Forgan.) The Controllers of the five radio networks, alongside those of the two television channels, would in future work to Will Wyatt as Chief Executive of a commissioning and scheduling division, to be called BBC Broadcast, while radio producers would be lumped with television production in bi-media departments answering to Ron Neil as Chief Executive, BBC Production.

Radio 3 therefore approached the fiftieth anniversary of the Third Programme acutely uncertain as to whether this new split structure of separate commissioning and production – accentuating the split between those two functions of the BBC which had already been introduced by Producer Choice – would enable the character of the network to survive. But Kenyon said he was confident: 'It's the programmes that count, not the structure, and we have some of the most talented and creative producers in the BBC. I look forward to working more closely with television – as we pioneered during the Purcell celebrations – while keeping the best traditions of radio alive.'

*

In 1976 Sir William Haley gave a talk on the Third Programme to mark its thirtieth anniversary. During it, he said:

> It is not only broadcasting that has changed. People have changed. Society has changed. The world has changed. Information, education, entertainment – these requirements in the BBC's Charter remain. The BBC's mission is to enhance awareness of the richness of life, to support moral leadership in the nation, to raise public taste. The Corporation would be otiose and sterile without it. That mission has to be accomplished by ever-evolving methods. It is the will that must stay constant.

The BBC and its third radio network have altered more in the last twenty years than they did between 1946 and 1976. It is doubtful whether Haley would feel at home in the present-day Corporation, or be altogether in sympathy with the present-day Radio 3, which, at the time of writing, continues to be under fire for the changes Kenyon has made.[11]

Some long for the restoration of the old order. The author John Spurling, who worked as a Third Programme announcer from 1963 to 1966, writes:

> My millennial dream is to see the Third restored, not just to its old excellence but to a new glory as a real centre of international culture – tough, experimental, elitist, scholarly, argumentative, unmissable. Music would not dominate, as it does now, pushing everything else into gaps and corners, nor would the spoken material be PR chat *about* fiction or poetry, science, history, whatever, but the latest stuff itself plus serious discussion and evaluation. Impossible, of course.

Who, in the era of the sound-bite, would have the time and the commitment to listen to such a network? Alexander Goehr believes that the Third's typical listener of the 1940s, the 'hard-working, Labour-voting schoolmaster in Derby', still exists: 'I think there are still people very much of that type, especially outside the big metroplitan centres. In fact I *have* to believe they exist, because I compose for them. It's the relics of a liberal ideal to which one works.'

He may be right. Yet, if this fiftieth-anniversary history has done its job, it will have shown that there was no golden age of the Third Programme. From the beginning, it was a story of struggle. Haley formulates the dilemma and the challenge very accurately. Methods must evolve with changing times – providing the aim stays the same: to create the best possible kinds of public service broadcasting, whatever those may be at the moment, and to do it with self-confidence. The BBC's third radio network has often achieved that in the last fifty years. Despite its current critics, and its own present uncertainties, it stands a very good chance of doing so in the next half-century.

---

[11] During the spring of 1996 a Campaign to Preserve Radio 3 was organised by Ian Gordon of Folkestone.

As Robert Ponsonby has written,

What is unarguable is that the BBC should be unreservedly committed to a radio channel devoted to music and the arts at a discriminating level of quality, intelligence and articulacy. And if the philistines choose to call such a channel 'elitist', so be it: the BBC *must* be able to engage the best minds (from whatever background) as listeners and to purvey the best music (from whatever period, including the contemporary). It *must* experiment. It must take risks. It *must* – from time to time – be allowed to fail.

*

Nicholas Kenyon, looking back over the history of Radio 3 and the Third Programme, remarks that the current debate about the network is much the same as it has always been: 'the tension between highbrow culture and popular appeal, and between the cost of what we do and the number of people who make use of it'. And he has absolutely no doubt that 'the importance of Radio 3 is out of all proportion to either its audience or its cost. It is a crucial, central part of the BBC, but it must continue to earn that place.'

A few months before the fiftieth anniversary, this letter was received by Kenyon, from an address in Scotland:

Sir,
    Many years ago the Third Programme broadcast an early work of my father, the now-forgotten pioneer of aleatoric music, Piotr Zak.
    The piece was called *Mobile*, and anticipated, in a modest way, such works as Berio's *Circles* and the more visionary creations of Stockhausen, in being both peripatetic and improvisatory.
    These qualities were entirely characteristic of my father, who had come to Britain as a Polish exile in 1940. He disapproved of the interpretation given *Mobile* by your performers, saying it was a typical act of Viennese cultural imperialism – as though the Hapsburgs had never gone away. How could any Viennese understand Polish art? It was of no concern to him, therefore, that he was never paid for the piece ...
    Perhaps the tape of *Mobile* survives. Although I am aware of my father's strictures, I would like to hear it, nonetheless.
    Yours sincerely,
    Aleatora Zak.

Maybe, somewhere among Radio 3's fiftieth-birthday greetings, there is a card signed by Hilda Tablet.

CODA

A day in the life
of Radio 3,
April 1966

5.30 am

In Studio 1Q on the first floor of Broadcasting House, Penny Gore, who has short blonde hair and glasses and looks as if she might be a teacher or a doctor, is sorting out her script and CDs. There is half an hour to go before she presents *On Air*, Radio 3's first live programme of the morning.

1Q is the present home of Radio 3 Continuity: a cramped studio and control room ('cubicle' in BBC-speak) with the feel of a wartime bunker. The windows are tiny and darkened, presumably for security, making the dawn sky appear even more sombre than it is, and the height and width of both rooms are foreshortened by sound-deadening false floor, ceiling and exterior walls. Across the corridor is Radio 4 Continuity, and further along it are three suites for the Radio 2 disc jockeys. Radio 1 is over the road in Egton House and Radio 5 Live is across the landing, beyond the lifts. Access to the Continuity suites is restricted to the possessors of a plastic 'dongle' which unlocks a sliding glass door.

'I come in from Chiswick in a BBC hired car, and it only takes fifteen minutes at this time of the morning,' says Penny Gore. 'But I have nightmares about over-sleeping, and once the taxi driver did have to wake me.' She is standing in this week for Andrew McGregor, *On Air's* regular presenter. 'We choose all our own music for the programme. I'm not a musician, I'm a historian by training, so at the beginning that was quite a challenge.' *On Air* has an editor, Andrew Lyle, but he is also responsible for *Musical Encounters* and *In Tune*, and there is no producer invigilating Gore, McGregor, and the others who take turns on the dawn shift. From 6 to 9 am they have the freedom of the air.

'As I'm freelance now,' continues Gore, 'and as I also work in presentation at Channel 4 on weekday afternoons, I have to pick the records at weekends. It's difficult then, because the BBC Gramophone Library is short-staffed. They've got moveable shelves, and you're not allowed to browse without a member of staff, because someone might move them without knowing you were there, and you'd get crushed.' A headline comes to mind: 'RADIO 3 PRESENTER SQUASHED BY BACH CANTATAS.'

Gore settles down in the studio at the presenter's desk, a horseshoe of pale wood which holds (from right to left) a rack of three compact disc players, a Nagra reel-to-reel tape machine, a small display panel which operates a computerised audio-file, and a pair of gramophone decks. Facing the presenter are the faders which control sound levels and start the CD and tape machines. A plump microphone with foam-rubber windshield protrudes across the desk on a long arm. Beneath it, in a movable matte black box, is a small clock with red hands, fed (like all the clocks in the building) from a scrupulously accurate master-clock. Apart from the clock, the set-up is state-of-the-art disco.

Through the window which divides studio and cubicle, Nasser Pervez, the studio manager who has been allocated to Radio 3 Continuity this morning, is making his own preparations for *On Air*. Equipped with a large control desk with about twenty faders and equalisers, he will monitor and adjust the sound level and quality from Gore's microphone and other equipment. At the moment Gore is playing him excerpts from the CDs she will be using, so he can make a note of their levels.

On a low shelf to his right, the day's prerecorded programmes – *Composer of the Week* (Schubert), *The BBC Orchestras* (BBC Philharmonic on tour in Oman), *The Music Machine* and others – are waiting their turn, along with a batch of taped trailers. There are two sizes of tape box. The big ones contain ten-inch-diameter spools of analogue tape which will be played at fifteen inches per second, on one of the big reel-to-reel decks which stand opposite the control desk. The smaller boxes hold the tiny DAT cassettes, recorded and played back digitally on much smaller machines, which are superseding reel-to-reel because of quality and cheapness. DATs are so small that they are easily mislaid – entire acts of operas have occasionally gone missing – so they are sent for transmission in large clearly-labelled cardboard boxes.

When a programme is live, but is to come from somewhere other than Continuity – a London or regional studio, or a concert hall or opera house – the Continuity studio manager makes contact by telephone, to agree the handover procedure and check that the 'line' (programme circuit) carrying the programme has been connected. Some outside broadcasts have lines set up for the occasion by British Telecom; the London concert halls and opera houses are permanently wired to Broadcasting House. Formerly, these lines terminated on a board of jack-plug sockets known as a 'jackfield'; these days, they end their journey in a world of silicone chips inside the computer terminal which sits next to Nasser Pervez's row of faders.

5.45 am

For the last ten minutes, Pervez has been putting out 'tone', an electronically generated note (440 cycles, concert pitch 'A'), the first sound that early-bird listeners can hear on the Radio 3 wavelength each morning. This will soon change. At the back of the control cubicle, a brand-new

MasterControl computer terminal is waiting to begin work as Radio 3's all-night presenter, its disk drive and other hardware tidily out of sight on racks in a plant room at the back of 1Q. 'It'll operate entirely unattended,' explains Pervez. Will it announce programmes in a voice-simulated Californian-accent, like a mechanical impersonation of Classic FM? 'Oh no, everything will sound the same as usual. Programmes will be made in the normal way, then down-loaded into the computer, which will play them at the right time.'

5.50 am

The 'tone' stops, and Penny Gore slides open her microphone fader, activating a red light over the door. 'BBC Radio 3, good morning, and let's get the weather from Ian MacCaskill at the BBC Weather Centre.' Nasser Pervez starts a tape machine; the weather was recorded (from Television Centre, where the meteorologists are based) at 5 am. Any hurricane which has hauled itself out of bed in the meanwhile will not get a mention.

A computer printer in the corner of the cubicle hums into life, and from it slide two pages of news bulletin, with a brace of pronunciation hazards – 'Srbenica ... Lech Walesa'. But Penny Gore is well-armed against such tongue-twisters. Above the CD players is a shelf of pronunciation dictionaries (plus the two-volume *Oxford Companion to Music*), while against the wall stands a big card-index showing how to avoid about a thousand verbal booby traps. Continuity presenters are supposed to update this as new names appear in the news or the musical world. Failing that, they can ring Pronunciation Unit. Under Producer Choice, the BBC has retained this ancient institution, but insists that it charge producers £8 per pronunciation. An enterprising multilinguist might clean up a packet, touring the Radio 3 studios and giving cut-price demonstrations of umlauts and diphthongs.

'I used to work in Sound Archives,' Penny Gore explains. 'I was a Selector, picking programmes or items that I thought ought to be kept for posterity – Royalty and Weather were among the topics I had to handle. People kept saying, "You've got such a good voice, you ought to be an announcer."' She auditioned, and was accepted into the Radio 3 presentation team about six years ago – 'Paul Guinery and I were in the same intake.' She left for a while, and is slightly surprised to find herself back again, albeit as a freelance with no job security. 'I keep dreading that I'll say "This is Channel 4".' In 1995 an *In Tune* presenter absent-mindedly told Radio 3 listeners they were listening to Classic FM. He has not been heard on the programme since.

The weather forecast finishes. 'Ian MacCaskill there at the BBC Weather Centre. This is Radio 3.' Gore opens a CD fader, and a lilting waltz begins: one of Malcolm Arnold's *English Dances*, the network's current early-morning signature tune, suitably dreamy for this half-awake time of day.

She has written all her links for this morning's *On Air*, so as to have time to talk, but says she often does it partly ad lib. Checking her stopwatch-calculator (which adds up in minutes and seconds), she presses a talkback button which allows her to speak to Nasser Pervez in the cubicle: 'We are taking the GTS, aren't we?' She explains that the Greenwich Time Signal, at 6, 7 and 8 am, is slightly optional for *On Air*, but listeners tend to like it.

Pervez nods, presses a button labelled 'Time Signal On Line', and at 5.59 and 54 seconds, just as Gore has 'back-announced' the Malcolm Arnold dances (that is, named the piece and the performers), the pips begin. 'Radio 3, it's six o'clock, good morning, this is Penny Gore with *On Air*.' She gives a brief list of music to be heard during the first of the programme's three hours, then begins the news. The first item is about the ban on British beef, the last about a breakthrough in the development of a male contraceptive pill – it is now said to be 'almost ninety-nine per cent effective'.

6.02 am

Gore's first musical choice of the morning is Frank Bridge's First String Quartet. While it is playing, she goes into the cubicle to look at the morning papers, which have just been brought by a messenger. She has to write a summary of the arts stories in them, and read it at about 8.15. But *On Air* contains much less speech than in its early days. 'People hate too much chatter at this time of day,' she says. 'And you get some weird letters: "Will you stop saying *And now the weather*. Just say *The weather*." Of course it's only the obsessive ones who bother to write.'

6.32 am

'Frank Bridge's First String Quartet was played by the Brindisi Quartet. And now something of a cultural shift . . . ' Gore gives a brief introduction to Khachaturian's First Suite from the ballet *Spartacus*. Her style seems plain, but after a while you realise how skilful she is, perfectly balancing formality and friendliness, the personal and the generalised. And she keeps her spoken links short.

7.10 am

Breakfast arrives in Continuity: grapefruit, yoghurt, croissants, orange juice, toast encased in silver foil. Penny Gore checks a prerecorded trailer by Brian Kay, who is taking over Richard Baker's *Comparing Notes* on Radio 4. The trailers can either be played on the Nagra tape recorder or fed into a computer, and activated by the small panel on the presenter's desk. 'There's something wrong with it,' Gore says on the talkback to Nasser Pervez. 'He sounds as if he's got a heavy cold.' 'And there's something rumbling in the background,' agrees Pervez. 'I'll see what I can do.' He fiddles with the jackfield – there is still one among the computers – and, after manipulating a couple of plugs, cures Kay's throat infection. He and Gore tuck into the grapefruit.

7.45 am

Gore comes back from the loo. 'We're not supposed to go, but in a three-hour programme you have to.' She has started Liszt's symphonic poem *Les préludes* rather later than she intended. 'Oh dear, it'll be too tight for the pips. Let's give them a miss this time.' The music stops only a few seconds before eight o'clock, and the Time Signal is omitted before the news.

When she has finished newsreading and has put on a Monteverdi motet, she prepares to read her summary of the newspapers. Outside, as far as it is possible to tell through the smoked glass windows, the sun is shining energetically.

On a notice-board in the control cubicle is a picture postcard of a donkey. Someone has drawn a speech bubble coming out of its mouth: 'Ah shure lurve your show, Mister Gambaguinery.'

8.30 am

Half a mile from Broadcasting House, the morning sunshine is obscured by fumes from delivery motorbikes roaring through the heart of London's filmmaker-land, Wardour Street. Buildings announce PARAMOUNT, WARNER, MGM, MENTORN. This intruder among the American giants is the independent TV, film and radio production company which was awarded the contract for *Morning Collection*, Radio 3's 9 am Monday to Friday record show.

Past a reception area reminiscent of the Hard Rock Café, in a windowless room towards the back of the ground floor, the owner of the most controversial radio voice in Britain is going through his script with his producer. Five minutes later, the producer emerges: none other than Tony Cheevers, formerly a senior member of Radio 3, and Andrew Lyle's predecessor as editor of *On Air*, *In Tune* and *Musical Encounters*. 'I don't miss running a department,' says Cheevers, who was poached by Mentorn to produce Gambaccini. 'It's nice to listen to the music again.'

The *Morning Collection* studio and control cubicle are modest versions of Radio 3 Continuity. Gambaccini, whose close-cropped head and aquiline nose have become almost as well known as his voice, thanks to the BBC publicity for the show, is visible through the glass, sitting at the presenter's desk, with compact disc machines and faders. The cubicle, on the other hand, has the simplest of mixing desks – an amplifier with just one fader, a primitive-looking knob. But there is no shortage of people.

Dave Thomas, a young fair-haired former BBC studio manager, is in charge of the knob. At the moment, Gambaccini is playing his discs to Thomas (just as Gore did to Pervez), and Thomas is making a note of the levels. But of course here there is also a producer. Cheevers sits at a table with a talkback facility to Gambaccini. And in walks Paul Frankl, a third BBC refugee who worked for Cheevers on *In Tune*.

Gambaccini relaxes for a few minutes before going on air. Why does he need so much back-up for this very simple one-hour programme – today there are four pieces of music? 'Tony chooses all the music in the strands,' explains Gambaccini. Here, that ubiquitous 1990s radio word 'strand' means a series of records within the programme; this week they are playing the Tchaikovsky Suites. Gambaccini continues: 'I pick the tracks for the features, which is what I wanted to do, because anybody who knew my style would expect it.' Features? He explains that on Monday they feature 'a bestseller of years gone by', on Tuesday a piece of music associated with a film, on Wednesday a current British classical bestseller, on Thursday a current American one. 'Friday's programme we prerecord, because I'm on GMTV.' Apparently Friday has no 'feature'.

But what does Paul Frankl do? 'He's the researcher,' answers Cheevers. Gambaccini's two-and-a-half-page script for today's programme seems unlikely to have required a great deal of research, but Frankl is certainly making himself useful, trying to discover whether drilling noises upstairs are penetrating to the studio.

Why does Gambaccini do the programme live, considering that it contains no up-to-the-minute material, and could easily be prerecorded in batches? He has a well-honed answer to this: 'Live is always best. I always quote Arletty in *Les enfants du paradis*: "I'm not beautiful, I'm alive." Live is alive.' Nevertheless his 9 am commitment has required 'the successful rearrangement of my own time. I used to go to the gym three days a week, in the mornings. But by ten, when I have finished here, the day has *begun*.'

Naturally, he has a large postbag. 'People think I can perform any feat for them – "Please will you introduce me to Barry Manilow?" The letters that come to *me* are almost always constructive – the people who write angrily to *Feedback* don't write directly to me. Shows you what cowards they are!'

He is fairly philosophical about the press attacks: 'In the very first week, I became aware that I was the symbol of Nick Kenyon's changes. You can't draw a cartoon of *Composer of the Week*, but you can of me.' But he and Cheevers are angry about the inaccuracies they claim have peppered articles by Gillian Reynolds and the other radio critics – misrepresentations (they say) of what the programme is actually doing. 'We're *not* like Classic FM,' says Cheevers. 'We play music they wouldn't touch.'

Does Gambaccini miss Classic FM? 'I don't miss the ads, and the computer you play them on. One set of ads for Britain, another for Scotland. You get them both on your headphones, one in each ear.' On the other hand Cheevers speaks a little wistfully of the American classical stations he and other Radio 3 staff visited at Kenyon's behest in 1992. 'There was one where they didn't bother to do any advance programme planning. When the presenter realised that, in about twenty minutes, she needed to fill a forty-minute slot, she just consulted the computer, then went and found the records it had told her to use.'

9 am

The voice of Penny Gore comes over the Mentorn loudspeakers, back-announcing Rossini: 'I do hope you can join me tomorrow. This is Radio 3, now it's nine o'clock, and here's Paul Gambaccini with *Morning Collection.*'

'Thanks, Penny, and goodbye,' reads Gambaccini from his typewritten script. 'I'm not being dismissive, it's just that before we get to Tchaikovsky's Suite Number Two, and a Reverie and Caprice by Berlioz, we're going to hear the Chopin Waltz known as The Farewell. It was composed in the spirit of *unrequited love*' (this said with the characteristic Gambaccini emphasis) 'for the sixteen-year-old Maria Wodzinska. Upon hearing the work, she knew what it must be called: L'Adieu.' Adieu to all the traditions of the Third and Radio 3, one might think. Yet Gambaccini's delivery of a script is curiously formal and old-fashioned.

In the other room, while Dave adjusts the knob, Tony Cheevers is following the sheet music of the Chopin. He has the scores of the other items in the programme waiting in a pile, all of them labelled 'BBC Music Library'. Why does he do this? 'Just so I know where we are.'

Inevitably, the talk turns again to the attacks on *Morning Collection* and its presenter. 'I've never had so much mail about a programme,' says Cheevers, 'and I was the person who started *On Air* and *In Tune*, and they were incredibly unpopular at first. I'd say seventy-five to eighty per cent of the mail we get is basically pro Paul – while Nick Kenyon seems to get all the hate mail.'

Gambaccini is introducing the Berlioz: 'Here is one case where you will never wish to be in the position of the character described in the score ... he is drowning.' Next comes Lucia Popp with an aria from *Rusalka*, and then the Tchaikovsky, which is timed to run for thirty-six minutes. Most presenters stretch their legs during long pieces, and fetch coffee or talk to the production team, but Gambaccini sits by himself in the studio, reading a listings magazine. 'Sometimes he makes a few phone calls,' says Dave, making a small adjustment to the knob.

Cheevers himself telephones, to Radio 3 Continuity, checking the ten o'clock handover from Gambaccini to Andrew Lyle, who will be presenting today's *Musical Encounters*, or as it is called by Radio 3 staff, with Birtism in mind, 'Musical Accountants'. When ten o'clock comes, Lyle picks up smartly from the handover, says, 'We're off to the hunt', and goes straight into a bouncy piece of horn music. 'Too quick,' says Cheevers disapprovingly.

11 am

While Lyle is still on the air, several of his colleagues arrive at Nicholas Kenyon's office, three floors above Continuity, to discuss Radio 3's next big venture, an extended season of masterpieces of the twentieth century, to run from February 1997 until the eve of the millennium. 'The idea,' says Kenyon, with his usual puckered grin, 'is to outdo even *Fairest Isle.*' The BBC orchestras will bear the brunt of the series, but outside orchestras will be encouraged to take part too, with modest financial inducements to give all-twentieth-century concerts. 'We want them to do pieces they've always wanted to, but couldn't afford. They won't get the cheque if they just do a token *Portsmouth Point.*'

Somebody asks if orchestras which have *already* planned twentieth-century programmes will get the cash too. 'It's a bit unfair if they don't.' Kenyon promises to think about this.

The composer George Benjamin has been brought in as a consultant for the series. Slightly built, and with a mild, self-effacing manner, he is no match for the wisecracks of the somewhat world-weary BBC men. 'The nearer you get to the end of the century,' he says eagerly, 'the more living composers there are to talk about their work.' Martyn Westerman, Radio 3's Commissioning Executive, snaps back: 'Is that good or bad?' and the meeting explodes in guffaws.

Kenyon winds up the proceedings at 12.15 with: 'I want what's been said this morning to inform the next offers round.' He promises to explain this BBC lingo to Benjamin, and adds: 'We need a series title.'

12.50 pm

The audience for today's BBC Lunchtime Concert is trickling up the steps beneath the neo-classical portico of St John's, Smith Square. Among them is John Sergeant, the BBC's Chief Political Correspondent, whose Westminster office and studio is just round the corner. 'I've been coming to these broadcasts for more than twenty years,' he says, 'and paying for my ticket – I remember when it used to cost seventeen shillings.'

In the vestry, the producer, Willie Robson, is eating a sandwich, while string players wander about the south aisle, tuning up. There has been a late change of artists: the Brindisi Quartet (last heard playing Frank Bridge at 6.02 am) have recently changed cellists, and a week ago, despite being billed in the *Radio Times*, told Robson they would rather not broadcast live at the moment. 'That's nothing,' he says. 'What I dread is the singers who ring up the evening before – "I've got a sore throat."' What does he do when that happens? 'There are lots of pianists in London, keen to stand in. And I ring round the agents. It's a good programme to be heard on – the actual audience here is small' (there are about a hundred people waiting now, on metal-framed chairs which fill the body of the church) 'but, if you include the Sunday repeat, there are nearly a quarter of a million listeners.'

Donald Macleod – like Robson, a lightly-bearded Scot – puts finishing touches to his script, while Robson moves on to an apple. Macleod, one of the most familiar voices on the network, will be heard even more in future – though chiefly in the insomniac hours. He has been put in charge of the all-night broadcasts, and will be presenting many of them himself, prerecorded. He makes a face when the computer is mentioned.

1.01 pm

Macleod comes on to the stage, which is backed with red velvet curtains hiding the altar, and takes up his position at a pair of stereo microphones. He welcomes the audience. Sixty seconds later he is on air, explaining the change of artists, and welcoming to the stage the Guildhall String Ensemble. They walk on, looking young and enthusiastic, and wearing day clothes.

With the exception of the two cellists, they play standing up, beginning with an enthusiastic performance of Mozart's Divertimento in B flat. The sound is big and fresh, and easily fills the large church. Next come Grieg's *Two Elegaic Melodies*, with spotless intonation in a tricky *divisi* passage for violins, then Mendelssohn's String Symphony No. 9 in C, which finishes at 1.52. Applause and Macleod's closing announcement take the programme up to 1.53. 'A bit of an under-run,' says Robson, who has telephoned Continuity to warn Susan Sharpe, the afternoon presenter. 'We more usually have over-runs – things tend to stretch in live performance.' The audience, who had expected a quartet and got eleven accomplished young players instead, dissolves happily into the Westminster afternoon.

2.50 pm

The sound of the string section of the BBC Symphony Orchestra penetrates through the Victorian stained glass of St Augustine's Church into Kilburn Park Road, to mingle with the noises of traffic and schoolchildren. 'There's some noise getting in, too,' says Ann McKay, Chief Producer of the Symphony Orchestra, who is struggling to record Lutosławski's *Funeral Music*. 'I'm sure we're picking up birdsong. Or is it an ambulance? That would be appropriate for this piece.'

The string players, a vast number compared to the eleven at St John's, are ranged across the nave of the gothic church. White plastic cases for the double basses line one aisle like sinister sarcophagi – the image, of course, is suggested by the eerie music. A young American, Joseph Swensen, is on the rostrum, looking relaxed, with a Coke tin on his music stand, but he is not letting anyone slack. He takes the cellos and violas through the sombre opening bars again and again, note by note, until the intonation is perfect.

'What's happened is that the wind and brass and percussion, and a lot more people, are spending a fortnight rehearsing *The Mask of Orpheus* for the South Bank Birtwistle Festival,' explains Ann McKay. 'So rather than give these guys the time off, I thought we'd do some string pieces. We had to come here because there was no big studio available at Maida Vale. We did the Dvořák *Serenade* this morning.' The recordings will go into the pool of tapes which presenters can draw on for *On Air, Musical Encounters* or *In Tune* – after McKay has edited them. Certainly the Lutosławski will need plenty of edits. Swensen, recently appointed Chief Conductor of the Scottish Chamber Orchestra, is having difficulties achieving more than about twelve satisfactory bars at a time, chiefly due to the birds. McKay's production assistant makes a series of increasingly desperate phone calls on a mobile, to the BBC department responsible for allocating music studios, begging for a real studio tomorrow.

The sound-balance is in the hands of Neil Pemberton, one of the small elite of studio managers who take charge of live concert and opera broadcasts, and he leaves the DAT machine running between takes, in the hope of picking up the odd bar or two which he might need for splicing. Not that music editing is usually done with a razor blade now: the digitally recorded notes are manipulated on the screen of a computer named by an acronym, SADIE. Frequent training courses on SADIE are offered to producers, but they are a little frightened of it, just as their 1950s predecessors were frightened of cutting up tape.

3.45 pm

Swensen puts down his baton. 'Thanks, everyone.' The string players express their appreciation of his conducting by tapping their music stands with their bows. But Ann McKay is still gloomy about extraneous noise: 'I'm sure we picked up a pigeon.' The phone calls have borne fruit, and she gets on the talkback to the orchestra: 'You'll be glad to know we're back in Maida Vale tomorrow – Studio 2.'

4.30 pm

'I'd like a few arses around here,' says drama director Hilary Norrish to the cast of David Edgar's *Pentecost*, in Studio 6a, Broadcasting House. The play will be broadcast on Radio 3 in two months' time, and Edgar is sitting inconspicuously behind Norrish and the studio manager, viewing the proceedings with the manner of a world-weary don observing his pupils running riot.

Actually it is only Norrish who is a little over the top. She has short red hair and a tight black dress, waves her arms manically, and tends to ignore BBC No Smoking signs. '*Lots* of arses, in fact,' she shouts on the talkback. Edgar explains that she's using a Drama Department acronym. 'It's "ARS", which stands for "A Radio Sound" – a grunt or sigh or some other wordless noise she wants the actors to make.'

Has he changed the play, first staged by the Royal Shakespeare Company, for this radio production? 'Not really, apart from the necessities of the medium. And a few cuts.'

Being more verbal than visual, it is coming over well on the Studio 6a loudspeakers. The setting is an abandoned church in an unnamed Eastern European country soon after the ending of the Cold War, where a British art expert is shown a wall-painting that could lead to a re-dating of the Renaissance. Oliver Ford Davies, playing the Brit, is the only member of the cast not obliged to impersonate Slavs speaking English.

Visually, drama is the most unglamorous activity in radio. Orchestras and other live music groups look good in any context; presenters can be interestingly better or worse looking than their voices might suggest; but there is no less rousing spectacle than a bunch of actors in their own clothes standing casually around a microphone, scripts in hands, while a studio manager clinks a teacup.

Actually the clutter of sound-effects junk in Studio 6a – which includes an antique gas cooker, to which an anglepoise lamp has been incongruously attached, and an equally elderly safe – rather suits the unglamorous setting of *Pentecost*. The actors have been at it since 10 am. 'You cocksucker!' screams Sian Thomas, whose character has just gone loco on discovering the truth about the painting. But when not acting, she has a mild, detached look, as if she's thinking about what to buy for supper. The plump, slightly baggy, benign Ford Davies, on the other hand, is indistinguishable from the mild-tempered Englishman he is playing, who happens to be called Oliver too.

'That's it for today, folks,' chirrups Hilary Norrish into the talkback, precisely at six o'clock. 'Your arses were *magnificent*.'

6.10 pm

Eight floors down, in Studio B12, Natalie Wheen is surrounded by bits of paper. The speech content of *In Tune*, Radio 3's drive-time record programme, includes announcements of concerts, ad libbed from brochures and fliers, which get scattered all over the studio table, among the CD sleeve-notes. 'It's tragic,' muses Wheen, one of the most experienced of Radio 3's broadcasters, who looks like a tough headmistress but has a sly smile. 'Look at the amount of live music that's going on out there, with such *tiny* audiences – "*Please* will you advertise our concert?"'

Wheen once said 'fuck' on the air by mistake, and seems in danger of doing so again. 'There's some farts near the beginning,' she says into the talkback, to someone who is lining up a tape of the Gordon Jacob Trombone Concerto, from last night's *BBC Young Musician of the Year*. When Humphrey Burton, co-founder of the competition, arrives to be interviewed about it, Wheen describes the National Youth Orchestra (who were backing the soloists) as 'starchy and middle class'. The very polished Burton hits this sort of stuff effortlessly for six: 'What's wrong with being middle class?'

When she is not reading off her bits of paper, Wheen talks into the mike with extraordinary fluency, her eyes half shut, gazing smilingly into the middle distance. Radio could have been invented for her.

She introduces an Elizabeth Söderström track, then gets on the talkback: 'Did I say Sodastream?'

7.15 pm

Chris Marshall, Chief Music Producer for Radio 3 in Birmingham, is in the doorway of Dressing Room 17 of Pebble Mill, the BBC's Birmingham headquarters, asking soprano Valdine Anderson and violinist Rebecca

Hirsch if everything is all right. There are fifteen minutes to go before this evening's live chamber concert – a Glock-like mixture of Brahms and contemporary works. It's easy to forget that Radio 3 relays live music almost every night of the year.

'Fine,' says Hirsch, looking tense, 'but I think I'll go and get some air.' 'The Brahms lasts half an hour, doesn't it?' checks Anderson. Marshall corrects her hastily: 'God, no, it's only about five minutes. Don't disappear anywhere. You'll be on very quickly.'

Hirsch is standing in for a violinist who has hurt his hand. 'Consequently we've had to drop the Ligeti Horn Trio,' says Marshall, 'which is a pity, as I built the whole concert around it. But we've put in the Maxwell Davies *Sea Eagle*, an unaccompanied horn piece which fits in very well.'

The audience, few of them under sixty, are being admitted to Studio 1, which was built to house the BBC Midland Light Orchestra, now long defunct. Too small for a symphony orchestra, it is rather barn-like for recitals and chamber music, which Birmingham contributes to Radio 3 about twice a week. Do Marshall and his colleagues mind not having their own symphony orchestra, as do Cardiff, Manchester and Scotland? 'Not at all. Orchestras are lovely objects, but hellishly difficult to manage. We prefer having our local band, the CBSO, down the road for us when we want them.'

Chris Wines, Birmingham's regular concert presenter, takes a yellow tie out of his pocket, puts it on, and goes in to warm up the audience. He seems to be paying little attention to his headphones, which will give him the handover cue from *In Tune* in London. But when the cue comes, he responds instantly with: 'Good evening from Birmingham . . . ' He explains the change of artist and programme, and says that in the interval two horn players 'will be disgusting the difficulties of their instrument'. 'I think he means "discussing",' laughs Marshall in the cubicle. The audience seems not to have noticed.

The pianist Barry Douglas opens the concert with Brahms's *Ballade* in D, and then Valdine Anderson, Rebecca Hirsch, the horn player Richard Watkins and the flautist Sebastian Bell embark on Harrison Birtwistle's *Monody for Corpus Christi*. 'Ooh, they're in for a surprise,' mutters Marshall sadistically, looking through the cubicle window at the elderly audience.

In fact, for Birtwistle, it's quite a gentle piece, and seems to go down well. Wines then introduces *Sea Eagle*, and Watkins's unaccompanied horn begins to soar aloft, emitting angry bird-cries. At the end of the first movement, he has to empty a great deal of saliva from the instrument. 'We ought to have brought a bucket,' murmurs Steve Postnoi, the studio manager.

8.10 pm

The applause for the Maxwell Davies is the most enthusiastic so far. Wines cues to the interval tape – the horn discussion was recorded in Birmingham, but is being played in by Radio 3 Continuity in London –

and the audience adjourn to buy tea from an urn outside the studio, while the programme team drink coffee in a passage. Richard Watkins joins them, and the talk gets round to Maxwell Davies. 'I did one of his *Strathclyde Concertos* for horn and trumpet, with John Wallace, at the Golders Green Hippodrome,' says Watkins. 'There was a huge audience – but they were utterly dismayed, because it was a Friday night recording, and they thought they were coming to *Friday Night is Music Night.*'

Liz, the Production Assistant, looks at her watch. 'Whoops, only two minutes.' No one had noticed the time was going so fast. Steve rushes back to his control panel and Chris Wines to his presenter's microphone. A matter of seconds later, the concert resumes.

10.20 pm

Night Waves, the last live programme of the day, goes out from Studio B14 in the basement of Broadcasting House. Wine bottles and mineral water are set out on the rectangular table, alongside a microphone for each of the four guests, plus two (in case one breaks down) for the presenter, who this evening is myself.

I have been spending the last two hours at the London Coliseum, watching the English National Ballet in *Giselle*, which we are reviewing, having written and timed my script during the afternoon. The greater part of the programme will be unscripted – live interviews and a discussion. I have mapped these out in advance as much as possible, but you have to keep your mind open to what people are actually saying, and not just follow a prepared course.

One of the guests has already arrived when I get back from the ballet: John McClelland from Nottingham University, who has written the eight-hundred page book on the history of Western political thought that we are to discuss this evening. I have been wrestling with it intermittently over the last ten busy days, but there was no hope of reading every word, and in any case if I did, I would probably be over-prepared for an eighteen-minute discussion – this is the amount of time that Julian May, the producer, estimates we will have. It's believed that Roy Porter, who has often presented *Night Waves* himself, and is taking part in the discussion, didn't open the book till last night. 'He's a fast reader,' says Julian.

John McClelland reminds me that we met at an Oxford party, and seems to be in a party mood himself: 'No, I won't have any wine yet, I've been drinking port at Simpson's.' Anthony Howard, also taking part in the discussion, rolls up with ten minutes to go, accepting white wine, and Roy Porter materialises shortly after, looking comfortably knowledgeable about political thought. I pour myself a glass – well, a BBC plastic cupful – and check that my digital wristwatch is synchronous with the studio clock; I find it easier to read digits at a glance, though Julian will be talking me through the timing of the interviews and discussion on my headphones.

No sign yet of Alistair MacAuley from the *Financial Times*, who is going to review the ballet. Act Two of *Giselle* began less than an hour or two ago, so he may be late. I mark my script at the points where we will have to change the running order if necessary. Robert Dawson Scott comes on the line from Scotland; he is to preview this year's Edinburgh Festival (its programme was announced today), and Julian asks if I want to chat to him before we go on air. Not really. It's fatal to rehearse an interview, and I try to avoid revealing my plans for the discussion. The aim is to make people think as they talk.

'I'll give you Radio 3,' says Jill the studio manager into my headphones, meaning that she'll let me hear the end of the programme that precedes us. Chamber music clicks on abruptly. Forty seconds to go. 'Alistair MacAuley's arrived,' says Julian into my headphones.

The chamber music ends with applause, and the voice of Fiona Talkington, who is on duty in Continuity tonight, says 'It's ten forty-five, and now *Night Waves*.' An orange light comes on to indicate that the studio is live to network. A red light glows to show that my microphone is faded up. A green light flashes to tell me to start.

Bibliography

1. THE BBC's ARCHIVES

(a) Written Archives

Papers dating from the founding of the BBC until the 1970s are kept at the BBC Written Archives Centre (WAC) at Caversham, Berkshire. Those referred to in the source notes chiefly begin with the prefix 'R' (standing for 'Radio'), e.g. R53/298/1. This is the number of the file in which the document quoted is to be found. In the remainder of the reference, the document is identified, in the case of an internal memorandum, by its title and date, or, where there is no title, by the name of the correspondent and recipient and the date.

Papers relating to outside contributors to the BBC – writers and performers – are held in a different series of files at the WAC. Most of those quoted in the book are in the 'RCONT1' series (standing for Radio Contributors 1). They generally consist of letters, and are identified by the names of the correspondent and recipient and the date.

The WAC also holds scripts, mostly on microfilm and microfiche, and BBC press handouts. Where these have been quoted, their location within the WAC is specified.

BBC internal files from the mid-1970s until the early 1990s, when not still in use, are held at the Corporation's Records and Programme Information Centre (RAPIC), awaiting transfer to WAC. These bear a number without any prefix, e.g. 10028153. When these files are transferred to WAC they will be renumbered according to the WAC's own system, but the RAPIC reference number can be used to trace them.

WAC is open to outside researchers by prior arrangement (and fee). RAPIC is not open to users outside the BBC.

(b) Sound Archives

The BBC Sound Archives form part of the Sound Library at Broadcasting House (with some material stored elsewhere). Where material has been quoted from this, disc or tape numbers are given. The Sound Archives are not normally open to outside researchers.

2. INTERVIEWS

Two series of interviews have been drawn on for this book:

(a) The BBC's Oral History Project

Interviews conducted on tape with the intention of recording the Corporation's history for its own use; not available to outside researchers. Those quoted in the book are as follows (with the prefix used in the source notes):

OH/Glock	Sir Willliam Glock interviewed by Frank Gillard, London, March 1983.
OH/Haley	Sir William Haley interviewed by Frank Gillard; transcript corrected by Haley and dated by him 4 April 1978.
OH/Grisewood	Harman Grisewood interviewed by Frank Gllard, 1977.
OH/Newby	P. H. Newby interviewed by Frank Gillard, 6 March 1990.

(b) Interviews recorded for this book by the author

These are identified in the source notes by the prefix HC:

HC/Amyot	Etienne Amyot, London, 3 May 1994.
HC/Baker	Richard Baker, London, 9 January 1995.
HC/Barnes	Anthony Barnes, Norwich, 1 July 1994.
HC/Berkeley	Michael Berkeley, telephone, 27 January 1996.
HC/Berlin	Sir Isaiah Berlin, Oxford, 9 January 1996.
HC/Burton	Anthony Burton, London, 20 September 1995.
HC/Cleverdon	Nest Cleverdon, London, 26 October 1995.
HC/Crowe	Tom Crowe, London, 4 August 1995.
HC/Drummond	Sir John Drummond, London, 19 December 1995 and 16 January 1996.
HC/Esslin	Martin Esslin, London, 11 January 1996.
HC/Evans	John Evans, London, 16 January 1996.
HC/French	Philip French, London, 25 July 1995.
HC/Glock	Sir William Glock, Brightwell-cum-Sotwell, 20 November 1995.
HC/Goehr	Alexander Goehr, Cambridge, 12 February 1996.
HC/Grisewood	Harman Grisewood, Eye, 1 July 1994.
HC/Gueroult	Denys Gueroult, Oxford, 19 September 1995.
HC/Hearst	Stephen Hearst, London, 29 September 1995.
HC/Holme	Anthea Holme, Oxford, 1 August 1995.
HC/Hughes	Patricia Hughes, London, 26 October 1995.
HC/Hurwitz	Emanuel Hurwitz, London, 7 February 1996.
HC/Johnson, A.	Arthur Johnson, London, 26 October 1995.
HC/Johnson, G.	Graham Johnson, London, 27 February 1996
HC/Kenyon	Nicholas Kenyon, London, 12 December 1995 and 4 January 1996.
HC/Lade	John Lade, London, 16 February 1996, and letter to the author, 5 March 1996.

HC/Laslett	Peter Laslett, Cambridge, 7 February 1995.
HC/McIntyre	Ian McIntyre, Radlett, 25 September 1995.
HC/Manduell	Sir John Manduell, London, 30 March 1995.
HC/Muir	Frank Muir, Thorpe, 24 October 1994.
HC/Newby	P. H. Newby, Garsington, 24 May 1995.
HC/Pinter	Harold Pinter, London, 20 June 1994.
HC/Plowright	Piers Plowright, London, 7 February 1996.
HC/Ponsonby	Robert Ponsonby, London, 7 February 1996.
HC/Rigby	Cormac Rigby, Oxford, 26 May 1995.
HC/Smith	Prudence Smith, Oxford, 6 July 1995.
HC/Spenser	David Spenser, London, 14 June 1994.
HC/Stevens	Denis Stevens, London, 15 November 1994.
HC/Tippett	Sir Michael Tippett, Calne, 22 September 1994.
HC/Tydeman	John Tydeman, London, 11 January 1996.
HC/Winder	Anne Winder, London, 16 February 1996.

3. BOOKS AND OTHER WRITTEN MATERIAL

The following is a list of books and other printed material quoted frequently in the text, together with the prefix used in the source notes:

Briggs	Asa Briggs, *The History of Broadcasting in the United Kingdom*, Oxford University Press: Volume ii, *The Golden Age of Wireless*, 1965. Volume iii, *Sound and Vision*, 1970. Volume iv, *The War of Words*, 1979.
Brinnin	John Malcolm Brinnin, *Dylan Thomas in America*, Readers Union/J. M. Dent, 1957.
Bridson	D. G. Bridson, *Prospero and Ariel, the rise and fall of radio, a personal recollection*, Victor Gollancz, 1971.
Cleverdon	Douglas Cleverdon, *The Growth of Milk Wood*, J. M. Dent, 1969.
Coulson	Barbara Coulson, *Louis MacNeice in the BBC*, Faber & Faber, 1980.
Dylan Thomas Letters	Constantine Fitzgibbon (ed.), *Selected Letters of Dylan Thomas*, J. M. Dent, 1966.
Ferris	Paul Ferris, *Dylan Thomas*, Hodder & Stoughton, 1977.
Glock, *Notes*	William Glock, *Notes in Advance*, Oxford University Press, 1991.
Grigson	Geoffrey Grigson, *Recollections: mainly of artists and writers*, Chatto & Windus, The Hogarth Press, 1984.
Grisewood	Harman Grisewood, *One Thing at a Time: an autobiography*, Hutchinson, 1968.
Hall	Barrie Hall, *The Proms and the Men Who Made Them*, proofs of unpublished 2nd edition kindly lent by the author (first edition published by Allen & Unwin, 1981).
Harries	Meirion and Susie Harries, *A Pilgrim Soul: the life and work of Elisabeth Lutyens*, Faber & Faber, 1969.

Heppenstall	Rayner Heppenstall, *Portrait of the Artist as a Professional Man*, Peter Owen, 1969.
Hibberd	Stuart Hibberd, *This – Is London*, MacDonald & Evans, 1950.
Keller symposium	*Musical Analysis*, vol. 5, number 2/3, July/October 1986: 'Hans Keller (1919–1985) – A Memorial Symposium'.
Kennedy, *Boult*	Michael Kennedy, *Adrian Boult*, Hamish Hamilton, 1987.
Kenyon	Nicholas Kenyon, *The BBC Symphony Orchestra: the first fifty years, 1930–1980*, BBC, 1981.
Laslett/*Granta*	Peter Laslett, 'Crisis in British Broadcasting', *Granta* (Cambridge), 18 October 1958.
Mehta	Ved Mehta, 'Onward and Upward with the Arts', *New Yorker*, 18 May 1963.
Morris	John Morris (ed.), *From the Third Programme: a ten years' anthology*, Nonesuch Press, 1956.
Ponsonby	Draft of memoirs by Robert Ponsonby, kindly provided by him.
Reed	Henry Reed, *Hilda Tablet and Others: four pieces for radio*, BBC, 1971.
RL/MacNeice	*Radio Lives: Louis MacNeice*, written and presented by Humphrey Carpenter and produced by Fiona McLean, BBC Radio 4, 1 July 1993.
Rowe	Joyce Rowe, *BBC Third Programme: the tenth anniversary*, typed and duplicated forty-four-page press handout, 1956; copy in WAC, R19/1932/1.
Warburton	Notes on the first draft of this book written for the author by Ernest Warburton, January 1996.
Whitehead	Kate Whitehead, *The Third Programme: a literary history*, Clarendon Press, 1989.
Wintle	Christopher Wintle (ed.), *Hans Keller: Essays on Music*, Cambridge University Press, 1994.

Three other books have been extensively consulted:

David Cox, *The Henry Wood Proms*, BBC, 1980; Jennifer Doctor, *The BBC and Ultra-Modern Music 1922–36: shaping a nation's tastes* (forthcoming from Cambridge University Press); and Ian McIntyre, *The Expense of Glory: a life of Lord Reith*, HarperCollins, 1993.

Notes on sources

These are identified by the first words quoted. When two or more quotations from the same source follow each other with little intervening narrative, I have generally only used the first quotation for identification. Abbreviations refer to the Bibliography.

Page xii 'Unlike France, which', interview with the author, London, 4.1.96.

Page 3 'Now there has', OH/Haley. 'highbrow education', R34/186/1, minutes of Control Committee, 23.9.24. 'Too many uninteresting', CO62/6, Burnham to Reith, 7.12.25.

Page 4 'He programmed Mahler', Harries 78. 'a really polite', ibid 82. 'an oily, unctuous', Mehta 109.

Page 5 'good nights when', R34/468, 'Minerva', 14.4.30. 'melodious', ibid. 'Home and Family', ibid. 'the radio-ridden', Humphrey Carpenter, *The Brideshead Generation*, Weidenfeld & Nicolson, 1989, 300.

Page 6 'the BBC's unerring', Harold Nicolson, *Diaries and Letters, 1939–45*, Collins, 1967, 314. 'A concert had', Rowe 1. 'the prime re-educative', Whitehead 10. 'a highly intelligent', R34/578/1, 'The allocation of wavelengths after the war (Home Broadcasting)', 16.3.43. 'it would frankly', R34/578/2, 'Memorandum by Mr Kenneth Adam', 27.8.43.

Page 7 'fixed points', R34/578/2, 'Home services: memorandum by Mr Nicolls', 28.10.43. 'simply could not', John Grant in *The Times*, 8.9.87. 'The one thing', OH/Haley.

Page 8 'Let it often', Mehta 110. 'The heart of', OH/Haley. 'In the end', Hibberd 216. 'put some more', R34/892/2, 'Royal Albert Hall Concert', 28.6.45. 'frenzied prestissimo', *Radio Times*, 27.9.46. 'Winn was most', Hibberd 277–8. 'Our concerts must', R34/892/2, 'Royal Albert Hall concert', 28.6.45. 'I said, "No, not on" ', OH/Haley.

Page 9 'until we are satisfied', ibid. 'Nicolls wanted', ibid. 'I have always believed', ibid.

Page 10 'give the home', R34/580, 'Post-war broadcasting', 28.11.44. 'And I said', OH/Haley. 'the third programme', R34/580, 'Press conference', 19.7.45. 'Mr G. R. Barnes', R1/1/13, 'Minutes of Board Meeting', 3.5.45. 'a tall, sandy-haired', Bridson 183.

Page 11 'You Oxford men', Mehta 111. 'something pedagogic', Bridson 183. 'The Cambridge world', HC/Berlin. 'a curious man', OH/Haley. 'about half', R34/580, Haley to Robert Spicer, 6.4.45. 'frequency modulated', R53/298/1,

'Radiation of "C" Programme', 9.10.45. 'medium-wavelength 514', R1/1/13, 'Minutes of Board Meeting', 18.10.45. 'for the institution', R34/615/5, 'Programme policy meeting', 5.1.46. 'Programme C to', R34/890/1, 'Date for Programme C', 2.8.45. 'one year after', R53/184, Ashbridge to the Director of Telecommunications, GPO, 25.1.46. 'The Programme is', R34/602, 'Programme C Terms of Reference', 16.1.46.

Page 12 'assuming that', R34/890/1, 'Programme "C"', 1.3.46. 'Third Programme', R34/615/5, 'Programme policy meetings', 7.5.46. 'I am afraid', R34/602, 'Overseas currency transactions', 14.6.46. 'will not actually', R34/890/1, 'Offers for Third Programme', 23.7.46.

page 13 'The Programme', R34/890/1, 'The Third Programme', 29.7.46. 'Title of the', R34/602, Haley to Ashbridge and Nicolls, 20.6.46. 'Various names', OH/Haley. 'Many suggestions', R1/1/13, 'Minutes of Board Meeting', 4.7.46. 'were all delighted', OH/Haley.

Page 14 'The official Programme', R34/890/1, 'Programme "C"', 30.8.46. 'The Third Programme was', HC/Goehr.

page 15 'very suave', HC/French. 'My father died', HC/Amyot. 'into a thing', ibid. 'You don't get a job', ibid.

page 16 'this was more exciting', ibid. 'Highly intelligent', ibid. 'You would have preferred', Grigson 140. 'but we all came', HC/Amyot.

Page 17 "I think we thought', ibid. 'The heads of the Programme', R34/580, 'Post-war sound broadcasting', 24.7.45. 'absolutely crazy system', OH/Grisewood.

Page 18 'we should rely', R27/500/1, 'Music: Programme C', 17.5.46. 'not up to our programme', R34/602, 'Music Festivals', 30.5.46. 'e.g. Vaughan Williams', R27/500/1, 'Music: Programme C', 17.5.46. 'tight fit', R34/890/1, 'Programme C requirements', 29.12.45. 'the right sort', ibid. 'There are not many', ibid. 'If the music policy', ibid.

Page 19 'Anthony was wonderful', HC/Amyot. 'such a standard', R27/500/1, 'Music: Programme C', 17.5.46. 'on the contrary', R27/500/1, 'International artists', 11.6.46. 'We should propose', R27/500/1, 'Music: Programme C', 17.5.46. 'bring back the', R27/500/1, 'Mr Stanford Robinson and Programme "C"', 21.5.46. 'should solve', R27/500/1, '"C" Programme music meeting', 20.6.46.

Page 20 'starved of performances', HC/Amyot. 'should take the initiative', R27/500/1, '"C" Programme music meeting', 20.6.46. 'no more than', R27/500/1, 'Music: Programme C', 17.5.46. 'If the Marx Brothers', *Evening News*, 6.8.46. 'Sophisticated Revue', R34/890/1, 'Variety suggestions for Third Programme', 12.7.46. 'When there is', R19/933/2, 'Poetry in the Third Programme', 17.7.46. 'not be planned', R27/500/1, '"C" Programme Music Meeting', 20.6.46. 'one can hum', R27/500/1, 'Music talks for the Third Programme', 24.7.46.

Page 21 'Madame Renata Borgatti', R34/890/1, 'The Third Programme', 21.9.46. 'His brother was', HC/Amyot. 'producing on Bognor Pier', R34/890/1, 'Meeting with Miss Martita Hunt, Mr Tyrone Guthrie and Mr Reginald Beckwith', 31.7.46. 'the sort of play', R34/890/1, 'Reginald Beckwith', 6.7.46. 'few plays', R34/890/1, 'Meeting with Miss Martita Hunt. . .'. 31.7.46. 'the great European', R1/3/59, 'The home programme policy of the BBC', 4.7.46. 'some of the younger', R27/500/1, 'Programme "C"', 14.6.46. 'I recommend', R34/890/1, 'News in the Third Programme', 20.7.46.

Page 22 'the great Christian festivals', R34/890/1, 'Religious broadcasts in the Third Programme', 10.7.46. 'a classical "First"', Grisewood 165. 'be managed on £7,000', R34/580, 'Notes of meetings to discuss post-war Home Service programme allowance', 25.10.44. 'The week seems', R34/890/1, 'Week 40: the Third Programme', 21.8.46.

Page 23 'The building of', R53/298/1, memo from press officer, 27.8.46.

Page 24 'NOTRE STATION', ibid, GPO to BBC, 27.8.46. 'TIMELESS RADIO', *Daily Mail*, 28.6.46. 'He is a Cambridge', *Sunday Pictorial*, 6.1.46. 'one of radio's', *Star*, 10.8.46. 'and most are under 40', *Sunday Times*, 22.9.46. 'Although the Russian', *Daily Express*, 20.9.46. 'considerably increased', *Manchester Guardian*, 20.9.46.

Page 25 'We may have', *Birmingham Mail*, 20.9.46. 'One of the big', *Star*, 25.9.46 'in order to', R34/602, paper by Anthony Lewis, 25.11.46. 'unfamiliar or difficult', R34/890/1, 'Policy of repeats in Third Programme', 5.12.47. 'the systematic repeating', R34/890/1, 'Third Programme planning: The Repertory Season', 30.6.49. *(Footnote:)* 'Repeat performances of', R34/890/11, 'The Third Programme', 29.7.46.

Page 26 'the cultural and political', *Tribune*, 27.9.46. 'venomously phrased', *Daily Worker*, 28.9.46. 'It is to be hoped', *Star*, 20.9.46. 'If the effect', *Times*, 20.9.56. 'Criticism of this venture', *News Chronicle* 26.9.46.

Page 27 'This is the BBC', BBC Sound Library T9487. 'He said, "I think"', HC/Amyot. 'Narrator (in a hushed tone)', BBC Sound Library T9487. 'We were terrified', HC/Amyot. 'Narrator: Are they ready?', BBC Sound Library T9487.

Page 28 'Housewife: Bottling apples', *Daily Telegraph*, 2.10.46. '. . .Admit me Chorus', BBC Sound Library T9487. 'The timing was slipshod', *Manchester Daily Despatch*, 30.9.46.

Page 29 'We are likely', *Birmingham Weekly Post*, 11.10.46. 'someone distantly', Briggs vol. iv, 68. 'We wanted the Third', HC/Amyot. 'cross-talk identified', R53/298/1, '"C" Programme – 514.6 metres, Droitwich', 2.10.46. 'very well', *Times*, 30.9.46. 'After Field Marshal', *Daily Dispatch*, 30.9.46. *(Footnote:)* 'What a lovely', Denys Drower to Nicholas Kenyon, 7.2.96.

Page 30 'It was a sticky', Kennedy, *Boult*, 207. 'It has brilliance', *Daily Sketch*, 30.9.46. 'problematic rehearsals', sleeve note to EMI EL 27 0263 1. 'It is impossible', *Times*, 30.9.46. 'Had our original', *Listener*, 3.10.46.

Page 31 'The handful of', *Star*, 30.9.46. 'The Third Programme', Haley's diary, 29.9.46, courtesy of Donald Haley. 'Haley's Third Symphony', *Daily Mirror*, 30.9.46. 'General verdict': *Daily Express*, 30.9.46. 'It would be unjust', *Evening Standard*, 30.9.46. 'It demanded no', *Daily Mail*, 30.9.46.

Page 32 'It has one drawback', Jeanette R. Taylor to BBC, 20.9.46. 'It was with the utmost', J. Vincent Carroll to BBC, 29.9.46. 'Today is the', S. J. Watson to BBC, 29.9.46. 'A dress designer', *Manchester Evening News*, 4.1.46. 'But he was absolutely', HC/Amyot.

Page 33 'Man and Superman riveted', *Manchester Sunday Chronicle*, 6.10.46. 'Shaw makes not', *Cavalcade*, 12.10.46. 'raises the question', *Irish Times*, 4.10.46. 'listened to the whole', *Irish Times*, 17.10.46. 'undue importance', *Daily Telegraph*, 3.10.46. 'These radio-mystique', *Cavalcade*, 12.10.46. 'the unseemly entrance', *The Bulletin & Scots Pictorial*, 7.10.46.

Page 34 'The...performance', ibid, 7.10.46. 'Huis Clos was banned', HC/Amyot. 'He was quite', interview with the author, 11.5.94. 'Every evening', *Birmingham Weekly Post*, 11.10.46. 'has not been as', *Irish Times*, 4.10.46. 'does not force', *Northern Whig*, 7.10.46. 'For the first', John Stonehouse to BBC, 10.10.46.

Page 35 'It is lamentable', *Newcastle Journal*, 5.10.46. 'There it is', *Newcastle Journal*, 5.10.46. 'I wonder', *New Statesman*, 5.10.46. 'given almost invariably', *Annual Register*, new series, 1946, 'Retrospect of Literature, Art and Science in 1946', 380. 'a very pleasing', *Spectator*, 4.10.46.

Page 36 'develop something new', R34/890/1, 'Light Entertainment in the Third Programme', 10.12.46. 'lost art ...', *Sunday Chronicle*, 6.10.46. 'You, being more', *New Statesman*, 23.11.46. 'Oh, by the way', *Punch*, 4.12.46. 'no apology', R34/894. 'Third Programme presentation', 1.10.46. 'I did feel', R34/894, 'Over-runs in the Third Programme', 8.10.46.

Page 37 'rather strongly', R34/894, 'Over-runs in the Third Programme', 19.12.46. 'You tuned in', interview with the author, Oxford, 18.3.95. 'I had met', HC/Amyot. 'you packed', RCONT1, Michael Tippett, Barnes to Tippett, 4.10.46.

Page 38 'Too much of it', *The Diaries of Evelyn Waugh*, Weidenfeld & Nicolson, 1976, 666. 'My father certainly', HC/Barnes. 'Mr Reed', BBC Sound Library 10132/3/4.

Page 39 'It is the most', quoted *Radio Times*, 22.11.46. 'you don't know half', RL/MacNeice. 'the George', ibid. 'none of us', Heppenstall 20–22.

Page 40 'a highly intelligent', RL/MacNeice. 'and if there are', ibid. 'The fact that', ibid. 'The pubs were', Douglas Cleverdon in conversation with J. W. Lambert, National Sound Archive, 15 February 1983 (transcribed from tape at National Sound Archive). 'He would stand', Ferris 205. 'used to come', HC/Amyot.

Page 41 'the thin puce', Dylan Thomas Letters 319. 'August Bank Holiday', *Dylan Thomas: The Broadcasts*, ed. R. Maud, J. M. Dent, 1991, 138. 'Dylan as an actor', *Book Week*, 24.10.65.*(Footnote:)* 'Good Lord', obituary of Cleverdon by John Wells, *Independent* , 3.10.87.

Page 42 'A whole masque', quoted Coulson 87. 'How many of', *Dylan Thomas: The Broadcasts*, ed. R. Maud, J. M. Dent, 1991, 146. 'the best all-round', Ferris 207. 'It was in', *Poetry*, November 1955, 112.

Page 43 'I ... found Dylan', ibid., 112–3. 'Had a good', RCONT1, Dylan Thomas, Thomas to Roy Campbell, 30.12.47. 'That was for', HC/Spenser. 'It was a lovely', ibid.

Page 44 'A sort of combat', Heppenstall 31–2.

Page 45 'which will show', R27/500/1. 'Third Programme: Foundations of Music', 8.10.46. 'In a few cases', ibid. 'Good', ibid. 'let us know', *Picture Post*, 30.11.46.

Page 46 'Repeat, even more', ibid. 'My own inclination', R27/500/1, 'Repeats of music', 31.10.46. 'it would be', R34/602, 'Music in the Third Programme, 25.11.46.

Page 47 'At two o'clock', HC/Amyot. 'the great Wagnerian', 'R34/602, 'Music in the Third Programme', 25.11.46. 'the Third Programme would', OH/Haley. 'How should Song', R27/500/1, 'Concerts and recitals', 9.12.46.

Page 48 'no doubt listening', R9/9/11, 'A Listener Research Report ... The Third Programme', 3.2.47. 'found reception', ibid. 'rather less', R53/298/1, 'Reception of Third Programme', 3.12.46. 'several schemes', ibid, 6.12.46. 'But this will take', ibid. 'like frying sausages', *Picture Post*, 30.11.46. 'could be heard', OH/Haley. 'It shows the old', *Sunday Times*, 13.10.46.

Page 49 'bold and imaginative', Haley's diary, 14.12.46, by courtesy of Donald Haley. 'You should consider', R34/890/1, 'Letter from Mr W. N. Weech', 13.11.46. '30% of the', R9.9.11. 'A Listener Research Report ... The Third Programme', 3.2.47. 'Nothing widened', Peter Hall, *Making an Exhibition of Myself*, Sinclair-Stevenson, 1993, 52. 'The Third Programme, when', interview with the author, Orkney, 23.7.94. *(Footnote:)* 'The ostrich has', RCONT1, Richard Strauss, Artist, 1944–62, 'Strauss Oboe Concerto', 11.4.46.

Page 50 'Enormously', HC/Pinter.

Page 51 'the Third Programme may', *Picture Post*, 30.11.46. 'There seems little', *Scotsman*, 22.2.47. 'we deserve', *Music Teacher*, December 1946. 'extremely bad' and 'On Monday', *Time & Tide*, 1.2.47. 'To someone living', *Tatler*, 22.1.47. 'third-rate poets', *Sunday Mercury*, 5.1.47.

Page 52 'A specious', *Time & Tide*, 4.1.47. 'a tirade', *Daily Worker*, 29.1.47. 'senior members', *Oxford Magazine*, 6.3.47. 'a series of', R51/5901/1, 'Third Programme Talks Meeting', 1.1.47. 'a very miniature', RCONT1, Geoffrey Grigson, Talks, 1946–8, Grigson to Mrs Horton, 'Tuesday' (September 1947). 'restricted panel', *Cavalcade*, 18.1.47.

Page 53 'monstrous that the', Miles Jebb (ed.), *The Diaries of Cynthia Gladwyn*, Constable, 1995, 32. 'It seems to be', R41/214, R. H. A. Powell to Director-General, 11.2.47. 'I have not missed', R41/214, J. A. Parsons to Postmaster General, 21.2.47. 'given on', *Times*, 19.2.47. 'Could not', R41/214, Mrs Thicknesse to BBC, 11.2.47. 'Shinwell decided', HC/Amyot. 'the BBC having', *Daily Telegraph*, 27.2.47. 'We're a small', *Radio Times*, 21.3.47. 'Poor we may', *Tribune*, 25.7.47.

Page 54 'He took me', HC/Amyot. 'a large scale', R27/500/2, 'Note of informal talk to Programme Builders ...', 21.1.47. 'When big singers', R27/500/2, 'Song recitals in the Third Programme', 10.3.47.

Page 55 'The principle', R27/500/2, 'Contemporary British Composers Series', 18.7.47. 'Delving among', *Radio Times*, 4.7.47. 'They wanted a', HC/Hurwitz.

Page 56 'Being the Third', ibid. 'Broadcasting can', R27/500/2, 'Music policy and procedure', 17.4.47. 'a good three', R27/500.2, 'Sir Adrian Boult and the Second Quarter Schedule', 5.2.47. 'the infrequency', R27/500/2, 'Musical masterpieces', 2.4.47. 'One orchestral', R27/500.2, 'Advance note on the Third Programme second year in general', 11.7.47.

Page 57 'Always think big', R27/200/1, 'Mr Barnes' meeting with Music Department', 31.3.47. 'Beecham would say', HC/Stevens. 'preposterously inadequate', RCONT1, Sir Thomas Beecham, Copyright, 1949–56, Beecham to Walford, 10.8.51. 'It is not my custom', ibid, Beecham to Candler, 16.8.51. 'no great composer', Glock, *Notes*, 40. 'I remember', HC/Glock. 'I think we', RCONT1, William Glock, Talks, 1938–59, in Barnes to Controller (Talks) and DG, 25.3.47. 'How could one', microfilm scripts, William Glock, *Music in Post-War Europe*, 1, 3.7.47. 'the best meal', ibid.

Page 58 'I'm not quite', ibid. 'the best orchestra', ibid, 2, 5.7.47. 'more scores', ibid. 'made an unforgettable', ibid. 'I'd hoped', ibid, 3, 7.7.47. 'Be patient!', ibid, 4, 8.7.47. 'whether the greatest', ibid. 'at least one', R27/500/2, 'Third Programme dinner: music', 11.2.47.

Page 59 'look like copies' and 'Diagonalisation of', R27/400/2, 'Diag-onalisation with Home Service', 11.3.47. 'It swamped Milton', *Listener*, 30.10.47. 'MacNeice continues', L1/285/2, Left/MacNeice, 21.3.47. 'sti-mulating outside', ibid. 'Haley came in', HC/Amyot.

Page 60 'These are performances', *Listener*, 25.9.47. 'He is in real', RCONT1, Richard Strauss, Artist, 1947–62, 'Richard Strauss', 21.6.47.

Page 61 'foreign orchestras', R27/500/1, 'Music in the fourth quarter, 1947', 6.8.47. 'we must not', R2/500/2, 'Third Programme schedule', 17.11.47.

Page 62 'They are almost', RCONT1, William Walton, Composer, 1940– 47, Walton to Barnes, 31.1.47. '*PLEASE* do *NOT*', RCONT1, Ralph Vaughan Williams, Composer, 1947–57, Vaughan Williams to Lowe, 21.2.47. 'a double concerto', R27/500/2, 'New works for the first anniversary of Third Pro-gramme', 10.3.47. 'I think he might', RCONT1, Francis Poulenc, Composer, 1941–62, 'Francis Poulenc: proposed commission for Third Programme anni-versary', 25.2.47.

Page 63 'play and sing', ibid, 'Poulenc and Bernac', 26.3.47. 'really sails', ibid, 'Poulenc and Bernac', 28.3.47. '*Catastrophe!*', ibid, Poulenc to Lockspeiser (translated by Lockspeiser), 18.8.47. 'I am down', RCONT1, Michael Tippett, Composer, 1947–55, Tippett to Barnes, 13.7.47.

Page 64 'so strongly moved', RCONT1, Michael Tippett, Artists, 1942–51, Barnes to Tippett, 25.8.47. 'already arranged', ibid, Barnes to Tippett, 9.9.47. 'We have been considering', ibid, Barnes to Tippett, 25.2.47. 'I had not realised', Microfilm, Talks Scripts, Betjeman, 'Aberdeen Granite', 28.7.47.

Page 65 'There were two', Morris 76–7. 'She became', HC/Cleverdon. 'He'd be about', Dylan Thomas, *Quite Early one Morning*, J. M. Dent, 1954, 75–6.

Page 66 'more or less', HC/Tippett. 'one of the most', HC/Amyot. 'an "explorer"', Grisewood 164. 'spoke all the', Grisewood to the author, 12.8.94. 'if an idea', OH/Newby. 'He had been', HC/Tippett. 'My wife was very', HC/Amyot.

Page 67 'I did exceedingly', *John Bull*, 17.2.51. 'In the evening', OH/Grisewood. 'not BBC' and 'Beatrice Harrison', ibid. 'so far to', ibid.

Page 68 'He just said', ibid. 'He did used', OH/Haley. 'Harman was somebody',

HC/Amyot. 'It was a charming', Grisewood 160. 'mixture of improvisation', Grisewood 161. 'Next door', HC/Grisewood.

Page 69 'exercising a great', OH/Grisewood. 'Kirkpatrick's harpsichord', R34/894, 'Timing of music programmes', 13.10.47. 'This period', R34/892/3. 'Timing of music programmes,' 20.10.47. 'the incompetence', ibid. 'well worth doing', R19/1295/4, 'Shakespeare histories', 14.10.47.

Page 70 'There is no doubt', R27/500/2, 'Repeats', 9.12.47. 'Must "serious" people', *Daily Express*, 25.9.47. '1. What was at', R34/890/1, 'Decrease of Third Programme audience', 5.12.47. 'dwindled because', *Penguin Music Magazine*, September 1947, 79. 'I must confess', R27/500/2, Haley to Barnes, 17.12.47.

Page 71 'a miscellaneous', R27/500/2, 'Third Programme Saturday concerts', 19.12.47. 'for academic reasons', R27/500/2, 'Chamber music: English quartets', 17.12.47. 'would be possible', R34/890/1, 'Decrease of Third Programme audience', 5.12.47.

Page 72 'Sir – how many', *Courier and Advertiser* (Dundee), 6.1.48. 'What enthusiasm', *Daily Telegraph*, 27.1.48. 'There are some', *Daily Telegraph*, 20.1.48.

Page 73 'A major new', *Radio Times*, 30.1.48. 'Slight, Drone', *Observer*, 3.10.48. 'Only recently', *Scotsman*, 9.3.48. '*Russell:* Certainly the question', Refilm 4 – Copleston.

Page 74 'our Control Room', RCONT1, Bertrand Russell, Talks, 1944–9, Basil Taylor to Russell, 19.1.48. 'perhaps a little', ibid, note by Haley, 29.1.48. '*Copleston:* Let us take', Refilm 4 – Copleston.

Page 75 'that face would', HC/Laslett. 'If you interfered', HC/Laslett.

Page 76 'One fears that', Hugh Walter to BBC, 26.1.48. 'will be devoted', R34/890/1, 'Third Programme extra hour', 12.1.48. 'Haley was anxious', Gerard Mansell, *Let Truth Be Told: 50 Years of BBC External Broadcasting*, Weidenfeld & Nicolson, 1982, 215.

Page 77 'a feeling that', HC/Barnes, 'short, eager', *John Bull*, 17.2.51. 'I was talking', HC/Grisewood. 'He was an expert', HC/Grisewood. 'in most of', HC/Holme. 'But I didn't, HC/Grisewood. 'The attacks on', ibid.

Page 78 'did the Third', OH/Haley. 'When Harman was', HC/Newby. 'He was very', HC/Holme. 'the lack of', R19/4925/5, 'Original writing for radio', 27.2.48. 'I undertake all', Dylan Thomas Letters, 322. 'outsider' and 'publicity is', R27/500/3. 'Serenade Concert', 7.4.48.

Page 79 'Third Programme music', R27/500/2, 'Preliminary suggestions', 3.12.47. 'We play tonight', R27/500/3, 'A serenade', 6.4.48. 'I enjoyed the', ibid. 'This difficult', R27/500/3, 'Serenade Concert: April 23, 1948', 26.4.48. 'I do not know', R27/495/2, 'Report on music in the Third Programme', n.d., 1949.

Page 80 'the Third Programme audience', R9/9/12, 'A Listener Research Report', 16.4.48. 'concentrate on listening', ibid. 'Our sonata recital', *John O'London's Weekly*, 6.8.48.

Page 81 'Will the BBC', *Musical Express*, 18.6.48. 'I know nothing', R27/500/3, 'Week 26', 4.5.48. 'an aggressive', HC/Grisewood. 'either I should',

R27/500/3, 'Programme supply from Music Department', 26.5.48.

Page 82 'altogether too great', ibid. 'I cannot accept', R27/500/3, 'H.M.'s memo of 26th May', 1.6.48. 'need to make', R34/890/1, 'Third Programme resources', 1.6.48.

Page 83 'the performance will', R27/130, 'History in Sound of European Music', 14.3.47. 'Each broadcast', ibid, 16.5.47. 'It has been worked out', *A History in Sound of European Music*, BBC pamphlet, n.d. [autumn 1947]. 'incompetent', R27/130, 'Notes on relations with Gerald Abraham', n.d. [1948]. 'seriously deficient', R27/130, Administration of History of Music', 20.2.48. 'the presentation and', R27/130, 'History of Music in Sound', 4.3.48.

Page 84 'It is a pity', R27/130, 'History of European Music in Sound', 28.10.48. 'the ultra-mincing', *Daily Mirror*, 8.11.48. 'I was one', Films T375, Nicolson.

Page 85 'after March', *Manchester Guardian*, 29.9.48.

Page 86 'a series of' and 'a good deal', R27/500/3, 'Light music in the Third Programme', 29.9.48. 'should not' and 'very sound', ibid. 'What is the', R27/500/3, 'What is light music?', 30.11.48.

Page 87 'I was sent', HC/Grisewood.

Page 88 'Mr E. M. Forster', R27/500/3, 'Record of interview ... with Mr E. M. Forster', 8.12.48. 'I spoke with', HC/Grisewood. 'We are none', R25/500/3, 'Suggestions from music critics' luncheon', 14.12.48. 'it would probably', R27/500/4, 'Music schedule: second quarter', 18.1.49. 'six weekly', *Daily Herald*, 19.11.48. 'almost a disaster', *Birmingham Mail*, 20.11.48. 'our interest', R27/500/3, 'Jazz in Third Programme ...', 27.10.48.

Page 89 '*Third Division*, with', R44/586/2, 'Third Division', 23.12.48. 'Until then', HC/Muir. 'We have now', R46/521/3, 'Third Division', 30.11.48. 'EFFECT: DING DONG DING DONG', Light Entertainment Scripts, LE 411/412.

Page 91 'It was wonderful', HC/Pinter. 'achieved an outstanding', R1/3/70, 'The Third Programme', 11.11.48. 'experiments', R34/890/1, 'The Third Programme: note by the Director-General', 5.11.48.

Page 93 'experiments', ibid. 'considered that, R34/890/1, 'The Third Programme', 23.11.48. 'in effect a cut', R20/189, 'Rising costs', 28.2.49. 'the plain fact', R20/189, 'Rising costs', 2.3.49.

Page 94 'exceptionally heavy', R27/223, 'Opera policy', 21.3.49. 'The performance', R27/495/2, 'Report on music in the Third Programme', n.d. [spring 1949]. 'That the criticisms', ibid. 'Should we not', R27/500/3, 'Schedule: first quarter 1949', 18.10.49. 'the opportunity', RCONT1, Mátyás Seiber, Composer, 1941–62, Seiber to Lowe, 18.3.49. 'Quite frankly', ibid, Murrill to Seiber, 28.3.49.

Page 95 'a rather sad', ibid, Seiber to Murrill, 4.4.49. 'PRETENTIOUS CULTURE', *Evening Standard*, 7.3.49. 'evenings when I', *BBC Quarterly*, vol. 7 no. 4 (1952).

Page 96 'rumours from', R44/586/2, 'Third Programme publicity', 8.6.49. 'a period which', R34/890/1, 'The Third Programme in 1950', 28.6.49.

Page 97 'repertory season', R34/890/1, 'Third Programme Planning: the Repertory Season', 30.6.49. 'I remain convinced', R27/500/4, Lowe to Grisewood, 30.5.49. 'What is at stake', 'The Third Programme and its Audience', typescript lent by Harman Grisewood.

Page 98 'A high proportion', Publications A/476, 'The Third Programme Plans for 2 October-31 December 1949. 'well below the', R27/130, 'History in Sound of European Music', 3.6.49. 'caused considerable', R27/130, 'Editorial contributions to History of Music', 6.7.49. 'we should stop', R27/130, 'Copy of extract of letter from C.T.P. to H.M.', 4.8.49.

Page 99 'The opera completely', RCONT1, Michael Tippett, Artists, 1942–51, Tippett to Newby, 25.10.49. 'Is anything', RCONT1, William Walton, Composer, 1948–62, Haley to Nicolls, 29.9.50. 'On the whole', ibid, Walton to Wilson, 1.3.50. 'Most of the works', Composers' Guild of Great Britain, *Bulletin* no. 6 (July 1950).

Page 100 'a most shocking', R27/245/3, Isaacs to Head of Music, 1.9.50. 'they are apt', ibid, Murrill to Isaacs, 2.10.50. 'the BBC have had', RCONT1, Elisabeth Lutyens, Composer, 1940–62, Lutyens to Vowles, 27.11.50. 'the unrelieved "coldness"', RCONT1, Mátyás Seiber, Composer, 1941–62, Reading Panel Reports, 31.1.49. 'I certainly', RCONT1, Mátyás Seiber, Composer, 1941–62, Boult to Seiber, 3.5.50.

Page 101 'The BBC was', OH/Haley. 'draw up', Kennedy, *Boult*, 214. 'do not object', R27/500/4, 'Music meeting minutes: 23rd November 1949', 13.12.49. 'What right', ibid, 5.12.49. 'offensive', ibid, 13.12.49. 'Wilson came along', OH/Haley.

Page 102 'I said to Nicolls', OH/Haley. 'injustice', OH/Haley. 'Obvious instances', R34/894, 'Timing of programmes', 22.9.49. 'we find it', ibid, 3.10.49.

Page 103 'a thoroughly responsible', R34/894, 'Third Programme timing', 6.1.50. 'cannot provide', R27/500/5, 'Third Programme timing', 11.1.50. 'This sort', R27/500/5, 'Vivaldi oratorio "Juditha Triumphans"', 23.1.50. 'The Schutz', ibid, 1.2.50. 'specifically in charge', HC/Stevens.

Page 105 'one fairly big', R27/500/5, 'T.P. planning', 28.3.50. 'act as a planning', R19/1295/7, 'Third Programme poetry arrangements', 15.1.50. 'On the whole', R41/214. 'Comments on the Third Programme', n.d.

Page 106 'thinking the frequency', R53/298/4, 'Daventry Third Programme transmitter – 647 kc/s', 8.3.50. 'late Bomber Command', R53/298/4, 'New Third Programme transmitter at Daventry', 20.11.50. 'since there was', R53/298/5, untitled memo, 22.5.51. 'ample volume', R53/299/2, 'Third Programme reception in Manchester', 12.4.51. 'good reports', *Universities Quarterly*, August 1951, 373. 'Signal strength', R53/299/2, 'Third Programme reception tests', 15.5.51.

Page 107 'It gives musicians', *Manchester Evening News*, 25.4.51. 'Music from the', R34/831/1, 'Special contributions from R.B. Department in 1951', 9.2.51.

Page 108 'Everything which you', *Radio Times*, 20.4.51. 'fine planning', R34/890/1, Lowe to Grisewood and Holme, 3.5.51. 'devoting each evening', R9/9/15, 'The Third Programme 1851 Week', 5.6.51.

Page 109 'the odd result', *Economist*, 24.10.53. 'in the neighbourhood',

R4/1/21, *Report of the Broadcasting Committee,1949*, 20.

Page 110 'a quite impracticable', R53/298/5, 'Third Programme Reception', 20.4.51. 'since it began', R4/1/21, *Report of the Broadcasting Committee,1949*, 21, 51. 'The Third Programme, positively', ibid, Appendix H, 364. 'So he was', HC/Laslett.

Page 111 'Tonight I want', Morris 268. 'One Saturday night', *Cavalcade*, 20.5.50. 'the agnostic', *Evening Argus*, 22.9.50. 'forthright', *Church Times*, 22.9.50. 'establish a closer', *Universities Quarterly*, August 1951.

Page 112 'Here was a chance', *Spectator*, 2.2.51. 'I have an excellent', RCONT1, Iris Murdoch, Talks, 1946–62, Smith to Assistant Controller (Talks), 17.11.49. 'I couldn't believe', HC/Smith. 'Dear Prue', RCONT1, Iris Murdoch, Talks, 1946–62, Murdoch to Smith, 8.11.49.

Page 113 'I don't think', ibid, Smith to Murdoch, 24.11.49. 'It's high level', ibid, Smith to Assistant Controller (Talks), 17.11.49. 'These are people', Talks Scripts T351.

Page 114 'Michael Ventris worked', HC/Smith. 'For a long time', script lent by Prudence Smith.

Page 115 'Not at all', HC/Smith. 'I believe our', R51/128/2, 'Record Review', 12.11.52. 'I am astonished', R51/128/2, 'Record Review', 14.11.52. 'The Third Programme . . . is', *The Times*, 29.9.51. 'NOBODY agrees', *Evening News*, 2.10.51. 'sounded like aristocrats', *Twentieth Century*, November 1951. 'the Board expressed', R34/890/1, 'Meeting of Board of Governors, 25.10.51', 1.11.51.

Page 116 'is really beginning', R44/586/2, Simon to Grisewood, 4.2.52. 'The coming of', R9/9/16, 'Recent trends in listening', n.d. [1952]. 'Ah, if only', *Evening Standard*, 6.8.51. 'I was introduced', OH/Haley.

Page 117 'This is a pernicious', RCONT1, Arnold Schoenberg, Composer, 1943–62, Isaacs to Head of Music, 21.6.51. 'oldest pupil', ibid, Stein to Murrill, 26.8.51. 'subservience to', R27/500/6, 'Schönberg Commemoration', 11.9.51. 'I wasn't Schoenbergian,' HC/Tippett. 'He is very', RCONT1, Arnold Schoenberg, Composer, 1943–62, 'Schoenberg Opus 16', 2.1.52.

Page 118 'It is a little', ibid, 5.1.52. 'The works of', *Spectator*, 4.1.52. 'Searching my mind', 910, Thomas Mann, 1941; 1946–55, Mann to Kallin, 27.11.51.

Page 119 'Like Freud', Michael Tippett, *Moving into Aquarius*, Paladin, 1974, 35, 37, 42. 'not a Schönbergian', *New Statesman*, 22 March 1952. 'I admire', R27/500/8, 'Report on Third Programme', March 1953. 'OSKAR ADLER NEVER', RCONT1, Michael Tippett, Artist, 1952–5, Keller to Tippett, 21.3.52.

Page 120 'Mr Tippett referred', ibid, Keller to editor, *Radio Times*, 21.3.52. 'Fortunately Dr Adler's', ibid, Keller to Tippett, 21.3.52. 'What an unforeseen', ibid, Tippett to Keller, 22.3.52. 'Speaking off the', ibid, Tippett to Grisewood, 22.3.52. 'In the second', R44/586/2, 'Schoenberg and his Time', n.d. [autumn 1951].

Page 121 'a kind of', 910, Thomas Mann, 1941; 1946–55, Kallin to Mann, 23.1.52. 'if it isn't as flawless', ibid, Mann to Kallin, 15.5.52. 'You do not sound', ibid, Kallin to Mann, 22.5.52. 'a ticklish theme', Scripts T321.

Page 122 '7 April: J. Enoch Powell, MP', R34/890/1, 'Noel Annan's Report: Third Programme', 25.4.52. 'I have never yet', *BBC Quarterly*, vii/3, autumn 1952, 143, 145.

Page 123 '*Jourdain:* We've often', Sound Archives MT 14207.

Page 124 'genuine extemporary', RCONT1, Arnold Toynbee, Talks, 1940–51, Toynbee to Kallin, 29.3.51. 'At present', R19/1359, 'Editing of tape: setting up facilities', 20.10.54. 'In the first', R27/500/8, 'Report on Third Programme music', March 1953. 'What I would', RCONT1, William Glock, Talks, 1951–9, Glock to Fiske, 28.7.54.

Page 125 'The trouble about', ibid, Fiske to Glock, 30.7.54. 'still gave the impression', Glock, *Notes*, 58. 'Producers used', OH/Glock. 'musical underground', Glock, *Notes*, chapter title. 'like ourselves', R34/890/1, 'Noel Annan's Report: Third Programme', 25.4.52.

Page 126 'She said her', HC/Newby.

Page 127 'about the fact', HC/Berlin. 'I have nothing', R44/1130/1, Berlin to Grisewood, 3.7.51.

Page 128 'From the tone', microfilm scripts, Kingsley Amis, 'Literary Opinion', 9.6.54. 'it would be', RCONT1, Kingsley Amis, Talks, 1954–62, Amis to Newby, 9.5.54. Newby's reply is drafted on Amis's letter. 'When recently', *Time & Tide*, 14.3.53.

Page 129 'George will hire', Grigson 140. 'I suppose we', HC/Newby. '800–odd', RCONT1, Oxford University Delegacy of Extra Mural Studies, Panel of Consultants, 'BBC General Trainee Scheme', 10.6.55.

Page 130 'He was a nice', HC/Grisewood.

Page 131 'evidently by Menotti' and 'What a magnificent', R19/1295/9, 'Announcers' comments', 8.1.53. 'I had fiddled', HC/Baker.

Page 132 'the opposite of', HC/Baker. 'Mrs Blunt was', R34/1503/1, 'Haydn and Mendelssohn series: presentation', 18.8.65. 'in which I played', HC/Baker. 'I always try', HC/Crowe.

Page 133 'It was very', HC/Hughes. 'I always look', R34/890/1, Eliot to Morris, 3.7.53.

Page 134 'You will notice', R34/890/1, 'Third Programme autumn plans', 12.5.53. 'a provisional estimate', R20/189, 'Third Programme', 22.9.53.

Page 135 'Henry was a', HC/Cleverdon.

Page 136 'My mind would', Reed, dedicatory letter. 'Henry was already', HC/Spenser. '*Reeve:* The late', Reed 11.

Page 137 'I am not ill', Reed 14. 'A lunch party', HC/Spenser. '*Reeve:* I never', Reed 21–3. 'A fair number', Reed, dedicatory letter. 'Good God', quoted *News Chronicle*, 4.12.53. 'a grave error', ibid. 'full frontal', Reed, dedicatory letter.

Page 138 '*Hilda (distant, behind door)*', Reed 65–6. 'They had been', Harries 142.

Page 139 'It is important', Harries 142–3. 'knowing that he', Cleverdon 18. 'we also', ibid 19. 'What Laugharne', ibid 1. *(Footnote:)* 'By chance', Hall.

Page 140 'most of the', ibid 16. 'At what stage', ibid 18. 'I suggested the', ibid 19. 'He'd written about', HC/Cleverdon. 'its effect', Cleverdon 20–21.

Page 141 'the Black Book', ibid 3. 'too good', ibid 35. 'Dylan arrived', ibid

35–6. *(Footnote:)* 'I am aware', R19/1359, 'The Village that was Mad (alias Llareggub): by Dylan Thomas', 26.8.52.

Page 142 'his immense', Brinnin 209. 'His body', *Radio Times*, 22.1.54. 'Had Dylan lived', Cleverdon 41.

Page 143 'innocent children', ibid 43. 'I have gone', R19/1359, 'Under Milk Wood', 19.1.54. 'at the discretion', ibid, 21.1.54.

Page 144 'two tits', Cleverdon 43. 'wriggle her roly', R19/1359, 'Under Milk Wood', 26.1.54. 'I was spellbound', *Listener*, 4.2.54. 'If this is', *Daily Sketch*, 29.1.54. 'As the last', *Tablet*, 30.1.54. 'a major', *Radio Times*, 22.1.54. 'radio's greatest', Bridson 206.

Page 145 'running a private', R19/1295/9, 'Drama offers: first quarter 1955', 19.10.54. 'prefers Cleverdon', R19/1295/9, 'Third Programme drama', 9.11.54. 'Third Programme Specialist', R19/1295/9, 'Liaison between Third Programme and Drama Department', 19.11.54. Morris's mention of Cleverdon's productions, R19/1931/1, 'Two inserts for European Service feature on Third Programme', 7.9.56. '*Hilda (confidingly):*', Reed 63. 'last resort' and 'On December', R27/852/1, 'Isaac Stern, Igor Markievitch and the Philharmonia Orchestra', 5.1.54.

Page 147 'any ambitious', R34/890/1. 'Third Programme: forthcoming plans for autumn and winter', 13.8.54. 'established', *Musical Opinion*, August 1953.

Page 148 'I have never believed', RCONT1, Elisabeth Lutyens, Composer, 1940–62, Reading Panel Reports, 5.5.52. 'My own experience', ibid, Lutyens to Isaacs, 22.11.52. 'Your work for', ibid, Howgill to Lutyens, 30.11.53. 'should prefer a', ibid, Lutyens to Howgill, 19.2.54. The BBC is not', ibid, Isaacs to Howgill, n.d. 'increasingly difficult', R34/890/1, 'Third Programme: forthcoming plans for autumn and winter', 13.8.54.

Page 149 'In order to', R34/1306/1, 'Talking points on *Lord of the Flies*', 8.8.55. 'considerable reputation', RCONT1, William Golding, Scriptwriter, 1952–62, Morris to Peter Duval Smith, 20.10.55. 'It seemed to', ibid, Golding to Campbell, 23.10.55. 'I'm glad of', ibid, Golding to Carne-Ross, 23.2.57. 'Giles didn't look', HC/Cleverdon. 'At Mathry Beacon', RCONT1, Giles Cooper, Scriptwriter, 1955–6, Drama Script Reader's report, 'Mathry Beacon', 11.2.55.

Page 150 'the most gruesome', ibid, Greenhalgh to Script Editor, Drama (Sound), 8.3.55. 'A brilliant', ibid, Drama Script Reader's report, 'Mathry Beacon', 11.2.55. 'Donald was', HC/Cleverdon. 'a very silent', HC/Newby. 'Fantasy about', RCONT1, Giles Cooper, Scriptwriter, 1955–6, Greenhalgh to Bray, 28.5.56.

Page 151 'It is hardly', ibid, McWhinnie to Controller, Entertainment, 20.11.56. 'Mr Ebony', ibid, Greenhalgh to Bray, 7.12.56. 'The synopsis', MS note on previous memo. 'a dialogue between', RCONT1, John Mortimer, *The Dock Brief*, 1956–62, Mortimer to Pain, 31.10.56. 'I think it', ibid, 2.11.56.

Page 152 'The first part', RCONT1, Samuel Beckett, Scriptwriter, 1953–62, Reeves to McWhinnie, 17.3.53. 'in French', ibid, King Bull to McWhinnie, 15.4.53. 'quite interested', and 'basically "phoney"', ibid, Play Library to McWhinnie, 2.2.54. 'we ... feel', ibid, McWhinnie to Greenhalgh, 3.2.54.

Page 153 'far less funny', ibid, King Bull to Stokes, 24.5.54. 'At the worst', Deirdre Bair, *Samuel Beckett*, Cape, 1978, 454. 'Let me say', RCONT1, Samuel Beckett, Scriptwriter, 1953–62, Raikes to Gielgud, 29.9.55. 'immediate enquiries', ibid, Morris to Gielgud, 18.6.56. 'an elusive', ibid, Reeves to Gielgud, 21.6.56. 'As I explained', ibid, Beckett to Reeves, 4.6.56.

Page 154 'As arranged', ibid, Morris to Gielgud, 18.7.56. 'It calls for', ibid, Beckett to Morris, 27.9.56. 'delighted', ibid, Morris to Beckett, 5.10.56. 'I find it', ibid, Beckett to Morris, 18.10.56.

Page 155 'His ideas', ibid, Beckett to Morris, 16.11.56. 'I have finally', ibid, Beckett to McWhinnie, 18.12.56. 'I may be', ibid, Beckett to McWhinnie, 18.12.56. 'The production', *Daily Telegraph*, 14.1.57. 'an extremely', *Spectator*, 18.1.57. 'Donald McWhinnie's', *Time and Tide*, 19.1.57.

Page 156 'Bien travaillé,' RCONT1, Samuel Beckett, Scriptwriter, 1953–62, Beckett to McWhinnie, dated '14.12.56' for 14.1.57. 'if you yourself', ibid, Morris to Beckett, 11.2.57. 'I am afraid', ibid, Beckett to Morris, 16.2.57. 'He feels', ibid, McWhinnie to Beckett, 21.2.57. 'They are, of course', ibid, McWhinnie to Beckett, 19.3.57.

Page 157 'Incidentally, John Morris', ibid, 23.4.57.

Page 158 'quite incorrigibly', David Cecil, *Max: a biography*, Constable, 1964, 491. 'No duty-listening', R9/13/116, 'Third Programme Panel Member's Guide', December 1954. 'The announcers', R9/9/20, 'General questionnaire – week 14', 1.5.56.

Page 159 'As a member', *Daily Worker*, 11.3.55. 'undemocratic and', *Times*, 4.2.55. 'I suggest we', R19/1931/1, 'Tenth anniversary of the Third Programme', 3.8.55. 'In December', R27.852/1, 'Celebrations for a festival', 8.2.56. 'Hilda: Musique concrète', Reed 130–1.

Page 160 'I understand', RCONT1, Henry Reed, Scriptwriter, 1955–7, '*A Hedge, Backwards* by Henry Reed', 28.2.56. 'merely the latest', ibid, Gilliam to Standing, 29.2.56.

Page 161 'I share your', ibid, Standing to Gilliam, 2.3.56. 'the best way', note written on previous memo. 'My dear', ibid, Cleverdon to Reed, 19.3.57. 'The script was', HC/Spenser. 'I am persuaded', R19/1932/1, Russell to Cleverdon, 31.8.56.

Page 162 'I am familiar', *Times*, 11.8.56. '*all* the songs', Rowe.

Page 163 '*Ustinov:* Well, Peter', Sound Archives T45233.

Page 164 'It all began', micofiche scripts. 'It was hoped', *Times*, 22.8.56. 'the opportunity', R34/992, 'Leading article: the Third Programme', 24.9.56.

Page 165 'superficially pleasant', R34/992, 'The tenth anniversary of the Third Programme', 11.10.56. 'and indeed by lowering', press cuttings files, 'Department of Mass Communication, UNESCO, December 1956.'

Page 166 'Haley said', R34/1033/3, 'Thoughts about "Ingredients"', 28.9.55. 'radio would last', HC/Newby. 'However much', R34/1022/2, untitled memo signed by R. Marriott, July 1956.

Page 167 'I believe', ibid, 'Notes, 5.10.56. 'The whole output', ibid, 'Future of Sound Broadcasting, 18.10.56.

Page 168 'A starting time', ibid, 'The Future of Sound Broadcasting', November

1956. 'the Third Programme does', ibid, 14.11.56. 'a personal slight', R34/1022/5, 'Sound Broadcast Working Party', 27.11.56.

Page 169 'They are fair', R34/1639/1, 'Correspondence about the Third Programme', 12.12.56. Listeners' letters are filed with the above memo. 'I would be', R34/12022/3, unsigned and undated memo to Director of Sound Broadcasting. 'ought to be', R34/1021, 'The Future of Sound Broadcasting in the Domestic Services: Report of the Working Party . . .', January 1957.

Page 171 'adjustment of', *Sound News* (Sound Broadcasting Society newsletter), June 1957.

Page 172 'said in a foreign', *Daily Mirror*, 25.3.57. 'only a little', *Birmingham Post*, 26.3.57. 'heavily weighted', *Manchester Guardian*, 28.3.57.'Now the time', *Tribune*, 20.3.57. 'shortened to', *Sound News* (Sound Broadcasting Society newsletter), June 1957. 'a retreat', ibid. 'They must', *Times*, 9.4.57.

Page 173 'bureaucratic double-talk', *Daily Telegraph*, 9.4.57. 'a policy which', *Sound News* (Sound Broadcasting Society newsletter), June 1957. 'an inescapable', R34/1639/1, 'Third Programme', 5.6.57.

Page 174 'the dangers of', R34/1639/1, 'Third Programme fourth quarter programme plans', 27.6.57. 'There were only', Laslett/*Granta*. 'The Third Programme is', *Scotsman*, 19.7.57.

Page 175 'I . . . allowed myself', Mehta 116. 'Eliot made a', HC/Laslett. 'impressed', *Scotsman*, 19.7.57. 'Shall we beat', *Evening News*, 18.7.57.

Page 176 'said that in his', R34/1022/6, 'Minutes of the meeting of the BBC Advisory Committee [*sic*]', 17.7.57. 'It is . . . particularly', R34/875/2, Hoffnung to Cadogan, 15.8.57. 'No useful purpose', *Times*, 16.8.57. 'the chief victim', *Times*, 27.8.57. 'making the best', ibid. 'apologised for not', *Times*, 30.9.57. 'It is a pity', ibid.

Page 177 'Let's look', *Cambridge Review*, 12.10.57.

Page 182 'They paid you', HC/Lade.

Page 183 '1. Wine making', R34/1020/2, 'Network III: "In Your Own Time"', 7.8.57. 'Here you can', Laslett/*Granta*. 'at least one', *Radio Times*, 29.9.57.

Page 184 'the lack of', Heppenstall 77–8. 'The purpose', R34/1555, 'Third Programme Committee', 17.6.57. '*Molloy* by', R34/1127/1, 'Third Programme Committee', 24.6.57.

Page 185 'the multiplicity', *Radio Times*, 3.1.58. 'refugees from', press cuttings P83, 'Sound Broadcasting Society . . . Report on Sound Broadcasting in the Last Quarter of 1957'. 'The Third Programme has', *Daily Telegraph*, 3.2.58. 'The man who', *News Chronicle*, 20.2.58.

Page 186 'If it would', RCONT1, T. S. Eliot, Scriptwriter, 1935–68, Eliot to Bridson, 14.12.57. 'convinced that feeling', press cuttings P83, *Sound News*, March 1958. 'if we were', RCONT1, Samuel Beckett, Scriptwriter, 1953–62, McWhinnie to Morris, 14.1.58. 'If we were', ibid, Marriott to Wellington, 19.1.58. 'Having read', ibid, Jacob to fforde, 3.2.58. 'I think he,' ibid, fforde to Jacob, 3.2.58.

Page 187 'He feels', ibid, Stokes to Marriott, 26.3.58. '0.1% of', ibid, Audience Research report LR/57/2036, 14.1.58. 'Miss Kallin', R34/1127/1, 'Third Programme Committee', 8.7.57.

Page 188 'Fade in the bells', Reed 154. 'Third Programme that', Reed 200. 'The BBC Third', *Times*, 21.8.58. 'only further weaken', *Manchester Guardian*, 4.9.58. 'late night', R27/847/1, 'Late night serious music', 20.11.57.

Page 189 'a rumpus', Laslett/*Granta*. 'Uncommon egghead', *Manchester Guardian*, 4.11.58. 'Newby is more', Mehta 119.

Page 190 'On first acquaintance', Warburton. 'There are few', Val Gielgud, *Years in a Mirror*, Bodley Head, 1965, 174. 'Now about myself', RCONT1, P. H. Newby, Talks, 1946–62, Newby to Radley, 12.11.46. 'I look back', HC/Newby.

Page 191 'very quiet', HC/French. 'He'd read a', OH/Newby. 'in a state', ibid. 'sound out their', *Manchester Guardian*, 4.11.58.

Page 192 'When I succeeded', Newby 119. 'abominable no-men', R19/1931/2, 'Third Programme', 18.3.59. 'The whole energy', HC/Newby. 'Everybody in Talks', HC/French.

Page 193 'I had rarely', ibid. 'used to come', HC/Smith. 'She had been', HC/French.

Page 194 'When it was', Kenyon 278. 'Please come to', OH/Glock. 'in a state', Glock, *Notes* 97. 'campaign of insurrection', ibid, 86. 'You're a bloody', OH/Glock. 'I don't know', Glock, *Notes*, 99. 'Richard Howgill', OH/Glock. 'What had gone', ibid. 'Many times', ibid.

Page 195 'dissastisfaction and boredom', and other details about the Proms in the 1950s: Hall. 'narrow horizons', Glock, *Notes*, 101. 'likeable', ibid. 'a Hitler', OH/Glock. 'What we tried', ibid. 'the old segregation', Glock, *Notes*, 116. 'you might have', RCONT1, Peter Maxwell Davies, Artists, 1959–62, Glock to Davies, 14.11.61.

Page 196 'I think he', OH/Glock. 'a fine musician', ibid. 'rejuvenation', Glock, *Notes*, 205. 'We wanted to', HC/Goehr. 'No doubt', Glock, *Notes*, 103. 'Indeed when one', Keller symposium 344. *(Footnote:)* 'low-grade', telephone call to the author, 23.2.96, and David Drew to the author, 23.2.96.

Page 197 'engaging in free', Wintle xiv. 'He defined', Keller symposium 346–7. 'The striking', Wintle 83–4. 'Hans could not', Keller symposium 347. 'positive aggression', Wintle xv. 'adolescent', William Glock, 'Benjamin Britten', Third Programme, 29 January 1953, microfilm scripts. 'Could have been', Glock, *Notes*, 103. 'invariably aggressive', ibid.

Page 198 'pronouncements which', Keller symposium 379. 'over my', ibid 358. 'in charge of', ibid. 'I don't think', HC/Glock. 'He had no interest', HC/Newby. 'I wasn't in', 10022154, 'Presentation', 6.7.71. 'Tautology is', *Music Review*, 17 (1956), 48–58.

Page 199 'bits of so-called', *Musical Times*, January 1960. 'brilliant', ibid. 'Now, while this music', Hans Keller, 'The Thirteenth Festival of the International Society for Contemporary Music', Third Programme, 19.7.56; microfilm scripts.

Page 200 'DISAPPOINTING MOBILE', *Times*, 6.6.61. 'The first performance', *Daily Telegraph*, 6.6.61. 'was arranged by', ibid, 1.8.61. 'banging about', *Daily Express*, 1.8.61.

Page 201 'Miss Susan Bradshaw', 'The Strange Case of Piotr Zak, Third Programme, 5.8.61, transcript filed under 'Keller' in microfilm scripts. 'if one had tried', ibid. 'I took a', HC/Newby. 'The revelation', *Daily Telegraph*, 12.8.61. 'There are many', 'The Strange Case of Piotr Zak, Third Programme, 5.8.61, transcript filed under 'Keller' in microfilm scripts. 'sandwiched between', Glock, *Notes*, 113.

Page 202 'I had tried', ibid, 111. 'It was in', HC/Goehr.

Page 203 'planned only', Glock, *Notes*, 113. 'The programming of', HC/Goehr. 'is ... as much', R27/945/1, 'Thursday Invitation Concert in Bristol', 7.3.62. 'the only person', R27/945/1, 'Third Programme Invitation Concert from St Andrews University', 10.11.67. 'and Deryck had', HC/Manduell.

Page 204 'I'm a great', ibid. 'The names', *Radio Times*, 2.5.60. 'The function', R27/852/7, 'The Innocent Ear, 19th January 1954: Berwald Septet', 21.1.64. 'unjustifiable exclusion', Robert Simpson, *The Proms and Natural Justice*, Toccata Press, 1981, 30. 'What do you', HC/Glock. 'Bob was a', HC/Newby. 'ninety per cent', HC/Goehr. 'I think we', R27/945/1, 'Thursday Invitation Concert: Manchester 13th October'.

Page 205 'I am quite', R27/945/1, 'Thursday Invitation Concerts, North Region', 8.9.60. 'entitled to some', ibid, 13.9.60. 'Thank you for', ibid. 20.9.60. 'bearing local', R27/945/1, 'Thursday Invitation Concerts', 22.9.60. 'You must not', ibid, 28.9.60. 'On an issue', R27/852/6, 'Gershwin', 15/11/62.

Page 206 'What kind of', R27/847/2, 'Maxwell Davies: Worldes Blis: Promenade Concert: 28.8.69'. 'There was cheerful', HC/Goehr. 'become a considerable', *Listener*, 5.12.63.

Page 207 'We met socially', OH/Newby. 'William took', ibid. 'the offers that', OH/Newby.

Page 208 'I ... hope you', RCONT1, Harold Pinter, Artist, 1950–62, Pinter to Smith, 24.1.51. '1. Not much', ibid, audition report, n.d. 'I think you', ibid, Smith to Pinter, 24.1.55. 'A very bleak', ibid, Pinter to Smith, 3.5.54. 'I find it', RCONT1, Harold Pinter, Scriptwriter, 1957–62, McWhinnie to Pinter, 21.1.58.

Page 209 'The play has', ibid, Pinter to McWhinnie, 21.5.58. 'I think we', ibid, Bakewell to McWhinnie, 3.6.58. 'Pinter is just', ibid, McWhinnie to Marriott, 8.7.58. 'I agree that', ibid, written on Bakewell to McWhinnie, 3.6.58. 'Both these authors', ibid, Marriott to Morris, 11.7.58. 'whatever the individual', ibid, Gielgud to McWhinnie, 19.8.58.

Page 210 'no amount of', *Listener*, 6.8.59. 'very effective radio', RCONT1, Harold Pinter, Scriptwriter, 1957–2, Bray to McWhinnie, 26.6.59. 'Mr Pinter is', ibid, Izzard to Bray, 20.7.59. 'Please go ahead', ibid, Newby to Bray, 31.7.59. 'I am most', ibid, McWhinnie to Gielgud, 28.1.60. 'too obscure', ibid, Barry to McWhinnie, 1.9.59. 'I think I', ibid, Newby to Gielgud, 26.10.60.

Page 211 'incomprehensible', ibid, Gielgud to Newby, 28.10.60. 'I believe *The Dwarfs*', ibid, Newby to Gielgud, 31.10.60.

Page 212 'there was no', Anthony Thwaite to the author, 3.1.96. 'The programme will', R19.1931.3, 'Third Programme suggestion', 28.9.61.

Page 213 'We had arranged', R34/1503/1, 'Henry Reed', 18.10.71.

Page 214 'rivalled in our', *Guardian*, 10.12.86. 'He begs us', R28/469/1, 'Third Programme news', 13.8.63. 'significant news', R28/469/1, 'News on Third Programme', 14.8.63. 'the whole of that', ibid, 23.8.65.

Page 215 'becoming a magazine', R28/469/1, 'News in Third Programme', 30.10.63. 'I take the view', R28/469/1, 'Third Programme news', 25.11.63. 'We have, to date', ibid, 26.11.63.

Page 216 'I completely failed', OH/Newby. 'a coherent picture', *Third Programme Quarterly Plan*, October-December 1964. 'It was decided', HC/French.

Page 217 'the most taciturn', Anthony Thwaite to the author, 3.1.96. 'suddenly seemed to', *Independent*, 17.2.92. 'George always wore', HC/French. 'Wherever there is', R19/933/1, 'Programme C: poetry programmes', 22.3.46. 'I think that', R19/1822/2, 'The broadcasting of poetry', 29.8.57.

Page 218 'Mr Gittings asked', R19/1822/2, 'Poetry Committee', 8.2.63. 'The important thing', quoted in obituary of MacBeth, *Daily Telegraph*, 17.2.92. 'If you write', *Bluff Your Way in Literature*, Wolfe Publishing Ltd, 1966. 'This phrase ... is', ibid. 'very much part', HC/French.

Page 219 'I'd be happy', RCONT1, Ted Hughes, Talks, 1956–62, MacBeth to Hughes, 12.4.60. 'the single most', *Times*, 17.2.92. 'lack of distinction', R51/893/1, 'New Comment', 30.1.63. 'David Edge', Mehta, *passim*.

Page 220 'Somebody said it', interview with the author, Oxford, 18.3.95.

Page 222 'almost doubled' and 'consistently bigger', R34/1035, 'Network Three listening figures', 20.1.59. 'The present Network', ibid, 20.2.59. 'Before we give', R34/1035, 'Network Three: third quarter 1959', 21.4.59.

Page 223 'I favour ... putting', R34/1035, 'Network Three', 17.6.59. 'Objective: To please', R34/1035, 'Music in Network Three: Saturday afternoon'. 21/7/59. 'I checked this', R27/847/1, 'Music output', 21.8.59. 'used to their', R34/1585/1, 'Area and local broadcasting final report', 1959.

Page 224 'the unused time', R27/818/1, undated, unsigned typescript beginning 'The idea of an extension of sound broadcasting ...'. 'throughout the daytime', R34/1585/1, 'Area and local broadcasting final report', 1959. 'though known as', R27/847/1, Canadian music stations', 28.4.60. 'it may be', R27/847/1, 'Music: Home Service day-time', 3.11.60.

Page 225 'I thought that', R27/847/1, 'Music on Third Network: December 26th and 27th', 2.1.61. 'programmes of serious', R4/4/21, *Report of the Committee on Broadcasting*, 1960, 216. 'I didn't like', HC/Glock. 'danger of musical', OH/Glock. 'on balance', R4/4/21, *Report of the Committee on Broadcasting*, 1960, 251. 'But as the weeks', R27/818/1, 'New Music Programme: start', 26.11.62. 'The Union say', R27/847/1, 'Extract from Programme Contracts Digest no. 21, February 1963'.

Page 226 'We shall have', R27/847/1, 'The BBC's Music Policy', February 1963. 'He was a brilliant', OH/Glock. 'the slavery of', ibid. 'started going abroad', ibid.

Page 227 'very frustrating', HC/Manduell. 'a time of energy', R34/1034/1, 'Music Programme (first draft) statistics and observations', 27.3.63. 'The point has', R27/847/1, 'Extension of sound broadcasting – proposed music service', 9.10.63. 'for the foreseeable', *Music and Musicians*, August 1964.

Page 228 'If we fail', R34/1034/1, 'Music Programme', 30.7.64. 'the new Music Programme', BBC Press Service handout, 'The new Music Programme', n.d., probably August 1964. 'A SERIOUS SOUND', *Birmingham Post*, 31.7.64. 'a widespread weekly', *Radio Times*, 27.8.64. 'I felt as the', HC/Manduell. 'too much talking', R34/1034/1, 'Proportion of speech in Music Programme Phase One', 3.9.64. 'the delivery and', R27/819/1, 'Music Programme: music meeting', 8.9.64. 'absolutely vital', R34/1034/1, 'Music Programme: speech content, 10.9.64.

Page 229 'Is it not', R27/827/1, 'Opera on the Music Programme', 12.10.64. 'One of the most', R27/818/1, 'The Music Programme', 11.11.64. 'while inevitably the', R27/818/1, 'The Music Programme', 11.11.64. 'broadcasting a quantity', *Times*, 27.11.64.

Page 230 'usually overpowered by', *Strad*, November 1964. 'four programmes devoted', *Third Programme Quarterly Plan*, April-June 1963. 'Anna was marvellous', HC/Lade.

Page 231 '*Music Magazine* was', HC/Manduell. 'The listener ... risks', *New Statesman*, 25.12.64.

Page 232 '(1) Mr Drew raises', ibid, 8.1.65. 'Voices have been', *Sunday Times*, 14.2.65.

Page 233 'There were striking', LR/63/358, 'A study of the musical tastes, interests and behaviour of the adult population', March 1963. 'the comparative distaste', LR/64/1378, 'The public for "serious" music', 1964. 'I have arranged', R27/818/2, 'Music Programme trailing', 8.1.65. 'Sunday is supposed', R27/818/2, 'The faceless Music programme', 12.1.65. 'a psycho-socio-anthropological', R34/1621/1, 'Third Programme Committee minutes', 1.3.64.

Page 234 'There is substantial', R34/1034/2, 'Music Programme: the Beatles', 26.1.65. 'not an acceptable', R34/1034/2, 'Music Programme: the Beatles', 27.1.65. 'This memo', R27/818/2, 'Franz Schmidt/Leo Wermser' [*sic*], 14.4.65. 'A corner cannot', R27/818/2, 'Franz Schmidt/Leo Wurmser', 13.5.65. 'light music of', R34/1034/2, 'Music Programme: 2.00–3.00 pm weekdays', 9.4.65. 'virtually no audience', R27/818/2, 'Music Programme: 2.00–3.00 pm', 6.5.65. 'and it is hoped', *Times*, 12.3.65.

Page 235 'we used to scan', HC/Manduell. 'music of the', R34/1034/2, 'Notes of a meeting ...', 11.5.65. 'Light Programme uproar', *Daily Mail*, 23.7.65. 'find another wavelength', *Times*, 31.12.65. 'the audience for', R34/1–34/2, 'Ball-by-ball commentaries and Music Programme', 4.7.67. 'I put the Bartók', HC/Lade. 'There is a steady', R34/1034/2, 'Jazz', 3.11.66.

Page 236 'the afternoon schedules', R27/818/2, Gillard to Mansell, n.d. 'a somewhat mechanical', R27/818/2, 'A personal reaction to Music programme', 8.9.65. 'There are days', *Financial Times*, 11.1.66. 'Only a musical', *New Statesman*, 18.6.65. 'I thought we', R27/818/2, 'Music announcing', 29.10.65. 'This is the BBC', *Punch*, 1.9.65.

Page 237 'This morning seems', R27/818/2, 'Attached copy of notes', 3.12.65. 'fairly regularly', R9/9/30, 'The Music Programme', March 1966. 'a comforting assessment', R34/1034/2, Gillard to Silvey, 19.10.67. 'no measurable audience', R34/1034/2, 'Music Programme: afternoon programmes', 25.10.65. 'not for us', R27/818/2, 'A personal reaction to Music Programme', 8.9.65. 'Only a minority', R9/9/30, 'The Music Programme', March 1966.

Page 238 'A million and', *The Third Programme: a lecture by P. H. Newby ... in the Concert Hall at Broadcasting House, 20 October 1965*. 'I was very', HC/Newby. 'We broadcast more', *Radio Times*, 19.8.67. 'subjects for "open-end"', R34/1621/7, 'Third Programme Committee, 30.1.67. 'shortfall', R34/1503/1, 'Third Programme documentaries', 2.2.66.

Page 239 'the lack of', R34/1621/1, 'Third Programme Committee, 9.8.65. 'a study of', *Third Programme Quarterly Plan*, January–March 1964. 'it was a talk', RCONT1, Bill Naughton, Scriptwriter, 1960–62, Naughton to Newby, 10.1.62. 'I remember being', HC/Newby. 'radio drama', HC/French.

Page 240 'arrived in an', HC/Esslin. 'I would always', HC/Tydeman. 'Dear Mr McWhinnie', RCONT1, Tom Stoppard, Scriptwriter, 1961–62, Stoppard to McWhinnie, 7.12.61. 'A diffuse, wordy', ibid, Hardwick to Bakewell, 8.1.62. 'There is a', ibid, Bakewell to Ewing, 22.6.62. 'In a mad', RCONT1, Tom Stoppard, Scriptwriter, 1963–67, Cottrell to Imison, n.d.

Page 241 'Little plot', ibid, Pughe to Tydeman, 9.12.63. 'The basic idea', ibid, Stoppard to Williams, n.d. 'the one about', ibid, Williams to Stoppard, 19.2.65.

Page 242 'Not my sort', ibid, Play Library to Esslin, June 1965. 'This is a very', ibid, Esslin to Powell, 25.5.67. 'the uneasy feeling', Whitehead 87. 'like shouting into' and 'If I write', ibid 86, 90. 'Oh no', HC/Newby. 'Portland Place dignifies', ibid, Stoppard to Imison, 5.2.66.

Page 243 'We never had', HC/French. 'In 1968 Norman', HC/French.

Page 244 'Howard and I', HC/Manduell. '*Wednesday 4 September*', diary extract kindly supplied by Cormac Rigby. *(Footnote:)* 'Peter Gould', Ponsonby.

Page 247 'not happy', R34/1621/1, 'Third Programme Committee', 23.10.67. 'Hitherto our main', *Daily Telegraph*, 9.8.68.

Page 248 'within budget limitations', R1/23/1, 'Improving the Management of Resources', report of McKinsey & Co, September 1968. 'for information and', R34/1621/1, 'Third Programme Committee', 4.11.68.'an unfinished job', R78/568/1, Gillard to Curran, 5.2.69. 'spiral upwards into', R78/568/1, 'Working group on the future of radio', January 1969.

Page 249 'I thought it', HC/Newby. 'If rising costs', R78/948/1, 'Policy Study Group, the Future of Network Radio, second progress review', 24.3.69. 'The term "Third Programme"', R78/548/2, 'Board of Governors presentation', 22.5.69.

Page 250 'the lack of', R34/1621/1, 'Third Programme Committee', 13.1.69. 'a whole series', ibid. 'Few people have', ibid. 'was very happy', HC/Cleverdon. 'probably inspired by', *Guardian*, 7.2.69. 'scotch the rumour', *Sunday Telegraph*, 16.2.69. 'a wide-ranging', R34/1621/1, 'Third Programme Committee', 17.2.69. 'always been difficult', R9/9/33, 'The patronage of Radio 3', March 1969.

Page 251 'rarely touches 200,000', *Guardian*, 9.4.69. 'distrust, mounting rumour', *Sunday Telegraph*, 1.6.69. 'our apprehension about', *Times*, 4.6.69.

Page 252 'The BBC is', *Broadcasting in the Seventies*, BBC, 1969. *(Footnote:)* 'too small to', R1/23/4, 'Improving the Management Resources' (report of McKinsey & Co), February 1970.

Page 254 'the future of', *Daily Telegraph*, 11.7.69. 'What about the', *New Statesman*, 16.7.69. 'the tiny nibbling', *Observer*, 20.6.69. 'the quiet and somewhat', ibid.

Page 255 'We are going', R101/box 14, 'Campaign for Better Broadcasting', September 1969. 'a private playground', R101/Box 14, 'Draft', 5.9.69. 'two immense piles', *Daily Telegraph*, 9.1.69. 'further action', 7/1267/1534, 'Broadcasting developments', 16.10.69.

Page 256 'If people say', 7/1267/1534, 'The future shape of the networks', n.d. 'It is D. G. Bridson', *Guardian*, 19.11.69.

Page 257 'uneasy and unconvinced', R101/box 14, 'Campaign for Better Broadcasting', 6.1.70. 'a higher proportion', R34/1503/1, 'Radio 3 in second quarter', 6.1.70. 'What is left', R101/Box 14, 'Statement following the new radio schedules', January 1970. 'The feeling among', ibid. 'The consumers' confidence', *Times*, 25.2.70. 'further discussion of', ibid, 23.1.70. 'Why does Mr', ibid, 29.1.70.

Page 261 'the very first', *Radio Times*, 2.4.70. 'What remains', ibid.

Page 262 '*The Third Programme label*', R78/549/1, 'The BBC's plans: a fact sheet', 12.2.70. 'The programming remains', *Radio Times*, 2.4.70. 'Radio 3 will', ibid. 'other forms of', ibid. 'The keystones of', ibid.

Page 263 'no idea how', ibid. 'about 80% middle-class', 10028153, 'Radio 3 Committee, 21.8.72. 'for the Yahoos', Bridson 331. 'Michael Young and', HC/Laslett.

Page 264 'The Third Prgramme was not', ibid. 'Peter is using', HC/Smith.

Page 265 'My role was', HC/Newby. 'I play renaissance', RCONT2, David Munrow, Artist, 1966–7, Munrow to Lam, 18.11.66. 'People had been', HC/Johnson, A.

Page 266 'music programmes aimed', 10028153, 'Radio 3 Committee', 15.2.71. 'We'd initially planned', HC/Johnson, A.

Page 267 'therefore I've always', HC/Hearst. 'was not initially', HC/Newby.

Page 268 'People like Alisdair', HC/Hearst. *(Footnote:)* 'more or less', HC/Esslin.

Page 269 'They thought I', HC/Hearst. 'an enthusiast who', HC/Rigby. 'Stephen was tremendously', HC/French. 'Since something like', R34/1503/1, 'Radio 3 trails', 7.12.71. 'narrow and constricting', *Catholic Herald*, 30.4.93. 'I opened the', HC/Rigby.

Page 270 'Radio 3 would', *3: The Radio Three Magazine*, December 1983. 'What I was joining' HC/Rigby. 'On my first', ibid. 'this dance-informed', *Dancing Times*, September 1985. 'By the time', HC/Rigby.

Page 271 'announcements much too', 10022154, 'Two points about music presentation', 19.5.72. 'would expect to', HC/Rigby. 'I did the', ibid. 'I can't exaggerate', HC/Johnson, G.

Page 272 'I remember hearing', HC/Burton. 'My audition was', Anthony Rolfe Johnson to the author, 30.9.95. 'As Chief Producer', Warburton. 'Eleanor Warren did', HC/Johnson, G.

Page 273 'Paul was not', HC/Rigby. 'One was encouraged', HC/Burton. 'My first broadcast', HC/Johnson, G. 'the most successful', HC/Rigby.

Page 274 'much more relaxed', HC/Hughes. 'He took me', HC/Rigby. 'and even the numbers', interview with the author, London, 21.11.95. 'The divine Tom', HC/Rigby. 'When I came', HC/Crowe. 'Good morning to', 10022154, 'Presentation', 18.6.71.

Page 275 'The best of', HC/Rigby. 'Occasionally one played', HC/Crowe. 'There are his laborious', *Listener*, 23.4.81. 'I used to tease', HC/Hughes. 'a great scare', HC/Rigby. 'You would get', ibid.

Page 276 'It became a', ibid. 'What I wanted', HC/Hughes. 'virtually invented the', HC/Berkeley. 'Remove her', HC/Rigby.

Page 277 'an institutional nightmare', HC/Hearst. 'it was very difficult', HC/Newby. 'when I arrived', HC/Burton. *(Footnotes)* 'Peter was a', Warburton. 'inspired, intuitive re-creator', Ponsonby.

Page 278 '15 songs in', 10022154, 'Early despatch of scripts for weekends', 17.2.72. 'My wife and', 10022154, Keller to Rigby, 15.7.75. '75% of programmes', R34/1503/1, 'Overruns in Radio 3', 7.3.72. 'a delicious finale', 10022154, 'Music presentation', 21.2.72. 'Is music an', 10022154, 'Presentation', 3.3.72. 'masterly', 100927995, 'The key system of *Fidelio* ...', 17.7.72. 'I myself, who', 10027995, 'Technical language in music talks', 18.7.72.

Page 279 'Stephen H. may', ibid. 'C.R3 said that', 10028153, 'Radio 3 Committee', 14.2.72. 'the desirability of', 10028156, 'Symposium of music talks', 19.10.72. 'I asked Cormac', HC/Hearst.

Page 280 'You had Basil', ibid.

Page 281 'the fact that', HC/Esslin. 'much greater supporters', HC/Tydeman. 'my (personal) weekly', 10022154, 'Music in Our Time', 30.11.72. 'eminently reasonable', ibid, 8.12.72. 'personal weekly nightmare', ibid, 5.12.72. 'I think we can', ibid, 4.12.72. *(Footnote:)* 'Stephen Plaistow is a', Warburton.

Page 282 'The presentation of', ibi, 6.12.72. 'The entire score', Kenyon 350–1.

Page 283 'a dialogue with', *Radio Times*, 13.1.72. 'rambled slightly', Kenyon 370–373. 'This is a central', ibid, 5.12.72.

Page 284 'very tall', Warburton. 'While William was', Ponsonby. 'the administration of', HC/Newby. 'Stephen was a', ibid. 'There was a', HC/Hearst.

Page 285 'I found that', HC/Hearst. 'Why should we', 10022158, 'New Music Committee', 9.9.70.

Page 286 'desirable to have' and 'inviolable', 10028153, 'Radio 3 Committee', 9.10.72. 'There was a', HC/Hearst.

Page 287 'entirely devoted to' and 'We can no longer', 10022146, 'Newspaper summary', 2.1.73. 'We read that', 10022146, 'Radio Three plans', 3.1.73. 'I sympathise with', 10022146, 'C.R3', 2.1.73. 'normal practice', 10022146, 'Radio Three plans', 4.1.73. 'The public ... are', ibid, 8.1.73.

Page 288 'a kind of', *Listener*, 28.12.72. 'the first time', 10028153, 'Radio 3 Committee', 8.1.73. 'few women composers', ibid, 5.2.73. 'a wry look', *Listener*, 27.9.73. 'the theme of', 10028153, 'Radio 3 Committee', 1.10.73. 'I think that's', HC/Hearst. 'A weekly two-hour', *Listener*, 29.3.73. *(Footnote:)* 'My friends, this', HC/Crowe.

Page 289 'Radio Three, a channel', R101/333, telex from Margaret Hale, BBC Bristol, 2.4.73. 'simply and clearly', 10028159, 'Music Division Control Committee', 7.4.73. 'highly critical', R101/333. 'Sunday mornings on Radio 3', 25.4.73. 'the callers had', HC/Lade. 'I have not encountered', R101/333, 'Sunday mornings', 10.4.73. 'I regard this', R101/333, 'Memo from Hans Keller', 12.4.73. 'could not muzzle', ibid. 'disadvantages', 10028159.

Page 290 'Music Division Control Committee', 30.8.73. 'crackly voices', *New Statesman*, 27.2.76. 'the phone-in', 10028153, 'Radio 3 Committee', 29.10.73. 'not felt to', ibid. 'it should not', ibid, 5.5.75. 'I said, something', HC/French. 'I never had', ibid. *(Footnote:)* 'I wanted better', HC/Esslin.

Page 291 'Clive James paid', ibid. 'the sacramental lunch', Robert Carver (ed), *Ariel at Bay: reflections on broadcasting and the arts; Critics' Forum Festschrift for Philip French*, Carcanet, 1990, 8. 'a memorable hand-to-hand', ibid, 76–7. 'Where, in all', 10022158, Newby to Hearst, 12.4.74.

Page 292 'For myself, I', *Daily Telegraph*, 6.12.74. 'rejected not just', 10022158, 'Modern music and all that', 8.5.74. 'television would have', ibid. 'wondered how often', 10028153, 'Radio 3 Committee', 10.6.74. 'said she rarely', ibid, 3.2.75.

Page 293 'lack of communication', ibid, 16.9.74. 'the cult of', 10022154, 'The cult of personality in announcers', 18.11.74. 'hideously limp-wristed', 10022154, 'Don Carlos', 25.9.74. 'screwed down', *Listener*, 13.2.75. 'emerged almost unscathed', 10028153, 'Radio 3 Committee', 8.12.74. 'When Isaiah Berlin', HC/Hearst.

Page 294 'an increase in', 10028153, 'Radio 3 Committee', 5.5.75. 'Lassus; Josquin; and', 10029827. 'Early music', 11.3.75. 'from about £3,000', HC/Ponsonby. 'The EBU international', ibid.

Page 295 'In 1977', HC/Johnson, G. 'in order to', R92/76/1, Capon and others to Newby, 26.6.75. 'a lack of', 10028153, 'Radio 3 Committee', 13.10.75.

Page 296 'short of criminal', R92/76/1, 'Departmental inadequacies', 4.11.75. 'neither the serious', 10028153, 'Radio 3 Committee', 13.10.75. 'that muzak', *New Statesman*, 27.2.76. 'a brilliant essay', George Fischer to the author, 1.1.96. 'a convenient solution', 10028153, 'Radio 3 Committee', 13.10.75.

Page 297 'return to the', *Report of the Committee on the Future of Broadcasting*, March 1977, Cmnd. 6753, 86.

Page 298 'largely responsible', HC/Newby. 'What was proposed', Ian McIntyre to the author, 21.1.95. 'to create smoother', ibid. 'a formidable debater', *Times*, 13.10.83

Page 299 'I reflect that the outfit', *Daily Telegraph*, 26.8.92. 'strong peasant constitution', *Evening Standard*, 1.3.78. 'Wearing blue serge', *Sunday Telegraph*, 8.7.79. 'very bad', *Observer*, 1.7.79. 'Taking over Radio 3', 10120750, 'Pleasure and Enlargement', 17.5.79.

Page 300 'Should we be concerned', R92/69/1, 'Radio Programme policy', 7.12.78. 'What was being', Warburton. 'altering verbs', *Harpers and Queen*, March 1982. 'so that it can't' and 'self-indulgent', *Observer*, 1.7.79. 'a dodgy start', HC/Rigby. 'Of course many', HC/Burton. 'They didn't like', HC/McIntyre.

Page 301 'What I did', HC/Hearst. 'had a fuckometer', HC/Tydeman. 'Ian could be', Warburton. 'I got on', HC/Plowright. 'He had a temperament', HC/Newby. 'politically, very', HC/French. 'George was', HC/McIntyre.

Page 302 'One of the things', HC/Burton. 'good manners', 10116540, 'CR3', 10.8.78. 'a person of', HC/McIntyre. 'When Ian Trethowan', 'Robert Mayer Concerts', 11.6.85; copy supplied by Anthony Burton. 'Many thanks for', 'Robert Mayer Concerts', 12.6.85; copy supplied by Anthony Burton. *(Footnote:)* 'And it is shameful', HC/Ponsonby.

Page 303 'as an awful', Anthony Burton to the author, 8.1.96. 'It is snobbishly', 10122632, 'Discussion paper on Radio 3', 13.9.78.

Page 304 'programmes should not', 10073196, 'Music Division Liaison Meeting', 3.12.80. 'if anyone were', 8/1170/1, 'Radio Weekly Programme Review Board', 31/1/79. 'I already hear', 10022156, 'Classical music programmes', 15.5.79. '*Homeward Bound* was', Warburton. 'A lot of people', HC/Burton. 'the Open University', 10022156, 'Classical music programmes', 2.7.79.

Page 305 'a sensitively compiled', 10022156, 'BBC Radio 3 – new programme – Mondays to Fridays 1700–1900', 29.10.79. 'inane', *Listener*, 27.1.80. 'My first decade', *Spectator*, 30.6.79.

Page 306 'He was the only', Wintle xiii. 'the light of battle', Ponsonby.

Page 307 'outraged' and 'They threatened', Ponsonby. *The Atkinson People* script was broadcast on 30 April 1979.

Page 308 'Week by week', *Observer*, 18.11.79. 'the failure of Radio 3', R78/1176/1, 'Submission to Radio Network Working Party by Ernest Warburton'. 7.10.80. 'Some of the programmes', Robert Simpson, *The Proms and Natural Justice*, Toccata Press, 1981, vi, 13f.

Page 309 'The whole structure', HC/McIntyre. 'personality problems', 10116540, 'The proposed re-organization of Music Division', 29.10.80. 'music producers', ibid, 30.10.80. 'It is a very', 10120766, 'Orpheus', 10.10.85. *(Footnote:)* 'There were so', HC/Lade.

Page 310 'In the current', 10073196, 'Music Division Liaison Meeting', 18.11.81. 'In future the output', 10116540, Board of Management minutes (extract), 23.11.81. 'makes it impossible', 10028676, 'Huddersfield Contemporary Music Festival', 3.11.80. 'what I dislike', *The Third Dimension*, Stourton Press, 1983, p. 136.

Page 311 'As I went', ibid., 109. 'the exact moment', ib. 112. 'Do I really', ibid. 12. 'It was a period', Fraser Steel to Anne Winder, 23.02.96. 'a dedicated populariser', *Observer*, 31.1.82. 'Ian got me', HC/Gueroult.

Page 312 'the sunlight of', *3: The Radio Three Magazine*, October 1982. 'The audience has', ibid. '*This Week's Composers*', ibid. '*Friday:* Getting increasingly', ibid.

Page 313 'pack away her', *Times*, 28.1.94. 'Well now,' 10022154, Simon Emerson to McIntyre, 22.3.83. 'a considerable', 10029598, '3', 24.2.84. 'appears to be', *Times*, 13.10.83. 'Those meetings were', HC/Crowe. 'too stodgy' and 'the one who', 10122632, 'Radio Three presentation', 8.3.84.

Page 314 'given Russian arts', *Sunday Times*, 29.9.85. 'someone from Radio 3', 10029644, Semenov to McIntyre, 14.10.85. 'one of Radio 3's', *Listener*, 27.2.86. 'her delivery', *Listener*, 20.2.86. 'It's the first', 10029644, 'Russian Season', 22.12.86.

Page 315 'I rather think', 10029644, McIntyre to Sir Curtis Keeble, 9.12.86. 'caused quite a', 10029644, 'Radio 3 Russian Season', 8.12.86. 'could well be', 10029644, McIntyre to Sir Curtis Keeble, 9.12.86.

Page 316 'It happened because', HC/Drummond. 'I was not', ibid. 'He is a formidably', *Independent*, 24.7.95. '200 words', *3: the Radio Three Magazine*, September 1983.

Page 317 'It was the', HC/Drummond. 'Alisdair Milne rang', ibid. The time to', HC/McIntyre. 'I had a', HC/Drummond. 'It didn't mention', ibid.

Page 318 'It didn't mention', HC/Drummond. 'bloody-minded and', ibid. 'more than any', *Independent*, 13.6.91.

Page 319 'Glock had had', HC/Drummond. 'It's a constant', HC/McIntyre. 'off-putting', 10028704, 'Radio 3 Committee', 11.3.87. 'galling', ibid. 'would not provide', ibid. 'a tetchy little', Ian McIntyre to the author, 21.12.95. 'I was thought', HC/McIntyre. 'disloyal', Singer to McIntyre, 30.10.81 (lent by Ian McIntyre).

Page 320 'The Board of', 10116540, 'Radio Directorate', 9.4.87. 'I had accepted', HC/Drummond. *(Footnote:)* 'Ian McIntyre's search', Piers Burton-Page to the author, 26.02.96.

Page 321 'Few deny', *Observer*, 26.4.87. 'not the soul', *Daily Telegraph*, 30.4.87. 'a bit of a charade', HC/McIntyre. 'They organised this', HC/Drummond.

Page 322 'The Board of Governors', 10028804, 'Controller, Radio 3', 22.5.87. 'although I did', Ian McIntyre to the author, 10.1.96. 'in the middle', HC/Drummond.

Page 323 'a fine job', 10116540, 'Music', 25.10.88. 'Michael Checkland, when', HC/Drummond. 'The fact that', *Independent*, 24.7.95.

Page 324 'He immediately abolished', HC/French. 'Philip French may', HC/Drummond. 'I went to', Philip French to the author, 3.1.96. 'I had some', HC/Drummond.

Page 325 'Yes, I did', George Fischer to the author, 1.1.96. 'During the time', HC/Drummond.

Page 326 'hand-outs from', *Independent*, 24.7.95. 'He was inspirational', HC/Winder. 'warm, encouraging, chatty', HC/Plowright. 'went along to', interview with the author, 26.1.96. 'a late night', Hall.

Page 327 'Piers Burton-Page', HC/Drummond. 'I have been doing', 10065962, 'Readings on radio', 22.6.89. 'a daily strand', 10120750, 'Radio 3 – the next 5 years', 17.7.87. 'The initial plan', HC/Drummond.

Page 328 'somewhat lacking', 10029650, 'What is a radio play?', 7.9.87. 'That is hardly', ibid. *'Billy and Me'*, *Listener*, 4.1.90. 'I found Drama', HC/Drummond. *(Footnote:)* 'very appreciated by', HC/Tydeman.

Page 329 'The public are', 10120750, 'Radio 3 – the next 5 years', 17.7.87. 'My local shop' and 'I have been using', 10120759, transcripts of telephone calls to the BBC circulated at FM Steering Group Meeting, 7.12.89. 'I had no', HC/Drummond.

Page 330 'special projects', 10120750, 'Radio 3 – the next 5 years', 17.7.87. 'McIntyre had been', interview with the author, London, 21.11.95. 'I think that's', HC/Drummond. 'John Drummond took', HC/Berlin. 'I can remember', HC/Drummond. *(Footnote:)* 'I caused a', HC/Drummond.

Page 331 'We had a', ibid. 'broadcasting history', 10120745, 'Radio 3 presents "Twin Cities Weekend" from Minnesota', 8.5.91. 'many quiet delights', *Sunday Times*, 9.6.91.

Page 332 'reflect the way', BBC press handout, May 1995. 'never quite caught', HC/Drummond. 'The [Continuity] studio', *Observer*, 7.8.88. 'so small', *Observer*, 7.8.88.

Page 333 'the heritage industry', *Scotsman*, 12.11.88. 'a vampire bite', *Daily Telegraph*, 12.6.91. 'For how long', *Independent*, 12.6.91.

Page 334 'Meanwhile ... the new', *Daily Telegraph*, 15.6.91. 'will not be a rival', *Guardian*, 5.9.90. 'He gets up', *Guardian*, 11.6.91. 'They asked me', HC/Drummond. 'Mr Drummond has', *Independent*, 11.6.91.

Page 335 'The conference', *Independent*, 12.6.91. 'drift on the Pavarotti', *Times*, 20.8.91. 'everybody knows', *Guardian*, 3.8.91. 'Radio 3 broadcasts', *Daily Telegraph*, 6.4.92. 'of unbelievable idiocy', HC/Drummond.

Page 337 'two sharply honed', *Independent*, 22.1.92. 'I had thought', *Observer*, 15.3.92. 'I do remember', HC/Kenyon. 'I don't see it', *Independent*, 22.1.92. 'lack of any', HC/Kenyon. 'Can't we find'

Page 338 'I tended', ibid. 'He has never', *Sunday Times*, 15.3.92. 'broadcasting professionals', HC/Kenyon. 'inclined to lope', *Independent*, 22.1.92. 'And the biggest', HC/Kenyon. 'I have an enormous', *Independent*, 22.1.92.

Page 339 'I felt it', *Sunday Times*, 15.3.92. 'I think its', HC/Kenyon. 'not all of their', *Daily Telegraph*, 26.3.92. 'A third of all', *Sunday Times*, 26.4.92.

Page 340 'Radio 3's *Music Weekly*', *Sunday Times*, 21.6.92.

Page 341 'Am I taciturn', *Times*, 30.6.92. 'two weekday programmes', 'BBC Radio 3 FM's New Look', Radio 3 publicity handout, 29.6.92.

Page 342 'a quarter, not', *Times*, 3.7.92.

Page 343 'To clear up', 10116540, Scotland to Kenyon, 30.6.92. 'rather badly handled', HC/Kenyon. 'who feel that', *Guardian*, 30.6.92. 'Nicholas Kenyon...has', *Independent*, 30.6.92. 'Let Classic FM', *Times*, 9.7.92.

Page 344 'grotesquely saccharine', *Times*, 3.9.92. 'curious double identity', *Guardian*, 7.9.92. 'One star means', *Classical Music*, 27.3.93.

Page 345 'My heart was won', *Evening Standard*, 8.9.92. 'Of course the main', *Times*, 9.9.92. 'Classic's recipe', *Independent*, 20.1.93. 'Radio 3 has never', ibid. 'If we are successful', *Classical Music*, 27.3.93. 'Radio 3 still has', *Western Morning News*, 30.1.93.

Page 346 'truly distinctive and', *Extending Choice*, BBC, n.d. [1992], 45. 'high quality programmes', 10118648, 'BBC orchestras', 30.3.93. 'Diminished Third', quoted *Independent*, 3.12.94. 'a real shock', HC/Kenyon. 'Our presenters', *Daily Telegraph*, 25.2.93. 'My own experience', HC/Kenyon.

Page 347 'I myself look', HC/Evans. 'will certainly get', HC/Kenyon. 'demonstrate both to', Peter Cloot, *BBC Producer Choice: a Case Study*, Templeton College, Oxford, 1994, 7–8.

Page 348 'When I joined', HC/Evans. 'we really had', conversation with the author, March 1996. 'half-baked Thatcherite', interview with the author, London, 4.1.96. 'I think it had', HC/Winder.

Page 349 'the absolutely vertical', HC/Kenyon. 'Nick Kenyon wants', HC/Evans. 'It's certainly introduced', HC/Kenyon. 'We assemble programmes', ibid.

Page 350 'There's a limit', HC/Evans. 'I can't help thinking', *Listener*, 22.8.79. 'I think it's', HC/Kenyon. 'too many people', *Observer*, 4.7.93.

Page 351 'We are part', HC/Kenyon. 'It's all strategy', *Independent*, 24.7.95. 'I remember at', HC/Burton. 'I think the discipline', HC/Evans. 'All that "strategy"', HC/Kenyon.

Page 352 'expected to meet', 10118648, 'B[oard] O[f] M[anagement] paper by M[anaging] D[irector] N[etwork] R[adio], suggested draft', 21.4.93. 'our orchestras', 10118648, notes by Kenyon on meeting with John Birt and others, 29.6.93. 'But I have absolutely', HC/Kenyon.

Page 353 'I am not going', *Sunday Telegraph*, 18.7.93. 'concerned with opinion', 'Music Matters on BBC Radio 3', Radio 3 press handout, 9.9.93.

Page 354 'a tweak here', *Guardian*, 10.9.93. 'holy minimalist', *Sunday Times*, 10.10.93. 'helped to boost', *Sunday Times*, 26.12.93. 'sampler', *Independent*, 2.2.94. 'Classic FM encourages', ibid. 'We haven't yet', ibid. 'Whatever next?', *Daily Telegraph*, 10.2.94.

Page 355 'Nicholas Kenyon', *Guardian*, 16.8.94. 'The idea for', *Independent*, 3.12.94. 'a series of', ibid. 'Three of the biggest', HC/Kenyon.

Page 356 'I outlined', ibid. 'welcoming to', *Guardian*, 7.7.95. 'frankly elitist', ibid.' 'Every BBC', HC/Kenyon.

Page 357 'long before', ibid. 'classical greats', BBC publicity handout, n.d. [autumn 1995]. 'refraining from any', *Independent*, 11.8.95. 'The outrage', *Daily Telegraph*, 21.10.95.

Page 358 'the deliberate degradation', *Guardian*, 13.10.95. 'I entirely disagree', HC/Kenyon. 'accountability, accessibility, what', HC/Drummond. 'Kaufman is right', *Guardian*, 20.10.95.

Page 359 'The BBC is', 'BBC Radio to launch new digital service in 1995', BBC press handout, 24.11.94. 'Nick was uncertain', HC/Drummond. 'Structurally, it is', HC/Kenyon.

Page 360 'CDs are very', ibid. *(Footnote:)* 'There are now', HC/Johnson, G.

Page 361 'The golden age', HC/Winder.

Page 362 'Of course much', HC/Kenyon. 'It's the programmes', HC/Kenyon.

Page 363 'It is not only', '30th anniversary of the Third Programme', 29.9.76; script kindly lent by Prudence Smith. 'My milennial dream', John Spurling to the author, 15.2.96. 'the hard-working', HC/Goehr.

Page 364 'What is arguable', Pasenby, 'the tension', HC/Kenyon.

Acknowledgements

My first thanks must be to John Manger, who suggested to Nicholas Kenyon that I might be the right person to write this book. Piers Burton-Page of Radio 3 Music Department had already proposed that the network's half-century should be commemorated by a chronicle of its history, and I am very grateful for his generous support and encouragement when he learnt that I was to compile it. Nick Kenyon himself has given me every possible kind of help and encouragement, and his personal assistant Yvette Pusey has been a tireless and supremely efficient aide in the project. Radio 3's Managing Editor, Brian Barfield, has encouraged and helped me with his usual good humour. My agent Felicity Bryan cleverly found the perfect publisher for the book, Ion Trewin at Weidenfeld & Nicolson, where Elizabeth Blumer, Cassia Joll and Nick McDowell have provided congenial and skilful support in the final stages.

The book could not have been written within three very busy years without the substantial help of Jennifer Doctor. Author of *The BBC and Ultra-Modern Music 1922–36: shaping a nation's tastes* (forthcoming from Cambridge University Press), she was already a highly experienced user of the BBC Written Archives Centre when she began to pilot me around its thousands of files. She has also done her best to keep me from error when dealing with the intricacies of the musical world of the last fifty years. Sins of omission in that area of the book are, however, entirely my own.

At the Written Archives Centre, Jacquie Kavanagh and her staff, especially Gwyniver Jones, Jeff Walden and Trevor White, provided skilled help, and heroically undertook the answering of about a hundred queries, some of them very difficult to research. Pam Edwards of the BBC's Records and Programme Information Centre (RAPIC) kindly made it easy to investigate more recent papers, while Miranda O'Brien of the BBC Picture Archives and Liz Hamilton of Radio Picture Publicity provided the majority of the illustrations. Gratitude is also due to Sally Hine, Mark Jones, Christine Marsh and Simon Rooks of BBC Sound Library, Rita Bennett of BBC News Information, and Susann Smith of Radio 3 Publicity. Piers Burton-Page, Emma Kingsley and Fiona McLean helped with production of the interview material.

My remaining thanks must be chiefly to the many people who have worked for the Third and Radio 3 in the last fifty years, and who have given generously of their time and recollections. Most of their names are listed in the catalogue of interviews in the Bibliography, but I should also mention Barbara Bray, Lord Bullock (Alan Bullock), Mary Crozier, Sir Peter Maxwell Davies, David Drew, Denys Drower, George Fischer, Milein Cosman Keller, Barrie Hall, Anthony Rolfe Johnson, Gerard Mansell, Dame Iris Murdoch, John Spurling, Fraser Steel, Martin Starkie, Ernest Warburton and Bernard Williams.

Meirion Bowen helped in many ways with Sir Michael Tippett's contributions to the book, as did Henry Hardy with Sir Isaiah Berlin's. Donald Haley kindly provided excerpts from the diaries of his father, Sir William Haley. Alison Garnham and Christopher Wintle assisted with my research into Hans Keller's radio career. Fr Cormac Rigby lent to me lavishly from his personal archive. Leonard Miall provided advice and addresses.

Many present-day BBC staff talked to me, on and off the record; particular thanks are owed to Derek Drescher, Adam Gatehouse, Jeremy Hayes and Gwen Hughes.

Permissions to quote from unpublished letters were kindly given by the following people: Shirley, Lady Beecham (Sir Thomas Beecham); Edward Beckett, for the Samuel Beckett Estate; Mrs Valerie Eliot and Faber & Faber (T. S. Eliot); Dr Caroline Grigson (Estate of Geoffrey Grigson); John Mortimer; David Higham Associates (Estate of Dylan Thomas); Mrs Annetta Hoffnung (Gerard Hoffnung); John Mortimer; Dame Iris Murdoch; Glyn Perrin, on behalf of the Estate of Elisabeth Lutyens; S. Fischer Verlag GmbH, Frankfurt am Main (Thomas Mann); Harold Pinter; Bertrand Russell Archives Copyright Permissions Committee; Tom Stoppard; Mrs Ursula Vaughan Williams (Ralph Vaughan Williams); and Lady Walton and the William Walton Trust. I am very grateful to WATCH (Writers And Their Copyright Holders), at the University of Reading Library, for supplying names and addresses of some copyright holders.

My last thanks are to Alec and Susan Hamilton for the generous loan of their flat, forty yards from Broadcasting House, into which I could collapse when it all became too much.

Index